C000147428

APOPHATIC BODIES

TRANSDISCIPLINARY THEOLOGICAL COLLOQUIA

Theology has hovered for two millennia between scriptural metaphor and philosophical thinking; it takes flesh in its symbolic, communal, and ethical practices. With the gift of this history and in the spirit of its unrealized potential, the Transdisciplinary Theological Colloquia intensify movement between and beyond the fields of religion. A multivocal discourse of theology takes place in the interstices, at once self-deconstructive in its pluralism and constructive in its affirmations.

Hosted annually by Drew University's Theological School, the colloquia provide a matrix for such conversations, while Fordham University Press serves as the midwife for their publication. Committed to the slow transformation of religio-cultural symbolism, the colloquia continue Drew's long history of engaging historical, biblical, and philosophical hermeneutics, practices of social justice, and experiments in theopoetics.

STEERING COMMITTEE:

Catherine Keller, *Director*
Virgina Burrus
Stephen Moore

APOPHATIC BODIES

Negative Theology, Incarnation, and Relationality

EDITED BY CHRIS BOESEL AND CATHERINE KELLER

FORDHAM UNIVERSITY PRESS ⁂ NEW YORK 2010

Copyright © 2010 Fordham University Press

All rights reserved. No part of this publication may be reproduced, stored in a retrieval system, or transmitted in any form or by any means—electronic, mechanical, photocopy, recording, or any other—except for brief quotations in printed reviews, without the prior permission of the publisher.

Fordham University Press has no responsibility for the persistence or accuracy of URLs for external or third-party Internet websites referred to in this publication and does not guarantee that any content on such websites is, or will remain, accurate or appropriate.

Library of Congress Cataloging-in-Publication Data

Apophatic bodies : negative theology, incarnation, and relationality / edited by Chris Boesel and Catherine Keller.—1st ed.

p. cm.— (Transdisciplinary theological colloquia)

Colloquium held at Drew University, fall of 2006.

Includes bibliographical references.

ISBN 978-0-8232-3081-5 (cloth : alk. paper)—ISBN 978-0-8232-3082-2 (pbk. : alk. paper)

1. Negative theology—Christianity. 2. Human body—Religious aspects—Christianity. I. Boesel, Chris. II. Keller, Catherine, 1953–

BT83.585.A66 2010

233'.5—dc22

2009025833

Printed in the United States of America

12 5 4 3 2

First edition

CONTENTS

ACKNOWLEDGMENTS

In a project such as this, which is not simply a volume of essays from a diverse and diversely gifted collection of scholars—a collaborative enough effort in its own right!—but a collection emerging from a colloquium that gathered, housed, and fed a host of flesh-and-blood bodies from points far and wide for three days of focused and lively conversation, there is quite simply not enough thanks to go adequately around. Nevertheless, we must risk the kataphatic gesture of articulating gratitude regardless of the inevitable inadequacy of such efforts. We are, of course, very grateful to the contributors whose work constitutes the visible body of this volume, for the gifts of their thought and work, as well as their patience, endurance, and responsive attention to detail throughout the process of publication. We are also indebted to those who brought their intelligence, wit, and sizable scholarly resources to the table of conversation at Drew University back in the fall of 2006 for the Transdisciplinary Theological Colloquium, from which this volume has emerged. Their efforts constitute the "invisible body" (invisible now, for you the reader, holding this book in your hands) of scholarly conversation that is here given flesh—made audible and visible—in these pages: Martin Cohen, Heather Murray Elkins, Peter Helztel, John Hoffmeyer, Walter Lowe, Stephen D. Moore, Laurel C. Schneider, Michael Sells, John J. Thatamanil, and Carol Wayne White.

As the needs, desires, and dignity of creaturely bodies—both in relation to the infinite and in their own form of infinite multiplicity and diversity—constituted the subject matter of our conversation over those few days, it is only right to remember with gratitude those who provided for the bodily needs of the colloquium participants by providing food, transportation, and hospitality. In addition to the fine housing and food service staff of Drew University, several of our graduate students committed a good deal of time and energy to the success of the gathering. The indefatigable Krista Hughes did a wonderful job of coordinating the event, ably assisted by Rose Ellen Dunn and Luke Higgins; in addition, the Herculean efforts of Dhawn Martin and Lydia York were indispensable to the editorial work of bringing this volume together in its final form—many, many thanks!

Our debt to and gratitude for the leadership, vision, and generosity of Maxine Beach, our dean, grow exponentially with each passing year and each successful colloquium. We also thank the amazing administrative staff that sustains our life and work at Drew. We are also grateful to Elliot Wolfson for allowing us to use his painting *Luminal Darkness* in the publicity materials for the conference and as the cover art of this volume. And finally, we thank again our colleagues at Fordham University Press, and especially Helen Tartar, under whose guidance the Transdisciplinary Theological Colloquia series continues to flourish—long may it be so!

APOPHATIC BODIES

Introduction

CHRIS BOESEL AND CATHERINE KELLER

Apophatic bodies. If the phrase stops the reader short, perplexes, provokes a pause, it will have begun to do its work. Indeed, the modifier "apophatic"—that which "unsays" or "says away"—presses toward the pause and the silence within language. It pauses before the unknowable infinity of: *bodies*?

Surely not! The ancient tradition of apophasis, or negative theology, concerns itself with the infinity called "God." It says and unsays talk about that God. It falls speechless before a mystery that inspires more speech in the next moment. Surely the paradox entailed in this traditional apophatic gesture is mind-bending enough—speaking as unspeaking, knowing as unknowing, darkness as light—to keep us occupied for all these pages. The apophatic mystics—Jewish, Christian, Muslim—do surely speak. They speak and unspeak volumes. With uninhibited *kataphasis* (the presumed affirmative opposite of apophasis), at once confessional and speculative, liturgical and philosophical, they speak about God. The more they speak, the more they unspeak; and yet because of the infinity of which they speak, it would seem they can never stop speaking. For without our finite images, images of the illimitable drawn from our bodily limits, would "God" exist *for us*? But without God as the self-giving source of all the embodied reality from which those images emerge, how would "we" exist—*at all*, let alone *for God*?

In one ear, we hear Meister Eckhart admonish: "[B]e silent and do not chatter about God; for when you chatter about him, you are telling lies and sinning."[1] Yet there remains the divine referent of apophasis itself, the said that must be resaid if only to be unsaid ever again. "Of God we know nothing," writes Franz Rosenzweig. "But this ignorance is ignorance of God."[2] Thus, for instance, Eckhart, one of the most radical of theological unsayers, nonetheless does not cease to wax kataphatic. So in the other ear he whispers, for example, that "[w]hat God gives is his being, and his being is his goodness, and his goodness is his love."[3] "Silence," explains Elliot Wolfson, who has written voluminously on it, "is not to be set in binary opposition to language, but is rather the margin that demarcates its center."[4] This conundrum of creaturely speech about incomprehensible divinity runs so deep and is so stubbornly irresolvable that one can hear it echoing centuries later, and in the most unlikely places: in the unapologetically protestant voice of Karl Barth, for example, struggling with the perilous aporia facing the preacher ascending the steps of the pulpit, knowing that she cannot rightly speak of God and yet, nevertheless, that she must speak of God.[5] Indeed Barth affectionately likens theology, as appropriately ruptured and broken speech, to an "old woman's stammering."[6] The stammer, neither a pure silence nor a smooth proclamation, provides the alternative to the chatter.

AS IF THAT WEREN'T ENOUGH: APOPHASIS AND BODIES

Surely this predicament is dicey enough. Why make more trouble for ourselves? If this volume does, it may be in order to focus the light of scholarly imagination on a troubling effect of an invisible, unspeakable transcendence—trouble, that is, for bodies.

The traditional agents of apophasis evince little interest in the material body, beyond the disciplines needed to quiet its cravings so as better to hear "the mysteries of God's Word . . . in the brilliant darkness of a hidden silence."[7] They conjure for us the ascetic body, monkishly clad, itself writing bodies of light, angelic, saintly, or resurrected bodies, anchored perhaps in the singular incarnation, the only body whose fleshly vulnerability really matters for them. And however we may correct such a limited representation, there is no denying that the apophatic tradition in Judaism and Islam as well as Christianity is steeped in Neoplatonic sensibility. The hierarchical ascent to the immateriality beyond finite form—"simple, absolute, and unchangeable," to return to the poem of Pseudo-Dionysius—aspires beyond every bodily being, beyond being itself, *hyperousios*. If we are looking for bodies, surely negative theology would seem to point us in the wrong direction. Ascending to that hidden silence, apophasis seems to *say away* the language of the bodily, the creaturely.

And today we are indeed looking for bodies. For we have become painfully cognizant of the long history of Christian looking beyond the body, as if we could hardly wait to escape the limits of our living flesh. We are today learning to consider instead the toxic consequences of spiritual disembodiment—a history of both theological and metaphysical thought whose wake is strewn with . . . well, bodies. Out of concern for the dignity, beauty, and well-being of bodies, for the endangered ecology and all things creaturely, we have endeavored to keep the body rather stubbornly in the cross-hairs of the apophatic gesture and desire. In so doing, we are very aware of ratcheting up the paradoxical tension of apophasis a notch or two—or actually three. The first notch of heightened paradoxical tension is that of a split obligation. As if speaking—and unspeaking—of God were not problematic enough, we want to know how we might speak (and unspeak) of God without necessarily ceasing to speak of the body. Is there a movement of thought and language toward the infinity of the divine that is not ultimately a movement away from the concrete finitude of the body?

We need to proceed cautiously here. For this heightened tension entails a heightened complexity. The relation of the classic apophatic traditions to the body, and therefore to this split obligation between divine infinity and embodied finitude, may not be as straightforward as it appears at first blush. For the apophatic movement of negative theology—a seemingly provisional interest in bodily life eclipsed by a concern for commerce with and within the disembodied life of infinite divine reality—is not the only theological gesture that spells trouble for the embodied life of creatures. The problem posed by the apophatic gesture is also one of too great a distance, too radical a separation, between divine and creaturely reality; too absolute a sense of divine transcendence in relation to the finite realm of creaturely embodiment. This transcendence smacks of indifference (and so, ethically, of quietism) in the face of the needs, desires, and unjust sufferings of an embodied life.

There is, however, a problematic theological gesture toward the divine that appears when we try to move in the opposite direction. This problem arises when the difference and distance between divine and creaturely reality is not big or radical *enough*; when creaturely finitude assumes too cozy a relation with the divine infinite, as if the former—creaturely concepts, categories, language, texts, persons, communities—could comprehend and so contain divine reality. And when an embodied creaturely reality identifies itself with and so presumes to grasp and control an infinite mystery, it is time to start passing out the crash helmets and flak jackets to protect the bodies of neighboring but differing creatures. Mastery over divine mystery routinely results in a body count.

In the latter gesture, we are dealing with the storied problem of idolatry. And this is where it gets interesting. For the problematic gesture of a body-transcending mysticism might actually yield some fairly compelling resources with which to resist and remedy the other problematic theological gesture, that of an idolatrous identity between the creaturely and the divine. If we read carefully, might we find in the arguments of negative theology—albeit beyond its historically determined assumptions about embodiment—a supplement for contemporary commitments to the body? A close reading of these texts reveals that the traditional apophatic gesture negates our embodied finitude only inasmuch as finite forms are mistaken for the divine infinite. Divinity comes, after all, encumbered by the projection of all manner of finite images derived from our bodily life: images of a lord or a warrior, a friend or a father, a humanoid love, and minimally, an inconspicuous little personal pronoun (as in "He is not a person, He is beyond gender . . ."). Or, as some of us may prefer to phrase it, in coming to us, divinity submits—quite problematically—to bodily encumbrances while nevertheless remaining irreducible to them.

With varying degrees of self-critical consistency (and the merest hint of a proto-feminist consciousness), the negative tradition peels away the linguistic accretions, like barnacles, of finite images. The very word "God" cannot be uttered without these accretions, helpful as far as they go. But encrusted in pious certainty or unquestionable orthodoxy, habituated in propositions and attributions, any God-talk can harden, it was recognized, into the smuggest of idols. So Meister Eckhart, in an outburst of reverent iconoclasm, utters the single most succinct moment of apophasis in Christian literature: "I pray God to rid me of God." At its negative edge theology recognizes its own jeopardy—the intimate temptation we may call *theolatry*.

The creaturely body as such, then, may not be the problem for apophasis. It is wary of the creaturely body *as idol*. Put differently (in anticipation of the second level of heightened tension), it is not so much talk of the body that is problematic, but talk of God.

Apophasis, in other words, does not negate bodies as such. Rather it targets our false knowledge, the idols formed in our confusion of the finite with the infinite. "Therefore," writes Cusa, "the theology of negation is so necessary to the theology of affirmation that without it God would not be worshiped as the infinite God but as creature; and such worship is idolatry, for it gives to an image that which belongs only to truth itself."[8] The image, the projection, is ipso facto drawn from creaturely life. And this inevitable work of the imagination is for these mystics made both more perplexing and promising by the overflow of divinity's self-giving in, through, and to living bodies.

For "the transcendently originating Life" itself "teems with every kind of life. It may be contemplated and praised amid every manifestation of life." So this God "is rightly nameless and yet has the names of everything that is."[9] Because none fit, all may be worn. As Cusa argued, following Dionysius, and as this volume's engagement in the cosmology of the apophatic tradition attests, all the names are appropriate because that infinite divinity is present in everything, every body of the universe, as its animating source, life, breath, and goal. The circuits of theological language threaten to blow in the struggle to express the relation of anybody and everybody, the plenitude of finite bodies, to their infinite source. It is a relationality whose denomination circulates within the apophatic tradition between the classically theist dualism of transcendent creator/material creation on the one hand, and the risk of a monism, a pantheism, that kept mystics under suspicion, on the other. The third way of an eirenic panentheism, congenial to many authors represented in this volume, may or may not solve the problem. It does, however, hint at one overarching way that negative theology folds into—and has always in a certain sense folded into—a relational *affirmation* of bodies. Does a radically widened incarnationalism begin to appear in the void of the radical negation? If so, our presenting enigma of apophatic bodies would signify more than a simple oxymoron.

The agents of apophasis do not doubt the necessity of humanly comprehensible terms for the inhuman infinity of the divine, a necessity they believe to be accommodated by the excesses of divine self-giving in, through, and to creaturely reality. Indeed, the most bodily of metaphors of God may be the most appropriate (Dionysius again: eyes, face, hands, feet . . . all Bible citations) precisely because they bring us up short. They reveal the metaphors as metaphors, indispensable for analogies, icons, praise, and prayer. The negation thus exposes the "fallacy of misplaced concreteness."[10] The problem is not the concreteness of bodily reality, nor its metaphoric displacement onto the infinite. The problem is the abstraction of a metaphor into the false concreteness of our unquestionable knowledge of God. In the process of this abstraction a familiar Western rationality masters both the concrete bodies and that for which they offer metaphors. Apophasis, for all its Neoplatonically charged speculation, cuts against this idolatrous certainty, this pseudo-knowledge. *Si comprehendis non est deus,* entones Augustine: if you understand it, it isn't God.[11]

Indeed, in deconstructing the names of God in the name of God—if only for a moment, if only at its Zen-like Western extremities—negative theology attracts a growing and varied flock of scholars today. It offers a balm for the discomfort with God-talk suffered by so many contemporary thinkers, especially those who are drawn, even after atheism, even "after the death of God," to the questions of theology, but disappointed by the answers.[12] "The divine has been ruined by God," says Jacques Derrida;[13] and many who make their living from the questions of theology say "amen."

A select handful of these discomforted contemporary thinkers attracted to the questions of theology and a group of equally discomforted theologians have been drawn together into this volume. They consider the possibility that apophasis may be good medicine for bodies threatened by concepts of "God" that also threaten the divine. Amid the tension, then, between the demands and desires of real mattering bodies and the austere transcendence that looks away from bodies even as it says away God, we ask if the apophatic might yet do a double-take? Might it look back to bodies with a fresh gaze, even as it speaks afresh of the divine?

Yet this conversation takes with equal seriousness the fact that even the most radical of these ascetic authors do not do justice to what we mean, or hope we mean, by "bodies," now, today, in contexts of progressive politics and theology. For we mean the embodiment of justice; we mean an attention to the animal imperatives of food and health and shelter; we mean an environment where the water is potable and the air breathable, where the trees and the ocean and the birds and the bees are not dying. We also mean to do justice to the defining human sexualities and social markers of the body. By "bodies" we signal a care for all these dimensions of an embodiment that cannot be reduced to biological, sociological, or for that matter theological abstraction without again confusing the abstract with the concrete.

Such signals of eco-socio-sexual respect for our interdependent creaturely life express a wide and still emergent theological mood for which no strong antecedent can be found amid the classical or neoplatonizing traditions. We may, however—and through the waves of liberation, feminist, queer, postcolonial theologies, actually *do*—find biblical and countercultural antecedents. And we may then relate the ancient epistemic radicalism of negative theology to the still emergent theologies of embodiment, "theologies that matter" (Darby Ray). For instance, in her trinitarian theology of Sophia, Elizabeth Johnson affirms the classical way of negation as key to challenging exclusively masculine images of God. She affirms that "no name or image or concept that human beings use to speak of the divine mystery ever arrives at its goal: God is essentially incomprehensible."[14] And therefore the new names, new concepts, new strategies—arising, in Johnson's argument, from women's distinctive historical and bodily experiences—cannot be disqualified simply for their unfamiliarity among the family insignia of Abraham.

The coupling of apophasis and bodies, then, forges a heightened, ethically nuanced tension of obligation split between linguistic gestures toward a transcendent divinity on one hand, and flesh-and-blood commitments to the embodied life of creatures on the other. Within the conversation embodied in the present volume, this tension calls forth creative engagements with the variegated possibilities of the apophatic gesture in a wide range of periods, contexts, and disciplines, for the sake of embodied life caught in the imperialistic teeth of idolatrous discourses. And these engagements at the same time attend to the shadow of an austere and indifferent transcendence that those resources themselves can cast across the life of embodied creatures.

EVEN MORE: GOD, "GOD," OR NOTHING OF THE SORT?

There is a second notch of heightened tension encountered in this collection of transdisciplinary reflection on the paradox of apophatic bodies, and it folds out of the first. It is the tension between the various ways in which the split obligation treated above is approached and resolved and the respective assumptions those approaches and resolutions entail. Is this split obligation, in the first instance, an ethical or a theological predicament? Which inheres in the other? Does the theological gesture constitute the necessary context for an ethical commitment to the well-being of bodies, or does it, in fact, constitute an obstacle for, or even a rupture of, such a commitment? Does the ethical concern for colonized bodies demand the critical transformation of *idolatrous* desire for God or of desire for God *as such*?

Reconstructing the gesture toward divinity in such a way that it does not ultimately leave the body behind is not the only way to resolve the tension of split obligation. One quite obvious alternative is to simply remove transcendent divinity from the equation altogether. Indeed, much of the current interest in negative theology, the revival of its radical potential, stems from its affinity with atheism. Deconstruction, for example, brings to the surface the hyperousiology, the Neoplatonic hierarchy, the ontotheology that leaves its traces even in the beyond-being. It ceaselessly searches out the radical limits of an epistemic certainty lodged somewhere near the top, under cover of that luminous dark. Deconstruction, then, can be, and has been, interpreted theologically as a structural movement that performs the corrective service of saving the name of God from theology itself—a postmodern, non-appropriable apophatic gesture ridding us of God for the sake of God. However, it can also be, and has been—earlier and more widely—interpreted as a structural movement that simply rids us of God, or rids us of notions of a God behind "God," such that the sign "God" can now be employed more appropriately and less toxically as a name we use for the structural conditions of possibility. These latter interpretive options are advanced as one of deconstruction's ethical contributions to anti-imperialist commitments to embodied life within the radical limits of finitude. And a growing number of theologians are finding it harder and harder to argue against these interpretations.

If it is through the leadership of Kevin Hart and John Caputo, variously related, happily or not, to the Roman Catholic tradition, and then eventually Derrida himself, admitting to "passing" for an atheist to the end, that the deconstructive reconstruction of apophasis has become hip within the classrooms and conference halls of the academic study of religion—across all the messy distinctions attempting to separate, negotiate, and police the nontheological and the theological—this genealogy obviously does not resolve the tension but intensifies it. So, while thinkers from various disciplines have been drawn together with theologians to this conversation out of a shared wariness in relation to bad theology's consequences for embodied life, we bring with us different assumptions about what might constitute good theology in relation to bodies—or whether there even is such a thing.

Not surprisingly, this tension appears less self-consciously in conversations with poststructuralist or indeed postcolonial texts that have no reason to occupy themselves directly with God-talk. For instance, Trinh Minh-Ha, the postcolonial Vietnamese American filmmaker and feminist theorist, kindled the interest of one of us long ago, before any engagement of this arcane dialogue between poststructuralism and historical apophaticism. In that encounter, Trinh was narrating a remote village gathering, a discussion with the women, men, and children, going late into the night, with problems addressed, music played, naps taken. And so much listening. She says of the story that "it never stops beginning or ending. . . . Its (in)finitude subverts every notion of completeness and its frame remains a non-totalizable one."[15] This postcolonial apophasis—mindful of "differences not only in the . . . play of structures and of surfaces, but also in timbre and in silence"—she would later call "critical non-knowingness."[16]

And yet (as the other of us points out), this infinite, this unknowability, is strictly oriented to the inter-human. To read into its opening a mystical divinity, or a postcolonial third space for God, is to burden it with alien concerns. It would not respect Trinh Minh-Ha or theology. It would involve us in a kind of shell-game of language. But yet again (the complexities confronting us here have no end; expectations of a final word will be disappointed), we also recognize Trinh's allusion to the Asian analogue to apophatic theology; interestingly, she ends the above discussion by quoting Laozi, "who used to say, knowing ignorance is strength, ignoring knowledge is sickness."[17] The parallel with Cusa's "knowing ignorance," or *docta ignorantia*, is striking and altogether inadvertent. In the context of this book we cannot adequately pursue the intriguing questions of comparative theology (though Philip Clayton makes an adventurous contribution in this direction). The Asian sense of the ultimate has been perhaps more consistently addressed in apophatic terms, certainly in terms resistant to humanoid projections and anthropomorphic metaphors. "The Dao that can be spoken is not the true Dao." The anthropocentric infinity opens into a greater mystery, inasmuch as it opens into the Dao, the Way. With this transcultural negative tradition in play, it becomes impossible to draw a fixed boundary between an Asian American, secular feminist "critical non-knowingness" and the Western apophatic tradition. The difference remains profound but perhaps just for that reason and in the present global context—porous.

LAST BUT NOT LEAST: APOPHASIS *OF* BODIES

The contributors to this book write their solidarity with bodies very differently from each other—as differently as they approach the traditions and themes, methods and desires of negative theology. Yet they may all be said to be preoccupied with the *crux of embodiment*: the turning point where bodies may be said to emerge into our fields of perception, meaning, language—into a world. At that point, language—our own daily referentialism, or our poetic indirection, or our *theos logos*—makes contact with its world, becomes body, becomes flesh. These authors notice the quantum uncertainty of the transition back and forth between meaning and flesh. And the crux of that oscillation has repercussions for theologians as well as for the historians and philosophers who interpret the effects of theology. For it is not just a matter of an obvious, objectively knowable and therefore readily speakable materiality contrasted, in our presenting enigma, with an unspeakable divinity. None of these authors rehearses a simplistic style of emancipatory materialism.

The promised third notch of heightened tension, then, comes by way of the dissolution of the hierarchically ordered binary—infinity / finitude—that is traditionally assumed to pertain in the relation between incomprehensible divinity and the material, creaturely world. This dissolution is simultaneous with the disorienting yet promising discovery that material embodiment may entail a strange and mysterious infinitude all its own. In other words, the apophatic unsaying that is interrogated and employed in these essays unsays *bodies* too. It speaks away objectifying speech about bodies at the same time and in the same spirit with which it speaks away objectifying speech about God. A materialist positivism may have superseded the claims of positive revelation as culturally hegemonic at a certain stage. It indeed continues to empower itself in resistance to the authoritarian claims of religion. Yet at the same time it may have absorbed the ontotheological—even theolatrous—habit of the absolute. Deification and reification converge. The negativity of negative theology in our current conversation thus cuts against materialist as well as theological positivism (though this is not to suggest an identity without remainder between the possibilities of "positive revelation" and an authoritarian, absolutist theological positivism). This critical resistance of the negative is all the more compelling today given the way in which theological and materialist positivism can be recently seen to overlap, not only in the gross forms of the "name it and claim it" strategy of the so-called prosperity gospel but in the identity politics that progressive Christianity struggles to outgrow. "Apophatic discourse," according to Michael Sells, "yields an open-ended process by which the original assertion of transcendence continually turns back critically upon itself."[18] Analogously, an apophatic body will necessarily turn against the positivism of the current discourse of the body that stimulates our "apophatic body" project in the first place.

The unsaying of the body in the name of the body—like the unsaying of God in the name of God—commissions the apophatic body not only as an enigma but as a concept. Some authors in this volume may unsay apophasis itself less out of fidelity to its own self-implicating discourse and more because they prefer other approaches to mystery, including the unaccountably embodied approach *of* and *by* divine mystery. Yet all articulate some sense of an unspeakable body. All would protect the complex vulnerable bodies from theological, political, or epistemological mastery. Indeed, all might subscribe to a nonparochial version of what Graham Ward in his contribution to the concept of the apophatic body calls "the politics of postmaterialism." The "subtle embodiments" that Patricia Cox Miller finds in Late Antiquity, for example, make contact with the "apophatic bodying" that Roland Faber proposes by reading Whitehead and Deleuze together with the mystical tradition. His reading of the Deleuzian "body without organs" almost parallels Virginia Burrus's and Karmen MacKendrick's "bodies without wholes." These subtle, or in David Miller's theopoetics, "evanescent," bodies morph across our pages into an "apophatic panentheism" in some of our readings—as in Catherine Keller's, of a Renaissance cardinal, or as in Elliot Wolfson's, of a recent kabbalistic master.

That is to say, the trope of apophatic bodies suggests at once a sympathetic retrieval of the subtle panentheism of the mystical negation and its supplementation by contemporary affirmations of materiality. If these concerns are driven by a complex of feminist and ecosocial justice discourses, those discourses still need liberation from the positivisms, the reductionisms, by which the just cause of the material body has been advanced. The unsaying of the body implies an unsaying of the impermeable boundaries and ontological—indeed ontotheological—fixities of a modern body. Yet that body formed itself in reaction to a certain Christian repression—and, complicatedly, as some of us may want to argue, as a repression of a certain Christian affirmation. We would not hope to negate the positivism only in order to return to those particular flesh-negative versions of Christianity that have always accompanied and often overwhelmed that tradition's more affirming resources. The subjugated flesh that modernity at once negates and reproduces will not be emancipated by any simple negations or affirmations.

The deconstructive labors of this volume expose, as in John Caputo's essay, the specifically Christian danger of advancing "bodies without flesh." Indeed the resurrection of a fleshless body may remain not only a Christian self-contradiction but a peculiar risk posed by our own volume's exploration of more subtle, indeed spiritual, bodies. The feminist essays, and in particular that of Sigridur Gudmarsdottir, keep us conscious of the risk of mystical disembodiment—as well as of the risk of a facile feminist dismissal of potentialities that many women find liberating. And from another point of view, we entertain cautionary questions about the ethical limits of deconstruction itself to protect anybody, together with their bodies, and especially the body of the neighbor, the "other" in whose name deconstructive readings are often claimed to be undertaken. Thus Chris Boesel warns of an illusion of epistemological mastery ricocheting right through our finest deconstructions. Yet to heed this warning is not to transcend or even to try to transcend the radical limits of finitude so effectively and persistently—indeed, maddeningly—traced by the non-appropriable movement of deconstruction.

All the essays in this book engage the poststructuralist interest in and challenge to apophatic theology. Indeed we have among us perhaps the single most prolific and influential voice in the current philosophical "return to religion." Caputo's readings of Eckhart may have prepared him to read Derrida and to help Derrida overcome a mere negation of the affinity of deconstruction to negative theology. But no essay in this book acquiesces in the deconstructive potential of apophasis (as deconstruction itself does not acquiesce in deconstruction). In dramatically differing ways and styles, each practices unsaying in order to say better, to construct and to reconstruct, a theory of affirmative embodiment. So the possibility of an iconic body, taking, in our book, Advaita and Jewish as well as Christian incarnational forms, emerges "in the image of the invisible" that Kathryn Tanner proposes.

Readers, of course, will judge for themselves whether the differences both generating and generated by the various tensions entailed in the coupling of apophasis and the body facilitate or impede the continuation beyond this volume of the transdisciplinary conversation which the authors here perform. At the very least, we believe the essays collude in a systematic disruption of the conventional binary opposition of transcendence and materiality; and they conspire by drafting as agents of the disruption historical movements conventionally assumed to carry the dualism. Certainly none of the essays in this volume would pretend to escape or finally resolve the mutually stimulating tensions in which they are here embroiled.

OUTLINING APOPHATIC BODIES: UNFOLDING TRADITIONS OF NEGATIVE THEOLOGY

As the first part of the book demonstrates, our interest in negative theology expresses at once a contemporary theological unfolding of a historical tradition and a contemporary historical unfolding of a theological tradition. We begin indeed with the master text of the fold, that of the early Renaissance *Docta ignorantia*, in which Cusa explicates the idea of God as the infinity that unfolds—*explicatio*—into and as the world of finite bodies, which also gets enfolded—*complicatio*—in God. This pre-empiricist cosmology leaps rather stunningly ahead even of Copernicus and Galileo in its vision of a boundless universe not only *not* earth-centered but *not* sun-centered, and so like the postmodern universe, acentric. Here the panentheism of classical Christianity develops its first systematic reference to the interconnectedness of all bodies within each other and ipso facto within God. Keller reframes Cusa's image of the "cloud of the impossible" as a meditation on the limits of Derridean impossibility in the face of Cusa's own kataphatic image of *posse ipsum*, possibility itself. The aporetic is interrupted by the spiritual porosity of bodies within the material conditions of the "dignified star" Cusa considers the earth to be.

This dignity of a matter capable of divinity was intensively practiced in early Christian asceticism. In her luminous essay, "Subtle Embodiments," Patricia Cox Miller shows how ancient Christian representations of the bodies of saints already dignify "matter" as "a locus of spiritual presence." She investigates the tension between the problem of idolatry, or the overinvestment of bodies with transcendence, and the transfiguring presence of the holy on the human level. Her discovery of the apophatic body in late ancient hagiography contributes not only to the revision of early Christian studies but also to the opening of the "signifying space between transcendence and immanence"—which would be a superb transcription of the signifying space of this entire anthology.

This third space between apophatic excess and its material bodies, between transcendence and immanence, might seem more readable upon the transfigured bodies of saints than in the Neoplatonic texts of their community. Dionysius the Areopagite, sometimes called Pseudo-Dionysius, the apparent originator of negative theology as such, was writing during the same period. Charles Stang makes a compelling argument for reading Dionysius' negative theology, by way of Paul's influence, as negative anthropology. In "Being Neither Oneself nor Someone Else," Stang finds a resonance between the deconstructive displacement of the subject in writing and the Pauline negative anthropology of Dionysius' own authorial subjectivity. The upshot of the argument is the surprising discovery of an affirmation of embodiment, going right against the grain of current critiques of negative theology as simply capitulating to hierarchical hostility to the creaturely body.

INCARNATIONS: BODY/IMAGE

Speaking of subverting hierarchical hostility to the creaturely body, Virginia Burrus and Karmen MacKendrick analyze Augustine's struggle to get his mind around an embodied relation to divinity upon arrival at that faraway country of heavenly rest. The result is a strong case for a bodily excess that Augustine attempts to encompass and comprehend while seeming never to exhaust. Bodies themselves, then, are rendered by Augustine's text as excessive to the point of incomprehensibility, thereby constituting their own apophatic operation of, or upon, language. Burrus and MacKendrick suggest that this is an apophatic operation wherein we as well as God become lost beyond the sayable, in the excessive unsayability of bodies. This bodily apophasis can be seen to resist what is often critiqued as the traditional—including Augustinian—apophatic tendency to denigrate embodiment, with suggestive implications for theological and ethical engagement with the materiality of creation, assumptions about beauty, and discourses desiring repressive control over the body.

Caputo also tackles the difficulties presented by the very notion of a resurrected body, but he focuses on the theological rendering of one resurrected body—that of Jesus of Nazareth. Caputo interrogates the problematic gap between the Christian tradition's accounts of Jesus' resurrected body and the inescapable finitude of material embodiment creatures are resigned to endure while within this mortal coil. Under Caputo's critical gaze, the impossible characteristics of the resurrected body as portrayed by the Christian theological imagination appear to express a desire to escape the limits of embodied finitude. He discerns a desire fundamentally hostile to embodiment, which masquerades as a theological affirmation of the same by way of testimony to bodily resurrection. Caputo calls for a chastened theological imagination that can fully embrace the limits of radically embodied finitude, conceiving "God" as the name for the aporetic structural conditions of that finitude—a postmodern rendering of "God with us"—rather than a Being expressive of hostility toward the mortality born, and shared, by creatures.

Echoing the notion of excess in Burrus and MacKendrick, Kathryn Tanner makes an argument for the openness and plasticity of human being. Tanner takes on the tradition of interpreting the *imago dei* in terms of fixed capacities—in some way characteristic of divinity—possessed by the human being. She proposes a radically relational alternative: human beings are in the image of God because of the unique relation with the divine in which they have been formed. Because the God with whom they are in relation is incomprehensible, the image of that God borne by human beings *is* precisely this incomprehensibility; in human, creaturely form, it constitutes the plasticity of open-ended possibility. *Imago dei* as radical plasticity functions two ways. It preserves divine incomprehensibility by disallowing the possession by human beings of divine likeness in terms of some fixed, permanent capacities. And because the image of God cannot be limited to, for example, the disembodied capacities of rationality and will, Tanner's argument resists the *imago dei* tradition's tendency to undervalue human embodiment, one consequence of which is an overemphasis on human exceptionalism in relation to other creatures.

MORE MYSTERIOUS BODIES: VEILS, VOIDS, VISIONS

Resonating with the themes of excess and plasticity, in Part III we spiral further into the enigmatic space of apophatic bodies, where the body itself seems to volatilize, to become stranger, subtler, more porous. Indeed, it becomes, in David Miller's mesmerizing theopoetics, "incandescent." Reading Bachelard reading Corbin on the Persian poets, he delicately raises, via Wallace Stephens, "no body to be seen." Miller argues that "the body itself is the problem," inasmuch as we try to fix it as an object of theory. On the path of a perspectival and linguistic body, Miller takes us on an eerie little detour. For this volume the detour is home: to the origin of "theopoetics" as a theological perspective, coined by his erstwhile colleague Stanley Hopper, in the context of a set of consultations at the Theological School of Drew University almost half a century ago. If new—and still radical—continental perspectives on language and divinity, poetry and hermeneutics were being considered and constructed, the current context of transdisciplinary theological consultation may perhaps begin to recognize its heritage, its debt, and its possibility.

The incandescence of the imaginal body leaps like a flame to Elliot Wolfson's profound commentary on "the light of the Infinite" in a living lineage of kabbalistic teachers. If the Chabad Lubavitcher tradition had been mistaken by some as little more than a popular messianic movement undergoing distress at the unexpected death of Rabbi Schneerson, its seventh master, Wolfson's disclosure of its brilliant textual tradition definitively lays to rest the misunderstanding. Here, as in the "luminous darkness" of the Areopagite, "light and darkness are made equal" in the

Infinite. Matter does not disappear, but rather the text—itself manifesting the text of the universe, composed of the tetragrammaton—will "transfigure materiality materially." In the play between *ha-olam* (world) and *helem* (concealment) Wolfson discerns an apophatic body "present in the absence of its absence," unveiling in its "feminine" locus a stunning "doctrine of incarnation that is the basis of Habad cosmology."

The mystery of the apophatic body deepens. If in Wolfson we read the "void that renders opposites identical in their opposition," in Roland Faber's essay we read that the "bodies of the void" perform a related dance of apophatic denegation. Faber argues that "apophatic negation works in two directions." While it risks negating the living body, the process of "bodying," it "can also negate what negates the bodying," thereby freeing the body to "an infinite embodying." Finding clues to the apophatic body in Judith Butler, John Damascene, and Cusa, Faber unfolds a conceptual matrix for a radically multiple, vital becoming of the body. It is especially by combining Whitehead's "entirely living nexus" with Deleuze's "body without organs" that he effects a "polyphilic bodying"—which unfolds finally its complicity, indeed its "theoplicity," with the divine apophatic activity.

APOPHATIC ETHICS: WHOSE BODY, WHOSE SPEECH?

Moving our attention from a "theoplicity" to a "theo-polity," Graham Ward attempts to construct a "postmaterialist" metaphysics by way of a theological account of the body politic. He critiques the reduction of the body to sheer materiality as a bad metaphysics, dramatically illustrated by the protagonist of the novel *American Psycho*. Ward finds a philosophical exemplar of this bad metaphysics of materiality in Hegel. Graham gives a critical reading of Hegel's "transcendence made fully immanent" with no remainder of "exteriority," demonstrating how Hegel fails to avoid this metaphysics with regard to the body politic, for example conceiving of the state as absolute religion. Ward then proposes that the Pauline Christic body politic provides the alternative to both *American Psycho* and Hegel, as a good, that is, postmaterialist, metaphysics of the body. Ward makes a strong case for how the Pauline Christic body politic is "apophatic," and so ethically resourceful, in a sense similar to Tanner's plasticity of the *imago dei*. The Christic body, for Ward, is irreducible to any particular, concrete political institution, process, or "throne" of this world, rendering impossible any identification of the state as absolute religion.

Engaging perhaps the most infamous critic of Hegelianism and its ethics of the established order, T. Wilson Dickinson gives a reading of a sermon pseudonymously penned by Kierkegaard. Focusing on its key refrain—that we are "always wrong before God"—Dickinson constructs an argument for a performative apophatics of confession that renders the subject riskily open and vulnerable in love to the divine, distinct from a relation of possession and control characteristic of the account-keeping of the ethical. This performative apophatic subjectivity challenges any medium calculative of ethics fixing and constricting of the open relationality of love within the closure of a metaphysical, speculative medium or of ethics. Dickinson suggests that an apophatic anthropology constitutes a performative doubling/duplicity that always risks complicity with, yet functions to resist, the ways a speculative metaphysics places the subject in a position of ethical mastery. The apophatic subjectivity is opened up to both God and the neighbor, but in distinctive ways, as for example, in joyful praise (to God) and embodied obedience of service (to the neighbor).

Explicating the ethical concern for the well-being of women's bodies, Sigridur Gudmarsdottir engages the differing voices of feminist theology with regard to the apophatic tradition. She cites Beverly Lanzetta's attempt to retrieve the mystical for feminist theology in response to the wariness of feminists toward negative theology's seeming uninterest in the body. While Gudmarsdottir believes Lanzetta's reading of the mystical tradition brings a needed resource to feminist theology that others have missed, she suggests that Irigaray might function as a supplemental corrective to her helpful but limited project, especially with regard to issues of embodiment.

Expressing a certain wariness of his own with regard to contemporary engagements with and employments of the apophatic gesture, Philip Clayton warns of moving too quickly to the apophatic in what he agrees is the ethically necessary critical response to narrowly possessive understandings of divine incarnational presence. While deploring the historical track record of incarnational theologies' (particularly in the case of Christianity) tendency to claim exclusive rights upon divine presence vis-à-vis a particular, locatable Incarnation—here, not there; this One, not that one; ours, not yours—Clayton also cautions against the theological and ethical relativism he believes are risked in the apophatic gesture, especially when seen in opposition to the kataphatic. He proposes a middle way, as it were, a theological rethinking of "knowledge and epistemic limit in a kataphatic context." Clayton employs a comparative reading of a Hindu devotional text and the Pauline *imitatio Christi*, to propose a kenotic epistemology of incarnational humility—the sign-post marking the way of a self-critical kataphasis necessary to any movement toward the apophatic.

LOVE STORIES: UNSPEAKABLE RELATIONS, INFINITE FREEDOM

The book concludes with several chapters that take the traditional issue of divine incomprehensibility and place it explicitly within the context of a love relation, tracking the consequences for an apophatic engagement with creaturely limits while keeping an eye on traditional habits of epistemological reduction and hierarchical ontology. Taking the deconstructive engagement with negative theology as a starting point, Chris Boesel notes that, in the "turn" to religion, practitioners of deconstruction express an apophatic desire of their own: a desire to save both the name of God and the creaturely neighbor from the clutches of human mastery. In response to certain deconstructive voices critical of negative theology for falling short in relation to this twofold desire, Boesel asks if an alternative theological tradition—the Reformation's evangelical focus on the freedom of divine word and deed as distinct from the infinity of divine being and essence—might constitute surprisingly fertile textual soil for deconstructive engagement with theology. Boesel borrows a mischievous Kierkegaardian thought experiment about a god who gives herself to be known in and for the sake of love to test the apophatic possibilities of free divine self-giving for the preservation of both divine mystery and neighborly integrity from the grasp of human mastery.

In keeping with the theme of divine-human love stories, Rose Ellen Dunn gives a phenomenological reading of the New Testament account of the Annunciation as a divine-human embrace in the union of love. She interprets this union as an apophatic moment of "letting be"—*Gelassenheit*—that transcends and transgresses the limits of language. Dunn employs Irigaray's work to read this moment of letting be as an event of egalitarian, interpenetrating, interdependent mutuality between the divine and human. This reading entails a feminist ethics of empowerment, as Mary is rendered a mutually active and agential partner with the divine in this co-creative event. In Mary's turn to Elizabeth, Dunn shows how her unity of mutuality with the divine spills over into and includes the embodied relation to the neighbor.

Krista Hughes opens her essay with another kind of love story. Hélène Cixous articulates the incomprehensibility of her very human lover, a flesh-and-blood creature ever escaping her attempts to render the lover in language. Hughes brings this passage from Cixous into confrontation with the Christian mystical tradition's tendency to leave out the body by focusing on the incomprehensibility of the divine, in radical alterity to the creature, as that which renders language limited and apophatics necessary. Hughes notes that the women mystics remedy this blind spot by setting the divine-human relation in the context of intimate love, which includes the body and the world of human-human relations in a more robustly incarnate vision. However, where the fulfillment of this divine-human love relation seems to ultimately eclipse the integrity of the human (woman) partner, and with it the embodied world, Hughes argues that the work of Cixous can function as a theologically fruitful supplement. Cixous may offer a vision of an embodied apophatic of intimate love that preserves the embodied integrity of both partners while rendering a poetics that might inform the speech of theology.

BEYOND THIS TEXTUAL BODY

Finally, then, apophatic bodies always signify at least the carnal reality, the spatiotemporal perspective, of anyone who is unsaying anything: the body, for instance, of the apophatic mystic. But that perspective turns knowingly upon itself, at the crux of embodiment, at the point where the inexhaustible excess, ever exceeding language, swerves into word even as word turns into flesh. The titular phrase retains its enigma within this volume, though an array of variously firm decisions and commitments will accompany it. It thus opens an interdisciplinary space, a space not mapped by disciplines so much as by decisions, a third space, indeed possibly a bit of *khora* or *chaosmos*—a space between the transcendently theological apophatic One and the immanent plurality of bodies. The many decisions of this book will not fall into line, we shall see. They will not evaporate into the undecidable but will breathe within its opening.

They will form the body of this text, and as such they will form a complex body, a body without a fixed center (this should be clear by now!), without a hierarchy of separate organs, perhaps even in Faber's sense a "polyphilic body."

The apophatic body project is part, indeed the sixth phase, of a series of annual symposia on the transdisciplinary potential of theological discourse. Sometimes biblical criticism, comparative religion or literature, sociology of religion, ecological and social ethics, feminist and queer, political and postcolonial theory have provided the main interlocutions. For the present consultation, theologically engaged philosophers and historians, ancient and medieval, joined a majority of theologians. At the originating event of conversation, the pauses—themselves palpable, full of listening and uncertainty, doubt and disclosure—did not swallow the words. We chattered and we stammered. But the words, which have been fruitful and multiplied in the subsequent silence, we now expectantly share.

Negative Theology: Unfolding Traditions

The Cloud of the Impossible: Embodiment and Apophasis

CATHERINE KELLER

Therefore I thank you . . . because you make clear to me that there is no other way of approaching you except that which to all humans, even to the most learned philosophers, seems wholly inaccessible and impossible. For you have shown me that you cannot be seen elsewhere than where impossibility confronts and obstructs me.
NICHOLAS OF CUSA, *De visione Dei*

*What would a path be without aporia? Would there be a way (*voie*) without what clears the way there where the way is not opened . . . ? Would there be a way without the necessity of deciding there where the decision seems impossible?*
JACQUES DERRIDA, "Sauf le nom"

THANKS FOR THE IMPOSSIBLE?

"Apophatic bodies." for instance. The phrase verges on the oxymoronic, lacking the oppositional elegance of, say, "languages of unsaying" or "brilliant darkness." Its multiplying bodies obstruct the path of a cleaner deconstruction, let alone the way of a higher negation. Just so it confronts us. We can't all be expected to voice a fifteenth-century Cusan enthusiasm: "[T]he more that cloud of impossibility is recognized as obscure and impossible, the more truly the necessity shines forth."[1]

Apophatic theology has little to (un)say about bodies, whereas it speaks volumes about that which it deems worthy of unsaying.[2] Bound inextricably to a Neoplatonic vector of transcendence, it treats bodies generally not as wicked or repulsive, but as sites of obstruction, suffering, distraction.[3] Left to its own devices, the negative way does not write a language of the body, of bodies in their multiplicity of fragile finitudes, but of the oneness of the infinite. By contrast, theologies that privilege the body—bodies in their own right, everybody, through and beyond the one exceptional incarnation—appear recent and raw. They voice such a confrontational worldliness that their passions appear foreign to the moods and motives of apophatic mysticism. Or obstructive.

Their suspicion about the conversation embodied in the present volume can be expressed through a paraphrase of a familiar rhetoric: Is it an accident that just as certain groups marked as bodies, long silenced for their bodily difference, begin to find voice within theological institutions a mysticism of transcendent silence becomes trendy? Since feminist theology as a collective comprises a critical mass of that body-affirming movement, and since some of us are also dangerously attracted to the apophatic way, the cloud of the impossible engulfs the present exploration from the start. Thankfully.

Of course these theologies that unfold contemporary interest in the body do not normally attend to embodiment as such, in its cosmological or biophysical dynamism, so much as to the systems, social and ecclesial, that enmesh everybody in networks of power, giving some bodies speech while withholding it from others. I for one would have no theological voice (*voix*) or way (*voie*) without these twentieth-century identity movements. They have called attention to the needs, the desires, the contexts of our constructed materialities; to the humiliations that distribute crucifixion more freely than any eucharist. In theological form they remain indelibly plural, solidaristic but stubborn in their differences, forming an inharmonious chorus that has too few or too many proper names: liberation, Black, feminist, womanist, mujerista, gay, and lesbian theologies. Each named God (S/He/It) anew, in the wounded image of a barely possible subject. As those identities became constricting, inhospitable to coalition, new names appeared: contextual, ecological, postcolonial, queer, counter-imperial theologies, a bit abstracted from the originary movements and infected by poststructuralism, yet bent on social change. The clumsiness of trying to name this rapidly shifting spectrum unavoidably besets all mainline theology. (Eco-social-feminist-euroamerican-postcolonial-poststructuralist process theology? Is that what "I" do?) This persistent intensity of politics and spirit, its self-naming as well as its own names for God bursting with conflictual revelation, may drive any theologian to the *via negativa*. Yet its rhetorical intensity, full of cultural negation, arguably has performed—by other names—its own apophasis.[4]

It may have been the considerable late twentieth-century Christian reaction against our unsaying of "God the Father" that surfaced a conscious feminist affinity with negative theology.[5] This affinity in turn exposes an aporia of "the body" itself. As feminist thought outgrows our sanguine "My Body/Myself" positivism, along with our victim-identification on the one hand and a callow erotic privilege on the other, the politically charged ways of "the body" (straight or not) have become ever less straightforward. The body becomes, we might say, cloudier. Distributed in its multiplicity of movements, disseminated by the discourse of poststructuralism, the decisive outlines of this body become hazy. The residues of an unproblematized, fixed Nature subdivided into smooth modern bodies break down. Early in this process, Luce Irigaray, exploring the folds of a "sensible transcendental," began to seek a spiritual flesh of the feminine, finding clues in medieval mystics.[6] On another path, Judith Butler early recognized the self-implicating elusiveness of the object of *Bodies That Matter*: "What about the materiality of the body, Judy?" When "woman" becomes "a permanent site of contest," we are on the way of an aporia.[7] Yet this contest offers no relief from the need to act, from—*pace* Derrida—the necessity of deciding. Thus the later Butler, in affinity with the Hegelian negativity, theorizes "moments of unknowingness" about oneself, any self, as a subject constituted in relations.[8] What makes bodies *matter* after all? At the edges of all the twentieth-century movements of emancipatory materialism, a haze of uncertainty—not unrelated to quantum indeterminacy, as we will see—surrounds the mattering body.

As such theoretical complications of the body slow down to the speed of theology—which, unlike faith, always comes after theory—might we recognize this unsaying of the body as a theological opportunity? Might such a connection, a fold linking the body-affirmative theologies (which never claimed to know it all anyway) and the mystical negation (which never stopped knowing its All) enhance the possibility of theology itself, now? Indeed, of an incarnation *that matters?* Might it strengthen the project of a widened incarnationalism—the development of a theology, even a Christian theology, that would not reduce the boundless diversity of bodies to that One and only Body that matters? Or does the apophatic gesture always already sweep the incarnational possibility, the chance for the enlivening of *every* body, into divine nothingness and human silence? Perhaps only a staunch, doubtless feminist, anachronism can loosen the mystical tradition from the bonds of its Neoplatonic, body-transcending patriarchy. It will at any rate not help in the present context to evade the tension between the progressive sensibilities of the "theologies that matter"[9] and the archaicism of the mystical unknowing. For the positive reading of the body privileges all the finite bodies of the creation, while the negative way finds everywhere the infinite.

Before such a daunting impasse, Nicholas of Cusa oddly appears as a mediator both of method and of content. He would plunge us not into an empty chasm but into "the cloud of impossibility." For it is there, where we acknowledge whichever aporia besets us, where we face our doubt, our incapacity, and our indecision, that we find ourselves in his language "at the wall": at a place "girded about by the coincidence of contradictories."[10] This *coincidentia oppositorum*, Cusa's condensed early Renaissance contribution to European thought, signifies in its impossibility both the impassable wall and the passage through it. I am suggesting that we imagine apophatic bodies as a fresh instance of the *coincidentia*. For here the method of *docta ignorantia*, knowing ignorance, folds into the dazzling affirmativity of his material cosmology.

Reading this abstruse cardinal of the earliest Renaissance rather closely, I consider in this essay the apophatic radicalism of his knowing ignorance. Does its specific negativity coincide in any meaningful sense with the current work of a positive theology of embodiment? Moving then through Cusa's negative infinity, as through a chiasmus, to its own affirmative side, we may discern a place for all bodies, a cosmological depth of both mystical theopoetics and progressive theopolitics. If the becoming-theologies of embodiment are to fulfill their own promise, indeed even to remain credible to their own authors, a dose of negative theology laced with deconstruction will tender, I suggest, a needed tonic. Far from silencing the outbursts of historically oppressed and unspeakable bodies, it might help us anew, to echo Nelle Morton, to "hear one another to speech."[11] Conversely, an earthier embrace of our diversely bodied creatureliness might call the mystical radiance out from under its bushel. The concurrence of apophasis and embodiment might then turn out to be no accident but a coincidence indeed: not an inevitability, not an impossibility, but an aporia turned porous. Like a cloud.

FOOD OF THE MATURE

In *De visione Dei,* Cusa pores over the aporia of the apparently impossible. "Hence, I experience how necessary it is for me to enter into the cloud and to admit the coincidence of opposites, above all capacity of reason, and to seek there the truth where impossibility confronts me."[12] This truth does not lie there waiting to be recognized, believed, had. It can *only* be sought in the cloud of contradictions. This aporetic truth challenges such familiar Neoplatonic oppositions as the eternal and the temporal, the infinite and the finite, the invisible and the visible. Apophasis and embodiment would count as such a pair. But Cusa's metaphors emit an existential intensity. This truth might take place wherever "the haze of indefiniteness with which decision must daily cope," as John Caputo puts it, becomes suddenly irrepressible.[13] The *necessity* of entering the "cloud of impossibility" is no mere metaphysical inevitability, but an all too familiar experience. Oppositions not only between warring ideas or conflicting doctrines but also between commitments, constituencies, and strategies obstruct me, when both poles *matter* to me, when both make a legitimate claim (as, say, in a classroom, between an evangelical Protestantism pushing toward progressive politics and an exploratory dance in the Nietzschean vortex; as in my church, between the priorities of combating poverty and homophobia). If we do not cling to a certainty whose oppositional purity we doubt anyway, we enter the Cusan cloud. Then we may relinquish the binary structure of the impasse itself.

Yet if we glimpse here a third way, a passage, it is a troubling one: "O Lord, you, who are the food of the mature, have given me courage to do violence to myself, for impossibility coincides with necessity, and I have discovered that the place where you are found unveiled is girded about with the coincidence of contradictories."[14] Strange apophatic eucharist: to feed on God in order to do violence to myself. How inviting is that?

Not that Cusa is speaking of mortifying the flesh (he does not; this is no hero for Opus Dei). His cloud is a complex metonymy of tropes about language, about epistemology. But when invited to hurt myself, my feminism raises its contrary head. "Communication," I then recall Karmen

MacKendrick musing, "occurs in bodies and in words too, in speaking and in the contact that requires an *impossible intersection* of impenetrable surfaces—that requires that we be cut open." The more sealed the boundaries of some established binary, the more violent their rupture. Poststructuralism, she elaborates, makes commonplace reference to cutting, wounding, laceration. Yet "it is hard to conventionalize what is always, definitionally, displacing and fragmenting, from which some measure of violence seems inextricable." A reading may be a rending, and "each rendition a violent tear in the stability, the solid fixed stolidity of language."[15] Of course to face one's own constitutive opacities and contradictions is, in Butler's later language, to come undone. Courage bolstered, I return to Cusa. For the promise of an impossible intersection seems to confront us within the porous cloud—just where the impermeable wall of contradictions looms.

The wall Cusa here is storming is the very "wall of paradise." He is seeking truth—"where you are found unveiled." Surely such unveiling, such conceptual *apokalypsis,* is the sort of truth that deconstruction deconstructs. So how would Cusa's sense of the obstruction amount to what for us is "the solid fixed stolidity of language"? It might, if we substitute for that fixity what in his day was called "reason." "The wall's gate is guarded by the highest spirit of reason, and unless it is overpowered, the way in will not lie open."[16] So the violence that is the gift of a mature spirituality (truly an acquired taste, this apophatic food) signifies the "overpowering" of our most entrenched logic, that is, of the rules of sociolinguistic construction that write our bodies, our selves. That "highest spirit"—Cusa's ironic allusion to Michael at the gate of paradise—invokes the late medieval reason, high indeed on its Aristotelian, Platonic, Catholic, and now early humanist confidence. Cusa himself embodied famously its mathematical and argumentative capacities.[17] For us those fixed stolidities may not be as high, its reason as spirited. It may indeed cave rather quickly under the pressures of postmodernism, which has produced some tenured guardian spirits of its own. However, by pressing through the contradiction between a too facile deconstruction and a stereotype of ontotheology, Cusa's self-critical violence seems to take on a deconstructive aura.

Might the wall suggest for us then, by way of what we must call a mindful anachronism, the deconstruction of whichever binaries immure our own thinking? Mystical unsaying and bodily voice, impossibility and the possible, deconstruction and theology? Cusa's painfully obstructive wall morphs, in that moment where conventional oppositions are recognized as constructions, into the momentarily open "wall of paradise." Within the cloud, the revelation of the closure is the opening. The wall becomes for a moment penetrable as a cloud.

If that opening however is reified, doctrinalized, stabilized, it forfeits its truth. It loses its radical edge. If it gets dislodged from Cusa's negative theology, the *coincidentia* may appear as some proto-Hegelian dialectic of necessary opposites, or proto-Jungian occidentalization of yin and yang.[18] "This cloud, mist, darkness or ignorance into which whoever seeks your face enters when one leaps beyond every knowledge and concept." With this chain of apophatic metonyms, Cusa links the *De visione Dei* back to the great engine of his earlier work, *De docta ignorantia* (1440). The "learned ignorance" comprises the epistemological register of the coincidence of opposites. And it may offer the most lucid definition of negative theology within the Christian corpus:

> Therefore the theology of negation is so necessary to the theology of affirmation that without it God would not be worshiped as the infinite God but as creature; and such worship is idolatry, for it gives to an image that which belongs only to truth itself.[19]

De docta ignorantia encodes the radicality of the apophatic gesture, heir at this point more to the Hebrew prophets than the speculative Platonists; its critique of idols is rooted in the Mosaic narrative as surely as Gregory of Nyssa's early apophatic exegesis of the "dark cloud."[20] And, as in the prophetic tradition, it aims principally at its own context. Here it is directed against the standard language of Christianity. Cusa's mimicry of the syntax of "give to Caesar" hints at the power dynamics and truth regime of the idolatry which would most concern him as a successful cardinal and reformer high in the ecclesial hierarchy. This negativity is not adequately characterized as iconoclasm—for the problem lies not with images themselves, not with personal metaphors, analogies, attributions, let alone icons, which Cusa found indispensable as hermeneutical devices.[21] But we are wondering anachronistically whether it can be called deconstruction and, in particular, a deconstruction helpful to the ongoing work, at once iconoclastic and iconoplastic, of feminist theology.

NEITHER THE ONE NOR THE OTHER NOR BOTH

The relation of deconstruction and negative theology needs here only a misty summation. It "is not that deconstruction is a form of negative theology but that negative theology is a form of deconstruction."[22] Deconstruction is not apophatic mysticism but has been irreversibly drawn into its cloud, whereas apophasis may be said to perform deconstruction *avant la lettre*. The latter is preoccupied with the God *avant la lettre, Dieu avant Dieu*, the God before truth, therefore captured in no truth claim. In the *Dialogue of the Hidden God* Cusa has his "Pagan" voice ask: "Is God truth?" "No," his "Christian" voice answers, "but God precedes all truth."[23] Whereas according to Caputo, "Deconstruction comes not . . . 'before' or 'over' faith, but after God."[24] The avant-God is not interchangeable with this après Dieu. The "after" already glosses the Derridean "without," the Dieu *sans* Dieu. Yet as Derrida gradually acknowledged, his "*Dieu sans Dieu*," who precedes and negates all language of God, is not alien to the God of Eckhart and Silesius.

Nonetheless the apophatic negation always releases something more than negation. That "more" may (or may not) hyperousiologically reinflate the changeless Truth that deconstruction lives to deconstruct.[25] However incomprehensibly, a truth is shining forth, a You is "found unveiled." The "truth itself"—does this language subserve the power drives of the apophatic theologian himself? Caputo gently warns that "in one of its voices, its most authoritative," negative theology "crowns the representations of metaphysics with the jewel of pure presence."[26] In the history of theology this truth can fall only before, *avant*, deconstruction, in the archaic and yet unrealized direction of an indeconstructible assumption, the pre/sumption of what we still might name "God."[27] Rosenzweig puts the paradox precisely: "Of God we know nothing; but this ignorance is ignorance of God."[28] Perhaps the following methodological *coincidentia* will hold: If a deconstructive apophasis calls into question its own *saying* of God, so an apophatic deconstruction will question its own *unsaying* of God.

If Cusa lacks the poetry of Silesius or the provocative pith of Eckhart, the discursive effect of the *docta ignorantia* is no less radical. It does not fail to turn upon itself. The above dialogue continues with Cusa's Pagan, perplexed by the refusal to identify God with anything nameable as true or truth, asking: "Do you not name God 'God'? *Christian*: We do. *Pagan*: Are you saying something true or something false? *Christian*: Neither the one nor the other nor both."[29] This self-implicating logic—with no influence from its Zen contemporaries!—displays the performative intensity by which Michael Sells distinguishes "apophatic discourse" from "apophatic theory."[30]

Indeed Cusa's apophatic logic performs an infinite deconstruction, spun from the negativity of the in/finite itself. As the infinite, that "object" autodeconstructs, possesses no predicates, cannot be possessed even as truth: "[N]othing other than infinity is found in God. Consequently negative theology holds that God is unknowable either in this world or in the world to come." This negation never erases, it merely relativizes the traditional affirmations.[31] Saving God from the positivism of faith, it would save orthodoxy—an orthodoxy in which Cusa, like Silesius or Pseudo-Dionysius, is immersed—from its own closure.[32] Casting all the personal names of God on the waters of unknowing, it receives them back manifold. For the infinite unfolds into the bodily manifold of the world. In the sun it is what the sun is, in persons what a person is, that is, personal.[33] Thus—precisely at the fold of embodiment—it exceeds its own impersonality: "I see that *you* are infinity itself."[34] Cusa often shifts into the second person appellative—a "you" rather than an *it* or a *he*. We are invited to relate to the incomprehensible infinite not in ignorance of our own ignorance of its unknowability—but as a *you* nonetheless.

"SHE" MATTERS

The pronoun "she," needless to say, did not need to be unsaid. Indeed the semantic force field linking mystical apophasis to a deconstructive demystification is considerably stronger than any intra-Christian fold between feminism and the male mystics. The thrusting of the "she" as both subject and object of theology—quite apart from the subsequent deconstructions of subjects and their objects—into the discourse of God stimulates an unavoidable bodily difference, if not dismay. Nonetheless the power of Elizabeth Johnson's *She Who Is* springs from its feminist recourse to the negative tradition. Exposing as idolatry not all masculine images of God but their deployment "exclusively, literally, and patriarchally," she insists on the divine *mystery* as no other feminist or theologian of embodiment had done.[35] She draws mainly on Thomas of Aquinas (whose *via negativa* may more properly fit Sells's characterization of apophatic theory) and has the strategic advantage of an unquestionable orthodoxy. His Aristotelianism helps her to leverage a positive evaluation of embodiment that would remain occluded by the Neoplatonism of more radically apophatic thinkers, at least before Cusa.[36] Johnson's interest has been to move beyond every negation (either political or mystical) into the inauguration of alternative affirmations. Yet already in the oracular teachings of Nelle Morton in the late 1970s, such iconoplastic innovations came accompanied by the iconoclastic proviso that these female images can in turn also become idols if rendered absolute.

The ability to denounce theological idolatry in rigorously Christian terms is the *sine qua non* of the feminist and other body-affirmative incarnationalisms. Yet these movements in theology have drawn their motive force mainly from the Hebrew prophetic tradition and from its New Testament and then secular offshoots. Only with the Roman Catholic and mystically tinged work of Johnson did the iconoclasm of feminist theology get systematically linked to the *via negativa*. Yet we saw above in the example of Cusa the convergence of the prophetic denunciation of idols with apophatic discourse. This is not the context for an exploration of the relations of feminist thought to mysticism or to apophasis.[37] I am wanting to surface the depth relation between the apophatic discourse and the wide affirmation of embodiment of which in U.S. theology feminism has been one, perhaps the major, manifestation.

This widened incarnationalism in its contemporary form has unfolded an ecological vision so pressing as to morph a critical mass of feminist theology into *ecofeminist* theology.[38] So—despite the powerful influence of the "denaturalizing" impulse of Butler and the generally acosmic discourse of poststructuralism—we have witnessed the surprising translation of the linguistic and institutional anthropocentrism of an earlier feminism into the currency of a cosmology tuned to the environmental crisis, to the postcolonial potential Gayatri Spivak calls "planetarity."[39] The tensions internal to feminist theory, needless to say, remain forceful, drawing us ever again to the edges of language. Perhaps we are learning to pause at that edge as at Cusa's wall, to enter that cloud, despite its costs, with curiosity and occasional gratitude. I am suggesting that if the finite body and the apophatic infinite will fruitfully coincide, after long contradiction, it may be because of a peculiar opening in Cusa's wall: not into God *tout court*, but into the space of the creation, not as a singular event but as an eventive cosmos.

FOLDOUT GOD

Piercing the wall of contraries, Cusa proceeds to violate the principal boundary of classical theism, that between the creator and the creation. To pick up where we left him off: "I see that you are infinity itself. Therefore, there is nothing that is other than, or different from, or opposite you."[40] For if God is infinite—or at least not what Hegel would dub a bad infinite—how can we conceive of any boundary where God ends and the world begins? But God's difference is not diminished but heightened in this meditation. The infinite is so different, so other, from any and all creatures as to be *non aliud*, not-other.[41] Aha, one mutters, whether in inquisitorial or conspiratorial glee: pantheism after all. But the apophatic engine is roaring, with a rather formidable logic of its own. "Infinity is incompatible with otherness; for since it is infinity, nothing exists outside it. . . . [I]nfinity . . . exists and enfolds all things and nothing is able to exist outside it. Consequently, nothing exists that is infinity's other."[42]

In other words once you grant the altogether orthodox proposition of the divine infinity you might choose to skirt around its implications by simply abstracting it from its spatial and therefore cosmic associations. Or you might, like Cusa, explicate from it a universe. His universe—all creatures, all bodies, the universe of bodies—unfolds from the divine infinity even as all beings and things within it are simultaneously enfolded. "God, therefore, is the enfolding [*complicatio*] of all in the sense that all are in God, and God is the unfolding [*explicatio*] of all in the sense that God is in all."[43] Cusa's *complicatio/explicatio* order comprises the heart of his doctrine of creation, his theo-cosmology. The folding together of all bodies in the infinite is their complication—which is explicated in the finite bodies of the world. Thus the "explicit complications" express the inseparability of God and the world in their very distinctness from each other.[44] Its semantic oscillation of enfolding/unfolding at once reflects and enacts the asymmetrical fluctuation of affirmation/negation.[45]

The dynamism of folds is Cusa's riff on Plato's concept of participation. God then *is* not all things, God *is* not the universe—except in this restricted sense of the copula: when something is *in* God, it participates in God, and so it is *part* of God. For God in the presumed ontology remains always simple, one, noncomposite. Cusa does not question that presumption so much as twist it outside in. As "in a stone all things are stone . . . in hearing all are hearing . . . in reason all reason . . . and in God all are God. And now you see how the unity of things, or the universe, exists in plurality and, conversely, how plurality exists in unity."[46] This I do see: in the stone the organism has become fossil; in my hearing all things register as sounds; in my mind you dwell as a thought. But you remain still *other* than my thought, a sound, or a fossil, indeed registered as other within the internal relation of the thought, the sound, the stone. The universe as *un*folded, is not-God; but as *en*folded in God *is* God. For that which participates in God cannot by the classical presumption be a composition of separable *parts*. Otherwise God would be an aggregate. The slippage of language toward pantheism is, it seems, ironically necessitated by the dual orthodox convention of God's noncomposite and infinite nature! Only by failing to think these attributes together does classical Christianity maintain its dualism of creator and creation.

In other words, the apophatic proximity to heresy may be described as an effect of orthodox logic pushed to its own limit. Unity can no longer be opposed to plurality, if it is the divine one; nor by the same logic can the creator be disentangled from the creation. The classical Christian apparatus of divine as opposed to other "natures" rests on the metaphysics of substance, the essence of "reason." Cusa can destabilize, even deconstruct—via the *coincidentia*—the indivisible unity of a changeless essence. If he stepped neatly *out* of ontotheology he could no longer "overpower" the guardian angel of eternal truth. The repeated risk of anathema evinces the chutzpah—Cusa's "violence to myself"—of his unsayings of such unquestionable presuppositions: "the courage and the dissidence, potential or actual," as Derrida says of the apophatic masters.[47]

The boundary of creator and creature comprises not just a nonnegotiable premise of classical orthodoxy but, trickily, the wall of resistance of orthodoxy to its own Platonism. Derrida, contemplating Silesius, senses this tension. "But isn't it more difficult to replatonize or rehellenize creationism?" Remarking that "creationism" (the mimicry of the language of U.S. fundamentalism may be inadvertent) "belongs to the logical structure of a good many apophatic discourses," he notes the images of God's pouring forth "in creation" *(ins Geschoepf)*. Indeed this pouring, the *bullitio* or boiling and bubbling over, in Eckhart would have influenced Cusa's *explicatio* (though his cosmology is dramatically more embodied, more physical, than Eckhart's). Derrida then wonders—with a gesture toward modern materialism—if this might signify, "in place of being a creationist dogma, that creation means expropriating production and that everywhere there is ex-appropriation there is creation." On that rather opaquely emancipatory note he pivots into a meditation on the "*n'importe,*" the serene "it doesn't matter," of Eckhart's *Gelazenheit*.[48] Derrida turns the mystical indifference back on the question of creation itself. The radicality of the aporia of creation in the apophatic heritage is passed over; cosmology does not matter (here, yet) in deconstruction, not even in its warmer affirmations of a shared negativity.[49] And indeed with Eckhart one cannot yet trust the possibility of an ecologically hospitable cosmology.

What if we were to linger over the aporia of the infinite and the creation as though it does in fact matter? *N'importe quoi:* the in/difference, the non-aliud, of equality: all things matter, no matter which. Cusa equalizes all things, which matter all-together, in the apophatic divinity. "For the being of creation cannot be other than a resplendence, but not a resplendence positively received in something other but one which is *contingently different.*"[50] The "contingent difference" signifies Cusa's attempt to keep the difference of creator/creature, of the infinite and its bodies, without reifying it. In such passages, clogged by the metaphysics of substance, startling observations continue to occur. "The infinite form is received [unfolded] only in a finite way." This reception refers to his argument against the platonic, mediating hierarchy of forms in favor of the "equality of being." Consequently, "every creature is, as it were, a *finite infinity or a created god.*"[51]

Lo: bodies appear on the stage of apophasis. Their finitude blazes with the aura of the infinite. Perhaps anachronistically reverberating with this metaphysical affirmation is the protest on behalf of current bodies: of bodies humiliated as female or disabled, gay or dark; bodies human and nonhuman threatened with mass extinction. All of them, every body, all creatures, appear here in an ontological equality amid difference, "as much like God as possible."[52] Not just prelapsarian human beings in *imago dei*. These finite infinities, all embodied in one another and in God, make up the universe. God—as "the absolutely maximum" (Cusa's loan from Anselm) is "negatively infinite." By contrast the universe "embraces all the things that are not God," so it "cannot be negatively infinite, although it is *boundless* and thus privatively infinite, *and in this respect it is neither finite nor infinite*."[53] The universe is not negatively (divinely, absolutely) infinite but boundless, a virtual but not an actual infinity. The confrontation with Christian "creationism" can hardly be exaggerated.

The potential of the apophatic tradition to support the resymbolization of materiality appears most concretely in its relation to natural science. "Our bodily eye findeth never an end, but is vanquished by the immensity of space. . . . There is in the universe neither center nor circumference. For our bodily eye findeth never an end, but is vanquished by the immensity of space presented before it, and confused and overcome by the myriads of stars ever multiplying, so that our perception remaineth uncertain and reason is forced to add space to space, region to region, world to world."[54] Thus said Bruno, repeating Cusa's line of thought. Our prosthetic eyes still find never an end of this universe. The expanding immensity threatens us today with a nihilism from which the inquisitors of the sixteenth century tried to protect us. Over a century after the cardinal died in an honored old age, Bruno would burn at the stake for the claim of the universe's infinity and its pantheistic implication.[55] Cusa had proposed precisely this radical decentering of the universe: "[T]he world machine will have, one might say, its center everywhere and its circumference nowhere." Recall that neither Copernicus a hundred years, nor then Galileo two hundred years later, had gone beyond setting the earth to spin around a fixed sun; they had not decentered the cosmos, nor yet put every one of its bodies in motion. Cusa leaps light-years ahead in his vision of a centerless cosmos, in which every body is in perpetual motion around the center which is everywhere. Of course it is

Cusa's mysticism as much as his math that allows him to conceive of this boundless and centerless cosmos: "[F]or its circumference and center is God, who is everywhere and nowhere."[56] Moreover, the Cusan boundlessness (the contingent or "contracted" rather than negative infinity) may be read as anticipating the conundrums of cosmic immensity characteristic of contemporary astrophysics, with its speculations on the inflationary universe, the multiverse, the mind-busting quantities that constitute various *relative* infinities. If it exercised little influence on the course of modern science, Cusa's cosmology may be all the more suggestive now, as science explores the irreducible uncertainty at the edges of its own comprehensibility.[57]

While science has been newly encountering bottomless mystery (whether in the form of quantum weirdness, spooky action at a distance, dark matter, dark energy, or the cosmic vibrations of string theory), theology has during the same century adventurously reconnected to science. All the while the Punch and Judy show of scientific versus fideistic positivisms intensifies, fueling the culture wars where fundamentalist mistrust of evolutionary science has bolstered corporate resistance to ecological reform: a great contemporary cloud of the impossible. I sense that the passageway from the negative infinity to the boundlessness of the universe has strategic potential. It may at least help us make ourselves at home spiritually in our runaway galaxy universe, 93 billion light-years across. For the learned ignorance lets the universe be read as a finite "image" of the infinite—not a faceless totality but a mysterious infinity. In a Christian context, we may with Cusa address this infinity appellatively, doxologically, as You, God, triune Love. It may thereby support the delicate work of translation between science and religion needed for the rescue both of democracy and ecology.

The *coincidentia oppositorum* of the infinite and the finite suggests a spiritual discipline of suspended certainty, in which the space of the cosmological imagination may reopen.[58] That space calls into the cloud the reductionisms of mere bodies in a void, to be exploited, pampered, or ignored. And at the same time it obstructs the inflation of disembodied minds rising to the Eternal. How does the enfolding of the universe in God and the unfolding of God in the universe, cultivate a greater *intercreaturely* solidarity? Not without quantum leaps of translation. Why bother, wonders a theology of embodiment? *Qu'importe?* The answer lies in the entangled interrelatedness—at once social, ecological, and cosmological—of all creatures. Or as Cusa recognizes, perhaps before any other theologian, "that all are in all and each is in each."[59] This vision of the radical interdependence of all creatures as entailed by the God/world relation—and vice versa—constitutes an achingly rare theologoumenon:

> Since the universe is contracted in each actually existing thing, it is obvious that God, who is in the universe, is in each thing and each actually existing thing is immediately in God, as is the universe. *Therefore, to say that "each thing is in each thing" is not other than to say that "through all things God is in all things" and that "through all things all are in God."*[60]

Cusa has in this passage put apophatic bodies into language. Busting through the wall of the impossible, into the coincidentia of complication and explication, Cusa opens at the same time a *multiplex* spatiality of folds. Everybody is in every body; but no one body is the same as any other, nor could "each thing . . . be actually all things." For this reason, he argues, "there is a diversity and a connection of things."[61] Evident as the plural connections of matter may be, it is rare that this diversity and this connection *mattered* in theology, let alone materialized in and as God. "That all are in all and each is in each" does not pose a foreign thought for ecofeminist theology, which draws on various panentheisms, on the metaphor of the universe as God's body, or on process cosmology.[62] Whitehead, a mathematical cosmologist involved in the earliest cultural explication of quantum and relativity theories, put it thus: "[I]n a certain sense everything is everywhere at all times."[63] He thus spookily prepared the way for the quantum physicist David Bohm's implicate order—apparently named in innocence of Cusa. In distinction to the explicate, Cartesian order, "in terms of the implicate order one may say that everything is enfolded into everything."[64]

All in all and each in each: this vision perhaps only comes into its exoteric own now that we see it all too physically, in a de/faced negativity. Our species has in the meantime so aggressively lodged itself "in each thing" that each molecule in the earth's atmosphere is now affected by our CO_2 emissions. We are folding into each thing with violence, and all things are unfolding back into us with menace.

The willful ignorance—the know-it-all ignorance that ignores its own ignorance—cuts down that All that the learned ignorance cuts open. Whether in Christian or secular certainty, the willful ignorance ignores the sacred fold of the infinite.[65] It creases the finite body with a denial of finitude that ipso facto occludes the finite infinities. For they circulate only through the mutual contractions and enfoldments of all creatures. The effects matter all too materially. They plunge us in our new millennium toward the incomprehensible indeed: the unspeakable horror rather than the complicating ecstasy, the all too calculable apocalypses rather than the incalculable apophasis.

FREE FOLDS

Speculation about the infinite and the finite will not of course solve the aporia of unspeakable bodies. And the *coincidentia oppositorum* may unveil after all a gilded cloud of postmodern retro-renaissance. But it may offer some of us—so diverse and so entangled—a monastic moment, from which we may better confront the concrete impossibilities of the unfolding present. What is the opposite of an aporia? A new way? A new voice (*voix*)? But, to return to Derrida, "[W]ould there be a way (*voie*) without what clears the way there," where the way is not yet opened?[66] Every Way—even that of Christ, for Cusa the unique conjunction of the opposites of infinite and finite, the apophatic and the bodily—threatens continuously to close up again. As to the infinite itself—"the inaccessible light, the beauty, and the splendor of your face" to "be approached without veil"—may reinscribe the hierarchy of changeless light and bodily darkness, the very contradictories that in the unveiling of the *complicatio* coincide.[67] The very pores of that shining face get clogged by the christocratic history of kitsch, murders, and certainties. What is the alternative to mere aporia?

Decision, on one level. Archie, the sub-hero of Zadie Smith's comic apocalypse, unimpressed by the Sartrean conundrum of equal and conflicting imperatives put to him by Dr. Sick, says it thus: "Well, he better just do one and get on with it."[68] On this, the deconstructive undecidability doesn't differ. It may defer the particular decision. And in that lull, that silence—some of us do pray. For God to solve, fix, indeed just *do* it for us? Worth a shot. But not even a long one, with Cusa.

"And when I thus rest in the silence of contemplation, you, Lord, answer me within my heart, saying: 'Be yours and I too will be yours!'" I should first be my own? The dawn of early modern individualism? Perhaps, read anachronistically. But it also sounds like feminist or womanist insistence on getting a self before giving it away. "Hence, unless I am my own, you are not mine, for *you would constrain my freedom since you cannot be mine unless I also am mine.* And since you have placed this in my freedom, you do not constrain me, but you wait for me *to choose to be my own.*" In other words the necessity you lay upon us is: to be *free*? A Sartrean deity? Inescapable freedom? So what about sin? "[Y]ou . . . allow us to depart and to squander our liberty and our best substance. . . . Yet you do not wholly forsake us, but you are present continually urging us. And you speak within us and call us back to return."[69] Freedom is not relieved by grace but intensified.[70] The "urging," indeed the speech and the call, signifies no coercive power, no control of the outcome.[71] If we prodigal sons and daughters squander both our freedom and our best stuff, those gifts that mark our singularity, grace does not cease thereby its calling.[72] We will unfold God in our bodies, our selves. Whether I make my decisions with or against the grain of that "urging" depends on me. But this is an "I" precisely not as separate, or autonomous, ego but as one among all the creatures participating at every moment in each other. And so also in the infinite actualizing itself in the contractions of the finite bodies. Possibility is "contracted" as actuality. For Cusa God's favorite name will finally become *Posse Ipsum*, possibility itself.[73] It cheerfully defies the reigning Aristotelian *actus purus* that froze the responsive biblical God into an unmoved Mover, into the impassive One whose impassible omniscience guarantees an impassable transcendence.

The *explicatio/implicatio* pattern reads as a beginningless and endless process of foldings rather than as a set of eternally ironed and prefolded creases. "To say that 'each thing is in each thing'"—in a universe where all things move, is this not to say that each thing *passes* into each thing? Once we cut through the impasse of substantialism, the "is in" itself shifts into motion—as in the "rheomode" of Bohm's implicate order.[74] The complication of all in all is not a static containment, like Chinese boxes, but a ceaseless flowing of events in relation. In such porosity of pan-participation, each thing is prehended by each thing, in-fluencing, minimally or maximally, delicately or turbulently.[75] The folds enfold an open and unpredictable universe; they unfold spontaneously, differently and dangerously. Their effects gather and amplify in the fractal folds of "each thing in each thing."

I unfold in this moment of decision, saturated by the influences I enfold; what I become unfolds in the world that enfolds me. My passages matter. They materialize in you-all. We-all, all of us bodies, actualize; we "explicate," possibility itself. In the explication of a *non aliud* that becomes freely other, in the inseparable difference of boundless diversity, then, at the other edge of the moment, we fold back into—infinity. *You?* The fold is by definition not an ontological break, as between the changeless and the changing, the eternal and the temporal, the immaterial and the embodied. Therefore these ranked binaries also reveal themselves in their *coincidentia* as constructions of high Reason. The learned ignorance brought these ontotheological presumptions into the cloud. If other impossibilities cloud our horizon now, if an altogether other cosmopolitics beckons, still, the anachronistic possibility of the *complicatio* has not yet unfolded the gift of its possibility.

APORETIC POROSITY

What then is the alternative to an aporia? How might an impossibility coincide with the *posse ipsum*? Knowing my ignorance I turn to etymology: perhaps the passageway through the impossible is not freedom in a void but in the *porous*, the literal opposite of an *aporia*.[76] Passages blocked in the moment of doubt, of defense, clear and open like pores. Bodily and metaphoric, the openings in the skin, the leaf, or the rock through which the world passes, the passages of breath, air, food, mucus, moisture, fold one life into another. We are made this way, alarmingly porous, vulnerable in our flesh and in our hearts of flesh, dependent in every breath on the *ruach—the breath of the creation, the spirit*—that connects us all. Everybody is coming in and out of us. Our thoughts, if they take flesh, barely hold form and body, so porous are they to the thoughts of others, the feelings, the obstructions, the distractions, the refractions of too many others. Always too many to know, too many to say. The holey boundaries of our materialization, metonyms of the shared body of the planet, its own atmosphere a great vulnerable cloud of porosity, become increasingly the matter of theological contemplation. To "pore" over something, to contemplate, comes from that same root as "going, passage."[77]

The folds are pores, passages in and out of becoming creatures that have no substantial boundaries. Yet in their singular freedoms they expose endless layers of porous surface, faces of the deep. We might say quasi-cusanically: the divine is unfolded as *posse ipsum*, pure possibility, the power that makes possible, but does not unilaterally *make*—everybody. All of which are enfolded in and as the boundless body of the otherwise infinite. There would be something in it for this God, something gloriously indeterminate, like surprise, vulnerability, adventure, like the wild creativity of Job's whirlwind. Like true love. "From the power to love infinitely and the power to be loved infinitely arises an infinite bond of love."[78] Cusa explicates that bond as the Holy Spirit of connection. It will take all the negative capability of our most affirmative practices to embody that interconnectivity. In love of this little finite world of ours, porous to the infinite, in love of the Love that is infinitely porous to every body.

Does the "splendor of your face" not shine through its pores?

Subtle Embodiments: Imagining the Holy in Late Antiquity

PATRICIA COX MILLER

From the fourth century through the seventh, late ancient Christianity fostered the development of three remarkable movements—the cult of the saints, the cult of relics, and the production of iconic art—all of which were premised on the conviction that the material world—particularly in the form of the human body—was a locus of spiritual presence. This dignifying of "matter" raised what became urgent issues: the problem of idolatry, understood as investing the material world with too much meaning, and the consequent need to articulate how the holy could be present in the contingent order in a nonidolatrous fashion.[1]

One of the themes addressed by essays in this book suggests that the phrase "apophatic bodies" disrupts the conventional binary of transcendence and materiality. My essay addresses this disruption by exploring ancient Christian representations of the bodies of the saints. In so doing it focuses on a particular problematic in late ancient Christianity that developed in the course of the burgeoning of the cult of the saints in the fourth and fifth centuries: How might human holiness be depicted without either transgressing the prerogatives of divinity or undermining the earthy humanity of the saint? The problem, briefly put, was how to conceptualize transfiguration enacted on the human level.

From Patricia Cox Miller, *The Corporeal Imagination: Signifying the Holy in Late Ancient Christianity*. Copyright 2009. Reprinted by permission of the University of Pennsylvania Press.

As the later iconoclastic controversy of the eighth and ninth centuries made very clear, the transfiguration of both Christ and human beings could be understood in two quite different ways: on the one hand, as the triumph of spirit over matter, and on the other, as the triumph of flesh over human fallenness. In art, the primary battleground of the iconoclastic controversy, these different understandings of transfiguration had direct implications for the representation of human holiness. In Marie-José Mondzain's succinct summary of the issue, the iconoclasts' position that transfiguration signaled a triumph of spirit over matter rendered "the portrayal of that triumphant and radiant immateriality useless and impious," while the iconophiles' understanding of transfiguration to mean "the triumph of the flesh over sin, suffering, and death" entailed an affirmation of art. "Portrayal [of saints as well as Christ] is therefore the *portrayal of life* itself."[2] The two sides of the debate could not be clearer: either the body is glorified, or else it is beside the point.

In the three centuries prior to the outbreak of the iconoclastic controversy—centuries that witnessed a "growth industry" in hagiographical literature as well as what Averil Cameron has termed an "extreme proliferation of religious imagery"[3]—the battle lines drawn between "radiant immateriality" and "the flesh" were not quite so stark, and yet there *were* indications that religious investment in human holiness carried certain risks. In part this was because embodying the holy in the form of saints posed a new problem in terms of imagining the relation between the human and the divine. For centuries, the Greco-Roman cosmos in which Christianity developed had been densely populated with mediating spirit-beings (daimons, *genii*, guardian angels) that functioned as invisible friends and protectors of human beings. As described by Peter Brown, such a protector "was an invisible being entrusted with the care of the individual, in a manner so intimate that it was not only the constant companion of the individual; it was almost an upward extension of the individual."[4] Brown is correct to add "almost" here, since the personal spirit-guardian did not render the human being in its care "holy," nor did it enable that person to function as an intermediary between the divine and earthly realms. Contact with the divine was the province of a decidedly *im*material being.

The difference between this older model of divine-human relations and the newer one signified by the phenomenon of saints is striking:

"[T]o seek the face of a fellow human being where an earlier generation had wished to see the shimmering presence of a bodiless power is no small change."[5] It was in fact a momentous change, involving alterations both in notions of what was possible for an embodied self and also in possibilities for divine intervention in the world. Now a human being (or that person's body-part or picture) could play an active role in the physical or spiritual salvation of a fellow human being: as a woman in need of a cure says of St. Symeon Stylite the Younger, "[I]f only I might see his face [*homoiōsin*: his painted likeness], I shall be saved."[6]

As celebratory as the cult of the saints seems to have been in terms of dignifying the material realm with a touch of transcendence, it was also accompanied by a certain pause or holding back, and in that hesitance lies the phenomenon of the "apophatic body" as it applies to human holiness. In an essay titled "Disruption, Hesitation, Silence," which is about her favorite kind of poetry, Louise Glück wrote,

> I do not think that more information always makes a richer poem. I am attracted to ellipsis, to the unsaid, to suggestion, to eloquent, deliberate silence. The unsaid, for me, exerts great power: often I wish an entire poem could be made in this vocabulary. It is analogous to the unseen; for example, to the power of ruins, to works of art either damaged or incomplete. Such works inevitably allude to larger contexts; they haunt because they are not whole, though wholeness is implied.[7]

As I will argue, this particular kind of commitment to "less is more" was characteristic of late ancient Christian constructions of what I will eventually designate as the "subtracted self" of the saints. Using a variety of strategies when they wrote about and depicted saints, hagiographical authors and artists relied not so much on the "unsaid" as on what Michael Sells calls an apophatic "speaking away."[8] Ellipsis, then, and suggestion and allusion to the hauntings of (un)wholeness: these are modern ways of describing the ancient presentation of the ephemeral solidity of the saints.

In this essay, I treat hagiography not as a discrete genre limited to literary lives of saints but rather as a set of discursive strategies for presenting sainthood.[9] Hence anecdotes in collective biographies of desert ascetics and miracle stories in full-fledged saintly *vitae* will all fall under the purview of late ancient hagiography, whose primary purpose lay in the materialization (and not simply the memorialization) of saintly presence in the world. Because saints were *a*—if not *the*—major conduit for the activity of the divine in everyday life, strategies for understanding the sensible world as sustaining, however subtly, traces of holiness, of the suprasensible, were crucial to religious sensibility.

As necessary as they were, however, such strategies were also delicate—delicate because collapsing the transcendent into the immanent, as compared with maintaining a tensive relation between them, would be idolatrous. Late ancient Christians were cautious about investing the material world, including the human bodies that once or still inhabited that world, with too much spirit. At the same time, however, convictions that the material world was saturated with divine presence and that the human body could be a locus of sanctity, were central to the late ancient Christian mind-set.[10] Hence the need, when representing human holiness, to tread lightly, avoiding both a spirituality devoid of earthy contact and an idolatrous materialism.

Approaching this problematic with a more contemporary vocabulary, one might say that, in the process of materializing saintly presence, Christian hagiography developed techniques for the animation of lifeless objects. Saints might be considered to be "lifeless objects" because they were, of course, physically dead. Yet, when the hagiographical tradition sought to convey the spiritual aliveness of the saints, it did so not by emphasizing their immaterial presence but by endowing them with bodies that flirted with material substance without quite achieving corporeal solidity.

An example of this "speaking away" of literal physicality without losing the body is the following anecdote from a seventh-century hagiography, the *Life of Saint Theodore of Sykeon*. Returning to his monastery after performing miracles in local villages and successfully routing an evil sorcerer, Saint Theodore falls ill and lies weeping underneath an icon of Saints Cosmas and Damian. Eerily, the saints emerge from the icon "looking just like they did" in the painted image. Coming close to him "like doctors do," they take Saint Theodore's pulse, determine that he is indeed desperately ill, ask the saint a series of questions, and finally offer to go to heaven to plead with Christ on Theodore's behalf. Returning, they announce that his life has been extended, and they vanish—presumably back into the icon whence they came.[11] In the uncanny moment when Saints Cosmas and Damian emerge from their own iconic portrait as animate presences in the life of Saint Theodore, the reader experiences what material-culture theorist Bill Brown describes as ontological instability: Are these saints somehow "inside" their own portrait, or is it just a picture? Can bodiless saints really take someone's pulse? What is the status of these figures who seem to have a privileged relation to divine power?

In one of his studies of "things," Brown has analyzed the "ontological ambiguity" of animated objects: human or thing?[12] What interests Brown is the "ontological instability" of such artifacts, namely, their "oscillation between animate and inanimate, subject and object, human and thing."[13] According to Brown's analysis, this oscillation is what makes such artifacts uncanny, uncanny in the sense developed by the psychologist Ernst Jentsch, who linked uncanniness with intellectual uncertainty about "whether an apparently animate being is in fact alive; or, conversely, whether a lifeless object might not in fact be animate."[14] The hagiography devoted to Saint Theodore certainly does present the reader with a form of intellectual uncertainty. Indeed, I suggest that this text is playing with—perhaps, even, intentionally straining—the reader's credulity for a pedagogical purpose: to teach the reader how to "see" or apprehend that saintly presence does (not quite) incarnate divinity.

The feature of Brown's argument that strikes me as most relevant to hagiographical representation is the phenomenon of ontological instability and the uncanny oscillation that it produces. Consider another anecdote from the *Life of Saint Theodore of Sykeon*. While visiting a monastery in Constantinople, Theodore is subjected to the following ruse: unbeknownst to him, the monks and their abbot, desiring to have a memorial of the saint's stay with them, hire an artist to paint Theodore's portrait. On the sly, the artist produces a good likeness, and one of the monks shows Theodore the portrait and asks him to bless it. Smiling, Theodore says, "You are a fine thief, what are you doing here? We must see to it that you don't run off with something."[15] As Robin Cormack has observed, "[W]ith his remark [Theodore] had betrayed a belief that an icon which copied a person could somehow take away something of the original and have a reality of its own in his image," the implication being that "the icon might function independently of Theodore."[16] Yet Theodore made his remark with a smile—was he joking about the theft of his own "substance," or was he dead serious? Which is the real Theodore, and what kind of body does he have?

The fact that this anecdote (and others like it) raises such questions is not, I think, an accident. This form of subtle embodiment, which refuses to take a final stand on the reality—the concrete solidity—of the saintly body, had theological warrant, because only an ephemerally solid body could allude to the larger context of Christic power without in effect replacing it or claiming identification with it. As Rowan Williams has explained, "[O]nly in Christ is the flesh fully and lastingly saturated with the indwelling divine power," and he notes the development, beginning in the fourth century, of "a picture of holiness that is wary of anything like a fusion between the fully and unambiguously holy on the one hand and the created human agent on the other."[17] This development did not, however, simplify the hagiographical task of constructing images of human holiness that maintained a "dialectic of immanence and transcendence,"[18] such that hagiographical representations matched the delicate balance of human and divine in the saints themselves.

How then can one have a truly material (because humanly physical) sign of the presence of the spiritual world in this earthly world without reifying the holy? The beginning of the early Christian journey toward answers to this question can be found in the hagiographical literature of the late fourth century to the sixth century devoted to desert asceticism. Much of this literature was written in the form of collective biographies (or, more appropriately, hagiographies), compendia of anecdotes compiled by admirers who had gone out into the deserts of Egypt and Syria to observe the lifestyles of the men (and a few women) who practiced an austere form of Christian devotion there.[19] One of the striking features of these hagiographies is their presentation of the ascetic practitioners' emaciated and mutilated bodies as angelic bodies full of light.[20] The literature of desert asceticism, that is to say, developed a rhetoric of the holy body that focused the reader's attention on the vulnerable physicality of the saint while deflecting attention away from it at the same time.

Although one might think that the angelic body would eclipse the human one, there is no doubt about the insistent physicality of the phenomenon of desert asceticism and the reportage about it. This hagiographical literature is dominated by reports of practices of extreme fasting, repetitive praying and singing, wrapping the body with chains and ropes, and so forth.[21] What might seem, to a modern sensibility, as negative results of such practices—the ulcerated feet of Symeon the Stylite, the sun-blackened body of Saint Mary of Egypt, the sunken eyes of Saint Pelagia of Antioch—were positioned by hagiographers as positive signs of spiritual transformation.[22] As Peter Brown has argued, it was in the desert that the transformative implications of the Incarnation for human beings were put into practice: "Through the Incarnation of Christ, the Highest God had reached down to make even the body capable of transformation."[23]

And transformed their bodies surely were, especially given their practices of eating (or not). Fasting produces a body that looks different from conventional bodies, that is, bodies marked by their ties to normal social and domestic contexts. Yet, despite the obsession of such collective hagiographies as the *Historia monachorum* with ascetic bodily practices like fasting, there is very little actual physical description. On the basis of such texts, one cannot visualize those desert saints who had "attained a God-like state of fulfillment by their inspired and wonderful and virtuous way of life."[24] Instead, hagiographers used metaphors of light to describe these exemplars of the saintly self. According to the *Apophthegmata Patrum*, for example, the face of Abba Pambo shone like lightning, and Abba Sisoes's face shone like the sun.[25] The author of the *Historia monachorum* observed that Abba Or "looked just like an angel, and his face was so radiant that the sight of him alone filled one with awe."[26] The entire body of Abba Silvanus shone like an angel, while another old man appeared "entirely like a flame."[27]

These metaphors of light were useful for evoking the subtle bodies of the desert saints because they allowed hagiographers to materialize the holiness of the saint without reifying it. One cannot, after all, "see" light. In these texts, there is a "speaking away" of literal physicality without losing the human body, which persists alongside the shining angelic body as the disfigured ascetic body—"the disfigured [that] was figured as desirable," as Geoffrey Galt Harpham has said.[28] By aligning images of mutilation and disfigurement with images of light, hagiographers of desert ascetics maintained their subjects in a tensive perch between transcendence and materiality.

It is true, however, that these texts constantly strain after inferences to wholeness or spiritual completeness. Along with their emphasis on ascetic practices, collective hagiographies prominently feature the various charisms granted to the denizens of the desert on the basis of their ascetic efforts. Many of these spiritual gifts are decidedly Christomimetic: exorcising demons, healing the sick, even raising the dead and walking on water.[29] And in addition to tales about spiritual gifts, there are the stories about ascetics whose bodies negotiate the spirit/human divide with astonishing ease. For example, one old man, Patermuthius, flies through the air, passes through closed doors, and was once "transported physically to paradise," whence he brought back "a large choice fig" as proof of his journey.[30] For three years another monk, Abba Or, ate only heavenly food, which was placed in his mouth by an angel.[31]

Such textual materializations of desert saints gave human materiality a hefty push toward transcendence, indeed toward what Harpham has called the most insidious temptation of the ascetic life: "the illusion that one had reached an ideal or perfect identification with Christ the Word."[32] Even the literary form of such collective hagiographies as the *Historia monachorum* and Theodoret's *Historia religiosa* supports the divinizing tendencies just noted. The stories that form these collections are not full, chronologically organized biographies that situate their subjects in richly detailed sociocultural contexts. Instead, they are rapid, staccato accounts of the saints in action, taking the form of snapshots endlessly repeated. The collections thus place the desert saints in an extended "middle" that helps accentuate their heavenly status by subverting conventional biographical narrativity and depriving their angel-like ascetic characters of history. For angels, "untainted by historicity," "do not have biographies," as Stephen Crites once remarked.[33]

But there is in these hagiographies a countermove to this tendency to allow the embodiment of desert saints to slip wholly into the luminosity of the saints' holiness, and herein lies another kind of "hesitance," one that curbs the divinizing tendency of these portrayals of human holiness. In order to maintain a tensive balance between divinity and humanity, the kind of "speaking away" referred to earlier must "unsay" transcendence as well as materiality. Texts like the *Historia monachorum* avoid the blasphemy of complete identification of their saints with the ultimately holy, Christ, by presenting the ascetics as constantly in motion. This is the other side of the staccato format of these texts, most of whose anecdotes present their subjects performing one ascetic feat after the other. As Harpham argues, this kind of restless activity is one of the central features of asceticism, defined as "a quest for a goal that cannot and must not be reached, a quest with a sharp caveat: 'seek but do not find.'"[34] Living out a Christomimetic dynamic in which he is "constantly progressing but never arrives," the ascetic may be defined as an "emergent person" or an "evolving subject" ever in motion toward a divine paradigm.[35] As Abba Poemen said about Abba Pior, "[E]very day he made a new beginning."[36] Thus is the saint subjected to the hesitance that even the exuberance of this kind of incarnational thinking cannot dispel.[37]

Collective hagiographies were among the earliest Christian attempts to imagine the (near) triumph of flesh over human fallenness. Their version of the "subtracted selves" of the saints, inhabiting bodies radiant and ravaged at once, displays the difficulty of bringing human and divine together by the way in which their representations of the desert ascetics veer from one pole of the transcendence/materiality binary to the other. This kind of textual anxiety over endowing human beings with too much divinity was not limited to collective biographies of saints. Hagiographies devoted to single figures also worried about how to present the relation between the spiritual and the material: Were holy people passive channels of divine activity, or was there an active synergy of human and divine at work in them, and how was it to be pictured?[38]

In his paradigmatic *Life of Saint Antony*, written a quarter century before the earliest of the collective hagiographies, Athanasius tried to chart something of a middle course in answer to these questions. Although he was wary of localizing the divine, whether in holy places like Jerusalem or in relics, he was willing to portray the body of Antony as a perfectly toned reflection of his spiritual prowess.[39] Still vigorous and youthful after decades of fasting and combat with demons, Antony is a prefiguration of the incorruption that humans will enjoy in the resurrection. Yet Athanasius emphasized that Antony achieved what he did, not by virtue of his own agency but through Christ. As David Brakke has argued, "[F]rom Athanasius's perspective, it is correct to call Antony's body 'holy,' but only in the sense that it has been restored to its original (prefall) condition through the divinizing work of the incarnate Word. Antony's body is not holy in the sense that it transmits or mediates holiness to others."[40]

For hagiographers of later centuries, however, the problem of God's presence on earth, and particularly in the saints, had become more acute. Not far in the background lay the Christological debates of the fifth century, since Christ was the supreme instance of divinity enfleshed.[41] In the course of these debates, extreme care was taken not to compromise the transcendent divinity of Christ. However, as Peter Brown has put it, this elevation produced

> a need to show that so high a God was truly implicated in human affairs. . . . Often seeming to be tragically absent, Christ needed to be "represented" on earth, and it was as "Christ-bearers," as those who imitated him and consequently carried his power within them, that holy persons—alive or in their tomb—gave human density to the urge to find a joining of heaven and earth, which the rise of monotheism, despite the Christian doctrine of the Incarnation, had placed in jeopardy.[42]

This way of thinking about human holiness prompted the development of new hagiographical strategies for materializing the presence of the holy in human bodies.

In the hagiographical literature devoted to individual saints that developed in the period from the late fifth century through the seventh century, a biographical sketch of the life of the saint is often merely a prelude to the explosion of the saint into action, as miracle succeeds miracle in rapid-fire, almost incantatory fashion.[43] Here again is the staccato format found in the collective hagiographies, yet in these (mostly later) *vitae* that are essentially collections of miracles, the saint is not presented as an "emergent person" or "evolving subject." The point of these hagiographies, such as the *Life of Saint Theodore of Sykeon* discussed above, is not to present the reader with a snapshot of an imitable saintly life, as in the literature on the desert ascetics; the point is, rather, to teach the reader how to see that everyday life is saturated with palpable saintly presence. Now saints are not aligned with angels. Instead, they are themselves theophanic vehicles of the highest degree.

Because Christ had become more remote as intercessor between heaven and earth, there was an urgent need for figures that could mediate divine presence.[44] Hagiography satisfied this need by fashioning the bodies of the saints as transcendent bodies, their "matter" charged with religious power. Instead of being exemplars of spiritual progress like the desert ascetics, these later saints' lives are stages for the display of divine action in the world. Understandably, the theological pressure that the idea of intercession placed on saints posed a problem for conceptualizing and then narrating their embodiment. What exactly was the difference between the human and the divine? In other words, how might one portray spiritual presence in the saint without idolizing the human and circumscribing divinity?

Hagiographies such as the *Life of Saint Symeon the Stylite the Younger* developed what I discern to be techniques for rematerializing the saint as a subtracted self, an "enigma of corporeal substance."[45] We have already seen an example of such enigmas in the ephemerally solid bodies of Saints Cosmas and Damian as they interact with the ailing Saint Theodore of Sykeon. Mediation of the divine by a human body requires, not *de*materialization, but precisely *re*materialization in verbal images that convey how a body touched by transcendence can be palpably present in the world.[46] On the one hand, to construct a truly *material* sign of the presence of the spiritual realm in the here and now the hagiographer could not overemphasize the indwelling of spirit in the saint for fear of erasing the humanness of the saintly *persona* as intercessor. On the other hand, overemphasis on the humanness of the saint would detract from the status of the saint as a genuine epiphany of a specifically *transfigured* human presence.[47]

One of the most interesting hagiographical techniques for keeping saints in such a tensive balance between two worlds was the *dis*placement of the reality of saintly presence and power onto images. As with the (near) identity of Saints Cosmas and Damian with their own icon, such animated images may, like apophasis, accomplish a "momentary liberation from referential delimitation," which is precisely what the phenomenon of saintly flesh demands.[48] An apt example of this technique is in the late sixth-century *Life of Saint Symeon the Stylite the Younger*, which is one of those hagiographies marked by a profusion of miracle stories. In Miracle 231 (!), a priest has brought his ailing son to the foot of Symeon's column for healing. Having blessed the son, Symeon tells the priest and his son to go home. The priest begs that they be allowed to stay in Symeon's vicinity, since "being close to you will guarantee us a complete cure." As Charles Barber remarks, Symeon's next move is to "extend the notion of his presence": "The power of God is effective everywhere," says the saint. He continues: "So take this *eulogia* [token] made of my dust [*tēs komeōs mou*], depart, and when you look at the imprint of our image, it is us that you will see."[49]

Not only does Symeon extend his presence, he extends his body by scattering it in the form of clay tokens imprinted with his physical likeness. Yet even the dust has an ambiguous referent: Is it some actual shedding from the saint's real body (an allusion, perhaps, to the creation of human beings from the dust of the earth in Genesis), or is it the dust from around the saint's column, rendered holy due to its contact with Symeon's body and to its use as image-bearing token? And what of the priestly petitioner? It would seem that Symeon's gift of the *eulogia* and his command to depart are intended to deprive the priest of an idolatrous attachment to the saint's very flesh—except that the dusty token *is* (possibly) his flesh. The saintly body has a persistent vitality that defies categorization: Is it an entity, or is it an event?[50]

Stories like this one are full of deflections and oscillations. Symeon's location seems truly undecidable. At the very least, the displacement of Symeon's powerful presence onto his material artistic image dignifies the "matter" of the world as a site of divinity, but at the same time this displacement disrupts the reader's (and the priest's) singular focus on the saint's body. Yet, while seeming to opt for a two-dimensional Symeon, simply a figured seal on a clay token, the text is also a powerful affirmation of the saint's holy touch. Is he a figure in the round, or not? Like the icon of Saints Cosmas and Damian, Symeon's figured token partakes of that ontological instability, an oscillation between subject and object, human and thing, that teaches the reader to exercise a certain hesitance in regard to the phenomenon of human holiness.

In fact, this sort of hesitance—a disruption of expectations of divinity straightforwardly embodied—seems built into the apophatic bodies of the later hagiographical tradition. As Sells argues, at the heart of apophatic unsaying is a dialectic of transcendence and immanence. One of the results of this dialectic is that, "when the transcendent realizes itself as immanent, the subject of the act is neither divine nor human, neither self nor other."[51] We have just seen Symeon's identity turn on an imaginal displacement or disruption of his presence. This "neither-nor" (which is also a "both-and") seems characteristic of the hagiographical presentation of saintly bodies, especially when the corporeal solidity or wholeness of the saint is implied, and then questioned. Paraphrasing Glück, quoted above, one might say that such hagiographical constructions of holy bodies "allude to larger [heavenly] contexts"—but "they haunt because they are not whole, though wholeness is implied."[52]

A final hagiographical technique pertains precisely to this "haunting" whereby the saint's textually reconstituted body flits in and out of focus, tantalizing the reader with intimations of complete divine-human synergy. My exemplary text is the fifth-century *Life and Miracles of Saint Thecla*, which presents the holy body of its saint as ambiguously corporeal.[53] Saint Thecla's body is a visionary appearance that is nonetheless tangible, as in the following anecdote. In Miracle 38, Thecla, described as a great friend of the literary arts, decides to help a gravely ill scholar named Alypius, who has come to her compound seeking a curative dream. She visits him (in the form of a dream) at night; but the text, instead of emphasizing the saint's phantom-like appearance, insists that "she showed herself in her real form." This tangible wraith then asks the scholar what ails him, and he replies with a Homeric tag. Charmed by the appropriateness of the verse to the situation, "[T]he martyr [Thecla] smiled and gave the man a pebble," which she ordered him to attach to his neck, saying that it would cure him. When the scholar woke up, the pebble had vanished, and he was still ill. Meanwhile, his son, on the way to visit his father, came upon the pebble lying in the road and, "seduced by its beauty," picked it up, took it to his father and placed it in his hands, and he was immediately cured.[54]

This is a holy body that is both starkly physical and utterly phantasmal, as is the pebble that she proffers. Materiality is inflected with divinity, but uncannily so. Stories like this one abound in the hagiographical tradition, although they are especially striking in the case of Saint Thecla, who, for another example, once spent an entire night with her arms wrapped around an emotionally fragile female suppliant and then, at evening's end (and as observed by the suppliant's roommate), flew out of the room.[55] Interestingly, even though Thecla tends to interact physically with her venerators, the most commonly used verb to describe her appearances (*epiphoitáō*) means to visit or to haunt.[56] Thecla's haunting presence implies wholeness but does not reify it. Literally "fleeting," this ambiguously corporeal body of the saint enacts the "referential openness" that an apophatic body needs to survive.[57]

In the light of such images, I think it is fair to say that late ancient hagiography accomplished the transformation of the literal body into a deeper truth. Holy bodies like Saint Thecla's are epiphanies of transfiguration that occupy a signifying space between transcendence and immanence; and just as they avoid idolizing the material, so they also deconstruct naive or insipid notions of spiritual presence in the world. Theophanic and human at the same time, the subtle embodiments of late ancient hagiography were supremely indirect, and in that indirectness lies their unsaying, their sidestepping; in short, these subtle embodiments are the hagiographical version of apophasis.

"Being Neither Oneself Nor Someone Else": The Apophatic Anthropology of Dionysius the Areopagite

CHARLES M. STANG

Recent interest in the negative, or apophatic, mystical tradition prompts us to consider that tradition's foremost late antique spokesman, Dionysius the Areopagite, or, as he is often called, "Pseudo-Dionysius."[1] This is not the first time that Dionysius has seemed peculiarly relevant to contemporary concerns: in the sixth-century Christological debates, in the eighth-century Iconoclastic controversy, in the fourteenth-century Hesychast movement, and in the Italian Renaissance, thinkers turned to the Areopagite and submitted his small corpus—four short treatises and ten letters—to rigorous attention.[2] To these periods we may add our own, when the burning interest in Dionysius is reflected in the fact that even the late Jacques Derrida felt compelled to explain how his own deconstructive project did and did not relate to the writings of this nameless monk from Syria.[3]

But the recent and widespread interest in Dionysius follows on the heels of more than a hundred years of specialized scholarship, much of which has been devoted to assessing the nature and extent of his debt to post-Plotinian Neoplatonism. By reading him largely against this Neoplatonic backdrop, scholars have often characterized Dionysian Christology

---

I acknowledge and thank those who have read previous drafts of this essay, including Sarah Coakley, Ryan Coyne, Benjamin Dunning, Amy Hollywood, Sarabinh Levy-Brightman, István Perczel, Paul Rorem, and the editors of this volume. I acknowledge and thank the anonymous reviewers for Fordham University Press for their helpful comments.

as an "exceedingly thin veneer,"[4] a "cosmetic"[5] disguising his true commitments to the realm of the eternal and unchanging at the expense of this fleeting world.[6] Not only does this reading do great disservice to Neoplatonic views of creation and the body—views that are as diverse as they are subtle[7]—but this approach obscures the influence of Paul on Dionysius and consequently misunderstands some of the central themes of his theology, including his Christology. The entire *Corpus Dionysiacum* [hereafter *CD*] is in fact animated by the figure and writings of Paul; after all, this late fifth-century author chose to write under the name of the Athenian who was converted by Paul's speech to the Areopagus, as mentioned in Acts 17.

This essay traces Paul's influence on Dionysius' "apophatic anthropology" and Christology. In the first and second sections, I offer a brief review of the Dionysian universe, giving special attention to the themes of body and creation. The third section takes up the question of Paul's influence on Dionysius' "apophatic anthropology" and his corresponding Christology. The fourth section considers how this anthropology helps explain why our author wrote under the pseudonym of a disciple of Paul and argues thereby that writing pseudonymously is integral to the aims of the corpus. Finally, in the fifth section, I ponder whether and how this practice of writing stands outside the purview of the celestial and ecclesiastical hierarchies and thereby leaves open the possibility that we might access deifying union with the unknown God in ways other than those permitted by the hierarchies.

BACKGROUND: *THE CELESTIAL HIERARCHY* AND *THE ECCLESIASTICAL HIERARCHY*

In order to focus on the apophatic anthropology and the question of pseudonymity, it is necessary to set the stage and review the main features of the Dionysian universe, while giving special attention to the themes of body and creation. The first two treatises of the *CD*—*The Celestial Hierarchy* and *The Ecclesiastical Hierarchy*[8]—concern the hierarchies, specifically the sacred order of the celestial and ecclesiastical ranks. The aim of the hierarchies is the deifying union of each rank or order with the divine source that both permeates and escapes the created hierarchies.[9] Deifying union consists in each of us, in our established rank, becoming "co-workers with God" (*theou synergoi*), that is, ciphers through which the activity (*energeia*) or the work of God (*theourgia*) moves.[10] Such movement presumes space, and so creation—insofar as it is a series of interlocking hierarchies—is the arrangement of distance that makes possible proximity. Despite the prevalent descriptions of ascent, deification and union are achieved not by our moving closer to the divine source, or ascending the hierarchy rank by rank, but rather by allowing the source to move more fully through us.[11] Insofar as there is ascent, therefore, it is assent—the assent of each individual member of the hierarchy to the work of God. Creation can be understood, then, as a circuit, and the choice facing every creature is whether and how well it will conduct the current that runs out from (*proodos*) and back to (*epistrophê*) the divine source. We neither ascend nor transcend creation, as if it were a great chain of being or something from which we must flee. On the contrary, we flee *into* creation, *into* our established order in the hierarchy of embodied creation.[12]

For Dionysius, our access to this deifying union seems to be restricted to the liturgy, for it is only in the liturgy, specifically the rite of baptism, that we meet Jesus and assent to conduct the activity that runs out from and back to the divine source. Jesus is not only our access to this activity; he is in fact that very activity, most often figured in the *CD* as light and love. For any rank in the hierarchy, deifying union consists in this: receiving the light and love of Jesus and allowing it to pass through us on its way to the next rank, be that rank above or below us. Thus the hierarchies ensure that deifying union is a "corporate" enterprise in both senses: "corporate" insofar as it is a collective endeavor concerned with the assent of our neighbors in the hierarchy *and* "corporate" insofar as it necessitates a flight into our particular rank in that hierarchy of *embodied* creation.

Once we assent in the liturgy to conduct light and love, we come to lead a split existence: on the one hand, we remain firmly established in our rank in the hierarchy of embodied creation and, on the other, we are carried outside ourselves as the luminous and loving activity of the ultimately other and ineffable divine source—the work of God (*theourgia*)—courses through us. This split existence reflects the split existence of God, who processes into creation and simultaneously calls that creation back to God, all the while somehow remaining in perfect repose: "always proceeding, always remaining, always being restored to itself."[13]

For Dionysius, God "is, as it were, beguiled by goodness, by love, and by yearning and is enticed away from his transcendent dwelling place and comes to abide within all things, and he does so by virtue of his supernatural and ecstatic capacity to remain, nevertheless, within himself."[14] Creation answers this ecstasy with its own: "[A]ll being derives from, exists in, and is returned toward the Beautiful and the Good."[15] Dionysius, however, is concerned with a particularly recalcitrant sliver of embodied creation, namely humanity, "who freely turned away from the divine and uplifting life and was dragged down instead as far as possible in the opposite direction and was plunged into the utter mess of passion."[16] Laden with passions, humanity refuses to answer the divine ecstasy and remains in its place, thinking itself whole and self-sufficient. In order to be freed from these passions, however, humanity must reawaken its passionate yearning (*erôs*) for the divine. For just as it was through yearning that God suffered ecstasy and so brought forth all of creation, so too it is only by our yearning that we may now suffer ecstasy and thereby both sink deeper into that creation and allow to flow through us what is ultimately other to that creation.

BACKGROUND: *THE DIVINE NAMES* AND *THE MYSTICAL THEOLOGY*

Within this sacramental and liturgical context in which we assent to be ecstatic ciphers of the divine current, the next two treatises—*The Divine Names* and *The Mystical Theology*—insist on a complementary program: that one "say" (*kataphasis*) and "unsay" (*apophasis*) the "divine names" (*ta theia onomata*) in perpetuity in order to solicit union with the divine. But how do we know which are the "divine names"? On the one hand, insofar as God is the cause of all creation, "to praise this divinely beneficent Providence you must turn to all of creation."[17] On the other hand, Dionysius insists, we must limit ourselves to the divine names that were revealed to the scripture writers.[18] Dionysius follows Paul in insisting that our speech about God echo God's speech about God—in other words that worship echo revelation.[19] It is more fitting that God graciously descend to us than that we recklessly reach beyond our limits, for insofar as God is the "Cause of all existence and therefore itself transcending existence, [God] alone could give an authoritative account of what [God] really is."[20] Therefore revelation is prior to any affirmation of the divine names, which in turn is prior to any negation of those same names. Ten chapters of the *Divine Names* (*DN* 4–13) are devoted to the "conceptual" divine names as revealed in scripture. Each of these ten chapters takes up one or several related names and contemplates their many and hidden meanings. The "sensory" names are treated in *The Symbolic Theology*, a treatise Dionysius mentions several times but which is probably fictitious, although possibly genuine and lost.[21]

In *The Mystical Theology*, Dionysius explains that our contemplation of these names should follow a strict cyclical order: a progressive affirmation (*kataphasis*) of the names most like the divine (the conceptual names) to those most unlike the divine (the sensory names) followed by a regressive negation (*apophasis*) of the names most unlike the divine to those most like.[22] At the peak and valley of this cycle, Dionysius offers two further and complementary movements: (1) the negation of negation and (2) the contemplation of "entirely dissimilar names." The aim of this entire contemplative program—in which "saying" and "unsaying" are inextricably bound together—is to heighten the tension between divine immanence and transcendence to such a point that the "unimaginable presence"[23] of God may break through all affirmations and negations and the "unknowing union" (*henôsis agnôstos*)[24] with "the unknown God" (*ho agnôstos theos*)[25] may descend.

At first glance it may appear that this contemplative cycle gives short shrift to embodied creation, since priority is given to the conceptual rather than the sensory names. Several details, however, should complicate this impression. First of all, although Dionysius does refer to names as more "like" or "unlike" God, he also insists that God is immanent in all things, from angels to earthworms. Furthermore, the fact that God is also and always absolutely "beyond all things" raises the question of whether the ultimately other can be properly understood as more or less like or unlike any of those things to which it is ultimately other. Second, the contemplative program does not merely ascend from the sensory names to the conceptual names. On the contrary, at the height of the contemplation of the conceptual names—presumably those names most "like" God, such as "Good" and "One"—Dionysius sees a peculiar danger. For such conceptual names are more likely to become idols precisely because we suppose them to be so like as to be sufficient stand-ins for the ineffable name of God. Chief among these idols, of course, is the very name "God."[26] Even when we negate or "unsay" such names, however, we are not safe, for then a new danger arises: that we will settle on the negation or "unsaying" as somehow sufficient to free God from our cramped categories.

In order to shake us free from such conceptual complacency and the temptation of the negation, Dionysius insists on the negation of every negation. This unsettling procedure derives from Proclus, who terms it a "hyper-apophasis."[27] It is definitively not a discrete operation, for a second negation would merely repeat the fault of the first.[28] Rather, it is a commitment to perpetual unsaying: "[L]anguage when conversant with that which is ineffable, being subverted about itself, has no cessation, and opposes itself."[29] Although the term "hyper-apophasis" never appears in the *CD*, that very commitment to the ceaseless unsaying of even what is unsaid pulses through the *Mystical Theology*: "We make assertions and denials of what is next to it, but never of it . . . for it is beyond both every assertion . . . and also beyond every denial."[30] At the peak of the contemplative cycle, then, the negation of negation dethrones not only those conceptual names most "like" the ineffable source but even the negations of those names.

Dionysius, however, insists on at least one significant departure from this contemplative cycle in which we affirm what is most like the divine, carry on affirming all the way to what is least like the divine, deny everything in opposite order, and then deny those denials in turn. Into this cycle Dionysius introduces something of a twist: "dissimilar similarities."[31] In attempting to explain the anagogical value of the crass imagery in which scripture describes angels, Dionysius insists that "scriptural writings, far from demeaning the ranks of heaven, actually pay them honor by describing them with dissimilar shapes so completely at variance with what they really are that we come to discover how those ranks, so far removed from us, transcend all materiality."[32] Later in the chapter, Dionysius explains that "the mysterious theologians employ these [dissimilar similarities] not only to make known the ranks of heaven but also to reveal something of God himself."[33] Both affirmations and negations run the danger of idolatry, but "the sheer crassness of the [incongruous] signs is a goad so that even the materially inclined cannot accept that it could be permitted or true that the celestial and divine sights could be conveyed by such shameful things."[34] Examples of such goads include naming God a worm,[35] a drunk, even someone suffering from a hangover.[36] Strictly speaking, these "dissimilar similarities" are names that we must say because they reveal God as much as any other. And yet these names, however crassly kataphatic they seem, contain within them the seeds of their own denial. In fact they hover between saying and unsaying, transcendence and immanence, and resemble, in this regard, the negation of negation. If at the peak we come closest to freeing God from all affirmations and negations by negating the negation of the name most like the divine, such as the Good, in the valley we do so by holding in our mind the notion of God as a worm. This is further evidence that Dionysius would not have us flee the hierarchy of embodied creation, merely ascend from the sensory to the conceptual names, but rather find those sites in embodied creation which so tax us that what remains ultimately other to all creation may break through to meet us precisely in and through creation.

This meeting is best understood as the descent of what Dionysius calls an "unknowing union,"[37] that is, a union with "the unknown God." We say and unsay the divine names precisely in order to solicit this unknowing union, which delivers us, if only momentarily, from the impasse of how God is both present and absent. We do not achieve this unknowing; rather we wait for it at the tense cusp between our affirmations and negations, where our perpetual saying and unsaying calls out to the God beyond being. So Jesus—"the Light of the Father" and "the work of God"—condescends to us, and, in a fleeting state of unknowing, we enjoy such union as we are able.

PAUL AND APOPHATIC ANTHROPOLOGY

For Dionysius, the aim of the hierarchy of all creation is none other than deifying union with "the unknown God." Not surprisingly, then, the self who is united to the unknown God must also become unknown, that is, suffer "an absolute abandonment of [your]self and everything, shedding all and freed from all."[38] Thus an apophatic theology assumes an apophatic anthropology, wherein the self is progressively unsaid, or, to use another favorite term of Dionysius, "cleared away" (*aphairêsis*).[39] The way of negation is then a practice of transforming that self who would solicit an unknowing union with the divine. Apophasis is, for Dionysius, a sort of asceticism, an exercise of freeing the self as well as God from the names and categories that prevent it from being divine.[40] And so when Meister Eckhart prayed, "[T]herefore pray God to free me of God," he might also have prayed, "Therefore pray God to free me of *me*."[41]

This mutual disclosure of God and self as unknown has long been acknowledged to be the case with both Eckhart and his joint heir to the Dionysian fortune, John Scottus Eriugena. Bernard McGinn has written extensively on both figures and has made the connection explicit.[42] For Eriugena, because the human self is the only true *imago dei*, like the God of whom it is an image it does not know *what* it is (that is, it does not know itself as a *what*). Thus "the primacy of negative theology in Eriugena is complemented by his negative anthropology."[43] For Eriugena, negative theology and negative anthropology are grounded in the conviction that divine and human subjectivity are one and the same in essence. One important conclusion of this conviction is that God is the subject in all human knowledge of God—that is, God comes to know God through humans knowing God. Corollary to this conclusion is what McGinn calls the "negative dialectic of the divine nature": "To know humanity in its deepest hidden darkness is to know God."[44] Meister Eckhart follows Eriugena here, insisting that God and soul enjoy a union of indistinction owing to the fact that they share the same ground, or *Grunt*. If the soul is united to God in its ground, then it must be as completely unknown and unknowable as God. Consequently, to know the unknown God one must know the unknown self. For Eckhart too, then, negative theology calls forth what McGinn terms a "negative mystical anthropology"[45] in which is acknowledged "the priority of unknowing in the search for God."[46] McGinn rightly credits this anthropology and the primacy of unknowing in Eriugena and Eckhart to Dionysius.

The most obvious place to turn for Dionysius' "apophatic anthropology" is the *Mystical Theology*, where he advises his friend Timothy "to leave behind you everything perceived and understood, everything perceptible and understandable, all that is not and all that is, and, with your understanding laid aside, to strive upward as much as you can toward union with him who is beyond all being and knowledge."[47] He warns his young charge that there will be those who refuse to lay aside their faculties and "who think that by their own intellectual resources they can have a direct knowledge of him who has made the shadows his hiding place."[48] These "uninformed" provide the foil to his apophatic anthropology: they cling to the efficacy of their noetic powers, confident that their *nous* can meet God as *Nous*.[49] Dionysius does not advise Timothy to lay aside his senses or his reason in favor of another faculty, such as certain later medieval mystics will do.[50] Quite to the contrary, Dionysius insists that there is no refuge for the self that seeks union with the unknown God: it must be entirely "cleared away" along with our most cherished categories for the divine. In *The Mystical Theology*, the model for this apophatic asceticism is none other than Moses, who, atop Mount Sinai "plunges into the truly mysterious darkness of unknowing."[51] Here Dionysius refrains from his usual terminology for un-selfing—namely *apophasis* (unsaying) and *aphairesis* (clearing away)—and instead says of Moses that "he is neither himself nor someone else."[52]

This condition recalls Dionysius' discussion of eros and ecstasy in *Divine Names* 4, where Dionysius describes how God's love for the world is best understood as *erôs*, or "yearning." God creates because God is "beguiled by goodness, by love, and by yearning and is enticed away from his transcendent dwelling place and comes to abide within all things, and he does so by virtue of his supernatural and ecstatic capacity to remain, nevertheless, within himself."[53] Just as the ecstatic deity once stood outside itself to create, so now that same deity graciously stands outside itself calling us to answer with our own ecstatic yearning. Ecstasy should answer ecstasy, according to Dionysius. Thus the self that would suffer union with God must learn how to yearn to such an extent that it suffers ecstasy, that it becomes literally beside itself for God. This is the same anthropology as described in *The Mystical Theology*, but from another angle. There, the process of un-selfing is figured as a stark clearing away that renders the self neither itself nor someone else. Here, that same process of un-selfing is figured as the self yearning to the point that the self splits, somehow remaining in its place and returning to its source simultaneously. And so if apophasis of the self is for Dionysius a sort of asceticism, it is equally a sort of eroticism.

Whereas the model for this pursuit in *The Mystical Theology* is Moses, here in *The Divine Names* it is none other than Paul, who, according to Dionysius, "was truly a lover and, as [Paul himself] says, was beside himself for God, possessing not his own life but the life of the one for whom he yearned, as exceptionally beloved."[54] Dionysius is quoting from

2 Corinthians 5:13, where Paul famously asserts: "[I]f we are beside ourselves—[literally: "if we are in ecstasy"]—it is for God; if we are in our right mind, it is for you." Paul emerges then as the model of the ecstatic lover of the divine beloved. And lest we suppose that this single mention of ecstasy was an isolated indiscretion for the apostle, Dionysius reminds of Galatians 2:20: "This is why the great Paul, swept along by his yearning for God and seized of its ecstatic power, had this inspired word to say: 'It is no longer I who live, but Christ who lives in me.' "[55] By Paul's own admission, then, he has been ecstatically displaced to the point where, like Moses in the cloud of unknowing, he is "neither himself nor someone else."

This apophatic anthropology is crucial for understanding Dionysian Christology. Recall that according to the two treatises on the hierarchies, Christ not only gives us access to the divine activity—the work of God—through the rite of baptism, but he himself is that activity, the light and love that cascades down and rises up through the ranks of the hierarchies. Deifying union consists in our assenting to be ecstatically displaced by this light and love. Dionysius situates Paul's ecstatic confession that "It is no longer I who live, but Christ who lives in me" in this hierarchical scheme, such that Paul's confession in Galatians 2:20 is understood as his assent to the ecstatic intrusion of the divine other. And this is the crux of Dionysian Christology: Christ is he who intrudes and interrupts the self that mistakes itself for whole. For Dionysius, Paul is the preeminent witness to this fact, for he teaches and suffers precisely this truth.

One could say—although Dionysius himself does not—that each time someone assents to this divine intrusion, Christ becomes incarnate once again. Christ displaces another self and thereby takes up residence in a new body. Meister Eckhart will describe this event as the "Birth of the Son in the Soul"[56] and suggest thereby that the Incarnation is not only a singular actuality, but an eternal possibility. Although Dionysius never makes precisely this claim, his description of Paul should give pause: "that guide in divine illumination, that light of the world by whom I and my teacher [Hierotheus] are led, the one great in divine things."[57] Here Dionysius dares to speak of Paul in language usually reserved for Christ: "the light of the world" (John 8:12). It seems that for Dionysius, at least Paul—though perhaps not all of us—is capable of becoming a Christ on earth, firmly placed in the hierarchy of embodied creation and yet ecstatically displaced by the light and love of the unknown God.

PSEUDONYMITY AND WRITING

With this understanding of Paul's relevance to Dionysius' apophatic anthropology and Christology in place, we can now venture an explanation as to why this late author wrote under the name of a disciple of Paul. Modern scholarship has been nearly unanimous in its explanation.[58] Enthralled by later Neoplatonism, the story goes, our author sought out a pseudonym by which to clothe his dangerously pagan philosophy with apostolic authority. With such an apostolic pedigree, the corpus could be assured a wider readership. One of the many problems with this explanation is that it pretends that Paul is entirely exterior to the content of the corpus, dismissing the countless quotations from and mentions of Paul as mere additions made after the fact to improve its chances of being read.[59] Furthermore, this explanation fails to consider why this author chose this *particular* pseudonym, that is, a disciple of Paul rather than any of the other apostolic pseudonyms that would have provided the same pedigree.

There is, however, another, perhaps better, explanation. Paul provides our author an apostolic account of apophatic anthropology, that is, he witnesses to the apophasis of his own self as he suffers union with the divine. Our author in a sense apprentices himself to the Paul who suffers a blinding vision of Jesus on the road to Damascus (Acts 9:3–9),[60] the Paul who stands atop the Areopagus and insists that we worship the "unknown God" "through unknowing" [*agnoountes*] (Acts 17:23),[61] the Paul who was caught up to the third heaven (2 Cor 12:2).[62] Our author assumes the identity of a disciple of Paul not merely for these extraordinary moments of intimacy with the divine, but because Paul reveals that such intimacy comes at the cost of his kataphatic self, the self whom he knows and has known his whole life, the self that cannot break free from its sobriety, the self who bears a name, or even two (Saul and Paul). Paul understands that this "said" self must be "unsaid," suffer the ecstatic intrusion of the divine, and suffer the incumbent loss so as to know salvation.

But our author's decision to write under a pseudonym may be even more relevant to the apophasis of the self. The author does not merely sign the name of Paul's disciple Dionysius the Areopagite to his corpus. He goes much further and literally assumes the identity of this figure from the past.[63] He writes not treatises but letters addressed to other apostles and disciples;[64] he imagines himself into this apostolic community, to the point that he is present at the Dormition of Mary;[65] he counsels John sequestered on Patmos.[66] And yet all the while the author is also somehow in the fifth century: quoting—sometimes at great length—from Proclus' works,[67] treading dangerously close to contemporary Christological controversies,[68] describing the ceremonials of Byzantine churches rather than the home churches of the New Testament. The author is, in other words, "neither himself nor someone else," neither the monk from Syria scholars assume him to be nor the Athenian judge under whose name he writes. Like the ecstatic God with whom he seeks to suffer union, as a writer he simultaneously remains where he is and stretches outside himself.

Perhaps then the craft of writing itself—specifically writing in such a way that one is "neither oneself nor someone else"—is an apophatic *askêsis* in the service of soliciting deifying union with the unknown God. Perhaps pseudonymous writing is for our author a practice that renders the self unsaid, that is, unseated from its knowing center, unknown to itself and so better placed, because displaced, to suffer union with "him who has made the shadows his hiding place."[69] This interpretation of the craft of writing finds corroboration in recent scholarship on authorship in the late antique Christian East.[70] Although his attention is focused on hagiography and hymnography, Derek Krueger convincingly argues that this place and period—precisely the provenance of the *CD*—witness the emergence of a new understanding of the practice of writing, what he calls "a highly ritualized technology of the religious self."[71] This "technology" of writing "is not so much a proprietary claim over literary output as a performative act, a bodily practice," the aim of which is nothing less than the salvation of the writer.[72] Thus "writing itself [was] figured as an extension of the authors' virtuous ascetic practice" and "exemplified emerging Christian practices of asceticism, devotion, pilgrimage, prayer, oblation, liturgy, and sacrifice."[73] Krueger thereby recasts writing as a form of devotion itself, whose aim—as is the case with any *askêsis*—is a "reconstituted self."[74] In the case of our unknown author, however, writing under a pseudonym, that of Dionysius the Areopagite, and thereby neither himself nor someone else, writing serves as an embodied and ecstatic devotional practice that aims to deliver precisely a *de*constituted self. As such, pseudonymity is absolutely vital to the aim of the entire Dionysian enterprise: deifying union with the unknown God.

Modern scholarship on Dionysius has not considered whether the very practice of writing pseudonymously might serve the ends of the apophatic enterprise. It comes as something of a surprise, then, that Jacques Derrida has on this point made some very suggestive remarks. These remarks are made in a characteristically elliptical fashion in the opening of his essay "Sauf le nom:"

> . . .
>
> —Sorry, but more than one, it is always necessary to be more than one in order to speak, several voices are necessary for that . . .
>
> —Yes, granted, and par excellence, let us say exemplarily, when it's a matter of God . . .
>
> —Still more, if this is possible, when one claims to speak about God according to what they call apophasis, in other words, according to the voiceless voice, the way of theology called or so-called negative. This voice multiplies itself, dividing within itself: it says one thing and its contrary, God that is without being or God that (is) being. [. . .].[75] I would like to speak to you, don't hesitate to interrupt me, of this multiplicity of voices, of this quite initial, but interminable as well, end of monologism—and of what follows.[76]

Often scholars interested in the encounter between Derrida and negative theology—and especially Dionysius the Areopagite—fix their attention on his long essay, "How to Avoid Speaking: Denials."[77] For my purposes, however, that essay is less interesting than this brief opening exchange from "Sauf le nom." His insight that "it is always necessary to be more than one in order to speak" leads him to take up several voices in "what follows," and to write a dialogue between a nameless and indeterminate "multiplicity of voices." This is "necessary" when "speak[ing] about God according to what they call apophasis" not merely because apophasis "says one thing and its contrary," but even more so because the self who would speak of "the God that is without being or God that (is) being" must "multipl[y] itself, dividing within itself." The refusal to do so constitutes "monologism" and would collapse this "initial, but interminable," dialogue into a monologue.

The multiplication and division of the self that Derrida effects through writing this dialogue corresponds to the multiplication and division of the self that Dionysius effects through writing under his pseudonym. The preeminent witness to this "multiplicity of voices" is for Dionysius none other than Paul. But that divine intrusion and corresponding loss of the monological self that Paul suffers on the road to Damascus is what both Dionysius and Derrida seek to solicit through the practice of writing. Into his dialogical address ("I would like to speak to you") in a "multiplicity of voices," Derrida invites the other to intrude: "[D]on't hesitate to interrupt me." So too Dionysius, "being neither [him]self nor someone else," invites the luminous intrusion of his divine addressee: "Let us, then, call upon Jesus, the Light of the Father."[78] Derrida, in attempting to distinguish deconstruction from apophasis, famously takes issue with the fact that for Dionysius the addressee is predetermined, the other is thereby not given leave to be other, and thus negative theology fails to be sufficiently negative.[79] Despite this irreconcilable difference, Derrida succeeds in suggesting not only that an apophatic anthropology requires that one "be more than one"—that is: divide within oneself and speak in several voices—but also that this multiplication and division is effected by the practice of writing so as to invite interminably the interruption of the other.

WRITING AGAINST THE HIERARCHIES? BEING OUTSIDE AND AHEAD OF ONESELF

In this final section, I wish to offer the fruits of this investigation to contemporary, constructive theologians, especially those who may understandably balk at the fact that in the Dionysian universe, each of us is firmly fixed in our respective rank in the hierarchy of embodied creation. According to Dionysius, we do not ascend that hierarchy, but assent to have the divine source stir in and through us. Deifying union consists in simultaneously sinking into the hierarchy and standing outside ourselves—suffering ecstasy—in union with the ultimately other. For Dionysius, to rebel against the divinely ordained order of things is to forfeit salvation. As he tells a rebellious monk: "Everyone must look to himself and, without thinking of more exalted or more profound tasks, he must think only about what has been assigned to his place."[80] For Dionysius, we must accept our assigned place in the hierarchy precisely because it is there and only there that we can be *dis*-placed by the light and love of the divine.

But even this construal of hierarchy may not satisfy contemporary theologians, since the insistence that each of us accept his or her assigned place presumes a rank order that privileges certain creatures over others. And the historical privileging of some over others on the basis of gender, race, class, or even species understandably sits ill with contemporary theological concerns with justice. Many readers today will reject the notion that access to the divine—in this case, Jesus, the light and love of the Father—is granted only in the rites of the liturgy, as overseen by ecclesiastical ranks whose authority we are bound to obey or risk forfeiture.[81]

I am therefore offering this interpretation of pseudonymous writing as an ecstatic devotional practice in hopes that such readers will find in it a productive site for their own constructive theological enterprises. On my construal, writing is an embodied practice in the service of the apophasis of the self and deifying union, but one that stands outside the purview of the ecclesiastical hierarchy. Writing is a technology of the self whose power to de-constitute cannot be contained in the hierarchical universe that that very writing describes. Dionysius, of course, does not explain how his peculiar practice of writing fits into the smooth circuit of the celestial and ecclesiastical hierarchies. How could he? Were he to reflect on the aim of writing under a pseudonym he would not only give himself away but also instantly dispel the productive and ecstatic tension that such writing strings taut. We have inferred from his peculiar practice of writing that neither the choice to write under a pseudonym nor the choice of pseudonym is incidental. Would the fifth-century author acknowledge this interpretation of his writing practice and the challenge it poses to the hierarchies? It is of course impossible to say for certain, but it seems unlikely, given his efforts to shore up the seams in the order of things.

I submit that what we have here is an instance of an inauguration that brings with it its own resistance. Odd as it may seem, this will be made clearer by appeal to the historiography of psychoanalysis. Jacques Lacan and Jean Laplanche, each in his own way, read the history of psychoanalysis as the history of the resistance to its greatest insight: the unconscious.[82] More recently, Arnold I. Davidson has argued persuasively that while Freud's work on the sexual drive challenged the reigning notion of a teleological sexual instinct, he nevertheless continued to appeal to that teleology and the consequent concept of perversion.[83] According to Davidson, Freud emerged from and remained loyal to his *mentalité*, that "set of mental habits or automatisms that characterize the collective understanding and representations of a population"—in this case a commitment to a teleological view of human sexuality.[84] At the same time his work challenged that very *mentalité*, such that Freud often seems as if he were at cross-purposes with himself. Just as Davidson "wonder[s] about the accessibility of this achievement to Freud himself," so we might wonder about the accessibility of this understanding of writing as an ecstatic devotional practice to the very author who practices it.[85] This question of how accessible an innovation is to the innovator, however, does not determine the value of that innovation. For just as Davidson esteems Freud's "conceptual innovation worthy of the name of genius"[86] and insists that "genius is always ahead of itself,"[87] so we can esteem Dionysius' ecstatic writing worthy of the name of genius and entertain the possibility that with regard to this innovation Dionysius is ahead of even himself. The work of Lacan and Laplanche on the history of psychoanalysis may be especially relevant here, for they contend that any inauguration works to repress its own constitutive insights. In the case of Dionysius, it seems that the very inauguration of the hierarchical vision contains within it the potential to challenge its supremacy, or that the very articulation of the hierarchies requires a mode of discourse that implicitly questions its authority. Our author, then, might very well resist the destabilizing potential of this new mode of discourse.

There is, however, an important difference in the case of Freud and that of Dionysius. There is a fundamental incompatibility between the *mentalité* to which Freud was loyal and his own insights about the sexual drive unmoored from its procreative end. There is no such *fundamental* incompatibility between the Dionysian hierarchies and the practice of writing as an ecstatic devotional exercise. Indeed, our very understanding of writing as an effort to displace the self, to become unknown to one's own self and thereby to solicit union with the ultimately other, only makes sense against the backdrop of the hierarchies. That is to say, we can infer this understanding of writing precisely because Dionysius explains that this displacement of the self in the service of deifying union is the very goal of the hierarchies themselves. And so while writing has the same goal as the hierarchies, it stands outside the purview of the hierarchies. And insofar as writing stands outside the purview of the hierarchies, it leaves open the possibility that we might access the work of God (*energeia* or *theourgia*)—for Dionysius none other than Jesus as light and love—*otherwise*, that is, in ways *other* than those ordained by and through the celestial and ecclesiastical ranks. These different modes of access—the hierarchical and the otherwise—need not be mutually exclusive. Nor need our fifth-century author have acknowledged the possibility of access otherwise for us to explore that possibility today. My hope is that contemporary constructive theologians may be able to find ample resources in both the traditional, hierarchical account of access *and* the possibility that, through writing, we might chart a different, and perhaps complementary, course as a way to the divine.

Some will complain of distortion, infidelity to the tradition of the "Fathers" and *eisêgêsis* of contemporary concerns. But they forget—or more likely, they choose to forget—that such exploration and exploitation of latent possibilities within a manifest tradition is the only thing that makes a tradition a tradition. The early reception of the *CD* witnesses to precisely this process, wherein each side of the theological divide finds in it evidence in support of its own position. Thus the *Scholia* of John of Scythopolis and Maximus the Confessor helped facilitate the "odyssey" of the *CD* from the heretical to the orthodox fold, and they did so largely by using parts of the *CD* as leverage against other parts.[88] I would have contemporary theologians to do the same, that is, explore the fissures within the Dionysian universe, not in order to bring the whole down, but in order to set the author against himself, the text against itself, ourselves against ourselves, and thereby to accept the ecstatic invitation.

Incarnations: Body/Image

Bodies without Wholes: Apophatic Excess and Fragmentation in Augustine's *City of God*

VIRGINIA BURRUS AND KARMEN MACKENDRICK

One can easily discover in Augustine "the elements of a negative theology," as Vladimir Lossky observed in 1954.[1] Yet if the North African theologian positively embraces a *docta ignorantia*,[2] this ignorance is not without limit, as Lossky also notes. A forgotten knowledge limns Augustine's unknowing.[3] His is a queer apophasis, then—an apophasis of confession, not least. In confession, there is always more to say—and to unsay. One never gets to the bottom of it all, for no utterance is ever quite right. The self eludes language as surely as God does.

David Dawson writes regarding the necessary inadequacy of theological language that its breaks, the "ontological and moral fissures between human intention and expression," have two sources: the "insurmountable qualitative division between God and creation"—in other words, God's always-excessiveness in relation to us—and the fallen urge to tell lies,[4] which, as Augustine's multiplying confessions suggest, may get themselves all tangled up in our often-excessive telling (or making) of truth as well.[5] The fragmentation, the break not only between intention and expression but also between human and divine in the fallen world, produces excess, not merely by adding on lies to the truth, but by keeping us talking (perhaps fictively) toward a God our words can never reach:

The arguments of this essay emerge out of deeply pleasurable collaborative conversation, the text out of combined efforts of inscription and erasure, both painful and pleasurable. Our names are listed in merely alphabetical order, of course.

there is always more to say. We hope, here, to read Augustinian apophasis as a matter of excess and fragmentation, of the always-more and the breaking-apart.

Denys Turner argues for the interconnection of negative and affirmative theological speech, the necessary inherence of each within the other, through an argument about a body. Christ, he says, is not only "the Way" to knowing God, but at the same time the way to the unknowability of God. "For in that catastrophe of destruction, in which the humanity of Christ is brought low, is all the affirmative capacity of speech subverted: thus it is that through the drama of Christ's life on the one hand and death on the other, through the recapitulation of the symbolic weight and density of creation in this human nature on the one hand, and its destruction on the Cross on the other, is the complex interplay of affirmative and negative fused and concretely realized."[6] Perhaps at the limit of unsaying, where our multiplying words fall silent, we find not only God but also the body, which speaks and yet eludes being-said.[7] Or: we find God becoming body. In the body of God rendered susceptible to destruction—even, just possibly, in the God destroyed in becoming body—are both the ultimate theological negative (unsayable, even unthinkable) and the most concrete theological affirmation (the flesh-which-is-the-word itself, present among us)—an affirmation that turns negation around on itself by unsaying the divine unsayability, giving itself as if to be said, while continuing to elude our language in its very presence.[8]

In Augustine's texts, bodies consistently evade wholeness, produce excess, affirm, and negate—and approach a God who likewise does all of these things. In *Confessions*, Augustine seems to be in constant struggle with excess and with his own (perhaps rhetorically exaggerated) excessive behavior; with the excessive temptations of his somatic desires, which must somehow be moderated without eliminating the use and appreciation of those senses; and with the burning self-exceeding desire for God, in whom we might finally rest (in fullness of satisfaction and knowledge), though we never quite do. Compared to *Confessions, City of God* is more didactic and tends (size notwithstanding) to feel more restrained; Augustine is less prone here to the gorgeous outbursts of either praise or pleading that frequently irrupt in *Confessions*. This work, however, has its own excessive modes. A wearied reader might be inclined to find them simply in its length, but in fact there are other forms of excess within the bounds of this strange text as it tries to find or make the truth, and some of these, as they attempt to stretch language (laid out in time, one word after another) before and after itself, also draw the excesses of the textual or discursive and of the somatic together in revelatory ways.[9] Augustine strains to remember a paradise that never was, so as to imagine a heaven that just might be—and all by observing closely the infinitely weird world that is ever emerging.[10]

City of God describes several modes of what we might call corporeal excess—and in so doing, not only tends to textual versions as well, but pushes into the conceptual excess of paradox. Saying (about God, about bodies, about God's body) is cut through by the unsayable (God, bodies, God's body). In the passages on bodies, even more than in the rest of the text, Augustine seems unable to restrain the urge to go on and on, to make extensive lists that nonetheless cannot be exhaustive (and one wonders if he might have been frustrated by this incompletion, by the insistence of bodies on overflowing the descriptions that try so hard to contain them). In the kind of *apophasis*-by-*kataphasis* most famously demonstrated by Pseudo-Dionysius, the overflowing text gestures toward what it cannot capture, the overwhelming presence of incarnation and Incarnation. Like the *City of God* more broadly, the mortal bodies within it offer glimpses both of an "original," unfallen "past" and a redeemed, transfigured "future" that takes up and resembles (also reassembles), but does not re-create, that past. Like the incarnate God, the mortal bodies of the text twist the intellect past comprehension.[11]

Thus we find pages and pages, chapter after chapter, describing bodies that go beyond the "normal" boundaries of fallen nature, whether by proportion (as in the case of giants), duration (longevity associated with gigantism), type (the various forms of "monstrosity" Augustine discusses), or will (unusual abilities to control various parts of the body, or, on the flipside of this, the capacity of the body to rebel against the will or the inadequacy of the will to control the body). Augustine in the face of this overflow seems quite unable to contain himself—he, too, is too much. We'll suggest that even the beauty and desirability of bodies, about which he also has plenty to say, might be regarded as exceeding necessity. In his discussions and descriptions of body, we are led into Augustine's (never quite successful) efforts to reincorporate and reinscribe excess, to reintegrate it into a properly contained text, a neatly bounded body, a whole clearly distinguishable from a collection of fragments. In particular, the resurrected or glorified body—the body most closely modeled on God's own risen flesh—appears repeatedly as the body restored to order, freed from excess as from fragmentation.[12] But this freeing, as we shall see, not only fails, it actually leads to a deeper breakage, a more dramatic spilling-over. As our bodies become more like God's body, in this resurrection modeled on that of Christ, they, like God, break open and overflow our capacity to say.

We begin with the case of bodies that go beyond the limits apparently set by nature. Antediluvian humanity, Augustine assures us, was both longer-lived and larger than the present version. Taking his first evidence from Virgil's *Aeneid,* he also cites the evidence of "bones of incredible size" and enormous human molars uncovered in tombs (*City of God* 15.9). He argues that even when humans in general were larger (as he assumes they once were), there were exceptions, giants among them, just as there are humans today who are giant in comparison to most. Similarly, while he is uncertain about the nature and status of the "sons of God" who are said in Genesis 6 to have mated with human women, he is not perturbed by claims about their giant offspring, saying to those who doubt them: "There had been giants on earth when the sons of God took as wives the daughters of men. . . . It is true that giants were also born after this happened. . . . Thus there were giants both before and after that time" (*City of God* 15.23).

These humans who take up an exceptional amount of space are also credited with taking up an exceptional amount of time. Granting that material evidence cannot prove duration as it can size, Augustine nonetheless declares, "we should not for that reason call in question the reliability of the sacred narrative," adding that "Pliny also states that there is to this day a nation where men live for two hundred years" (*City of God* 15.9). He goes on to give numerous examples of long-lived biblical figures, noting minor discrepancies in the reporting of their ages but deciding that these are not significant and do not affect the truth of the claim that people once lived very long lives.

In addition to these long-lived giants of both past and present, there is among humans a multiplicity of corporeal types that can only be called excessive. Ostensibly concerned with the relatively succinct point that anything human is a descendent of Adam, Augustine here cannot resist the multiplication of examples:

> There are accounts in pagan history of certain monstrous races of men. If these are to be believed, the question arises whether we are to suppose that they descended from the sons of Noah, or rather from that one man from whom they themselves derived. Some of these monsters are said to have only one eye . . . ; others have the soles of their feet turned backwards behind their legs; others have the characteristics of both sexes. . . . Then there are men without mouths, who live only by inhaling through their nostrils; there are others whose height is only a cubit. . . . We are told in another place that there are females who conceive at the age of five and do not live beyond their eighth year. There is also a story of a race who have a single leg attached to their feet; they cannot bend their knee, and yet have a remarkable turn of speed. . . . There are some men without necks, and with their eyes in their shoulders. . . .
>
> What am I to say of the *Cynocephali*, whose dog's head and actual barking prove them to be animals rather than men? (*City of God* 16.8)

Nor does he stop here,[13] though these examples should suffice. It is hard not to be drawn into his obsession with the wholly unnecessary, utterly fascinating variability of human phenotypes, even if we don't quite share his credulity. Similarly, it is difficult to the point of impossibility not to be drawn into his enthusiastic descriptions of peculiar bodily abilities, excessive both in sheer number and in going so far beyond utility.

> Some people can even move their ears, either one at a time or both together. Others without moving the head can bring the whole scalp . . . down toward the forehead and bring it back again at will. Some can swallow an incredible number of various articles and then with a slight contraction of the diaphragm, can produce, as if out of a bag, any article they please, in perfect condition. There are others who imitate the cries of birds and beasts and the voices of any other men, reproducing them so accurately as to be quite indistinguishable

> from the originals, unless they are seen. A number of people produce at will such musical sounds from their behind (without any stink) that they seem to be singing from that region. I know from my own experience of a man who used to sweat whenever he chose; and it is a well-known fact that some people can weep at will and shed floods of tears.
>
> Far more incredible is the phenomenon which a great many of our brothers witnessed in recent times. There was a presbyter in the diocese of Calama, named Restitutus. Whenever he pleased . . . he would withdraw himself from all sensations, to the accompaniment of cries like those of someone making lamentation, and would then lie immobile, exactly like a corpse. When pinched and pricked he felt nothing whatsoever, and even when he was burned by the application of fire he was quite insensible to pain, except later on from the resulting burn. (*City of God* 14.24)

In each of these cases—excesses of size, duration, type, and ability—Augustine rhetorically performs too-muchness even as he so eagerly describes it; in each case, even the too-much is not exhaustive, and the bodies overflow the text, refusing capture by their descriptions, always leaving more to say.

The flesh also exceeds the will—both God's will and ours, disobeying our very own commands. This disobedience, the split of the body from its perfect harmony with will, is for Augustine the consequence of an original disobedience, better known, of course, as original sin. Humans willfully disobey God in a fleshly act (eating) that manifests the split between human and divine wills, and find in partial consequence that their own flesh, formerly altogether docile to will, becomes disobedient, not only to God, but to their own intentions. Disobedience multiplies: "Who can list all the multitude of things that man wishes to do and cannot, while he is disobedient to himself, that is, while his very mind and even his lower element, his flesh, do not submit to his will?" (*City of God* 14.15). As a result, humans find themselves driven by contradictory desires. Indeed, somatic insubordination links flesh to desire so strongly that many readers are convinced that the original sin is sex, and not the distraction and insubordination of the will. In this fallen world, desires multiply outrageously, scattering among beautiful objects and worldly pleasures. The Augustinian ideal is desire reunified such that it is solely directed to God. The will thus reintegrated would harmonize not only with itself and with God's will but with the flesh as well.

Augustine writes of the flesh as obedient or disobedient, yet if flesh is not will, it is unclear exactly how these terms apply. Disobedient flesh seems to be more than merely recalcitrant matter. When my body responds contrary to my will or fails to respond to my will, I experience a different kind of failure and disharmony than I do when I cannot move a very large rock or get it to float on water. The resurrected flesh that is to be reintegrated with will turns out to be not only conceptually slippery but also conceptually excessive—always slipping out of place, always spilling over.

It is in Augustine's attempts at a conceptual reintegration (a reincorporation or reinscription) of our not-so-docile bodies that the unsayability of bodies most evidently fragments and exceeds the text. Here too we may begin with the phenomenon of very large bodies. The effort to reintegrate excessive size comes about indirectly, in the discussion of a problem that arises in considering the resurrection of the body, to wit: What about the leftover bits?

The problem of the leftover bits is this: if our bodies are raised whole (as Augustine claims), what becomes of all those parts—he mentions nail clippings and cut hair—that once belonged to a given body?[14] Do they simply disappear? Are we resurrected into our glorified bodies with yard-long toenails? What happens?

Augustine's solution is weird, but elegant. He declares:

> All that is required is that the whole pot should be re-made out of the whole lump, that is, that all the clay should go back into the whole pot, with nothing left over.
>
> Now the hair has been cut, and the nails have been pared, again and again. And if the restoration of what has been cut would disfigure the body, then it will not be restored. But that does not mean that anything will "perish" from the person at the resurrection. Such constituents will be returned to the same body, to take their place in its structure, undergoing a change of substance to make them suitable for the parts in which they are used. (*City of God* 22.19)

In other words, as long as all the "stuff" that was ever of the body is gathered, it needn't retain exactly the form it once had. This, we have to assume, would make all of us enormous—if, not insignificantly, well-proportioned. That is, in our resurrected, glorified bodies, we will all be giants.

Or maybe not. Having presented this intriguing solution, Augustine seems less certain of it in the text's next section, where he writes that

> in the resurrection of the body for eternal life the body will have the size and dimensions which it had attained, or was to attain, at maturity, . . . with its appropriate beauty preserved also in the proportions of all the parts. If, in order to preserve this beauty, something has been taken from a part displeasing by excessive size, and if this is dispersed throughout the whole body, in such a way that this material is not lost, while the congruence of the parts is kept, then there is no absurdity in believing that there may be some addition to the stature of the body as a result of this. . . . On the other hand, if it is maintained that every person is to rise again with the precise stature he had when he departed this life, there is no occasion for violent opposition to such an opinion. (*City of God* 22.20)

Faced with the potential excessiveness of risen bodies, Augustine does not so much backtrack as multiply his options. Perhaps we are all to be giants. Perhaps we rise the same size as we lived, but well-proportioned (with the added matter of our too-big bits redistributed—if we were too large overall, whatever that might mean, would we become unusually dense, excessive in weight but not in volume?). That we might have the stature we *would have attained* at maturity is also startling: evidently a body may acquire, not merely all the matter it ever had, but matter that it never incorporated. Resurrected bodies must take account not only of the material accumulation of the past but of the material potential of the future. Not just descriptively, but conceptually, an excess of body seems again to produce an excess of text. Even if we allow multiple possible answers to the problem of size, however, a few puzzles remain.

First, while we might prefer to join him in not thinking about it, it does seem problematic that Augustine gives little consideration to waste matter. (Even in his excessive thoroughness, he cannot reincorporate everything.) The body always is, always wants, and always makes too much. There is an indirect mention of waste in the discussion of cannibalism, where Augustine writes, "Now surely no one is going to maintain, with any show of truth or reason, that the whole of a body so eaten passes straight through the intestinal tract without any change or conversion into flesh of the eater" (*City of God* 22.20). Presumably waste matter is what passes through the body without becoming a part of it as the rest of one's food does. Are we then to exclude from reassemblage everything within us that could without harm have been eliminated from us? And how would we know just what that would be? The puzzle of waste raises the puzzle of boundaries, of what counts as body, of what is properly internal.

The issue of cannibalism raises other puzzles, as bodies overlap, overflow into each other. Augustine grants eternal "possession" of the body's meat to the one whose body it first was, rather than to the one who is nourished by consuming that body (*City of God* 22.20). This leaves unaddressed the question of the body of the one who ate human flesh and gained mass by so doing: Is such a person resurrected as smaller, thinner, or less dense? Cannibalism is admittedly rare, but (though Augustine does not mention it in this context) we do ingest one another, from the time that we are infants at the breast (cf. *Conf.* 1.6). Again, the flesh exceeds; our bodies overflow and forget their bounds. This confusion is not merely spatial but temporal; the analysis of cannibalism suggests that I get the flesh if it was mine first, but it is not at all clear whether mother's milk, safely exuded, would be resurrected with mother or child.[15] It becomes impossible to figure out just what can be, or what ought to be, contained "within" the body. The very insistence on bodily integrity, on re-incorporating everything that was ever of the body, runs into multiplicity (matter shared among multiple bodies); the boundaries of interiority and exteriority do not hold, in space or in time. It becomes difficult to say what is broken or whole, excessive or insufficient. It becomes difficult, too, to say the body, to know where we are saying too much.[16]

Time is a central question in boundary issues, as Augustine struggles with first possession of matter, matter once possessed and later discarded, and matter that would at some future point have come into one's possession. Certainly there is something unusual in the time of resurrected bodies. They seem to reintegrate extreme longevity by making even longer—indeed, sempiternal—lives the bodily norm. Just as we will all be giants (maybe), so too we will all live a long time—so long that length of time will cease to make sense (if we lived forever, would we still keep count?). Time is more shareable than space: each body can take up all that remains of time in a way that it can't take up all of space, which is part of what creates the problems with size (how to cram eternal flesh into a finite place?). But the very time of that heavenly, infinitely extended "future," the fleshly living-again, is excessive; again, it takes up the paradisiacal past (before sin earned its wage of death) and yet goes beyond it to a mysteriously greater glory. All of time's sweep seems to be not merely unfolded here, but infolded, gathered—again, as in eternity—not only because paradise is taken up and transfigured but also because, as we've seen, the very matter of the body must be very strangely regathered from its various distributions across time. These bodies are indeed made, not (only) to last, but (also) to be eternal, to share in God's eternity.[17]

The beauty of these eternal bodies has already been emphasized in the necessity that they be well-proportioned. It plays another, slightly different, role in Augustine's effort to explain the monstrous multiplicity of forms that we find in the human bodies of this world.

> The explanation given for monstrous human births among us can also be applied to some of those monstrous races. [That is, the same explanation holds for individual and group monstrosity.] For God is the creator of all, and he himself knows where and when any creature should be created or should have been created. He has the wisdom to weave the beauty of the whole design out of the constituent parts, in their likeness and diversity. The observer who cannot view the whole is offended by what seems the deformity of a part since he does not know how it fits in. (*City of God* 16.8)

The argument here is of a familiar form, a variant on the argument from the greater good, which holds that what from a particular perspective seems evil, wrong, or bad (even aesthetically) turns out to be good or beautiful if we can take a greater perspective. In this case, Augustine argues, the apparently monstrous multiplicity of types actually contributes to the beauty of the world. He does not, to be sure, precisely clarify how—but perhaps such clarity can only be attained from the perspective of God. Yet this argument, dependent on the whole, demands multiplicity, declaring it necessary to God's design for goodness. The whole, however constructed, cannot be a totality, or singular, or seamless.

Beauty as an argument continues to appear in Augustine's efforts to reintegrate bodily excesses. It is not merely the case that beauty is a characteristic of the resurrected body; it is a characteristic by which that body is distinguished from, by which it in fact transforms, the mortal flesh: we will all be well-proportioned. But perhaps we ought to be a little suspicious of this: there is a kind of excess to the very fact of beauty, which goes beyond practical necessity. Augustine (notoriously the Augustine of Book 10 of *Confessions*) is himself suspicious of beauty, not least because it provokes desire. But what happens to desire in the resurrection?

To consider this, we can return to the discussion in *City of God* regarding the startling range of human ability. Far from being a difficulty for which Augustine must account, this range is presented as evidence in favor of the hope that humanity might someday find its collective will in harmony with that of God. This hope is presented in a curious parallel to humanity's edenic obedience:

> We observe then that the body, even under present conditions, is an obedient servant to some people in a remarkable fashion beyond the normal limitations of nature; this is shown in many kinds of movements and feelings, and it happens even in men who are living this present troubled life in the corruptible flesh. If this is so, is there any reason why we should not believe that before the sin of disobedience and its punishment of corruptibility, the members of a man's body could have been the servants of man's will without any lust, for the procreation of children? (*City of God* 14.24)

The maximum of bodily control by the will in the present world gestures back toward the perfect obedience of Eden and forward to the perfect harmony of the world redeemed. Perhaps, in the kingdom to come, as our bodies harmonize with our wills as with God's, we shall all be able to wiggle our ears.

This nostalgically recalled (or creatively invented) capacity of the will to control the body is in contrast to the body's persistent capacity to exceed the will—that is, to our hereditary somatic disobedience, the incapacity of the will and body to harmonize perfectly such that to will an act is to do it. The paradigmatically disobedient flesh of the genitals (that which most often inconveniences us by countering our good intentions, and where, presumably, "disturbance" was first felt) is aesthetically reintegrated into the resurrected and glorified body. The context this time is the question—startling to contemporary readers—of whether women will remain female in the resurrection.

> While all defects will be removed from those bodies, their essential nature will be preserved. Now a woman's sex is not a defect; it is natural. And in the resurrection it will be free of the necessity of intercourse and childbirth. However, the female organs will not subserve their former use; they will be part of a new beauty, which will not excite the lust of the beholder—there will be no lust in that life—but will arouse the praises of God for his wisdom and compassion, that he not only created out of nothing but freed from corruption that which he had created. (*City of God* 22.17)

This is a very full little paragraph, well beyond exegesis within this essay, but a few points stand out for our purposes. The resurrected body is free from necessity as imposed by use-value (no longer disobedient, the genitals are no longer useful either), free from distracting desire (that is, any desire that might turn us away from the divine), and so beautiful that it arouses in the viewer the praises of God. Augustine insists on the beauty of even mortal bodies, of which he says that "one would be at a loss to say whether utility or beauty is the major consideration in their creation." What functions well and harmoniously is beautiful, but beauty may also be nonfunctional. Some of the body is simply aesthetic and impractical, he argues, "for example, the nipples on a man's chest, and the beard on his face." In resurrected bodies, however, beauty clearly trumps use value: "For practical needs are, of course, transitory; and a time will come when we shall enjoy one another's beauty for itself alone, without any lust. And this above all is a motive for the praise of the Creator, to whom the psalm says, 'You have clothed yourself in praise and beauty' [Ps. 104.1, LXX]" (*City of God* 22.24). These are the bodies that most nearly approach the body of God, not only in their form but also in their speaking, as they praise the world, seeing that it is good.[18]

Granted that form need not follow function, we nonetheless come to suspect something odd in the insistence on the unnecessary beauty of risen bodies; it is hard to see where or why anything unnecessary would *stop,* how its proper and proportionate place could be defined or determined. Perhaps more important, it is even harder to see what beauty (or for that matter praise) might mean in detachment from desire. Even Kant, who Germanically insists on removing "interest" from aesthetic sensation, insists equally that the response to beauty must be a kind of desire.[19] Desire is not self-limiting; it may be cut short by satisfaction, but on its own it often tends to excess, most of all when it desires the divine. Fiery desire, too, draws us back and forth in time, back toward memory, forward toward rejoining divinity. But by now we must suspect even more strongly that this time is not so simply a before, now, and after; the before of this memory is rather more ontological than temporal, the after as much an eternity as an indefinite endurance, a fullness of life in time. Overfull life, life in awe and joy at beauty, life in search of God, is life in desire.

And beauty does create for Augustine a particular kind of desire: the desire to praise. This might reintegrate beauty neatly, were praise itself not excessive speech, already full to bursting. As any reader of *Confessions* knows, praise spills forth sensuously, repetitively, not always voluntarily, often in fragments rather than sentences, often in sentences that keep on going. It imparts no information and performatively accomplishes no deed. If beauty's "function" is to draw forth praise, it is most excessive of all, as Augustine himself suggests. In *City of God,* having finished his recitation of all the beauties and utilities of creation, he adds: "I have here made a kind of compressed pile of blessings. If I decided to take them singly, to unwrap each one, as it were, and to examine it, with all the detailed blessings contained within it, what a time it would take! And these are all the consolations of humanity under condemnation, not the rewards of the blessed" (*City of God* 22.24). The praise of God for the blessings of the resurrected life would surely push language to its limits, and then past them. Most present in the flesh—in Incarnation and in the beauty of glorified bodies—God becomes most apophatic, most boundary-burstingly unsayable.

The scattered wills of worldly desire are drawn together in this direction of the will toward God, with the flesh delighting (through) the senses. But the neatness of this unity, the sense of wholeness and propriety as if in the perfection of self-control, slips again. The redeemed will is one with the flesh but also restored to its proper harmony with God's will—a harmony of complete subordination. Autonomy, just when it seems to be perfected, is overwhelmed, and so it must be: self-will is the original sin. Thus to attain this perfect control is not to be in control at all, but to give the will over. Praise is given not as to an admired or beloved object, but within a loop of divine self-delight. More, desire thus drawn together, thus concentrated, is explosive, a single spark bursting the boundaries of the autonomous self. The praise of God drawn forth from all these gorgeous bodies is also God's own joyful desire, concentrated in the flesh. Will, flesh, and God are in perfect harmony, but only by undoing the sense of all three terms, only in the bursting forth of irresistible praise, surely not "voluntary" in the deliberative sense we commonly attribute to the term.

In *Confessions*, Augustine seeks neither to repress nor simply to redirect desire but to intensify it further, once he has turned desire to God; he asks God to set him on fire, burning hotter than the Carthaginian cauldron of unholy loves: he asks that the desire for God usurp his will.[20] *City of God* concerns itself differently with desire in excess of will and struggles to glorify that desire right out of existence, just as it endeavors to transfigure the too-much, the left-over, that which is in excess of both nature and will, into the beautiful, the fitting, the proportionate, the proper. But the too-much of size keeps on overflowing; there is always more to incorporate until we come to the blurred boundaries of bodies incorporating each other. We face the question not only of where the body ends, but when, as eternity folds the past of paradise into an infinite future. The too-much of beauty persists in linking itself to desire, which bursts out into praise for the creator of those beautiful bodies, yet is somehow not supposed to touch the bodies themselves, for they can never be possessed. But it remains the beauty of bodies that draws us in and the excess of desire, divinely overwhelming the autonomous will, that breaks us apart.

The beautiful body *is* apophatic: whether sensuous or spoken, it at once overfills, overspills the event of its manifestation. The superlative beauty of the embodied divine, Word made flesh and mortal flesh glorified, is the paradoxical maximum of coherence and breakage, excess and fragmentation, saying and unsaying in an infinite un-vicious circling. Michael Sells elegantly points out three characteristics of classical Western apophasis. It is characterized by the metaphor of overflowing[21]—here rendered still more complex by the mutual overflow of body and language, the mutual divinity of which and into which they seem to come and to break. It is "dis-ontological," struggling to avoid reification of the transcendent[22]—as the God, the body, the words that would say them explode into multiplicity and negation in the very act of making nouns; where there was just about to be one neatly gathered, suddenly there are more than we can re-collect. Finally, in apophasis is found "a distinctive dialectic of transcendence and immanence in which the utterly transcendent is revealed as the utterly immanent."[23] God, the slippery always-becoming always-more that cannot quite be nominalized, transcends all corporeality and all saying only and exactly by being all corporeality and all saying, all of each and more than either, shattering both. Not only language, but we who would use it, we who are made by it, are lost here; at the asymptote of the approach, God too is lost in the only places we find God: both in saying and in flesh.

Bodies Still Unrisen, Events Still Unsaid: A Hermeneutic of Bodies without Flesh

JOHN D. CAPUTO

Only those who are unfamiliar with theology would be surprised to hear that theology is all about bodies, very corporeal bodies, mystical bodies, bodies politic, but also what Saint Paul called the *soma pneumatikon* (1 Cor 15),[1] a certain "spiritual body," which, if there is such a thing, is my special interest here. Of all these visible but slightly immaterial and insubstantial incarnations one body in particular stands out, the "risen body" in the New Testament, which I treat as a focal body. It is upon just such a body that Christian theology has turned from of old. It marks both its *arche*—"the first fruits"—and its *eschaton*—our "faith is in vain" (1 Cor 15:20, 14), for the whole end of our faith is that we too will be risen. As such, this body is, in one way or another, theology's bottom line, the final payoff of a certain strong theology, the sum and substance of its faith. I agree with Paul that if there is not some sort of hope in transformation as is figured in this body, then what is the use of our faith (in the event)? Of what can we dream? In what can we hope? (1 Cor 15:14). What would there be still to come? I want to answer that question by way of a hermeneutics of the risen body as figure of what I am calling an event. I make this proposal, then, not as a contribution to the exegesis of the relevant New Testament texts, although I will certainly rely upon historical-critical commentary, but as a way to answer Paul's question, which was probably, in his mind, a rhetorical one.

BODIES WITHOUT FLESH

The risen body is a distinct phenomenon that should not be confused with other related phenomena.[2] The risen body is not the same as the immortality of the soul, where immortality is gained by separating the soul from the mortal and corruptible body. The risen body represents a refusal to be separated from the material body. It refuses to abdicate the body and insists on the reinstatement of the body even after death and in such a way as to transcend death. The risen body is not a resuscitated body—Lazarus and the daughter of Jairus are resuscitated, but they do not have risen bodies. Rather, in being brought back to life, they reassume their mortal or corruptible bodies, subject all over again to suffering and to death at a later date. Snatched from death once, their final death is but deferred; exceptionally, they actually have to die twice. The risen body is not a matter of reincarnation, in which an imperishable soul migrates from one corruptible body to another. The risen body is not matter of eternal recurrence, in which one passes through the cycle of birth and death, living this same corruptible life over and over again, being born and dying over and over again.

According to Paul, who comes the closest to giving us an account of it, the risen body refers to rising again from the dead in such a way as to put all mortality and corruptibility behind it once and for all. For this transformation to occur one would not even, in principle, have to die—since it was Paul's expectation and that of the early Church that Jesus would return in their lifetime, and they would then all put on this immortality. I will tell you a mystery—we will all be transformed, but we will not all die (1 Cor 15:51). The body that is risen, reinstated, and resurrected is "imperishable" or incorruptible (1 Cor 15: 35–54), released from suffering and death. One might also speculate that it is blocked from sensual pleasures, since pain and pleasure are seated alike in self-feeling; if it cannot feel pain, it cannot feel at all. It would in fact be a body without flesh—"flesh and blood" (*sarx kai aima*) cannot inherit the Kingdom of God (1 Cor 15:50).

That makes for a quite unusual body, which is why it provides an inviting and suggestive occasion for the exploration of the event. The risen body readily rises above bodily limitations. It is able to pass through walls, to appear instantly in distant places and just as instantly to disappear (Luke 24: 31; John 20:19–29), which is effectively to have no containing place and to show no signs of being limited by temporal conditions. Such a body effectively contradicts the central features of embodiment, of spatiotemporal limitation, which is why it has the look of a body that is no less immaterial than the immaterial soul, that seeks to separate itself from the body no less than does such a soul. Indeed, in the risen body, the distinction between the soul that has escaped its body and the body it escapes begins to weaken, and it raises the question of the extent to which the notion of the risen body is a repudiation of the body, which in one sense it certainly is and in another sense it is not.

In one sense the risen body certainly does not repudiate the body.[3] The risen body is visible and in some texts identifiably the same as the mortal body, although in another text the disciples on the road to Emmaus did not recognize Jesus. It is not supposed to be a soul that has escaped its body and been set free to lead a purely immaterial life, as in the *Phaedo*. Nor is it supposed to be a ghost, as in *Hamlet*, which means a body that is quite dead but with still unfinished business on earth which requires that a phantom, replica, or simulacrum of itself be sent back to tidy up its affairs. A soul is not a body at all, and a ghost is a bodily remnant or afterglow, whereas the risen body is a completion or perfection of the body. The risen body is the same body restored and extended to perfection, a "spiritual body" (1 Cor 15:44) without the limitations of the body, related, Paul says, as the seed (the corruptible body) is to the fruit (incorruptible body) (1 Cor 15:35–37). One is reminded of the medieval Franciscans who explained angelic life by means of an "immaterial matter," a kind of prime matter that when given form issues not in a material substance but an immaterial one, which was a lighter, thinner, more light-suffused, airy, aerial, ethereal stuff, capable of a kind of absolute velocity and of passing through solid substances (passability). These bodies are "swift, hot and light, like the stars," which is why they can ascend to heaven.[4] The risen body is something like these Franciscans angels, pictorially represented by the angels in Fra Angelica's murals in San Marco, the Dominican friary at Florence, with their wispy transparency. One is also reminded of some medieval accounts of the body of Mary, which shared in these properties. Not only was she penetrated by the power of the Holy Spirit, which required a Spirit to pass through her bodily walls without damage to her virginity, but even in some of these accounts the newborn baby Jesus was able to traverse the birth canal without rupturing the hymeneal membrane.

The risen body is the restoration of the body but this time marked by passability, absolute mobility, luminosity but—above all—"incorruptibility" (Paul). These appear to be virtual and upwardly compatible possibilities, so that on any given occasion, a given power may not be exercised and the body remains subject to certain normal bodily limits or conditions. Thus in two post-Easter stories Jesus appears as a humble gardener (John 20:15), and on the road to Emmaus the appearance is unexceptional enough that the disciples do not even recognize him, and when they do he disappears (Luke 24:16). The risen body can make itself visible or rise to invisibility as the occasion demands. And just as it can make itself seen, it can make itself felt. So Jesus invites the skeptical apostles to feel his wounds, his flesh and bones; but at the same time he can pass through the walls of a locked room. So the risen body enjoys both passability and palpability! That is, it can pass through other physical objects that do not offer it resistance, but if need be, it can offer a palpable mass that can be felt, which requires resistance—otherwise, the apostles' hands would pass right through his risen body and they would not feel anything. It is, in short, a completely magical body. The risen body is a body (not an angel, soul, or ghost) whose highest defining feature is its freedom from corruption and death. While it seems able to suspend every other feature in any given situation, if the occasion calls for it, the one thing it cannot suspend is its incorruptibility—it could not die to prove a point. In this way the body is not only restored to its status in the second creation myth—where our bodies were not supposed to die and incurred mortality only by sin—but it is raised to a higher and more ethereal life.

If the idea of the risen body closely skirts the outright rejection of the body—by rejecting bodily limitations—it cannot be simply reduced to such a rejection, otherwise the construction would simply have been abandoned in favor of a soul freed from the body. The risen body is not so much the rejection of the body as its projection, the body carried to idealization or completion or fruition, as Paul says, just as in a transcendental illusion, when an empirical concept is brought to its limit or carried out to its idealized conclusion, the way an empirical circular thing is perfected in an ideal geometric circle. The risen body is not a soul without a body but a perfected body, which Paul describes as a body without suffering or corruptibility. Of course, it is to that extent unavoidably and importantly also a rejection of the body. One need only recall the Nietzschean affirmation of the body in which the test of affirmation, of the yea-sayer, is whether we are prepared to affirm the entire circle or cycle of life—of suffering no less than pleasure, of sorrow no less than joy, of the midnight darkness no less than high noon. To affirm life one-sidedly, trying to extract the joy without paying the price of sorrow, trying to extract life without its partner and attendant death is, for Nietzsche, the very definition of the nihilism of belief in the Christian afterlife. If there is to be any myth of afterlife at all for Zarathustra it is the myth of the eternal recurrence of the very lives we have, which means not only living but also suffering and dying an infinite number of times. For Nietzsche, the ring dance of eternity is a dance with the body that brought you life in the first place.

The doctrine of the risen body is thus an affirmation of the body, of incarnation, but in rather a half-hearted and qualified sense, rather like a faint-hearted friend. The doctrine affirms bodily life just so long as it is completely immunized against every bodily limitation but rejects the body when the going gets rough. When the doctrine is examined closely, it turns out that it affirms life, not the body, because the body implies suffering and death; and it affirms the body just insofar as it is a vehicle of life and not a living thing as such, which means one that also suffers, corrupts, and dies. It is not exactly an affirmation of the body but of life, and not exactly of life but of a certain life, that is, life without death. That is not *the* impossible that we dream of but the simply impossible, because it breaks the tension between the possible and the impossible. It is not a body exposed to the possibility of the unimaginable but a simply impossible body.

The risen body is at best a *figure* of the event where the event is the event of life and life more abundantly. That is why I practice transcendental suspicion on any possible spectrology. On my more hauntological accounting, the risen body, held suspect as a literal fact, is an attempt to release the *event* that stirs within the body, to release the sense, or at least a sense, of the body. The risen body is an idealization of the empirical body which is trying to express the truth of the body, the event that takes place in the body—as an event of mobility, velocity, light, power, and incorruptibility. Empirical bodies, immortal souls, ghosts, and risen bodies are so many ways to actualize or instantiate events, in words and things that are variously material or immaterial, hauntological, literary, or religious. The difference between the empirical body and the spectral risen body does not lie in the event but in the mode of realization of the event, in the figure in which the event is expressed. In the one case, it is subject to bodily limitations, in the other not; in the one case corruptible, in the other not. In the one case, it is dull, heavy, plodding, and encumbered; in the other, it is brilliant and unencumbered.

The risen body is able to rise above the limitations of space and time, illness, weariness, frailty, aging, injury, and death itself. It is a body from which all real risk and vulnerability have been removed but not without a trace. The New Testament makes a point of insisting that the "trace" of the vulnerability of the perishable body remains, as do the visible wounds in the body of the risen Jesus which doubting Thomas wishes to see and feel (John 20:26–28). Thus the passage shows a continuity of the crucified and risen body of Jesus. In short, the very "flesh" that defines the bodies that so massively populate the New Testament vanishes in the risen body. The risen body of Jesus at the end of the gospels is the opposite of the blind, lame, leprous, and paralyzed bodies with which the gospel narratives open. The risen body of Jesus is the "firstborn," the first of the bodies to be transformed by the event, which all other bodies, our bodies, are to follow. The sparks the agent body gives off, the surge of power, agility, mobility, the sway and swagger of being on the move are all magnified, intensified, and concentrated in a single entity whose characteristic status is to be neither mere matter nor pure spirit, neither immaterial soul nor merely material body, neither/nor, and thus to be the slash between the two. The risen body signals the event which is expressed in words and realized in things as a kind of non-thing or no-thing of particular brilliance and effulgence. Nothing more perfectly betokens the event than a no-thing that cannot find a firm place on the side of either souls or bodies. It is a construction peculiarly tailored to embody the event whose proper place is nowhere, whose time is always to come or lodged long ago in the irrecuperable past, whose power is the power of the impossible, of the unthought of, undreamt of, unimaginable bodies still to come.

Deleuze undertook his study of *Alice* unencumbered by any background problem of the search for the historical Alice or by an institution hovering in the background monitoring the interpretation of the text and armed with the disciplinary weapons of heresy and excommunication. Deleuze was not trying to establish the empirical probability of the things that occur in Wonderland but to explore the range of the event, the free-floating character of the exercise of the event of sense, to examine how the event is released in an exemplary text, in which events were set free in a special way. Without in any way conflating the nature and the intentions of these texts, the New Testament displays the workings of the event in a suggestively parallel way. In both texts, bodies—both spectral and literary—are emancipated from the laws of physics, and meaning is emancipated from the laws of signification. In the New Testament, the result is a phenomenology of the spectral body as a thing of beauty, power, and incorruptibility, marked by qualities of shining whiteness and glowing incandescence.

The unique character of the risen body of Jesus is brought out clearly in a fascinating episode. After his appearance on the road to Emmaus, according to Luke, Jesus appeared to the disciples assembled in Jerusalem, seemingly out of the blue, who were startled and "thought that they were seeing a ghost (*pneuma*)." He reassured them and urged them to look at the wounds in his risen body, and urged them to touch him: "[F]or a ghost does not have flesh and bones as you see that I have." Then, as a pièce de résistance, he took a piece of broiled fish and ate it to allay their doubts (Luke 24:36–43), after which he led them out to Bethany, blessed them, and "was carried up into heaven" (Luke 24:50). That is an episode that surely requires a gloss. If it is left to stand as it is, its implications would overwhelm the narratives of the risen body. It would imply a functioning digestive tract and consequently the production of waste products, a heavenly food industry, requiring farms, a favorable climate, and a waste-management industry, to put it all rather circumspectly.[5] What is foolish or amusing about this, of course, is that we have literalized and reified an event, conflated an event with some sort of heavenly or otherworldly fact of the matter, where not only the world is everything that is the case, as Wittgenstein said, but heaven is too. That would be the equivalent of taking seriously what sort of housing, food supply, and waste-management system would be required to accommodate Alice's surprising change of size in Wonderland, or where the Mad Hatter purchases his tea.

Thomas Aquinas proposed a way out of this dilemma by offering a typically ingenious metaphysical gloss on this amazing episode, in which he relied on an analogy adopted from the Venerable Bede about the contrasting ways the earth and the sun consume water. The earth is "thirsty" for water, meaning that it consumes water by absorbing it from defect or need, while the sun is higher than or in excess of water, and does not "need" water, and so it consumes water by burning it up or evaporating it. The mortal body is like the earth—it needs food—but the risen body is like the sun—it does not need food but consumes it by evaporating it or burning it up. The food is not transformed into the risen body of Christ (which would create the need for heavenly plumbers) but evaporated, reduced from an actual object to its primal potency. But, since Aquinas does not allow for annihilation, which contradicts God's purpose in creation, then where did the broiled fish that Jesus ate go? If not into the resurrected digestive tract of the risen body of Jesus, then where? The same place water goes when it is evaporated by the sun. So Aquinas thinks the fish was disseminated into minute and undetectable particles into the atmosphere, just the way water is by the sun. Those particles, which could in principle be recombined by the power of God to reconstitute the food, are the "preexisting matter" or potencies from which it was assembled in the first place.

From the point of view of a historical-critical view of the Scriptures, Aquinas is not far off, but with this difference: the resurrected body is not analogous to a heavenly body; it *is* a heavenly body, of the same stuff. Of course, the problem here is that, as Dale Martin says, there is "no fixed tradition as to the exact nature of the resurrected body of Jesus" in the New Testament.[6] Luke and John make a point of emphasizing that resurrection is a resurrection of the flesh, that the hands of Thomas could feel the soft tissues of Jesus' wounded side, that Jesus could eat broiled fish, have breakfast of fish with the disciples on the shores of the Lake Tiberias, and share bread with the disciples in the inn at Emmaus, and that he was no "ghost" (*pneuma*). Paul, who knows nothing of these later narratives, explicitly rejects that possibility in advance, almost verbatim, which seems like just the sort of thing to bring down ridicule upon the whole idea of resurrection as patently mythical and magical, and about that I think Paul is right. If one took Luke and John literally, one would then face the problem of coming up with something to avoid the paradoxes of heavenly waste disposal.

To avoid such ridiculous consequences, while not giving up on the idea of the resurrection of the body completely, as Martin shows in a close analysis of 1 Corinthians 15, Paul took pains to distinguish the features of corruptible and incorruptible bodies. Corruptible bodies are strictly earthly bodies, made of earthly dirt, while heavenly bodies are made of a purer, finer astral material. Paul distinguishes not between body and soul (Plato), or body and mind (Descartes), but between gross bodies and refined bodies. Human bodies are composed of elements of both. As descendants of Adam, we are possessed of the lower elements, which Paul characterizes as *sarx,* flesh, the soft tissues of the body responsible for feeling, and *psyche*, a "soul," or in Latin an "*anima*," which is responsible for its animate vegetative and sentient life, which it shares with the animals on land, sea, and air. Finally, it has the element of *pneuma,* which is responsible for the higher acts of cognitive and intelligent life; this is nothing "immaterial" in the modern sense, but consists in the finest, most refined, and ethereal of material substances, out of which the sun, the moon, and the stars are made. So the natural place of *pneuma* is not the air but the heavens. These are heavenly bodies, *somata epourania*. The first two elements, *sarx* and *psyche*, belong to the sphere of *hyle*, which is commonly translated as "matter," but which meant the grosser, heavier side of matter, while *pneuma* means ether, fire, and air, more refined and lighter materialities. Now while we today would say that fire and air belong to the "material" world, they were not in Paul's vocabulary hyletic (*hyle*) or "material" (in the "gross," or narrow, sense) like wood or dirt. In the resurrected body, it is *pneuma* that survives, but not *sarx* or *psyche*. The resurrected body is still a body (*soma*), not a gross-hyletic body but a "pneumatic body," one that sheds its grossness and is resurrected in a highly refined ethereal body whose function is one of higher intelligent life but not lower biological or zoological life. One gets a sense of this in contemporary debates among theoretical physicists who point out that in the sphere of particle physics, one is no long dealing with "matter" (in the gross sense) because of the minuteness of the particles, by which the physicists do not mean to say that they are studying spiritual substances.

To be sure, many questions arise about this fine-grained, ethereal, and delicate body. Would a resurrected pneumatic body have an organic structure? It would have no need of organs to perform the functions of digestion and reproduction, which are functions of death and corruptibility. We eat because otherwise the individual body would die; we reproduce because otherwise the species would die. So it would seem that part of the ridiculousness Paul was trying to avoid was the idea of resurrecting useless but incorruptible and immortal bodily organs of digestion and reproduction. Of course, one might imagine that such a body could continue to "breathe" since that is an operation performed among the finest airy-ethereal elements of which it itself is composed—and hence that such a body would have a respiratory system. Possibly—but if so, this could not at all imply the possibility of being suffocated or choking to death, which would expose the risen body to corruption and death. But, then, again, it might also be that such a body would not have *particular* respiratory "organs" because the entire body, the resurrected body as a whole, would be a piece of airy stuff and hence capable in its entirety of airy respiration. Then one might speculate that its respiration would consist entirely in a kind of ethereal inspiration, which would be the basis of its higher heavenly noetic life, so that it would breathe with the very life of God and the saints, or shine with their glory. One could plausibly speculate, then, that this would be a body without organs, a body of an entirely and homogeneously airy substance.

When one compares Paul's account with that of Luke and John, the latter seem to take a magical, mythopoetic, or a theopoetic view of the risen body as—implausibly—palpably risen flesh, with risen but incorruptible bodily functions like eating and drinking, while ignoring—if indeed they even knew—the way Paul had forestalled those problems in advance and explicitly ruled out risen flesh from the kingdom of God (1 Cor 15:51). Paul, who was worried about the learned despisers of resurrection among the Corinthians, avoids all such magical concoctions. He cleans up the account of the resurrected body by defining it as a body without flesh, possibly even without organs, treating it as a body made of an astral stuff that even the learned members of the ancient world would agree is incorruptible.[7] While the *hoi polloi* at Corinth would swallow almost anything, Paul was hearing objections from the educated.

The Pauline account would cause Aquinas to make some further distinctions, because he used an idea very similar to Paul's—a body made of air—to explain how the risen human body differs from the purely apparent bodies of angels, that is, the bodily forms that the angels assume when they appear to human beings. For Aquinas, angelic apparitions are only apparent bodies, assembled from condensed air, like clouds, and shaped into human form by God; they are not living bodies. These phantom angelic bodies neither take in food by need nor evaporate food from above. They do not consume food in either manner and in fact they perform no vegetative or sentient operations at all.[8] The only thing that is alive in these angelic apparitions is the immaterial angel, not the body. Risen bodies, on the other hand, are real living bodies that have been reunited to their souls—Paul does not have this Platonic and Aristotelian distinction—and what is alive in them for Aquinas is the composite of body and soul, so their bodies perform life functions, but only higher-order ones that do not imply any biological need, dependence, or corruptibility.[9]

If Deleuze could speak of the body of a schizophrenic as a body without organs, we might offer a parallel hypothesis of the risen body as a body without flesh, a body without the physics of density and volume, without the biochemistry of organic functions, and without the affective structure of vulnerability and mortality. I myself think it is also best thought of as a body without organs, not because I do not see any earthly use for organs but because I do not see any heavenly use for them! This is a body that is all function, all action and agency, all life and intelligence, without flesh, vulnerability, wound, passivity or sensuous pleasure, because if it could feel pleasure it could feel pain. The construction skirts perilously close to, but should not be confused with, a Cartesian "consciousness," which is a series of conscious experiences that could in principle take place without a real physical body, which is what Bishop Berkeley concluded about perceptual life in general.

But the idea is to avoid crossing over that Cartesian line and to retain the bodily life as an integral component, remembering that bodily resurrection was just that in first-century Judaism, which did not have a Platonic conception of the soul or a Cartesian concept of mind or consciousness. But it is a body of a more spectral sort, an astral body not only comparable to but of the same stuff as the fiery or airy ethereality of the astral bodies described by Paul, Bede, and Aquinas. The pneumatic Pauline risen body of Jesus was not hungry, did not have the pleasure of satisfying his hunger, and did not produce waste, no more than the body of Jesus could have been cut by the knife with which the broiled fish was cut, no more than he could have bled from this cut or would have had to brush his teeth after eating. His body could not suffer hunger or take nourishment, be cut or wounded, grow weary or need exercise. It is a body without flesh.

On my account, the risen body is a construction woven out of events, a literalization of an event. It imaginatively projects a body that represents the crowning triumph over the body that was crowned with thorns, that is now invulnerable to Roman swords and Roman nails and the blows of the soldiers. If the prelapsarian body of Adam is innocent of desire, naked, and uninjured, if the fallen body is wounded, mortal, and wracked by desire, and if the crucified body of Jesus is almost all flesh, then the risen body is a triumphant flash of power and beauty without flesh and the desires of the flesh. It does not get exhausted, sweaty, constipated, hungry, erotic, senescent, or stuck in traffic jams; it does not have blood pressure or a temperature; it is not lowering the risk of high cholesterol by eating fish or running the risk of getting overweight with a bad diet. It does not sink back in happy exhaustion, unable to move a limb, after a strenuous but exhilarating physical exertion. It cannot sink like a rock into bed at night. It does not need a bed or house at all, or umbrellas to protect it from the rain, where in fact it does not need to rain, and so on. It is a life without work or rest, sleep or dreaming, without food, shelter, or clothing, marrying or divorcing (Luke 20:35), virtually without everything we know as life—except the powers of relocation, ethereal visibility, luminosity, speech (*la parole soufflée*) and intelligence. It is "swift, hot and light"[10]—and intelligent.

The risen body is all agency without flesh, all action without vulnerability, all function without substance, all form without the weightier conditions of matter, all play without work, all light without density and weight, all life without death. The risen body is a body freed from this body of flesh and death. It is a body whose powers of agency have been extended or allowed to run to completion beyond all the limitations imposed by flesh, like an ideal circle in geometric space. But this body is found not in geometric space but in literary space, the space of what I call theopoetics. It instantiates the event of agency, the agency of the event, without restriction, in a body of pure action, vision, light, intelligence, and power, like the sun itself, which is why Bede and Aquinas could compare its "digestion" to the evaporative power of the sun, and why Paul thought it really was made of the same stuff as the sun. In it, these qualities, or the qualities of these events, are released or put on display, allowed free play in paradigmatic fashion.

There is even a curious connection between the risen body and technology, between these spectacular scenes in the New Testament and the literature of science fiction, between the miracles of the New Testament and the miracles of techno-science. Has not science always been dreaming of resurrection and immortality, and does not science dream of it even more today when certain impossible things have become possible? We today cannot avoid noticing how much the risen body imagines bodily possibilities that are progressively realized by medical science and contemporary robotics, bionics, and biotechnology—the possibility of moving through the air in flight, curing disease, straightening and even replacing limbs and organs and even the ultimate possibility of downloading consciousness into new bodies. We even find a high-tech equivalent of the way the risen body of Jesus was able to appear and disappear instantly, behind closed doors, in the famous "Beam me up, Scotty" scenes in the TV series "Star Trek," which project the technological possibility of instant bodily relocation. On the horizon of this techno-body is the ancient dream of the elimination of death, perhaps as an ideal limit to be approached asymptotically—right now we would all settle for an average lifetime of several hundred years—and maybe even on a transformed earth, cleaned up and protected from the right wing. There is, moreover, the interesting parallel between these astral bodies of the first century and contemporary particle physics, where the lines between the material and the immaterial get fuzzy, where we are no longer dealing with gross-hyletic matter but something quite different. Theologians like John Polkinghorne, equally at home in particle physics, offer us new theories of resurrection.

In the spectral body, like the biotechnical body, we imagine the body beyond the present, beyond the actual, beyond the possible. We imagine impossible bodies, bodies that will never die, bodies which will trump every material setback or limitation, counter every blow with a triumphant counterblow, supersede every mark of mortality with immortality; where there is death, the reduction of death; where there is death, new life. The point of the multiple bodies that populate the New Testament is the event they harbor, and the event they harbor on my accounting is summarized under the name *metanoetics*, that is, the transformability of body and heart, which turns on a logic of repetition, where every death is trumped by rebirth. The risen body, the transformed heart, are symbols of life in the Kingdom, of hearts and bodies that have come under the event of God's rule. They are symbols of a new life, a new being, a new creation, ways of dreaming of a transformed life, of reimagining the event that unfolds in life itself, in bodies still unrisen, in events still unsaid.

GRAMMATOLOGICAL AND SACRED ANARCHY

The phenomenology of the spectral body, this spectral phenomenology, is the work of a religious imagination that is structurally parallel to the work of the literary imagination of Lewis Carroll and others like him. One might even define the spectral body as a body that has suffered the event of the divine, a sacred or sacralized body, in the same way that Carroll tries to imagine a body that has been drawn into a world of logical paradoxes, that has learned to dance in a world of logical dilemmas. Both visualize, embody, incarnate, or incorporate the effect of this preternatural or extranatural force on bodily life, not as way of predicting that such bodies could or would actually happen, but as a way to write large, to visualize or illustrate, the *events* harbored by the body. *Alice* and the New Testament embody events that are thereby released, magnified, and visualized, the way a Venn diagram visualizes logical relationship of class inclusion and exclusion. When Alice grows alternately taller and shorter she embodies the relativity built into "longer than" and "shorter than" which express the "event" (sense) of magnitude or extension, just the way a "half cup of tea" exploits the ambiguities of language. Carroll's events belong to the logical and grammatological anarchy of words and meaning. They put on visual and narratival display all of the ambiguity, paradoxes, dilemmas, disseminations, and undecidabilities of language and logic. The goal is not to make a mockery of language and logic, no more than it is to suggest that this is a world that would or could come about. It is rather to suggest the ambience of life and language, the ambience of the event. It suggests the flexibility, the undecidability, or what Derrida calls the unprogrammability of life. The rule that logic and language exert over us is not tyrannical, absolute, rigid, or deterministic. Logic and language do not close our lives off, determine or predetermine them, or bind them in. On the contrary, they harbor the possibility of the surprise, of the unforeseen twist, of what would otherwise have seemed impossible.

To the logical and grammatological anarchy of Lewis Carroll there corresponds the sacred anarchy of the New Testament, which depicts a world of bodies undergoing no less marvelous metamorphoses. Seen in terms of the event, the point is not to determine whether such bodies enjoyed factual existence or could come about in the future—but to keep the horizon open, to keep open the hope of what is coming, when things will come under the rule of God, which is a Kingdom not of magic or standard-form poetics but of theopoetics. Its point is to imagine the ambience of the life of grace, of God's rule, of life that flows under the rule of God. Then—in the Kingdom—we shall be as if we were angels or astral bodies. We shall pass through solid substances, glow with God's light, move with God's power, see as if with God's eye, act but not suffer, love but not die. Our bodies will be all velocity and light, all agency, action, and power, all airy and ethereal activity. This is what we imagine it is like when God rules. That is how we visualize the new time, the new creation, the new being. We will all be transformed; that's the secret, yes, yes.

In a theology inspired by events, less literalizing and more literary, chastened by transcendental suspicion, resistant to the end to reification, all this is not to be construed as a physical or metaphysical description of what things will be like at some point in the future, nor does it represent some possible future course that things may take. This does not have to do with a prediction but with a promise. It is not a prediction of the future but an imaginative visualization of the events that stir and simmer within the name of God. The name of God is not the name of a separate substance, enjoying existence outside space and time, but the name of a promise. It is a name that harbors events that are manifest in the body of Jesus, events of unfathomable suffering on the cross, events of weakness, of the power of powerlessness, that can be transformed and transfigured into events of transforming glory, of grace-filled and Spirit-filled life, of light and joy and free play. There, in the rule of God, the events are sacred and the world is one of sacred anarchy, which is summarized under the name of the "Kingdom of God."

What the New Testament and Lewis Carroll both describe is a certain free play of paradoxical events, of play without weariness or work. In the case of Carroll the events are primarily cast in terms of humor and incongruity, whereas humor is not a prominent feature of the New Testament. That is perhaps a function of the limits of the imagination of the evangelists or of the historical information we have about Jesus. It is easy to imagine that an oral genius of the sort Jesus must have been, who, from all we can tell, could turn a sharp and memorable phrase, would also have been capable of a considerable wit and that he would have used that wit to advantage in his critique of religious authorities. After all, he was criticizing hypocrites and what better weapon for that than satire and wit? Be that as it may, the free play of paradox in the Kingdom is not the play of humor but the play of grace, the grace of marvelous bodily transformations and the grace of love beyond rigid prescriptions, of prodigious mercy and forgiveness.

If the operative figure of forgiveness is release from sin, and if the first bodily figure in which this release of the spirit is displayed is release from paralysis and disease, then its final figure is the risen body, which is released from the deepest and darkest limitation of the flesh. First the frailties of the flesh are mended and healed, and then they are abolished altogether, removed in principle. First we are healed, and then we are set free from all possible sickness. The risen body restores and even exceeds the prelapsarian body. It is the higher counterpart to the mythic bodies of Adam and Eve, which never would have incurred death and illness at all but for their fatal fall, their fateful disobedience. Religious myths are populated by spectral and spectacular bodies; they describe conditions in which events are released, and where everything about the name of God is meant to be the occasion of releasing the event. The risen body is a way to imaginatively visualize the event even while, in the real world, the only one there is, we must work and suffer, grow ill and die. Our bodies are frail bearers of the event, but they remain the only way events can be actualized. The name of God is the name of an event. The Kingdom of God is the name of that scene in which the events that name contains have been released and set free, which is what I have called a sacred anarchy.

I WILL TELL YOU A SECRET: DESIRING AND DREAMING OF THE BODY TO COME

I will tell you a secret (*mysterion*)—we will all be transformed (1 Cor 15: 51), and if we are not transformed, what good is all this? (1 Cor 15:14).

What would be the point of having faith or hope in the event, in what is coming? It would make more sense to find a way to make a lot of money, to eat and drink (1 Cor 15:32), instead of allowing ourselves to be troubled by these specters in which we hope there are transformative powers. I tell you a secret, which is the event, the secret of the event: the event is not what exists, but what is coming, the ghost specter of what is coming, and the dangerous memory of the dead. What is coming is the stuff of which dreams and desires are made, the stuff of unforeseeable transformations to come. Spectral bodies give imaginative form to events, which means they "embody" our dreams and desires, having been woven out of them in the first place. But the events haunt us, events lead us down the corridors of spectral imagination, events strive to take shape in these spectral forms. Spectrology, the panorama of spectral forms, without an idea of events is naive and superstitious; hauntology, the theory of the events that haunts us, without spectrology is ineffective, disembodied, unimaginative, deprived of its dreams. So one must always search spectral bodies for the events that animate them, for the dreams and desires that haunt them. Events are not garden variety desires but desires beyond desire, for what eye has not seen, nor ear heard, taking the step/not beyond (*le pas au-delà*). There is something intrinsically apophatic about dreaming and desiring because we do not know what we desire when we body forth our desires in dreamy spectral forms; we do not know what is coming or where events are urging us. The image of our life that I have is this: someone hears a call off in the distance, in the night—is that someone calling, like Mr. Rochester calling "Jane!" or is it perhaps just the wind?—and sets off to follow it, full of expectation, on the one hand, and trepidation, on the other, never knowing whether with each step the danger grows. Life is risky business, but a beautiful risk. What calls is the event, which is what I mean by the event. Events are inexhaustible, possessed of an unforeseeable future, an inner restlessness and dynamic, in virtue of which the event is never given a final expression in words and never reaches a final realization in things, even and especially spectral things of which we can only dream:

> And as imagination bodies forth
> The forms of things unknown, the poet's pen
> Turns them to shapes and gives to airy nothing
> A local habitation and a name.[11]

When I cite this text, you have to understand it is not a criticism for me to say that something is a dream. The one without dreams would be the one to deserve criticism. I say all this in praise of a vocative imagination, by which I mean the power to imagine what is calling and to give it body, form, and shape.

Events, which are very mysterious stuff, provide the basis of a general vocative apophatics. Whatever is in any way apophatic is so in virtue of the event. If a word or a thing lacked the event, it would instantly volatilize into a completely transparent surface. The opposite of the apophatic is not precisely the overt or manifest but the spent, the used up, something whose string has run out, something that has exhausted all its possibilities, whose life is over, even if it is not actually dead. For example, a word in a "dead language" is a word that has only a past but no future metaphoric deployments, reinvention, transferences, or transformations. One could completely spell out its meaning if one had a record of all its past occurrences. A word without an event, where there is no more unused event, is a word that will no longer be redeployed in new and unprecedented circumstances. A dead word has no future. It is like an extinct species whose evolutionary string has run out. The opposite of the apophatic is whatever is spent, deprived of the future, deprived of the event, deprived of "truth" in the sense of its becoming true, its concealed heart entirely exposed to view and withered by the sun of knowledge.

The event drives an ongoing process of becoming—or it is nothing and there is no event. The event is the incessant unfolding or taking shape in words and things, even spectral things or nothings—or there is no event. The event has a future; the event is the future; the future of the event is the event of the future—or there is no event.

There is a future I can foresee and plan for and a future I cannot. I can and should plan for my own future, or that of my family, and that is called the future present. This is the future I can reasonably predict—for example, the need to plan for anticipated expenses for my children's education or for my retirement—the future that it is only a matter of time until it becomes present. I would be foolish, improvident, and shortsighted if I did not see this future coming; it is the future that savings banks, pension funds, and life insurance companies depend on to turn a profit. Here the event follows a more or less predictable course, the future of things that were all along quite possible, and possible to the point of probable, and probable to the point of inevitable, and I am expected to make provisions. There is more planning here than dreaming, more a matter of following a map than venturing into the unknown.

But there is also a future that is a secret, a mystery, one that takes me by surprise, that I could not have seen coming, for which I could not have prepared. That is called the "absolute" future, meaning that it is absolved or detached from the ordinary course of things, more free-floating and spontaneous, the sphere of improbability, unpredictability, chance—or grace. Chance or grace—death or God. Whether it be chance or grace, not unlike what the insurance companies call an "act of God," by which they do not mean to express their piety but to say they do not want to pay for it, which leaves us without a prayer. Acts of God—that would be an event. This is the sphere in which when something happens we are astonished, reduced to asking, "How was that possible?" The absolute future is *the* impossible, something that shatters the horizon of expectation, of what was assumed to be at all possible.

The absolute future emerges from the deeper recesses of the event, from its most unforeseeable possibilities or, alternately, from the most unforeseeable concatenations of events, where it enters into combinations that are entirely unpredictable. The absolute future arises from the defining feature of the event, its potentiality, its simmering possibilities, its restlessness and stirring, its *dynamis*. Exposure to the absolute future is beyond preparation and exceeds all possible readiness. This radical exposure is well described in James Joyce's neologism "chaosmic." In a chaosmos the event is sustained by the tension between chaos and cosmos, order and disorder, *arche* and *anarche*, where neither one nor the other can get the upper hand. In a chaosmos, the future is kept open.

Spectral bodies are a "mystery," a secret (*mysterion*); they are apophatic figures, indeed, ways to imagine or body forth, ways to dream or desire what is coming, to depict the transformations to come. If we are not transformed, there is no point to concerning ourselves with the event. One of the defining and uncircumventable features of the figure of the spectral body is that it is a striking image that is virtually without an intelligible account. It is all surface, all imagination, all picturability, but it has almost no rationale superstructure, like a fantastic drawing or a

Chagall painting of bodies floating in midair. The risen body is a spectacular image, but every attempt to make sense of it is so far-fetched it just collapses. Faced with explaining itself, theology throws up its hands, feels called upon to warn us against curiosity, and quickly has recourse to what I will call a "Mystery," capitalized in the sense of Strong Theology, which is one of the most treasured methodological resources for dodging the conundrums Strong Theology weaves. The Mystery runs afoul of foolishness or simple unintelligibility, like dealing with resurrected digestive tracts, because one has reified, transliterated, or literalized the event into a visualizable embodied figure. But in the account given in my more spectral, weaker, hauntological theology, the spectral figure of the risen body is a figure of the event of the unimaginable future, of transformations whose course we cannot foresee, of the event that haunts us with the future, an uncapitalized mystery, which is what Derrida calls an absolute secret. That is why my attention is directed to the event that takes place in this figure and why I invoke the principle of transcendental suspicion, which respects the distinction between the event and any literal embodiment of the event, which suspects any identification of the event with a particular proper name or privileged incarnation.

The event harbored within the body is the secret of the future it holds for the body, the secret it withholds from the body, what the body is capable of, the future we cannot possibly know or foresee. The absolute future is what we cannot imagine, or rather what we can only imagine. The final and most radical veil in life, and the scene of the most radical apophasis, the veil of absolute mystery, is death. Death is at once completely foreseeable, one of our most elemental certitudes, and yet the very definition of mystery, of the absolutely unforeseeable. It is a common and everyday occurrence, and yet nothing is more unknowable, more unimaginable, more apophatic. This event of absolute unimaginability, the absolute apophatic unimaginability of this event, is the most basic overlapping feature shared by "God" and "death," by the *deus incognitus* and the veil of death.

In just the way that words have a history, undergo metaphoric transformation and a history of meaning, so bodies have a future and a history. The *risen* body is a figure not of a relative future but an absolute one; it imagines not the transformation of life in this or that order, but the absolute transformation of life. I will tell you a secret—we will all be transformed! The risen body attempts the step/not beyond, tries to go where we cannot go, to make the movement beyond the grave, to pierce the absolutely impenetrable veil—God or death—to imagine the unimaginable future of the body. In this sense, there is no more perfect and thoroughgoing figure of *the* impossible, of going where you cannot go, of seeing what you cannot see, than the risen body. There is no more striking or powerful apophatic figure, or figure of apophasis, no more powerful way to imagine the possibility of the impossible, than the risen body. It is a concept of the inconceivable, a representation of the unrepresentable, an icon of transcendence.[12] The defining feature of transcendence is movement beyond a horizon or line of sight. The notion of absolute transcendence *stricto sensu* makes no sense, since one would always have to specify transcendence beyond or relative to *what*. Absolute transcendence makes no more sense than saying "absolutely longer." Transcendence is always a relative term, tethered to the corresponding sphere of immanence. Transcendence is a movement beyond that is relative to what is not beyond, beyond the known toward the unknown.

The transcendent element of bodily life is the extension of the body that we know to a dimension presently forbidden and unknown. It is a figure of the bodily life we can only dream of, for which we pray and weep (or which we fear). "Death" (God or death) is the absolute barrier, the line beyond which we cannot, dare not cross, from which no one ever returns or reports back—at least, not without some controversy about the reliability of the reports coming from the other side. Just as the many relative limits we face are summarized, recapitulated, and absolutized in the limit which is death, so the many versions of transcendence we seek are concentrated, summarized, and absolutized in the transcendence of death. Just as life is a movement of transcendence, of rising above the many daily deaths which we defy or at least with which we must deal, the transcendence of death itself, of God or death, hovers before us like a ghost, a specter, a spirit—or the dream of a risen body.

In the end, I take the risen body to be an imaginative figure of our love of the future, of what is coming, of a desire for transformation—and if we are not transformed, what is there to desire? It is a figure of repetition and rebirth, and if we are not reborn—what is there to dream of? In the risen body, relatively accessible and empirical figures of rising again are brought to completion, allowed to run to the end beyond any empirical fulfillment, like a transcendental illusion. There are several figures in which the body "rises" not absolutely but relatively, reborn not from death but from something death-like. The body "rises" each morning from sleep as from a certain sweet and transient death, especially from a deep sleep, untroubled by disturbing dreams or restlessness, when one was "dead to the world." One rises, refreshed, ready for a new day, in a kind of quotidian resurrection from a sleeping nondeath. Death is like a deep sleep; a deep sleep is like a death from which one rises. The morning itself, the rising sun, is such a figure for every rising again. The early morning hour combines the quiet of a night that has not yet been disturbed with the light of a new day; it is as quiet as the night, but blessed by the light of day; it is a moment when there is light but we are temporarily spared the assault of daily action, allowed a moment for quiet reflection or silent contemplation. One rises again—from a sickbed, which is a kind of death, which even threatens death, and one says one has one's life back; life has been restored after having been taken away. In a larger sense, we rise again from defeat, from stunning setbacks, which are a kind of death, when everything says the cause is dead, but we refuse to give up. We rise from the death of the other, the *dimidium animae meae,* the death of the better half of our souls, when the better half of us dies with the beloved, and we think ourselves quite dead but then must find some way to come back to life, a way to go on. The body rises from the dead when someone dies but we refuse to let their work or their cause die with them, when we resolve to let them live again in us, who have resolved to carry on their work, and everyone who engages in this work can feel the breath of their spirit. That I think goes a long way toward explaining the impossibility of the death of Jesus in the hearts of the disciples.

The risen body is a figure of the absolute future, which is fundamentally apophatic. The risen body is the most radical way to imagine metamorphosis, *metanoia*, rebirth, transformation. It is the most fundamental way to image a new life, a new creation, a new being, which means to carry the event to a new level of actuality, vitality, energy, and life.

The future is the horizon of new possibilities yet unrealized. As a living being, the body is always rising, again and again, in an upward trajectory turned toward the future, toward its many rebirths, resurrections, and repetitions. Before it is the name of a purported episode in history, some factual or literalized occurrence confirmed or unconfirmed that is submitted as evidence in apologetics, the risen body is an event, or harbors an event of repetition, of rebirth and restoration, and beyond restoration, transformation. The future is the horizon of possibilities yet unrealized, of events for which we lack the vocabulary and the grammar, of apophatic bodies, of transformations whose comings and overcomings are as yet unimagined.

The event is the absolute potency of the beyond, of the to-come, of the open-endedness of the future. The spectral body is the figure of the step/not beyond, of surpassing the unsurpassable, of surviving death itself, of the impossibility of death, of the death of death, of living on, *fortleben*, surviving countless skirmishes with death, defying death's relentlessness, its irreducible menace. The absolute future stretches out before us like an infinite expanse, beyond the horizon, projecting an unimaginable future. The risen body is a figure of an unfigurable future, of impossible bodies, of the event of the future, of the future of the event, of bodies still unrisen, of events still unsaid.

The event of repetition—the repetition of the event—is in constant contention with death, which is the end of the event, the event of the end, and is, alas, as real as real can be and all around us, with God or death, with the secret, with the mystery that we are. We are all dreaming of being transformed, and if we are not transformed, our faith in the event is in vain.

In the Image of the Invisible

KATHRYN TANNER

Christian theologians often maintain that God is incomprehensible, beyond human powers of positive explication through concepts and speech, because God is without limits or bounds. God is without limits of time, being framed by no beginning or end. Existing in perfect simplicity, God is without internal limits or boundaries dividing the divine nature into manageable component parts or aspects for our comprehension. The absolute fullness of being and goodness, God transcends all divisions between kinds and exceeds all bounds of a particular nature or mode of being that might allow God to be set alongside others or encompassed by anything it is not. The divine, in short, cannot be comprehended or contained in any respect; it is simply not anything that we can get our heads around.

Christian theologians, following verses in Genesis to this effect, also commonly claim that human beings are created in God's image. Putting the two ideas together, one might expect them therefore to develop just as commonly the way in which human nature reflects divine incomprehensibility. Theological discussion of what it is about humans that makes them the image of God frequently moves, however, in the opposite direction: such discussion often simply amounts to the effort to find some clearly bounded human nature of quite definite character that both reflects the divine nature and sets humans off from all other creatures. Humans are created in the image of God because, unlike other creatures, they have reason, free will, or the ability to rule over others as God does.

Given this interest in well-defined and well-bounded characteristics that are ours by nature, theological anthropology runs afoul of a number of contemporary intellectual trends. Biotechnologies, particularly interspecies gene transfers, call into question the fixed boundaries of natural kinds. Violence bred of ethnic and religious division in our world familiarizes us all too well with the bellicose potential of narrowly drawn, closely guarded identities. Feminists remind us of the way appeals to fixed and given natures help solidify unjust social arrangements and disguise their contingency. Postmodernists of various stripes caution against the insistence on a self-identical, coherent character, rigidly predicated on the exclusion of others so as to promote protective postures that degrade and sever human connection with them. And they lead us to question the ethical priority of self-discovery, as if the truth about oneself—an already established nature or identity—could determine all by itself what one might become, one's place within the world, and the character of one's responsibilities, in sovereign independence of any unpredictable entanglements beyond one's control with human and nonhuman others.

The intent of this essay is to move theological anthropology away from this sort of fixation on a fixed human nature, this preoccupation with established capacities and given identities, by diagnosing its theological underpinnings, and by developing an alternative account of the way humans image God in conversation with early Christian thought. I show, thereby, how an apophatic anthropology is the consequence of an apophatic theology. If humans are the image of God, they are, as Gregory of Nyssa affirmed, an incomprehensible image of the incomprehensible: "If, while the archetype transcends comprehension, the nature of the image were comprehended, the contrary character of the attributes . . . would prove the defect of the image. . . . [S]ince the nature of our mind . . . evades our knowledge, it has an accurate resemblance to the superior nature, figuring by its unknowableness the incomprehensible Nature."[1]

At least in part, preoccupation with a well-bounded and clearly defined human nature seems fomented by theological anthropology's isolated attention to humans in and of themselves, as if the image of God could be located *in* them, in abstraction from their relations with others, particularly the God they are to image. The underlying problem is simply the presumption that human beings have a definite nature to begin with that could be considered in itself and perfectly well specified in its own terms.

What Augustine attempts in books 8–11 of his *De trinitate* would be a prime illustration of such a problem—at least if one considers the influence those particular books have had on theological anthropology in the West. Augustine tries to support the intelligibility of rules for trinitarian speech—e.g., the rule that persons of the Trinity are really distinct in virtue of their relations with one another but one and equal in their divinity—by finding analogues for those rules in the more familiar character and dynamics of the human mind and heart. The effect of this, however, is often in these books to turn attention away from human consciousness in relation to God—indeed, to turn attention away from its relations with anything not itself, whether above the human (God) or below it (sense objects). Only the internal dynamics of human consciousness—the self's relations with itself—can mimic, for example, the perfect equality and union of distinct things which is the rule for the Trinity; in relations with anything else there is, if not distance or disunity, then at the very least a marked lack of equivalence among the things related. For these reasons, Augustine goes so far as to suggest that the mind is a *better* image of God when knowing itself rather than God.[2] The strong impression from such discussion is that human consciousness is the image of God all by itself, in an ideally self-enclosed self-sufficiency—e.g., when the self is knowing, loving, or remembering only its own pure productions.

The alternative would be to consider human nature an essentially relational affair, indistinct apart from and clearly definable only in terms of its determination by what it is related to. Human beings would therefore become the image of God only in an actual relationship with God, bringing with it the only real correspondence with divine life and action to be found in human existence. Humans would be the image of God, properly speaking, only, say, when actually contemplating God face to face in heaven, as Augustine himself avers in the culminating books of *De trinitate*. Considered apart from such a relationship, there would be nothing much to say about the reflection of God in human nature per se. Humans would at most be only in a secondary, less proper sense the image of God in virtue of whatever it is about them that is a prerequisite for such a relationship (e.g., in virtue of the cognitive capacities that when suitably expanded by God's grace enable them to see God in that fashion). Were one to read books 8–11 of Augustine's *De trinitate* through the lens of what he says in later books about the true or proper image of God in knowledge of God face to face—something that the West typically fails to do—then this simply becomes Augustine's considered opinion to begin with.

A more radical deflection, however, of concern for a well-bounded and well-defined human nature comes about in theologies for which human beings are not the primary image at all. If one reads the Genesis passages through the lens of the New Testament, especially Pauline texts, it is possible for the image of God to take on a primarily intra-trinitarian sense.[3] The image most properly speaking—the express or perfect image of God (following Hebrews 1:3)—is the second person of the Trinity. And what that image is to mean for us is then most properly demonstrated in the human life of the Word Incarnate. If we are to image God, we have to be formed according to God's own image—the second person of the Trinity—in something like the way Jesus was.[4]

The Genesis discussion of human beings' creation in the image of God can be viewed then in Christologically focused trinitarian terms. Humans are not simply the image but "in" or "after" it, as the verses say (Gen 1.27), because the image referred to here is itself divine—either the second person of the Trinity or the Word Incarnate. Which one makes little difference since in the latter case the primary image is still the second person of the Trinity and the second person of the Trinity only becomes applicable to us in becoming incarnate. Since the Holy Spirit is thought to unite us to Christ and allow us thereby to be made over in his image, often a great deal of interest is directed to Genesis passages that could be taken to refer to the Holy Spirit—the spirit hovering over the waters (Gen 1.2), or the living soul breathed into Adam (Gen 2.7). The Holy Spirit itself was given to humans when they were created, in order to form them according to the image of God that is the second person of the Trinity; they thereby became a human image of that divine image like (but not exactly like) the Word Incarnate to come, Jesus Christ. The theology of Cyril of Alexandria sees the full and explicit development of such a view: "[I]n the beginning . . . the Creator of all, taking dust of the ground and having formed man, breathed upon his face the breath of life. And what is the breath of life, save surely the Spirit of Christ . . . ? But since He [the Spirit which is able to gather us and form us unto the Divine Impress] fled away from the human nature . . . the Savior gives us this anew bringing us again into that ancient Dignity and reforming us unto His own Image."[5]

With this more radical loss of a primary preoccupation with human nature per se as the image of God comes an odd refocusing of what is of interest about human beings, both when they actually image God in Christ and when considering their "capacities" for it. In theologies that deny the possibly subordinationalist import of talking about the second person of the Trinity as the image of the first—i.e., "image" does not mean any lesser degree of divinity—the second person of the Trinity is not comprehensible while the first is incomprehensible, but images it in its very incomprehensibility. And this holds for the incarnation of the second person of the Trinity too. The second person of the Trinity—whether the firstborn of creation by being the one through and for whom the world was created, or the firstborn of the dead by becoming incarnate for our salvation to everlasting life—remains in a strong sense an "image of the invisible."[6] Jesus is not the comprehensible stand-in or substitute for an incomprehensible divinity but the very exhibition of the incomprehensible divinity of the Word in a human form or medium.[7] Jesus displays in his life what it means to be an incomprehensible image in the flesh of an incomprehensible God.

There would be something then incomprehensible about human nature as it is shaped by a relationship with God that makes it like God, and, secondarily, even something incomprehensible about it from the very start, one might say, which renders it capable of being worked over into a divine form. Like God who is incomprehensible because unlimited, humans might have a nature that imitates God only by not having a clearly delimited nature. Every other creature imitates God by expressing the goodness that God is in a limited form; they are good by being a definite something—a pig or a rock—indeed the best pig or rock they can be. Humans are a definite sort of creature distinct from others and in that sense of course still have a particular nature; they are not God who alone is different from others by not being a kind of thing. But humans can still stand out by their failure to be clearly limited by a particular nature as other creatures are. Failure of definition by remaining ill-defined is not so much the point; what is primarily at issue here is a failure of definition through excessive love. Humans seem to have an underlying concern for what is absolutely good per se—for God—for what is not merely good in certain respects but fully good in a perfectly unlimited way. They want in some sense to *be* that absolute good rather than any particular sort of thing, rather than the specific sort of creature they are, by being formed in and through a relationship with the absolute good—for example, by knowing the absolute truth that is God, the absolute good for human cognition, that comes by way of God's very presence to the mind. The weirdly unlimited character of human nature and drives would then be the fundamental reason for traditional theological preoccupation with human intelligence and will when discussing the way humans are the image of God. These "faculties" are of interest because of their excessive openness, one might say, because of their attraction to formation through what exceeds their own or any limited nature.

Otherwise expressed, if humans are to be made over in God's image—so radically reworked as to be deified in the way Jesus' humanity is—then what is of interest about human nature is its plasticity, its openness to formation through outside influences, and the unusually wide range of possible effects of such a process of formation. For humans to come to be in the image of God is an extreme case of coming to be oneself in relation to what one is not—God, what is most unlike creatures generally. All creatures are formed in relation to what they are not, but humans do this in an exaggerated way that opens them to a radical sort of reformation from without in the divine image. Irenaeus expresses this essential malleability to divine formation well: "Offer to Him thy heart in a soft and tractable state, and preserve the form in which the Creator has fashioned thee, having moisture in thyself, lest, by becoming hardened, thou lose the impressions of his fingers. But by preserving the framework thou shalt ascend to that which is perfect, for the moist clay which is in thee is hidden [there] by the workmanship of God. His hand fashioned thy substance; He will cover thee over [too] within and without with pure gold and silver, and He will adorn thee to such a degree, that even 'the King Himself shall take pleasure in thy beauty (Ps 14.11).'"[8]

All living creatures become themselves by taking in things from outside themselves; seeds, for example, require food from without in order to germinate. Humans, because they are made to be in the image of God, require God for their nourishment. In heaven, indeed, God will be our only food and drink, as Gregory of Nyssa maintains: "[W]hile our present life is active amongst a variety of multiform conditions, and the things which we have relations with are numerous, for instance, time, air, locality, food and drink, clothing, sunlight, lamplight, and other necessities of life, none of which, many though they be, are God—that blessed state which we hope for is in need of none of these things, but the Divine Being will become all [1 Cor 15.28], and instead of all, to us, distributing Himself proportionately to every need of that existence. . . . God [will] become . . . locality, and home, and clothing, and food, and drink, and light, and riches, and dominion, and everything thinkable and nameable that goes to make our life happy."[9]

In the case of all other livings things, whatever they take in is formed according to the limits of their pre-established natures. For example, the natural resources assimilated by a plant for its nourishment—light, water, nutrients from the soil, and so on—are transformed to conform to the plant's nature. The plant remains itself, becoming merely a bigger and better version of itself, where there was genuine nourishment for the plant's good. When human beings take in God as their proper nourishment, they come out, to the contrary, as God. They are turned thereby into the matter, so to speak, for a new divine organization of what they are. They become God's image, rather than God's becoming theirs; humans are reworked according to God's pattern of living, rather than God being reworked according to a human one. Humans when they are formed in the image of God take on Christ's identity, in short. Like what happens to light, water, and soil—but now with a peculiar reversal of consequences from the usual scenario—men, women, children, Greek and Jew, free and slave—all go into the process of reformation and come out in the form of Christ. "This is the purpose for us of God . . . to raise our flesh and recover his image and remodel man, that we might all be made one in Christ . . . that we might no longer be male and female, barbarian, Scythian, bond or free (which are badges of the flesh), but might bear in ourselves only the stamp of God, by Whom and for Whom we were made, and [having] so far received our form and model from Him, that we are recognized by it alone."[10]

To generalize from this, one might say human beings are unusually impressionable, in a way that the language of image often unpacks in a quite concrete way: they are like soft wax on which a vast variety of seals might impress images; they are the mirror of whatever it is upon which they gaze. They take their identities from the uses to which they put themselves, like vessels that gain their character from whatever they are made to carry. Earthenware or pure gold, what goes into them for certain purposes establishes what they are; whatever their fundamental constitution as vessels, when full of shit (for example), they can only be shit pots.[11]

Less graphically speaking (and in a more contemporary idiom), one could say that human life takes a variety of forms depending on what it is that people care about.[12] "Such is the strength of love, that the mind draws in with itself those things which it has long thought of with love, and has grown into them by the close adherence."[13] Human beings exercise self-reflective powers; they are able to make an object of themselves in projects of self-fashioning and re-fashioning, following changeable judgments about what is most important to them—fancy cars, the respect of their peers, wisdom, and so on. They attach themselves to these objects of desire and draw them into themselves, so to speak, as variable organizing principles of their lives. "Human nature adapts itself to the direction of thought and it changes according to whatever form it is inclined to by the impulse of free choice."[14] This means—to return to a previous metaphor—that "[h]uman nature is in fact like a mirror, and it takes on different appearances according to the impressions of free will. If gold is held up to the mirror, the mirror assumes the appearance of gold and reflects the splendor of gold's substance. If anything abominable is held up, its ugliness is impressed in the mirror—for example, a frog, toad, centipede, or anything unpleasant to behold."[15]

Reflective capacities of self-judgment mean humans can try to reshape in a self-critical fashion even those desires they cannot help having by nature. One may have the natural desire to eat, but one need not shape one's life around the importance of food—asceticism is a case in point. Humans have the capacity to use the passions of their animal natures (as Nyssa would term them)—their natural attraction, for example, to what benefits them—as instruments of either virtue or vice.[16] That attraction may be the energy propelling them toward, say, profligacy—or God. Humans have the power to cultivate or discourage those natural drives and tendencies that they start out with whether they like it or not, making efforts, for example, to alter their intensities through stimulation or neglect, or efforts to rework the way they figure in one's life as a whole. Indeed, these self-reflective powers account for why human lives can become so horrible, much more horrible than those of other animals; the anger, for example, that an animal might fleetingly feel when faced with an opponent can be husbanded by the human mind—dwelt upon—so as to pervade all one's dealings with others, in a host of variable forms—envy, malice, conspiracy, deceit—with the result that one's whole nature is traced anew after that design.[17]

Human beings have plastic powers, self-formative capacities, and it is the fact that those capacities are not determined to one thing as natural desires are—the fact that those capacities need not incline in a predetermined direction according to the givens of one's nature or essential definition (following a Thomistic understanding, for example, of natural desires)—that accounts for the heightened variability of their effects in operation. People turn out in wildly different ways, for better or for worse. Or, one might say the self-formative capacities of humans do have a nature, but the particular nature of rational volition is just to have no definite nature to be true to, in the way that animals are true to their natures when acting properly, for their own good. Humans can think of a variety of things that it would be good to do in certain respects or for certain purposes, and what they decide about what is most important to them in the course of such deliberations decides in great part the character of their lives, the identity they come to exhibit in their acts—*that* is just their nature.

The early Eastern church's stress on free will as the image of God—or often secondarily, rule in the sense of self-rule—could now be taken in a new light, not as the promotion of some vaunted power in a positive sense, an imitation of divine omnipotence, but as an interest in the unusual plasticity of human lives absent any predetermined direction by nature. Free will is an indication of variability. Their unusual powers of self-determination mean humans can become anything along the continuum of ontological ranks, from the bottom to the top. Humans, it is true, are determined to God—being formed in the image of God is their good, by nature. But that is just *not* to be determined in any particular direction as other things are, since God is the absolute good and not a limited one.

All the qualities of humans typically highlighted by the theologians I am interested in here have something to do with their rational capacities, and there is probably a good reason for this even from a more modern point of view (as I have implied) if indefinite plasticity, the nature that is no nature, is what these theologians are trying to get at. Especially in the early church figures I am drawing on, however, such a focus often dovetails with a marked matter-versus-spirit dualism and with an exaggerated disjunction between human and nonhuman which often accompanies that dualism. It is therefore important to see the way that plastic or non-natured *bodies* are the ultimate issue even for these early church theologians. At the end of the day it is our bodies that are to be remade into Christ's body.

Mitigating any matter-spirit dualism for all these figures (who generally hold a hylomorphic anthropology in any case) is the fact that souls are influenced as bodies are (e.g., through the incorporation of outside factors and influences) and the fact that the object of self-formation includes the body. It is very easy therefore to express what they are getting at in a more contemporary idiom not, so obviously at least, bound up with any need to distinguish spiritual from material: Human beings form themselves with reference to a whole host of outside influences—people, places, animate and inanimate influences, what have you—and what is formed is their whole lives, irrespective of any division between the material and the spiritual. When our minds are therefore formed according to the divine image, so are our bodies: when the mind is "adorned by the likeness of the archetypal beauty . . . the nature which is governed by it [i.e., the body] . . . is adorned by the beauty that the mind gives, being, so to say, a mirror of the mirror."[18]

When it is the plasticity of human lives before the divine that is at issue, blurring the boundary between spirit and matter is often a primary gambit. See, for example, the use of the oxymoronic notion of "spiritual matter" in Augustine's treatment of Genesis: rational creatures have an essential character like unformed matter (the abyss)—i.e., they exhibit matter's lack of form per se—when considered apart from the well-being—that knowing well—that results from their being informed by God's own image.[19] They are fluid wax in need of sealing; they are mirrors, otherwise empty, to be made light by light.

Moreover, human materiality is essential to the image of God so as to take the whole of existence, irrespective of any division between spirit and matter, to God. (This is why angels or disembodied pure intelligences are not the image.) Only in virtue of the fact that they have bodies can the whole world hope in humans. Humans demonstrate that, appearances to the contrary (especially in the cultural and philosophical milieu of the early church), the material world itself is plastic—by extension just as plastic to divine influence, one might hope, as human lives. God formed humans out of the dust of the earth so that when formed in the image of God humans might show that the earth too can be made over in God's image: both matter and mind are made for a single grace.[20]

Understanding the image of God as the second person of the Trinity deflects attention from the character of human nature for a final reason: because there is a sense in which humans, considered in and of themselves, never become a proper image of God at all even when formed according to it. The image of God in a proper sense is just God, the second person of the Trinity. Not being God, humans can therefore never simply become that image in and of themselves through any process of transformation. Since there is no ontological continuum spanning the difference between God and creatures, one cannot hope to become the divine image, this perfect or proper image, by approximating divine qualities—for example, by improving one's mental capacities in some gradual approach to God's own perfect rationality.

And yet, without abolishing or mitigating the difference between God and humans, humans do become the divine image—by attaching themselves to it. It is by being identified with what they are not that the divine image becomes their own. Humans become the image of God in the strongest sense (not imaging the image but simply identified with it) when they are not trying to be it at all, not trying to image the divine image in a human way, but when they are brought near to it, so near as to become one with it.

Humans, one might say, are never sufficiently fluid or flexible simply to be the image in and of themselves, to be made over into some good approximation of it; they cannot hope, therefore, to achieve a simple reproduction of the divine image in some perfect human imitation considered on its own terms. Humans, instead, have the image of God only by clinging to what they are not—that divine image itself—in love. There is only one perfect or express image of God—the second person of the Trinity—and that perfect image becomes humans' own only through their exceedingly close relationship with it—e.g., by its own actual presence within them, made their own by the first person of the Trinity through the power of the Holy Spirit on the basis of second person's incarnation in human flesh. Humans show off, so to speak, the light that is the divine image itself—and are in that sense good images of God themselves—by exterior illumination, by glowing with a light that remains another's and not by some phosphorescent assimilation of that light into their own natures as some now human property.

All creatures can do this same showing off or shining back of the divine glory. Plasticity is not a prerequisite for it. Even now creatures can glorify God, glow with a kind of divine penumbra by pointing to, and in that sense making manifest, the goodness of the God who made them: the wonders of the world speak of the wonders of God. In the reformation of the world to come, when, for example, death will be no more, all creatures and not just humans can image the divine in the way we have just been talking about by living off, for example, the very eternal life of God, by drawing on powers that remain divine, in virtue of a close relationship or oneness with God, that makes those powers their own.

Because of its fluid character, the character or identity of human nature itself is remolded in the process—that is its peculiarity. Something, in other words, happens to human nature when it reflects the image of God. To switch metaphors, human nature is not like iron that simply glows when the divine flame is applied to it without any fundamental change in its character; were the iron to cool it would show its usual properties. It is more the nature of nonhuman things to be inflexibly themselves like that, even when feeling the divine heat. Human nature is not made for resistance and therefore humans are more like wood set ablaze by God in that their character will never be the same. For example, their defects might be purged of everything short of the good in the process. Human nature is itself reworked in the image of God so as to become humanly perfect—e.g., perfectly virtuous or perfectly pious.

This refashioning is not the divine image per se but specifically human perfection, and as such forms only a dim, distant analogue of divinity. Human perfection, which follows from union with the divine image, is always an image of an image (Christ) of an image (the second person of the Trinity), in a radically inferior medium—indeed, before the eschaton in which perfection is achieved, an image of an image of an image in a thoroughly corrupted medium (e.g., one hard and unimpressionable to divine imprint). The image of God remains, properly speaking, a divine image and before that image any difference between humans and nonhumans pales in significance.

The perfect form of imaging found in the second person of the Trinity is beyond anything achievable in human life. The divine image is perfect because it is not an image by participation, by sharing, that is, in something that it is not in some imperfect fashion. The second person of the Trinity is like an image in that it both has a relation of origin with the first person of the Trinity (it comes from the first person, begotten by it) and reproduces in itself what makes the first person divine. But this is a perfect imaging—everything that is divine about the first person is found again in the second—and therefore not an imaging by participation: an image by participation is not its archetype but a mere image of it in virtue of some inferiority. Unlike things that become images by participating in what they are not, the second person of the Trinity simply *is* what it images and therefore does not become an image by participating in what it is not. Unlike other images, it does not acquire the capacity to image something by, say, being impressed by it. Being an image cannot be an accidental acquired characteristic of that sort in the divine case since in divinity accidents are identical with essence—that is, divinity simply is everything that is said about it. The second person of the Trinity does not in any sense borrow from the first what it does not itself have; one cannot say that the second person of the Trinity "is made illustrious by the mere addition to Himself of features that were not originally His own, so that He shines as it were by reflected light from glories bestowed upon him, and not by his own natural luster."[21] Instead, whatever the second person gets from the first is properly its own by nature; the second person of the Trinity is divine in and of itself and not simply in virtue of being the image of the first person. What is "the very Image and Likeness and Effulgence" of the Father must be "bearing innate within Himself the proper characteristics of His Father's essence, and possessing in all their beauty the attributes that are naturally the Father's."[22] Finally, unlike things that participate in what they are not, the second person of the Trinity does not participate in the divinity of the first in any variable degree (more or less is not applicable to its imaging of the first, being a perfect image) and whatever it images of the first person of the Trinity it does not stand in danger of losing (like, say, dry sand that is in danger of losing the imprint of one's foot when one walks away). The relation between the second and first persons of the Trinity is for these reasons analogous to an imaging relationship that comes about in virtue of a shared nature. The second person, in other words, is something like a natural image of the first in the way a son might be the spitting image of his father (this is taken to be the point of "son" language in the Bible), and nothing like an image produced in a medium foreign to the original—say, the way a flesh-and-blood person might be reproduced with paint on a canvas.

Contrary to all that has just been said for the second person of the Trinity, human beings are mere images of God by participating in God. They are fashioned by God so that they image what they are not—God—in an imperfect fashion. They receive what is not their own and therefore they do not have it in the way God does, in a perfect or divine fashion—fully, unchangeably, and without susceptibility of loss.

Human beings are images of God by participation, moreover, in two major ways. At the very lowest level, human nature itself is an image of God—not just our rationality, free will, or plastic capacities—but everything about us that is given to us by our Creator. And the same holds for every other creature. Everything that creatures are or have for their good is received from God, and constitutes a kind of image of God in a created form, if what God is always trying to give to others in creating them is the goodness of God's own life. Creatures form created versions or approximations of God's own goodness, following (for example) the principle that a cause contains its effects in a superior fashion: creatures image God in that God as their cause contains in a super-eminent divine fashion what they are.

Participating in God is just what it means to be a creature. God is (for example) life itself, life through itself, while everything else receives its life from God, without simply being it, in and of itself. Any creature therefore has life in some degree or fashion and can lose it. Expressing much the same thing in a Thomistic way, one could say God does not participate in being but *is* it: to be *God* just is to *be*; in God there is no distinction between what God is (essence) and the fact that God is (existence). To participate in being is, by definition, not to be it, if participation means participating in what one is not; and therefore with participation arises a distinction between essence and existence, the very constitution of created things.[23]

Although we image God in and through what we are as creatures, we do not do so independently of God. That is indeed one of the points of saying that we image God through participation. This is not an accidental mirroring of God, by chance or happenstance in virtue of what we have become independently of God, on our own steam apart from any relation to God, the way a pumpkin might by chance or happenstance have grown of itself into the image of a human face. We image God because we have been fashioned by God. Indeed, we are the image of God only by participating in God, by continuing to receive what we are from God. To be a creature means to lead an insufficient life of oneself, to lead a kind of borrowed life.

Creatures can be more or less the image of God in virtue of their particular created characteristics. We have seen this in the case of human beings—the way they are more the image of God than animals and more the image of God in certain respects than others—in virtue primarily of the peculiar plastic capabilities that open them to re-formation according to an absolute rather than merely partial or relative good. But this is still participation at the lowest level—participation in virtue of the character of created qualities themselves, participation by way of imitation in an ontologically inferior, because nondivine, medium.

Even what we are to become by being formed in Christ's image is a low-level image of God of this sort—insofar as the end product, so to speak, is a human state—a most excellent state indeed, but still a human one. The reflection of God in humans, when the Spirit conforms them to Christ, is in this sense like the reflection of the sun in a mirror: the reflection is not at all like the sun itself in most respects—it is extremely small, relatively cool, quite dim so that we can look at it without being blinded, and so on.

Indeed, the difference between God and creatures is the primary problem for this first sort of image through participation. The difference in medium, so to speak, between the human image and its divine archetype makes too big a difference here; the divine simply cannot be imitated, strictly speaking, in what is not divine. Because God is their source, creatures must be imitating God in what they have of the good, as we have said; but the difference between God and creatures—the fact that they do not both figure within the same ontological continuum—nonetheless forbids the idea of any real approximation to the divine on the creature's part. There is nothing in between God and creatures, as the idea of imitation, particularly when used to discriminate between one sort of creature and another, might suggest. One is either one or the other. There is only one true image, then—the divine image—which perfectly reflects its archetype. Anything short of that is hardly an image at all.

In a second, much stronger sense of being an image by participating in what we are not, what we are not itself becomes part of us, an ingredient of our constitution. We are the image of God not by way of a human imitation of God, not by way of what we are ourselves, but in virtue of some sort of incorporation of what remains alien to us, the very perfection of God that we are not. God becomes part of us, an ingredient in our faculties, as a prerequisite for the excellent exercise of human operations. Cyril, for example, and Augustine, too, distinguish between our existence and our well-being and claim that the latter is a function of God's own entrance within us. We are rational creatures, say, and that is a sort of image of God—the low-flying kind—but when we know well, then we are the image of God in a stronger sense in virtue of the fact that the truth itself, God, has entered within us to give us the truth. The excellent functioning of our native capacities is not a self-sufficient operation, then, in the sense of simply unrolling from our own capabilities, but requires a strong dependence on the very powers of God which have become ours for the taking—in some extraordinary gift of God to us of what is not ours by nature. The perfection of human living that is Christ's and (to a lesser degree) ours in him would be the supreme case of this sort of thing—of human powers elevated through the entrance of God's own powers, through the gift of the Holy Spirit itself forming humanity according to the image of the second person of the Trinity.

Here we image God by living off God, so to speak, in the way a fetus lives off the life of its mother, living in and through or with her very life. This is the mirror that is bright not by anything that is its own but only through the presence of the sun's own light. This—to use the more common biblical imagery perhaps—is the branch that lives on the alien sap of the vine to which it has been engrafted.

These two senses of image by participation—the weaker and the stronger—are obviously bound up with each other. The first sense of image by participation is the presupposition for the second: one cannot participate in God in the strong sense, have God within one, unless there is something to one apart from God—unless one is an image of God in the weak sense by having an existence and nature of one's own as a creature. Those created capacities that image God (in a weak sense) more than others also provide the openings through which one becomes an image in the strong sense. Those capacities, one might even say, are the prerequisites for being an image in the very strongest sense. All things can come to live off the eternal life of God, when, say, that is the only life left to them. But God's gift of God's own self can become a true constituent of only certain sorts of created natures—ones whose functions are not limited by nature, those that inherently have room for God internal to them. The strong sense of image by participation is, finally, what enables the strongest version of the weak way human acts can be the image of God: by having the one whom we are not, Christ, the very incarnation of God, for our own, we should one day be able to live a human life that imitates God's own in the most perfect way possible for mere humans.

To conclude, we are then—body and soul—an incomprehensible image of the incomprehensible both in our natural capacities and in what we become in relation to the true image, the Word Incarnate. Human capacities imitate God's incomprehensibility in only a negative and prospective way in virtue of their not being limited by a predetermined nature. Rather than being unlimited through inclusiveness, through unbounded fullness, as God's perfection is, we are unlimited in our powers through lack, through a failure of predetermination, by not being anything in particular to start.

We might one day come to imitate in our humanity the inclusiveness of the absolute being and goodness of God but only when aided by God to become what we are not. Formed by the Word when that day comes, humans may imitate the incomprehensibility of God in a positive sense, e.g., by becoming incomprehensibly good as God is good. Like what happened in Christ's own human life, the new pattern of human lives will then be ultimately comprehensible according to an archetype that cannot be understood—according to the incomprehensible pattern of the Word's own relations with the other members of the Trinity. Because he is the Word Incarnate, Jesus' life follows the pattern of the Word's own relations with the other members of the Trinity and ours will too, united with him.

Incomprehensible in its own fullness of goodness, this archetypal divine pattern will remain, moreover, invisible in its divinity even as it surfaces as the organizing principle of human life. The divinity of Jesus' life is an inference, hidden behind the fact of human acts that save; all one sees is a human life with unusual saving effects, unimaginable apart from divine powers, which one consequently must affirm by faith rather than sight. In much the same fashion, what is responsible for making our lives this way will not appear *as* itself or per se, in any part of them, but will appear invisibly, only in and through the unusual character of a human life otherwise inexplicable in merely human terms.

We will come to be more than an imitation of the incomprehensible only by assuming or taking on the identity of what we are not, the alien identity qua divine of the Word Incarnate itself. By attaching ourselves to the incomprehensible that has attached itself to us (in becoming incarnate for this very purpose—so that we might attach ourselves to it), we become in the strongest sense incomprehensible ourselves. One with Christ, incomprehensible in his divinity, we take on the very incomprehensibility of the divine rather than simply running after it, working to reproduce it in human terms. This is the hidden incomprehensibility behind the visible incomprehensibility of a new human pattern of living. Christ's own life provides, not just the pattern of a new human way of life for our imitation, but the cause of that pattern in us, by our assimilation within it. The second person of the Trinity not only shows forth the true image in human form by becoming incarnate but makes us like that image by uniting human nature thereby with the very incomprehensibility of the divine life. It is by being bound to the incomprehensible in and through Christ—and thereby gaining a new identity in him apart from anything one is oneself—that one comes to live a boundlessly full and good life.

More Mysterious Bodies: Veils, Voids, Visions

"The Body Is No Body"

DAVID L. MILLER

The body is no body to be seen
But is an eye that studies its black lid.
WALLACE STEVENS, "Stars at Tallapoosa," in *Collected Poems*

THE BODY . . . APOPHATICALLY SPEAKING

The problem with the thematic of "aphophatic bodies"—even if one could in some way manage to conceptualize the near oxymoronic nature of the phrase—is not the word "apophasis," which is well known from the tradition of mystical or negative theology.[1] What is really problematic is the so-called body. Presumably, if the "body" is truly apophatic, like resurrection bodies, ethereal bodies, and subtle bodies, it must be, as Wallace Stevens has said, "no body to be seen." Then to what does the word refer?

Sarah Coakley has observed that an "obsessive interest in the 'body,'" which is a feature of a recent "explosion of thought and literature," has, at the same time raised the "question of definition, which is not so easily grasped, let alone answered." She notes that there is a seeming clarity about the "cultural obsession," but far from security "about its referent."[2] Coakley cites two very different witnesses to this point, Judith Butler and Mary Douglas. The former had written: "I tried to discipline myself to stay on the subject, but found I could not fix bodies as objects of thought."[3] And the latter said: "Just as it is true that everything symbolizes the body, so it is equally true that the body symbolizes everything else."[4] "Body," it would seem, has a way of eluding intellectual grasp.

The Venezuelan psychoanalyst Rafael López-Pedraza has written an insightful essay on Picasso's later etchings in his book *Hermes and His Children*, an essay that indicates something about the nature of the "body" problem psychologically.[5] The Galerie Louise Leiris showed 347 etchings by the eighty-two-year-old Picasso in 1968 and 1969.[6] Many of these showed an old man (painter) and a young woman (model) in wildly strange positions of sexual coupling. In the corner of the etching was a third figure, typically a cardinal or a priest, peeking voyeuristically through a small opening in a curtain. To imagine it from the standpoint of the cleric as taboo or sinful, crazy, excessive, fragmented, or perverse—that is, from a religious or moralistic perspective as sinful—immediately gives "body" to the body, that is, it gives an embodied perspective, perhaps like Stevens's "eye that studies its black lid." "Body" in López's work does not refer to an object in some outer world; rather, it is a perspectival metaphor, as in the "body" of the wine or the hair that has "body." "Body" here refers to a quality and not to an object. It would seem that López's point is that imagination is crucial to the body; otherwise the body may be experienced as docetic and disembodied, that is, not "saturated with itself." López's psychological insight is that some sex, though physical, has no "body" in it.

The point here is that the problem of the "body," apophatically speaking, is perspectival and linguistic. It is a problem of language, a language whose nature petitions a discourse that gives quality without concretizing that value in an object. What may be needed is an apophatic (nonliteral) manner in which to speak of bodies in order that the discourse itself be apophatically "speaking away" without being less expressive. An example of this kind of discourse can be seen in the writing of Wallace Stevens, for whom poetry is such an apophatic "speaking away." Here are a few of his figurations of poetry as apophatic discourse: "Poetry is a pheasant disappearing in the brush,"[7] or like a great cat that "leaps quickly from the fireside and is gone,"[8] or like the disappearing of a "meteor,"[9] or like "a woman writing a note and tearing it up."[10] This sort of apophatic discourse as fundamentally metaphoric and poetic is reflected in the words of Plotinus, who said, "One should understand 'as if' [*hoion*] with each of one's words" that attempt to speak of transcendental matters,[11] that is, when speaking of apophatic bodies the discourse, if it be itself apophatic, is metaphoric.

THE BY-WORD

Jacques Derrida addressed the problem of an embodied discourse that is not at the same time fixating or idolatrous in an essay, "Comment ne pas parler" ("How Not to Speak"),[12] in which he petitioned assistance from Meister Eckhart. The latter, in his twenty-sixth sermon, *Quasi stella matutina*, argued that "soul" is a *bîwort*, a "by"-word, which in Latin would be *adverbum*, an "adverb."[13] Contrary to conventional understanding, "soul" is not a noun because it does not name some-*thing*. Rather, it qualifies, modifies, gives quality and value to every-*thing*, as does an adjective or adverb. On this perspective it would be appropriate to say "soul-music" or "soul-food" but inappropriate to say "the care of the soul." Further, the soulful quality of music or food in, say, New Orleans, is sensed only by and through the body. Used properly as *bîworts*, according to Eckhart there is no body / soul opposition. It is not that apophatic discourse *should* be adjectival; it is that it *is* always and already, and only, adjectival—even if it employs nouns. It does not refer to things, even when it seems to. It refers to qualities and values.

This "adjectival" nature of imaginal and poetic, not to mention apophatically theological, discourse has nowhere been more insisted upon than by Gaston Bachelard. In this section, I should like to do two things: (1) to explicate Bachelard's notion of "adjective" or adjectival perspective, and (2), with the aim of relating this notion and its perspective to theology, to demonstrate a connection between Bachelard's literary theory and the history of religions perspective of Henry Corbin, a connection that has not been made public until now. I begin with Bachelard on the notion of "adjective."

In 1957, Bachelard wrote in *The Poetics of Space*: "A gloomy life, or a gloomy person, marks an entire universe with more than just a pervading coloration. Even things become crystallizations of sadness, regret, or nostalgia. And when a philosopher looks to poets . . . for lessons in how to individualize the world, that person soon becomes convinced that the world is not so much a noun as an adjective. If we were to give the imagination its due in the philosophical systems of the universe, we should find, at their very source, an adjective. Indeed, to those who want to find the essence of a world philosophy, one could give the following advice—look for its adjective."[14]

Bachelard in this period was working on the imagination of matter, the material imagination, especially its fundamental mythic and poetic tropes: earth, air, fire, and water. His perspective was that these words do not name some-thing(s), but that they—if I may put it this way—"adject." They speak of qualities: earthiness, airiness, fieriness, and fluidity. A person does not look at something when looking imaginally at material imagery; rather, one looks through the image at everything, which is thereby given its quality and value. Bachelard's observations concerning this are consistent, and stretch from 1940 to 1960, from his book *The Philosophy of No* through works on each of the mythic and poetic elements to late writings on light and candles. Typical of Bachelard's observations are the following: "Mass [in the physics of post-quantum mechanics] is an adjective."[15] "[T]he qualities of light and air [in Goya's paintings] are *adjectives*, which can help us to know the true *substance* of the countryside."[16] "Each adjective has its privileged noun which material imagination quickly retains. *Coolness* [*fraîcheur*], accordingly, is an attribute of water. Water is, in a sense, embodied coolness. . . . When the substantial root of a poetic quality has been discovered, when the *matter* of the adjective on which material imagination works has really been found, all the well-rooted metaphors develop by themselves."[17] "One fine adjective, clear, well-placed, assonant—and voilà! substance."[18]

Bachelard believes that in conventional literary theorizing (and I would add, theology), "adjectives came to be absorbed into nouns,"[19] that is, qualities were objectivized; what was substantive was now seen to be concrete substance. Bachelard's hermeneutic strategy is the reverse: namely, to absorb nouns into adjectives, nominalism into imagination. "When imagination places an attentive sensibility within us," he writes, "we note that qualities are not so much states as processes."[20] This implies that adjectives have more a verbal than a nominal force, or, as Bachelard says it, "red [*rouge*] is nearer to redden [*rougir*, lit. 'to be embarrassed or ashamed'] than it is to redness [*rougeur*, lit. 'a blush']."[21] So, "fire is not itself the true fire; it is only the fire flaming, burning, fuming, ashening."[22]

There is an additional matter that Bachelard attributed to adjectival function, a matter of special significance to the religious or theological imagination, namely, verticality. "Adjectives . . . that convey the power of the imaginary," he wrote in *Air and Dreams*, "live vertically."[23] In *The*

Flame of a Candle, nearly twenty years later, just a year before he died, Bachelard put the matter this way: "An upright form soars up and carries us along in its verticality. . . . To communicate with the verticality of an upright object through the imagination is to . . . participate in the hidden fire that dwells in beautiful forms, forms self-assured of their verticality."[24] Similarly, and much earlier in *Earth and the Reveries of Will*, he had written: "Verticality is so impressionable a human dimension that it occasionally permits an image to be elongated, stretching it in two directions at once, both upwards [*vers le haut*] and downwards [*vers le bas*]."[25] And later in the same work, Bachelard, citing Schelling, wrote: "Only the vertical axis has an active spiritual significance; width [*largeur*] is purely passive and material. The meaning of the human body resides more in its height [*hauteur*] than in breadth [*largeur*]."[26]

In a section on "the verticality of flames," Bachelard wrote in relation to the poetry of Novalis: "The most diverse beings are made substantive by [the verticality of] the flame. Only an adjective is necessary to make them more specific. A cursory reader will perhaps see no more here than stylistic play. But if he participates in the inflammatory intuition of a poetic philosopher, he will understand that the flame is the source for a living creature. Life is a fire. To know its essence one must burn in communion with the poet. To use an expression of Henry Corbin, we could say that Novalis' formulas tend to raise meditation to incandescence."[27] Corbin, for his part, had written earlier: "[I]deas have a substantial, transcendental, angelic existence, and the relation of terrestrial persons with ideas is ordained according to the length (verticality) of the world, not according to its breadth"[28] So, what is the point about verticality? And what is the connection to the work of Henry Corbin? I will return to the matter of verticality and incandescence in the concluding section of this chapter. But first I want to demonstrate the extent of the connection between Bachelard and Corbin.

The relation between the thought of the literary theorist and the historian of religions is revealed in a correspondence between the two men, or at least from a series of letters from Bachelard to Corbin.[29] Bachelard wrote to Corbin in the latter's role as director of the collection *Bibliothèque Iranienne* on 31 December 1955. These are his words: "Henry Corbin, whose articles in the Eranos Jahrbuch I have read with attention, gives to me in these writings proof of a beautiful depth of meditation.

. . . I do not wish to put down your book on Avicenna. . . . All of its pages captivate me. They make me think and dream."

In August of the same year, four months earlier at the Eranos Conference in Ascona, Switzerland, Corbin wrote: "Just as in the *Dialectic of Love,* one takes one's departure from sensible beauty in order to be elevated even to a meeting with the unique principle of all beauty and all ideas, so the adepts of hieratic science take for the point of departure precisely these apparent things and the sympathies as that have manifested between them and the invisible powers. Observing that all is in all, they have situated the foundations of the hieratic, being astonished to see and admire in initial realities the ultimate venues of being and in such ultimates also the proximate realities; in the sky there exist the terrestrial things according to a fortuitous and celestial mode, and on the earth there exist heavenly things in a terrestrial condition. What other reason could one give for the fact of a heliotrope following by its movement the movement of the sun, and the selenotrope the movement of the moon, making a procession in the measure of their ability, with the cosmic flames?"[30] This is striking, because the line about the heliotrope was the very same sentence that Bachelard would cite in *The Flame of a Candle* to be published six years later.[31]

The connection between the thought of the two men was confirmed by Stella Corbin in a personal letter to me (10 October 1983).[32] "When Bachelard wrote *Flame* he had tried to see Henry in order to inquire about Persian poetry, but in those years Henry sought few contacts. So it was I who had taken *Terre celeste* to Bachelard. On that evening he showed me with emotion his copy of *Avicenne et le récit visionnaire,* a copy well used, pages scribbled with notes, phrases underlined." Two letters from Bachelard to Corbin demonstrate the fidelity of the emotion and the connection. On 13 May 1956, he wrote: "Your Avicenna never leaves my table. But with each re-reading, I see in it more complexity. If you have the occasion of passing Place Maubert, knock at my door."[33] And on May 17, five years later, Bachelard wrote to Corbin: "Dear Monsieur. For a long time I have been wanting to write to you. . . . Your book has such an importance that I would like to study it without ceasing in order to be able to speak to you about it in an appropriate manner. When I spoke to your belle-soeur [*sic*] of the usefulness that it would have for me to see the Iranian religion of fire, I believed that then I was touching the poetry of fire. . . . But where are the poems of the Persian poets? . . . In this deficit of little works, how important for me was the discovery of your book? It is the *élan* of verticality that I received from each page of *Terre Céleste*. If I had known your work twenty years ago, what stronger tone would I have given to my book *Water and Dreams*? Reading you, I imagine that I yet could have the power to speak of the dynamicity of human verticality."[34]

So it would seem, then, that it is no incidental matter when Bachelard says: "To use an expression of Henry Corbin, we could say that Novalis' formulas tend to raise meditation to incandescence"—shimmering consciousness, radiation, resonance, iridescence. Indeed, it was in that very book—the one that never left Bachelard's table and in which he had scribbled—that Corbin had written: "What is certain is that, in Avicennan terms, the contemplative intellect, Absâl, is ordained to the illumination that it receives from the Angel, but this illumination, the irradiation of Forms that it received, is also the very same light of which it is itself made. . . . Thus it is its own light that grows more intense, its own being that is progressively brought to incandescence."[35]

THEOPOETICS

What I am proposing is that the word "body" in the phrase "apophatic bodies" be seen as adjective, even if it is not an adjective in the literal grammatical sense. It does not denominate something. It is—in Stevens's words—the body that is no body; it is an adjective in Bachelard's and Corbin's sense. Body is *de*-nominated by being viewed as adjectival: bodying and embodying, not body.[36] To be sure, this makes of body a metaphor, and it implies that apophatic theological discourse is theopoetics, using this term, not in the ancient sense of *theopoiesis* (assimilation to the divine),[37] but rather in the sense employed by Amos Wilder in his book *Theopoetic*.[38]

Wilder noted the recent history of the term, saying: "I believe that I had picked up the term 'theopoetic' and 'theopoiesis' from Stanley Hopper and his students, no doubt in one or another of the remarkable consultations on hermeneutics and language which he had organized at Drew and at Syracuse to which many of us are indebted."[39] Wilder is alluding to conferences at Drew University in 1962,[40] 1964, and 1966,[41] and a fourth conference at Syracuse University in 1970.[42] These consultations were located intellectually at the intersection of left-wing Bultmannian biblical interpretation, the thought of the late period of Heidegger's existential philosophy, and the Religion and Literature movement. The first conference focused on hermeneutic and biblical interpretation and featured Gerhard Ebeling and Ernst Fuchs. The second, a follow-up to the first, was more theological, and Fritz Buri and Heinrich Ott made presentations. In the third conference, literary and philosophical perspectives were added, and the speakers included Beda Allemann, Owen Barfield, Norman O. Brown, Kenneth Burke, and Julián Marías. And the fourth, following up on the third in theme and perspectives, featured Henry Bugbee, Richard DiMartino, Hans-Georg Gadamer, Keiji Nishitani, Wolfgang Zucker.

Because of the centrality of Heidegger's perspective on language and poetry (citing Hölderlin, he had written "poetically human beings dwell upon the earth"), Stanley Hopper and Karlfried Froelich visited with Heidegger before the second consultation and invited him to attend. He agreed. But because of illness he could not attend. Rather, he sent a letter in which he urged three questions upon the deliberations: (1) What is the nature of the referent of theological utterance? (2) What is the nature of thinking that is objectifying? and (3) Is a non-objectivizing thinking and speaking possible?[43]

The problematic of objectivizing discourse is theologically the problem of idolatry, and it may well be that all speech reifies its subject in some manner. But it does not follow—or so it was the experiment of these consultations to probe—that language may not thereby perform an entirely different function, namely, to use Heideggerian language, to bring Being to appearance, to allow the unveiling of Truth (*a-letheia*), and to let that which is appear *as* that which it is.

The "as" is crucial. Already in *Being and Time*, Heidegger had argued that all language has an *as*-structure. In the third Drew consultation, this was interpreted as poetry, as radical metaphor. Allemann referred to such radical metaphor as "anti-metaphor" or "absolute metaphor."[44] Hopper,[45] following Philip Wheelwright, called it "diaphor" as opposed to "epiphor."[46] That is, one is not viewing poetry as mere metaphor, simile without the word "like," which would be the expression of the likeness of like things, ignoring difference. It would still be a reinscription of objectivization and of the ontometaphysical tradition in which Being is viewed as a being.

Hopper saw this move in the direction of a radical poetic consciousness as "theopoetical," and he wrote, in his introduction to the third consultation: "What *theo-poiesis* does is to effect disclosure through the crucial nexus of event, thereby making the crux of knowing, both morally and aesthetically, radically decisive in time."[47] Amos Wilder was surely correct in his judgment, and he himself carried on the theopoetical perspective in religious discourse, de-nominalizing and de-objectivizing theological referents in a manner consistent with apophatic intentionality, that is, a "speaking away."

AN AMORIST ADJECTIVE AFLAME

I have been implying that poetry, like Bachelard's and Corbin's adjectival discourse, gives vertical perspective (i.e., height and depth) to what it describes. Poetry—like adjectives—carries meditation and thought to incandescence, to use the word borrowed by Bachelard from Corbin, a word to which I now return.

Coincidentally (or perhaps not so coincidentally), the American poet Wallace Stevens also mentions "adjective" in a poem having to do with the verticality of fire, a poem that implies an incandescence.[48] Perhaps this poetic witness, a little closer to home than the German hermeneutic theologians or the French historians of religion and myth, can serve as conclusion to the point that an apophatic body is no body, and that every body is potentially an apophatic body when imagined incandescently.

Stevens writes the following in his poem "The Man with the Blue Guitar":

> The pale intrusions into blue
> Are corrupting pallors . . . ay di mi,
>
> Blue buds or pitchy blooms. Be content—
> Expansion, diffusions—content to be
>
> The unspotted imbecile revery,
> The heraldic center of the world
>
> Of blue, blue sleek with a hundred chins
> The amorist Adjective aflame.[49]

On 25 June 1953, Stevens wrote to Renato Poggioli, his Italian translator, responding to a question the latter posed about these lines. Stevens explained: "In this poem the amorist Adjective means blue (the amorist Adjective) as a word metamorphosed into blue as a reality."[50] But four days later, apparently Stevens had a second thought, and so he wrote another letter, saying: "The other day I commented on 'amorist Adjective aflame.' Perhaps my explanation was a bit too expansive. The poem in which this appears is a poem that deals with the intensity of the imagination unmodified by contacts with reality, if such a thing is possible." And then comes the surprising sentence: "Intensity becomes something incandescent." Stevens goes on: "I took a look at this poem after I had written to you and thought that the metamorphosis into reality, while a good enough illustration, was misleading. The poem has to do with pure imagination."[51] Here Stevens uses the very same words that Bachelard fastens on in Corbin, and apparently without knowledge of the work of either, at least as far as I have been able to determine.

Eight years after Stevens's letter, Bachelard wrote: "The flame is an inhabited verticality. . . . Everything vertical in the cosmos is a flame. . . . The fire flowers [*feu fleurit*] and the flower lights up [*fleur s'illumine*]. These two corollaries could be developed endlessly: color is an epiphany of fire; and the flower is an ontophany of light."[52] And, concerning precisely what this color is, Bachelard had concurred in advance with Stevens. The following had been published in 1938, fifteen years before the American poet's letter to his translator: "You may object that Novalis is the poet of 'the little blue flower,' the poet of the forget-me-not tossed as a pledge of imperishable memory over the edge of the precipice in the very shadow of death! But go down into the depths of the unconscious, find there with the poet the primitive dream, and you will clearly see the truth: the little blue flower is red!"[53]

So it is with the apophatic body that is no body. It is an embodying perspective that can give valence to life and meaning, a vertical dimension in which ordinariness incandesces, flaming and flowering. The body that is no body is incandescence.

Revisioning the Body Apophatically: Incarnation and the Acosmic Naturalism of Habad Hasidism

ELLIOT R. WOLFSON

In Bodhi there is no tree,
Nor a mirror bright,
From the beginning not a thing is,
Where can the dust alight?
HUI-NENG

The expression "apophatic body" strikes the ear as a pairing of words that do not sit together so easily. What, after all, is it to speak of a body about which nothing can be spoken? From both the commonsense and more erudite perspectives, it would seem that the body, however we are to conceive it, presents itself with a gravitas that makes it hard, if not impossible, to depict it apophatically. How would we take hold of such a body? How would such a body take hold of us?

In considering the matter more circumspectly, however, one comes to appreciate that not only is there no contradiction in lumping these terms together, but it is precisely their juxtaposition that opens a unique path to contemplate the matter of embodiment. In speaking of body, the body spoken is no longer the lived body of which one has (un)spoken. The body, one might say, is precisely what cannot be spoken but as the no-longer-spoken-once-spoken, an incarnality spoken in its unspokenness. Alternatively expressed, the texture, the touch, of what we confront and what confronts us in our materiality, however we are to construe the latter, resists the reduction of the corporeal to the linguistic. We face the somatic and name it, but in so naming, we discern the opposition of that which we face, the discreteness and distinctiveness of what must remain other to consciousness as it is part of consciousness as the other just as consciousness is part of it as other. One may be critical of thinking consciousness in terms of the structure of intentionality, the for-itself and for-the-other, but there seems to be no way around the taint of the mirror image. Language, on this score, is not a bridge that connects mind and matter, a communication of the linguistic being of things, in Benjamin's telling formulation;[1] it is, rather, an open enclosure—a circumscription—that reveals the double inflection of the apophatic body. To mull over a matter so ponderous in its immateriality, one would be wise to calibrate one's thinking in accord with contemporary quantum physics, as the mundane orientation is not amenable to rendering the stuff of being most abstract at the basest level of concreteness and most concrete at the highest level of abstraction.

In this essay, I consider the theme of apophatic body as enunciated in the contemplative mysticism of the branch of east-European Hasidism known as Habad or Lubavitch. The former name is an acronym for *ḥokhmah*, *binah*, and *daʿat*, "wisdom," "understanding," and "knowledge," a reference to the three upper aspects of the ten enumerated divine emanations[2] and their corresponding psychological faculties, *nefesh*, *ruaḥ*, and *neshamah*, which constitute the triadic nature of intellect (*sekhel*);[3] the latter designation is the Yiddish version of Lyubavichi, the town in Russia where the headquarters of the movement were established by Dov Baer Schneersohn (1773–1827), son of and successor to Shneur Zalman of Liadi (1745–1812), one of the prominent disciples of Dov Baer, the Maggid of Mezeritch (1704–1772), himself a follower of Israel ben Eliezer (1698–1760), the *Baʿal Shem Ṭov*, "master of a good name," generally abbreviated as the Besht, the man to whom credit is given for spearheading and inspiring a revivalist pietism that flowered into a vibrant social phenomenon in the late eighteenth and early nineteenth centuries.[4] As of this moment, no replacement has been named for Menachem Mendel Schneerson (1902–1994), still referred to, long after his physical demise, by the honorific title "the Rebbe," the seventh master in a lineage that can be traced to Shneur Zalman, the Alter Rebbe.[5]

Habad is distinguished in many respects from other hasidic dynasties that evolved in these centuries, but, as scholars have noted, one of the most distinctive ways that this is so is the emphasis it places on cogitation as the supreme form of mystical piety, a point encoded in its very name.[6] This emphasis can be discerned in the mandate of Habad from its inception to render esoteric teachings rationally, to cast the secrets in a style that is intellectually demanding and responsive to the seemingly perennial curiosity of the human mind to gain knowledge of the sensory world and beyond.[7] I shall return to this theme below, but suffice it here to emphasize that this scholastic orientation has yielded a truly impressive literary output. The library compiled by, or on the basis of the oral discourses and written documents of the seven Habad masters, not to mention other peripheral figures who expounded their teachings, is stunning in size and breathtaking in scope. Accordingly, the documentation in this study is necessarily selective. I have not attempted an exhaustive historical or philological analysis of all the relevant sources, surely a worthy task, but the limited number of textual samples that I offer from this voluminous corpus should be sufficient to establish the constructive theological contribution that these thinkers can make to the larger philosophical question with which this book is engaged, the phenomenon we are calling (without taxonomic certainty) "apophatic embodiment."

INTELLECT BEYOND INTELLECT: FAITH, VIA NEGATIVA, AND VISIONARY GNOSIS

The philosophical piety promulgated by the proponents of Habad eschews any conflict between mysticism and reason. Lubavitch masters have uniformly endorsed an epistemological agnosticism, acknowledging the inherent inability of the human reason to ascertain knowledge of the divine essence, but they nonetheless viewed it as the means to attain the gnosis that is a transrational state also identified as faith (*emunah*).[8] Here it is pertinent to recall that Shneur Zalman and his fraternity were criticized by other Hasidic masters, led by Abraham of Kalisk in 1797, for emphasizing the role of intellect as a vehicle of contemplation instead of affirming as the pietistic ideal a pure and simple faith that is not only beyond but also antithetical to reason.[9] The matter was, as one might expect, more complex than the polemical condemnations would suggest, for according to Shneur Zalman, and those who followed and elaborated his teaching, the highest level that one can attain in worship relates to the attribute of faith that does indeed exceed the limit of intellect and language.[10] The following statement from *Torah Or*, the anthology of Shneur Zalman's discourses on Genesis, Exodus, and Esther committed to writing by his brother, Judah Leib of Yanovitch, and compiled by his grandson, Menachem Mendel Schneersohn (1789–1866), commonly referred to as the Tzemach Tzedek, can be considered representative: "To comprehend the matter of blessings . . . all of Israel believe . . . that which the philosophic sages and scientists tire of understanding by their intellects, for faith is above comprehension and the intellect, even above the comprehension that is in the root of the divine soul that is in Israel . . . for thought cannot grasp it."[11] Faith is connected intrinsically to blessing, as the latter consists of the efflux of light that overflows from the fountain of life, the essence of the Infinite (*aṣmut ein sof*), beyond rational comprehension and even beyond the comprehension that is unique to the Jewish people who are imprinted with the divine soul in a singular way.[12] The mystical import of the liturgical utterance is "to draw down the disclosure of this faith, so that the being of the light of the Infinite, blessed be he, will be blessed and will issue forth in the disclosure below. The order of concatenation, the drawing forth of the disclosure, from the first was so that the Lord would be our God, the disclosure of the light of the Infinite, blessed be he, in the souls of Israel, to be 'our God' actually in the aspect of annihilation, for they are from the interiority of the worlds."[13]

We can detect in this passage the intricate interweaving of the theosophic, cosmological, and anthropological threads, which inform the warp and woof of Habad thought: faith denotes the divine light that transcends intellect, the emanation of that light in all that exists, and the form of worship by which the Jewish soul[14] attains mystical gnosis of the light and is annihilated in its impenetrable source. What is conventionally referred to in Western metaphysics as the "chain of being" is designated in Habad speculation (based on earlier kabbalistic sources) as the "order of concatenation" (*seder ha-hishtalshelut*),[15] which shows itself as the "drawing forth of the disclosure" (*hamshakhat ha-gilluy*). Philological precision is warranted here, as it sheds light on the spot where the ontological and phenomenological collude—the truth of being (*mahut*) is the being of truth, the truth of the essence (*aṣmut*) is the essence of truth,[16] determined from the vantage point of what appears, the manifestation of the essential light (*or ha-aṣmi*) that must remain hidden and thus can be revealed only through the drape of darkness,[17] the "aspect of the concealment of the essence that is above the aspect of light" (*beḥinat heʿlem ha-aṣmut she-lemaʿlah mi-beḥinat or*),[18] the "supernal dark" (*ḥoshekh elyon*) whence there was a disclosure of the light of the Infinite (*gilluy or ein sof*),[19] the "supernal light" (*or elyon*) too radiant to be revealed as light but through the veil of light, just as the splendor of the sun becomes visible only as it is refracted through layers of the atmosphere. In a noteworthy passage from *Torah Or*, Shneur Zalman refers to the "Infinite in itself" (*ein sof be-aṣmo*) as the "aspect of the luminescence that is the source of the light and from which the light emanates" (*beḥinat ha-maʾor she-hu meqor ha-or u-mimmenu nimshakh ha-or*).[20] In other Habad sources, the distinction between the concealed essence and the manifest light is made even more sharply. The discussion in one of the treatises of Shalom Dovber Schneerson (1860–1920), the fifth Rebbe, known as the RaShaB, is demonstrative of the point. On the one hand, insofar as light by nature entails disclosure (*gilluy*) and the essence is too hidden (*heʿlem*) to be included in the category of disclosure (*be-geder ha-gilluy*), it is reasonable to presume that the aspect of light is "like something added to the essence" (*kemo davar nosaf al ha-eṣem*). On the other hand, it is not apposite to speak of the light as something supplemental, since it is the "disclosure of the essence" (*gilluy ha-eṣem*) and not some "other substance" (*mahut aḥer*).[21] Grappling with this philosophical quandary, the seventh Rebbe astutely observed that the "light that is comprised in the essence is not in the category of disclosure, for all that is comprised in the essence is like the essence," whence it follows that "the light as it is comprised in the luminescence is not in the aspect of the existence of light at all [*ha-or kemo she-hu kalul be-ha-maʾor eino bi-veḥinat meṣiʾut or kelal*], since it is not in the category of disclosure, but it is only in the aspect of possibility [*bi-veḥinat yekholet*]."[22]

I shall return to this insight regarding the essence whose actuality it is to be pure possibility, but at this juncture what needs to be underscored is that ritual performance in general, and the act of blessing in particular, has the effect of drawing this possibility, the light that is contained in the essence, from concealment to disclosure,[23] albeit a disclosure that perforce is a concealment, as the concealment that is disclosed cannot be disclosed but through being concealed, the paradox that holds the key to understanding the incarnational dimension of Habad.[24] According to

Shneur Zalman, the liturgical act, epitomized in the formulaic *barukh hu*, "blessed be he," empowers one "to draw down from that which is above place to the aspect of place . . . to draw down from that which is above time to the aspect of time."[25] Drawing down the effluence of light into the corporeal and stripping away the corporeal to liberate the sparks of light entrapped therein are two ways to view the self-same phenomenon. One can arrange these matters sequentially, so that the drawing down is posed as consequent to the stripping away, but it is also possible to reverse the causal order, and to pose the stripping away as consequent to the drawing down.[26] The basic monotheistic tenet of Judaism is transposed in Habad into the quietistic ideal of abnegation (*biṭṭul*) or sacrifice of self (*mesirat nefesh*),[27] referred to in various other ways as well, including debasement (*shiflut*) , submission (*hakhnaʾah*), great love (*ahavah rabbah*), and desire of the heart (*reʿuta de-libba*): to believe in one God is to be conjoined to, indeed incorporated within,[28] the will (*raṣon*) or supernal holiness (*qodesh ha-elyon*) that is "ontically extinguished in the light of the Infinite" (*ha-baṭel bi-meṣiʾut be-or ein sof*). Just as the natural inclination of the flame is to rise and to be integrated in its source, the elemental fire, so the impulse of the will and desire of the human soul—represented paradigmatically by the Jew[29]—the aspect of wisdom in which there is the light of the Infinite, "yearns in its nature to separate and go out from the body, to cleave to its root and source in the Lord . . . so that it will be nothing and nil [*ayin wa-efes*] and its existence will be entirely eradicated there [*titbaṭṭel sham bi-meṣiʾut legamrei*], and nothing will remain of its first substance and essence."[30]

Many passages could be adduced to illumine further the aspect of wisdom in the divine soul that is "above knowledge and intellect,"[31] but I will mention only one other particularly poignant discourse from 1805 delivered on the Sabbath known in the rabbinic calendar as *shabbat naḥamu*, literally, the "Sabbath of comfort," the Sabbath that always follows the Ninth of Av, the fast day that commemorates the destruction of both Jerusalem Temples, and on which Isaiah 40 is read as the prophetic section, a chapter that begins with God's call to comfort the people of Israel. Shneur Zalman's exposition is framed as a meditation on the verse "Know this day, and consider in your hearts that the Lord is God in heaven above and in earth below, there is no other" (Deut 4:39), a verse from the Torah section that is always read liturgically on that very Sabbath. Reflecting on the scriptural command to know that the Lord (YHWH) is God (Elohim)—the mystical intent of which alludes to what kabbalists have long referred to as the mystery of the androgyne (*sod du-parṣufim*), the coupling of mercy to the right and judgment to the left, the sacred union of male and female, the potency to bestow and the capacity to receive[32]—Shneur Zalman distinguishes between knowledge (*daʿat*) and faith (*emunah*): the former entails discernment of the immanence of the divine light in the world, the enclothing of soul in body (*hitlabbeshut nefesh be-guf*), signified by the technical expression *memalle kol almin*, "filling all worlds," and the latter, the transcendent dimension of that light that is marked linguistically as *sovev kol almin*, "encompassing all worlds."[33] One apprehends the immanence of God through an intellectual vision (*reʾiyyah sikhlit*), which shares something of the tangibility of the physical sense of sight (*reʾiyyah ḥushit*),[34] but the transcendence of divinity, the light that is "above the aspect of being garbed in the worlds" (*lemaʿlah mi-beḥinat hitlabbeshut be-olamot*), is known through contemplation (*hitbonenut*) that is "beyond the intellect" (*lemaʿlah min ha-sekhel*),[35] an apophatic contemplation, we can rightly say, since what is contemplated is what we cannot contemplate, not an incomprehensible something but the limit of all possible comprehension, that which thought cannot grasp at all, *leit maḥashavah tefisa beih kelal*, to use the zoharic dictum employed by Shneur Zalman and repeated often in Habad sources.[36] I will return to this particular affirmation of apophasis below, but for now the crucial point is to appreciate the distinction that is upheld between knowledge and faith. Only through the latter does one ascend to the hidden Wisdom (*ḥokhmah setimaʾah*), the "supernal will that is above knowledge [*raṣon ha-elyon she-lemaʿlah min ha-daʿat*], which in the human soul is the aspect of *yeḥidah*, the aspect of abnegation [*beḥinat biṭṭul*] in relation to him, blessed be he, above knowledge and comprehensible understanding [*lemaʿlah mi-daʿat we-haskalah ha-mussag*] . . . the incomposite will that is without any comprehensible reason or intellect [*raṣon pashuṭ beli shum ṭaʿam wa-sekhel mussag*], which extends from the aspect of the Supernal Crown [*keter elyon*] . . . the aspect of nullification with respect to the light of the Infinite, blessed be he [*beḥinat biṭṭul le-or ein sof barukh hu*]."[37]

One could dedicate a whole chapter, perhaps an entire treatise, to unpacking all that is implied in this text and to do justice to all the sources upon which it is based. Of necessity, however, I must be brief, and hence I will only signpost the points that are most germane to the analysis of apophatic embodiment. First, the transcendent aspect of the godhead, the dimension that is not subject to representation of any sort, whether mental or physical, corresponds pneumatically to *yeḥidah*, the aspect of the soul that is beyond individuation and in virtue of which the line separating divine and human may be crossed in contemplative ecstasy (*hitpaʿalut*). What is implied in Shneur Zalman's words is made more explicit in the formulation of his son Dov Baer, also known as the Mitteler Rebbe: "This is the aspect of *yeḥidah* that is in the soul whose root is in the aspect of the essence [*beḥinat ha-aṣmut*]. Therefore, it has an aspect of essential nullification [*biṭṭul aṣmi*] that is above *Ḥokhmah*."[38] Second, the attainment of this unity beyond apprehension—technically speaking, the language of attainment is problematic as there is nothing to attain (t)here but nothing that is not (un)attainable, and yet we have no choice but to employ the term metaphorically to denote this quest to reach, both upwardly and inwardly, the place above place and the time above time[39]—comes about through ceremonial observance, which is grounded ultimately in faith rather than in knowledge. Indeed, even the minimal halakhic routine should and can be endowed with this mystical valence predicated on the consubstantiality of God and the Jewish soul. As Shneur Zalman put it, "[T]he worship of the Lord in the human soul [*nefesh ha-adam*] is the aspect of the disclosure of the light of the Infinite in the aspect of *yeḥidah* in the divine soul, which is far above the aspect of any comprehension and understanding."[40]

The commandments are the means by which one achieves a state of conjunction (*devequt*), a merging of the human and divine wills, the abnegation of self and its integration into the unified One (*yaḥid meyuḥad*) that results in drawing down the infinite light into the veneer of a world of differentiation.[41] The commandments can serve this role because they are, kabbalistically imagined, limbs of the body of the Torah, a notion of corporeality that is not inconsequential to understanding the apophatic embodiment we are seeking to articulate in these reflections.[42] A rudimentary axiom of the kabbalistic worldview is the belief that the Torah is the linguistic body, the body made of the twenty-two Hebrew letters, which are contained in the name YHWH.[43] In Habad thinking, the name is identified, moreover, as the "aspect of the light of the Infinite that is in his essence . . . which is the aspect of the disclosure, that is, what can be revealed and disseminated like the ray of the sun from the sun."[44] Insofar as the Torah is the name, we can say that the "essence of the Torah is unified in his essence . . . in the interiority of the light of the Infinite."[45] Through the agency of the Torah, therefore, one can serve as a conduit for the emplacement of the light that exceeds all limitations in the world of delimitation, to transfigure materiality (im)materially, or, in the rabbinic idiom,[46] which is often employed by Habad masters, to make a habitation for the divine below (*dirah ba-taḥtonim*).[47] To cite Shneur Zalman again, "The fulfillment of the commandments is verily from his essence . . . he gave of his essence to us, as it were, so that we could verily draw down his essence."[48] This idea, which is emphasized repeatedly in Habad teaching, provides the ontological foundation for moral action—in line with the older kabbalistic tradition, Habad thinking does not separate ontology and ethics[49]—as the good is determined on the grounds that the very possibility of there being something rather than nothing is due to the paradoxical identity of transcendence and immanence.[50] But perhaps we should speak of meontological in place of ontological, as the basis for the ethical demand to be nothing is the nihility that is the ultimate void of being. In the formulation of the Mitteler Rebbe, the essence of the soul's self-sacrifice consists of "the nullification and integration into the aspect of the nothing of the Infinite itself in an essential nullification [*ha-biṭṭul we-hitkallelut bi-veḥinat ayin de-ein sof aṣmo be-viṭṭul aṣmi*] . . . and not merely the aspect of the nullification of something to nothing [*beḥinat biṭṭul ha-yesh le-ayin*]."[51] Implicit here are the two forms of annihilation distinguished by Habad masters, the "nullification of existence" (*biṭṭul bi-meṣiʾut*) and the "nullification of something" (*biṭṭul ha-yesh*), which correspond to the two gradations of the "aspect of the nothing," the "essential nothing" (*ha-ayin ha-aṣmi*), which is the "nothing of the concealment of essence" (*ayin shel heʿlem ha-aṣmut*), and the "nothing of the something" (*ayin shel ha-yesh*), that is, the nothing that is not in relation to anything but to its own nothingness and the nothing that is nothing only in relation to something other that comes forth from the nothing, though that other is nothing other than the nothing of its own nothingness.[52] The nullification of existence, which is also marked semantically as the "essential nullification" (*biṭṭul aṣmi*), the nullification of essence, completely obliterates all differentiation; the one assimilated into the "essential nothing," the "nothing of the Infinite," has no sense of self at all (*eino margish et aṣmo kelal*).[53] As Dov Baer describes what we might call the dissolution of an egocentric consciousness in another passage, "This is the aspect of the actual nothing [*ayin mammash*] and this is the aspect of humiliation [*shiflut*] and modesty [*anawah*], which is called the essential nullification [*biṭṭul aṣmi*], for his soul is essentially like dust in relation to everything."[54] Moses, who is described scripturally as the humblest of all human beings (Num 12:3), represents the archetypal realization of this ideal: "From the perspective of his being conjoined to the essence, the nullification of his self was through an intense integration to the point that he did not feel his self at all."[55]

In emulation of Moses, one can become the actual nothing that one is through self-effacement, which in turn restores everything into nothing; the one who attains this nondual consciousness, the consciousness in which even the distinction between dual and nondual is eradicated, mimics the "essential nothing of the interiority of *Keter*," where opposites coincide, a mystery that is referred to as the "supernal wonder" (*pele ha-elyon*),[56] the *mystery of mysteries*, as it is the mystery that encapsulates the paradoxical characteristic of all mystery, though essential to the nature of mystery is an indeterminacy that renders its imprint constantly different, *a genuine repetition that erupts from an originary transformation*, to appropriate the language of Heidegger,[57] always having already been the retrieval of what is yet to come. To avail myself of another Heideggerian turn of phrase, the integration of opposites is not "the coalescence and obliteration of distinctions," but rather "the belonging together of what is foreign" (*Zusammengehören des Fremden*).[58] The supreme expression of this belonging together—the conundrum that is the origin, the *pele* that is the *alef*—is the manifestation of the infinite light beyond nature in the time-space continuum of material nature, the mystery of incarnation that is the secret of the garment.[59] The unmasking of this secret consists precisely of an aporetic withholding, a not-wanting-to-be-transparent, lest the lucidity obscure the concealing of the concealment that uncovers the nonbeing of being in the recovery of the being of nonbeing.[60]

The point is repeated in numerous passages from the Habad corpus, but I will translate one relevant citation from the RaShaB, not because of the novelty of his words, but on account of their clarity: "It is known that the purpose of creation and the generation of the worlds, and the purpose of the intention of the descent of the soul to the body, is to draw down the disclosure of the light of the Infinite in the worlds by means of the Torah and commandments, and this is the matter of the unity of the light of the Infinite that encompasses all worlds in that which fills all worlds [*yiḥud or ein sof ha-sovev kol almin be-memalle kol almin*] . . . for this is the matter of drawing down the disclosure of the essence of the light of the Infinite, as this is the purpose of the intent in the generation of the worlds and the descent of the soul in accord with the dictum that the holy One, blessed be, desires to have a habitation in the lower beings."[61] The unity of the transcendent and immanent is beyond the range of the lower knowledge (*daʿat taḥton*), which relates to our propensity to differentiate opposites—*zeh leʿumat zeh*, "one vis-à-vis the other"[62]—a dual consciousness that rests on a binarian logic, a depiction obviously inspired by the scriptural image of the tree of knowledge of good and evil.[63] From this vantage point, we posit spirit in opposition to matter, even though all our efforts may be to unify the two. By contrast, faith "reaches that matter that the eye of the intellect cannot comprehend at all, as it is said, 'no thought can grasp you at all,' the meaning of 'you' is your actual being and your essence; the thought of the vision of wisdom cannot grasp it at all, but only the power of faith through which one actually believes in his being and in his essence. Even though one does not see with the eye of the intellect or with the vision of the eye, the might of faith is so strong that it is as if one actually saw with one's eyes his being and essence, which no thought can grasp."[64] Faith is thus a gnosis of the higher knowledge (*daʿat elyon*), the knowing that exceeds the dichotomizing conceptualization, a vision of the "aspect of the incomposite will [*raṣon ha-pashuṭ*] that is above reason and knowledge and above the aspect of the lights being garbed in vessels,"[65] the "aspect of the essence of the light of the Infinite"[66] wherein light and darkness are made equal (*shaweh u-mashweh or we-ḥoshekh*),[67] the "single equanimous light" (*or eḥat shaweh*),[68] the light that is the surplus of light, the one that is more than what is less than one, the holiness that has "already been purified," that is, the holiness purged of all unholiness and hence beyond being holy. Faith, therefore, provides access to that which the seventh Rebbe dubbed as the "without boundary that is above being without boundary" (*beli gevul she-lemaʿlah mi-beli gevul*).[69] Based on the older kabbalistic principle of *aḥdut ha-shaweh*, the "equanimous one,"[70] in Habad the term *hashwaʾah*, "equanimity" or "indifference," is applied "to the essence of the light of the Infinite," the luminosity that is "beyond the perimeter of the concatenation" (*heqqef de-ha-histalshelut*),[71] as it transcends both the light that "encompasses all worlds" and the "illumination that is garbed in the world . . . in the aspect of that which fills all worlds."[72] As was his wont, the seventh Rebbe expressed the complex philosophical issue in straightforward and comprehensible terms: "[H]is essence, blessed be he, is simple in absolute simplicity and it is devoid of all forms, and it is not fitting that there be anything opposing him."[73]

Here we both note an important affinity and mark a significant discrepancy between the leaders of Habad, beginning with Shneur Zalman, and the medieval sage Maimonides, who clearly functioned as their spiritual mentor: just as the *via negativa* embraced by Maimonides served to augment rather than to abolish physical and metaphysical inquiry of a scientific nature[74]—the former designated as *maʿaseh bereʾshit*, the "account of creation," and the latter as *maʿaseh merkavah*, the "account of the chariot"—so the perspective expounded by Habad encourages the exercise of intellect to plumb the depths of the universe and to probe the unfathomable mystery of God.[75] Shneur Zalman set the tone by insisting that the acquisition of knowledge of the *seder hishtalshelut*—the technical term for the standard four worlds of kabbalistic ontology, emanation (*aṣilut*), creation (*beriʾah*), formation (*yeṣirah*), and doing (*asiyyah*)—is the "great commandment" proclaimed in the verse "Know this day, and consider in your hearts that the Lord is God in heaven above and in earth below, there is no other" (Deut 4:39). By attaining such knowledge one acquires a "perfect heart" (*lev shalem*) and ascertains that the comprehension of existence entails divesting it of corporeality (*hassagat ha-meṣiʾut hu lehafshiṭ mi-gashmiyyut*).[76] To apprehend reality, one must strip it of its materiality, a reversal of the process of creation, "the annihilation of something into nothing" (*ha-biṭṭul yesh le-ayin*),[77] to the point that "corporeality is eradicated into nothing in the extreme" (*ha-gashmiyyut baṭel le-ayin be-takhlit*).[78] As Shneur Zalman put it elsewhere, "The aspect of the nullification of something [*beḥinat biṭṭul ha-yesh*] is the opposite of the root of the matter of the break [*shevirah*],[79] which was for the sake of the disclosure of the light precisely in the aspect of something [*hitgallut ha-or li-veḥinat yesh dawqa*]." Yet, it is this inverse mirroring that facilitates the causal connection between the "nullification of something to nothing" (*biṭṭul ha-yesh le-ayin*) and the "drawing of nothing to something" (*hamshakhat ayin le-yesh*).[80] Only when one sees from the vantage point of this double annihilation—the nothing becoming something that is nothing—does one comprehend the philosophic meaning of the verse from Deuteronomy proclaiming that apart from God there is no other, that is, appearances notwithstanding, there is no being (*mahut*) but the "actual nothing" (*ayin mammash*)[81] that everything is apparently. In the essence of this void, the substance of discriminate beings, including the personal God of biblical and rabbinic Judaism, is rendered insubstantial. Not to advance to this stage is to allow theism to elide into idolatry.

FROM SOMETHING NOTHING BUT NOTHING OF SOMETHING

The paradoxical nature of Habad cosmology leads to the assertion that "it is impossible for something to come to be from something,"[82] an explicit rejection of the well-known philosophical maxim *ex nihil, nihil fit*, "from nothing, nothing comes," since the source of all that exists is the "aspect of the true nothing of the essence of the light of the Infinite in actuality" (*beḥinat ayin ha-amitti de-aṣmut or ein sof mammash*).[83] With regard to this *true nothing*, Habad plainly deviates from Maimonides, for while the latter also identified ultimate human felicity as a state of conjunction whereby the intellect rids itself of its bodily encasement and is united with the Active Intellect, the last of the incorporeal intellects that emanate from God, he did not advocate a cosmology that would disrobe the world of its material investiture. For Maimonides, there is no logical principle that would allow for the dialectic inversion of being into nothing, and even his commitment to the dogma of *creatio ex nihilo* is suspect; by the logic of the aforementioned principle *ex nihil, nihil fit*, the presumed traditional doctrine of *yesh me-ayin*, the creation of something from nothing, is a marvel beyond the comprehension of created beings,[84] but it still falls short of the absurdity implied in the paradoxical identification of *yesh* and *ayin* that overwhelms Habad thinking. I will not enter into a discussion of the earlier sources that doubtlessly influenced Habad, though I hasten to add that these sources, which go as far back as the thirteenth century, are not irrelevant, and a proper treatment of this topic well demands a suitable delineation that would illustrate the importance of this motif to the kabbalistic sensibility more generally. Instead I will emphasize that, for Habad, it is this paradox that undergirds the mystical duty of purifying the "materiality of the world and its density [*ḥomriyyut ha-olam we-gassuto*] . . . so that it will not be in the aspect of something and a separate thing in and of itself [*beḥinat yesh we-davar nifrad bifnei aṣmo*], but rather everything will be comprised in the aspect of nothing [*ha-kol yukhlal bi-veḥinat ayin*], for the purpose of the creation of the worlds from nothing to something [*takhlit beriʾat ha-olamot me-ayin le-yesh*] is to transform the aspect of something into the aspect of nothing [*le'ahafkha mi-beḥinat yesh li-beḥinat ayin*], and then 'the Lord shall be my God' (Gen 28:21), for 'God' [*elohim*] is the concealment and withdrawal so that there will be worlds created from nothing to something [*ha-heʿlem we-ha-ṣimṣum lihyot ha-olamot nivraʾim me-ayin le-yesh*], and the 'Lord' [*yhwh*] is the aspect of the interiority of the light of the Infinite, blessed be he [*beḥinat penimiyyut or ein sof barukh hu*], that sustains and brings into being."[85]

The secret pronounced in this text is expressive of the wisdom encapsulated in the daring postulate of the *coincidentia oppositorum*—a logic of the middle excluded by the logic of the excluded middle—as it relates to the primary ontological binary: *creatio ex nihilo* is cast in a mystical vein, as we can speak of the drawing out of something from nothing to the extent that we comprehend that everything amounts to and is integrated in this nothing, a matter that is not simply a cognitive insight but a way of seeing that alters reality, a specularity that divests the universe of its gross physicality, restoring the multiplicity of all being to the indistinct and indifferent one that comprehends everything in the nothingness of its (not) being every nothing. The paradox is expressed as well in terms of the traditional unification of the divine names YHWH and Elohim, which correspond respectively to the attributes of mercy and judgment. In Habad symbolism, YHWH denotes the essence that is above nature (*lemaʿlah min ha-ṭeva*) and Elohim its appearance in nature (*ṭeva*).[86] Shneur Zalman already expressed the matter in *Shaʿar ha-Yiḥud we-ha-Emunah*, the second part of *Tanya*, as an exegesis of the verse "For the Lord God is sun and shield" (Ps 84:12): just as the sun has a shield that makes it possible for created beings to endure its light, so the name Elohim "protects" the name YHWH, that is, the name Elohim, the veil of nature, makes apparent the essential name YHWH, which signifies that the essence brings everything into being from nothing (*mehawweh et ha-kol me-ayin le-yesh*).[87] "Thus the name Elohim is the name of the attribute of strength and contraction, and therefore it is also numerically *ha-ṭeva*[88] because it conceals the light above that generates and sustains the world, and it appears as if the world stands and is governed in the way of nature. The name Elohim is a shield and sheath for the name YHWH, to conceal the light and vitality that emanates from the name YHWH, so that it will bring forth from nothing to something, and it will not be revealed to created beings, which result in their being annihilated in existence."[89] Commenting on this seminal text, the seventh Rebbe wrote, "the coming-into-being of the world is from the name YHWH . . . but if the coming-into-being of the world were only from the name YHWH, the world would be annihilated in existence. Therefore, the actual coming-into-being was by means of the name Elohim."[90] The harnessing of the names, therefore, alludes to the "matter of the garbing" (*inyan ha-hitlabbeshut*), the paradox that the concealed light of the Infinite is revealed in the garment that is the world through which it is concealed, for had it not been concealed, the beings of the world would be "utterly eradicated" (*beṭelim be-takhlit*) like the ray of sunlight that is completely obliterated by the radiance of the sun.[91] The matter of the enclothing can also be cast in the image of the light being constrained in the vessels. "The explanation for the unification of the lights and the vessels is from the perspective of their root in the names YHWH and Elohim, for YHWH is the source of the lights and the name Elohim is the source of the vessels, as it is written "For the Lord God is sun and shield" (Ps 84:12), for the shield has two functions—first, it conceals the light of the sun, and second, through concealing the essence of the light, it reveals the light below, and thus it is with respect to the names YHWH and Elohim, for the name Elohim conceals the light of YHWH and reveals it in the vessels."[92] The conjunction of YHWH and Elohim bespeaks the mystery of incarnation (*hitgashshemut*), the pairing of ostensible antonyms (*hafakhim*), which is sometimes referred to as the "inscrutable power to act" (*koaḥ mafli laʿasot*),[93] as the spiritual beyond space and time is combined with the corporeal that is bound by space and time, and, as a consequence, the "aspect of the light that is above the aspect of being garbed in the vessels [*beḥinat ha-or she-lemaʿlah mi-beḥinat hitlabbeshut be-kelim*] will enter the vessels, and, moreover, it will extend to corporeality [*gashmiyyut*], and then the corporeality will be in a different manner."[94] Again, we note the confluence of the ontological and phenomenological—to be is to appear, to be seen, though what is seen is the unseen, the limitless light delimited in the constriction of the vessels, the concealment (*heʿlem*) that makes possible the manifestation (*gilluy*) of transcendence, that which encompasses all worlds (*sovev kol almin*) and which shines without boundary (*beli gevul*), through its occlusion in the aspect of immanence, that which fills all worlds (*memalle kol almin*) and which shines through the measure of contraction (*ṣimṣum*).[95] The one who apprehends the collusion of these opposites in the identity of their opposition will discern the immateriality of the material in and through the materiality of the immaterial, an acosmic naturalism that is conceptually quite far from the naturalist cosmology accepted by Maimonides.[96]

In spite of this obvious difference, Shneur Zalman adopts a fundamental tenet of the Maimonidean approach, maintaining—against his critics—that one could not worship God wholeheartedly unless one first attained knowledge of divinity, an idea linked exegetically to the advice David offered to Solomon: "[K]now the God of your father, and serve him with perfect heart and eager soul" (1 Chron 28:9). On the one hand, love of God is "beyond the limit of comprehension and thought cannot grasp it at all," but, on the other hand, the only way to achieve this level is for one "to accustom one's intellect and one's understanding to comprehend the supernal intelligibles that are abstracted from corporeality. . . . By faith alone one's soul is not actualized [*we-al yedei ha-emunah levadah lo yitpaʿel be-nafsho*] . . . for there is no entry into the interiority of the heart, so that the heart will be aroused, except by knowledge, as it says 'know the God of your father, and serve him with perfect heart.'"[97]

Apart from the obvious matter of influence, it is plausible to say that Habad has been informed by a distinctive way of reading Maimonides. Rather than viewing him as an advocate of a rationalism that stands in opposition to mystical devotion, Habad masters look upon the "great eagle" of medieval Jewish society as articulating a "rational religion" that is at the same time a "philosophic mysticism,"[98] terms that well apply to their own kabbalistically inspired ruminations. Consider, for example,

Shneur Zalman's depiction of the "soul that comprehends and contemplates constantly and apprehends the light of the Infinite, blessed be he, and it has no other comprehension."[99] This wisdom is further characterized as the "supernal knowledge" (*daʿat elyon*) in relation to the "lower knowledge" (*daʿat taḥton*), which is delineated further as the human intellect that is aligned with the animal soul and which comprehends the corporeality of the world. The ultimate felicity consists of joining these two forms of knowledge, the knowledge of a unity beyond differentiation and the knowledge of a unity predicated on the pairing of what has been torn asunder, a conjunction that is presented in the explicitly heteroerotic terms of the Song of Songs. Leaving aside the importance of the erotic symbolism, the conjoining of the two kinds of knowledge indicates that contemplation of the Infinite that is above nature is contrasted with, but also set in homology to, the apprehension of nature. Here, it seems to me, we come upon a familiar esoteric trope, the only way through the veil is the veil.

The point is epitomized in a passage in *Derekh Miṣwotekha*,[100] a treatise penned by Menachem Mendel, the third Rebbe, and the namesake of the seventh. Philosophy or "Greek wisdom" (*ḥokhmah yewanit*) and kabbalah or "divine wisdom" (*ḥokhmah ha-elohit*) are contrasted on the grounds that the former is a mode of comprehension (*hassagah*) that always has as its object a discrete, comprehensible form (*ṣiyyur ha-mussag*), whereas the latter is an "intellectual vision" (*reʾiyyat ha-sekhel*) in which there is a "disclosure of the Infinite" (*gilluy ein sof*), and hence it is symbolized by the letter *yod*, the subtle point (*nequddah daqqah*) that comprises in its infinitesimality the totality of all that was, is, and shall be—a compresence of the three tenses of time in the timeless time, which is the mystical connotation of the Tetragrammaton, the one true being that is both above and within the order of concatenation[101]—an excess of totality that exceeds even the totality of excess. The wisdom of the divine tradition (*ḥokhmat ha-qabbalah ha-elohit*), which is the prophetic legacy of the Jewish people, is an intellectual vision, a seeing of intellect (*reʾiyyat ha-sekhel*), but one that is nonetheless characterized as belief (*emunah*), a faith that surpasses, even if it does not contradict, discursive reason. We are told, therefore, that the true tradition (*ha-qabbalah ha-amittit*) is "to believe in the Lord and in his commandments, for he fully transcends the aspect of wisdom and comprehension, and 'thought cannot grasp him at all,' even the supernal wisdom. When the Lord wishes it for the community or for an individual, he makes known through prophecy, which is above the intellect, the disclosure of his divinity, blessed be he, and the goal of the wisdom is the belief in the interiority of the Torah and in its secrets, and this was the miracle of Hanukah with divine wisdom prevailing over Greek wisdom, which is philosophy."[102] As the conclusion of the passage makes clear, the inner intent of the festival of Hanukah is the overpowering of kabbalah over philosophy, divine wisdom over Greek wisdom, faith over reason. The final purpose of the traditional wisdom is to believe in the interiority of the Torah and its secrets, a belief that imparts gnosis about the divinity, but a gnosis that transcends knowledge, an apophatic ideal that is expressed in language drawn from a discourse on the nature of God placed in the mouth of Elijah in the introduction to *Tiqqunei Zohar*, *leit maḥashavah tefisa beih kelal*, "thought cannot grasp him at all."[103] The zenith of the contemplative ascent is to discern the inherent inability of the mind to fathom the divine, and yet this mystical state of learned ignorance, to know that one cannot know, is described as the "aspect of the illumination of wisdom" (*beḥinat heʾarat ha-ḥokhmah*), which is described further as the "gaze of the intellect that is above comprehension" (*seqirat ha-sekhel she-lemaʿlah min ha-hassagah*)[104]—above comprehension, but a gaze of intellect nonetheless.

Numerous other texts could be cited in support of this claim, but suffice it here to mention the words of the seventh Rebbe in a letter from 21 Shevaṭ 5716 (3 February 1956) that both "simple faith" (*emunah peshuṭah*) and "inquiry and knowledge" (*ḥaqirah wa-daʿat*) are necessary on the path of devotion. He adds that it is not only that "there is no contradiction [*setirah*] between the two, but, on the contrary, the one completes the other."[105] The ultimate rationale for pious worship is faith, but, as Schneerson is quick to point out, quoting Maimonides from the beginning of the laws concerning the fundamental principles of the Torah, which he placed at the commencement of his code of Jewish law, the *Mishneh Torah*, the "foundation of foundations and the pillar of wisdoms" (*yesod ha-yesodot we-amud ha-ḥokhmot*) is to acquire knowledge of God, a point substantiated not only by the aforementioned text of Maimonides but by reference to a corresponding passage from the zoharic stratum known as *Piqqudin*,[106] so-called because it deals with the kabbalistic interpretations of the commandments. In the tradition of medieval Jewish philosophers, epitomized by Maimonides, Habad masters affirm that it is a religious obligation to strive for this knowledge[107] even as they concede that this knowledge is above intellect and understanding.[108] To apprehend the essence that is beyond reason, therefore, one must rely on faith. From neither the Maimonidean nor the Habad perspectives, however, is this blind faith, or faith that is opposed to reason; it is, rather, a suprarational faith, a faith that reaches the "intellect hidden from every idea" (*ha-sekhel ha-neʿlam mi-kol raʿyon*),[109] the "intellect-that-is-beyond-intellect" (*sekhel mi-lemaʿlah min ha-sekhel*), in the felicitous locution of Dov Baer,[110] or in the language of the Tzemach Tzedek, the "supernal knowledge" that "is garbed in the souls of Israel in a discernment without any comprehensible knowledge" (*mitlabbesh beḥinah zo be-nishmat yisraʾel be-hakkarah beli shum daʿat ha-mussag*),[111] the disclosure of which promotes the awareness that "above the substance and below it everything is verily considered as if it were not [*kolla ke-lo ḥashiv mammash*]."[112] Accordingly, there is no conflict between the unremitting demand to know and the inescapable inability to know. In pursuing knowledge about God, the supernal knowledge that is above wisdom and understanding, one comes to know that one does not know. The degree to which the orientation of Maimonides is synchronized with Habad on this issue is exemplified in another passage from Dov Baer wherein the philosophic characterization of divine knowledge as the indivisible unity of knower, knowing, and known[113] is presented as an exact parallel to the mystical insight that there is nothing outside of God (*ein ḥuṣ mimmenu*). To say that there is nothing outside of God means not only that God comprehends all that is, but that there is no being independent of God, a truth that can be discerned only from its opposite, that is, from the fact that the being of God is veiled in the guise of that which seems independent, a mystery that the mind cannot comprehend and the mouth cannot articulate.[114]

TORAH AS PRIMORDIAL PARABLE: DEFERRAL AND THE RETRACE OF LITERAL METAPHORICITY

A shared thread that allows for the blending of the Maimonidean and kabbalistic perspectives is the *via negativa*. Thus, we read in a passage from Shneur Zalman's *Liqquṭei Amarim*, the first section of *Tanya*: "As it says in the *Zohar*,[115] 'the Torah and the holy One, blessed be he, are entirely one,' that is, the Torah is the wisdom and will of the holy One, blessed be he, and the holy One, blessed be he, in his glory and in his essence, is one, for he is the knower, the knowledge, [and the known], as we wrote above in the name of the Rambam.[116] But the holy One, blessed be he, is called Infinite, 'his greatness cannot be fathomed' (Ps 145:3) and 'thought cannot grasp him at all.' "[117] The final assertion, which we have already discussed, is paired with the identification of the Torah and God, a belief that has been affirmed axiomatically by kabbalists since the thirteenth century, though there is solid textual evidence that it is indeed much older. In kabbalistic lore, as I briefly noted above, the equation of God and the Torah is corollary to two further identifications, God and the name, on one hand, and the name and the Torah, on the other. What is most crucial for our purposes is Shneur Zalman's use of this equation to distinguish the aspect of the divine essence that is garbed in the Torah and the aspect that is not garbed; the apophatic utterance, *leit maḥashavah tefisa beih kelal*, applies only to the latter, for when the essence is garbed in the Torah, it can be comprehended. Indeed, this act of enclothing (*hitlabbeshut*), epitomized in the zoharic sentiment that God and the Torah are one, is the kabbalistic way of articulating the mystery of incarnation, the paradox of the delimitation of the limitless, the nomian basis for the mystical ideal of *devequt*, of being conjoined to the divine through implementation of the commandments.[118]

Shneur Zalman alludes to this secret in a passage from *Shaʿar ha-Yiḥud we-ha-Emunah*, "the source of vitality [*meqor ha-ḥiyyut*] is the spirit of the mouth of the holy One, blessed be he, that is garbed in the ten sayings that are in the Torah."[119] Based on much older sources, the ten sayings of the Torah are correlated with the ten *sefirot*, which collectively make up the name (YHWH) by which the nameless (*ein sof*) is declaimed. The statement that the spirit (*ruaḥ*) is garbed in the ten sayings of the Torah is another way of expressing the idea that the light is configured in the ten emanations of the godhead. Elsewhere in the writings that preserve the Alter Rebbe's teaching, Torah is portrayed as the vessel through which the "light of the intellect" (*or ha-sekhel*) is revealed, and in which the "letters of thought" (*otiyyot ha-maḥashavah*), that is, the letters prior to any oral or written gesticulation, assume form through the "permutation of the letters of speech" (*ṣerufei otiyyot ha-dibbur*).[120] Commenting on the enigmatic opening to the *Zohar*, "in the beginning of the will of the

King, he engraved the engravings in the supernal luster,"[121] Shneur Zalman remarked that "the source of the letters is in *Keter* and the letters themselves in *Ḥokhmah*, that is, the disclosure of everything . . . and thus it is in all the worlds and in all the gradations up to the highest of gradations, for each and every thing is called by the aspect of letters, and there is an aspect of the letters of the Infinite [*beḥinat otiyyot ein sof*] as well, and they are also called the disclosure of the Infinite [*ha-gilluy shel ha-ein sof*]. Therefore, it is necessary for the letters to elevate the intellect and by means of them the intellect will change."[122]

All of reality can be viewed from this hyperlinguistic perspective: the substance of everything, from the highest to the lowest manifestation of the one essence, consists of letters, which articulate and thereby incarnate the word or wisdom of the divine, cosmically cast as the light of the intellectual overflow. The letters, consequently, are grist for the mill of contemplation, that is, the elevation and transformation of intellect comes by way of meditating on the letters as they reveal the light. This is the intent of the reference to "letters of the Infinite." But what does it mean to speak in this way? How could letters demarcate, or signify in any conceivable or imaginable way, the Infinite, the transcendent signifier that (in)essentially eludes signification other than perhaps as the sign that eludes signification?[123] And yet, the notion of letters of the Infinite brings the mind to the brink of just such a paradox. Influenced by the version of Lurianic kabbalah advanced by Israel Sarug and mediated through the *Emeq ha-Melekh* of Naftali Bachrach, Shneur Zalman remarked that the letters are the trace (*reshimu*) that is left behind in the space (*ḥalal*) after the removal (*histallequt*) of the light. Insofar as the trace marks both the absence and presence of that of which it is a trace—even if that is nothing other than a trace—the letters are compared to a garment that simultaneously reveals and conceals the absolute indeterminacy of the essential hiddenness.[124] It is in this sense that we can entertain the notion of the letters of the Infinite—the trace of the light that is retraced in the light of the trace. According to the striking formulation of Dov Baer, the mystery consists of knowing the "aspect of the letters of the primordial Torah that is actually in the essence of the Infinite."[125] Elaborating on this theme in a second context, he identifies the "supernal brain that is before the curtain that divides" (*moaḥ ilaʾah she-lifnei ha-parsa ha-mafsiq*)[126] as the "aspect of the holy Torah that at first was actually comprised in his essence," the "light that illumines the essence of the Infinite," the "light of the essence of Torah," which is garbed in a garment, the "primordial parable" (*meshal ha-qadmoni*).[127] Before the curtain was formed—a mythopoeic way to account philosophically for the division within the indivisible that results from the primary withdrawal (*ṣimṣum ha-ri'shon*)—the light of the Torah was incorporated in the essence of the Infinite, the indivisible will (*raṣon pashuṭ*) that is the source of life (*meqor ḥayyim*) of all that comes to be in the chain of becoming.[128] Habad cosmology builds on the platform of the Lurianic interpretation of the beginning as the contraction of the infinite origin that results in a space (*ḥalal*) emerging within itself devoid of itself, the vacuum that comes to be as what has already been within the plenum, as the plenum cannot not be but all-comprehensive and hence comprehending, in the nothingness of its being, even the being of its nothingness. In the beginning, the light of the essence is garbed in a garment that is the primordial parable of the Torah, the mantle of the name through which the nameless is revealed to the degree that it is concealed.[129] I note, in passing, that a likely source for Dov Baer's image is the comment of the eleventh-century exegete, Solomon ben Isaac, better known as Rashi, to the expression *meshal ha-qadmoni* in 1 Samuel 24:14: "The primordial parable of the world is the Torah, which is the parable of the holy One, blessed be he." But more to the point than Rashi's interpretation of the scriptural expression is its adaptation by Shneur Zalman:

> The Torah is also garbed in letters, for the source of the letters of the Torah is above the aspect of the Torah. The Torah comes forth from *Ḥokhmah*, and the source of the letters is above in the aspect of *Keter* . . . and the Torah is called the "primordial parable" [*meshal ha-qadmoni*] . . . for the matter of the parable is to analogize what is rendered parabolic in a manner that it will be understood from the parable [*inyan ha-mashal hu lehamshil et ha-nimshal be-ofen she-yuvan mi-tokh ha-mashal*]. The parable is thus another matter that is not the substance of what is rendered parabolic [*ha-mashal hu inyan aḥer she-eino mahut ha-nimshal*], but what is rendered parabolic is understood from it since it is comparable to it in some respect. And this is what is written "and in the hands of the prophets I will be imaged" [*u-ve-yad ha-nevi'im adammeh*] (Hos 12:11). And the sages,

blessed be their memory, compared the prophetic vision [*mar'eh ha-nevu'ah*] to a speculum [*aspaqlaryah*], for just as when one sees in a speculum it appears actually so in the likeness of the form, its semblance and its image, but it is not actually the body of the form itself. . . . Thus every comprehension of the prophets of the divinity, blessed be he, is naught but the aspect of likeness and image, and just like a parable whence is understood what is rendered parabolic. With respect to divinity, however, it says "no man shall see me and live" (Exod 33:20).[130]

The Torah displays the twofold structure of the parable, an outer shell revealing an inner core, albeit by concealing it. Rooted in older kabbalistic doctrine, Shneur Zalman inscribes the hermeneutical paradigm in an incarnational theology. The image of the "primordial parable" (*meshal ha-qadmoni*) conveys the idea that the Torah is the parable of the "primordial one of the world" (*qadmono shel olam*), identified further as the "light of the Infinite, blessed be he, in itself" (*or ein sof barukh hu aṣmo*), the one who is primordial to the world, the single and distinctive one (*eḥad u-meyuḥad*) signified by the essential name YHWH, the one "that was, is, and will be concurrently, above place and above time" (*hu hayah howeh we-yihyeh ke-eḥad lemaʿlah min ha-maqom u-lemaʿlah min ha-zeman*).[131] In order for there to be something other than the nothing-that-is-everything, the illumination that issues from the Infinite breaks into the binary of an "encompassing light" (*or maqqif*), which "surrounds all worlds" (*sovev kol almin*), and an "inner light" (*or penimi*), which "fills all worlds" (*memalle kol almin*).[132] The equation of God and Torah, the cornerstone of what I have elsewhere called "textual embodiment" and "poetic incarnation,"[133] is depicted in these parabolic terms to indicate that the Torah both remains other to the light it incarnates and serves as the medium through which that light is refracted in the limbs of the name, the letters of the Hebrew alphabet, which materialize differently on each of the worlds or planes of reality. As the parable of the primordial one, who cannot be represented, the Torah is the image of the imageless and thus it preserves the sense of difference it attempts to bridge. It is, we might say, the pretext, the showing that conceals in the very manner that it reveals. The mythopoeic axiom that God and Torah are identical—so central to the kabbalistic imaginary—presupposes that disparate matters are juxtaposed in the (dis)semblance of the name incarnate. In that respect, the Torah as primordial parable points to the inherent metaphoricity of language, the convergence of the literal and figurative.[134] The insight was voiced by the seventh Rebbe: "Therefore the Torah is called 'parable' because it is like this intellect that is concealed from its own perspective and it can be revealed only in a concealed manner."[135] The Torah is the primordial parable as it reveals the innately concealed essence of the primordial one by concealing it, for had it not been concealed, it could not have been revealed as the essence that is concealed. Schneerson affirms the duplicity of esotericism that has informed the kabbalistic hermeneutic from early on, the belief that the exposure of the secret, if it is the secret that is exposed, must itself be secretive, and hence the reproduction of secrecy is guaranteed even when, indeed especially when, the seal of mystery is undone. It seems to me that this crucial hermeneutical point has not been appreciated by the scholars who have written on the seventh Rebbe's commitment to the disclosure of secrets as part of his messianic campaign to reveal the new Torah or to publicize the inner meaning of the Torah.[136] While I do not deny that Schneerson understood the messianic mission of Hasidism in general, and of Habad in particular, to render the esoteric lore more exoteric, I maintain that there still must be something of the secret that persists in the divulsion of the secret, since the very nature of secrecy entails this reverberation. Simply put, there can be no lifting of a final veil, no defrocking of truth to an ultimate nudity, for in the eventuality of such an absolute exposure, there would truly be nothing to expose. Put even more simply, the most secretive of secrets is the open secret, the secret that is so fully disclosed that it appears not to be a secret. This, I presume, is the intent of the comment that the parabolic nature of the Torah requires that its concealed meaning can only be revealed in a concealed manner.

To cite Shneur Zalman again: "The first source and root of the Torah is the aspect of Wisdom . . . and it is called 'primordial parable,' for even though the light of the Infinite, blessed be he, is exalted and elevated manifold levels without end or limit above Wisdom . . . nevertheless within it dwells and is garbed the light of the Infinite, blessed be, for he and his wisdom are verily one. Therefore it is called the 'primordial parable,' just as a parable is a garment in relation to what is rendered parabolic and by means of which we can grasp it and comprehend it, so is Wisdom the garment for the Infinite, blessed be he . . . and through it and by means of it we can reach the Infinite, blessed be he."[137] It is this paradox that Shneur Zalman had in mind when he asserted that even the Torah of the pleroma of divine emanations (*torah de-aṣilut*),[138] about which it is said that "he and his lives are one" (*de-ihu we-ḥayohi ḥad*),[139] is still to be conceived as a parable in relation to the "supernal emanator" (*ha-ma'aṣil ha-elyon*).[140] Moreover, insofar as the Torah is rooted and unified in this light, the incomposite will of the (in)essential, which constitutes the (ir)reality of all that exists, it is reasonable to elicit the cosmological implications of this symbolism.[141] Externally, it may appear as if there is a reality outside of God, but, internally, this reality turns out to be merely apparent. The realm of differentiated being—the order of concatenation—is nothing but the one light of wisdom embodied in the twenty-two letters of Torah, which are branches of the tree whose trunk is the Tetragrammaton. All that comes to be in the chain of becoming is an instantiation of this parabolic dissimulation, the image of the hidden essence that appears to be apparent in the image of the apparent world that appears to be the hidden essence. Corporeality is to be measured from this textological perspective.

LIGHT BEYOND LIGHT: ACOSMIC NATURALISM AND APOPHATIC PANENTHEISM

It has been well noted that the doctrines and practices of Habad are deeply indebted to previous kabbalistic teaching, especially to the complex theosophic system cultivated by Isaac Luria and his disciples in the sixteenth and seventeenth centuries.[142] Of the many Lurianic ideas and expressions that have informed the Habad worldview, one whose influence surely cannot be underestimated is the topos of the shattering of the vessels (also referred to as the death of the primordial kings of Edom) in *olam ha-tohu*, the world of chaos that preceded the dissemination of the light in structured form, and the consequent dispersion of these shards to which are attached sparks of light. Just as Luria and the transmitters of his teaching had emphasized, exponents of Lubavitch lore—in line with other Hasidic masters who trace their way of thinking to the Besht—have repeatedly stressed that all of reality is infused with divine light, and that the telos of human existence, which is fulfilled most perfectly in the ritual practices of the Jewish people, is to liberate these holy sparks from their encasement in the demonic shells of the material word (a process that is referred to technically as *berur*) and to restore them to the light of the Infinite whence they emerged, the One in which opposites can no longer be differentiated but as opposites that are differentiated in virtue of being (in)different.[143]

From Shneur Zalman to Menachem Mendel, Habad masters (inspired by the orientation of the Maggid of Mezeritch) have interpreted the kabbalistic cosmology, which provides the ideational underpinning of the ethical pietism and messianic activism,[144] in a manner that hovers conceptually between pantheism and panentheism, that is, the belief that God is synonymous with nature and the belief that God is the One that is inseparable from and yet not quite identical with nature, that all being is in God but God is not identical with all being.[145] It would appear, however, that neither "panentheism" nor "pantheism" as such is adequate to render the Habad perspective, as both the transcendental and immanental aspects, *sovev kol almin* and *memalle kol almin*, are characterizations that are notionally and semantically meaningful only in relation to the world, but the light of the Infinite in and of itself, a transcendence that surpasses the distinction between transcendence and immanence, an infinity beyond totality, is "not in the category of worlds at all" (*eino be-geder almin kelal*), and therefore it is beyond the ontic splitting into the encompassing light and the inner light.[146] How, then, do we understand the passages that seem to affirm that the world and God are indistinguishable? Would these not clash with the insistence that divinity in its essence is above nature? We might propose that there is no discord, as those passages are not speaking about the unique one (*yaḥid, eyntsik*) unified in its essence (*meyuḥad be-eṣem*) but of the one (*eḥad, eyner*) that is characterized by a "division of particulars" (*hitḥallequt peraṭim*) manifest in the multiplicity of the four worlds of the kabbalistic cosmology, the world of emanation (*aṣilut*), which is the world of unity (*alma de-yiḥuda, olam ha-yiḥud*), and the worlds of creation (*beri'ah*), formation (*yeṣirah*) and doing (*asiyyah*), which together constitute the world of differentiation (*alma di-feruda, olam ha-perud*).[147] From another perspective, however, this response is not satisfactory, for even if we grant that the divine essence is the not circumscribable within the dual frame of the light-that-is-transcendent and the light-that-is-immanent, we would insist that it cannot be completely removed therefrom. Indeed, the vocation of the

Jew in giving witness to the oneness of the Creator (*aḥdut ha-bore*) underscores the point. The key expression in the declaration of faith "Hear, O Israel, the Lord our God, the Lord is one" (Deut 6:4) is "the Lord our God," *yhwh elohenu*, the two names that respectively denote that which is above nature (*lemaʿlah me-ha-ṭeva*) and nature (*ha-ṭeva*).[148] In proclaiming that "the Lord is our God," the worshiper gives verbal assent to and thereby participates in the conundrum of incarnation, the commingling of the metaphysical and physical, providing habitation for the light that exceeds the boundaries of time and place in the world that is bounded by time and place.[149]

> The name YHWH instructs that he is above time, for he was, is, and will be in one moment . . . and he is also above place for he brings about constantly the entire aspect of place from above to below and in the four sides. Even though he, blessed be he, is above place and time, he is nonetheless found below in place and time, that is, he is unified in the attribute of his kingship [*mityaḥed be-middat malkhuto*] whence place and time emanate and come to be, and this is the lower unity [*yiḥuda tataʾah*] . . . that is, his essence and substance, blessed be he, which is called the Infinite, blessed be he, verily fills the whole earth in time and place. . . . [E]verything is filled uniformly from the light of the Infinite, blessed be he . . . for everything is in the aspect of place that is ontically nullified in the light of the Infinite, blessed be he [*ha-baṭel be-meṣiʾut be-or ein sof barukh hu*], which is garbed in it by means of the attribute of his kingship that is unified in him, blessed be he. The attribute of his kingship is the attribute of constriction and concealment [*middat ha-ṣimṣum we-ha-hester*], which conceals the light of the Infinite, blessed be he, so that time and place will not be obliterated entirely from their existence.[150]

Material space can contain the immaterial beyond spatial delimitation, a possibility actualized in the Temple, which is imagined archetypically as the place above place.[151] By proclaiming the oneness of God, therefore, worshipers theurgically "draw down the disclosure of the light of the Infinite that is above the aspect of place so that it will be revealed in the aspect of place and the place will be annihilated, and this is 'the Lord is one.' "[152] In his inimitable style, the seventh Rebbe captures the paradox pithily, "[T]he disclosure that is above place, which shines in place, was from the perspective of place itself."[153] Elaborating in another context on what I called above (following Heidegger) the belonging together of the foreign, Schneerson put it as follows:

> The joining of nature with what is above nature is by means of the disclosure of the essence that is beyond both of them. . . . And this is also the reason why there must be a joining of the two matters of nature and what is above nature, for the root of each one of these matters is in the light of the Infinite, and by means of the joining of these two matters is the drawing down of the essence, that is, through this there is the possibility (from the perspective of the world as well) that by means of worship there will be in the world the drawing down of the disclosure of the essence, and through this the intention of the creation of the world (nature) will be perfected, for the blessed holy One desires that he will have a habitation in the beings below.[154]

The possibility of experiencing God's presence in nature (Elohim), therefore, is dependent on dialectically discerning the dimension of divinity that is absent from nature (YHWH). To appropriate the fecund neologism of Catherine Keller,[155] we can say that Habad cosmology espouses an "apophatic panentheism": the One is affirmed in everything to the extent that everything is negated in relation to the One, but the One is negated in relation to everything to the extent that everything is affirmed in the One. "Negated" is a careful rendering of *biṭṭul*, the technical terminology of Habad's contemplative praxis, which we can translate into the contemporary jargon of "denegation." By "denegate" I mean to eradicate, to uproot by clutching the root, or to efface, as effacing is always also a facing of what cannot be faced. To speak, then, of the One denegated in relation to everything and everything denegated in relation to the One, we must think of the space-between in which everything is nothing in virtue of being everything, and nothing is everything in virtue of being nothing. God's (non)being in all things is unutterable, an apophatic dictum, as it rests on presuming the capacity for the other in that which has no other, a capacity that kabbalists assign to the withholding that expands, the mystery of *ṣimṣum*, the concealment within the actual nothing that bears the potential to become every other nothing in actuality, the supernal Wisdom, *ḥokhmah*, which is decoded as *koaḥ mah*, the potential of what-is-to-become.[156] I note further that the word *mah*, which signifies the indeterminacy of this potentiality, is numerically equivalent to forty-five (*mem he* = 40 + 5), which is the same numerology as the Tetragrammaton when spelled out in full (*yw"d h"a wa"w h"a* = 10 + 6 + 4 + 5 + 1 + 6 + 1 + 6 + 5 + 1) and the word *adam* (*alef dalet mem* = 1 + 4 + 40). The linguistic and mathematical convergences are meant to communicate that the light of consciousness, the divine life force (*ḥiyyut elohi*) manifestly hidden in all that appears to be in the chain of becoming,[157] assumes the imaginal form of the human, the embodiment of the name YHWH, which is the Torah. In the space-between, the really apparent and the apparently real, actuality and potentiality, something and nothing, are identified in the opposition of their identity. We might say, therefore, that God is in the world exclusively to the extent that the world is in God inclusively, but the world is in God inclusively as what is other in relation to God, just as God is in the world exclusively as what is other in relation to the world. Apophatic panentheism, accordingly, presumes a reciprocal transcendence whereby God and world are preserved in the difference of their belonging-together, indeed they belong together precisely in virtue of the difference.[158]

Rehearsing an exegesis of *el olam*, the title by which Abraham addressed God (Gen 21:33), which can be traced to Shneur Zalman,[159] Shmuel Schneersohn (1834–1882), the fourth Rebbe in the Lubavitch dynasty, more commonly referred to as the Rebbe MaHaRaSh, enunciates the fundamental cosmological insight of Habad: "The souls of Israel join the world to the divinity, so that the world will not be a separate being and entity unto itself, but rather the world will be nullified vis-à-vis the divinity, as it is written 'and Abraham invoked there the name of the Lord, the everlasting God' [*el olam*], and not the 'God of the world' [*el ha-olam*], for the world and the divine are all one [*she-olam we'lohim ha-kol eḥad*], since the world is actually nullified vis-à-vis the divinity [*lefi she-olam baṭel mammash la-elohut*]."[160] On the one hand, God and world are proclaimed to be identical, but, on the other hand, they are presumed to be different, otherwise there would be no need for the Jew to conjoin them. There is no contradiction, however, as the identity of the difference depends on the difference of identity. As Shmuel's son, Shalom Dovber, put it,

> [I]t says *el olam* and not *ha-olam*, that is, the world is not a separate entity but the divinity, just as the substance of the fruit is the light (or substance) of the power of the plant that is materialized, and analogously, the vessels are the very light whence the vessels are made, which is the trace [*roshem*][161] . . . but this is like the light that is materialized . . . for all the created entities are the light and splendor that emanate from the divine potency that overflows on them and brings them into being, for the divine illumination itself materializes and becomes the aspect of the existence of something, and this is *el olam*; the world is the divinity in actuality [*she-ha-olam hu elohut mammash*].[162]

Tellingly, Menachem Mendel, the seventh Rebbe, included a similar observation in his inaugural address from 10 Shevaṭ 5711 (17 January 1951): "It is not *el ha-olam*, that is, the divinity as an entity unto itself and the world as an entity unto itself, but rather the divinity rules over and governs the world, for the world and divinity are entirely one [*she-olam wa-elohut hu kolla ḥad*]."[163] Rather than using the construct *el ha-olam*, "God of the world," which would suggest that the divine and the cosmic are separate, the two terms are placed in apposition, *el olam*, which can be decoded as the God who is the world. In the void of the radical denegation, there is no opposition—not even the opposition of no opposition—and hence alterity persists in the interlude between the one and the other, the hiatus wherein one is perpetually becoming, and therefore never is, the other. Here we mark the temporal implications of the miracle of creation (*ḥiddush*) as an apophatic incarnation, the constant renewal (*hitḥaddeshut*) of something from nothing to produce the generation (*hithawwut*) of something that is nothing, the same other that returns always as what has never been but as always other to the same.[164]

The negativity that doubly binds God and world yields what we may also call "acosmic naturalism." The adjective "acosmic" denotes that there is no world that is not enfolded in the essence that is the light of the Infinite, whereas the noun "naturalism" indicates that there is no unfolding without the enfolded, no manifestation but in the occlusion that is the world, an idea buttressed by the wordplay *ha-olam* and *heʿlem*, "the world" and "concealment." The calling into question of the independent status of beings vis-à-vis the one true being, which is central to Habad cosmological thinking, has to be seen from within the spectrum of this seemingly contradictory elocution. For example, in the *Tanya*, we read that

> all of the created entities in relation to him are actually annihilated in existence [*beṭelim eṣlo bi-meṣiʾut mammash*] like the annihilation of the letters of speech and thought in their source and their root, the substance of the soul and its essence . . . a physical example of this is from the matter of the annihilation of the splendor and light of the sun in its source that is the body of the sphere of the sun that is in the sky . . . for there it is annihilated in existence in its source and it is as if it is not in existence at all. And thus verily by way of analogy is the annihilation of the existence of world and its fullness vis-à-vis its source, which is the light of the Infinite, blessed be he.[165]

Just as the letters, whether spoken or contemplated, are obliterated in the soul that is beyond language, and just as the rays that reach the earth are extinguished in the sun in heaven, so all things in the created universe are nullified in the light that is the essence of the Infinite. I will cite another illustration from Shneur Zalman. The exegetical subtext is the description of the Torah based on the account of Wisdom in Proverbs 8:30 as "toying" (*mesaḥeqet*) before God:

> The matter is that the aspect of playfulness [*seḥoq*] is the aspect of the eradication of something into nothing [*biṭṭul ha-yesh le-ayin*], as it is written "God played a joke on me" [*ṣeḥoq asah li elohim*] (Gen 21:6), that is, the name *elohim* conceals and hides the light of the Infinite, blessed be he, so that the world will appear as a substance and as a separate being [*lihyot nirʾeh ha-olam le-yesh we-davar nifrad*], and it will not be ontically annihilated [*she-lo yibaṭṭel bi-meṣiʾut*] like the splendor of the sun in the sun.[166]

The toying around metaphorically denotes the negation of opposites, the crossing of boundaries, the nullification of something into nothing (*biṭṭul ha-yesh le-ayin*), a reversal of the process of creation of something from nothing (*yesh me-ayin*). The mystical nuance of this traditional notion is alluded to in the reading of Sarah's comment upon giving birth to Isaac, *ṣeḥoq asah li elohim*, "God played a joke on me." The name *elohim*, which signifies the attribute of judgment, conceals the light of the Infinite so that there is the posing of the world as an independent reality. The cosmic prank, so to speak, is the garbing of YHWH, the light of the Infinite, in Elohim, the veil of nature.[167] The contemplative's ability to turn that around in the act of *biṭṭul*, to see through the veil, is a mode of participating in this divine play, referred to as well as *shaʿashuʿim*. By the act of self-sacrifice, the all-consuming love that one has for God, the individual causes the descent of the "supernal delight" (*taʿanug elyon*)—the power of the boundless will through which the divine essence wills what it wills without internal desire or external compulsion[168]—to be garbed in the Torah, an act that is also troped, on the basis of earlier kabbalistic sources,[169] as God's bemusing himself in his own essence (*shaʿashuʿa she-be-aṣmuto*). The pietistic gesture is communicated in the verse "I took delight in your Torah," *ani toratkha shiʿashaʿti* (Ps 119:70): one augments the linguistic and erotic sport of *shaʿashuʿa* by means of *ani*, the "I," which consists of the same letters as *ayin*, "nothing," that is, "the aspect of the abnegation of substance [*biṭṭul ha-yesh*] as one makes *ayin* from *ani*, and thus even in the study of Torah there is not the aspect of substance but the abnegation of substance."[170] The pretense of an independent reality is fully disclosed in the messianic era when all sense of alterity is dispelled, a point made rhetorically by the promise that even the demonic other will be subjugated (*itkafya siṭra aḥara*) and the dark will be transformed into light (*ithapkha ḥashokha li-nehora*).[171] The terms *itkafya* and *ithapkha* in the Habad lexicon signify two modes of unification, the former involves sublimation of one thing by its opposite and the latter the transmutation of one thing into its opposite.[172] In the end the darkness will be transformed into light, as in the beginning, indeed in the origin before the beginning,[173] the essence of the infinite, light and darkness cannot be distinguished.

Echoing this theme, the seventh Rebbe commented in the sermon on the essence of Hasidism, which was delivered on 19 Kislev 5726 (13 December 1965):

> Also with respect to the aspect of the Torah that is united with his blessed essence, it is said "toying before him" (Prov 8:30), the bemusement (and joy) that is above comes by way of the purification [*berur*] and rectification [*tiqqun*] of the darkness—the darkness transmuted into light [*ithapkha ḥashokha li-nehora*]. And this is "toying before him": precisely through the aspect of the darkness being transmuted into light—"toying"—which is in the Torah, its interiority is expressed as it is united with the interiority of the light of the Infinite, blessed be he—"before him."[174]

The full intent of the motif can be culled from the discourse of Schneerson delivered on 23 Tamuz 5713 (11 July 1963):

> As it says "God joked with me," for it is precisely on account of the fact that the matter of the nullification [*inyan ha-biṭṭul*] is realized with respect to the entities that come from the name Elohim, which are in the aspect of something [*yesh*], the nullification of something to nothing [*biṭṭul ha-yesh le-ayin*], that the matter of the joke [*ṣeḥoq*] and pleasure [*taʿanug*] comes to be above, and similarly it is written "and Leviathan that you created to toy with" (Ps 104:26), for Leviathan is from the language of joining [*ḥibbur*][175] . . . and the matter of joining applies specifically when there are two things separate from each other. This matter is particularly in the work related to the nullification of something [*ha-avodah de-viṭṭul ha-yesh*], for something and nothing are two things that are separate from one another, and even so the nullification of something to nothing is realized [*poʿalim biṭṭul ha-yesh le-ayin*], and by means of this especially the matter of the joke comes to be.[176]

The playfulness of the divine is expressed in the dissembling of a world that appears to be independent of God, which is the esoteric intent of the traditional dogma of *creatio ex nihilo* (*beriʾah yesh me-ayin*). We can participate in the appearance of the nonapparent by turning the apparent something into the nothing that it really is not. The essence of worship is to reach the state of *ithapkha*, of transforming something into nothing, but this cannot be achieved without having realized the *itkafya*, the subjugation of something by nothing. Schneerson articulates this idea as well in terms of the distinction between two kinds of knowledge, which we have already encountered. Whereas the supernal knowledge is considered above as something but below as nothing, the lower knowledge is considered below as something but above as nothing. The contrast between the two kinds of knowledge occasions a corresponding difference in two forms of denegation. The lower knowledge brings about nullification of something (*biṭṭul ha-yesh*), the supernal knowledge nullification of existence (*biṭṭul bi-meṣi'ut*).[177] The former is an illustration of *itkafya*, the subduing of one thing by its opposite, the latter, an example of *ithapkha*, a total obliteration of the one thing becoming its opposite. In this state of annihilation, it is no longer meaningful to speak of permanence or transience, something or nothing, existence or nonexistence, and hence there is no need for pairing one with the other. Beyond effacing the creation of something from nothing by transforming the something into nothing, the nothing itself is negated, the annihilation annihilated.

The more effective nomenclature to capture the cosmological viewpoint of Habad in all of its subtleties and ramifications is either apophatic panentheism or acosmic naturalism. These terms imply that the world is not thought to be an illusion vis-à-vis the hidden essence as much as it is conceived to be a veil through which the illusion can be apprehended and thereby unmasked for the illusion it appears to be, an unveiling in which the hidden essentiality is (un)veiled. Nature, accordingly, is not denied real existence as if it were the "veil of Maya,"[178] but rather it is the veil that veils and thereby reveals the veil. The one who acquires this gnosis apperceives that the world is suffused with divine reality, as there is no place that is devoid of God. It follows that enlightened consciousness, which is a prolepsis of redemption, consists not in thinking that spirituality can overcome materiality, that the infinite essence is a negation of the phenomenal, but in the realization that the distinction between the two collapses in the identity of their difference. As the seventh Rebbe put it, "[S]pirituality and materiality are on a par."[179] A simple and succinct utterance—*ruḥaniyyut we-gashmiyyut shawin*—three words that challenge the binary that has prevailed upon so many thinkers through history. To speak of the parity between spirit and matter, however, is not to posit an equivalence that reduces one term to the other. On the contrary, the Habad viewpoint seeks to avoid either idealist or materialist monism. The issue, rather, is the parabolic replication according to which the spiritual is specularized through the prism of the corporeal and the corporeal through the prism of the spiritual. Herein is the alchemical basis for the ontic potential of a God that is really apparent and of a world that is apparently real. Thus, Shneur Zalman remarked that the "supernal mystery" (*seter elyon*) that enclothes the light of the Infinite is called *Arikh Anpin*, literally, the "long face," to indicate that "it can extend below as well . . . for before him, blessed be he, spirituality and materiality are equal [*ki qameih yitbarakh shaweh u-mashweh ruḥaniyyut we-gashmiyyut*], and thus the disclosure will be below in the lower unity as it is in the upper unity."[180] With respect to the Infinite there is no distinction between spiritual and material, as the two are rendered, philosophically speaking, indifferent, *shaweh u-mashweh ruḥaniyyut we-gashmiyyut*.[181] The transcendence that is above-nature is always immanent in nature as what is beyond the natural, mathematically depicted as the number eight and semiotically as the letter *ḥeit*, a symbolic complex that gathers round itself a kaleidoscope of images and themes strewn about the landscape of Habad, based on much older kabbalistic lore. The crucial point that may be elicited from these dense and convoluted texts is that God and world are identified in their mutual difference, the one that is in but still other to the other, the "wholly other" that embraces in its wholeness the possibility of being other to, and therefore both more and less than, the whole. Habad masters have long ago understood that sameness must be construed as neither identical with nor different from difference. To contemplate that God and world are the same is to apprehend the parabolic truth par excellence, a truth that affirms the identity of what is identified as different. The double mirroring is such that world appears as the image of God and God as the image of world, an apparent truth, the truth of what appears to be true, a truth that is called in kabbalistic and hasidic vernacular variously as *levush*, *malbush*, or *hitlabbeshut*, the secret of the garment related to the incarnational understanding of Torah as the primordial parable, the mark of (dis)similitude where truth appears in the image of truth.

The discerning of this truth is not the consequence of the return of all things to the essence, a "theosophic cosmology" based on the mystical ideal of *apokastasis*,[182] but rather it comes about through the indifferent essence being drawn into and hence garbed within the world of differentiation. The point is made incisively in the seventh Rebbe's description of the messianic realization of the materialization of the divine light in the physical domain: "[T]he truth of the matter of a habitation for him, blessed be he, in the lower beings is that there shall also be a disclosure that is above the emanation."[183] Could the paradox of the acosmic naturalism cut deeper against itself? To be messianically attuned is to perceive that the revelation of God in the cosmos is at the same time the highest disclosure of divinity, indeed the disclosure of the infinite light that is above the emanation of the *sefirot*, but such a disclosure inevitably must be an occlusion, as what is disclosed is completely divested of form and figure. The desire of the divine to have a habitation below is expressive of the essence, which is beyond all representation.[184] The façade of worldhood—or what is called nature, which includes the physical and the metaphysical—provides the ontic condition that makes possible the epistemic awareness that all that exists is naught but a veil by which the light beyond nature is manifest by being concealed. Translating this conception into a semiotic register, the transcendence that transcends transcendence, the "aspect of exaltation, the essence of the Infinite" (*beḥinat ha-romemut aṣmut de-ein sof*),[185] is symbolized by *alef*,[186] the silent letter that is the fount of all the other letters, which, according to an archaic kabbalistic belief, are comprised within and emerge like branches from the root-word, the name YWHW, the mystical essence of Torah, gesticulated concomitantly as phonic image and graphic sound—a crucial point that problematizes the privileging of either the visual or auditory in kabbalistic symbolism.[187] Reality—the essence that is hidden as the hidden essence—is this *alef*, the evolution of all that is, was, and shall be impressed in this letter, the mute resonance of the vacuum that is the plenum, the murmuring vibration of the nothing that is everything. Orthographically, as kabbalists were wont to point out already in the second half of the thirteenth century, the *alef* can be decomposed into three markings, a *yod* above, a *yod* below, and the *waw* in the middle, the numerical value of which is twenty-six (10 + 10 + 6), which is also the sum of the letters YHWH (10 + 5 + 6 + 5), the name that signifies the aforementioned compresence of the three modes of time. The *alef*, therefore, is the enigma (*pele*) that is the Tetragram, the stuff that philosophers call being.

In some measure, the terms "apophatic panentheism" and "acosmic naturalism" map onto the philological distinction used by Habad masters between the "upper unity," in which the world is effaced vis-à-vis the One, and the "lower unity," in which the One is effaced vis-à-vis the world.[188] Notwithstanding the significance of this distinction, the dialectical drift of Habad thought should give one pause from applying it too sharply—"lower and "higher" are themselves subject to the same undoing: what is attained through the lower is always already compacted in the higher, which is always already evolving in the lower. The depth of the paradox is exposed when the veil of being is lifted to reveal the being of the veil that is recurrently (re)veiled in the (un)veiling of the veil. Messianic consciousness, which is at all times a matter of the future attainable in the present as the past-that-is-perpetually-yet-to-come-as-what-has-already-been, turns on becoming aware that the real divergence between divine and cosmic is merely apparent, and the apparent divergence real. The theological presumption of either God or world independent of one another comes under suspicion with the proper attunement or vision to the nature of nature when considered from the perspective of the essence, the "divine light that shines above nature," as the second Rebbe put it,[189] or, in the language of the seventh Rebbe, the "light that is higher than being garbed in the world," the "light that is beyond the concatenation."[190] Surely, this unknowable and unnameable essence, the "aspect of the essential nothing that is the nothing of the concealment of the essence,"[191] cannot be essentialized because it points—allusively rather than indexically—to the one reality or substance to which neither being nor nonbeing may be attributed. For something to be, it must be nothing. The (in)essentiality is thus characterized as the "essential concealment that is not in existence at all as it is also concealed to itself,"[192] a concealment-of-essence that is the essence of concealment, an essence that is (in)essentially concealed, the *aṣmut* that is *heʿlem*. Insofar as the essence is defined as an essential concealment, the revelation of that essence must of necessity be a revelation of nothing, that is, a revelation in which what is revealed is the concealment, and hence a revelation that is in essence a concealment. Like many mystic philosophers from various cultural contexts, the Habad masters affirm that the essential hiddenness of the Infinite, the darkened light or the luminal darkness that precedes the fissure into light and dark, is comprehended apophatically;

on this score, the *via negativa* (*derekh shelilah*) winds its way to the awareness that there is nothing not to comprehend in the comprehension that there is nothing to comprehend but that there is nothing to comprehend.[193]

HA-OLAM HEʿLEM: CONCEALING THE CONCEALED

On numerous occasions Habad masters express the apophatic ontology by linking together two words that consist of the same consonants, *ha-olam*, "the world," and *heʿlem*, "concealment." Many passages could have been cited to illustrate the point, but I will mention a concise formulation offered by Yosef Yitzchak Schneersohn (1880–1950), the sixth Rebbe of Lubavitch, in a discourse from the night of Simḥat Torah, 23 Tishrei 5691 (14 October 1930):

> World [*olam*] is the language of concealment [*heʿlem*], for the root of the concealment is from the first withdrawal, as the intent of the withdrawal is for the sake of the disclosure [*gilluy*] . . . and if the matter of the withdrawals in the order of the concatenation is the diminution of light for the sake of disclosure, how much more so with regard to the first withdrawal, whose matter is the removal of the light entirely, is it clear that its intention is for the sake of disclosure.[194]

In this comment, one can detect the two principal ways that the juxtaposition of the words *olam* and *heʿlem* can be interpreted, both of them esoteric, to be sure, but the former overtly so and the latter more clandestinely, portending, as it were, the duplicity of the secret, the secret doubling itself, the secret of the secret, the secret secreted as secret.

In the first instance, the supposition that the world can be viewed from the vantage point of concealment suggests that the ontic chain can reveal the hidden light only by hiding it, for if it were not hidden, how could it be revealed as the light that is hidden? All of reality that proceeds from the essence—in Lurianic terms, from the Primal Anthropos (*adam qadmon*) to the physical world of doing (*olam asiyyah*)—can be viewed as the progressive concealment and disclosure of the light, indeed, a concealment that is a disclosure in virtue of being a concealment. The spatiotemporal universe is a place of darkness but a darkness that makes the light visible, the darkness where the light of God is manifestly concealed. As the seventh Rebbe put it, "[T]he concealment and hiddenness in the world is from the perspective of the essence of the existence of the world," and "for this reason it is called *olam* . . . which is from the expression *heʿlem*."[195] In another one of his discourses, the word *ṭeva*, "nature," is said to denote the

> divine vitality [*ḥiyyut ha-elohi*] that sustains the created beings, and it is the divine force [*koaḥ elohi*] that brings about the created beings from nothing to something . . . for the matter of nature [*inyan ha-ṭeva*] that is in it is also from the expression "submersion" [*ṭeviʿah*], since the being [*hithawwut*] is in the manner of withdrawal and concealment [*be-ofen de-heʿlem we-hester*], as the potency that brings into being is concealed and hidden in the created entities. . . . The reason for this is that the divine vitality is garbed in the created entities by means of the garments that conceal . . . but the divine force that brings the created entities into being is distinct from the created entities and is not garbed in them. [196]

The dialectic exploited in Habad sources is a central facet of kabbalistic ontology from the Middle Ages, but it was given explicit formulation and unprecedented emphasis in the sixteenth century when kabbalists commonly asserted the paradox that concealment is disclosure and disclosure concealment.[197] The cosmos appears as a reality separate from and independent of God, but the one who sees with the eyes of faith knows that this is mere appearance, as the garments of nature (*levushei ha-ṭeva*) are naught but the "concealment and withdrawal" (*heʿlem we-ha-hester*) of the divine.[198] "The world, which is under time and space, is as naught and nothing [*ke-ayin wa-efes*], and it is annihilated in the light of the Infinite, blessed be he, which is above the concatenation, for it is not in the category of time and space."[199] The world (*ha-olam*), therefore, is essentially a form of concealment (*heʿlem*)—it conceals the light so that it may be revealed, as there can be no extension without withholding, no showing without hiding, no presence without absence.[200] With respect to divinity, however, as Shneur Zalman already expressed it in *Tanya*, the concealment is no concealment, since we cannot speak of withdrawal in the plenum that is the Infinite, and hence "before him everything is considered as actually nothing [*qameih kolla ke-lo ḥashiv mammash*]."[201] The last statement, which is derived from a zoharic passage,[202] is frequently repeated in Habad literature as a slogan to impart what is often referred to as the acosmic ideal of the dissolution of the being of everything when viewed in relation to the Infinite, the nothing that actually is nothing actually. The concealment of which we speak, therefore, the concealment before the withdrawal of the light is a correlative term; its meaning can be evaluated only from the perspective of an impulse for the one to be related to another, an impulse that is ultimately inexplicable because it implies some degree of otherness within the essence that contains all things and hence in relation to which there can be no other. The incomprehensibility of this belief notwithstanding, the kabbalistic wisdom that "the disclosure of the light of the Infinite is for the sake of the worlds"[203] rests on the supposition that the potential for alterity is the aspect of concealment concealed in the concealment of the concealed essence, whose inclusivity includes the excluded even as its exclusivity excludes the inclusive. This capacity for otherness, the possibility of the divine donning the garment of the various worlds, is linked to the attribute of judgment, the quality of constriction that facilitates the emanation of light, the attribute of kingship (*middat malkhut*) or, more specifically, the "kingship of the Infinite" (*malkhut de-ein sof*),[204] the "capacity for exaltedness" (*koaḥ ha-hitnasse'ut*) that is not possible "without the other" (*beli zulat*).[205] As the seventh Rebbe put it in a discourse delivered on 24 Nisan 5712 (19 April 1952):

> The yoke of the kingdom of heaven [*ol malkhut shamayim*][206] is in the aspect of the essence that is also above that which encompasses all worlds. It has been explained elsewhere that in the light of the Infinite before the withdrawal there is also an aspect of the kingship of the kingship of the Infinite, as the withdrawal was in this gradation. . . . Hence, in the aspect of the kingship of the Infinite prior to the withdrawal, there is the matter of kingship.[207]

The potentiality for the (dis)semblance of the other is engendered as feminine; indeed, femininity is essentialized as the aspect of the essence that is the possibility (*yekholet*) of all that is to become, the name that is "the spark contained in the luminescence before the world was created, which is merely what is in the potentiality of the holy luminescence, blessed be he, to illumine from him an illumination when he desires to radiate."[208] To state the matter in slightly different terms, the feminine is the matrix of materiality, the infinite potentiality for finitude that expresses the creative actuality of the one true substance that is naught but naught. It is in this sense that the feminine dimension within the Infinite, *malkhut de-malkhut de-ein sof*, is the concealment (*heʿlem*) that makes possible the existence of the world (*ha-olam*). Commenting in another homily on the midrashic dictum that prior to the world God and his name were alone,[209] Schneerson remarked that the "name" contained in the Infinite[210] is "the aspect of delimitation in that which has no limit [*beḥinah shel hagbalah be-tokh mah she-ein lo gevul*], the root for there being a world, for there being the aspect of the other in relation to the Infinite that upholds everything [*shoresh lihyot olam lihyot beḥinah zulat legabbei ein sof ha-nose et ha-kol*]."[211] Inasmuch as the essence is the substratum of everything, it can have no genuine other, but precisely because this is so, the potentiality for disclosure vis-à-vis the other (*gilluy el ha-zulat*) must itself be contained in the concealment as the dimension of difference lodged in the heart of the indifferent, the aspect of the name embedded in the unnameable, the feminine capacity for limitation and boundary expressed in the concealed world (*alma de-itkasya*), which consists of the realm of emanation, and the revealed world (*alma de-itgalya*), which comprises the realms of creation, formation, and doing, the quaternity of traditional kabbalistic cosmology.[212]

HEʿLEM HA-OLAM: MEONTOLOGICAL DISCLOSING

There is, however, a second and deeper interpretation of the juxtaposition of *ha-olam* and *heʿlem*, and one that, in my opinion, may go beyond even the labels of acosmic naturalism and apophatic panentheism, indeed perhaps beyond any and every terminological taxon. As the sixth Rebbe put it, in contrast to all other attributes wherein concealment is connected to disclosure, in the case of *Malkhut*, the "concealment is more interior" (*heʿlem penimi yoter*), that is, the hiddenness associated with the feminine is not some latent power (*koaḥ neʿlam*) that will be revealed in a particular disclosure, which is consequently antecedent to the concealment, but the power of latency as such (*ha-koaḥ kemo she-hu be-heʿlem*), the concealment within the concealed essence that ontologically precedes disclosure (*qodem ha-gilluy*).[213] The pairing of the terms *ha-olam* and *heʿlem* intimates that what is concealed in the disclosure of world is not the divine light that is concealed but the concealment of that light, that is, the concealment of the concealment that is only further concealed in its disclosure. Worldhood partakes essentially of this inessentiality, a meontology that issues from the insight that "prior to the world having been created all of the gradations were annihilated and unified in the light of the Infinite in an absolute unity without any aspect of the existence of something."[214] The tangibility of the world is determined, therefore, from the standpoint of this annihilation, of its being something that is ultimately nothing, the reality of illusion, as opposed to its being nothing that is something, the illusion of reality. To deny that would be to conceal the concealment in such a way that the concealment would not be concealed. One of the clearest articulations of this subtle point is made by Aaron Halevi Horowitz of Staroselye, a disciple of Shneur Zalman:

> The essence of the unity and of the faith is that apart from him there is nothing at all [*she-ein zulato kelal*], and he is simple in utter simplicity [*pashuṭ be-takhlit ha-peshiṭut*] and equanimous in the utmost equanimity [*shaweh be-takhlit ha-hashwwaʾah*] on account of which all of the beings that exist in the world are all created from privation to actual being in a new being from nothing to something [*me-ayin le-yesh*], that is, their existence should not be described as a concealment of concealment [*heʿlem de-heʿlem*].[215] Therefore all of the worlds and existents were previously in the aspect of nothing [*beḥinat ayin*].[216]

There is only one reality, the one that is incomposite and indifferent, the-nothing-that-contains-everything-annihilated-in-the-nothing-that-is-everything. As Aaron Halevi put it elsewhere, "[O]ne must nullify the body from the perspective of the contemplation and faith in his divinity, blessed be he, that he is the root and source of all the worlds, and the physical worlds do not attain any substance in relation to him."[217] The "him" in relation to which the worlds are nothing is itself nothing. The double bind of this nothingness is the meontological truth one must come (not) to know.

To comprehend the Habad perspective, I have found it beneficial to adopt a form of logic akin to what in the Mahāyāna tradition is referred to as *madhyamaka*, the middle way, a logic that, in the locution I have availed myself of in previous studies, posits the identity of opposites in the opposition of their identity.[218] Translated in a more technical vein, the logic to which I refer is based on the tetralemmic scheme: S is P; ~P; both P and ~P; neither P nor ~P.[219] The middle of the four-cornered logic, which some scholars consider to be the core of Buddhist philosophy, should be conceived of not as a meridian point situated equidistantly between extremes, the venerated golden mean between excess and privation in the Western philosophical tradition, but as the indeterminate space that contains both and neither of the extremes, the absent presence that is present as absent, the lull between affirmation and negation, identity and nonidentity, the void that cannot be avoided. In this middle excluded by the logic of the excluded middle, ostensibly contradictory properties are attributed and not attributed to the (non)substance at the same time and in the same relation, whence it follows that the propositions (A · ~A) and ~(A · ~A) converge in the point of their divergence.

It goes without saying that I am mindful of the methodological difficulties that this kind of comparative analysis entails. Without obfuscating the semantic and conceptual discrepancies that divide these two cultural environments, I would argue that there is philosophic merit in applying the Mādhyamika presentation of emptiness (*śūnyatā*) and dependent origination (*pratītyasamutpāda*) as a heuristic tool to analyze the cosmological and metaphysical teachings of Habad.[220] The most important insight is already imparted by the Centrist school's purported founder, the Indian sage Nāgārjuna (c. 150–250): emptiness itself must be empty. The claim that all phenomena do not exist inherently ensnares the mind in a self-subverting paradox: it asserts a truth that is true only if it is false, but it is false only if it is true, in a manner analogous to the contention, "Everything I say is false"—if this statement is true, it must be false, but if it is false, it must be true.[221] Epistemologically, the doctrine of emptiness entails the discernment that the ultimate truth is that there is no ultimate truth, that the essential reality is that there is no essential reality, that nature is inherently devoid of an inherent nature.[222] The paradox is vividly disclosed in the following passage from Nāgārjuna's *Mūlamadhyamakakārikā*, considered a foundational text of the Mādhyamika tradition:

Whatever is the essence of the Thatāgata,
That is the essence of the world.
The Thatāgata has no essence.
The world is without essence. (XXII:16).[223]

If we substitute the term *Ein Sof* for Thatāgata, then we would have a perfectly apt formulation of what I have called the meontological perspective of Habad: the essence of the world is the essence of *Ein Sof*, but the latter has no essence, and hence the former is without essence. Most astoundingly, Habad speculation on the essence—the nothing that everything is in virtue of the everything that nothing will not be—bears an especially striking affinity to the logic of the middle explicated in the *Mountain Doctrine*, a treatise by Döl-bo-ba (1292–1361), considered to be the founder of the Jo-nang-ba sect of Tibetan Buddhism. From a vast array of sources, I have chosen one passage to illustrate what I take to be an astonishing conceptual affinity between the two contemplative paths. The text I will consider is initiated as a reflection on the characterization of emptiness in the *Differentiation of the Middle and the Extremes* (*Madhyāntavibhāga*) by Maitreya, the Buddha's regent: "The non-existence of the entities of duality / And the nature of non-entities is the character of emptiness."[224] Expounding this wisdom, Döl-bo-ba probes more profoundly into the contrast between ultimate emptiness and self-emptiness:

> Mere self-emptiness does not fulfill its role. Why? It is because that which is the ultimate emptiness not only clears away the extreme of non-existence—"not existent and not non-existent"—but self-emptiness does not clear away the extreme of non-existence. Concerning this, whereas conventional phenomena do not at all exist in the mode of subsistence, the extreme of existence is the superimposition that they do. Whereas the partless, omnipresent pristine wisdom of the element of attributes always abides pervading all, the extreme of non-existence is the deprecation that it does not exist and is not established and is empty of its own entity. That which is the middle devoid of those extremes is the basis devoid of all extremes such as existence and non-existence, superimposition, and deprecation, permanence and annihilation, and so forth, due to

> which it is the final great middle. It is non-material emptiness, emptiness far from an annihilatory emptiness, great emptiness that is the ultimate pristine wisdom . . . for the character of the emptiness that is the final mode of subsistence, the mere emptiness of non-entities is not sufficient. Rather, the emptiness that is the [ultimate] nature of non-entities [that is, emptiness that is the ultimate nature opposite from non-entities] is required.[225]

The closest philological analogue in the Habad lexicon appears to be the term *efes*. I cannot here properly engage the multivalency of this term, but let me state that it is applied by the Habad masters to the Infinite (*ein sof*), since, as Shneur Zalman put it, paraphrasing previous sources,[226] there "is no comprehension with respect to it" (*ki ein bo shum tefisah*)[227] and thus it is the "negation of thought" (*afisat ha-raʿyon*).[228] *Efes*, moreover, is often paired with *tohu*, the "abyss," as it is the voidness that is the essence of the Infinite (*aṣmut ein sof*)—the aspect of light whose very existence is nullification (*meṣiʾuto hu ha-biṭṭul*),[229] that is, for it to be, it must be not. And yet, the nothing of being-not is to be distinguished from the nothing of not-being; the former is marked linguistically by *efes* and the latter by *ayin*. Alternatively, the two aspects of nullification are designated as *biṭṭul ha-yesh*, the nullification of disparate beings, and *biṭṭul ha-ayin*, the nullification of nullification. It seems to me legitimate to think of *efes* as the semantic and conceptual equivalent to the emptiness that Döl-bo-ba described as the final mode of subsistence, the emptiness that is consummately empty and therefore empty even of the emptiness of which it is fully empty, the emptiness that is neither empty nor non-empty,[230] neither existent nor nonexistent, neither different nor the same,[231] the middle devoid of the middle, the ultimate lacking the ultimate.[232] The goal of the mystical path is to be zeroed, one might say, to dematerialize into the "consummate nil" (*efes gamur*)[233] that is the substance of all that is to become. Consider the formulation of the Tzemach Tzedek:

> In relation to the divine vitality [*ḥiyyut elohut*] that sustains us, we are eradicated from existence and in the aspect of the actual nothing [*anaḥnu beṭelim mi-meṣiʾut u-vi-beḥinat efes mammash*] like the ray of the sun when it is in the body of the sphere of the sun . . . there is

> no more existence at all apart from his existence, blessed be he [*she-ein od shum meṣiʾut kelal zulat meṣiʾuto yitbarakh*], and this is the complete unity [*ha-yiḥud ha-gamur*].[234]

The description here, as the Tzemach Tzedek himself states explicitly in another passage,[235] is necessarily limited, since the example of the sunlight in relation to the body of the sun is still too dualistic to capture the utter annihilation that pertains to one who has become the actual nothing (*efes mammash*), annihilated to the point of being nothing beyond the point of being nothing. Explicating the statement of the Tzemach Tzedek that "*efes* is a greater annihilation [*biṭṭul yoter*] than *ayin*,"[236] his son Shmuel commented that "*ayin* has the letters of *ani*, which is the aspect of something [*beḥinat yesh*], and it is only annihilated in the aspect of nothing [*raq she-hu baṭel bi-veḥinat ayin*], which is not so with *efes*, the aspect of the absolute annihilation [*beḥinat biṭṭul mi-kol we-khol*], for there is no existence of anything there."[237]

Döl-bo-ba's contrast of ultimate emptiness and self-emptiness corresponds to the distinction between *biṭṭul bi-meṣiʾut* and *biṭṭul ha-yesh*. The denegation associated with the former clears away the extreme of existence and the extreme of nonexistence, whereas the denegation of the latter clears away the extreme of existence but not the extreme of nonexistence. To occupy the space of the middle, the verbal and logical correlate to what is conceived meontologically as the void, one must pass beyond the *ayin* of *biṭṭul ha-yesh*, the nothing of the nullification of existence, to the *efes* of *biṭṭul bi-meṣiʾut* , the naught of the nullification in existence, the "actual integration" (*hitkallelut mammash*), which entails the annihilation of both existence and nonexistence as "there is no existence at all but only essence" (*she-lo yesh shum meṣiʾut kelal raq ha-aṣmut*).[238] The second nullification, therefore, is the nullification of nullification, a voiding of the distinction between being and not-being in an absolutely relative way. When the truth that the essence is neither existent nor nonexistent—in the infinite power, *yesh* and *ayin*, something and nothing, "are identical with no distinction at all" (*shawwin beli hevdel kelal*)[239]—is coupled with the traditional notion of creation of something from nothing, we are faced with another insurmountable paradox. The annihilation of all beings in the nothing makes possible the bringing forth of each discrete being as something from nothing, and yet, insofar as all beings persist in that nothing to the extent that they are annihilated therein, every innovation cannot but be a renewal of that annihilation. If one were to disavow either of these claims, one would be guilty of concealing the concealment that is the world.

The objective, then, is not to negate the negation, to discard the veil of nature, but to see through it and thereby discover that there is no seeing without a veil. Again, the Buddhist wisdom regarding emptiness as articulated by Nāgārjuna and his followers is helpful to understand the thinking on the part of Habad masters about the essence that is unthinkable even as the unthinkable essence. From the ultimate standpoint of emptiness the everyday world is nonexistent. The enlightened one knows, however, that this nonexistence does not imply a negation of the phenomenal world, but a reassessment of its existence, a shift from presuming that there are independent substances existing inherently to perceiving the relativity and codependency of all that comes to be in the chain of becoming.[240] The gnosis of awakening consists of discerning that the true nature of things (*tattva*) is emptiness (*śūnyatā*), a truth that is identical to or compatible with the cosmological principle of dependent origination (*pratītyasamutpāda*).[241] In the disclosure of this disclosure, one apperceives the world recovered in the formless void, whence everything comes to be in the nothingness of its being. The capacity to negate all beings in the emptiness of their being is thus to affirm them in the being of their emptiness, to realize the absence of their inherent existence. Analogously, in Habad philosophy, the essence functions as the substratum underlying the plethora of phenomena that constitute the world, but in this substratum all things subsist in the being of their nothingness to the degree that they are nullified in the nothingness of their being. The conceptualizing mind is always at risk of essentializing the essence, of clinging to the void as though it were something to which to cling, but this is to misapprehend the nature of the essence that transcends all empirical determinations and thought constructions and therefore cannot be reified as an inherently existing entity. If we are to speak of substance, it is the substance (*mahut*) that is the abyss (*tehom*), the substance that is nothing.[242] In this ground, which is the absence of ground, abiding and nonabiding are one and the same.

One might protest that Habad masters do speak of a full disclosure of the essence (*gilluy ha-aṣmut*) without any garment (*beli levush*),[243] a depiction that is linked especially with the messianic era. The prototype for the final redemption was the exodus from Egypt, which is understood symbolically as "an exit from limitations and boundaries" by means of "the disclosure of the essence of the Infinite."[244] As Shneur Zalman already expressed it, "in the days of messiah, the illumination will be from the aspect of naught [*beḥinat efes*], which is above the aspect of nothing [*beḥinat ayin*]."[245] I surmise, however, that the eschatological loosening of all limitations and disbanding of all boundaries must be interpreted esoterically, yielding the ultimate secret, the open secret, that is, the secret that hides itself in the shroud of there being no secret. Seeing without a garment consists of coming to see that there is nothing to see but the garment that there can be a seeing without any garment. Even the disclosure without a covering, accordingly, is another form of covering; redemption is this mode of re/covery, an uncovering of the covering, and hence the "vision of the substance of the essence" (*re'iyyah be-mahut ha-aṣmut*) is expressly a revelation of the light of the Infinite, the power of YHWH, in the corporeal body (*guf ha-gashmi*).[246]

Support for my interpretation may be elicited from the attempt on the part of the Habad masters to link the messiah to the state of mindfulness designated as *afisat ha-ra'yon*, the negation of thought, the (un)knowing of *efes*, the nil that is "more than nothing" (*mer eyder nisht*)[247]—more nothing than nothing—the essence voided of its essentiality, the indistinct beyond all distinction, even the distinction of being indistinct, the abyss before there was a before, before which there might be an after, the indifferent in which identity of difference and difference of identity are no longer distinguishable. From the vantage point of the lower form of denegation, *biṭṭul ha-yesh*, the spatiotemporal world is annihilated in the light of the Infinite that is outside of space and time,[248] but from the vantage point of the higher form of denegation, *biṭṭul ha-ayin*, the world of particularity is reconfigured as an expression of the void that is empty of being empty. In my judgment, the esoteric dimension of Habad, which is only amplified by the revelation of secrets, relates to a contemplative understanding of the traditional geopolitical messianic ideal along these lines. To be redeemed is to attain the highest level of nullification in *efes*, the *biṭṭul bi-meṣi'ut*, which ensues from the mind negating the negation of negation by being incorporated into the nothing-that-is-more-than-less-than-nothing. One of the key ways that this is expressed is as an interpretation of the passage from the morning prayers in the Sabbath liturgy, *efes biltekha go'alenu limot ha-mashiaḥ*, "There is naught but you, our redeemer in the days of messiah." Exoterically, the expression *efes biltekha* conveys the monotheistic belief that there is no divinity other than God, but, esoterically, it alludes to the meontological truth that even God is annihilated in the naught (*efes*) that is more than nothing (*ayin*), as nothing is still too much of a something to be naught. To drive this point home, the words *efes biltekha* are contrasted with the phrase that immediately precedes them, *we-ein zulatekha*, "there is none other than you." The RaShaB compared the avowal "there is none other than you" to the "nullification of the vessels" (*biṭṭul ha-kelim*), since it implies that "there is an existence but it is annihilated" (*she-yesh meṣi'ut ella she-baṭel*), and the assertion "there is naught but you" to the "nullification of the light" (*biṭṭul ha-or*), which suggests "that there is no other existence at all" (*she-ein meṣi'ut zulat kelal*).[249] Elaborating on this distinction, the sixth Rebbe commented that insofar as the light that issues from the essence is the "aspect of the nothing itself" (*beḥinat ayin aṣmo*) and the "nothing is nullification" (*ayin hu biṭṭul*), it follows that the nullification of the light involves three aspects, the "nullification of the privation of the orientation of place" (*biṭṭul de-he'der tefisat maqom*), the "nullification of there is none other than you" (*biṭṭul de-ein zulatekha*), and the "nullification of there is naught but him" (*biṭṭul de-efes bil'ado*). The disclosure in the future-to-come (*atid lavo*) relates specifically to the third aspect, as there will be the "discernment of the comprehension of the nullification of there is naught but you," that is, the ultimate principle of nullification (*efes biltekha*) will be nullified. The concealment of exile, the simulation of there being something other than nothing, is what prevents us from perceiving that God is "our redeemer constantly" (*go'alenu tamid*); in the future, however, when nullification itself will be nullified, and there will be no existence outside the essence, the nothing-that-is-more-than-less-than-nothing, that will need to be nullified, then this truth will be seen without any obstruction.[250] The soteriological secret harbored by the Habad masters (a secret that still seems to be hidden from those who think they have revealed the secret) is encapsulated in the awareness that the futurity of apocalyptic anticipation—waiting for the messiah to appear—is not a matter of time at all but a mental state whereby one realizes that what is to come is already perpetually present.[251]

In the annihilation of the annihilation, even the difference between time and eternity collapses, not however through the demolition of the world, but through an opening that allows one to see the world as the manifestation of the essence that is concealed, a revealing of the veil as veil, which is expressed in the rabbinic idiom of the divine presence making its habitation below. As Shneur Zalman wrote:

> In the days of messiah, there will be "none but you" [*efes biltekha*], that is, the perfection of the messiah [*sheleimut ha-mashiaḥ*] . . . for in those days there will be a disclosure of divinity in this corporeal world [*yihyeh hitgallut elohut be-zeh ha-olam ha-gashmi*], "and the earth will be filled with the knowledge of the Lord" (Isa 11:9). . . . In the days of messiah, there will be a disclosure of divinity in this lower world and there will be none but him [*efes bilʿado*], the naught that is higher than nothing [*efes gavoha me-ayin*], and he will not ascend to be higher since the essence of his dwelling will be in the lower beings.[252]

The paradoxical import of this idea is brought into sharper relief by the Tzemach Tzedek: "In the days of messiah, there will be a disclosure of the aspect of the naught [*gilluy beḥinat efes*], and thus the material reality will not conceal [*ha-yesh ha-gashmi lo yastir*], two opposites in one subject."[253] How can there be a disclosure of the naught? What is revealed when what is revealed is nothing, indeed a nothing that is even more nothing than nothing? The messianic ideal instantiates the paramount meontological *coincidentia oppositorum*; the full disclosure of the "aspect of the essence of the Infinite that is entirely above the aspect of manifestation [*beḥinat aṣmiyyut ha-ein sof she-lemaʿlah mi-beḥinat gilluy legamrei*]" is manifest in the multiple forms of the spatio-temporal world.[254] The material reality will no longer conceal because the garment itself will be exposed as a garment, and, consequently, the world of phenomena will not be considered a distinct substance that hides the revelation of divinity (*lo yihyeh ha-yesh davar nivdal we-lo yihyeh mastir le-gilluy elohuto*).[255] Playing with the same complex of ideas, the seventh Rebbe remarked that in messianic times the aspect of the negation of thought (*afisat ha-raʿyon*) would be revealed and "then the material reality will not conceal at all" (*ha-yesh ha-gashmi lo yastir kelal*), an idea anchored textually in the prophetic prediction, "The glory of the Lord shall appear, and all flesh, as one, shall behold—for the Lord himself has spoken" (Isa 40:5).[256] In the exilic condition, nature is a veil that conceals the light of the essence so that it may be revealed, but in the messianic state of mind, the veil is unveiled and what has been veiled is finally unveiled as the veiled.

"In the ultimate concealment," remarked the seventh Rebbe, "the concealment is not in existence" (*be-takhlit ha-heʿlem he ʿlem eino bi-meṣiʾut*)[257]—in the ultimate concealment even the concealment must be concealed. Messianic gnosis is linked precisely to this doubling of concealment in the disclosure of the world abiding always in the passing of its passing. Redemption is thus the time when the "concealment that is above revelation" (*heʿlem she-lemaʿlah mi-gilluy*) will be revealed below "in actuality" (*be-foʿal mammash*).[258] But how is the revelation of concealment that is above the concealment of revelation to be revealed? The response offered by Schneerson, which intensifies the paradox, relates to the compresence of the three dimensions of temporality connected to the advent of the messiah. Insofar as the time of redemption is hidden and concealed, it relates to the future, but the expectation of the redemption demands that one believe that it can occur in any moment, which transforms that future into the present, albeit a present that is always becoming past, as the time of redemption must always be a matter of futurity.

> The explanation of this—according to what was said that matters of redemption are from a level that is above the categories of concealment and disclosure, for by means of this the union of concealment and disclosure comes to be. An illustration of this relates to the time of redemption—it is above the dimensions of time, for by means of this the union of future with present and past comes to be, for the future redemption is from the moment of the present until the moment of the past.[259]

The concurrence of the three temporal modes in the messianic juncture, which, needless to say, betokens an imitation of the mystery of the Tetragrammaton, provides a path to comprehending the revelation of the concealment that is beyond revelation. What, then, is revealed? Let us consider carefully another account of the messianic revelation offered by the seventh Rebbe:

> The disclosure of the essence [*gilluy ha-aṣmut*] will be especially in the future . . . for there will be a disclosure of the essence above the name YHWH and above YHWH himself. Before the world was created he and his name alone were,[260] that is, YHWH himself and the name YHWH, and in the name itself there are two aspects, the disclosure for itself and the disclosure as it is appropriate for the worlds. However, in the future there will a disclosure of the essence that is above the aspect of "his name" and also above the aspect of "he." Hence, this disclosure will be equanimous for everyone, for even though then there will also be division of gradations, this will be from the perspective of the comprehension of the aspect of the name YHWH, but in the knowledge of the essence that is above YHWH they will all be equal. . . . For the matter of knowledge here is not to be explained from the language of cognition and comprehension, but it is the matter of knowing and union, the union of the soul with the essence.[261]

The ultimate revelation is the disclosure of the essence, which is even beyond the disclosure of the name. This disclosure is a form of knowledge (*yediʿah*) that is not a cognitive state but a gnosis that entails the "union of the soul with the essence and substance of the Infinite, blessed be he" (*hitqashsherut ha-neshamah be-aṣmut u-mahut ein sof barukh hu*),[262] a unified consciousness wherein all difference is overcome. Yet, as the above passage makes clear, the sense of difference will be preserved in the messianic future—which is already in the present because it has always been in the past—"there will also be a division of gradations" from the perspective of the name YHWH. Significantly, as we have seen, the name is linked symbolically to the aspect of the feminine demarcated within the Infinite, *malkhut de-ein sof*, as she personifies the potential for limit in that which has no limit, positioned as the midpoint of the void that renders opposites identical in their opposition. Preserving and overturning a long-standing hierarchical bias, the hylic character of the feminine is valorized as the locus of the concealment (*heʿlem*) that is the world (*ha-olam*), the apophatic body that is present in the absence of its absence.

The diasporic claim that the Jewish people will be dispersed to the "end of the entire world" (*ad sof kol ha-olam*) is applied esoterically to "the nullification (*sof*) of the concealment and hiddenness (*olam*), for an end and a conclusion to all the concealment and hiddenness comes to be, as the point of this matter is that by means of the descent of Israel in exile they come to the elevation that is in the redemption."[263] This play of projecting/ withholding—what is withheld is the projection that is the world projected as withholding—persists even in the eschaton, and thus the full disclosure of the essence in which all distinctions are eradicated cannot be severed from the disclosure of the name in which the distinctions are preserved. The doctrine of incarnation that is the basis of Habad cosmology and that also serves as the foundation for the ethical ideal of mystical quietism, the suffering of world through eradication of existence, rests on affirming that it is only through the garment that one can see without any garment.

Bodies of the Void: Polyphilia and Theoplicity

ROLAND FABER

What is an "apophatic body"? Is there a phenomenology of "apophatic bodies"? Probably not! Instead of an essentializing definition, let me try this: The "apophatic body" is a paradox that lives from a *negation*, an "un-naming" or "un-signifying" that is a twofold process of "negating bodying" and "bodying negating." What is negated? *What* is *un*-, and in this way, *em*bodied? It is the "What"—essence—itself! This *What* that cannot be named or signified, is *un*-bodied. However, in un-naming "essence," we do not negate the process of "bodying," but "what" is negating it, fixating it, pre-stabilizing it as the *That* of the body. *That* body is negated; and that *body* is un-said: its individuality as *this* body and its generality as *some* body. In this negation, what is embodied? What the *What was* before it was fixated, before it was identified as *that* body and that *body*. The double process of "negating bodying" and "bodying negating" does not negate the process of "bodying," but "what" negates its un-preformed singularity; and it does not embody negation (as such), but "what" negates its bodying (as such).[1]

The thesis is that apophatic negation works in two directions: It *can* negate the bodying itself, carrying with it the peril of a negation, which, embodied again, destroys the body; but it can also *negate what negates* the bodying, thereby freeing the process of "bodying." In uncovering the first apophasis as "peril" (especially of negative theology), I will mark some of the "characteristics" of the second apophasis as *pure affirmation*, especially with the help of Butler's, Derrida's, Deleuze's, Kristeva's, and Whitehead's respective accounts of concepts that indicate, imply, or can be directed toward an understanding toward what I mean by "apophatic bodies."

INFINITE UN-BODYING AND BODYING THE INFINITE

What is un-said in negative theology is any "attribute" that could grasp deity. Although we may start with positive characterization, for example, knowing, in un-saying knowing, we negate the finite character of knowing in which we live, and we project its absolute negation as the position of the deity: as absolute knowledge beyond any creaturely restriction. This method of negation is a process of "un-bounding," of "de-limiting," in proposing that the deity is in its "essence" un-bound and in-finite. In relation to the cosmos, the theology after 1277, the theological decisions published by the Parisian faculty about the orthodox notion of God in the medieval Church, named this the *immensity* of God, which led to a "spatialization" of the infinite deity and a deification of infinite space.[2] Although this "sea of infinite substance" has been conceptualized since Gregor of Nazians (*pelagos ousias apeiron kai aoriston*) and John Damascenus (*est enim deus pelagus infinitae substantiae et per consequens indistinctae*),[3] it was implanted at the heart of negative theology by John Duns Scotus. In his *Quotlibetal Questions*, he writes:

> Damascene confirms this corollary when he says that the essence is an infinite and limitless sea of substance. Substance, then, insofar as it represents what is absolutely first in the divine, he calls a sea, and as such it is infinite and boundless. But substance in this sense does not include either truth, or goodness, or any other attributable property. Therefore, infinity as such is a mode of essence more intrinsic than any other attribute it has.[4]

For Duns Scotus, this bound-less infinity is the "innermost attribute" of the essence of the deity, which is *in se* beyond *any* "character"—even Goodness or Truth. Its infinity is the expression of pure negativity, the negation of any finiteness. It cannot, therefore, be embodied at all. It is the negation of embodiment, of bodying, of the body. It is the expression of pure transcendence, unsaid, unheard, silent, empty of whatever it may characterize. Paradoxically, although it is without essence, its essence is Infinity itself. Whatever "embodies" this pure negativity must die! No body can "see" this infinite substance. And as Meister Eckhart has taught us, in the ecstasy of "mystical unknowing," which can be equated even with a "mystical death" of the soul, one may enter this silence, but only by losing any embodiment—be it that of World or God.[5] In his German sermon *Nolite timere eos*, Eckhart states that to enter the Godhead is to *un-create creation* and *un-god God*.[6] This negativity ends in *pure indifference*, pure un-bodying.

Yet, there is another way to look at this negating of bodying in negative theology. Rooted in a certain view of Plotinus and the Neoplatonic tradition, Nicholas of Cusa was not only engaged in the un-bodying infinity of the indifferent deity but also in the embodying of this infinity in the difference, which would be *deity's relation* to the world. Quoting Eckhart's *Sermo IV* of the *Sapientia Commentary*, he states that "*Deus autem indistinctum quoddam, est quod sua indistinctione distingitur*;"[7] that the indistinct God is precisely *distinct* by this indistinctness. But distinct from *what*? In order to be able to engage in the negativity of the un-bodying in mystical discourse, Nicholas insists that this is possible only if it is *already* constituted by a *relation* of God to the world, which, in the indifference of the Godhead, is not interrupted but rather *posited*. Here, the indifference of God is not a negation but an *affirmation* of the world as the creation of God.

With the "trinitarian formulary" of *De veneratione sapientiae*—a peak of apophatic unsaying—Nicholas states that the indifference is not nothingness beyond any bodying, but in the middle of its process: "The *non aliud* is *non aliud* than *non aliud*."[8] That the Non-Other is nothing other than the Non-Other, means two things: that the Non-Other is *before* the difference of anything, even the difference of "identity" and "difference"; and that, in its very relation to anything, it *creates* its identity and difference.[9] Thereby, the *non aliud* is even beyond (the difference and identity of) unity and plurality; and, of even more importance here, it opens a *process* of differentiation: The *non aliud* is *non aliud* than *non aliud* which is *non aliud* to *non aliud* . . . indefinitely differentiating. In proper Deleuzian terms, not being a differentiation of actual beings (between "things" already constituted as "unity"), because it is prior to "identity" and "unity"; this is a "differenciation" of the real—that which is not yet "identical" or "unified."[10] In other words, the *non aliud* is a process of *infinite embodying* of difference before identity, not against identity but rather actualizing itself as the identity and difference of subjects and objects of the world.

While the negativity of the first account is infinite un-bodying, the negativity of this second account is a process of *infinite embodying*. What does it negate, then, if it is *not* the positioning of bodying? It negates any identity and unity as being *prior* to the process of embodying. It negates any essentialism that understands the process of bodying in this world as the permanent positing of a substance or essence with accidental change; it negates any subject or object as the cause of its changing actions. Instead, it is an astonishing account of the *affirmation of the body* as being prior to any given "identity" or "unity." In this second sense, negativity does not negate bodying anymore; it negates the *presuppositions* that preform the becoming of the body; it frees the body in its bodying. The "negativity" becomes that of an embodied becoming before any indication, any being, any signification, any stabilization. It embodies the *event of becoming* of bodying.

NEGATIVE BODIES OR EMBODYING NEGATION?

It is, of course, not uncommon to characterize the poststructuralist tradition as emphasizing precisely this twofold critique of the "inscription" of allegedly pre-given structures of stability upon the body, which—for Michel Foucault more than Judith Butler—may indicate inevitable social power but—for Butler more than Foucault—may also hold resources of resistance.[11] Alain Badiou's critique may have been launched against the inability of this poststructuralist attack against the subject as *effect* of its (social) body, namely that it unsettles the ability to think of both the *identity* and *agency* of the so deconstructed subject.[12] But it forgets the poststructuralist's affirmation of a *body-apriori* as basis for *identity* and *unity* that, indeed, resembles the visionary thought of Nicholas of Cusa. However, it differs precisely in that now the apophasis is said and unsaid of the human (and social) body—unmediated by any deity.

With the *same* characteristic of the human "apophatic body" as its *becoming* (before identity) and its *difference* (before its unity) in both accounts—the theological and the poststructuralist—they also coincide in the *same* critique of negativity or "negating bodying." With Derrida's reconstruction of the *logocentric* negation of the body and Kristeva's *phallogocentric* localization of the universal negation of the body we enter the critique of the "metaphysic of presence"[13] with its seemingly neutral universals and its oppressive binaries, resituating the discourse on the body in the context of gender, race, and social power. The universality of the mind, ideas, and consciousness ever seeking identity and unity, cannot and does not want to undercut its own presuppositions of oppressive sexual and social inscriptions in the body.[14] Here the body itself becomes negated, bodying is substituted with the substantiation of universals of mind and consciousness. The body becomes "apophatic," a purely negative body, emptied of everything except Cartesian "extension,"[15] a hull of the Phallus/Logos. And in its connotation with the idea of the one, transcendent God, the master of infinite identity and unity, Derrida and Deleuze warn us that negative theology is afflicted with this negation of the affirmation of the body.[16]

Against this *active negating* of bodying in the interest of oppressive generalization, stabilized identity, and transcendent unity, various attempts have been launched to convert the apophasis of the "negative body" of phallogocentrism into an embodying of an apophasis. This embodying of apophasis, this "bodying of negativity" would not negate the body, dissolving it into mere generality but rather would deconstruct the structures that maintain the fake neutrality of phallogocentric negation of the body. There is Irigaray's reconstruction of the female that cannot be represented by male generality. Its subversive realm is beyond language at all—negative, but concrete bodying.[17] And there is Kristeva's reconstruction of Lacan's universal symbolic structure as "law of the father," which *negates* the matrix of the mother, a pre-symbolic realm of the body (of the mother). In equating this *semiotic* realm of irregularity, non-identity, and pre-unity, with the "poetic" account of concrete bodily processes and with Plato's *khora*,[18] she recovers bodying as the prevalent process of becoming and of the "un-coming" of male neutrality and generality. Very much does this recovery—as Catherine Keller has shown—also relate to Whitehead's discovery of the *body-apriori* in what he calls "causal efficacy," the often negated primordial mode of perception of our bodying:[19]

> It is evident that "perception in the mode of causal efficacy" is not that sort of perception which has received chief attention in the philosophical tradition. Philosophers have disdained the information

> about the universe obtained through their visceral feelings, and have concentrated on visual feelings.[20]

Instead of negating the body, the apophasis, now speaking through "causal efficacy," begins *positing* the body as the pre-conceptual, pre-signified, pre-identified mode of our existence in concrete difference. In Deleuze's conceptualization of Whitehead, the multiple vibrations of events in their interrelation, that is, their rhythmic pulsating, is the bodily pre-conceptual connection of this "causally effective" nexus, "us" being the *effect* of its *vibrating multiplicity of becoming* from which is extracted what we call "my Self (Moi)."[21] "Bodily experiences, in the mode of causal efficacy," happen to us when we lift those negations of bodying, when

> in the silence, the irresistible causal efficacy of nature presses itself upon us; in the vagueness of the low hum of insects in an August woodland, the inflow into ourselves of feelings from enveloping nature overwhelms us; in the dim consciousness of half-sleep, the presentations of sense fade away, and we are left with the vague feeling of influences from vague things around us.[22]

In this "visceral philosophy"[23] of Whitehead, Deleuze, and Kristeva, we encounter the other side of apophasis, the embodying of a negativity that erases not the bodying but the oppressive unifications and identifications that hinder understanding and politically demands its liberating difference, its unoccupied diversity and indispensable becoming-differently. The "great divide" of the "apophatic negation of bodying" and the "apophatic positing of bodying" is where generality negates becoming and becoming embraces difference, where multiplicity negates pre-given identity and unity.

In his analysis of Heidegger's ontological difference as a sexual difference, Derrida gives an important account of a common ground for the departure of both directions of apophasis from the profound *neutrality* of *Dasein*.[24] When Heidegger understands *Dasein* as prior to sexual difference, or any difference (except the ontological difference by which it is constituted), for that matter, he proposes its

> peculiar *neutrality* [to be] . . . essential, because the interpretation of this being must be carried prior to every factual connection. . . . [However, its] Neutrality is not the voidness of abstraction, but precisely the potency of the origin, which bears in itself the intrinsic possibility of every concrete factual humanity.[25]

On the one hand, this seems to say that a negating generality is at work here, which instantiates precisely the phallogocentric apophasis of bodying as the neutrality of *Dasein* in relation to any difference, especially sexual difference: it erases the sexual difference in the ontological difference. On the other hand, this neutrality does not want to "abstract," to "void" (sexual) difference; rather, it wants to open a path for the *positing* of Dasein as *pleroma*, as the origin of potency for indefinite differentiation. *This* neutrality "strongly [indicates] a negativity,"[26] that, as Derrida notes, is itself an apophatic process of *affirming* apophatic bodying.

> By means of such manifestly negative predicates there should become legible what Heidegger doesn't hesitate to call a "positive," a richness, and, in a heavily charged code, even a power. Such precision suggests that the a-sexual neutrality does not desexualize; on the contrary, its *ontological* negativity is not unfolded with respect to *sexuality itself* (which it would instead liberate), but on its differential marks, or more strictly on sexual duality.[27]

Other than the neutralization of difference, this apophasis is pure affirmation of the multiplicity of the process of bodying as pure *excess*, the pleroma of potency. Its negativity erases the generalizing binaries, thereby liberating the event of the bodying for infinite differentiation. Its negativity removes the oppressive oppositions and dualities that stabilize identity and unity, thereby un-creating "transcendence" as a possessive unity under a Law and re-creating it as that which becomes only "in difference." Following this *second* apophatic negation as affirmation of bodying, Derrida now envisions "a multiplicity of sexually marked voices . . . this mobile of non-identified sexual marks whose choreography can carry, divide, multiply the body of each 'individual,' whether it is classified as 'man' or 'woman.'"[28]

BODYING THE APOPHATIC

It is ironic that although the logocentric reduction of the body is part of Kant's transcendental approach, in his early work (and largely forgotten and not even taken up later by himself) he already had made first steps for a fresh philosophical recognition of the body. In his mature *Critique of Pure Reason* he followed Hume's *Treatise* in reducing the body to a mere constituent of consciousness in which bodying is transcendentally reconstructed as a mere condition of space and time for thought, devoid of any "causality" or effective and affective reality. In his early dissertation *On the Form and Principle of the Sensible and Intelligible Word* (1770), however, and in his essay on "The Ultimate Ground of the Differentiation of Regions in Space" (1768), Kant already had re-discovered a *body-apriori*. Following the old philosophical axiom of Archytias that "to be is to be somewhere," Kant realized the body to be *the* precondition for any discourse on the sensible and the intelligible, phenomena and noumena.[29]

Yet, it was Whitehead who (among a number of other philosophers of his time) contested *systematically* the negation of the body in philosophy. His "philosophy of organism" is, indeed, a *philosophy of the body*.[30] In his vision of infinite nested hierarchies of bodies and their environments, which are themselves bodies in other environments and altogether an interfused multiplicity of bodies, the (human) body becomes the presupposition of all knowledge and experience of the world. In *Science and the Modern World*, Whitehead states that

> we have to admit that the body is the organism whose states regulate our cognisance of the world. The unity of the perceptual field therefore must be a unity of bodily experience. In being aware of the bodily experience, we must thereby be aware of aspects of the whole spatio-temporal world as mirrored within the bodily life.[31]

The bodily life is so important for everything we might be inclined to substitute for it (and which we cannot substitute, therefore) that *all* of our knowledge, internally and externally, is mediated by our body. It is the membrane of both our "direct knowledge of the relationship of our central intelligence to our bodily feelings" and our understanding of "other sections of the universe [which] are to be interpreted in accordance with what we know of the human body."[32] It is the membrane of perception, which

> takes place where you are, and is entirely dependent on how your body is functioning. But this functioning of the body in one place, exhibits for your cognisance an aspect of the distant environment, fading away into the general knowledge that there are things beyond. If this cognisance conveys knowledge of a transcendent world, it must be because the event which is the bodily life unifies in itself aspects of the universe.[33]

This "event which is the bodily life" is a becoming of the whole world in it so that the "world for me is nothing else than how the functionings of my body present it for my experience;" and yet, "the body is merely one society of functionings within the universal society of the world."[34] The reason for *not* recognizing this "mutual immanence"[35] of the body and the world and all nested organisms in one another is precisely the substantialism that haunts the history of philosophy—a symbol of the phallogocentric generalizations and abstractions that fulfill Heidegger's "voidness of abstraction" and Derrida's "a-sexual neutrality" as the apophatic negation of bodying (in the first sense). Whitehead conceptualizes his critique with the *Fallacy of Misplaced Concreteness*, which does not point to the use of (neutral) abstractions as such but to our "mistaking the abstract for the concrete."[36] A basic indication of this replacement of concrete difference by abstract oppositions is what Whitehead calls "simple location," which takes everything just to be where it is in space and time. Whitehead, instead, proposes

> the entire abandonment of the notion that simple location is the primary way in which things are involved in space-time. In a certain sense, everything is everywhere at all times. For every location involves an aspect of itself in every other location. Thus every spatio-temporal standpoint mirrors the world.[37]

While the generalizations of "simple location" indicate the "neutrality" of the phallogocentric "bifurcation of nature" into static binaries (of male/female, mind/matter, soul/body) that indicate the vanishing point of the body, their entire abandonment frees (our recognition of) the body from pre-stabilized stability and recovers it as a *universally defused becoming of the multiplicity of the world.* It establishes the other apophasis (in the second sense) of a pure affirmation of the plenitude of differentiation before and beyond any identification, unification, or stabilization, of its existence and meaning by negating its priority.

Part of the problem of the first apophasis lies in the constitution of the subject, part in the social determination of the body. If the body is subjected to a (private) subject, this subject becomes unable to understand itself as the body's emergent *effect* and instead projects itself as its *possessor* (I and my body) or even *origin* (my soul as original and actual form of my body). Yet, substantializing itself, this subject follows only the social power that inscribes itself by internalizing the pre-formation of environmental societies. While Foucault saw the soul as a mere surface effect of this social inscribing of the body,[38] Butler deconstructs the (socially logocentric) "matrix of intelligibility" that erects the regulative boundaries of identification and unification of which the self-identifying identity of persons is an effect.[39] But Whitehead deconstructs the substantiation of the subject in relation to its body in a reconstruction of consciousness, namely, the effect of the same bodily life that undercuts its socially preformative character.

The bodily paradox of consciousness and life unfolds when we hold them together as "contrasting opposites." Consciousness, for Whitehead, is a *late evolutionary product* of bodily life that *heightens its intensity* by *interrupting its stability*; but the "stream of consciousness"[40] is also *cloaking* the "infinite complexity of our bodies" by "the selectiveness of enjoyment" through which structures of the environment are highlighted, while consciousness, at the same time, negates "its dependence on detailed bodily functioning."[41] The body becomes apophatic in the *first* sense: It loses its visceral dependence and the multiplicity of the causal efficacy working in it as pure multiplicities of myriad processes. Life, on the other hand, develops for Whitehead where the "defining characteristic" of a society, which is the body and the social (and natural) environment sustaining it, is *interrupted* by non-determination arising from the difference of bodily actualization in differentiation from what is or could have been otherwise.[42] Then, it is precisely the interruption of "conformity" that elicits consciousness as effect of the originality of bodily life.

> Life is a bid for freedom: an enduring entity binds any one of its occasions to the line of its ancestry. The doctrine of the enduring soul with its permanent characteristics is exactly the irrelevant answer to the problem which life presents. That problem is, How can there be originality? And the answer explains how the soul need be no more original than a stone.[43]

With this bodily view of life and consciousness in Whitehead, we need a critique of the "negating bodying" of consciousness in its stabilizing, unifying, and identifying effect, which (through consciousness!) regains the multiplicities veiled behind its creation of seamless unity, of identifying things and oneself as subject. Such "vivid conscious experience is a return to the concrete"[44] multitude of becoming. This is the regaining of the "bodying of the apophatic." In Butler's words, it is the uncovering of a "subversive matrix of disorder" and the "heterogeneity" of the body that liberates to new and alternative potentials.[45]

MULTIPLICITIES AND THE VOID

With the differentiation of the two forms of negation operating in this reversal of apophasis, namely neutralization *as* abstraction, on the one hand, and neutralization of the *negation* of abstraction, on the other, we can now see how both modes of apophasis correspond to the "bodies" they instantiate or liberate. The first apophasis can be found to be articulated by the atomism of Epicurus, Democritus, and Lucretius; the second apophasis may reveal itself by the "interconnected emptiness" of the "place" in Plato's *Timaeus*.[46] Both traditions address the two kinds of negativity their bodies populate, respectively: The atomistic approach presupposes "simple location" and, therefore, negates the becoming of the body; it knows only of external relation of identified "units" in "empty space," the void, the *kenon*. It is precisely this approach which lived on in Descartes's "extension" and Newton's "geometrical space." In its phallogocentric negation, it neutralizes all relation except that of "pushing." The Platonic approach situates everything in its becoming in an unidentified space of vibration, of *pre*-symbolic *non*-identity, and *ante*-unified multiplicity. This negation is the *khora*, the "origin (without origin)" of *becoming—becoming as such*.

It is not without reason that Whitehead, Derrida, and Kristeva attacked the first apophatic negation of bodying as being simply the located, presented, and symbolized realm of the Phallus/Logos, and adopted the second apophatic negation of unity, identity, and stability in the image of the *khora*. While the *khora* names the pre-symbolic, semiotic, concrete, material poetic for Kristeva[47] and the un-signifying of the negativity of *différance* for Derrida,[48] for Whitehead it names unpreformed, unidentified "mutual immanence."

> In itself, with the various actualities abstracted from it, the Receptacle participates in no forms, according to Plato. But he designates it as "the fostermother of all becoming." Later in the same Dialogue he calls it "a natural matrix for all things." It receives its forms by reason of its inclusion of actualities, and in a way not to be abstracted from those actualities. The Receptacle, as discussed in the *Timaeus*, is the way in which Plato conceived the many actualities of the physical world as components in each other's natures. It is the doctrine of the immanence of Law, derived from the mutual immanence of actualities. It is Plato's doctrine of the medium of intercommunication.[49]

In being the *negation* of the "form" as medium of identification and unity and in being the *negation* of the stabilization of "being," it frees the body as *pure becoming, differentiating*, and process of *intensity*.[50] While the first apophasis creates a stabilized being *out of* or *in* the void (*kenon*), the second apophasis fosters bodying as becoming *of* the void (*khora*). While the negation of bodying presupposes an *empty void* of pure externality and transcendence of everything in it—indicating sheer plurality—the negation of abstraction as affirmation of the bodying, on the other hand, is embraced by the *void of pure intensity and immanence*—indicating pure multiplicity. *Becoming* is the *multiplication of this (second) void*.

When Deleuze invokes Nicholas of Cusa's and (following him) Giordano Bruno's concept of *complication/explication* to indicate the understanding of his pairs "difference/repetition," "intensity/extensity," and "enfolding/unfolding," he follows the second apophasis of plenitude for which identity is neither prior to difference nor the point of reference in its understanding—for example, as difference between "identified" things.[51] On the contrary, it relates to Cusa's series of notions for the deity that are *apophatic affirmations* of becoming and multiplicity. This can be witnessed by the relentless overthrowing of his terms of apophasis by increasingly stripping away any negation that would create opposition. From the *coincidencia oppositorum* and the *non aliud* to the *possest*, his way ended with the *posse ipsum*, the pure *potential for complication and multiplication*.[52]

There is, however, another approach to the void as introduced by Badiou in his *Being and Event* (2005), which I refer to here to highlight an important aspect of the void introduced here, which would otherwise go unnoticed, namely that it indicates that which is "unaccounted for" in any form of unification. For Badiou, the ontological difference is that between unification—"counting-as-one"—and a sheer multiplicity that is unified. In the process of unifying, becoming a being, the Being (multiplicity) is always already unified, although in itself it must be considered an *inconsistent multiplicity*, devoid of any unity—it is multiplicity of multiplicity all the way down. This "void" is a "nothing" that

> [b]y itself . . . is no more than the name of unpresentation in presentation. . . . The nothing names that undecidable of presentation which is its unpresentable, distributed between the pure inertia of the domain of the multiple, and the pure transparency of the operation thanks to which there is oneness.[53]

What in the counting-as-one is "not there" but is the "nothing" that ontologically allows for it to "be" is therefore the *uncounted* multiplicity and the *act* of uniting. This void is "present" as "nothing" in the counted one. In this sense, *every* "being" is an "apophatic being," a creature in and of this void; everything is a body in and of the void; everything has an apophatic *aspect*.

The problem with Badiou's void—in contrast to those of Whitehead and Deleuze—is that it *presupposes* unity and identity as given for events to happen. Although it hints at the *process* of counting-as-one, it voids this process in the light of its "being (already) counted." This is important: what goes "uncounted" in Badiou, but is aimed at in Whitehead and Deleuze, is the *becoming* of this being (one); and what is postulated is that this becoming is always *intending* unity and identity.

Whitehead's account of the same "ontological difference" as presented by his *Category of the Ultimate* avoids the presupposition that we find in Badiou because the *act of becoming* is, at the same time, creative uniting *and* creative multiplying—the "becoming-one-of-many" and the "increasing-many-by-one." Its aim, now, is not only *unification*—as in Badiou—but also *multiplication*.[54] Other than the way "being" is for Badiou, for Whitehead "being" here is a *disjunction*, a potential, an infinite divisibility of infinite perspectives, an infinite depth of the multiplicities from which the becoming is the *process* that is *not* countable.[55] It is not countable ("counting-as-one"), because in Whitehead's ontology, *becoming* is neither in space and time, nor *is* it at all, that is, "one" or "identical." It does not per se create *identity* because it is always a unique becoming *and* perishing. It is only "countable" insofar as it "accounts for" a unification in space and time that is a *repetition of attainment* (of becoming) in building a "defining characteristic" (counted-as-one) which is that of a "society," an "organism," a "body." Only as *counted*, the character of "becoming" *in a nexus* will *define identity*.[56] With Kristeva, its "pattern" may now function as the *symbolic structure* that creates identity (an identical subject) in negating (or neutralizing) the *process of becoming*, the semiotic disorder, that underlies this "being."

Consequently, although Badiou's void enables us to speak of the apophatic nature of *every* body, what—in the light of the contrast between Badiou and Whitehead—happens in such an apophasis must be *differentiated* into the void of the "apophatic negation of bodying"—the *empty void* of the atomists (that Badiou favors)—and the void of the apophatic negation of this "*dualistic* marking of identity"—the *plentiful void* of Plato (that Whitehead favors). To say it in terms of multiplicity: while the first negation Badiou employs neutralizes difference (counting-as-one), the second negation, the one we find in Whitehead's concept of becoming as multiplication (which always goes unaccounted) seeks multiplicities in their depth, their becoming, their heterogeneity, their intensity, in their radicality "*before*" any counting of unity as identity.

APOPHATIC LIFE

In Whitehead and Deleuze, there are two *direct* accounts of such "bodies of the void," that is, of "apophatic bodies," that conceptualize the "bodying of the apophatic" (in the second sense). One is Whitehead's strange notion of an "entirely living nexus,"[57] and the other Deleuze's odd notion of a "body without organs."[58] Both concepts undercut any negation of bodying, but negate its dualistic construction of identity and unity.[59] Furthermore, in sensitivity to Derrida's "multiplicity of sexually marked voices," we may even recognize their complex sexual connotations: In a fundamental sense, both concepts in their recovering of the "orgiastic" over against the "organic" are seeking pure "life" and indicating pure "desire."[60] Like the "body without organs," which "discovers in itself the limits of the organized,"[61] the "entirely living nexus," although it can arise only in a highly structured society, "is not properly a society at all, since 'life' cannot be a defining characteristic. It is the name for originality, and not for tradition."[62] Freed from any social "defining characteristic," its pure intensity may be

> perhaps some thread of happenings wandering in "empty" space amid the interstices of the brain. It toils not, neither does it spin. It receives from the past; it lives in the present. It is shaken by its intensities of private feeling, adversion or aversion. In its turn, this culmination of bodily life transmits itself as an element of novelty throughout the avenues of the body. Its sole use to the body is its vivid originality: it is the organ of novelty.[63]

It is pure apophatic negation, since it has no "correspondences" to any identity, unity, or fixation by "character" or "form." It is not defined by its possibility (as pre-formation). It is the negation of any unification that may substitute its multiplicities of becoming. It is "apophatic life." Since it does not "correspond" (or repeat) any "origin," it is, indeed, the expression of *pure becoming*—thereby only "responding" to the "*Eros* of the Universe" of which originality, novel potential, and creative intensity is an incarnation.[64] It is the incarnation of pure life! They are pure *intensities!*[65] This is the singularity of "apophatic body" we may look for when we try to understand the "resurrected body."[66] This might also direct us to the singularity of an apophatic deity that is not negating bodying but, as in Cusa, is the pure *posse ipsum* of apophatic life.

We would, however, misunderstand the "orgiastic" and "erotic" nature of this "pure life" of an "orgiastic body" or an "entirely living nexus," if we become tempted to equate or identify it with pure *subjective* life or pure subjectivity (devoid of any objectivity). On the contrary (and maybe counter-conceptual at first glance), "pure life" is always beyond, before, and after subjectivity. The pure becoming of the "entirely living nexus" is always *satisfied* by its (subject's) death—as is true for any organic becoming.[67] Its "orgiastic" striving is not "possessed" by any subject; it is pre-subjective. Herein, it functions quite similarly to the pre-subjective process of *desiring* and *intensity* of the "body without organs" in Deleuze and the pre-symbolic *semiosis* in Kristeva. What Kristeva, Deleuze, and Whitehead indicate is the *body of the void*. A better way of phrasing it might be that they uncover bodying in its apophatic dimension of becoming, and they insist on multiplication as the veiled event in all structuring and subject-creating of the body. This void is pre-subjective and pre-objective, it is all-relative and non-exclusive, it is non-formal and in a plentiful sense "neutralizes" its phallogocentric binary markings. In this void, both the "entire living nexus" and the "body without organs" are unpossessed and unrepresented by the social constructions they un-structure or de/construct—both *de-* and *con*struct at the same time, ever new, ever the event of their becoming-multiple. In bodying the apophatic, these bodies live only by the traversing multiplicities of their becoming. Apophatic bodying, hence, is the caring about multiplicity, the love for the multiple. Its event of becoming is *polyphilic*.

With polyphilic bodying we may encounter the pre-subjective, pre-occupied dimension of our bodily relationship to the world as *pleromatic* and the *world* in all its interrelatedness as *the bodying of the void*—as a moving, fluid concourse of forces, emotions, feelings, energetic movements, rivers of tensions—what Merleau-Ponty names "the flesh"[68] and Glen Mazis calls "e-motion," that which "neither [is] just matter or spirit, neither physical nor mental, but something between and in motion,"[69] and that is the experience of Whitehead's non-localizable, all-relational body insofar as it "is to be conceived as a complex 'amplifier'"[70] of an all-pervading vibration of apophatic energy. Bodying the plentiful void of the *khora*, the "body without organs . . . [reveals itself as] an effective, intensive, anarchist body that consists solely of poles, zones, thresholds, and gradients."[71] In the freed movement of the event-field of polyphilic bodying the body exhibits a "complex energy" of becoming, at the same time physical and "emotional and purposeful,"[72] which is the *apophatic event of becoming*. Because it cannot be restated as "being" with its unity and identity, the *apophatic event of polyphilic bodying* can never be reconstructed from either the subjective/objective or the individual/social binaries. In the void, it is always traversing all bodying as Life—personal, cultural, ecological, or cosmic.

Polyphilia, the practice of the *pure life of the body*, however, is *dangerous*. Since this life is apophatic by being "*non*-social," as in Whitehead, it always corrupts the "organic" by becoming "orgiastic." It is dangerous, because it "answers to the notion of 'chaos'"[73] and "tumult, restlessness and passion underneath apparent calm. It rediscovers monstrosity."[74] It is dangerous because it is its "existence" to *interrupt* unification for unoccupied multiplicities. It can, indeed, *destroy* the organic (natural, cultural, or social) matrix that allows it to proliferate. But neither Deleuze's nor Whitehead's (nor Kristeva's) apophatic negation in the concepts of a "body *without* organs" or an "entirely living nexus" (or the poetic semiotic body) negates the organic body or the social organization of life (or the symbolic body) as such by indicating the becoming of an "un-social body" or an "un-organic body" or "organless body" (or a purely non-symbolic body). They urge, however, for an interruption that denaturalizes the account of this "organicity" as expression of the pre-given Law they understand as the secondary process of sedimentation.

That is to say: against any dualistic account of the first and second apophasis, which to differentiate was necessary conceptually, it is now important to see their intricate interaction: Because of its *endangered fragility*, the *apophatic body of pure life* exists only *with* the "organic body" (the "social body," the "symbolic body"), and its unifications of subjectivity; and its polyphilic practices come only *with* a certain ontological *neutralization* of itself. This is to say that the first and the second apophasis may after all not be viewed as dualistic alternatives (they are not forming a new binary), but in bodily practice only as interwoven *directions of bodying*. While the "organic" bodying aims at unification, thereby exercising the *unifying bodying* (with the danger of oppression), the "orgiastic" seeks the multiplication beneath, before, and after all unification, thereby exercising the *polyphilic bodying*. The "orgiastic" direction may become ecstatic, but it can never become undifferentiated and existing on its own (in Cartesian self-sufficiency).

Polyphilic bodying realizes pure difference, but its actualization is never "pure." This is also the reason that the organic, and with it the apophasis as neutralization of bodying, can never be totally overturned, nor might we wish to overturn it. Pure life would be instant death! Nevertheless, the uncovering of this bodying of multiplicity or the bodying of the apophatic plenitude, or the seeking of the "orgiastic" (in this sense) may be understood, as Deleuze does, as the "greatest effort of philosophy."[75] And it is here that we enter the mystical tradition again: Only the dead can "see" the "living God"[76]—only in the "mystical death," beyond subjectivity, beyond the difference of God and Creation, are we approaching the apophatic life of God. However, as in Eckhart, the "un-godding" of God, the indifference of God and World *in* the Godhead, is always already a process of self-differentiating, of the creative differenciation *of* God and the World *out* of the Godhead: creating and "godding"—polyphilic bodying.

MINING POLYPHILIA OR BODYING IMMANENCE

One of the most interesting aspects of Deleuze's and Whitehead's treatment of polyphilic bodying—which differentiates them equally from mystical monists and Cartesian dualists—is *how* they conceptualize the pre-structural and pre-subjective voidness of apophatic life *in relation* to the organic and unified construction of (natural, human, social, and cultural) bodies. By a bold move against any hermetic isolation of apophatic negation, they intimately interlock the organic and the orgiastic dimensions of bodying by indicating their abstract *incompleteness* for themselves and, hence, their *mutual* determination. Especially in their last essays, Deleuze's "Immanence: A Life— . . ." (1995) and Whitehead's "Immortality" (1941), they distinguish the polyphilic Life as the apophatic dimension *of* bodying, which is "pure immanence" and "value"—realities of non-subjective importance and meaning.

Instead of the negating bodying inherently related to *real* individuals and their *possible* generalities (first apophasis), Deleuze differentiates apophatic bodying in terms of *virtual* singularities and their *actual* universality (second apophasis). Instead of the individual with its subjective unity and objective (general) identity, in the (second) apophasis, we learn to experience the pre-individual singularities that in constant becoming reformulate the event of unique existence with its universal importance.[77] With this differentiation and the restatement of the "body without organs" as "field of consistency"[78] or "plain of immanence" that "traverses the organism,"[79] Deleuze enables us to discriminate the *subjective* life, which is individualized and possessed, from the *apophatic* life, which is "absolute immanence."

> Absolute immanence is in itself: it is not in something; it does not depend on an object or belong to a subject. . . . [T]he plain of immanence [cannot] be defined by a subject or an object that is able to contain it.—We will say of pure immanence that it is A LIFE, and nothing else. It is not immanent to life, but the immanent that is in nothing is itself a life. A life is the immanence of immanence, absolute immanence: it is complete power, complete bliss.[80]

What we encounter in the event of such singularities is that they appear only in the *indefinite* form of the verb—of "bodying" (going, smiling, greeting, and so on). This indefinite verbal process resonates with the *infinitive* form of Whitehead's "values." In his differentiation of a "World of Multiple Activities" from a "World of Value," Whitehead sought to articulate that neither the orgiastic nor the organic direction of bodying can be separated because "[e]ither World considered by itself is an abstraction." But while in Deleuze the virtual and the actual are both "real" and don't lack anything in relation to each other, Whitehead's "Worlds" of subjective life and apophatic life must for their "adequate description include . . . characterizations derived from the other, in order to exhibit the concrete Universe."[81] While the one World articulates "the multiplicity of finite Acts" (Deleuze's actualizations of the real), the other World is "grounded upon the unity of active coordination of the various possibilities of Value"[82] (Deleuze's virtual potentials).[83]

In Whitehead's view, however, Infinitive Values (abstract potentials) must become "*realized* values," that is, become *actualized* in multiple becomings. They must become *events of valuation* in order to become what they are: singular, important, immortal. In this "persuasive coordination of the essential multiplicities of Creative Action,"[84] it is Value, and not the Creative Act, that represents the *singularity* (and universality) of "*a* life" over against the individuality (and generality) of *the* subjective life. In its "*active* coordination," Value actualizes the singularity of Creative Acts. Whitehead's World of Value, again, in its "modification of creative action,"[85] which realizes the apophatic life rather than the subjective life of creative action, begins to unravel its uniqueness when we see it through the eye of the pre-individual and pre-subjective singularities of Deleuze's "Virtuals."

> A life is everywhere, in all the moments that a given living subject goes through and that are measured by given lived objects: an immanent life carrying with it the events or singularities that are merely actualized in subjects and objects. The indefinite life does not itself have moments . . . it offers the immensity of an empty time where one sees the event yet to come and already happened, in the absolute of an immanent consciousness. . . . The singularities and the events that constitute *a* life coexist with the accidents of *the* life that corresponds to it, but . . . they connect with one another in a manner entirely different from how individuals connect.[86]

For Deleuze the apophatic life takes place in the "immensity of empty time," in *connecting* intense singularities (which are neither subjective nor objective) in a *virtual event* that might become actualized in an extensive individual, and for Whitehead "the essential character of the World of Value . . . [is intensive] *coordination*."[87] But, while for Deleuze the virtual and the actual do not *change* one another although they *become* as virtual and actual event, for Whitehead Value and Actual *determine* one another mutually—as *activity*. Thus Values resonate with Deleuze's "timeless immensity" or are otherwise of *immortal intensity*, but since, other than in Deleuze, they require *mutual determination* with the "World of Active Creativity,"[88] this determination is also an

> activity [that] consists in the approach to the multiplicity by the adjustment of its many potentialities into finite unities, each unity with a group of dominant ideas of value, mutually interwoven, and reducing the infinity of values into a graduated perspective, fading into complete exclusion.[89]

Both thinkers conceptualize *polyphilic* bodying. The Virtuals and the Values are pre-individual, pre-subjective, and immense or immortal realities, which represent singularities of universal importance that group together in the event of virtual or actual becoming. In other words, the bodying of the singularities *in the event* is the apophasis of the bodying. It *becomes* a constantly changing "coordination" of singularities/intensities which is profoundly veiled in the substantiated individual/extensive body. In this insistence of the *event* of the constantly changing coordination of immortality and immensity of Virtuals and Values lies the character of the second apophasis as plenitude, as the *event of polyphilia*.

Nevertheless, both thinkers conceptualize *different* polyphilic events of apophatic bodying. Deleuze understands the event as the virtual reality of groupings and changing regroupings of singularities as potentials of becoming, whether they are actualized in an actual becoming or not.[90] Whitehead, on the other hand, allows for the *event* of polyphilia to occur only in *mutual* completion of Value and Actuality. In other words, this event occurs in *both* Worlds, as in Deleuze, but only in their mutual determination so that in both Worlds the event is an *activity* of realization, not an activation of a virtual reality.

If there is a deeper difference between their understandings of the event of polyphilic bodies it is that for Deleuze *becoming is a change in the event* (which is virtual),[91] and for Whitehead the *event is a change in becoming*.[92] While the virtual event is pure immanence and in its virtuality is independent of actualization, Whitehead's event needs to be *actualized* in becomings of which it is a *nexus* that exhibits no social character. But since such an event can be said to be either "the *difference* between actual occasions comprised in some determinate event"[93] or to be taken in as "a nexus in its formal completeness,"[94] the *form* of an "entirely living nexus" will precisely be its *formlessness*, its being a body (out) of the void. Hence the Values of the event are the togetherness of *actualized* singularities in the difference of each of the becomings of the event—its actualized Immortality as Void or as actualized Multiplicity. They *are* not just Multiplicity, but are driven by its actualization. In the Void, the actualized multiplicity of singular event-valuations, they become the event-field of polyphilia.

THEOPLICITY

The difference between the conceptualization of polyphilic bodying in Deleuze and Whitehead implies that Deleuze's Virtuals are real but not actual, that they need nothing, are pure immanence, and remain in their empty time of pure consciousness, and that Whitehead's Values, although also in immortal timelessness, only "exist" as immortal *activity*, an activity he names God: "The World of Value exhibits the essential unification of the Universe. Thus while it exhibits the immortal side of the many persons, it also involves the unification of personality. This is the concept of God."[95]

While the event of virtuality of the togetherness of singularities is Deleuze's polyphilic bodying, or the bodying of the apophatic, which happens in pure immanence and timeless, empty time, this togetherness of Values is immortal in the *activity* of God. Neither can, for Whitehead, the "character" of a living person nor the "character" of the "living nexus" of any society (cultural or ecological) be restated as a "defining characteristic" (of a soul or a world-formulary) so that the "maintenance of character is a way in which the finitude of the actual world embraces the infinitude of possibility."[96] Rather, it is the togetherness of singular Values without organization, the "orgiastic nexus," which is then, in the realm of Value, "immortal." As in Deleuze, this timeless Virtuality or Immortality is neither about subjectivity (e.g., of a person's immortality) nor any objectivity (e.g., the life of an event beyond itself or the permanence of a world-structure)—immortality is unpossessed—but about its *apophatic life*! It is "*a* life" that becomes immortal or, in other words, is the *event of immortal becoming*. That for Whitehead this World of Value, which is determined by the "concrete values" attained in the actualization in the World of Creative Action and Change, not only constitutes the "immortal side of the many persons" but also "involves the *unification* of personality" as such (in its *event*!) is a consequence of the immortal event as *activity*, which "is the concept of God."[97]

This difference is so profound that for Deleuze a concept of God arises only when the pure immanence is broken by a "One" that is a "transcendent that might contain immanence."[98] Then, it would be precisely the apophatic body of pure life, the "'body without organs' that God has stolen from us in order to palm off an organized body without which his judgment could not be exercised."[99] With this transcendent, the first apophasis would reappear as an "*Omnitudo realitatis*, from which all secondary realities are derived by a process of division."[100] For Whitehead, on the other hand, apophatic life would be broken if we destroy the *mutually determining activity* of the two Worlds, which in "mutual immanence" is *pure immanence*—not transcended by a deity but insisted on by the *activity* of the pure *posse ipse*.

God, for Whitehead, is not the transcendent One, not the "apophatic body" *of* the World of Creative Action (first apophasis). Rather God, in Whitehead's account, is *the* apophatic body *of the World of Value*. In "seeking intensity, and not preservation,"[101] God, then, is the *immanent* bodying of the apophasis of Immortality *of* the World of Creative Action *in* the World of Creative Action; that is, God's bodying immortalizes its "pure life" beyond its subjectivity or objectivity (second apophasis) only by becoming the polyphilic "Eros of the Universe," the *lover of the multiplicity* of the World of Active Creativity. This Divine apophatic activity I would like to name "theoplicity." In God's *apophatic activity*, God is the event of theoplicity, of insistence on multiplicity, in being the apophatic bodying of multiplicity, in being the polyphilic Eros of *initiation* and, at the same time, the polyphilic *salvation of the self-created multiplicity of the World of Creative Act*, thereby (by the Immortality for the World of Change) insisting on its *diversity*. Indeed, this invokes Cusa's apophatic "bodying" of God (the World of Value) and the World (of Change) with the pair of *complication/explication*, which is the *event* of becoming-God and becoming-World in the *same* act, which, in Whitehead, appears as the *mutual, completed activity* of the two Worlds.

Whitehead's biblical association of this activity with the "kingdom of heaven"[102] is easily misleading: It is not the collection of the subjective life (*the* life) in its individuality but the immortality of the Value, the *singularity* of the *apophatic* life (*a* life) of our bodying. And it is not a fugitive collection *out of* and aiming *beyond* the World of Creative Activity, but the activity for *its* intensity, *its* importance, *its* Immortality as *event of its becoming*. It is the activity of *theoplicity*: the insistence on *its* "essential multiplicities of Creative Action."[103] It is with the "kingdom of God" as with "*a* life" of "very small children [who] all resemble one another and have hardly any individuality, but they have singularities: a smile, a gesture, a funny face—no subjective qualities. Small children, through all their suffering and weaknesses, are infused with an immanent life that is pure power and bliss."[104]

Perhaps it is this apophatic life, this immanent life of "our" singularities, in which we are bodying the void, pure life, pure immanence, pure unique connectivity—thereby, in this apophatic bodying, becoming immortal *as* the event of God's activity. Perhaps the becoming-immortal in the "kingdom of God," then, is our unique importance for the World of Active Creativity, in which "the kingdom of heaven is with us," because "the love in the world passes into the love in heaven, and floods back again into the world."[105] And perhaps, this is the meaning of the biblical saying that it is to such as little children "that the kingdom of God belongs,"[106] because "a life" is the becoming of the apophatic body, the body of apophatic life—a smile, a gesture, a funny face. It is perhaps here that we might begin to understand the *activity* of God: the "coordination of the many personal individualities as factors in the nature of God"[107] and "the transformation in God's nature . . . beyond our imagination to conceive."[108] Perhaps it is this "power [that] lies in its absence of force,"[109] this "suffering and weakness"[110] of "a life," that is God's "pure power and bliss"[111]—"the Tragedy, the Sympathy, and the Happiness."[112] And perhaps this is the "resurrected body," the *soma pneumaticon*,[113] the apophatic body of pure life, that is immortal, infinitely important beyond objective death and subjective life.

Apophatic Ethics:
Whose Body, Whose Speech?

The Metaphysics of the Body

GRAHAM WARD

[To] be no part of any body, is to be nothing. . . . At most, the greatest persons, are but wrens, and excrescences; men of wit and delightfull conversation, but as moales for ornament, except they be incorporated into the body of the world, that they contribute something to the sustentation of the world.
JOHN DONNE, quoted in *Donne: The Reformed Soul,* by John Stubbs

What I am intending in this essay is to make some moves toward the construction of a metaphysics of the body. I embark on such a venture rejecting the dualism of physical and metaphysical, materiality and spirituality, nature and culture. What I mean by metaphysical with respect to the body is the system of values pertaining to embodiment *through which* embodiment is viewed, shaped, and performed. These are moral values such as goodness, social values such as justice, aesthetic values such as beauty, and claims to truth or the way things are. There is no materiality as such, then; materiality is always imbricated in conceptual evaluations. That does not mean that there is no difference between matter and thought, only that they cannot be separated in any inquiry into either. As Judith Butler pointed out a number of years ago now, "matter *matters*."[1] How matter *matters* is related to how it is made to speak, how it speaks, and what it speaks. Recently, we have been reminded that "[b]odies only speak if and when they are made heavy with meaning."[2] To be made "heavy with meaning" concerns the events in which the body presents itself, announces itself, and performs its meaningfulness. This is a series of operations that enacts a metaphysics. While one would have to admit that the dualism of matter and thought announces (rather than enacts) a metaphysics, it does so by creating a false clinical space in which materiality can appear as itself, shorn of any values, naked under the clinician's objective gaze. The body becomes an object, and its nakedness announces a metaphysics of the unveiled real. This is how things are: the God's-eye view. The creation of such a falsehood constitutes a bad rather than a good metaphysics. Ironically, the philosophical implications of this falsehood provide the foundations for a purely empirical view of any material object that deems itself anti-metaphysical! A good metaphysics, on the contrary, is one that avoids such falsehood-creating reductions, acknowledges the co-implication of meaning and matter, and recognizes that this co-implication is not epiphenomenal or a contamination of one by the other, but rather points to the necessary cohabitation of the material and the metaphysical.

Why does it seem absolutely critical that we move toward constructing a good metaphysics of the body, and bodies made "heavy with meaning"? Because of a cultural devaluation of the body that is shockingly ironic given the attention to fitness and diets. It is a devaluation that parallels the plethora of material goods that flood our high streets and the attention to branding which idealistically elevates the name above any material content. But let Bret Easton Ellis's novel *American Psycho* open up this contemporary phenomenon for us.

This is not a novel for the squeamish, but to my mind it is a parable of the reductions brought about by rapacious free-market capitalism. Bateman, Ellis's protagonist, is a high-earning young executive with a perfectly toned body who lives in New York. He is film-star handsome. He moves among a similar kind: people with what Ellis calls "hardbodies," clothed from socks to tie in designer-wear, continually on the lookout for new, expensive, and exclusive restaurants, people who look so alike and are so accustomed to using others that they frequently fail to identify each other. Bateman is also a sadistic killer who carves up and sometimes eats his victims with little show of emotion. "In my locker at Xclusive lie three vaginas I recently sliced out of various women I attacked in the past week. Two of them are washed off, one isn't. There's a barrette clipped to one of them, a blue ribbon from Hermès tied round my favorite."[3]

The book was written in the 1990s, and it points to a fascination with embodiment that has emerged with postmodernity and continues up to the present day with the public exhibition of dead bodies in a plastic coating.[4] We might call this "the return of the flesh," using the Pauline understanding of *sarx*: human beings reduced to their sheer physicality.[5] But *American Psycho* is a testimony to the hell of such a reduction—in fact Dante's *Inferno* echoes throughout the text, along with ads for *Les Misérables*. Bateman is the dark side of our fascination with the body. What concerns me amid this bourgeois cultural obsession with fitness, cooking, sex, and bodily fluids is its unapologetic materiality, a materiality that in fact cheapens the body. The overproduction of the body not only commodifies it, it dehumanizes it. And that's what Ellis's novel plays out. The body is just a billboard for an accumulation of brand names. Beneath it there is nothing, a void. Bateman senses that neither he nor anyone else is anything: "[W]here there was nature and earth, life and water, I saw a desert landscape that was unending, resembling some sort of crater, so devoid of reason and light and spirit that the mind could not grasp it. . . . [T]his was how I lived my life, what I constructed my movement around, how I dealt with the tangible."[6] Action is "movement," not agency, and only constructed; the tangible is only an image from a war with Afghanistan, Iraq, Lebanon, Darfur. The bodies are not persons, only screens for the commercialized world of labels. Ellis's novel presents us with the experience of contemporary nominalism.

I want then to "humanize" the body by arguing that the body can be valued positively only when it is viewed metaphysically and made "heavy with meaning." Again, in Pauline language, I want to put the *soma* back into the *sarx*, because the danger is not just mass murder in the name of a no one; the danger is the disintegration of the social into the cultural. Ellis's novel, I argue, depicts a final stage in atomism and alienation. Beyond the rampant and competitive individualism of *laissez-faire* capitalism lies the marketing of people as products; beyond the reduction to materialism lies the omnipresence of the image and the virtually real. In the past I have employed phenomenological analyses by thinkers such as Merleau-Ponty, Michel Henry, and Jean-Louis Chrétien and explored the nature of touch, for touch cannot reduce the body to an object seen, to a visible surface, in the way sight can. I have also examined the Eucharist as a site in Christian theology for rethinking embodiment, and rethinking

Jesus Christ's body and the ecclesial body in terms of displacement and transcorporeality. But it strikes me that beginning with the human body, even if it belongs to Jesus of Nazareth, only capitulates to the modern moment. It isolates this body as this object to investigate and prevents an understanding of the body as multiple: the body as enacted within a diverse range of scenarios that each stages different meanings and values that elude neat and stable identifications. The body as object, as Giorgio Agamben has observed, "is the new subject of politics. And democracy is born precisely as the assertion and presentation of this "body: *habeus corpus ad subjeciendum*, 'you will have to have a body to show.' . . . This new centrality of the 'body' in the sphere of politico-juridical terminology thus coincides with the more general process by which *corpus* is given such a privileged position in the philosophy and science of the Baroque age, from Descartes to Newton, from Leibniz to Spinoza."[7] In this essay, therefore, I want to begin from another perspective entirely, not with the human body but the more amorphous and fluid body politic.

THE BODY POLITIC

Influenced no doubt by Hellenistic thinking about parts and whole, there is a tendency to understand the word "body" in "body politic" as a metaphor: the physical body is an organized whole made of various interdependent parts, and so we extend this understanding of embodiment to a political organization. And so the body, either physically or politically, is a homogenous entity. Some commentators view this as Paul's use of the body analogy for the church in the First Letter to the Corinthians: the body is used properly with respect to the physical and metaphorically with respect to the ecclesial (or political). I will argue here that that is wrong. In fact, Paul uses *soma* to speak of sin (Rom 6:6), humiliation (Phil 3:21), dishonor (1 Cor 15:43), and death (Rom 7:24) as well. It is these other uses of the word "body" that can reorient our thinking of embodiment and open up our thinking about the human body in terms of the body politic.

In political thought, the body politic has had a long history. How long is still a matter of debate among Bible scholars and historians of late antiquity, though there are landmarks such as John of Salisbury's twelfth-century text *Policraticus* and Christine de Pisan's fifteenth-century *Livre de corps de policie*. Hobbes, of course, famously describes the State as an "artificial man." Hobbes, in fact, signals a new development in our understanding of the body, and so this is where we will begin. The medieval world recognized an analogical relation between human embodiment and social embodiment, an ontological continuity between personal and political corporeality. This relation was grounded in the ecclesial and sacramental understandings of body and the doctrine of the incarnation. The perfect form of embodiment (of being human) was Jesus Christ, and then, following the ascension of Christ into heaven, the Church was understood as being a kingdom of God but not yet fully realized, what Augustine termed the *ecclesia peregrinans* on its way to the *civitate Dei*. In *Corpus Mysticum*, Henri de Lubac details the development and complexities of this understanding of the body—although, unfortunately, because his emphasis is on the development of Eucharistic theology, he does not relate it to the body politic.[8] He could well have uncovered another significant layer in his excavation of the theological nexus with John of Salisbury's *Policratus* and Christine de Pisan's *Book of the Body Politic*, but he doesn't. The work of Ernst Kantorowicz in *The King's Two Bodies* charts much more of this story.[9] Nevertheless, Hobbes announces a new distinction between the natural and the artificial; the ontological relation no longer holds, and the "artificial man" is a human construct, a contracted relation, to rein in the murderous lusts of the natural man. There is no longer a controlling sacramental world order analogically related to a transcendent principle. Corporate living in which, as for Augustine, the private was related to the Latin "privatio"—a sin because a lack of something substantial to being human—was now a matter of convention. The social, from *socius*—a friend, a relation, an associate, a fellow human being—now divorced from a theological account of grace-bound nature was subjected to the cultural. As Bruno Latour points out: "From the myth of the social contract onward, the body politic has always been . . . a *problem*, a ghost always in risk of complete dissolution."[10] There is now no political body as an attestable fact. There is only an image and a series of actions which point to the event of that body, that make manifest a body. But it is not substantial and therefore only open to analysis in tracing the points at which it acts, politically.

Communities were on their way to being imaginary—in Benedict Anderson's understanding of that process:[11] voluntary associations in which certain cultural vehicles (a map, a museum, a national newspaper) create the means for reinforcing a collectivity and homogeneity. And this process advances as advances in communications take place.

My question is: What happens to the body—political and personal—when communities become imaginary and the body as a specific focus in a designated locality begins to disappear? Recently Michael Hardt and Antonio Negri expose a suggestive genealogy in the move from the body of the nation state to what they term the contemporary Empire. "The traditional army thus forms an organic fighting body, with generals for its head, lieutenants for its midsection, and the common soldier and sailors for its limbs," they write.[12] But in the move toward Empire there is a "command shift from a centralized model to a distributed network model."[13] They proceed to examine what this shift entails for the political body; I want to extend their analysis to include the personal, physical body. My suggestion is that in this shift toward the motile and the imaginary, bodies become virtual, disposable, because dispersed across networks of symbolic exchanges, enmeshed in the march of metaphors (to cite Nietzsche). And this situation, I would argue, is implicated in a bad metaphysics.

How then do we go about examining and therefore producing a good metaphysics of the body politic? Of course, we could reconstruct the analogical worldview; reimagining bodies from a certain Catholic theological perspective. And in *Cities of God* this is what I was attempting to do. But I want this time to examine the metaphysics of the State—the State conceived, after Hobbes, Locke, and Hegel, as the body politic. For the State is a metaphysical entity. Fascism recognizes this. Keynes, writing in 1915 about Germany, could speak of "a sort of idealism. The nation will grow into a 'closed unity,' "[14] a monad in which all parts constitute a whole. The fascist state as a collectivist state demands the commitment, even sacrifice, of its members for the good of the Fatherland. There is something ultimately Spinozistic about this—there are no individuals, only modifications of the transcendent One. The body figures forth this oneness, this "closed unity." For Spinoza that one body is God's: Spinoza's is the ultimate monotheism, the dissolution of all difference. With the fascist state the polity of the radical immanence of Spinoza's metaphysics is made plain, but now monotheism has become an imperial *Volksgemeinschaft*—the State as a religion.

But let us not suppose that liberal democracy avoids the metaphysics of the State. In theory political liberalism has required the minimalization of the State for the maximization of individual freedom, but in practice the minimalization of the State has meant merely concealing the State's intervention in civil society. In fact, from Habermas[15] through to post-democratic thinkers such as Colin Crouch,[16] political philosophers have pointed to the way in which the rise of the neoliberal state from the mid-seventies onward has increasingly eroded the public sphere and both subjected private freedoms to governmental surveillance and sought to fashion the society it governs. It does not speak of a "closed unity" but rather of being inclusive of difference, embracing plurality positively. But ultimately, any government has to govern, has to command a sovereign obedience. The State in liberal democracy hides its transcendent sovereignty by working through juridical systems and even, when necessary, declaring states of exception. For both Margaret Thatcher and Ronald Reagan and certainly for the two Bushes, the neoliberal State went hand in glove with fostering national allegiance to a religion of the State.

The thinkers of the liberal democratic state are the ones who tend to view the body with respect to the political as a metaphor, whereas fascists such as Mussolini accepted, like Hobbes, that political corporatism was the body macro made up of the bodies micro. But the metaphysics of Mussolini's and Hitler's understandings of corporatism were wrapped in the pseudoscientism of natural law, *Blut und Boden*, whereas Hobbes's corporatism was linked to mechanics. Again, the seeming lack of such a correlation between the political and physical body in the liberal democratic state might well be related to the hidden sovereignty in such a polity. That is, liberal democracy likes to portray itself as a political organism without a head; or with a head who is only *primus inter pares* and accountable to his or her cabinet, party, and the electorate. The head can be removed—impeached, for example, or voted out next time. But there is a headship; hung parliaments and coalition governments are always weak parliaments and weak governments. And the stronger the leadership given by the head, the more realized is a complete political vision for the State. This headship is frequently, it seems to me, expressed in terms of spearheading the nation's destiny: a nation's messianic mission. F. A. Hayek, in his famous and highly influential 1944 book against socialism, *The Road to Serfdom*, quotes the English political historian Paul Lensch, who wrote in a book published in 1918 about German socialism fulfilling "her historic mission of revolutionising the world."[17] The rhetoric is there in Lenin, as it was in Hitler and Mussolini: not just that certain nations have to be the political and economic avant-garde idea of nationhood, but this is their destiny. But how frequently have we heard this same rhetoric in more recent years in the speeches of leading liberal democratic leaders ? Since the 1980s decisionist leadership is a major style of neoliberal politics. I like to call this the return of the king.

Let me take this argument one step further before focusing explicitly on the metaphysics of the body. To return to Hobbes: the physiology and fluid mechanics of the body were just beginning to emerge when Hobbes was writing, and one of the key figures in that emergence was Hobbes's Oxford friend Richard Harvey. The mechanical body was then both a political and a physiological phenomenon at the same time. A similar correlation held between eugenics and an understanding of the State in fascism. The physical body or the way in which embodiment is understood and fashioned is then directly related to the body politic. I don't want to say one is the cause of the other. As I pointed out above, the distributed networks composing the new political "body" of Hardt and Negri's Empire must affect our conceptions of physical embodiment; the cultural and social forces that produce both discursive knowledges are very complex (and something I wish to analyze in the future). But while the Third Reich was being constructed, while its mythology was being cultivated, films were made that presented models of the Aryan body and its healthy physical development. The Fatherland was to be composed of sturdy, energetic, well-formed blonde and blue-eyed men and women. Foucault would call this biopower, a key aspect in modern methods of governmentality. And biopower is just as strong in liberal democracies, demonstrated by such phenomena as the enforced bans on smoking in public places and the suggestion in Britain that if patients do not follow their doctor's instructions and persist in bad habits—overeating, for example—they may be refused treatment by the same doctors in the future. But rather than biopower, I prefer the term used by Althusser (that Foucault adapted to his own end): state apparatuses.[18] The body politic works out its ideology through various state-informed practices acting through various state-related institutions—schools, universities, religious bodies supportive of state policy, the army, the police force, the courts, and so on. These apparatuses not only promote certain values and views of the bodies political and physical, they shape them through specific disciplines imbued with specific values (usually said to be moral values). By this means the metaphysics of one kind of body produces the metaphysics of another, and vice versa.

I hope it has now become evident why I thought it important to sketch the cultural appearance of the body in *American Psycho* as the trigger for my present examination.

HEGEL'S METAPHYSICS OF THE BODY POLITIC

It is time now to examine more closely these metaphysics, bearing in mind what I said earlier about the rejection of the dualism that pitches the materiality of the body against its spirituality, matter against thought. Hegel also rejected this dualism (though not the nature/culture distinction): the actual is the rational; the concept and its existence are two aspects of the same thing. Philosophical inquiry, either with regard to individual human bodies or the state itself, seeks to discern "in the semblance of the temporal and transient the substance which is immanent and the eternal which is present."[19] The word "eternal" points to Hegel's conviction that the metaphysics of the body implies a theology of the body. We will develop this later. For now it is important to understand that Hegel begins his treatise on the body politic with an analysis of human embodiment, leading eventually, in the closing section of the book to a study of international law and the world spirit.

> The concept and its existence [*Existenz*] are two aspects [of the same thing], separate and united, like soul and body. The body is the same life as the soul, and yet the two can be said to lie outside one another. A soul without a body would not be a living thing, and vice versa. The existence [*Dasein*] of the concept is its body, just as the latter obeys the soul which produces it.[20]

To some extent this could have come straight from Aristotle's *De Anima*, but what Hegel does explicitly is develop the logic of existence (body), concept (soul), and their interrelationship into an account of the content and form of the state and the operation of reason that governs both of them: "For *form* in its most concrete significance is reason as conceptual cognition, and *content* is reason as the substantial essence of both ethical and natural actuality."[21] For Hegel, then, the political body can only be understood in terms of a *thinking about* and a *reasoning concerning* the body.[22] The body politic is for Hegel, as we argued in the opening of this examination, inseparable from "concepts of truth and the laws of ethics."[23] The state is a metaphysical entity because it is an "inherently rational entity,"[24] that is, its form and content, its soul and body, participate in the great dialectical reasoning of *Geist* as its moves toward the actualization of the Absolute.

> The states, nations [*Völker*], and the individuals involved in this business of the world spirit emerge with their own *particular and determinate principle*, which has its interpretations and actuality in their *constitution* and throughout the whole *extent* of their *condition*. In their consciousness of this actuality and in their preoccupation with its interests, they are at the same time the unconscious instruments and organs of that inner activity in which the shapes which they themselves assume pass away, while the spirit in and for itself prepares and works its way towards the transition to its next and higher stage.[25]

A nation, composed of individuals in families, particular estates organized into corporations, and a governing class of professional civil servants, becomes a state. A group of individualized states, freely consenting to an international law code and under the sovereignty not of any single ruler but governed by the dialectic of the "universal spirit, the spirit of the world,"[26] gives way to the final state which is the actualization of that universal spirit. In terms of feeling and the ethical life this final state is the embodiment of faith, love, and hope. This is the point where the metaphysics of body becomes inseparable from a theology of the body. For the final embodiment of faith, love, and hope, a triad Hegel takes from the First Letter to the Corinthians (13:13), is the Christian kingdom of God, Christianity being the highest expression of the spiritual and the rational: "heaven down to earth in this world, to the ordinary secularity of actuality and representational thought."[27] This is the end of history, though not the end of time.

Francis Fukuyama is right to read Hegel as announcing a final consummation, although Fukuyama emphasizes that the key virtue of such a realm is individual freedom, rather than faith, love, and hope, expressed in a universal democratic condition.[28] He misunderstands the nature of freedom for Hegel. Because Hegel would not concur; he is no liberal. The individual, as he makes plain in the Introduction to his *Phenomenology of Spirit*, loses his or her identity as such. An individual's freedom is sublated to the freedom of the whole in the actualization of the freedom of the Absolute *Geist*. The only true freedom is the "free infinite personality."[29] The state is the end in itself, everything else, everyone else, is sacrificed to the logic of the state. This is hardly Fukuyama's apotheosis of free market liberal democracy. In fact, though Hegel's account is evidently communitarian, there is a question over whether it is democratic at all. A whole crowd of commentators have believed that he provides the philosophical basis for totalitarianism. This is wrong. Hegel positively endorses constitutional monarchy—"the achievement of the modern world, in which the substantial Idea has attained infinite form."[30] This is as far as he goes in his last major work, *Elements of the Philosophy of Right*, but in view of Hegel's theology and the working of the universal spirit beyond the particularities of nationhood, constitutional monarchy would find its consummation in a Messianic rule. "[T]he usual sense in which the term 'popular sovereignty' has begun to be used in recent times is to denote *the opposite of that sovereignty which exists in the monarch*. In this oppositional sense, popular sovereignty is one of those confused thoughts which are based on a *garbled* notion [*Vorstellung*] of the people. *Without* its monarch and that *articulation* of the whole which is necessarily and immediately associated with monarchy, *the* people is a formless mass. The latter is no longer a state."[31] The constitutional monarchs of nations must give way, in the final actualization of *Geist*, to the absolute monarch; the realization of the kingdom of God is the realization of the rule of Christ whose Spirit was given totally to the world following the death of God on the Cross. We will return to the "formlessness" of popular sovereignty at the end of this essay; for now it is important to understand that Hegel cannot easily be secularized in the way Fukuyama, after Kojève, attempts. In fact, secularization is the final achievement of the coming down of heaven to earth, of the laboring of faith, love, and hope; only then is the transcendent principle made fully immanent.

In one sense, that Fukuyama reads Hegel badly is not the point. The point here is that Hegel's state as the body politic is a thoroughly metaphysical notion, and those individuals whose wills and desires are sublated to the logic of the state's development participate in a spirituality that refuses the sheer materialism and its consequent irrationalism announced in Ellis's novel. It is because bodies are spiritual that they are free and must be political. One observes in *American Psycho* that there is no political action. In fact, there cannot be when all action and agency is reduced to the anonymity and moral anesthesia of "movement" in an infinite Sierra Nevada. "Hardbodies" are consumers, customers, or clients; they are not citizens. Nevertheless, there is a certain symmetry between Bateman's world and Hegel's. For, with Hegel, one has to understand that the language of the infinite, the truth, the eternal, the universal, and the absolute are defined within the dialectic circles of the immanent. His speculative philosophy is a metaphysics, announcing, in Kantian terms, a transcendental logic, but it has nothing to do with transcendence itself. For Hegel this is a theological point that turns on a conception of the Trinity in its working in the world. Christ on the Cross dissolved the transcendence of God the Father into the immanent operations of the spirit of Christ within the world. Two important corollaries issue from this philosophical theology.

First, there is no alterior standpoint beyond the dialectics of this world. The salvation this effects results from a relation between the mental (*geistliche*) contemplation that goes on within this world, such as the philosopher's speculative logic, and the movement of absolute mind (*Geist*). The relation does not admit alterity, a fundamental and unsublatable difference such as might be possible in the analogical worldview. Instead, there is a univocal relationship between the spiritual (*geistliche*) operations within human beings and the Absolute spirit (*Geist*).

Second, the theological dynamic for the dialectic of history is the way of the Cross. The work of the Spirit is a work of negation. The trajectory along which the politics of the state moves toward the ultimate kingdom is constituted by negativity. Hegel analyzes this work of negation in terms of the will and desire in determining the particularity of the "I." There are two moments in this particularization. In the first moment the "I" emerges from "the element of *pure indeterminacy*," from a negative freedom that Hegel describes as "the freedom of the void, which is raised to the status of an actual shape and passion."[32] At this point what is posited to the "I" in its self-contemplation is a representation, an abstraction. But Hegel is not content, in this analysis of the "I," to restrict himself to psychology. There can be a collective "I," a corporate personality. Hegel then immediately adds: "[I]f it turns to actuality, it becomes in the realm of politics or religion the fanaticism of destruction, demolishing the whole existing social order, eliminating all individuals regarded as suspect by a given order, and annihilating any organization which attempts to rise up anew."[33] What we glimpse here is Hegel's positive evaluation of the French Revolution as it appears more clearly in his letters: the pure destructiveness and iconoclasm that characterized the Reign of Terror. This is Hegel's account of a negative or apophatic body politics. But the second moment in the determination of the "I" is not a cataphatic reversal. The actual *positing* of this determinacy and differentiation "is just as much a *negativity* and cancellation [*Aufheben*] as the first—for it is the cancellation of the first abstract negativity. Just as the particular is in general contained within the universal, so in consequence is this second moment already contained within the first and is merely the *positing* of what the first already is *in itself*."[34] Indeterminacy is negated to become the determined and the determined then is overreached in a further dialectical sublation, and so on. Speculative philosophy, then, as a political science, must "apprehend the negativity which is immanent within the universal."[35]

What are the consequences of this radical immanence driven by the universal laboring of negativity, for a metaphysics of the body politic? One first has to observe we are not treating monism as anything like the way it appears in Spinoza—exactly because Hegelian metaphysics is dynamic and differentiation is not epiphenomenal. If the fascist state can be associated with Spinoza's metaphysics, then with Hegel we approach something similar to Lenin's notion of the permanent revolution. The world spirit working in and as the human spirit continually transforms the cultural given. Hegel notes that modern society with its prevailing polity is an outworking of the Reformation and the French Revolution. But as we saw, this modern politics will also give way to what has yet to appear, though it remains concealed in the present as a potential. If there is one overriding polity it is a theocracy, only there is no direct rule by God; the operations of the Absolute are always and only mediations through concrete circumstance. Though Hegel's own representation of the state comes closest to being oligarchic—since the monarch is only a figurehead and the actual governing proceeds through bureaucratic leaders—the content of the state is never fixed. Its essential form is neither liberal democratic, communist, monarchic, fascist, or oligarchic; and yet potentially it is all these polities and more. Hegel did not celebrate the French Revolution because it was a move from absolute monarchy to democracy. He celebrated it because "the human spirit has outgrown like the shoes of a child" the ancien régime.[36] Although any state has specific content, then, it is continually subject to indeterminacy. There is always a body image, if you like, that gives shape to the body itself, but the image is governed by a prevailing iconoclasm, a political and theological apophaticism. This forestalls idolatry, as in a manner similar to the way the apophatic safeguards the mystery and transcendence of the divine for the mystic theologian. But it is with the mention of "transcendence" that we have to recall the immanentalism of Hegel's thinking on the body politic. The working of the negative in Hegel is a continual reminder of limitations, of finitude; but it is also, because it is an operation of *Geist*, a continual reminder of the infinite. One might suggest that Hegel has transposed the mystic's cosmological notion of transcendence into a historical one, except that history cannot be infinitely open for Hegel—he would then fall victim to his own analysis of the nihilism of the "bad infinite." A final state, an end of history, is presupposed. The system has a closure—and Hegel does not view the immanent development and exposition of *Geist* as a circle that endlessly repeats itself: what Nietzsche would call eternal reoccurrence.[37]

As with the mystic's apophasis, Hegel's negativity announces a limited understanding, the lack of a panoptic view. But Hegel is convinced that we develop a greater and greater understanding and discernment of the Absolute—that is what thought and rationalization are concerned with bringing about. The body (political or otherwise) does not understand itself fully, cannot grasp itself as an object. It is on a journey, collectively, through a long crucifixion, to an eternal salvation: a final disenchantment, an ultimate enlightenment which is a grand demystification. The laboring of the negative requires an ascesis, just as it requires a teleology, but does it also require a continual suffering? Is this why Hegel sees war as both inevitable and necessary? Why peace is viewed as stasis, as "people become stuck in their ways"?[38] Why, in the closing sections of his analysis is "sacrifice" the descriptor that is foregrounded? In the gospels the ascesis of the body demands also health, glorification, delight; the eschatology is both futural and present: the kingdom is not just to come, it is already here. I can see how Hegel would concur with this eschatology, but I wonder whether his anthropology (and by extension political science) remains too Lutheran: too oriented to the working of the crucifixion. The passage from Good Friday to Easter Sunday is a developmental and dialectical one. And my question is whether this metaphysics can adequately sustain a metaphysics of the body; whether a sustainable metaphysics requires an exteriority, a threshold of transcendence, a God otherwise than being that is not one with the operations of sublation? Does Hegel need a more adequate doctrine of analogy that would announce a sacramental politics of the body? How would this sacramental understanding of the body (political and otherwise) revise Hegel's thought?

These questions can best be sharpened when comparing Hegel's metaphysics of the body politic to that of Saint Paul. Although Saint Paul is strictly examining the nature of the church, the corollary of Hegel's argument is that the state is the church.[39]

SAINT PAUL'S METAPHYSICS OF THE BODY POLITIC

In recent years there has been much critical attention paid to Paul and the political. This has only partly come from the New Testament critical industry itself—through the work of Richard Horsley,[40] Neil Elliot,[41] and Bruno Blumenfeld.[42] It has also come from philosophico-political voices concerned with examining and responding to where we are culturally situated today—through the work of Alain Badiou,[43] Giorgio Agamben,[44] and Slavoj Žižek.[45] But there remains an interesting reticence in both the New Testament cultural historians and interpreters with respect to examining the major model organizing Pauline ecclesiology—the body. Blumenfeld recognizes "the critical, foundational role that the body of Jesus plays."[46] He comes closest to breaking through that reticence when, in his exposition of the political subtext of Paul's Letter to the Philippians, he observes Paul's "wide body-language register" and concludes: "The *polis* reaches the depths of physicality."[47] The *ekklesia* is for Blumenfeld the heart of the new political community (the *polis*) Paul is committed to forging. But he adds little more to these observations, given how critical and foundational the body is, later in his book, in his detailed analysis of the Letter to the Romans (one of the four major texts employing the body analogy). We are told again that "[t]he idea of Christ as the body of which the people are members, connects again with the idea of the *polis*," that Paul is abandoning the older "*polis-psuche* similarity" (of Plato and Aristotle) and this "could have been mediated by the Hellenistic Pythagorean pseudepigrapha, which used both political similes" (e.g., Pseudo-Archytas).[48] Earlier in the book, Blumenfeld has taken us exhaustively through every one of these political pieces of pseudepigrapha. Where these new analyses of the political Paul, by both New Testament scholars and cultural theorists, leave us is very unclear. For Badiou, Agamben, and Žižek, in quite different ways and with different agendas, Paul is a revolutionary, a left-wing radical *avant la lettre* and able to offer us victims of both modernity and liberal democracy a way forward. To Blumenfeld, Paul is a conservative supporter of Roman Imperialism (a precursor to the famous example of Jewish accommodationist policy by Josephus) and a defender of the Pax Romanum. For Elliot, Paul is a pragmatic thinker whom we should not expect to find having "a clear, consistent, univocal 'pro-Roman' or 'anti-Roman' posture."[49]

To this celebrated collection of critics excavating the political Paul should be added a second group of New Testament commentators working with *traditionsgeschlichtlich* interests in the Pauline body going back to at least 1919 and Traugott Schmidt's *Der Leib Christi*.[50] From this scholarship, two theologies of the body as a *societas* are evident, the first found paradigmatically in Paul's First Letter to the Corinthians and the second found paradigmatically in the Letter to the Ephesians. The latter has Christ as "the head of the church, his body" (Eph 5:23); the former has the church as an ancephalous body. Critical opinion is divided as to whether these two theologies cohere, and much of the argument revolves around whether Paul can be recognized at the author of the Letter to the Ephesians. For myself, on the basis of the undoubted Pauline authorship of the Letter to Philemon and the Letter to the Colossians, and the profound relationship between these two letters and the Letter to the Ephesians, I accept Ephesians as Pauline and view the two theologies as constituting one coherent line of thought.

> For just as the body is one and has many members, and all the members of the body, though many, are one body [*onta en estin soma*], so it is with Christ [*outos kai o Christos*]. For by [*en*] one Spirit we were all baptised into one body—Jew and Greeks, slaves and free—and were all made to drink of [*en*] one Spirit. For [*kai gar*] the body does not consist of one member but of many. If the foot should say, "Because I am not a hand, I do not belong to [*estin ek*] the body," that would not make it any less a part of the body. And if the ear should say, "Because I am not an eye, I do not belong to the body," that would not make it any less part of the body. If the whole body were an eye, where would be the hearing? If the whole body were an ear, where would be the sense of smell? But as it is, God arranged the organs in the body [*etheto ta mele*], each one of them, as he chose. If all were a single organ, where would the body be? As it is, there are many parts, yet one body. The eye cannot say to the hand, "I have no need of you" nor again the head to the feet, "I have no need of you." On the contrary, the parts of the body which seem to be weaker are indispensable, and those parts of the body which we think less honourable we invest with greater honour, and our unpresentable parts are treated with greater modesty, which our more presentable parts do not require. But God has so composed [*sunekerasen*] the body, giving greater honour to the inferior part, that there may be no discord [*schisma*] in the body, but that the members have the same care for one another. If one member suffers, all suffer together; if one member is honoured, all rejoice together. Now you are the body of Christ and individually members of it [*kai mele ek merous*]. (1 Cor 12:12–27)

There are several points to observe about this passage: first, its predominantly ontological tenor—the repeated use of *estin* and *onta*. The verb "to be" is not used merely as a copula; it is employed emphatically in the sense of "to participate" as the prepositions "*en*" and "*ek*" emphasize. Hence the translation "belong to," in this Revised Standard Version (RSV) (the Authorized Version translates more literally). But the ontology announced here is not one which is concurrent with the natural order: we do not grow into becoming members of this body; we are initiated into it through baptism. By inference, then (and this would be a second point) this body "which is also Christ" (*outos kai o Christos*) is both related to and yet different from other physical bodies. *Kathaper* is the Greek term introducing a similitude, but the similitude does not have the grammatical logic of simile where the predicate intrinsically and ontologically belongs to the substantive ("as white as snow").[51] *Kathaper* has the grammatical logic of analogy where the properties of two substantives (in this case the human body and the body of Christ) share properties but in a way that neither admits of their being intrinsically related or extrinsically associated. I concur with the New Testament scholar John A. T. Robinson: "Paul uses the analogy of the human body to elucidate his teaching that Christians form Christ's body. But the analogy holds because they are in literal fact the risen organism of Christ's person in all its concrete reality. . . . It is almost impossible to exaggerate the materialism and crudity of Paul's doctrine of the Church as literally now the resurrected *body* of Christ."[52] As I argued in *Cities of God* the body of Christ becomes the governing body, and the condition for the possibility for a new ordering of the human body. I grant this is a theological rather than a philosophical argument. In the grammar of analogy the attribution of properties proceeds from the primary to the secondary analogate. What I am suggesting here is that the transcendent body of Christ redefines the human body from a more exalted, in fact, glorified position—so that the properties co-abiding in Christ's body are communicated to the human body. This does not merely boil down to the statement that I do not naturally as a human body belong to the body of Christ. Nonetheless, baptism "by (*en*) the one Spirit" marks an ontological shift from being in the world to being *en Christo* (a favorite use by Paul of the dative of location).[53] But then neither members nor even Christ is translated out of this world—the use of *en* suggests rather another level of ontological intensity available in this world but not concurrent with it. There is an incorporation effected by baptism, and this incorporation does not leave the human body as such unchanged. The character of that change we will pursue below and conclude here that the incorporation is made possible because of the analogical relation.

This incorporation brings about two changes that seem to be antithetical to life in the world. The first change is with respect to social and racial differences: Jews, Greeks, slaves, free are indicators of social tensions and hierarchies. In the Letter to the Galatians, Paul will add "male and female" and characterize the socio-sexual tensions and hierarchies. Each of these positions was embedded within value systems concerning the human body—class notions of embodiment, ethnic notions, sexual notions, and so on. But incorporated *en pneumati* and *en Christo* a new social order is announced. The Christocentric body politic constitutes this order. It is not an order where difference is elided—the body is not one organ but many different functions. This is not then Spinoza's monism. But the differences, functioning as such, live out this polity. Paul does not equate this body with a group of people, not even the church in Corinth. It is a not an object visible in the world. This is not a collection of people so much as a coordination of operations. The body is made manifest in those events in which it is seen to be working. Its only location (which is not a location with either spatial or temporal coordinates that can be mapped) is in Christ and the Spirit. There are not necessarily any institutions—no estates, no civil society—although the institution of the church necessarily presents a visible representation of the notion "church." (How else would the people learn about the church, its meaning and its values?) But there is governance. The governing is an inner composition (*sunekerasen*) effected by God. The word *sunekerasen* is the aorist active of the verb *sugkerannumi*, a highly unusual word for Paul. Although it is found in Plato, the verb does not occur in the Septuagint (LXX) at all and is only found twice in the New Testament, here and in Hebrews 4:2. In both cases it means to mix, temper, or be united with, though in the passive it can describe very close relationships between people. It is related to the verb *parakolutheo*—"to follow closely," "to follow beside" (as in discipleship)—and *sudzeugnumi*—"to yoke" (again used in the Gospels with respect to discipleship). The tense and voice here with Paul suggests that God put together this body at some definite point in the past and that this action continues until now. Commentators seemed to fight shy of this verse, but I would suggest that what Paul is referring to here is the making of the primal human being. For the verse has shifted from the body of Christ to the physical body itself—in the context of Paul's wider theological interests, from the second to the first Adam. The body then, human and divine, does not issue from Bateman's void, therefore without meaning. It is created by an act of God and preeminently significant, "heavy with meaning." The politics of incorporation in the body of Christ fashion an understanding of the body as God first created it. Again, to go back to what I said above—the Christic body becomes the model for understanding all embodiment. The act of discipleship, which is the operation of a Christic politics, realizes these coterminous bodies—the human and the divine.

Let us take this further. Earlier, I mentioned Althusser's notion of state apparatuses that fashion ideologies which we live out, often unconsciously, ideologies that have implicit within them value systems. As I said, Foucault examined such apparatuses in terms of "technologies," particularly technologies of the self. And Talal Asad, in two of the essays collected in *Genealogies of Religion*, examines these technologies in terms of medieval monastic institutions[54]—extending Foucault's analyses of confession, for example. But I want to go further, on the basis of this relation exposited by Paul. Of course, the human bodies constituting the ecclesial community at Corinth will be fashioned by specific institutional practices. In fact, Paul will go on later in the letter and in other letters to outline a number of those practices—and Dale Martin, among others, has helped us see the understanding of the human body with respect to these practices and their context.[55] Martin enables us to see the human body as a cultural product. I want to enable us to glimpse the human body as a product of the Christic polity, the product of a fundamental realignment that goes on in the incorporation into the body of Christ. For no doubt also the Greek, the Jew, the slave, and the freeborn will each be fashioned by the dominant practices defining their own cultural situation. The Greek will live out her Greekness, and all that is culturally entailed; the Jew will live out his Jewishness, with all that is entailed. The slave will live out his slavery, and the freeborn what was then valued and expected of one who is born free. But institutions or state apparatuses aside, when the Greek, the Jew, the slave, and the freeborn are incorporated into the body of Christ, these fashionings are transposed by a further working of the Spirit. Paul's language describes that transposition. For the Greek, the abrupt contrast between the things of the soul (*psuchikos*) and the things of the spirit (*pneumatikos*) in 1 Corinthians 2:14 or the phrase "the mind of flesh" (*tou noos tes sarkos*) in Colossians 2:18 is nonsense. For the Jew the phrase "in the flesh" (*en sarki*) in Romans 7:5 and 8:9 brings confusion because human beings *are* flesh; they are not *in* a domain that is fleshly. The language of freedom and bondage equally overturns what either of these terms might mean to one born free and another born into slavery. *En Christo*, Greek, Jew, slave, and freeborn become something else. They live out and become produced as hands, feet, eyes, ears, honored parts, inferior parts, weaker parts, and stronger parts within this new body. They become incorporated into other forms of behavior, other value systems, other conceptions of embodiment and pneumatic movements that fashion their bodies anew—in accordance with the living, that is, operational body of Christ. Hence Paul's elliptical phrase "the Lord for the body [*o kurios to somatic*]" (1 Cor 6:13)—where "Lord" is a political title. The human body is fashioned by the politics of the body of Christ and the position of that body with respect to other cultural corporations that make up "the world." What does this signify?

Any possible democratization in terms of equality—as individual members within one body, ruled over by one Spirit, equally valued before God, and so on—does not occur necessarily in terms of social, sexual, or racial status. It occurs through the new politics of living in Christ and being governed by a command to love one another. Love in the thirteenth chapter of the First Letter to the Corinthians constitutes the great erasure of statuses of any kind because it "bears all things, believes all things, hopes all things, endures all things" (13:7). What being a member of the body of Christ entails, in other words, is a political discipleship that does not readily translate into institutions or even modes of political activity in this world. Of course, this discipleship and the politics it enacts take place in and with respect to this world, but its import lies in the operations of God with respect to salvation understood as becoming truly human, truly embodied. This is important for understanding the apophaticism of the body of Christ. The New Testament scholar John A. T. Robinson sums up why, commenting on the First Letter to the Corinthians 13–20: "It is in their [Christians'] 'bodies' (v.15)—as *somata* and not merely 'spirit'—that Christians are members of Christ . . . so there is no real line between the body of His [Christ's] resurrection and the flesh-bodies of those who are risen with Him."[56] *Sarx* or mere flesh dies; it is mortal, weak, corruptible, and prey to sin. But since there is only one body, *soma*, composed of many bodies, *somata*, and that body is a glorified and resurrected body; *soma* is immortal, eternal. This "[b]ody is not among the things that are seen (*ta blepomena*, i.e., the *sarx*) and belong to this age only (*proskaira*), but is *aionion* [eternal], belonging to the age to come," Robinson concludes.[57] The human body participating in the risen, eschatological body politic of Christ, lives in a transpositional state. It has only liminal identity. It lives physically in this world and equally as physically in the world to come. We can observe this liminal condition in the verbal tenses of Paul's description in the Letter to the Ephesians: God "raised us up with him [*sunegeiren*—aorist active] and made us to sit with him [*sunekathisen*—aorist active] in the heavenly place in (*en*) Christ" (Eph 2:6). The verbs are newly coined by Paul to emphasize our con-formity in the one body. Just as, in Paul, there is a continuity between the physical and historical body of Jesus the Christ and his resurrected body, so there "is therefore no ultimate distinction between the individual resurrection and the one resurrection Body."[58] The cataphatic body, that which is visible (after the Greek *kataphasis*—that which can be spoken about) is also, in Christ, apophatic (after the Greek *apophasis*—a denial, a negation), that which is beyond the powers of human beings to conceive or think. According to Liddell-Scott, *phasis* is often in Greek associated with *phainomai*, appearance. Hence Paul has to invent a new language in which to sketch his theological conception of this body.[59] For what individual *soma* can say "I am a hand . . . or a foot . . . or an eye . . . or an ear"? No one can identify their function. And if they cannot identify their function, then their functioning is hidden from them also. Maybe not hidden entirely insofar as they have a sense of vocation, but the events in which they enact the church as a "foot" or a "hand" or an "ear"—those events into which they are identified as the operative body of Christ—are only graspable as acts of faith. Their identity within the body of Christ is worked out in Christian terms of practices of faith, hope, and love that go beyond the naming and labeling in this world. While remaining a Greek, a Jew, a male, a female, a slave, or a freeborn, one is also and more significantly a member of the body of Christ. A body which is "heavy with meaning" that is not possible to translate. One condition or identity is not necessarily effaced in the other, but it is transformed in ways beyond telling. One discovers one's somatic nature in the tranquility of recollection; it is not self-evident. It is discovered not discretely but by continuing to work within the body of Christ, a new polity, with new relationships and new distributions of power that can never find their full realization in any political system in this world, which therefore resist accommodation with the politics of this world and offer possibilities for an alternative politics. The altar on which Paul asks the Roman Christians to present their bodies as a living sacrifice can never be identified with a particular throne. The body is continually being given, continually moving out and enacted elsewhere, and as such it continually transcends strict identifications that it imposes on itself or that are imposed on it. The body is never there as such (as if a static object in a freeze-framed still); the body is there only because it moves, it circulates, it acts, it disseminates its knowledges, rejecting, absorbing, and adapting itself to new knowledges. It is in this way that it can be deemed apophatic.

It is because *soma* is apophatic that it is for Paul always and only a theological and metaphysical entity. Hence there is a body of sin and a body of death. These are metaphysical conditions of embodiment effecting *sarx*, conditions *sarx* has little or no understanding of, because *sarx* is the secularized, demystified body. This is the body that can be viewed as a physical and, politically, artificial machine for Hobbes and a worthless, political nonentity dressed in designer labels that bear no relation to the products they are labeling for Bateman. *Sarx*, even though it possesses for Paul a psychic nature (the "fleshly mind" of Col 2:18), is a materialist reduction of embodiment, not necessarily bad in itself, for it is the purely natural condition for humanity, although to be human is have a body, not just to be flesh. *Sarx* cannot inherit the kingdom of God (1 Cor 15:50), and it is the body, not the flesh, that is redeemed. The bodies of sin and death, are, like the body of Christ, realms; but they are realms of enslavement. They too are metaphysical and operate transcendentally in this world; but they constitute a bad metaphysics. The good metaphysics is only arrived at through enacting the body in and through the body of Christ, through the politics of discipleship, through the eternal life of the Spirit. Which returns us to Hegel.

What is immediately apparent is that the working of the negative in Hegel is quite different from the operation of the living Spirit in Paul. For Hegel, God has given Himself entirely to this world through the death of Jesus Christ on the Cross. Through the work of the "inwardness of this principle is the . . . reconciliation and resolution of all opposition."[60] For Paul, the immanent logics of this world have to bow to the power not of the death of God but the resurrected Christ. There is no reconciliation and resolution of all opposition; those not participating in the body of Christ are sundered from the life of God. Any reconciliation and resolution is on the basis of total commitment to a new covenant between God and human beings. Paul speaks of an end to "discord [*schisma*] in the body . . . [when] the members have the same care for one another" (12:25). But opposition for Hegel is the dialectical encounter with the other, and resolution is the sublation of that otherness, an incorporation. The body politic, like the human body, is caught up in temporality, desiring and willing an eternal condition of rest beyond representation in the absoluteness of the Idea. There is something Gnostic in this desiring—a yearning to be beyond the materiality of state institutions, religions, and sciences in an unbounded universalism. And yet it is never so simple with Hegel, who to the end affirms the concrete and the actual in what can only be the development of this world into the kingdom of God. The Christian body politic for Paul is already constituted in the risen Christ—it can never be then a development from within this world. Furthermore, in the incorporation into Christ otherness and difference remain and are unsublatable. The Greek will continue Greek, the Jew, Jew; the hand will not be the eye; the ear will never be the foot. The difference and materiality of *somati* are guaranteed by the one transcendent *soma*. Not being of this world, and yet enabling the world to participate in it, this body can be truly metaphysical in a way that makes possible a postmaterialist condition. It enables a true apophasis of the body that guarantees its mystery and its sanctity through a politics of redemption.

Emptying Apophasis of Deception: Considering a Duplicitous Kierkegaardian Declaration

T. WILSON DICKINSON

Beginning a series of supposedly edifying remarks with the declaration that one is always wrong is likely to raise suspicion. Yet this is the central thrust of the text that will be the primary concern of this essay, the sermon of Kierkegaard's pseudonym, the Jutland Pastor. The central meditation of this subversive supplement to the multivoiced *Either/Or* is that "The upbuilding lies in the thought that in relation to God we are always in the wrong."[1] For an audience of discerning listeners, this might serve as a good indication to stop listening or abruptly exit. Such an admonition may lead the listener to one of two conclusions: that the speaker's insights will inevitably lead to failure or, perhaps, that it is a smokescreen for a great deception. That is, perhaps, by declaring an unending condition of "being in the wrong" the Preacher has undertaken a mystification par excellence, gaining what he has claimed to deny by finding an unmovable point in which his own discourse stands in the right above all others. In a time of televangelists—who are often little more than self-interested salesmen, shrouding their greed with the comforting cloaks of humility, forgiveness, and salvation—the contemporary reader quite likely understands the duplicitous possibilities that accompany the pretenses of piety. The assertion of such an extreme position

---

I thank Christopher Boesel, John D. Caputo, Catherine Keller, and Edward Mooney for their comments on this essay. I wish only that I could have more adequately responded to the call of their criticisms and insights.

might lead one to wonder if this apparition of self-doubt is not a dissembling declaration that disguises one who truly holds the opposite. One may be right to be suspicious of such a performance, yet in this essay I hope to disrupt the structure of performer and spectator that underlies this suspicion and one's relationship to texts more generally. That is, I do not want to view the performance of this text merely in terms of a dissembling operation, behind which one can find what is real; rather I want to consider the manner in which the pastor, his declarations, its hearers, and readers are all caught up and co-implicated in dynamic practices. Therefore, the Preacher's performance does not seem to merely demand the demystifying activity that can sniff out the man behind the curtain and expose his fraudulent show of smoke and lights as so many buttons and levers. Instead of adding yet another layer of self-assured discourse that criticizes, but in its reduction repeats, the very dilemma that it claimed to overcome, it is my hope to hesitate before assuming that the truth of such a sentiment can be revealed by merely removing a mask. This hope is not directed toward a simple suspension of suspicion, but rather it opens in the swerve of self-reflexivity in which criticism doubles back to question the ground on which the observer with a cocked brow stands, or even more accurately, the way that he or she moves. Though much of this essay will be an activity of demystifying analysis[2] that turns its questioning gaze to such extreme claims, the discourse that follows cannot itself assume a place above the fray of ambiguity and deception.

The rhetorical and conceptual excess of the Preacher's central meditation and the dilemmas that surround it seem to be paralleled by or analogous to that which is called "apophatic theology." The Preacher's utterance engages in its own form of unsaying, as its concluding word, "wrong," undermines the very capacity that would be necessary to make such a universal declaration. Apophatic theology, if such a thing exists, is also often subject to the same suspicions of mystification and deception, as its excess is often read as only a momentary deferral of the metaphysical grounds that it appears to deny. This critical reading frames the issue in epistemological terms as apophatic theology's delimitation of one's rational capacity is taken to be its primary gesture. So long as apophasis is viewed in this way, the invocation of the unsayable logically necessitates a bait and switch in which the human conceptualization of God and the descriptive power of language is not blocked *from* but even more absolutely conferred *to* the possession of the apophatic theologian.

This problem is displaced, if not overcome, when one questions the parameters of the trial to which the apophatic declaration is being brought. That is to say, perhaps it is the imposition of the heading of "apophatic theology" as a coherent category or theoretical position that has created the problem. Michael A. Sells has argued that it is largely the reception history and the ensuing generations of interpreters, rather than the "apophatic" texts themselves, that often make this apparent mystification most pronounced.[3] Filling in the gaps of excessive and poetic passages, systematizing texts into a coherent formulation of doctrine, and forgetting the practice and embodiment that surround these texts, these later interpreters and scholars are often the ones who, in seeking clarity, twist the discourse back around into a deceptive and static theory.

Sells distances apophasis from these largely epistemological limitations by making a distinction between "apophatic theory" and "apophatic discourse." In the former, one can rest assured knowing precisely what one does not know (and oftentimes, because one is then able to contain what one does not know, then one can quarantine such problems away from all of the other things that one does know). An apophatic discourse, however, is reserved for "those writings in which unnameablity is not only asserted but performed. In those writings, the effort to affirm transcendence leads to a continuing series of retractions, a propositionally unstable and dynamic discourse in which no single statement can rest on its own as true or false."[4] Such a distinction, however, must merely be employed as a heuristic device. Otherwise it would threaten what it presumes to protect, as the distinction is itself a theory of apophasis. Accordingly, if apophatic discourse is to elude the charges of mystification brought against it, then "apophasis" cannot function as a clearly distinct category or heading but will itself be caught up in the struggle with and against the dilemma of deception. This does not necessitate the exclusion of the term from this analysis, but as William Franke quips: "The attempt to delimit and define apophasis so as to avoid promiscuous and indiscriminate use of the term has strong scientific motivation, but apophasis remains recalcitrant to all definition and simply does not lend itself to being made a useful and well-behaved scientific term."[5] In following this ambiguity and resistance, apophasis can largely be considered not as a technical scientific term, but as a performative activity. Such a shift exceeds the static predication of metaphysics, moving into a space of practice.[6] Resituating the problem in this manner, however, does not alleviate the concern of mystification, but opens it into a realm in which merely rational claims have always exercised their sway—the body. Therefore, in this space, apophasis begins a liturgical dance with an askesis that is fraught with the risk of a denial of autonomy and power, only to regain it in an even more absolute form.

The looming possibility of a deceptive and mystified return to a discourse of static metaphysical claims will remain a risk that haunts all efforts against it. In the space of these pages, this difficulty is most directly pronounced in the dual meaning of the term "duplicity." On the one hand, this term functions to differentiate between the *deception* that I am seeking to avoid, while on the other it denotes a *doubling* that drives simple and straightforward positing beyond itself. Yet, as both senses are folded into one word it also marks the coupling of opposites, forming an aporia. This marks the doubling of a demystifying analysis with apophatic performance, prohibiting the activity of the former to settle into a supposedly neutral, transparent, and static space, as discourse is caught up in an unending activity whose duplicity cannot gain the assurance of truth or falsity.[7] Without the performative disruption or the discursive dynamism, one could imagine, perhaps, three movements, each of which left us with a very similar result: The first would be the typical metaphysical or speculative declaration against which the Preacher appears to be protesting, which would straightforwardly make absolute claims about the absolute. The second would be the deceptive activity of the Preacher that claims to undermine his own ethical and epistemological position, but in doing so employs a mode of speaking in which he is absolutely right. The third movement, which threatens to consume this essay, would then criticize the Preacher in the name of a demystified piety, which claimed to finally tell the truth about absolute truth claims once and for all. While these are modes of deception that I will seek to resist, their duplicity might very well be wrapped up in the doubling activity that I am trying to highlight. Simply put, I accept the problem of mystification, but do not accept the binary between the misty realm of deception and the demystified realm of metaphysical truth, or the frame of philosophizing that reduces dynamic practice to axiomatic predication. Accordingly, I can provide no assurances or guarantees against deception, but can only begin to travel down the path of an apophatic and, perhaps, duplicitous mode of thought and performance.

These gestures of performance are not pure because they are largely understood within the context of criticism and interpretation.[8] Though this essay will emphasize the activity of the Jutland Pastor's sermon which undertakes a dynamic doubling, the risk of mystification remains. Yet this dilemma is not debilitating, as one need not limit one's discourse to the assertion of static propositions or the formulation of an entirely stable position. One could instead embrace the contingency of one's own writing and speaking by emphasizing the extent to which it is a practice that is always only just getting under way. Accordingly, while the Preacher speaks *of* and *at* the impossible intersection of divinity and humanity, finitude and infinity, transcendence and immanence, his words do not have to be read as hardening over or reducing one side to the other. If it is read in this manner, the sermon enacts an apophatic discourse that confronts aporias rather than proposes axioms. In hopes of this possibility, the analysis that follows will highlight a rhetorical duplicity that attempts to resist this problematic by troubling not only the spheres of language and embodiment but also subjectivity and ethics.

The attempted performance of this essay follows four acts. In my initial interpretive move, I consider the sermon not as establishing epistemological claims, but as advocating for a self-giving practice of love. This shift in emphasis toward an apophatic performance will serve to reframe the issue from being considered in a primarily epistemological sense to an ethical register. Pursuing the manner in which the caricature of the apophatic and the reductions that enframe and arrest the play of the Sermon's discourse are undermined and exceeded, the next section considers this radical ethical context in terms of a demand for responsibility which does not reduce activity to a legalistic application within fixed parameters, but into an ongoing practice that is constantly faced with trials of love. In the third section, these ethical reflections and their relationship to the deceptions of speculative claims are continued around the trope of *kenosis*, which opens both the duplicitous and risky coincidence of the divine and the human, but also forces the discourse into the space of embodiment. Finally, the essay concludes with a brief consideration of another layer of duplicity, the pseudonymity of the Jutland Pastor and the dilemmas and openings that this provides.

JUDGING EPISTEMOLOGICAL MYSTIFICATION

The relation of the Jutland Pastor's Sermon to the heading of "apophatic discourse" is, perhaps, greatly strengthened by the apparent tensions between its dynamic message and the manner in which it is framed by the one from whom it is received, Judge Wilhelm—the pseudonymous author of the two voluminous letters preceding its insertion into *Either/Or*. Much like the redactors of other apophatic theologians, the spectacles of the Judge place the dynamism of the Preacher's discourse at risk. In his introductory remarks, the Judge writes, "In this sermon [the Preacher] has grasped what I have said and what I would like to have said to you; he has expressed it better than I am able to."[9] The Judge not only passes the letter on with approval, but also seems to imply an accord between what the pastor says and what the Judge has tried to say. Even a cursory reading of the sermon, however, seems to highlight profoundly different, rather than similar, sentiments. Though one could perhaps understand the Judge's comment to mean that the sermon has caused the Judge to reconsider his own position, there remains an immense tension between the letters and the sermon, which, if covered over, transforms the apophatic performance of its central utterance into a mystified axiom. In order to find these two figures in agreement one would not only have to read the central declaration as a proposition but also assume that this statement necessarily implied the axiom that "God is right." Under such an understanding, God's transcendence would seemingly be asserted as always being over and above our own capacities. Yet, insofar as it is rendered axiomatically and given over to knowledge with certainty, such an assertion of God's transcendence would serve as a bait and switch that knows what is unknown (not unlike an "apophatic theory"). So long as one can glean such certainty from the sermon, the parameters of identity, knowledge, and justice—to which the Judge clings—hold. It is the coherence of these efforts and domains of thought and action, however, that the Preacher's sermon seems to contest rather than ground. The declaration that "The upbuilding lies in the thought that in relation to God we are always in the wrong" seems to be articulated *against* the background of positive claims regarding identity, knowledge, and justice.

This is illustrated by the Preacher's interpretation of the scriptural passage from which the sermon opens. The sermon begins with Luke 19:41–48, in which Jesus mourns Jerusalem,[10] ostensibly addressing the city in general and those singular selves within it, saying, "Would that even today you knew the things that make for peace! But now they are hid from your eyes. For the days will come when your enemies will cast up a bank about you and surround you and hem you in on every side, and then will dash you to the ground and your children within you and will not leave one stone upon another in you, because you did not know the time of your visitation."[11] The Preacher does not interpret the passage in terms of the *just* punishment that Jerusalem will receive, but the fall of a schematic of *justice* and the epistemological claims that underlie it. Seen as prophecy, the passage can be read as the prediction of retributive justice exacted upon the city for his death. Jesus, then, would merely lament the actions of the city, but seemingly uphold the order of justice that must be carried out. To understand the destruction of the edifice of Jerusalem as the historical fall of the Temple, however, encounters the dilemma of the suffering of the righteous and unrighteous alike. Therefore, such retribution would not be particularly just. Expanding beyond the exceptional situation of Jerusalem, the Preacher articulates this problem into the more general terms of theodicy, asking if this is a unique gap within the economy of justice, or is this "experienced" by everyone, if "on a smaller scale"?[12] That is, does the collage of destruction and disaster in history indicate such "unjust" suffering to be unique or is it quite common? If the latter is the case, and God is both provident and right, how can these situations be resolved within the structure of justice? A self or a people confident in its possession of knowledge of the Good, the pastor notes, will not give up on justice; rather, they "will contend with God, and hold on to him," refusing to let God escape without receiving God's blessing, its proper wages.[13] Such an orientation implicitly considers itself and its order to be above God in that it obligates the divine to the self, it makes God into a subject and subject to its order. This form of subjectivity knows that it is right, and it will exercise its rights, even over God. God, then, is below the order; or more accurately, the divine is the infinite mechanism that allows it to run absolutely, a component that elevates the system above contingency, while remaining in absolute dominion over all things contingent.

The figure of Jerusalem and its possession, as both a locus of identity and the residence of the sacred, is used by this mode of thought, which seeks to possess the transcendence of God and absolutize its claims to knowledge. Jacques Derrida has often noted that the name of Jerusalem can be invoked so as to empower a theological discourse[14] and political machinery.[15] Jerusalem, employed in this way, is the place of the promise where presence and possession "will take place fully. It will fully be a place."[16] If one, however, lacks the Archimedean point of the ontotheological Jerusalem, the very basis of knowledge seems to be brought into question. This seems to be the Preacher's point, as he asks, "Does not [the destruction of Jerusalem], that it has happened, have the power to make everything else unexplainable, even the explainable?"[17] This destruction seems not only to break one's expectations but also to rupture the very parameters of knowledge and the enclosed boundaries of what one thought to be one's own, the self. Rather than finding an absolute ground upon which one can know and affirm particulars, through the figurative destruction of Jerusalem, the self is opened *within* its situation and emptied in its relation to God. Such an opening, however, does not yield the direct knowledge of a self-evident finite economy, or the evacuation of all content, but demands the rigors of a self-emptying, or kenotic, practice.

The tension, therefore, between the declaration of the upbuilding character of the relation to God and the prophecy of the tearing down of Jerusalem in the passage from Luke can be read not as mutually exclusive, but as two movements of the same activity. As such, the problem is displaced from being a matter of the righteousness of God to calling into question the mode of rationality that frames this understanding of justice and a chosen people. If Jesus' declaration of the destruction within the ambiguous "you" is read not as a prophecy of a historical event but as the composition and constructions of those selves who attempt to possess God, then this passage announces the self-effacement and emptying that is not threatened but promised. Furthermore, this very ambiguity does not lead to utter abstraction but oscillates between the singular and the plural. The self continues to reside within the city, but, through its singularity, opens its eyes to its contingency. The wisdom wrought by this perspective does not allow for the positing of systematic truth, but is instead caught up in an admission or a prayerful utterance that in relation to God one is wrong. In this manner the wisdom of God is not only madness to those who seek control and autonomy,[18] but something that eludes our efforts to translate it into our own idiom. Following Jesus' lamentation, the scriptural passage recounts the episode of his entering into the Temple and chasing out the money lenders, showing a direct conflict between a den of robbers, whose task it is to exchange human wealth into a divine currency, and a house of prayer.[19]

This reinterpretation of the passage marks a shift from the speculative problematic of theodicy into the self-emptying practice of love. In the stead of self-possession the Preacher speaks of a relation of love and, to my ear, echoes Paul's declaration that "'knowledge' puffs up, but love builds up."[20] The Preacher argues that if you were in love with someone and perceived yourself to be wronged by this other, then you would undoubtedly try to find a way in which you were wrong, or could be held accountable. If, furthermore, you could not by your reasoning find a means to establish that you were wrong, then "you would tear up the accounting in order to help you forget it."[21] Acting as a lover rather than an accountant, one would give up in the struggle for calculation and control, becoming opened and vulnerable. This self, then, would freely cry out, "I am wrong!" from a passion that pours forth, giving what it cannot possess.[22] Such a declaration would deny both the hold over the other and the self, thrusting it into the vulnerability and risk of a relationship outside the fixed parameters of control and expectation. This love, however, should not be misdirected merely to being an affair between an other and the self, but rather the upbuilding love of which the Preacher speaks is the relation to God. In this case, how could we possibly but say that "I am wrong"? The Jutland Pastor asks: "Would not he who is in heaven be greater than you who live on earth; would not his wealth be more superabundant than your measure, his wisdom more profound than your cleverness, his holiness greater than your righteousness?"[23]

Yet one cannot reply to this majestic challenge of one's own worth and boundaries by declaring that "God is right."[24] This simple proposition is problematic as it would strip the loving hope of being in the wrong of its freedom, making the conclusion wrought by this definitive knowledge claim necessary. This reply shows its inadequacy by its reduction of the infinite to the finite, as God is circumscribed within the boundaries of right and the epistemological parameters that can define and discern it. To declare "God is right" would be to make it into an axiom over which one could have control.[25] Understanding God as the provident ruler of right causes the divine to be doubled into the servant and ground of a calculable economy of assurances and earned certainties. Even if this order is declared to be inscrutable to our present capacities, God is still said to operate with a plan that will bring out a positive balance in relation to the necessities of right. The declaration that "God is right" serves not only to positively attribute the predicate of right to God but also solidifies God as a subject who is subject to the grammar of attribution and the knowing logic of propositions.

Judge Wilhelm's letters seem to advocate just such a position. Addressing a young friend whose intellectual capacities and self-involved sensibilities lead him to doubts about God's providence and justice, the Judge strongly advocates a faithful choice. Against the arbitrary and individualistic concepts of a notion of choice that keep the internal will separated from the external world, Wilhelm speaks of a choice that binds the two in the absolute through the universal position of what he calls "the ethical."[26] He writes, "I choose the absolute that chooses me, I posit the absolute that posits me."[27] In this manner, one does not make this decision outside or in spite of one's history or the institutions one inhabits; rather, this choice is also a reception of one's context.[28] Through repentance and humbling oneself before humanity and God, life is sanctified, binding the infinite and the finite, opening the eternal in the moment. Judge Wilhelm declares that it is "a sign of a high-minded person and a deep soul if he is inclined to repent, if he does not take God to court but repents and loves God in his repentance."[29] While this might seem to resemble the central meditation of the Jutland Pastor, it is founded upon this essential difference: the Judge does not take God to court because God exceeds courts but because God is right. God, for the Judge, seems to be the ground upon which ethics and our selves can be founded. In direct opposition to a meaningless world characterized by doubt and wandering, the Judge has found an assurance in his surroundings. He writes that the ethical position founded through the faithful choice "gives life peace, safety, and security, because it continually calls out to us: *Quod petis, hic est* [What you are seeking it is here]."[30]

One could, perhaps, contend that the Preacher's statement, "The upbuilding that lies in the thought that in relation to God we are always wrong," does much the same. Thought of as a propositional claim, this statement enacts the very mystification with which this essay is concerned to call into question: it founds autonomy by naming the entities of "God" and an "I" in relation to which it stands in a constant position. Read in this manner, the statement does not undermine human knowledge, but gives it infinite purchase on its own existential situation, knowing precisely where it stands. Through the affirmation of the continuous condition of being wrong, one knows this as a reality that is stabilized between God and the self.

The Preacher, however, resists such a reading. The declaration is not "a truth you must acknowledge, not a consolation that alleviates your pain, not a compensation for something better, but it is a joy in which you win a victory over yourself and over the world, your delight, your song of praise."[31] Put within the context of a performative utterance, the internal logic of the sentence exercises a radical dynamism. The statement and its activity, therefore, are characterized by irresolvable tensions that lead to an ongoing deferring rather than a simple assertion. Both the fleeting character of its utterance and its negative and uncertain concluding word "wrong" undermine a static reading. Furthermore, the metaphoricity of the sentence begins to slip from abstraction into a situation as the words "lies" and "in relation"[32] indicate spatial relationships and activities. A more literal translation of "in relation" would be "against," even more strongly denoting an activity rather than a static or resolved proposition. Forced into this space of practice and utterance, the ironic iterability of "always" becomes clearer. Slipping past the lips or across the eye within the matter of a brief moment, "always" demands an infinite extension that infects all other moments before and after, and yet here, it evaporates as it enters the air. It acts as a performative contradiction that ruptures our speculative capabilities, opening the concluding word "wrong" rather than closing it. At the end of the sentence we are left to return to its beginning and consider the upbuilding that comes from the destruction of our efforts to construct and contain the truth of the infinite. Accordingly, those very entities whose existence and integrity was implicitly posited by their very articulation, "God" and "I," are ruptured through the activity that comes from a place that claimed to draw the two into relation.

In contradistinction to positing that "God is right," the Preacher exhorts one to prayerfully utter that in relation to God one is in the wrong.

"Wrong," does not function as a negative predicate, or even a dissimilar symbol for God. Nothing is said *about* or attributed *to* God, but instead the declaration turns to the relation to God. This relation does not settle around the polarity of the subject in a mystified acceptance of finitude nor does it solidify the divine in the placeholder of a conceptual infinity. The declaration is not a generalized description of our situation but an apophatic performance that seeks a loving relationship with God. This confession speaks of or to God without knowing exactly what it is doing or to whom it is speaking, without making God into an object of knowledge or a mechanism within our system. It is in this space of prayerful utterance or joyful singing that a self-emptying occurs, demanding a relationship to an*other* rather than autonomy, opening horizons beyond control and necessity, to response-ability.

ETHICS AND THE TRIALS OF LOVE

The call to respond, or a supposed lack thereof, seems to be the most contentious or neglected aspect of apophatic performance not only in general but also specifically by what Judge Wilhelm characterizes as "mystical." Since he recommends the sermon but condemns mystics, it would seem quite obvious that the Judge would not connect the two. If he had understood the sermon in the dynamic terms that are being opened here, however, the Judge might have leveled the charge of "mystic," and its corresponding deficiencies, against the Pastor. As Wilhelm has aligned himself with the "ethical," it would seem to be logically necessary that his opponents could be characterized as "unethical." Similarly one might suppose that given the criticisms of certain forms of ethics in the sermon, one could conclude that it is advocating an unethical quietism. The pseudonymous Judge's critique of the mystic, however, is slightly more nuanced, as he understands the mystic's ethic to be purely internal. Though he repents, the mystic is motivated by a disgust and boredom with the world. Therefore, "the distinctiveness of the mystical is not the religious but the isolation in which the individual, without regard for any relation to the given actuality, wants to place himself in immediate rapport with the eternal."[33] The mystic's position is built on "a metaphysical judgment" that existence "is vanity, illusion, [and] sin."[34] It is upon this basis that the Judge concludes that such a path of thought is "not only a dangerous road but a wrong road."[35]

If the charges just waged against the mystic were put to the Preacher, he would probably concede that he is wrong and that being such characterizes the path on which he treads, but he would also most likely object to the claim that he is advocating a disembodied narcissism that has simply rejected the world. Rather than being founded on a metaphysical assumption, the apophatic performance questions the road that traverses the pitfalls and difficulties of actuality and ethics with ease, assurance, and the knowledge that it has already come to possess precisely what it seeks. It is out of the concern for relation to the other that one questions oneself and the assurance of the place, which the poet Horace (quoted by the Judge above) has proclaimed to already be here. The Preacher seems to wonder if this Pax Romana is not a desiccated oasis made peaceful by the tranquillity of order.[36] The Judge, however, seems frightened by the disorder of the mystic, as his errant path "always takes revenge, and usually in the form of one's becoming an enigma to oneself." Furthermore, it is due to their failure to recognize the demands of actuality that mystics "encounter difficulties and spiritual trials that no one else knows anything about. It is as if they discovered an entirely different world, as if their nature were in itself double."[37] To this aspect of the charges waged by the advocate of ethics, the Preacher would, again, have to admit guilt or, put more simply, that he is wrong. However, such an utterance would not be demanded by necessity, but by love, as the trial would not take place in the courtroom but out in the "different world" of double nature. Accordingly, this begins to suggest that the presumed ethical deficiencies of apophasis can largely be attributed to the frames that define the parameters of the trial to which apophasis is being brought, as they are based largely on a series of presuppositions that not only limit its discursive capacities but also its performative and practical movements.

The duplicitous admission of one being wrong turns back around on the Judge's very claim and exceeds it. The Preacher notes that this doubling as the central meditation of the sermon "manifests its upbuilding power in a twofold way, partly by putting an end to doubt and calming the cares of doubt, partly by animating to action."[38] These two manifestations cannot be separated, as doubt is not calmed by being paired with certainty. For the Preacher, doubt and certainty are a complementary pair that accompany the pursuit of calculation and good conscience. It is the abandoning of such pursuits through the emptying of the resolute self that turns us away from the dialectic of certainty and doubt, and projects us into the trials of love and action. In the sermon, doubt is paired with the ethical assurance built upon the slogan, "one does what one can."[39] Such an understanding of ethics seeks an accounting scheme by which one can both discern one's own righteousness and also find a place of rest. In contrast, the Preacher begins the sermon with a prayer that declares rest can only be found in the joyful confession of being wrong before God.[40] Such rest is not the cessation of action but a transformation of toil and duty into service and praise. To be wrong is to live in faith, hope, and love, which calls one out of one's self and the universal structures of justice to live in relationship. In this relationship we can never hope to be right and, accordingly, we do not stand over the other in dominance. One can never find certainty in the actions of love. Love's very ambiguity and excess opens the closed circle of exchange. Thus, one does not act for the expectation of return or for the assurance of righteousness. He writes, "If you knocked but it was not opened . . . if heaven was shut and the testimony failed to come, you are still happy in your work."[41]

The tension between love and justice opened here does not lead to the rejection of the latter as such, nor to the mystified condemnation of those who passionately seek after it.[42] The apophatic performance does not escape language, nor does its loving activity escape the structures of right or justice. The Preacher asks, did not "the man who wished to be always in the wrong in relation to another man" do all he can "to be in the right and yet [wish] only to be in the wrong?"[43] One must still live with people, traditions, and laws, and struggle to think and act out of what is right. The apophatic utterance, however, seeks to chase the moneylenders out of the house of ethics, striving not to have hands that possess and exchange, but hands folded in prayer and calloused by service. Therefore, the Preacher admits that he is wrong and serves the Judge, not because of the latter's authority or for his affiliation with the right, but out of a self-emptying and joyful act of love.[44]

To be an enigma to oneself, to concede that one is wrong and lacks a transparent relationship to actuality, does not lead deeper into the recesses of an imagined inner self, but empties one to face God and to struggle with this relation out in the world. Therefore, the Preacher must concede and double one more point to the Judge: "The mystic also repents, but he repents himself out of himself, not into himself."[45] The Judge opposes this kenotic subjectivity with a self that chooses himself—an agent who looks more like a magistrate than a servant. By lifting up this structure of right, Wilhelm undertakes the mystification of God that the Preacher resists. This is perhaps most clearly illustrated in the manner in which the Judge employs the kenotic activity of Christ. Early in his first letter, the Judge reprimands his young friend, who the letters are meant to instruct, for lacking faith and subjecting God to intellectual scrutiny. By keeping his self and intellect separate from the world, the young man sees only the particular and accidental and is, therefore, left to conclude, fatalistically, that if there is a God he is absent from our world and his plan is unknown to us. The Judge replies that God's incomprehensibility is not a cause for sorrow, but of great joy, as it is God's love, and not God's detachment, that passes all understanding. On these grounds he makes reference to the Christological hymn from Paul's Letter to the Philippians, observing that Jesus did not curse his humanity or wish for it to be otherwise, but lived as a servant.[46] Serving as the ground of Judge Wilhelm's faith, such a rendering of the incarnation and the knowledge of God seems duplicitous in a deceptive sense. In emptying himself, Jesus becomes the servant of the ethical order, founded on a conflation between man and God. The servanthood of Christ is a fact that the Judge can admire and employ as proof of God's loving activity and his unifying function for the ethical self that the Judge implores others to choose. Rather than turning outside of the self and the societal structures that define it toward an imitation of service and self-sacrifice, the Judge stands at a distance, and admires Christ's humility. Instead of being challenged or transformed by Christ, he transforms the kenotic act into a speculative moment that grounds his system of thought.

EMBODIED APOPHASIS—A KENOTIC APPROACH

Departing from a different scriptural passage, the Preacher takes the promise of Christ not as a metaphysical fact, but as a call that provokes, invokes, and convokes the challenge of a kenotic subjectivity.[47] Through the acknowledgment that one is wrong before God and the illumined contingencies of the efforts at constructing and possessing the absolute (the destruction of the ontotheological Jerusalem), one is called to prayer and joyful action. This action is not organized around an autonomous subject that resides within its own interior certainty, or that brings things into its possession. Its dynamic activity, instead, forces it outside of itself into a relation that can neither be solidified nor controlled. Its efforts at speaking cannot be simply contained in static propositions, but all such sayings are also unsayings. Accordingly, one's relation to the divine is not characterized by certainty, but by an ongoing performance that can never rest and that is always called out of itself into service.

Considering this activity or subjectivity in terms of kenosis, however, which is usually a Christological matter, might seem to be a mystification par excellence, as self-denial conflates the difference between the human and the divine. Read in this way, the positive movement of kenosis in this essay is duplicitous in that it affirms precisely what it claims to deny, locating the divine within the boundaries of a subject or community.[48] Furthermore, one could question the significance of the almost seamless transition in the sermon from Christ to the believer after the initial passage from Luke. This would seem to raise the question: Has my formulation of kenotic subjectivity illuminated a deception in the sermon similar to that of the Judge's, that one comes to possess the means to discern authentic selfhood under the pretense of a self-emptying relation to God?

These concerns seem to be both raised and addressed by Kierkegaard's later considerations of the figure of Christ as the prototype. As articulated by the pseudonym Anti-Climacus in *Practice in Christianity*,[49] Christ is not an object for metaphysical speculation or idle admiration; instead, he issues an invitation for others to follow in his footsteps, imitating his life.[50] To place the ethical and existential activity of humans in such close proximity to the one whom Anti-Climacus refers to as the "God-man" might seem to be an equivocation between our own actions, structures, and desires and that of the divine. The incarnation, however, is "not the union of God and man"; it is not the speculative reality of a combined substrate of God and humankind but is God as an individual.[51] Christ does not simply represent a sign of a true metaphysical reality, whose truth may be inferred, understood, or abstracted; rather, Christ is a "teacher who is inseparable from and more essential than the teaching"—he is a "sign of contradiction."[52] As a sign, he points beyond himself; to be contemporaneous with him one would not be able to see or know his truth, and yet he is also the embodied fulfillment of his promise.

The sign of Christ does not directly correspond to a meaningful referent that we might possess and systematize. One cannot extrapolate a structure of activity, teaching, or any direct communication from Christ. The formulation of the God-man forces a contradiction that cannot be resolved, but nor can either side annul the other or force him into "an unconditional concealment."[53] One is not given the assured distinctions of a speculative Christology that would, under the pretense of maintaining a distance between the divine and the human, empower its own discourse and limit its subject to the frame of its categories. Rather, the sign of contradiction seems to remain duplicitous, as it seeks to empty itself, while remaining weary of the risks of deception and idolatry. The discourse *about* Christ remains dynamic and impossible, as this self-emptying activity unsays what is said. Through this discourse, one is confronted by the aporia of an indirect communication, with a language that does not seek to possess and control, but which is drawn out of itself into a practice. The sign of contradiction cannot be solidified by logical categories but forces thought into an apophatic performance.[54] It is not an object for consideration or admiration, but it forces us into a practice of self-emptying which flows into imitation. This imitation does not lead one back into himself or herself, but into a space of relation. Thus, we are brought into the activity of, and not the reflection on, prayerful utterance and joyful service. Anti-Climacus writes, "If anyone wants to have anything to do with this kind of communication, he will have to untie the knot himself."[55] Open, untied, and imitating the prototype of Christ, this subjectivity cannot form a placeholder or a site whereby it could begin to mistake itself or its constructions for God, nor could it conflate the distance between itself and the sign of contradiction.[56]

Similarly, the duplicity of the kenotic hymn in Philippians (2:6–11) stops short of a celebration of Christ's power and coronation as something that we can simply possess, as it makes reference not just to the incarnation but also to the crucifixion. The reading of the passage called for by both the pastor and Anti-Climacus draws the humble, suffering, and serving character of Christ into an inexhaustible tension with divinity. The text of the hymn in Philippians does not seem to give a simple doctrinal formulation, but carries out its own dynamic performance. The hymn begins with an identification of Christ with the divine as he was in the "form of God" (2:6) and in the "form of a slave" (2:7).[57] Then Christ proceeds deeper into the realm of appearance, being in the "likeness" and "fashion"[58] of humans (2:7), but returns to identification with the divine through the attribution of the name above all names, Lord (2:9). Traditional Neoplatonic readings sometimes place this string of terms on a line that undergoes a process of descent and ascent, whereby lowliness is replaced by or overcome through exaltation. The hymn is read as an account of Christ's life where he is one with God, made flesh in the incarnation, crucified, and then resurrected. Thus Christ is taken as a sign that refers to a metaphysical reality that can be given Christological representation. The tension between exaltation and lowliness, however, seems to be heightened, and not merely resolved, by the parallel drawn between Christ's "form" as both "God" (2:6) and "slave" (2:7).[59] The connection between humility and lordship seems to be more profound than being merely two separate events. Following a reading emphasizing practice rather than speculation, the play of attributes in the text does not settle into a metaphysical formula in which one can wrest Christ's glory from his servitude, but rather there is a doubling that undermines our constructions. The tension within the text between the divine and the human, glory and humility, is not resolved but pushes us beyond our efforts for control. The description of the serving practice of God exceeds propositional formulations, and ruptures the hopes of possessing and employing Christ in our economy. Therefore, this emphasis on service and love does not merely displace one descriptive account with another, but as divinity and slavery are drawn into an antinomy, our efforts at conceptualization are confounded, as the text enacts a performative force rather than just making a constative claim. Reading the text, our performance of praise does not find assurance but calls us out of ourselves.

The denial of this duplicitous character of kenosis, which only seeks to identify Christ in his glory, risks missing the call to action, so as to preserve its own expectations and structures. The attempt to affiliate Christ with these forms of worldly power draws us back to the initial scriptural passage in Luke, where Christ undermines the efforts of those who seek to regulate the house of prayer with a currency that can mediate or conflate the divine and human. John D. Caputo notes how such tendencies manifest in the philosophical and theological domains when he writes, "In Christendom, the call that issues from the bent body on the cross is converted into the coin of being and presence."[60] The sign of contradiction is not a word, heading, or figure that can be translated and converted into an object of exchange, but rather it seems to confound and exceed all such efforts, as it enacts what it means through the challenge of its aporia, calling us into the actions and struggles of loving relation, and not merely domination.

This self-emptying practice does not lead one into an immaterial remove or formless abstraction, but serves to radicalize efforts to understand embodiment. The duplicity, or the dual character of the movement of kenosis, is not an epistemological axiom and cannot settle safely into a category, but the utterance that "in relation to God I am wrong" is caught up in the singularity of a place that is open to the infinite and cannot reduce its relations to a finite economy of entities. Though the pastor's prayerful words can be repeated, generalized, and translated, its performance is embodied in a singular space that does not close itself off, but that exceeds its own capabilities. Much like the breath that gives voice to these words, this singular self is caught up in an ecstatic activity that empties out what it brings in. It is caught up in a practice that is necessarily related, and therefore this singularity cannot claim to clear away a space that is pure and pristine outside of the generalities that draw it out, nor can the particularities and historical indexes of the institutions we might try to choose or deem "chosen" be absolutized. Without properly being able to delimit a singular space or a generalized particular, the statement's central claim further complicates matters as it concerns a relation with the infinite. However, in doing so it denies any assurances that one might assume, as one is, instead, left with the upbuilding that lies in being wrong. The dynamic utterance makes the strict identification of the infinite with the finite impossible just as it makes their simple and assured separation equally as difficult. The duplicitous doubling of the practice of denial leads to, or perhaps more accurately, troubles a kenotic self drawn out of itself into relation.[61]

This aporia does not simply concern speculation regarding identity but also troubles the grounds of a supposedly self-evident materialism. The Jutland Pastor's sermon is itself seemingly ambiguous about embodied life. Nearing his conclusion, and at a point of great rhetorical effusion, the Preacher declares that the thought that one "is always in the wrong is the wings upon which he soars over the finite. This is the longing with which [one] seeks God; this is the love in which [one] finds God."[62]

Though this may appear to expose the pure interpretative invention of the latter part of this essay, such a declaration can be read as less "otherworldly" so long as one remembers the "double nature" that follows apophatic performance. Furthermore, the second sentence of the previously quoted passage echoes the sentiment of the opening prayer of the sermon, which seeks rest and peace, but finds them in action and service. Following from this, it would seem evident that the Preacher is not advocating an otherworldly escapism.[63] Rather, what is undermined here is a relation with material that reduces the world to being a space of knowledge, accounting, and the right.[64] Accordingly, the materialism that the apophatic utterance overcomes is a bare calculation, which lacks love. Embodiment cannot simply be reduced to a finite field of calculable objects, but as I have attempted to consider with my emphasis on the performative utterance, it is deeply connected with a discourse that exceeds conceptual control. As Jean-Luc Nancy[65] observes, the body is not an object that can be separated or held apart from discourse. Instead these two fields are joined, as writing and the body are not objects outside of which one can stand, conceptualize, or grasp but rather they are both caught up in an opening and rupture.[66] Furthermore, the singularity of the body does not only trouble abstracting claims of universalism but also the indices of particularity.[67] Nancy calls into question both a view of the incarnation that conjures away the body and the universalizing activity of what he calls "conquistador engineers," which under the pretense of materialism, reduce all things to the sterility of a lab or the abstraction of a blueprint.[68]

Therefore, the apophasis that undermines the simple acceptance of these particular forms of identity does not necessitate the imperialism of universalism, but opens relationships that cannot be subsumed by a closed economy of knowledge or self. The kenotic self enacted in the performative statement is not one that is disembodied, but one that struggles with the rupture and the opening that is the body, the languages, and cultures within which it thinks and acts. Though the Preacher questions the assurance with which one clearly draws the parameters of the world, he does not do so with the guarantee of another world, clearly divided from this one. Rather, the rest that is brought by apophatic striving and the peace that is given by loving service are caught up with the tension between the finite and the infinite, and through our loving relation not only to God, but also to others. Accordingly, it is out of the service and humility, enacted in the performance of being wrong, that this lowly matter doubles into exultation.

THE DUPLICITOUS MAN BEHIND THE CURTAIN

This final phrase of the preceding paragraph, however, is not left to rest. It does not bring the sermon to a close or give us the assurance that we will indeed be happy in the work that has been outlined within these pages. Rather, when one reaches the conclusion of the Jutland Pastor's sermon, another doubling occurs. As one closes the book one is reminded that the voice who just spoke was not real, but a pseudonym. Furthermore, the utterance of the central meditation doubles into a further dynamism, as it was never spoken aloud. The duplicity extends from the fact that it is a sermon that is read in the solitude of a study, not in the presence of a community, to its author, who is a fictitious projection of Kierkegaard. George Pattison notes that the difference between a "sermon" and a "discourse" is often an important distinction for Kierkegaard's writing, in that "the sermon is, after all, addressed to a congregation, to a general gathering. The discourse, however, is addressed to a reader, and the act of reading is always singular. I listen to a sermon as a member of a congregation. I read a devotional work as a discourse of my own." [69] In the case of the Jutland Pastor's sermon, however, this difference is elided as the reading of a sermon doubles back from a discursive form that is public and authoritative to one that is singular and personal. As such, the reader is imaginatively engaged to exceed any clear distinction between the two. Though the singular space of reading opens the façade of the public, its pretended context reminds one of one's situation within communities and of one's relation to others. This double genre pushes beyond an imagined individualism as the dialogical is combined with the sermonic, opening the aporia of the singular's connection to the plural.

Within the context of *Either/Or,* the multiple pseudonyms defer the authority of any of its polyvalent voices. As the final of three perspectives, the sermon does not seem to function as an answer or a hermeneutic key, but performs a deferral of such strivings.[70] This communication, then, is not the work of an all-knowing genius that hides behind a mask, deceiving so as to illumine and empower an autonomous self-same other.

The pseudonymous authorship, in this context, could be understood not as a description of the boundaries and content of a true self, but as a self-emptying practice that pushes beyond interior conflict into relation. Yet, elsewhere, in a work that bears his name, Kierkegaard offers his interpreters the promise of a true voice for his entire oeuvre, acknowledging that "the duplicity, the ambiguity [throughout the authorship] is a conscious one."[71] This would seem to mean that duplicity is the mask of deception that can be removed, admitted, and exposed; furthermore, that truth can be communicated in a direct way. However, even within the context of a signed confession the ambiguity of his duplicitous declaration remains. We are left to wonder how seriously we should take such an admission: Is this the trickster's ultimate prank? Is this the impossible confession of a compulsive liar? Or, is this a communication that defers direct categorization, acknowledging not dishonesty, but the impossibility of a speakable self-possession, of a doubling that ruptures, rather than resides in, closed categories? Is this the declaration that shows apophasis to be an *empty* deception, or does it dynamically overcome such a deception in an *emptying* activity? Faced with the doubling and mystifying character of such a question, the best answer seems to be that any closure that I might impose would surely be wrong. And yet such a declaration is hardly a conclusion, but more of a prayer.

Feminist Theology and the Sensible Unsaying of Mysticism

SIGRIDUR GUDMARSDOTTIR

The literary theorist Anne-Marie Priest argues that if poststructural scholars of religion have pointed out the connections between Derridean deconstruction and negative theology, the affinities between feminist theories of sexual difference and negative theology have been less explored. By reading the early texts of philosopher Luce Irigaray on alterity and sexual difference, Priest claims apophatic practices at the heart of contemporary feminism of difference. She maintains that for those feminists who affirm sexual difference, woman-as-the-Other holds a place similar to that held by God for apophatic theologians. Priest writes, "As an apophatic mystic of 'woman,' then, Irigaray sheds light on the 'womanliness' of God, suggesting that God is both a model and an agent for the disruption of patriarchy and the creation of feminine subjectivity."[1]

At first glance, Priest's mystical assertion may sound strange to feminist ears. Apophasis offers ways of detachment and denial of the divine affirmations, in whose image men and women are created according to Christian belief. If the Christian tradition that has channeled and held back women's mystical God-talk in ages past has lately relaxed its hold, do the ancient cataracts of apophasis then have anything to offer women as they rush forth for theological subjectivity in the beginning of the twenty-first century? How could the practices of unsaying or undoing render anything salient to bodies and materiality, to which women have traditionally been linked in the Western theo-philosophical corpus? For feminist theology, which is committed to the quest for the full humanity of women and to the end of their oppression within the Christian tradition, can anything sensible (that is to say both wise and pertaining to the senses) come out of this tradition of silence and unsaying? Have women not been silent long enough to afford a kataphatic moment? My intention in this essay is twofold: on the one hand, I intend to highlight some apophatic patterns within the field of feminist theology, and, on the other, to consider the prospects of apophatic feminist theology.

The theologian Laurel C. Schneider argues that feminist theology is shaped both by affirmation and negation, which produces creative images of the divine life and yet unmasks some of such transcendental claims. Using an image reminiscent of the mystical, bubbling flows of Neo-Platonism, Schneider likens feminist theologies to a river flowing from powerful sources.

> One source is the important and skeptical insight of the metaphoric exemption, producing and legitimating the transcendent core of metaphoric creativity. The other source flows from the embodied reality claims of women and men, who put theological metaphors into action, so to speak, and find that spiritual attention invokes a more profound substance than the metaphorical exemption allows.[2]

For Schneider, who argues for a divine plurality beyond the image of the Trinity, the time has come for feminist theologians to affirm to a greater extent the affirmative and the negative traditions of theology, "the heritage of negation that preserves divine greatness from idolatrous impulses and the heritage of sacramental attention that remembers—and honors—the presence of the divine."[3]

In *Power, Gender, and Christian Mysticism*, Grace M. Jantzen succinctly names some of the major problems with identifying mysticism as an emancipatory source for contemporary women. The mystical texts are, as Jantzen reminds us, always already embedded in an oppressive power dynamic that exalts some experiences and marginalizes others. However, for Jantzen the mystical traditions can also serve as channels of social justice, for they provide alternative tracts of discourses which may disrupt the ontological parameters of classical theism from time to time. Jantzen writes: "[W]hile oppressions run deep, it is also true that from within the mystical tradition, especially (but not only) from some of the women mystics, came creative and courageous efforts at pushing back the boundaries of thought and action so that liberation could be achieved."[4]

Like Jantzen, Amy Hollywood answers the question of possible positive affinities between feminism and mysticism in the affirmative:

> Feminism needs to find a place for the rituals that help human beings sustain loss and support subjectivity. At the same time, feminism requires a place for the apophatic, the ritual unsaying of those imaginary and symbolic supports that work to efface death's reality—and with it, the deep pleasures and pains of the speaking body.[5]

For Hollywood, this feminist apophasis, or "ritual unsaying," entails that women become aware of the oppressive structures that associate them and their bodies to death, dirt, and disgust. Hollywood maintains that apophasis draws out the differences and intricacies of the speaking body, "in all the complexities of its pleasurable and painful subjectification."[6] Following Hollywood's insistence on the speaking body, what would such an exploration of bodily complexities entail? If the main theme of this book is "apophatic bodies," whose bodies are they? Would they be free bodies or maybe silenced bodies, nobodies, raped, battered, and mutilated bodies, gendered, transsexual, queer bodies? Could the apophatic way perhaps help unravel those ideologies that oppress, silence, and batter those bodies, or heap them into a singular idealized body and its abjected other? Perplexed, yet titillated by the obvious oxymoronic trap of trying to answer apophatic questions in the affirmative, I would, with Hollywood, hesitantly and warily like to argue for the possibilities for a feminist apophasis, and with Jantzen identify deconstruction of Christian mysticism in the name of justice as a mystical task. *Pace* Hollywood, however, I don't think that such a method needs to choose between sexual difference and the sufferings and delights of bodies.

Mystical thought, and apophatic thought in particular, has often been considered to be metaphysically hostile to women, antimaterialistic, ahistoric, universal, hooked on transcendence, and unconcerned with bodies and particularity. If Betty Friedan launched the second wave of feminism by shaking women from the slumber of the suburban "feminine mystique" in 1963, Mary Daly's writings in the late seventies parody Christian mysticism by calling women from their slumber of patriarchal and theological "mystification." The patriarchal method of "mystification" for Daly consists of a fourfold procedure of erasing unruly women; of reversing their matrilineage by integrating them into the myths of patriarchy; by presenting resistance such as the feminist movement as evil and antimale, and finally by breeding token daddy-girls to ward off the more rebellious women.[7] In her *Wickedary*, Daly names the imposition of patriarchal myth as "misteries" and defines it as the "irrationality of the patriarchal male, projected onto women and nature, whom he archetypically brands as 'mysterious.'"[8] However, if Daly attempts to "demystify" and "exorcise" patriarchal myths and "misteries,"[9] she also notes a subversive power in mysticism. Thus, in *Beyond God the Father* (1973) Daly names feminist awareness as a "mysticism of sorority," and in *Gyn/Ecology* (1978) she likens the clearing of a patriarchal residue and the discovery of a more life-affirming reality beyond to "mystical journeys."[10] If Meister Eckhart once made significant apophatic contributions with his mystical vocabulary of the breakthrough into the Godhead beyond God, Daly sounds strangely Eckhartian when she declares: "When women break through this multiple barrier composed of deceptions ejaculated by 'god' we can begin to glimpse the true gateways to our depths, which are the Gates to the Goddess."[11]

If Daly holds a somewhat ambivalent relationship to mysticism, other feminists have distinguished sharply between feminist spirituality and the mysticism of patriarchal religion. For Charlene Spretnak in the early eighties, postpatriarchal spirituality likewise entails a union of all forms of existence and opens up dimensions of an embodied self linked with nourishment, interdependence, relationships with other living beings, humans, animals, plants, earth. Spirituality offered a sense of horizontality instead of a verticality, and entailed equality instead of hierarchical thinking. Spirituality for Spretnak thus serves to destabilize the soul/body dichotomy that so heavily characterizes Western thought. In sharp contrast to her friendly depiction of spirituality, Spretnak holds mysticism to be securely embedded in the parameters of established patriarchal religions, whether it be the Western hegemony over the masses or the Eastern esoteric form. Mysticism, however, entails something more sinister, morbid, and reeking of patriarchy, according to Spretnak. "In truth, there is nothing 'mystical' or 'otherworldly' about spirituality," Spretnak maintains. "The life of the spirit, or soul, refers merely to functions of the mind. Hence spirituality is an intrinsic dimension of human consciousness and is not separate from the body."[12] Spretnak links mysticism to that which is other than world, such as a fascination with resurrected bodies in the afterlife, the deferral of a union with the divine until death. If mysticism for Spretnak is built on a binary of body and soul, postpatriarchal spirituality seeks to heal this division between the somatic and the pneumatic. Spretnak emphasizes the negative aspects of the "otherworldliness" of mysticism, while Daly takes the word "otherworldly" and turns it on its head. "Otherworld journey" for Daly is both affirmative and negating for women; it unsays their oppression, as well as saying "yes" to women.[13] Thus, while both Spretnak and Daly emphasize matriarchal traditions—immanence and unity of body, earth, spirit, and the female—Daly seems in some ways to hold on to the transcendent, apophatic breakthrough of the Christian mystical tradition, an apophatic "otherworldliness" as it were, in the midst of patriarchal constructs.

In the last decades of the twentieth century, women started to doubt their own foundations of women's experience as one and universally given. Judith Plaskow and Carol P. Christ write in 1989: "[W]e can no longer speak of women's experience as if it were a 'Platonic form.'"[14] If feminists could to a lesser extent build their identity on the common ground of experience, why should mystical experience be any different? If time, intertexts, and places are considered intrinsic to mystical thought, the distinction between mystical experience and mystical theology can no longer be clear-cut. Strangely, the critique of experience can as well be directed toward the feminist embrace of spirituality and denial of mysticism, such as Spretnak's approach. If feminists can no longer speak about women's "experience" or "consciousness" in a unified way, if difference, standpoints, and locations have a meaning for feminists, then the case for the historical texts, such as Christian medieval mysticism, could provide potential fodder for feminist spirituality. This renewed interest in mysticism emerges, not because the texts are pure of patriarchal residue and not as a common root experience of all women. Rather the possibilities lie in their acting as openings and intertexts of resistance, on the edges and within the interstices of dominant discourses.

If feminist theologians display a renewed interest in mystical expressions, their interest may seem to focus more on the kataphatic affirmations of the divine, than the apophatic perspective. When apophatic markers and methods appear in their texts, they often serve more as a clearing for a feminist discourse than as an ongoing unraveling of language. For example, Rosemary Radford Ruether attends to apophasis as the clearing for new streams of kataphatic expressions of divinity in feminist thought when she argues that negative theology can be used to correct the hegemony of male-oriented names for God: "The tradition of negative or apophatic theology emphasizes the unlikeness between God and human words for God. That tradition corrects the tendency to take verbal images literally; God is like but also unlike any verbal analogy. Does this not mean that male words for God are not in any way superior to or more appropriate than female analogies?"[15]

Likewise, Elizabeth Johnson claims that the apophatic vision of the unnameable provides the dynamic to loosen up the patriarchal images and to pour in other God-talk crafted from the experience of women.[16] Johnson stresses the importance of kataphasis, women's right and need to name God with myriads of images, instead of the prevalent patriarchal ones. In a way similar to Johnson's careful balancing of the affirmative and the negative, Beverly J. Lanzetta addresses the need of speaking about patriarchal oppression from an angle which probes the spiritual no less than the structural. "In our various forms of contemporary analysis, we have yet to take a serious look at the spiritual dimensions of women's oppression," Lanzetta says.[17] She claims that feminism has not been attentive enough to the spiritual dimensions of domination and advocates feminist mystical theology as a remedy to the lack. Lanzetta maintains that the transformative power of mystical thought is capable of healing the wounds of the heart, which are caused by patriarchy.

In contrast to Daly's fight against "mystification" and Spretnak's repudiation of "otherworldly mysticism," Ruether, Johnson, and Lanzetta reside more comfortably within the Christian mystical tradition of saying and unsaying, and explicitly name apophasis as an important link in feminist God-talk. For Schneider however, as already stated, apophatic patterns do not merely appear in feminist theologies that openly discuss mystical methods, but rather have been indirectly at work in most feminist theologies of the eighties and early nineties. Schneider calls this modern form of apophasis "the metaphoric exemption" and presents it as a modern suspicion of idolatry that was developed in two distinctive ways by Karl Barth and Paul Tillich, the former characterized by rejecting important cultural assumptions of modernity, the latter by embracing culture as participating in symbols of divinity. According to Schneider, the metaphoric exemption has opened up new spaces of feminist God-talk.

> Theologians could begin to tend to culture for its life-giving, full humanity-affirming possibilities. Mary Daly offers "spirals" and "Verbs" for divine being; Sharon Welch contemplates the metaphor of beloved community; Delores Williams re-imagines black church and incarnation in women's bodies; Johnson envisions Christ as Sophia; Brock looks to the metaphor of the heart; Brown Douglas looks to the black Christ; Plaskow considers inclusive monotheism; and McFague explores the metaphor of the world as God's body.[18]

I argue that Tillich's and Johnson's predilection for symbols are closer to the mystical and medieval sensibilities of participation in religious language than, for example, Sallie McFague's metaphorical project. Johnson, expressing a more sacramental tradition than McFague's robust Protestantism, maintains the symbol language of Christian theology. Symbol for Johnson transfers to metaphor, but in my view endorses the social, collective, and organic persistence of Tillich's symbol.[19] However, while Schneider's argument of the multiplicity of feminist theologies might thus be made even more complex, her insight about the resemblances between feminist skepticism and negative theology is compelling. For Schneider, the metaphorical exemption that has produced the abundance of feminist theologies is also its greatest threat, because the metaphysical foundations which modern skepticism and its heir feminist theology rest on have not been altered. Schneider is claiming the negative heritage, deriving from Pseudo-Dionysius, Meister Eckhart, and Porete, to name a few, which challenged and disturbed the linguistic structures that bind the reality of God to human-made images. Likewise, Schneider's project aims at unsaying some of the modern metaphysical residue in which feminist theology is embedded. Thus, I am positing Schneider's theological project along similar apophatic lines as Priest's reading of Irigaray's mystical philosophy of alterity that I cited at the beginning of the essay.

Schneider maintains that feminist theology needs to get out of the modern impasse of the metaphorical exemption, which for her evokes skepticism about all language about divinity, but never alters the belief of the real entity that transcends finite language. Schneider suggests that feminist theology moves beyond monotheism and proposes divine multiplicity instead. "Divinity conceived as unlimited and multiple resists colonization by any one community and by any one identity, but offers itself to them without any hesitation. Divine transcendence as unlimitedness is incomprehensible in its scope, but infinitely comprehensible in its expression."[20] While agreeing with Schneider on the necessity of apophatic language which can express concrete experiences without enthralling the infinite to the finite, I am not convinced that such a project needs to go beyond monotheism. Those in the Christian mystical tradition, especially radical apophatic writers such as Marguerite Porete and Meister Eckhart, have always sought to say and unsay the strange paradox of *theos* and *monos* in Christian theology, the personal and the impersonal, the transcendent and immanent, the agent that is actively present in people's lives and the detached Godhead in which the soul and God are intimately known. If the Trinity is truly a mystery as the Christian tradition has claimed, this mystery should disrupt the standard notion of the divine household of father, son, and spirit. It might open up a bottomless apophatic, trinitarian discourse of multiplicity.

The recent mystical proclivities of many feminist theologies, especially but not exclusively toward the medieval female mystics and their experimental God-talk, open up interesting affinities between feminist theologies and "The French Feminists." Poststructural questions of materiality, subjectivity, particularity, and gender seem to move in curious affinity to the mystical tradition, poised as it is on the interstices of philosophy and theology. Like mystical theology, poststructuralism has often been accused of being self-absorbed, antipolitical, and antiethical. Poststructuralism and mysticism alike have been criticized for disregarding matter, dissolving everything and everybody into "textual play."[21] Poststructural thought has been criticized for relativism, even nihilism, as it seeks to destabilize the *cogito,* which Western thought has inherited from the Enlightenment. Likewise, mysticism in the Western world has sometimes functioned as a counterculture to Christian orthodoxies which shakes the ontological foundations of the divine relations, whether in connection with creation or other persons of the Trinity. Poststructuralist writings of continental feminist thinkers such as Julia Kristeva, Luce Irigaray, and

Hélène Cixous have especially in the English-speaking world been decried for their alleged "essentialism." Françoise Meltzer reminds us that each of the "French feminists" has her own characteristics, which become washed away when oversimplified with generalizations such as the term "French feminists." The "French feminists," who are stereotyped as "white, first world women of the latter part of the twentieth century, who have received an elite education in Paris and who work out of the '*métropole*' as their intellectual and institutional base,"[22] are thus criticized for being occupied with universals, stuck in old-fashioned, sexist, and racist ontologies of the enlightened self, and saturated with relativism.[23] If the criticism against the "French" has often moved in curious affinities to the criticism of mysticism in feminist discourse, the "French feminists" themselves keep an ambivalent attitude toward mystical discourse. Julia Kristeva has shown great interest in Mariology and Christian mystical affectivity, but views those discourses as imperfect sites for talking about motherhood, the female sex, and the narcissistic wounds of the psyche.[24] "*La mystérique*," Irigaray's strange neologism where the female gender, mysticism, mystery, and hysteria are liquefied into one word, is for her an appropriate way of speaking about mystical discourse within the Western philosophical framework. The promise of the negative way, for Irigaray, is that if apophatic theologians struggle to save the infinite God from finite language constructs, speaking about women in apophatic terms likewise evades the language structures of patriarchy. For Irigaray, the mystical epoch of women writers in medieval times is viewed with great appreciation as a singular moment in Western history of woman's public performance.[25] However, Irigaray also makes the threat and danger of the enterprise clear; for her, such a discourse risks the loss of self-identity or appropriation into a mirror of patriarchy.

If Irigaray thus binds together the threat and promise of mysticism in her concept of *la mystérique*, Jantzen and Hollywood likewise recognize the role gender plays in the construction of the modern notion of mysticism. Women have in the Christian tradition enjoyed limited access to theological and philosophical education as well as being barred from the holy order of the priesthood and from expressing scholarly erudition in writing or public speech. Thus, the general exclusion of women from certain forms of mysticism operates within the historical division between the affirmative and the negative in the sixth century and the corresponding split between the affective and the speculative types of mysticism in the thirteenth century.[26] Jantzen argues that the opportunities of expression that opened up for women in the twelfth and the thirteenth centuries through their mystical experiences also served to establish their gender as being closer to the body and the bodily passions than men are. If Jantzen is right, the abundance of women's texts of visionary affectivism and the scarcity of women's apophatic texts may therefore have more to do with women's social condition than with their alleged essential sensuality. However, as Hollywood claims in her responses to Jantzen's argument, the mystical binaries between male mysticism of cool intellect and philosophical erudition and the outpouring of female erotics of the body do not quite hold either. Hollywood maintains that mystics such as Meister Eckhart and Porete sometimes transcend boundaries of gendered exclusion: Eckhart by learning from and citing the beguines, directly or indirectly, and Porete for engaging in apophasis as the menfolk did.[27]

I am reading Irigaray's *la mystérique*, her figure of hysterical apophasis which mimics and is appropriated by Christian theology, as a twofold apophatic promise and danger to feminist theology. It threatens to rob women of their hard-won and fragile subjectivity in language. The mystical discourse is not an innocent method, but a tradition, "misteries" which have constructed, harnessed, mechanized, privatized, and opposed the theological projects of women. However, in all its vulnerability and claimlessness, it also gives the promise of an alternative language to essentialist deity and ontotheological constructs.

Daly prophesied "the true gateways to our depths, which are the Gates to the Goddess,"[28] and Irigaray also speaks of such ventures into the apophatic as abysmal:

> Now the abyss opens down into my own self, and I am no longer cut into in two opposing directions of sheer elevation to the sky and sheer fall into the depths. I know now, that both height and depth spawn—and slit each other in(de)finitely. And that the one is in the other, and the other is in me, matters little since it is in me that they are created in rapture. *Outside of all self-as-same.* Never the same—always new.[29]

What does this raptural, abysmal eros open up to other than this becoming flesh, becoming text, becoming difference, which endlessly transcends the limits of discourse and plunges into new cataracts of texts? "It is in this sense, then," Priest explains in her exposition on Irigaray and negative theology, "that 'woman' occupies the 'mystical' position of the unspeakable: the female sex cannot be spoken within a language given over to the representation of the male sex, just as the divine cannot be spoken within the language given over to the representation of the human." Priest continues: "To speak (of) 'her' is to subject her to logic and to forms of representation that are alien to her."[30]

For feminist theology, *via negativa* with its endless spirals of language is a tricky road. For women who are rising as speaking subjects in language after ages of silence and repression, such a disclosure of the vulnerability and wiles of language may feel profoundly disheartening. This important task of woman to name herself and her surroundings is duly noted by Irigaray when, with a Feuerbachian argument, she maintains that women need to name God according to their own gender: "We women, sexed according to our gender, lack a God to share, a word to share and become."[31] Irigaray's kataphatic assertion of women's divine becoming is made more complex by a series of apophatic statements.

> God is the other that we absolutely cannot be without. In order to become, we need some shadowy perception of achievement, not a fixed objective, not a One postulated to be immutable but rather a cohesion and a horizon that assures us of the passage between past and future, the bridge of a present that remembers, that is not sheer oblivion and loss, not a crumbling away of existence, a failure, simply, to take note.[32]

Irigaray's impossible emergence of an apophatic God produces fleeting images of memory, relationality, and touch. This Irigarayan spirituality of life and birth addresses a divine dimension which is not One, but insists like Spretnak on the unity of spirit and body. Serene Jones has criticized Irigaray for relying too heavily on Feuerbachian metaphysics. For Jones, "it would seem that female desire has consumed God."[33] Thus Jones maintains that Irigaray has reduced God-talk to the emergence of woman as subject and bearer of language. However, in her criticism of Irigaray Jones fails to note Irigaray's apophatic negations, the elusive trait that can possibly shield Irigaray's God from utter consumption. The ancient distrust of ontology slides through, licks and shakes even the most promising feminist constructs and metaphors of horizons, bridges, and passages.

If Jones considers Irigaray to go too far in her apophatic musings of woman's becoming, Lanzetta is more optimistic. For Lanzetta, feminist apophatic theological language could be addressed as *via feminina*, language of the feminine, the forgotten, the abused and the ridiculed: "Applying a feminist re-reading of the mystical journey, *via feminina* extends the apophatic process not only to language and conceptual ideas about God, but also to the gender parity codified within its spiritual practices and contemplative paths."[34] If Lanzetta's *via feminina* brings women through the wiles and miseries of gender oppression, she never tells us who gets to be "woman" in that scheme; the entity of woman and the power dynamic between one body and another are not deconstructed. The feminist apophatic practice that I am advocating would seek to unsay even that abysmal depth, and by doing so bring forth new gateways. Thus, if Lanzetta advocates an apophatic practice that unsays that which oppresses women, I am arguing that in her scheme categories such as "woman" and "God" still hold the same ontological status. The yearning that drives most radical apophatic discourse is not only to clear away some false statements about God in order to get to know the real God behind the idols, which would then be the real object of desire. Apophasis concerns itself thus not with distinguishing the true affirmations about divinity from the false ones. It is not about saying yes to some statements about God that are considered to be woman-affirming, and no to others that are more oppressive to women. Rather, apophasis seeks to disclose the liminality of every affirmation about God and seeks to destabilize any discourse that objectifies God. "The infinite is the finite name that negates itself. Thus it exercises a bottomless iconoclasm," Catherine Keller says.[35] The bottomless iconoclasm of the infinite that Keller evokes does not collapse all experiences into relativity or nothingness. Rather each discovery of a hidden bottom, each awareness of a bottomless depth below, behind, or between a hidden finitization of the infinite calls forth a new wave of language hitherto unknown or repressed.

For me this apophatic flesh of depth and divine inbetweenness holds a strong promise for feminist theology in spite of the ontotheological traps. Such becoming is fueled by the divine inexhaustibilities of abysmal negations and affirmations, a trembling praxis of opening, touch, withdrawal in language and undoing identities, genders, sexualities, racial, class, and heterosexual privileges, consuming yet consumed. With Priest, I affirm the connections between Irigarayan "mysticism" and negative theology. With Schneider, I argue that within the multiple tracts of feminist theology, apophatic practices have played an important albeit largely unacknowledged role. If Priest argues for similar movements within feminism and apophatic theology, I am claiming apophatic feminist theology as the sensible unsaying of mysticism.

The Infinite Found in Human Form: Intertwinings of Cosmology and Incarnation

PHILIP CLAYTON

Enough has already been said in praise of the Unsayable that I will not add my voice to the chorus—not that my silence on the merits of the Ineffable reflects any lack of conviction on the topic. In fact, *were* I to allow myself to write the panegyric on the virtues of the Unsayable that my fingers are even now itching to write, it would be driven above all by an ethical and political motivation: the drive to challenge literalists who transform holy mysteries into their own univocal possession. Incalculable social and political damage has been done wherever *incarnatio* has become Man's possession (I use the noun advisedly) and, having once become his, is transformed by his hand into a weapon against others. Possessing the incarnation of God into one's own image—God become *Man*—then becomes a ground for establishing the possessor's superiority over his inferior "opponents," that is, those who look or think differently. This book is published in a country where, sadly, the majority of those who think at all about "God became flesh" think of this as a doctrine that they know to be literally true, a doctrine that entails the falsity of most or all other religious traditions. "Neither is there salvation in any other: for there is none other name under heaven given among men, whereby we must be saved" (Acts 4:12, King James Version [KJV]). The

---

I dedicate this paper with gratitude to my teacher and doctoral advisor in the phenomenology of religion, Louis Dupré, professor emeritus, Yale University, for though it does not exegete his works, its spirit and approach is deeply influenced by them.

present publication would be worthwhile by itself if it could help to undercut that stance.

But I resist the temptation to write that essay. Other chapters here spell out the political implications of the said and the Unsayable; it suffices for me to add my (silent) endorsement of their arguments. This chapter instead asks a different question: Is it possible to preserve the strengths (ethical, political, and otherwise) of apophatic traditions both past and present, but to do so while working within a more strongly kataphatic understanding of religious language?

As we saw, the problem with much incarnational thinking, at least in the U.S. context today, is that its advocates take it to be a doctrine they *know* to be true. The experiment in these few pages is to see whether *a critique of their theory of knowledge* can have some of the same effects as endorsing an apophatic theory of religious language in toto would have, allowing me to keep my feet much longer on kataphatic shores than many of my fellow authors in this volume.[1] Put more boldly, I suggest that those who, for whatever complex reasons, wish to avoid a fully apophatic construal of theological language—and I count myself among that group—can achieve some of the same goals by combining a kataphatic understanding of theology with an appropriately revised theory of knowledge.

KATAPHASIS AND THE THEORY OF KNOWLEDGE

That it's possible to do interesting and productive apophatic theology at the intersection of deconstruction, poststructuralism, and theopoiesis goes without saying (no pun intended). But is it possible still to do *kataphatic* theology in the present context? To many it will seem obvious that, given the developments of the last few decades, only to the extent that theologians paint with apophatic brushstrokes does their work warrant our attention today—for reasons so well known that they do not need rehearsing here.

The present essay may be read as a plea for a more nuanced portrayal of theological language in all its complexity. Casting doubts on whether religious language is ever referential, as one does in moving from a kataphatic into an increasingly apophatic framework, is *one* effective way of adapting theological language to our late modern or postmodern context. But it is not the only way. (Would it not be ironic if the poststructuralist stance(s) gave rise to a new orthodoxy, and hence a new set of heresies and anathemas?) It turns out that one can reach a similar resting point by other means—for example, by rethinking the epistemic status that one attributes to theological theories. That, at any rate, is my quest today.

How radical should this rethinking be? How skeptical is its epistemology? When the epistemic bar is raised too high, it produces the view that all theological proposals are equally uncertain—that is, *completely* uncertain, utterly unknown—and hence that no formulation is to be preferred over any other. The limit case of epistemic limitation, then, confronts one with a claim for the complete relativity of all religious truth claims. The pluralism that results is so radical that, in its outcome and effects, it in fact maps one-to-one onto the *via negativa* of the radical apophatic tradition.

The negative constraints on one's view of religious language to which the *via epistemologiae* gives rise can be just as complete, it appears, as in the great apophatic works; both equally undercut all positive assertions made within the religious traditions. Note, however, that even in this limit case the epistemic route is not *identical* to the apophatic route; one may have arrived at the same place, but by a significantly different path. The differences matter.

If these were the only two options available to theology, I would choose the high road of apophaticism. After all, the great mystical writers write more beautifully and profoundly than any epistemologist I've ever read (Hume sometimes comes close). Moreover, the lowest-common-denominator relativisms that typically stem from assuming a complete epistemic equality among all theological proposals are less interesting, and less productive for constructive theology, than the mystical and apophatic traditions have been.

But of course total skepticism is not the only outcome of reflection on the nature of knowledge, and one is hardly required to accept a completely skeptical epistemology of religious language. What if we deny that the epistemic limitations really extend this far?[2] There are multiple reasons to pull back from the abyss of an "anything goes" incommensurability between religious truth claims. Elsewhere I've defended a pragmatic (Peircean) theory of knowledge, which provides an effective antidote against the flat-footed "who's to say" response that one often hears from one's first-year students in the study of religion. But recent work in fact offers a rather wide array of theories for understanding knowledge-in-practice, all of which move beyond the now outworn dichotomies between rationalism and skepticism.

To refute skepticism in a brief introduction is of course impossible. So you may, if you wish, take what follows as a hypothetical exercise, a thought experiment: How might we construe religious practice and the use of religious language if at least some of it qualifies as knowledge? What sort of knowledge might this be? More particularly, what happens when we combine a kataphatic theory of religious language with an appropriate humility about religious knowledge claims, a humility which, however, stops short of a self-destroying (or religion-destroying) relativism. Other chapters offer proposals for balancing apophatic and kataphatic elements in theological language; why not seek to move beyond despairing epistemic relativism and bald objectivism in the same way?

Indeed, a particular means suggests itself for this moving-beyond. There is something right, it seems to me, in the idealist quest for coherence between *what* one asserts and *how* one asserts it, including what epistemic status one attributes to it. Endorsing this quest suggests seeking a "reflective equilibrium" between the content of one's theological models and the epistemic status that one ascribes to them. (This is a standard with far-reaching implications, as the literature and a moment's reflection will make clear.[3]) When it comes to concepts as weighty as incarnation, cosmology, and the infinite, I will suggest, *kenosis* offers a powerful framework for mediating between content and epistemic status in this way. Indeed, what *kenotic kataphasis* allows one to say turns out to be rather more complex, and hence more satisfying, than certain uses of apophasis that one finds in the recent literature.

Before proceeding, one obvious objection must first be addressed. It might at first appear that epistemic humility and apophatic theories concerning language about ultimate reality go hand in hand, that they cannot be separated. Have not religious thinkers argued for epistemic limitations *because of* their conviction that the Ultimate lies beyond all religious language? Is this not the reason why the mystics have developed their various complex means for expressing the Ineffable, for *evoking* what cannot be said?[4]

As similar as the two approaches may be, they are nonetheless not identical. In particular, concrete religious life, devotional practice, and certain uses of religious language are characterized by significant and apparently irreducibly kataphatic elements—perhaps more clearly in Christianity than in many other of the world's traditions. (I can't here make the case that kataphatic language is *essential* for Christianity, though I suspect it is. For purposes of this essay it will suffice if kataphatic language, with its inevitably metaphysical overtones, is desirable in at least some religious traditions.) If this is right, it is all the more important to find a way to foster epistemic humility short of the full embrace of apophasis.

KENOTIC PHRONESIS IN FIVE STAGES: A HINDU-CHRISTIAN MEDITATION

As indicated above, my goal is to link a kenotic understanding of incarnation with a kenotic epistemology, thereby establishing the required link between what is claimed and how it is claimed. But because examples drawn from one's own tradition are often the most contentious and the most difficult to settle, I shall take my lead from a well-known text within the Hindu devotional (*bhakti*) tradition, and from the Sanskrit Vaishnavite notion of *sārūpya* in particular.[5]

In proceeding in this way, I seek a method that is adapted both to the problem under consideration and to the solution that will be proposed. Kenosis calls for a practice of self-humbling on the part of Christian theologians, a continual awareness of the hegemonic claims that their tradition has made—most painfully, perhaps, when it comes to the topic of incarnation. And yet Christianity has no corner on the market; questions of this sort are difficult enough that the Christian tradition can't afford to treat itself as self-sufficient. We desperately need the mystical and devotional writings of other traditions to help us overcome our blind spots—and nowhere more urgently, perhaps, than when it comes to our tradition's overly essentialized and triumphalistic doctrines of the incarnation.

Sārūpya occurs as one within a quintet of terms. The progression through the five terms expresses the growing closeness of the devotee to the object of her devotion. It is neither a movement from greater to lesser knowledge nor the opposite; *each* stage, it will turn out, brings with it its own form of knowledge *and* its own epistemic limitations.

Consider the text from *Śrī Caitanya-caritāmṛta*, by Śrīla Kṣradāsa Kavirāja Gosvāmī:

> sārṣṭi, sārūpya, āra sāmīpya, sālokya
> sāyujya nā laya bhakta yāte brahma-aikya. (Ādi 3.18)[6]

> (These liberations are *sārṣṭi* [achieving opulences equal to those of the Lord], *sārūpya* [having a form the same as the Lord's], *sāmīpya* [living as a personal associate of the Lord] and *sālokya* [living on a Vaikuṇṭha planet]. Devotees [*bhakta*] never accept *sāyujya*, however, since that is oneness with Brahman.)

Interestingly, the terms occur in different orders in different texts. Compare the words spoken by Lord Kapila, an avatāra of the Supreme Personality of Godhead: "My devotees do not accept sālokya, sārṣṭi, sārūpya, sāmīpya or oneness with Me—even if I offer these liberations—in preference to serving Me" (Śrīmad-Bhāgavatam 3.29.13).

In Vedanta there is rarely one right way to progress through the material; common themes invariably recur in ever-cycling permutations. So let me offer one pathway through the maze, without claiming it to be the only one.

Stage One, sālokya: living on the same planet as the Supreme Personality.[7] Or: entering into the space of the gods, living in the same domain as God. Perhaps also: entering into the temple. One might even paraphrase the Sanskrit term as entering into the *neighborhood* of the divine.[8]

Stage Two, sāmīpya: nearness or closeness to God. To be a personal associate of the Supreme Lord, or to be in constant association with the Lord.

Stage Three, sārūpya: taking on the form of the god; having features like those of the Lord. The root of the word is the Sanskrit word for form, *rupa*. Thus *sārūpya-mukti* means "having the same form of [as] Divinity."

Stage Four, sārṣṭi: In *sārṣṭi* liberation the opulence of the devotee is equal to the opulence of the Supreme Lord.

Stage Five, sāyujya: oneness with the Supreme Lord (from *yuj*, to unite); becoming one with God.

COMMENTARY

Recall that ours is the question of knowledge and epistemic limitation in a kataphatic context. *Neti, neti*—I assume that it's *neither* true that the religious traditions are incommensurable and have nothing to say to each other, *nor* that they are all saying the same thing. What happens if we approach our question using this Hindu text as the framework, yet adapting it to another context? In my case, that would be the context of contemporary liberal Christian theology. The result, I suggest, is an appropriately humbled, yet still largely kataphatic, incarnational theology.

1. Sālokya—*Entering into the neighborhood of the Divine*

Let's assume that the ultimate religious object, the ultimate reality, is experienced phenomenologically as the sacred or holy. For Otto this is the fascinating and frightening mystery, for Eliade it's that Other to profane reality that orients it and gives to it its focus.

Now if we have no ability to discern the sacred, if we cannot even tell when we are in the neighborhood of the divine, then there is no basis to begin either a theology or a phenomenology of the religious; we are finished before we begin.

So we must at least know when we are in the neighborhood. This knowledge suffices, on my view, for the birth of theology. Thus we might define theology, at least in its most nascent form, as that activity that begins as one struggles to describe the neighborhood in which she finds herself when she senses the presence of the holy.

Like many theologians today, and perhaps unfortunately, I have spent more of my theological career at this first stage than in theology's loftier realms.[9] Here one is concerned, for example, with the "intimations of transcendence" that Peter Berger has explored.[10] One explores the first tantalizing hints of a transcendent dimension that grounds all finite things. Here also one finds the sort of apologetics that one can try out without embarrassment with one's secular colleagues and scientist friends—an apologetics consisting of the first vague testimonies to the existence of a deeper dimension that upholds the world of our everyday experience. Here ambiguity abounds: some of the most powerful intimations could also be merely regulative ideas or Feuerbachian projections. After all, even the Kantian regulative ideas, and the regulative *ideal* of God, serve as hints (if one can call them even that) of something forever and intrinsically unknowable. There must be some knowledge, if the stage is to count as *sālokya* at all; and yet this (minimal) knowledge is deeply intertwined with what is as yet unknown, at least at this stage.

In short: certainly there is epistemic limitation in stage one, the limitation of not knowing. But some knowledge is also implied by this first religious location. Specifically, it's the knowing that is required in order to draw one for the first time into the neighborhood of the holy and to recognize it once one arrives—to know the presence of the holy.

2. Sāmīpya—*Nearness to God*

In the stage of *sāmīpya* one not only enters the neighborhood of the sacred but is ready to draw near to the object of devotion itself, to enter into its intimate space. Or, as the Vaishnava tradition understands it, one agrees to become a personal associate of the Supreme Lord. The Mystery that one now approaches is both *tremendum* and *fascinans*, and it evokes an equally two-sided response. The complex responses to nearness to God are well attested in the phenomenology of religion; one thinks, for example, of the famous passage from Isaiah:

> In the year that King Uzziah died, I saw the Lord seated on a throne, high and exalted, and the train of his robe filled the temple. Above him were seraphs. . . . And they were calling to one another: "Holy, holy, holy is the LORD Almighty; the whole earth is full of his glory." At the sound of their voices the doorposts and thresholds shook and the temple was filled with smoke. "Woe to me!" I cried. "I am ruined! For I am a man of unclean lips, and I live among a people of unclean lips, and my eyes have seen the King, the LORD Almighty." (Is 6:1–5, NIV)

Another translation of *sāmīpya* suggests "entering into the world (or space) of the divine." Here we might understand "world" as something like *die Welt* in Heidegger or like the living together in his later essay

"Bauen, Wohnen, Denken." This stage entails sharing values and a common living space. A shared world is a powerful reality; it helps explain, for example, that surprisingly similar energy (and even appearance) that one sometimes detects in close associates. Perhaps—to look to a more Jewish analogy—one might think of *sāmīpya* as similar to Levinas's notion of entering into the "home," the sphere of most personal interaction.

Increasing nearness is the precondition for transformation. It's not enough to hang out somewhere in the neighborhood of the divine, like the tourists who drive around Beverly Hills hoping to see one of their favorite stars. Sharing the space of the divine brings the experience of increasing nearness and growing familiarity.

But here's the point: growing familiarity stands in some tension with the "no knowledge" interpretation of religion. The knowledge may be more *kennen* than *wissen*, but it's not the throw-up-your-hands hopelessness of religious relativism. This stage, like each of the others, brings with it its own form of knowledge—limited, admittedly, but (phenomenologically speaking) vital to the practitioner and, I want to suggest, irreducible. Indeed, as we're beginning to see, the forms of knowledge grow deeper and deeper with each stage, most clearly perhaps during the first three stages. But we must not get ahead of the story.

3. Sārūpya—*Taking on the form of the Lord*

First, drawn by fascination and fright, one entered the neighborhood of the divine. But the allure was eventually too great; one could not merely stare from afar but wished to become an associate of the Lord (*sāmīpya*). Transformed from rubbernecker to practitioner, one begins to know (*savoir* more than *connaître*) something of the nature of the One to whom one is gradually growing closer.

And then the mystery: that one should not only be transformed toward the image (*Gottebenbildlichkeit*), but should actually begin to take on the very form of God. It's hard not to notice the parallels between *sārūpya* in the Hindu literature and Christian incarnational thinking. What happens when one juxtaposes the Vaishnavite notion of *sārūpya-mukti* (having the same form as Divinity) with the early Christian hymn of incarnation?

Your attitude should be the same as that of Christ Jesus:
Who, being in very nature [form: *morphē*] God,

did not consider equality with God something to be grasped,
but made himself nothing [emptied himself: *ekenōsen*; cf. *kenōsis*],
taking the very nature [from *morphēn*] of a servant,
being made in human likeness.
And being found in appearance as a man,
he humbled himself
and became obedient to death—
even death on a cross. (Phil. 2: 5–8, NIV)

Note that Paul places the hymn in an epistemic context: "Let this mind be in you, which was also in Christ Jesus" (KJV), or "Have this mind among yourselves, which is yours in Christ Jesus" (English Standard Version). It's actually a verbal notion (*phroneisthō*; cf. *phroneisis*): "be so minded." Paul's "frame" for the text is nothing less than *an overarching epistemology of religious practice*. In this Pauline epistemology, the core of Christian practice is *imitatio Christi*, and the emulation naturally entails some knowledge of the one being emulated.

In fact, the passage from Paul even suggests a label for this theory of knowledge: a *kenotic epistēmē*. The knowledge of *sārūpya,* of taking on the same form, is in the Christian tradition the knowledge of sharing in the practice of self-emptying. It's no coincidence that Paul again links epistēmē and kenosis in the next chapter, though now in the context of suffering: "I want to know Christ, and the power of his resurrection, and the fellowship (*koinōnian*) of sharing in his sufferings, becoming like him in his death" (Phil. 3:10, NIV).

But now for the epistemic limitation. In each of our two cases the knowledge is deeply tied to a particular practice: the practice of devotion in the Hindu *bhakti* tradition, and the practice of *imitatio Christi* in Christianity. The analogies hint at a deep reciprocity: knowledge of the nature of the divine depends on learning to "have the mind" of self-emptying; conversely, advancing in kenotic practice depends on participating within the life of the Godhead. In this epistemic/transformative project, knowledge claims about the divine are invariably blended with one's own practice of seeking to empty ego and deepen *bhakti*, or deepening Christ-mindedness and emulating the great Gethsemane determination, "Not my will, but Thine be done." In the epistēmē of Christian practice the incarnation of the Highest on the one side, and on the other side the *theosis* of the creation, this being drawn into the very life of God, are bound together—so deeply, in fact, that one's ability to know that a given statement or insight mirrors the divine kenosis appears to vary in direct proportion to how advanced one is in this practice.

With this interwoven reciprocity we encounter a third form of limitation on knowledge claims about the divine. The disciple knows something of a key event in the life of God, knows something of the incarnation, yet her knowledge is limited by the depth of her own practice. Insofar as one's only access to incarnational mystery is to strive to "have this mind which was also in Christ Jesus," the limitation is never completely overcome in practice, though it might be overcome *sub specie aeternitatis*. One's epistemic striving invariably hits the glass ceiling of the imperfection of one's own *imitatio Christi*. And yet the claim to growing knowledge remains intrinsic to the practice. In this sense, the call to "develop this mind-set" (*phroneisthō*, Phil 2:5) is reminiscent of the very practical quest for *phronesis*, practical wisdom, in Aristotle's *Nicomachean Ethics*—a quest that, again, is more kataphatic than apophatic in spirit.

4. Sārṣṭi —*Sharing the opulence of the Divine*

In the Sanskrit *sārṣṭi*, or sharing the opulence of the Divine, there are again resonances with the incarnational hymn of Philippians 2, but in this case more with the final three verses of the text:

> Therefore God exalted him to the highest place
> and gave him the name that is above every name,
> that at the name of Jesus every knee should bow,
> in heaven and on earth and under the earth,
> and every tongue confess that Jesus Christ is Lord,
> to the glory of God the Father. (Phil 2:9–11, NIV)

At this stage one's knowledge may encounter a more unbending limitation than at the previous stage of *sārūpya*. Yet here, I suggest, it's not the ineffability of apophasis, but rather a limitation driven by the connection between knowledge and a sort of ladder of power and powerlessness. The "therefore" with which this text begins gives the clue: only those who know more of the koinonia of suffering and powerlessness—

through personal biography, or perhaps through membership in an oppressed group—should feel the freedom to talk of their exaltation. One does not place the demand "Empty yourselves!" on those whom society and history have already emptied and tossed aside.

This limit, I suggest, is not "merely" political, as some have suggested, but also epistemic. Liberation theologians may sometimes have overstated the point in some of their claims for the epistemic privilege of the poor and oppressed,[11] as if poverty and the knowledge of truth always line up neatly together side by side. (Do such claims not threaten to romanticize the harsh realities of poverty?) Still, it seems incontestable that the ladder of power and powerlessness, and the social and political factors that create it, place limits on what one can and should say—however difficult it is to fold such factors into analyses of "justified true belief." The silence about *sārṣṭi*, about "sharing the opulence of the Divine," which is placed on those who already enjoy privilege in this world, is an effective epistemic boundary.

The kenotic humbling entailed by this new stage presents a strong limit to what I—the "I" characterized by labels such as "white," "male," "relatively affluent," "American," "North"—can know or say about exaltation. After all, the demands of kenotic epistēmē apply to theologians as well. The result is a crucial caution regarding certain topics, *especially those involving exaltation*, for certain persons and traditions. Given its history with Jews and Muslims, for example, Christianity needs to be eternally vigilant about the language of *Christus victor*[12] and its "superiority over its rivals."

Note that this call to silence is not the same as the ubiquitous nonsaying of mystical silence. It's the silence imposed by the upside-down world of Mary's realization:

> He has brought down rulers from their thrones
>   but has lifted up the humble.
> He has filled the hungry with good things
>   but has sent the rich away empty. (Luke 1:52–53, NIV)

Indeed, there may even be *political* reason to hold back from an overquick apophaticism, at least to the extent that a self-negating language can undercut the political effectiveness of (for example) the postcolonial critique of power structures. Political action must name the truths of injustice, and for this it needs kataphasis in its tool kit.

5. Sāyujya—*Becoming one with God*

Until now the limitations on speech about the divine have been driven mostly by praxis-oriented (ethical and, at least in this last case, political) factors. At each stage, language about the religious object faced epistemic limitations, without ever leaping the great divide from kataphatic to apophatic. But the title of this text requires us to consider a third term: incarnation, ethics . . . and infinity. *Sāyujya* (and *ekatva*, used synonymously in other passages) bring us to that final stage.

The response of the *bhakti* tradition to becoming one with God is unambiguous: "It is clearly stated herein that a pure devotee does not desire *ekatva*, oneness with the Supreme Lord, as desired by the impersonalists, the mental speculators, and the meditators. To become one with the Supreme Lord is beyond the dream of a pure devotee."[13] As it turns out, there is a somewhat greater ambivalence in the writings of the Christian mystics.[14] In their writings the drive toward unitive mysticism mingles in complex ways with the realization that human persons are finite, created rather than Creator—however strongly we may long to unite with our infinite source and ground. How is one to proceed through this "dark night" of competing instincts, longings, and claims?

Had language unraveled earlier, the devotee would lose the chance to formulate one final insight before the clouds of unknowing close over and one retreats (or perhaps better, advances) into poetry and practice—an insight into the nature of the finite-infinite relation. The impulse in this direction comes from a famous passage in Nicholas of Cusa's *De docta ignorantia.* Cusa recognizes why the God-world relation seems too great a mystery for us: "Who, therefore, can understand that God is the form of being but not intermixed with creation? . . . No one doubts that there can be no proportion between the infinite and the finite. . . . The curve cannot participate the essence of the infinite line by taking part of it, since the essence is infinite and indivisible. Who, accordingly, can understand how the one, infinite form is participated differently by different creatures?"[15] His idea for a solution comes from art:

> It is, perhaps, as if a work of art were to have no other being than that of dependency, for it would be totally dependent on the idea of

> the artist. From the artist it would take its being and under the artist's influence it would be preserved, like the image of a face in a mirror if we assume that before and after the image's reflection the mirror would be nothing in and of itself.[16]

Cusa does not stop with metaphor, however. In the same section he formulates the conclusion as an argument and a thesis, a position theologians would later come to call *panentheism*: "Because the creation was created through the being of the maximum and because, in the maximum, being, making, and creating are the same, creating seems to be no different than God's being all things. If, therefore, *God is all things and if this means creating* . . . ."[17] In *De visione Dei* Cusa further strengthens his case for this conclusion by basing it, as Hegel later would as well, on the logic of the notion of infinity:

> Lord my God, Strength of the frail, I see that You are Infinity itself. And so, there is not anything that is other than You or different from You or opposed to You. For Infinity is not compatible with otherness, because there is not anything outside it, since it is Infinity. For Absolute Infinity includes and encompasses all things. And so, if there were "Infinity" and something else outside it, there would be neither Infinity nor anything else. For Infinity cannot be either greater or lesser. Therefore, there is not anything outside it. For unless it included all being in itself, it would not be Infinity. . . . So if the Infinite is removed, nothing remains. Therefore, Infinity exists and enfolds all things; and no thing can exist outside it. Hence, nothing is other than it or different from it. Therefore, Infinity is all things in such way that it is none of them.[18]

Only the distinction of finite from infinite, in other words, and not some spatial distance imposed by creation, separates creature and Creator.[19]

In her chapter, Professor Keller ties these insights into the finite-infinite relation to "the apophatic engine." In the interest of dialectical tension, I would stress that they include a kataphatic dimension as well. Epistemic limitation and distance may blur our eyes and loosen our fingers' grasp, but they do not completely remove Cusa's insight from the realm of assertorical language—that is, as I've argued elsewhere, from an appropriately limited, hypothetical, and pluralistic metaphysics.[20]

There are many routes to Cusa's insight about the finite and the infinite. One can reach it (or variants of it) through the four stages of Hindu devotional practice (*bhakti*) that we have explored; or through analogous Christian practices; or through traditional metaphysical arguments; or historically, as I attempted to do in *The Problem of God in Modern Thought*; or by reflecting on the paradoxically self-transcending limits of reason, in dialogue with (but also in critical response to) Kant's critique of metaphysics. Each of these routes, I suggest, points to something like the following insight: the ground and source from which we stem and toward which we are drawn is infinite, not bounded by anything. We, by contrast, are unmistakably finite: limited, located, *geworfen in irgendeine Welt*, thrown into contexts not of our own making and choosing (and into some others that are). As such, we clearly are not ourselves the ground of our being, not *causi sui*. For most, Schleiermacher's "sense of absolute dependence" is the better phenomenological description. And yet we are *non-aliud* to the infinite ground of our being, as (following Cusa) it is not-other to us. How could we be fully other to that which continually grounds and embraces us?

Such is the (kataphatic) logic of the infinite, as the much-maligned Hegel spelled it out. An infinite that excludes the finite would be *eine schlechte Unendlichkeit*.[21] A finite placed outside the infinite would limit the infinite; and a limited infinite is, after all, not infinite at all. *Das wahrhaft Unendliche*, the truly infinite, must comprehend the finite,[22] including it, womb-like, within itself. Including within, yet not confused with—this is the dialectical nature of the finite's relationship to its infinite source.

Suddenly we find ourselves at the (frightening) intersection point of three major themes that this volume dares to set into motion and interconnection: creation, cosmology, and infinity. If finite and infinite stood *timelessly* in this dialectical relationship, one would not need to address questions of origin. But why would one then designate the finite, which in that case would be co-eternal with the infinite, as finite *rather than* infinite? Not to mention the problem of doing justice to the phenomenon of change, which a-creationism leaves unsatisfactorily thematized. Without process the very distinction is endangered (as Hegel also saw).

One is compelled, then, to include the language of source and origin to talk of Ground. When combined with the dialectical relation of finite and infinite just summarized, this mix immediately yields the famous twofold "in" of Book 2 of Cusa's *De docta ignorantia*, which Catherine Keller also quotes: "God, therefore, is the enfolding of all in the sense that all are in God, and God is the unfolding of all in the sense that God is in all."[23] All finite things are enfolded within the divine, distinct but never separated from their ground, in whom we "live and move and have our being" (Acts 17:28, NIV). The two "in"s are the "in" of origin and the "in" of destiny: Alpha and Omega, *implicatio* and *explicatio*, creation and telos, beautifully worked out (and in a recognizably Cusanian spirit) by Schleiermacher in the *Dialektik* as the intermingled interrelationship of *terminus a quo* and *terminus ad quem*.

Do we have here the germ of a theological cosmology? Yes and no. Locating the finite panentheistically within the infinite-divine simultaneously "locates" the cosmos, specifies its status, and links its fate with the history of God, or at least with God's salvific intent. But it is not a theory of origins in the sense of classical cosmology, or traditional cosmogenies, or the cosmological models in contemporary physics. This insight into the finite-infinite relationship is too formal for any of that—as one might already have assumed from the phrase "the logic of the infinite." If the relationship is formal, where will its material content come from? Well, myths, devotional practice, religious experience, the needs of political activism. . . . Pushed to say more, we can only tell stories. At *this* point, then—at this fifth stage, with the basic insight into the relation of finite and infinite behind us, standing now before the horizon of unitive longing or experience—kataphatic language does indeed dissolve into the apophatic. At the end of the day, the kataphatic thinker joins hands with the advocates of apophasis. It is right to do so here, standing before the light of the final horizon. But not earlier.

CONCLUSION: TOWARD AN INCARNATIONAL COSMOLOGY

The irony in my title should now be clear. The Infinite is never just "found" in human form, standing before us waiting to be grasped, *vorhanden*. The language may be kataphatic, but it does not therefore "possess" God in objective form. *Contemplatio* is always participatory: "And we, who with unveiled faces all contemplate the Lord's glory, are being transformed into his likeness . . ." (2 Cor 3:18, NIV, following the alternate reading). We are within that about which we speak; we may sometimes speak truly of it; but we do not thereby possess it. The fish does not own the water in which it swims.

Writing these pages, I frequently winced as I reviewed the various texts on incarnation—including some of the oft-cited biblical texts. One reads them through a *Rezeptionsgeschichte* that is laden with overtones of grasping, possessing, owning. Contemporary Christian literature is rife with a proud confidence that the church has located the place where "God became Man" and, having found it, is ready to interpret this fact for the benefit of the rest of the world. I recoil in horror that a notion so holy and elusive could ever be used in this fashion as a weapon for proselytizing—not to mention as a bulwark to justify a bellicose U.S. foreign policy. No wonder that one is wont to turn to apophasis as an antidote. Forced to choose between owning the doctrine of incarnation as a possession, one that would single me out as elect from the many who are damned, on the one hand, and declaring divine embodiment forever beyond the grasp of language, on the other, I too would side with ineffability.

But the point of this chapter has been that we are *not* forced to choose between those two options. Reflecting on the classic four elements of Hindu devotional practice, and reframing them in the context of the Pauline exhortation to "have the mind of Christ," suggested a *via media* where once an excluded middle was said to reign. Kenotic epistēmē, I labeled it. One could also speak of *kenotic phronesis*, the practice of self-emptying.

This middle way is deeply intertwined with epistemic limitations. But these limitations are not the global (self-)limitation of apophasis; they have the advantage of arising organically as one moves through the various stages. The five limitations I explored, taken together, serve a function perhaps not unlike the functions of the apophatic standpoint [*sic*]. But they arise in a differentiated fashion, linked phenomenologically and theologically with each particular stage of the practice of *imitatio Christi*. Nor are these limitations identical with one another; each one is motivated by ethical, political, and devotional factors in different ways. They reflect a logic, the logic of the finite-infinite relationship; they reflect a theo-logic, that of *Fleischwerdung*, the infinite found in human form; and of course they reflect a practice or set of practices: the exercise of self-emptying.

The two theological loci mentioned in my title are indeed "intertwined." In the end, however, incarnation trumps and limits cosmology. Theological cosmology, if there is to be one, can only be incarnational cosmology, a kenotic doctrine of creation.[24] We saw that the theology of incarnation grows out of the practice of *imitatio Christi*; these two sides then together constrain what the theologian may say about creation. If this is right, even the divine act of creation (and consequently, of course, the human one) must be seen as a voluntary self-limitation, mirroring the work of the one who "being found in human form . . . humbled himself." In the end, assertions about creation, at least those that would be theological, will be constrained by the same principle with which Paul framed the christological hymn: be minded as one who, though found in form divine, would exchange it for the form of a servant.

Love Stories: Unspeakable Relations, Infinite Freedom

The Apophasis of Divine Freedom: Saving "the Name" and the Neighbor from Human Mastery

CHRIS BOESEL

The general interest that provides the context for this essay emerges from what is often called, these days, the postmodern "turn" to religion and theology. This "turn" refers to a growing body of theologically minded work centered on the thought of Derrida and Levinas (but not to the exclusion of other postmodern thinkers), especially in the wake of Derrida's own deconstructive "turn" to the theme of religion. This is a theological current that is fast becoming a cottage industry, at least in the United States. What I find particularly interesting about this emerging arena of postmodern discourse, and what constitutes the entry point into this essay, is its engagement of the theme of incomprehensible divine mystery and the critical-constructive readings of the apophatic tradition of negative theology that that involves (apophasis being the method of negation—the *via negativa*—in which everything that can be said of God is denied in order to mark the transcendence of divine reality beyond the limits of creaturely language and concepts).

While I find this engagement not only interesting but compelling, I am also both dissatisfied with its current scope and suspicious of some of its central strategies. My dissatisfaction arises from my own bias, given my particular location as a systematic Christian theologian. It pertains to the way in which this epistemologically focused engagement often seems constrained within the orbit of the doctrines of God and creation, falling short of fully addressing the robust trinitarian activity of the Christian story (reconciliation, redemption, sanctification) in which God does some other very specific and very strange things. This is a story, after all, in which the act of creation is only the beginning, the prelude, the setting of the stage. It is a story of a God who is not content with being Creator and enfolding matrix of the cosmos but desires something more and in addition, a more radical relationality with creatures *in the midst of* creation—the communion of persons who love in freedom. Now, we may not like this story, or we may think it is problematic in precisely these ways, and for very good reasons. And it is certainly not the only religious narrative on offer calling for fruitful engagement with the post-modern discourse of deconstruction. But if, for whatever reason, the Christian story is among the various traditions, religious or otherwise, being engaged, it seems not unprofitable—at least from the point of view of a curious systematic theologian—to see what such an engagement might bring forth in venturing beyond the doctrinal cluster of God and creation.

My suspicion—what constitutes the critical edge of my thesis—is that there is an unstated assumption at work in these readings that we human creatures (or at least some of us) are ultimately *less* radically limited, less in the dark, *ethically* than we are *epistemologically* in relation to divine mystery. This suspicion has less to do with my particular trinitarian concerns as a systematic Christian theologian than with a sense of contradiction entailed in the deconstructive engagement in relation to its own stated desires (desires which I happen to share and affirm). I can't shake the feeling that, despite disclaimers to the contrary, someone is in charge here—and that it is *not* God. I get the sense that there is a subtle policing of the intercourse between divinity and created reality that attempts to ensure that both God and the creature are behaving themselves appropriately. The consequence is an ethical employment of the theological theme of divine mystery in the name of resistance to human mastery that may itself turn out to be a very subtle form of human mastery over divine mystery.

Maybe. That's the suspicion, at any rate.

The following is a basic roadmap of what I am attempting to do in these few pages. I first sketch out a very brief and very general characterization of a deconstructive reading of negative theology. I have in mind here, in addition to Derrida himself, the interpretations by John Caputo and Kevin Hart of Derrida's reading of Pseudo-Dionysius. It needs to be said that what I am calling negative theology, here, is, as all traditions, varied and multiform, and Derrida's deconstructive analysis and critique of one of its featured practitioners should in no way be taken as an authoritative representation of the tradition as a whole. Indeed, I am not assuming it is an authoritative reading even of Pseudo-Dionysius in particular. It is, in fact, not negative theology or Pseudo-Dionysius that primarily interests me so much as how they tend to be read by interpreters of deconstruction and how that reading entails what I think can be called a certain apophatic desire of its own: a twofold desire—*theologically*, to "save the name" of God from human mastery ("save the name" being a reference to a key text by Derrida on negative theology), and in doing so, to *ethically* "save the neighbor" from the always toxic consequences of said mastery.

I then suggest an alternative strand of the theological tradition that may provide resources for the apophatic desire of theologically minded interpreters of deconstruction. I have in mind the historically protestant (but not necessarily *exclusively* protestant) emphasis on the freedom of God's self-giving and self-disclosing Word. Now, you may be wondering how incomprehensible divine mystery is to be preserved if God actually shows up and introduces herself. Well, that is the rabbit I'm hoping to pull out of my hat in the following pages. And I attempt to do so in the form of a "thought experiment," drawing first on Kierkegaard and then on Barth.

After making the case that, *theologically*, divine mystery is indeed preserved from human mastery in the freedom of divine self-giving, I turn to consider the *ethical* dimension of what I am calling postmodern apophatic desire—the desire to save the neighbor. It is here that the freedom of divine self-giving, at least as I present it via Kierkegaard and Barth, runs into some trouble: divine self-giving "*to whom*," for example. So this third and final section of the essay struggles to tease out the complexity of the ethical implications of free, divine self-giving. And in the midst of this struggle we might find that the ethical offense caused by the apophasis of divine freedom reveals certain problematic fault lines in the postmodern turn to religion and theology and its engagement with the theme of divine mystery. We may finally find ourselves in a predicament of radical finitude (if not sin) wherein God's mystery confronts us as intractable problem rather than constructive resource, such that it is secured not by our self-critical method but by God's own self-giving freedom from all methodology, theological, philosophical, or ethical.

DECONSTRUCTION'S TWOFOLD APOPHATIC DESIRE: THE YES AND THE NO TO NEGATIVE THEOLOGY

Speaking very generally, the classical tradition of Christian negative theology, especially as articulated by Pseudo-Dionysius, could be said to express an apophatic desire to preserve the infinite, incomprehensible, and unknowable nature of God in the face of all particular, creaturely—and so finite—conceiving and speaking of God; it attempts, via the method of denial—i.e., apophasis—to (borrowing a Derridean shorthand) theologically "save the name"[1] of God from the grasp of all our finite, creaturely conceptual, and linguistic renderings of "God." The trick is, for this tradition at any rate, that such creaturely speaking (and so, conceiving) of God is appropriate and necessary to creatures, indeed, even commanded of creatures by God herself, given that they are created and sustained by said divinity precisely to give creaturely praise to and worship of God (appropriate to the diversities of nature and ability). The negative gesture of the apophatic, then, always accompanies the necessary and appropriate kataphatic—that is, positive—speech to and about God, in order to preserve or ensure its faithfulness and "truthfulness" as creaturely thought and speech in relation to its divine referent—a divine referent, of course, whose infinite nature exceeds all such creaturely thought and talk. As such, the apophatic itself—like the kataphatic—is seen as a response to divine command, the command against idolatry in all its guises: the confused reduction of God to, and identification of God with, a particular creaturely reality of whatever form—inorganic or organic bodies, the bodies of words, texts, traditions, canons, the bodies of ideas, conceptual bodies—wherein the divine might be presumed to be grasped, limited, contained, comprehended in thought and speech, as an object of our knowledge, and so brought under our control and mastery.

And speaking of Derrida. Given deconstruction's obsession with the radical limits of finitude with regard to knowledge, language, and meaning (well, with regard to everything, really), it is no surprise that an engaged critique of negative theology (that is to say, a critique that is not *simply* critical) constitutes a central moment of the deconstructive "turn" to religion and theology. Much of this engagement has been spent making the argument that deconstruction itself is *not*, in fact, negative theology, an argument made necessary because of their very real structural similarities—for example, deconstruction's ceaseless tracing of radical limits, the negative practice of trying to signify the impossible by writing "under erasure," and Derrida's attempt to articulate the "whence" (which is nowhere) of those limits, to signify "that" (which is no thing) by which they are determined. So, for instance, Caputo entitles a chapter of *The Prayers and Tears of Jacques Derrida*, "*Différance* Is Not God." But the engagement ultimately goes beyond clarifying the distinction between the two discourses. For while Derrida and his theologically minded interpreters are appreciative (given clarity on the distinction) of the resonance of negative theology with deconstruction's own ceaseless tracing of the limits of knowledge, language, and meaning, they (animated by an apophatic desire of their own) nevertheless find and follow a thread of critical reading.[2]

And here I'm going to give the barest sketch of this reading.

In *The Mystical Theology*, Pseudo-Dionysius advises his reader "to leave behind you everything perceived and understood . . . [and] with your understanding laid aside . . . strive upward as much as you can toward union with him who is beyond all being and knowledge."[3] Interestingly, this experience of union with the divine beyond the limits of creaturely knowledge and language would seem to provide, as a matter of fact, knowledge of a sort—a possession of those who have had this experience. It is a knowledge of God precisely as unknowable and incomprehensible; as well as knowledge of the limits of the creaturely in relation to the unknowability and incomprehensibility of God; as well as knowledge of the apophatic method of denying all kataphatic speech for the sake of its remaining faithful and true, as creaturely, in relation to its divine referent.

The problem for the interpreter of deconstruction, here, is . . . well, first of all, that that is *a lot* of knowledge, especially for a discourse committed to the negative marking of the limits of knowledge. Second, this experience of unity with the divine seems to constitute a kind of "arrival" outside of what Derrida calls "the text" (outside of which, nothing "is"); the experience of unity with the divine beyond knowledge seems to presume the possibility of escape, for certain human creatures, from the radical limits of (creaturely) finitude. And it is just such an escape from the limits and structures of finitude ("arrival" outside "the text") that the movement of deconstruction is said to render impossible. It will, for example, rigorously trace the inscription of *all* experience within the same radical structures of finitude as creaturely knowledge and language. And furthermore, the interpreter of deconstruction may suggest that a method of preserving divine mystery grounded in and governed by the assumption of such an experience of "arrival" and unity constitutes, contra its claim or intention, a form of totalized knowledge of the limits of finitude, and that such a knowledge of the boundary between finitude and infinity constitutes, in turn, a human fixing, locating, and even defining of the divine according to that knowledge (and thereby a kind of grasping, controlling, mastering).

The movement of deconstruction, then, suggests the nature and extent of negative theology's *theological* failure to fulfill its apophatic desire to preserve divine mystery. It might also, however, be interpreted to pick up traces of an *ethical* fallout from this theological failure. So, for example, you find Caputo saying that negative theology, in "managing to lift itself up into a pure presence above time and history, above language and the play of the trace . . . lends itself to a consummately dangerous political and ecclesiastical absolutism, to a politics of negative theology that is a threat to everyone." He concludes that negative theology, then, "would not save the name of God . . . but would endanger everybody with a dangerous absolutism."[4] I suggest that there are two ways in which this endangerment can be understood. First, the assumed "arrival" outside the text seems to suggest a denigration—even the destruction—of the creaturely itself in its material and historical particularity and finitude. For example, Pseudo-Dionysius describes the experience of unity as "break[ing] away from what sees and is seen, and plung[ing] into the truly mysterious darkness of unknowing. . . . Here, being neither oneself nor someone else, one is supremely united to the completely unknown by an inactivity of all knowledge."[5] Second, this experience of unity with the divine is clearly not for everyone, at least in this life. It is a privileged experience for the initiated, to be kept safe from those ill-prepared for it. Pseudo-Dionysius, again, after speaking of the mystical ascent in which one is "uplifted to the ray of the divine shadow which is above everything that is," immediately cautions his reader to "see to it that none of this comes to the hearing of the uninformed."[6] The mystical ascent would seem to constitute an "epistemological privilege"—that is, "I know and you don't"—in relation to those neighbors counted as "uninformed." In my reading of our contemporary context, the interrelated combination of these two dynamics—denigration of material embodiment and epistemological privilege—can be taken to constitute the unethical par excellence.

To conclude this section, then, I suggest that the apophatic desire of deconstruction, or at least of its theologically minded interpreters, is twofold, both theological and ethical: it is a desire not only to "save the name" of God but also to "save the neighbor" from all those presuming to grasp God in creaturely names and concepts. So you have Kevin Hart talking about deconstruction helping theology distinguish *God* from any "*concept* of 'God'," and in so doing, allowing "the possibility of re-thinking the divine in a discourse which . . . is no longer governed by metaphysics."[7] And Caputo following up, so to speak, by arguing that this deconstructive "saving of the name" of God functions to "save the name of God *for everybody*, not just the faithful in the determinable faiths."[8] The deconstructive method, or practice of reading, that ensures this twofold apophatic desire is the rigorous tracing of the limits of creaturely finitude, of "the text," *from "within"* those limits. Consequently, the *theological* desire to preserve the mystery of God by strictly observing the boundaries of creaturely finitude can be said to be *ethically* engendered in that such observance does not require and depend on a (1) *privileged* experience of (2) creaturely *disembodiment*, or *dis*-carnation. Or, we could state the same thing in this way: the *ethical* desire for an understanding of the divine that resists privileged experience and creaturely disembodiment can be said to be *theologically* engendered in that such an understanding functions apophatically to preserve divine mystery from human mastery. Again, the question of which desire—the theological or the ethical—is engendering which, lies at the heart of the complexity toward which I will be drawing us in what follows.

A THOUGHT EXPERIMENT: THE APOPHASIS OF DIVINE FREEDOM

I suggest that there is a quite different strand of Christian theology that nevertheless resonates strongly with (a) the twofold apophatic desire to "save the name" and save the neighbor, and (b) the conviction that the latter comes by way of the former.[9] Might this strand of Christian theology, represented here by "proto-postmoderns" (according to some), Kierkegaard and Barth, offer a fertile moment of engagement for interpreters of deconstruction in their—and the world's—recent "turn to religion"?[10] To test the possibilities of this question, I borrow a trick from Kierkegaard and put forward the following "thought experiment." If God *gives Godself to be known* by the materially and historically finite creature (note the protestant emphasis on a particular, determinate, incarnate Word from God to be heard and proclaimed), can divine mystery be apophatically honored? Is it possible to (a) theologically "save the name" of God, from all our finite, creaturely conceptual and linguistic "Gods," and (b) ethically "save the neighbor" from ourselves or from other more fundamentalist neighbors or, perhaps, from other more liberal, progressive, even postmodern neighbors, what with all our (and their) finite and creaturely conceptual and linguistic "Gods"? To anticipate where we are headed: *if* this is possible, it is a possibility that remains decidedly *God's*, and just as decidedly *not* our own—and *this* limit raises the specter of a problematic complexity to our postmodern—indeed, to all—apophatic desire (inasmuch as it is a human desire issuing in a human project and method).

I first use Kierkegaard to set out the dimensions of a kind of "Copernican revolution" that occurs when the question of divine mystery is set within a Reformation-Protestant context: divine self-giving *to be known* by the creature. I then turn to Barth to fill out the specific nature of this divine self-giving as the mystery of *free event*, and I attempt to make the case that there is entailed here a *theological* apophasis of divine freedom. In the last section I consider the *ethical* limits of this apophatic movement and how they point to the possibility that the postmodern employment of the theme of divine mystery might stumble over ethical limits of its own.

"LOVE'S UNDERSTANDING:" A COPERNICAN REVOLUTION OF SORTS

In *Philosophical Fragments*, the Kierkegaardian pseudonym Johannes Climacus proposes a thought experiment in which he sketches out an alternative to the Socratic assumptions about the human creature's relation to the truth (e.g., that we are born with a memory of the eternal by which we are always already in possession of truth: "the truth is within you").[11] Contra the Socratic, Climacus muses, "What if?" What if we, in our natural human state, are radically limited with regard to knowledge of the truth, the eternal. What if we are not in possession of the truth but are "in untruth." Consequently, we would need to be taught the truth, receive the truth, from another. And since no human being can do this for us, the required teacher would have to be "the god," who in teaching us the truth, gives us her very self, for the god *is* the eternal, *is* the truth itself, and so on. This is, of course, a mischievous sham; Climacus (or, at least, Kierkegaard) clearly has in mind the orthodox Christian doctrine of the incarnation.

It is Climacus's treatment of the why and the how of this little story that is most pertinent to our concerns.

First, the Why. Why does the god (the teacher) give herself (the eternal, the truth) to be known by the creature (the learner)? It must be for love—not by any necessity, but a free self-giving for the sake of the possibility of this relation itself.[12] And love has a twofold dimension here. It is not only out of the *god's* love for the creature that the god "makes his appearance as the teacher"; it is also *for the sake of love*, so that *the creature* might love the god, that the god and the creature might be joined in a relation of "love's understanding."[13]

Second, the How. How is the god to create the "equality," or "unity," necessary in order to "make himself understood" without "destroy[ing] that which is different," that is, the creature *as creature*?[14] How does the god give herself to be known by the creature in and for love without obliterating the beloved?[15]

Climacus rejects both the possibility of an "ascent," an exaltation of the beloved creature to the heights of heaven (à la mystical, negative theology, perhaps), and of a divine "appearing" in overpowering, sacred "splendor," on the grounds that they both would violate the integrity of the creature's existence, *as creature*.[16]

The "unity" of "love's understanding," then, must be "attempted by a descent." And a descent, by the god, to the level of "the lowliest" of all ("for if even Socrates did not keep company solely with brilliant minds, how then could the god make distinctions?!" Climacus asks. This will become important when we consider the ethical issue of "saving the neighbor"). Therefore, "in love [the god] wants to be the equal of the most lowly of the lowly," and so comes to the creature "in the form of the servant."[17] This "form," however, "is not something put on like the king's plebian cloak, which just by flapping open would betray the king . . . but is [the god's] true form." The god does not deceive, but in the "omnipotence of love," remains truly god while fully embodied as a particular human creature, just like any other human, even the lowliest of the low.[18]

I want to pause here and note the "change of context" that has occurred. Kierkegaard has taken the rarefied epistemological question of the possibility of our knowledge of the divine (the eternal, the truth) out of the philosophical, metaphysical, or even theological contexts in which it is typically addressed and set it within the context of a love story. (Doctrinally, this is the move beyond the cosmological sphere of the doctrines of God and creation, into the heart of the trinitarian engagement with the creatures of the cosmos.) I suggest that this change of context "turns the tables," so to speak—and rather significantly—with regard to divine mystery.

1. There is a change of direction. The problem of the limits of the creature with regard to knowledge of the divine is no longer the creature's problem, but God's. The issue is no longer the limits encountered by the human desire to "ascend" and escape—that is, transgress—the limits of creaturely finitude in order to lay claim to creaturely knowledge of the divine; the issue here is the limits encountered by *God* in God's desire to "descend" and enter—that is, transgress—the limits of creaturely finitude in order to be known by the creature, *as* creature (in and for love).[19] This change of direction has rather confusing consequences for the apophatic desire to preserve divine mystery. Rather than working to keep human knowledge *within* the proper limits of finitude, we would seem now to be dealing with something that looks an awful lot like keeping the divine *out*—schooling God on what is and what is not an appropriate way for divinity to behave. We will return to this in the final section of the essay. For now, we simply need to note that whatever "unity" occurs between the god and the creature in "love's understanding," occurs *this side* of the limits of creaturely finitude, within the realm of creaturely commerce, knowing, speaking, and so on. "*For love,* any other revelation," Climacus argues—any self-giving communication of

the god to the creature other than the god's own radical incarnation *as* creature, equal to the lowliest—"would be a deception."[20] It would not be in and for love of the creature, *as* creature.

2. The second element of our "Copernican revolution" is a "change of subject." What is it that is known in the descent of the god's self-giving? What is the referent of all the creature's consequent thinking and speaking of the god? It is no longer the *nature* or essence or being of the god in the primary instance but rather the specific, determinate *act* of incarnate self-disclosure in and by which the god gives her very self to the creature to be known in and for love.

And here we encounter the pivotal question. Is the incarnational and revelatory self-giving of the god to the creature *to be known* in and for love necessarily a self-giving unto *creaturely possession*, and thereby unto creaturely disposal, mastery, grasping? Does the "change of context"—to a love story wherein the god *wants* to be known and gives herself to be known in and for love—include a change from divine mystery to human mastery?

To pursue this question I turn our attention to Barth and his understanding of incarnational revelation as the mysterious event of free divine self-giving.

THE MYSTERIOUS EVENT OF DIVINE FREEDOM

For starters, Barth's answer to the above question is no; divine self-giving to the creature, as creature, is not a self-giving unto possession. In good Reformation style, Barth assumes that *what* is "known" by the creature in "love's understanding" is the divine self-giving of God in God's *Word* to and for the creature (rather than, in the first instance, God's *essence*, being, etc.).[21] He also assumes that the event of creaturely "knowing" *itself*—the event of faith, for Barth—is radically limited in relation to *what* is known, precisely in terms of the impossibility of grasping possession, control, and mastery on the part of the human creature. The event of faith constitutes, then, I suggest, a "knowing otherwise" than the human knowing of possession and mastery. "Invariably," Barth says, "faith is acknowledgment of our limit and acknowledgment of the mystery of God's Word," the mystery being, that in truly giving Godself to us in God's Word, God is "not giving Himself . . . into our hands but keeping us in His hands."[22] This means that the creature is prevented from thinking that "in thought and speech at least we are its [the Word's] master."[23]

Well, how is the creature so prevented, we might ask?

For Barth, the event of "knowing otherwise," in which God gives Godself to be recognized, *as* God, in the impenetrable creaturely incognito of equality with the lowliest of the low, is prevented from becoming a human knowing as possession and mastery by a "twofold barrier": (a) the "incomprehensibility" of God's Word "in itself," due to its nature as *event*, and (b) the incomprehensibility of God's Word in its "how," that is, due to its nature as *free* event. We will unpack these one at a time to get a sense of how they constitute an apophasis of divine freedom.

1. The Word of God as Event

Barth: "For one thing, as what it is it is only the content of the specific event of its being spoken to this man or that. Then again, as what this man or that receives and accepts and can give an account of as God's Word in the event of faith [Kierkegaard's "love's understanding" that occurs in "the moment"], it is no longer what the Word of God that is spoken to him is in itself, but only his recollection of what is said to him and his expectation of what will be said to him afresh."[24]

There are several things to consider here.

The present moment. The event nature of God's self-giving Word means that we cannot know it as it is "in itself," but only in the event of its occurrence, in the event of its being given—in the present moment. A present moment that is, however, not at our disposal but is, rather, one of utter receptivity (or, to borrow from Levinas, passivity) in relation to address from an other. It is a moment that *does* occur "in time" (contra Levinas, interestingly?[25]), the time it takes for creaturely words to be spoken and heard. But as receptivity to address, it is not a moment in time that stands before us as an object of our reflection, thematization, subject to the initiative and agency of our thinking and speaking. In "contemplating it," Barth says, "we no longer hear and we thus lose the reality."[26] For as God's Word to us, and not our own word, "we can only receive and have it in the act of receiving." Again: "We have it only as it gives itself to us *if* we have it."[27]

The past. It can be said, then, that *if* we "have" God's Word to us, and therefore God, in our "hands," it is only in the sense of the open-handed event of receiving. There is no possibility of closing our hands around it. Consequently, once the event is "over," there is nothing left of God in our hands to grasp and possess as if it was ours to wield. In the event of the self-giving of God's Word to be "known otherwise" by the creature, it "can never in any sense be our possession," to which we can "point *back* as to a datum." God's Word can never, "not for a moment or in any respect," become something we can "come *back* to," to "cling to . . . or build upon."[28] *We* always only *have* a fully human recollection.

The future. Because "we never have it," God's Word "can only be shared with us ever anew." Our "knowing otherwise," then, finds itself radically determined by and relative to an event that is always to come again (echoes of deconstruction?), to occur again, "as though nothing had happened before . . . as though it were ever totally new and quite foreign."[29] Even though, for Barth, it *has* come (again, contra deconstruction?[30])—that is, God *has* been with us as one of us (a lowly servant) and has been confessed as such by human testimony; God has spoken and been heard—because it is *God's* coming and *God's* speaking, it is always a coming as if for the first time, totally unexpected, unanticipated, surprising, strange, new.

The nature of God's Word as *event*, then, determines creaturely "knowing otherwise" as incapable of grasping possession and ownership of that Word.

2. The Second "Barrier": The Word of God as Free *Event*

When and Where. To reprise and paraphrase, we have God's self-giving Word, in the event of its coming, as "totally new and quite foreign," *if* it comes. In other words, "we cannot produce this event."[31] It "cannot be predicted . . . does not fit into any plan."[32] As the event of God's self-giving, it is God's act and not ours, and so occurs as "his unfathomably *free* act *at a given time*."[33] God is present to the creature in God's Word—that is, present to creaturely knowing in and for love—only "*when and where* [he] wills to be present."[34] Barth refers to this free nature of the event of divine self-giving as "the incomprehensibility of the fact that the Word of God is spoken to man." In relation to this occurrence, "no consideration . . . will ever help us to see how this reality comes to be." And just in case we have not yet grasped the point, he adds: "How it came about and comes about . . . will always remain incomprehensible to us."[35]

No method. Because the event of God's self-giving Word occurs in freedom from all human anticipation, manipulation, conjuring, power, influence, calculation, expectation, "one cannot lay down conditions which, if observed, guarantee hearing of the Word. There is no method by which revelation can be made revelation that is actually received. . . . There is nothing of this kind because God's Word is a mystery in the sense that [it is] only . . . *from God*."[36] Consequently, our creaturely, kataphatic "knowing otherwise" (and "speaking otherwise") of God in and for love is only a true, faithful knowing "*where and when* God . . . lets it become true."[37] That is, "according to his good pleasure," wherein "He wills at *specific times* to be the object of this talk" and this thought.[38] According to God's good pleasure, meaning in freedom from any external necessity (logical, structural, ontological, metaphysical, etc.) available to us and according to which *we* might then be able to judge, measure, calculate, anticipate, know. The nature of God's Word as *free* event, then, determines creaturely "knowing otherwise" as incapable of producing, calculating, anticipating, manipulating, influencing that Word.

THE APOPHASIS OF DIVINE FREEDOM: SUMMING UP

Whatever the nature of creaturely "knowing otherwise," it would appear to be incapable of control and mastery over that which is given it to know.[39] In knowing God's Word otherwise, in the free event of divine self-giving, "we have no power over it; it is not at our disposal."[40] Even as it is given to us, even as we know it, "God's Word is and remains God's." It never passes over into our possession, never becomes our own, even when given to us. Rather, it remains intractable, an undomesticatable mystery precisely in its self-giving nature.[41] The mystery of God's Word as free event, then, constitutes, for Barth, "a theological warning against theology, a warning against the idea that its propositions or principles are certain in themselves."[42]

I suggest, in the light of the above, that despite the significant "change of context" and its consequent "change of subject" (from God's unapproachable essence to God's active, self-giving Word), the theological theme of divine freedom does indeed address rather squarely the particular concerns of a postmodern desire to "save the name" of God from human mastery.

But what about the secondary (or is it the primary?) desire to "save the neighbor"?

CAN AN APOPHASIS OF DIVINE FREEDOM "SAVE THE NEIGHBOR"?

The (Partial) Ethical Resources of Free Divine Self-Giving

I have suggested that there are two elements in the ethical desire to preserve divine mystery: (a) a rejection of any kind of *privileged* experience or knowledge of the divine, and (b) a rejection of any creaturely *disembodiment*, or *dis*-carnation necessary to the God-creature relation. I believe that a rather clear case can be made for the apophasis of divine freedom with regard to the latter element. We just had a glimpse of this above, in the extent to which, in the "descent" of God's free self-giving to the creature, as creature, to be known in and for love, the creature remains thoroughly and at every moment "*within*" the creaturely—that is to say, historical, material—realm of radical finitude.

Cannot this desire of God's love for and commitment to the creature precisely as creature, in all the vulnerability and complexity of creaturely finitude, be seen as a radical affirmation of creatureliness—materiality, temporality, and so on—more generally? Is not the creaturely sphere affirmed precisely as that in which God chooses to meet the creature—as herself radically embodied and so radically immanent within the structures of creaturely finitude—and so to be with the creature, and remain with the creature, in loving relation? The sphere in which this God chooses to be God is not the "properly divine" sphere of the eternal darkness of unknowing, but the creaturely sphere of materiality and temporality wherein creatures see, hear, know, and love in a radically material and temporal way, within the finitude of particularity, for example, one by one, moment by moment, place by place.

We have to leave it there (due to strictures of finitude and particularity!). But I trust it is clear how a case can be made. As for the other element entailed in saving the neighbor from human mastery—the rejection of privileged knowledge and experience—the apophasis of divine freedom would seem to run up against a serious limit.

The Ethical Offense of Free Divine Self-Giving

Divine self-giving to concrete incarnation, as a particular, lowly human creature within the temporal-material particularity of creaturely finitude, is a giving that always, necessarily, entails a "to whom"—and this, in two different ways: in God's self-giving "there and then" and in God's self-giving "here and now." (Doctrinally, of course, divine freedom means we are dealing with that difficult notion of election, long anathema to all good ethical instincts, especially in the wake of the Enlightenment, but something Barth rather famously—and counterintuitively—affirmed as the very sum of the Gospel.)

Then and there. God's giving herself to be known by human creatures in and for love, by becoming *one* of them, appears to be ethically problematic (with regard to epistemological privilege: "I know and you don't") because precisely in becoming *one* of them, rather than *all* of them—or none of them, but simply diffused equally throughout creation and so present to all, equally—God gives herself to a particular time and place and so in a unique way to a particular group of historical witnesses, witnesses that just happen to be there (it could be argued) while all the rest of the creaturely population is located elsewhere on the globe or elsewhere in time. For Barth, of course, these witnesses are the biblical prophets and apostles.[43] This would seem to constitute a clear privileging on God's part of the knowledge or experience of those few who were encountered there and then by God in lowly human form, and to whose witness to that event and encounter the rest of humanity is in some sense dependent upon in relation to it. (How else do we hear or know of something that happened "then and there," if *it* occurred, and *we* remain, thoroughly inscribed within the structures of creaturely finitude?) Further, this witness upon which we—the rest of humanity—are in some sense dependent is a witness that itself never ceases to be fully human in all its creaturely finitude, limitation, vulnerability, and questionability (this includes vulnerability to the movement of deconstruction, for example, as well as vulnerability or susceptibility to do harm, e.g., via the patriarchal structures of language). In short, it is a witness that shares the impenetrable incognito of God's self-giving incarnation itself—no "sacred glow" to the witnesses or the witness. And this leads us directly to the second "to whom" entailed in the event of free divine self-giving.

Here and now. Due to the impenetrable, creaturely incognito of (a) the "original" event of the concrete incarnation of God as fully human, and (b) the fully human and so fully questionable report of the witnesses to that event, *God* must, to go back to Kierkegaard, "give the condition"—or, "open the eyes and ears" of faith—not only to those first witnesses but to those who hear their witness, in order that God might be recognized and known. (Doctrinally, with regard to the trinitarian activity of the Christian story, this giving of "the condition," the opening of the eyes and ears of faith, is traditionally understood as the work of the Holy Spirit.[44]) To whom, then, does God "give the condition" here and now? Whose "eyes and ears" get opened so as to *hear* God's own personal, self-giving address of love in what can only be understood as a crassly inappropriate, unworthy, and distorting human witness to this unfathomable and incalculable event of divine incarnation, of God with us in our very flesh? Even if the "knowing otherwise" that occurs in the free event of faith can be shown to be radically distinct from a knowledge of possession (because it is "event") and calculation (because it is "free"), and so radically distinct from creaturely control and mastery of the divine by those to whom the event of "knowing otherwise" occurs; even so, it is still an event of "knowing otherwise" that apparently occurs to some and not others, in specific times and places and not others (according to the incalculable freedom of divine good pleasure). As such, we would still seem to be dealing with a clear situation of epistemological privilege: for example, "I 'know otherwise' and you don't," or, "I *have 'known* otherwise,'" "I *have been* encountered and addressed by an event of divine self-giving, in the hearing of this strange, offensively unremarkable, and unworthy human reportage."

This would seem to be precisely the kind of ethically problematic epistemological privilege in relation to the neighbor that a postmodern apophatic desire wants to "save the neighbor" from. As a kind of open-ended conclusion, then, I am going to briefly suggest how one might respond to the problem of this ethical limit—without in any way trying to deny that it is indeed an ethical problem for us, especially for those of us in the West, living in the wake of the Enlightenment—and in doing so, note how this response points to a possible ethical limit entailed in the very apophatic desire that takes offense here.

THE ETHICAL DESIRE OF AN APOPHASIS OF DIVINE FREEDOM

Because we are dealing here with a case of *God's* free activity and movement—that is, because creaturely "knowing otherwise" of God, where and when and to whom it occurs, only occurs "from God," incalculably, according to the divine good pleasure—the first and final, and ultimately only response to the question of the justice of the "when and where" and "to whom"—that is, the question of the ethicality of the "I 'know otherwise' and you don't"—is nothing other than an appeal to *divine mystery*. (Think here of Paul's struggle in Romans with the apparent injustice of God's strange economy of election. "But who are you, a man, to answer back to God? Will what is molded say to its molder, 'Why have you made me thus?' " And later, as a final word on the matter: "How unsearchable are his judgments and how inscrutable his ways! 'For who has known the mind of the Lord?' "[45]) Because this is *divine* activity, the measure of it—*ethically*, and not only *epistemologically*—is precisely that which is and always remains radically beyond our ken and so radically beyond our ethical as well as epistemological grasp, control, and mastery: it is incomprehensible, unfathomable, impenetrable divine mystery. Again, the subject has been changed. The essential divine mystery (given the self-giving of God to be known in and for love) is not the nature of divine being or essence, but how and why God does what God does, which in this case, is to behave in a strange, inappropriate, "ungodly," and seemingly unfair, unethical way.

Now I assume that most of us, and I'm guessing probably all of us—myself included—who resonate with the twofold apophatic desire to not only "save the name" of God from human mastery, but to save the neighbor as well, find this response (which, is, after all, Paul's response) highly unsatisfactory. I want to quickly reflect, then, in closing, on what this ethical resistance to—Kierkegaard would say, offense at—the freedom of divine self-giving might mean. I am going to raise four questions.

1. Note that the ethically problematic epistemological privilege of "knowing otherwise"—God showing up incognito, in a certain time and place, encountering a few folk, who then go on to tell other folk, and so on—is the direct consequence of what was seen earlier to be the ethically resourceful divine commitment to relate to and love the creature, *as creature*, that is, thoroughly within and so vulnerable to the material, historical structures of creaturely finitude. Note the tension entailed in the two elements of the ethical desire itself: radical embodiment seems to undermine the possibility of a formal, universal equality of access.

Might not this mitigate somewhat the ethical problem of epistemological privilege particular to free divine self-giving? For example, in an ethics of love, which is the better news for the neighbor—that God has entered their concrete existence in such a radical way that they are encountered as the beloved of God in the very *vulnerability* of their creaturely particularity and finitude which nevertheless constitutes the possibility of the flesh-and-blood embrace of love (the consequence being that such an encounter occurs through the witness of another) or that God is immanently present to the creature in such a way that allows for God's simultaneous universal presence to all creatures in the same measure, that is, God is present to the creature precisely as incomprehensible divine mystery, and so significantly short of a self-giving to be known in the full flesh-and-blood embrace of creaturely love?

2. Does an ethical dissatisfaction with the apophasis of divine freedom suggest the extent to which an engagement with divine mystery is limited to the *epistemological* in distinction from the *ethical*? Does offense, here, signal an assumption that God is not, or should not be, incomprehensible to us ethically, or, more to the point, that we do not *want* a God who is incomprehensible mystery in that way, that is, who may come to us—or to our neighbor—in a way of which we do not approve? Note again the problematic structure. Do we use a form of respect for divine mystery in relation to the epistemological in order to domesticate the divine in relation to the ethical? Is the *ethical* employment of the theological theme of *epistemological* divine mystery, then, another expression of the human desire and attempt to master divine mystery? And isn't human mastery of divine mystery always precisely ethically problematic, in that, in whatever form, it always puts the neighbor at risk?

3. First, I will reiterate an observation. The creaturely witness to and hearing of God's self-giving incarnation shares in the latter's impenetrable incognito, and so is thoroughly creaturely knowing and speaking that takes place as rather hapless and completely questionable human witness (to an outrageous occurrence!—"Believe what I say as one believes in a miracle"[46]) in the midst and alongside of all the other greater or lesser ways, forms, and events of human knowing and speaking in the public square. And now, the question. Might not the epistemological privilege of "knowing otherwise"—and perhaps we could also say here, "speaking otherwise" (giving particular witness to this particular incomprehensible

thing)—be distinguishable precisely in its utter inability and lack of power to convince, contest, prove, impress, compel, persuade, urge, motivate, and so on, anyone with regard to its divine referent or subject matter (*Sache*)? To cite Barth, "[O]nly God Himself can provide the proof that we are really talking about Him when we are allegedly doing so."[47]

Could it not be argued that this is an epistemological privilege that is utterly unable, utterly powerless to master and control the neighbor in any way as a creaturely form of knowing and speaking? Might it be a knowing and speaking without undue violence, either rhetorical or material? The history of the Church and the Christian theological tradition, of course, is one of counter-testimony here, seemingly presenting all evidence to the contrary. It can only be said here that the Church has used these weapons—both rhetorical and material—precisely because the "knowing otherwise" is so uncertain and unsure, the most uncertain of all humanly speaking, and therefore as a rejection of the "knowing otherwise" proper to it, given to it, and as a betrayal and distortion of what it "knows otherwise." The Church's historical behavior is itself a rejection of God as God comes to the creature, and so a rejection of divine mystery.

In relation to the neighbor, then, all the creature can do in the wake of "knowing otherwise," *if it is faithful*, is to give witness. And this is to address the neighbor in such a way that puts oneself alongside of her and in the same position, facing the same direction, vis-à-vis divine self-giving to be known in and for love: awaiting an incalculable, unanticipatable, unproducible new event of divine address with open but empty hands. This, and no more. (Except, perhaps, to be with the neighbor in such a way that itself witnesses to the divine love of self-giving to and for the creature, for example, in a way that embraces, and yes, loves, the neighbor's creatureliness in all its materiality and temporality, particularity and difference, vulnerability and questionability, beauty and ugliness, promise and abandonment, goodness and badness, ethical and spiritual piety as well as unethical and crass dissipation, and so on.)

4. Finally, then, within the context of the "thought experiment," we have seen that the ethical dimension (when, where, and *to whom*?) of God's free self-giving is assumed to be part and parcel of divine mystery. The incomprehensibility of the divine that exceeds creaturely mastery has ethical as well as epistemological dimensions. Given that, does not

resistance to the radically incarnate (and so particular and vulnerable) way God chooses to give herself to the creature in and for love, on the basis of *ethical* criteria or sensibility that are somehow in the possession of the creature (e.g., within the grasp of finite, creaturely knowledge and deployment), take on the nature of a *theological* attempt to master divine mystery, or at least calculate and determine, even legislate what God can and cannot do (or be), how God can and cannot be God?[48] And, in the light of number 3, above, does this resistance to God's coming in incarnate particularity and vulnerability, subject to all the vagaries and distortions and inadequacies of human witness and testimony, actually betray a certain hostility and prejudice against such fragile speech in relation to things divine? Does this not, in fact, betray a longing for a more robust, secure, and proprietary form of knowledge required for the careful policing of such risky and incendiary talk? And this, for the sake of the neighbor. But does this not also mean, in turn, that I want to legislate what God can and cannot *be known or said* to do (or be), that is, to legislate what can and cannot be known or said of God *by the neighbor*? And this also, for the sake of the neighbor? Because I know what is best for the neighbor? I know and you don't?

And could this not constitute a form of epistemological privilege, expressing a presumed knowledge of the appropriate boundaries between the limits of the creaturely and the mystery of the divine that exceeds them? And therefore of what can and cannot be said of God by creatures, and how it can and cannot be said (and heard and understood)? An epistemological privilege in relation to the neighbor taken in the very name and for the sake of the neighbor? A desire to "save" her (and God) from her own uninformed, idolatrous tendency to mistake the encounter with frail, historically determined human witness and testimony as an encounter with the very Word and work of God herself?

For example, Derrida: "[O]ne will never, it is *impossible and it must not be done*, reconcile the value of a testimony with that of knowledge or of certitude. One will never, *it is impossible and it must not be done*, reduce the one to the other."[49] Can this not be seen as a kind of policing, an imposition of an ethical imperative, the final word of which is left thoroughly in Derrida's—or our—hands? Now consider Barth, who, in the reading I have given above, says pretty much the same thing as Derrida:

it is impossible, for us, to reduce testimony to, or replace witness with, a proprietary knowledge of certitude; and it must not be done by Christian theology. However, Barth will then *go on* to affirm, simultaneously, a "nevertheless," which takes the final word thoroughly out of his own or any of our human hands, that is, a "nevertheless" that keeps the human grasp on *divine* possibility in commerce with the neighbor (or with ourselves) irreducibly open and nonfinal. While agreeing with Derrida, then, that *we* cannot and should not reduce testimony to knowledge, Barth is nevertheless constrained (by his theological assumptions with regard to the apophasis of divine freedom) to make the astonishing affirmation—astonishingly *open* (with regard to both God and the neighbor)—that "the simplest proclamation [testimony] of the Gospel can be proclamation of the truth *in the most unlimited sense* and can validly communicate the truth to the *most unsophisticated* hearer, *if God so will*" (i.e., in the unfathomable mystery of divine self-giving).[50] Does the ethically problematic apophasis of divine freedom allow Barth, here, in some paradoxical way, an ethically fecund openness to the relation of God with the neighbor that Derrida might not be capable of on the grounds of an ethically driven postmodern apophatic desire? Is Barth constrained by the mystery of divine freedom to be open to the neighbor where Derrida can only legislate a rule of what can and cannot—what *must not*—be done?

A closing example (I promise). Mary returns from visiting Jesus' tomb and gives the following *testimony* to the other disciples (holed up, in fear and despair, behind closed doors), "I have seen the Lord!" The disciples, Peter, John, and the rest of the boys, respond (I am paraphrasing here): "Be quiet, you crazy woman. You are hysterical, out of touch with reality, and clearly do not know what you are talking about." Now, of the two corresponding laws—on one hand, a postmodern apophatic desire ("it is impossible and it must not be done"), and, on the other, an apophasis of divine freedom ("it is impossible and it must not be done; nevertheless, we must remain open to *God's* possibility to do the impossible")—which is more likely to determine a response echoing the exclusionary closure of the male disciples' response to Mary, and which is more likely to determine an open, more humble, more hospitable alternative in relation to such a neighbor?

Let It Be: Finding Grace with God through the *Gelassenheit* of the Annunciation

ROSE ELLEN DUNN

Who listens to the Annunciation that Mary makes?
To the memory or the experience she attests?
The excess to a certain God who speaks through her?
LUCE IRIGARAY, *Marine Lover of Friedrich Nietzsche*

In this essay I read the narrative of the Annunciation as a text that describes a phenomenological event, an event in which there is a manifestation of the divine to an experiencing subject. Using the understanding of releasement that flows from Meister Eckhart to Angelus Silesius to Martin Heidegger, I propose to create a theoretical framework for interpreting the Annunciation as a moment of releasement, or *Gelassenheit*. Since this reading is primarily phenomenological, the essay will begin with a discussion of the theological possibilities present in the phenomenology of Edmund Husserl and Martin Heidegger. These possibilities will then be interwoven with the work of Luce Irigaray, Jean-Luc Marion, and Jacques Derrida. Luce Irigaray's feminist interpretation of the Annunciation provides a foundation for thinking about Mary as a gendered subject, an example of a feminine incarnation of divinity. Jean-Luc Marion's phenomenology of givenness offers a means to think about the gift of possibility that is given in the event of the Annunciation. Jacques Derrida's interpretation of prayer and testimony invites further thought on the speech of the Annunciation as well as the speech of the Magnificat.

With this theoretical framework in place, I explore an interpretation of the Annunciation as an event of *Gelassenheit* which springs from a mutual gift of love. This essay will suggest that the text of the Annunciation is infused with possibility. Filled with grace, Mary is invited by the divine into possibility; responding in grace, she in turn invites the divine into possibility. Grace, springing from the desire of the divine as well as the responsive desire of Mary, draws both Mary and the divine into the very possibility that it creates—the possibility for an intermingling of the self and the divine in a mystical union of love. Transgressing the limits of language, this possibility slips into an apophatic moment of *Gelassenheit*, a mutual "letting-be" or releasement of both Mary and the divine, which then overflows into the song of the Magnificat.

PHENOMENOLOGY AND THE THEOLOGICAL: HUSSERL AND HEIDEGGER

The phenomenology of Edmund Husserl and Martin Heidegger provides possibilities for thinking theologically as a phenomenologist. Although much of Husserl's phenomenology suspends, or brackets, the question of the transcendence of God, there are suggestions in later manuscripts that Husserl himself allowed for an openness of the Transcendental *I* to the divine. As Richard Kearney observes, "The God of Husserl's phenomenology is . . . a God of an intuition so deep that it surpasses and overflows all our intentions . . . a God of testimony and empathy, of suffering and action, of passion and compassion."[1] The manifestation of the divine to an experiencing subject is, even for Husserl, an experience of excess, and of possibility.

Husserl's phenomenological method begins with the experience of the life-world. Phenomenology, for Husserl, is a descriptive science: the task of phenomenology is to describe what appears to consciousness in the manner in which it appears to consciousness. "I am conscious of a world endlessly spread out in space," Husserl observed, "endlessly becoming and having endlessly become in time. I am conscious of it: that signifies, above all, that intuitively I find it immediately, that I experience it."[2] The phenomenological method intuitively leads to the description of what Husserl calls the "wonder of all wonders": the pure *I* and pure consciousness ("Das Wunder aller Wunder ist reines Ich und reines Bewußtsein").[3]

In *Formal and Transcendental Logic*, Husserl suggested that "the subjective Apriori precedes the being of God and the world, the being of everything, individually and collectively, for me, the thinking subject. Even

God is for me what he is, in consequence of my own productivity of consciousness."[4] In Husserlian phenomenology, any understanding of God must be intuited through a manifestation of God to the experiencing subject in the absolute stream of consciousness of the transcendental *I*. For Husserl, as Steven Laycock suggests, to

> describe the God-phenomenon is to describe God *as experienced by me*. In this way, as Husserl maintains, "the I . . . bears its God in itself." The reflexive act, in virtue of which the first-order lived experience of God is apprehended, is *my* reflexive act. Only what is revealed *to me* through *my* act of reflection is phenomenologically admissible.[5]

Husserl's later writings, in the *Nachlass* manuscripts, suggest that there is a directedness of the human person toward God. "The life of humans," he wrote, "is nothing but a way to God. I try to reach this goal without theological proofs, methods, supports; namely to arrive *at God without God*."[6] To reach God without God, to reach God without theological proofs, while maintaining that the human life "is nothing but a way to God," is, perhaps, to suspend the transcendence of God through the phenomenological reduction, and reflectively turn, in the phenomenological attitude, to an intuitive manifestation of God experienced by the transcendental *I*.

The teleological goal of the phenomenological method is, Husserl suggests, the constitution of each individual transcendental *I* into the transcendental *We* through the experience of the world as an intersubjective world: "[W]ithin myself, within the limits of my transcendentally reduced pure conscious life, I *experience* the world . . . as an *intersubjective* world, actually there for everyone."[7] This *becoming* of transcendental intersubjectivity—the *becoming* of the transcendental *I* into the transcendental *We*, constituting the intersubjective world—is, for Husserl, an experience of the divine as ideal telos. Husserl suggests that:

> All absolute being is a stream of teleologically concordant becoming directed toward ideal goals. . . . This is the one stream of "divine" being; and God is the entelechy, or the pure form, toward which

> the ontological development strives in the drive of its *eros*. But this form is an idea but still the all present effective power in all being.[8]

The intuitive experience of the manifestation of the divine is the directedness of the transcendental *I* toward the ideal goal of the transcendental intersubjective community of *We*. As Stephen Strasser argues, for Husserl, "*the ideal telos is the Divinity itself*."[9] "God," Husserl wrote, "would be 'experienced' in each belief that believes originally-teleologically in the perpetual value of that which lies in the direction of each absolute ought and which engages itself for this perpetual meaning."[10] The divine, for Husserl, is an ideal: the ideal of an "absolutely perfect transcendental community."[11]

Divinity as ideal telos is experienced by the transcendental *I* in its directedness toward the ideal goal of the transcendental *We*. This *We*, for Husserl, is an intersubjective community in which the transcendental *I* (continually) becomes mutually interwoven with another transcendental *I* through love of neighbor:

> From each I (from me as I and from the other I who is Other as I to him) the way leads as the way proper to each; but all ways lead to the same trans-worldly and trans-human pole which is God. But these ways do not lead as separate ways converging together at a point. Rather the ways mutually penetrate one another in an indescribably spiraling fashion. This means the way of the neighbor, in so far as the way is the right way, belongs essentially, to an extent, to my way; the way is the love of neighbor.[12]

Husserlian phenomenology lays the foundation for understanding a certain openness and directedness of the Transcendental *I* to the divine that is realized in the love of neighbor.

With Martin Heidegger, the language of phenomenology begins to explicitly use not only the language of poetry but also the language of mystical theology. Heidegger inherits the understanding of *Gelassenheit*, or releasement, which he uses to describe the openness of *Dasein* to Being, from Meister Eckhart. In Heidegger's primarily secular insistence on the possibility of this openness of *Dasein* to the advent of Being, there is a corresponding openness to the Holy that is suggestive of an openness to the divine. Heidegger writes, "Only from the truth of Being can the essence of the holy be thought. Only from the essence of the holy is the essence of divinity to be thought. Only in the light of the essence of divinity can it be thought or said what the word 'God' is to signify."[13] While, for Heidegger, the thinking of the truth of Being frames the question of divinity and God, there is the suggestion of an analogous relationship between ontology and theology. As Richard Kearney observes, Heidegger "hinted that the ontology/theology relationship might take the form of an *analogy of proper proportionality*: namely, the believer is to God what *Dasein* is to Being."[14]

The later phenomenology of Heidegger turned from the question of the experience and disclosedness of Dasein as Being-in-the-world to the thinking of the presencing of Being (as Gift) through the event (*Ereignis*) of unconcealment (*Aletheia*). "Of all beings," Heidegger wrote, "only the human being, called upon by the voice of Being, experiences the wonder of all wonders: *that* beings *are*."[15] The essential nature of *Dasein*, for Heidegger, is meditative thinking, the thinking that is determined "by what there is to be thought about: the presence of what is present, the Being of beings."[16] Meditative thinking waits—in stillness—for the lighting up of Being in unconcealment; and, *Dasein*, by dwelling authentically in attentive waiting for the advent of Being, becomes itself a clearing through which Being can presence. Meditative thinking participates in and experiences the "wonder of all wonders," the giving of Being.

To think—to engage in meditative thinking—is to become attuned to the giving advent of Being. "Thinking," Heidegger writes, "is a listening that brings something into view."[17] As a thinking being, *Dasein* leaps into the play of *Aletheia*, the clearing and lighting of Being; the disclosure of Being through the play of the world—the play of concealment and unconcealment—the "disclosing that lets us see what conceals itself."[18] The essential task for *Dasein* is to wait in releasement (*Gelassenheit*) for the advent of Being. Heidegger suggests that this releasement is a listening for the silent address of Being that gathers *Dasein* into meditative thinking.[19] As John Caputo observes, for Heidegger, "The 'great being' of man lies in his cooperation with Being in bringing Being into its truth. Dasein cooperates with Being by 'letting Being be.' This is Dasein's fiat."[20]

This poetic understanding of *Dasein* as openness, or attunement, to the advent of Being, offers possibilities in an analogous manner for theological language and for a phenomenology of religious experience. Heidegger's later phenomenology, infused with a sense of wonder over the advent of Being and the releasement of Dasein, invites a sense of wonder regarding the advent of the divine. As George Kovacs suggests, the "recapturing of the sense of wonder about Being does not extinguish but rather reawakens the question of God, the sense of wonder about the sacred, divine horizon of human living."[21]

Heidegger's understanding of releasement, or *Gelassenheit*, is analogous to the understanding of *Gelassenheit* in the mystical theology of Meister Eckhart. For Heidegger, this *Gelassenheit* is the "letting be" of Being in the Event (*Ereignis*) of Truth (*Aletheia*); for Meister Eckhart, it is the "letting be" of the divine overflowing into the detached heart. The moment of *Gelassenheit* is comparable. As Caputo writes,

> [T]he relationship, the interchange, between God and the soul in Meister Eckhart is similar to the relationship between Being and Dasein in Heidegger. As God takes the initiative in Meister Eckhart, so Being takes the initiative in Heidegger. As the soul must stay open and receptive to God, so Dasein must stay open to Being.[22]

Caputo observes that the "god" of Heidegger's later work "is a cosmic-poetic god, not the ethico-religious God of the Hebrew and Christian scriptures."[23] Raising an important critique of Heidegger, Caputo suggests that "the later Heidegger understood that piety is *Gelassenheit* but he continued to miss the *kardia*."[24]

Turning to the narrative of the Annunciation in the Gospel of Luke, we find that what emerges from this text is not only the piety of *Gelassenheit* in the event of the Annunciation itself but also the *kardia* of ethico-religious concern which follows in the words of the Magnificat. While Heidegger provides the phenomenological means to think about the Annunciation as a moment of *Gelassenheit*, Husserl provides the means to think about the Magnificat as a directedness to an intersubjective community. Reading the texts of the Annunciation and the Magnificat through an interpretive lens informed by the work of Luce Irigaray, Jean-Luc Marion, and Jacques Derrida will encourage further thought on this moment of *Gelassenheit* overflowing into the *kardia* of love of neighbor.

THE ANNUNCIATION AS ATTENTIVE LOVE: LUCE IRIGARAY

Luce Irigaray's feminist interpretation of the Annunciation suggests that this spiritual event is an encounter between two subjects, each participating in the incarnation of divinity. For Irigaray, the Annunciation is "an engendering preceded by an exchange of breath and of words between the future lovers and parents."[25] To breathe—to take in the air—to share a breath: this, Irigaray argues, necessarily precedes a spiritual engendering, for "a spiritual engendering cannot take place without the coming into play of breathing and the controlled expression of this breathing between the lovers."[26]

Breath, for Irigaray, is pure spiritual being; shared breath is pure spiritual engendering. "The conception of a divine child," she argues, "depends on the quality of breathing and on the exchange of words that precede it—on its announcement."[27] The words of the Annunciation are proclaimed through the voice—and the breath—of the angel. The breath that follows is Mary's. Mary's breath is the breath of a "yes"—a "yes" that meant that the divine would be engendered in love.[28]

For Irigaray, this "yes" also proclaimed an annunciation of feminine divinity. Irigaray insists that it is a fundamental human obligation to become divine by fulfilling one's own gendered subjectivity and to incarnate divinity by fostering intersubjective relationships between gendered subjects. Irigaray maintains that becoming divine is a *feminist* project: a project that seeks the incarnation of feminine divinity in order to facilitate the becoming divine of women.

The divine, for Irigaray, is a horizon within this process of becoming. The divine horizon is present as the fulfillment and perfection of gendered subjectivity. A feminine divine, Irigaray insists, is possible through incarnation: "Does respect for God made flesh not imply that we should incarnate God within us and in our sex: daughter-woman-mother?"[29] Through her (re)reading of the narrative of the Annunciation as an encounter between two subjects, Irigaray develops a rich understanding of Mary as a divine manifestation participating in the incarnation of divinity—and becoming divine herself—by sharing the gift of breath.

Irigaray insists that it is breathing—and an understanding of breath as gift—that grounds the Annunciation as a spiritual event. Two subjects, the divine and Mary, breathing through a shared, spiritual breath, are gathered through the interpenetrating fluidity of the air that gives life to their breath. This sharing of breath, Irigaray insists, is preceded by a question: "[T]he question of the angelic messenger to Mary: 'Do you want to be the mother of the/a savior?' "[30] Without this question, Irigaray argues, the tradition of the Annunciation "forgets" and "silences" the "yes" of Mary's response; Mary is subjected to "an authoritarian power of a word that supposedly has to supplant the body and not make it divine as such,"[31] and the tradition becomes a statement, the insistence of a demand, "Mary, the Lord informs you that you will be the mother of his child."[32]

But with this question—"Do you want to be the mother of the/a savior?"—Irigaray argues that another interpretation of the Annunciation is possible: an interpretation that suggests that the breath of this announcement—the breath of the question and the breath of Mary's response—together foster a spiritual engendering. The breath of the Most High intermingles with the breath of Mary in the conception of this divine child: "And Jesus Christ," Irigaray writes "is born of a woman made fertile by the breath, the Spirit."[33]

Breathing, for Irigaray, is a gesture of sharing. The Annunciation, as an event of breathing, is also a gesture of sharing. The breath of the angelic greeting and announcement is a sharing of the breath of divinity with Mary. The breath of Mary's response is a "yes" that, breathing in divinity, becomes a sharing itself—the sharing of breath in a spiritual engendering. Through the Annunciation, "God's presence reappears in a different way. Having returned to earth, conceived and born by an attentive love, he manifests the miraculous power of that love."[34] The event of the Annunciation, for Irigaray is a manifestation of the advent of the divine reaching incarnation in a relationship of attentive love.[35]

THE ANNUNCIATION AS GIFT: JEAN-LUC MARION

Mary and the divine share the gift of breath, the gift of love, and the gift of self. This is a mutual giving: the divine gives to Mary, and Mary gives to the divine. Following the phenomenology of Jean-Luc Marion, the experience of giving and givenness that is present in the Annunciation can be interpreted as a phenomenological event.

Marion's phenomenology of givenness, while indebted to the earlier work of Husserl and Heidegger, reinterprets their work by proposing a third phenomenological reduction, the reduction of givenness.[36] Radically re-envisaging Husserlian "donation" and Heideggerian "possibility," Marion suggests that *donation* may exceed both the phenomenological horizon and the reduction to the transcendental *I*.[37] The reduction of givenness is exercised by a call that does not originate from either the object or Being, but rather originates from the "pure form of the call" itself.[38] For Marion, the thesis common to both Husserl and Heidegger, "[s]o much appearance, so much Being," presupposes a more essential statement "so much reduction, so much givenness."[39]

Marion suggests that the reduction of givenness "reduces to the *interloqué*, by leading every *I* or even *Dasein* back to its pure and simple figure as an auditor preceded and instituted by the call which is still absolute because indeterminate."[40] This reduction, Marion argues, "gives the gift itself: the gift of rendering oneself to *or* of eluding the claim of the call . . . [a]ccording to no other horizon than that of the absolutely unconditional call and of the absolutely unconstrained response."[41] The *I* is "given" as respondent to the absolute call.

What shows itself, first gives itself: it is the phenomenology of givenness—the sheer givenness of the phenomenon—that opens access to the self/itself.[42]

> The phenomenality of the given suggests that the phenomenon does not appear only when an other besides it (the I) constitutes it (Kant, Husserl), but first when it shows *itself* in itself and from itself (Heidegger). What remains is to take the most perilous step: thinking this *self/itself*—which alone permits the phenomenon to show *itself*.[43]

The self, for Marion, is the given-to; the self receives itself from the given: "[T]he given reveals itself to the given-to by revealing the given-to to itself."[44] Marion's reduction of givenness gives all that can call and all that can be called, and, by doing this, gives phenomenality as well.[45] Thus, for Marion, the phenomenon is the event of the call: "[I]t phenomenalizes the given-to through the same movement by which the given-to forces that which gives itself to show itself a bit more."[46] The call (given to the given-to/gifted) appears by its reception in the response (given to that which is called by the given-to/gifted): "[T]he response performs the call, and the gifted renders visible and audible what gives itself to it only by corresponding to it in the act of responding."[47] The response is, Marion suggests, "the first manifestation of the call."[48] The call becomes visible in the response: "The 'Here I am!' of the responsal is the only thing that can give the status of 'There you are!' to the call."[49]

The religious phenomenon, Marion argues, raises the question of the possibility of the phenomenon, and, hence, the phenomenon of possibility itself. In the light of Husserl's principle of all principles, Marion asks, "What would occur, as concerns phenomenality, if an intuitive donation were accomplished that was absolutely unconditioned (without the limits of a horizon) and absolutely irreducible (to a constituting *I*)?"[50] If, for Leibniz, metaphysics obeys the principle of sufficient reason; and if, for Kant, the possibility of a phenomenon is granted by the power of knowing; and if, for Heidegger, possibility stands higher than actuality, Marion asks:

> Can we not envisage a type of phenomenon that would reverse the condition of a horizon (by surpassing it, instead of being inscribed within it) and that would reverse the reduction (by leading the *I* back to itself, instead of being reduced to the *I*)?[51]

Marion understands this type of phenomenon as a saturated phenomenon. Similar to the Cartesian understanding of the idea of infinity and to the Kantian understanding of the sublime, the saturated phenomenon saturates and exceeds every horizon, giving itself as absolute. The saturated phenomenon, Marion suggests, poses the question of the phenomenology of religion in new terms.[52]

The terms, Marion would argue, are phenomenological, even though Husserl's principle of all principles must be surpassed by the possibility of the saturated phenomenon. For Husserl, the horizon and the constituting *I* were unquestioned presuppositions, but for Marion, "intention and meaning surpass intuition and fulfillment."[53] The saturated phenomenon is the possibility of the impossible: the phenomenon that exceeds the horizon and is irreducible to the constituting *I*. The appearance of the saturated phenomenon, Marion suggests, is "a *revelation*."[54] Marion understands this revelation as a "theophany, where the surfeit of intuition leads me to the paradox that an invisible gaze visibly envisages me and loves me."[55]

The saturated phenomenon is attested to in four different types of phenomena: a historical event, the work of art (idol), the flesh of the human body, and the face of the other (icon).[56] The phenomenon of revelation, Marion suggests, is itself a saturated phenomenon "that concentrates in itself the four senses of the saturated phenomenon."[57] Revelation, for Marion, is at once event, idol, flesh, and icon: "The saturated phenomenon therefore culminates in the type of paradox I call revelation, one that concentrates in itself—as the figure of Christ establishes its possibility—an event, an idol, a flesh, and an icon all at the same time."[58] Revelation saturates phenomenality and intentionality. The saturated phenomenon cannot be constituted by a transcendental *I*; rather the *I* is given to itself by the saturated phenomenon. Revelation, Marion argues, "provokes and evokes figures and strategies of manifestation and revelation that are much more powerful and more subtle than what phenomenology, even pushed as far as the phenomenon of revelation (paradox of paradoxes), could ever let us divine."[59] The saturating "givenness" of revelation operates at the limits of phenomenology and rationality; for Marion, revelation operates in possibility.

The possibility of the impossible: this theme is made explicit in Marion's discussion of the Annunciation.[60] It is the impossible, Marion argues, that is the means by which God allows Godself to be recognized: "[A]s soon as the impossible emerges, there God's proper realm emerges."[61] Radical possibility, for Marion, finds its point of departure precisely in the impossible, by transcending the impossible. In the narrative of the Annunciation, Mary's first response is a question: "How can this be?" She confronts the angelic messenger with the impossible. "To the angel who announces the possibility of motherhood to her," Marion observes, "Mary responds first with a factual impossibility."[62] The angel then answers Mary with the announcement of radical possibility: "For on God's part no saying shall be impossible."[63] Mary's second response accepts this possibility.

Mary's first response is limited by impossibility; it confines Mary to finitude and the impossible. As Marion suggests, the "experience of the impossible . . . unlocks as of yet no access to God's own proper region."[64] With her words "Let it be," Mary crosses into radical possibility; she crosses the threshold into "God's own proper region."[65] Mary accepts the "saying" of the angel that no "saying" is impossible with God.[66]

"God starts," Marion suggests, "where the impossible translates into the possible, precisely where the impossible appears as though it were possible."[67] Accepting the angelic word, Mary releases herself into divine possibility.

THE ANNUNCIATION AS PRAYER: JACQUES DERRIDA

Mary's response addresses the divine. She responds affirmatively, "Let it be," to the divine invitation. There is also a second address in the text of Luke's gospel, the Magnificat, in which Mary turns to Elizabeth and addresses Elizabeth on the basis of this experience with the divine. Reading these texts through the philosophy of Jacques Derrida enables a phenomenological approach to these addresses, these prayers that overflow from the divine invitation and the response of Mary.

The phenomenology of Husserl and Heidegger, particularly Husserlian intentionality and Heideggerian ontology, provided a lasting influence on the work of Derrida. Derrida's poststructural deconstructive readings of Husserl and Heidegger led to his critique of phenomenology and the phenomenological method. However, the relationship between the philosophical language of Derrida and the apophatic language of negative theology offers rich possibilities for a phenomenology of prayer. Deconstruction and apophasis meet at the limits of language, in their transgression of language, particularly in speech about God. For both Derrida and the negative theologians with whom he is in conversation, there is a certain apprehension in talking *about* God. There is however, for both Derrida and negative theology, the possibility of a prayer—a confession—a hymn—an address *to* God.

Derrida writes at some length regarding the twofold address that is present in the prayers and confessions of negative theology. The nature of the address is twofold since it proceeds in two different directions: namely, the address that is directed to God and the address that is directed to the listening, or reading, others. It seems that for Derrida, it is this address—the "I am addressing myself here to God" that is by its very nature shared with every listener or reader—that determines the theological moment in both apophatic language and the philosophical language of deconstruction.[68] Derrida's address is at the limits of language, working in a transgression of these limits by resting in a stillness—a silence—that simply waits, yearning, for the advent of the unnameable Wholly Other.

"The 'theological,'" Derrida suggests, "is a determined moment in the total movement of the trace."[69] The trace itself is neither a distinctive feature nor a simple presence or absence. The trace is set into motion by, and weaves its way through, *différance*. Derrida describes *différance* in terms of play and movement: "*[D]ifférance*, then, will be the playing movement that 'produces'—by means of something that is not simply an activity—these differences, these effects of difference"[70] *Différance* might be simply described as a series of playing movements within a given (con)text that produce difference and defer meaning. As Derrida argues, "[T]he border of a context is less narrow, less strictly determining than one is accustomed to believe."[71] There is a movement of play—of *différance*—at these (con)textual borders.

The "theological" is traditionally grounded in an understanding of God as a fixed origin, effectively eliminating the *play* of *différance* in the sign structures of theology, including the sign structure that is the name of God. Derrida insists that the name of God must be kept safe from univocal control, from orthodoxy, and from determinacy. A multiplicity of voices is needed in order to begin to speak about God; no one voice, no single context, Derrida insists, should attempt to circumscribe and limit the name of God.[72]

To save the name of God, for Derrida, is to keep the name of God *secret*: "The other as absolute other, namely, God, must remain transcendent, hidden, secret."[73] The secret is unconditional and absolute; it is "non-thematizable, non-objectifiable, non-shareable."[74] To save God is to abandon God in a moment of *Gelassenheit* that Derrida inherits from Meister Eckhart:

> The abandonment *of* this *Gelassenheit*, the abandonment *to* this *Gelassenheit* does not exclude pleasure or enjoyment; on the contrary, it gives rise to them. It opens the play *of* God (of God and with God, of God with self and with creation): it opens a passion to the enjoyment *of* God.[75]

The serenity of this abandonment—the abandoning of God to be God—opens a passion of enjoyment described by Eckhart:

> God is a Unique One; whoever wants to enjoy Him
> Must, no less than He, be enclosed in Him.[76]

The language of this passion is the apophatic language of negative theology. Perhaps "only a negative ('apophatic') attribution can claim to approach God, and to prepare us for a silent intuition of God."[77] The language of negative theology is an address that moves in the direction of God, while abandoning itself in the enclosure of God.

The apophatic experience, as an experience of *becoming*, especially interests Derrida: "[T]his becoming-self as becoming-God—or Nothing—that is what appears impossible, more than impossible."[78] Perhaps, for Derrida, it is the impossibility of this possibility of becoming that negative theology shares with deconstruction, "the very experience of the (impossible) possibility of the impossible."[79]

Exceeding language, resisting determination, opening a place for God and the *play* of God, saving (keeping secret) the name of God—these are themes that negative theology shares with deconstruction. Apophatic speech overflows language, moving theology to its limits—to silence.

> It is necessary to leave all, to leave every "something" through love of God, and no doubt to leave God himself, to abandon him, that is, at once to leave him and (but) let him (be beyond being-something). Save his name [*sauf son nom*]—which must be kept silent.[80]

This "leaving all" allows one "to respond to the true name of God, to the name to which God responds and corresponds beyond the name that we know him by or hear."[81]

Despite this move toward silence, Derrida identifies two concurrent (and competing) desires within negative theology: the first, the desire to guard the mystery, to keep safe the (divine) secret among those who honor and keep the secret, and the second, the desire to share this secret with the wider community.[82] The prayers of negative theology, these "words that carry themselves toward God,"[83] are addressed, Derrida argues, both to God and to the community through a movement of conversion.

To demonstrate this two-destination address, Derrida turns to the texts of Dionysius the Areopagite (*Mystical Theology*) and Augustine (*Confessions*). Dionysius begins his text with a prayer addressed to God. This same text is also addressed to Timothy, the disciple of Dionysius. Derrida writes, "[T]he address to God itself already implies the possibility and the necessity of this *post-scriptum*."[84] The apostrophe to God present in the prayer is linked with, and turned toward, the apostrophe to the disciple present in the instruction. Derrida observes, "The hymn [the prayer] and the didactic [the instruction] become allied here. . . . This conversion [the turning of the apostrophe] turns (itself) toward the other in order to turn (it) toward God."[85] The prayer has two destinations.

This conversion, Derrida suggests, is similar to the movement Augustine performs in his *Confessions*. Augustine's autobiographical text addresses both God and the (reading) community: "I need not tell all this to you, my God, but in your presence I tell it to my own kind. . . . And I tell it so that I and all who read my words may realize the depths from which we are to cry to you."[86] The two-destination address appearing in the confessional text of Augustine is similar in nature to the two-destination address appearing in the apophatic text of Dionysius the Areopagite.

The address asks God "to give the promise of His presence as other, and finally the transcendence of His otherness itself."[87] The address enables the one who addresses "to approach it [God, the Trinity, the Good], 'most intimately'—that is, to raise oneself toward it—and receive from it the initiation of its gifts."[88] At the conclusion of this address, the "one who asks to be led by God turns for an instant toward another addressee [without turning away from God, without changing direction], in order to lead him in turn."[89] The apostrophe turned to God that turns to the other allows the same text to speak to many others simultaneously. "The prayer, the quotation of the prayer, and the apostrophe, from one you to the other, thus weave the *same* text, however heterogeneous they appear."[90] Prayer as pure address remains "on the edge of silence," the bending of the apostrophe from God to the other enables the repetition of prayer to a multiplicity of addressees: "[I]f prayer did not bend, if it did not submit to writing, would . . . a theology be possible?"[91] It is the *post-scriptum* of the address to God that allows, for Derrida, the (impossible) possibility of theological language.

The prayer that addresses God is a theological moment of passion—the passion of desire, the passion of enjoyment—in the movement of apophatic language. It is in this moment of the address, that the one who prays also waits, passionately, in the silence of undecidability, in the silence of a *Gelassenheit*—an abandonment—that, abandoning God, is enclosed in the passionate enjoyment of God. The *post-scriptum* of the prayer or confession that is given to the community of readers celebrates the apophatic movement of the promised-becoming of the secret. The *post-scriptum* is an impassioned attestation; it is the confession or prayer that *testifies* to a passionate address to God. The wager of faith of the community then overflows—"becomes"—from the theological moment of this address to God.

Asking for nothing, yet asking for more than everything, the apophatic prayer "asks God to give himself rather than gifts."[92] *Give us the gift of yourself,* cries the apophatic prayer in its address to God: "If you don't give yourself to me, then you have given nothing."[93] This is the prayer of an impossible possibility of faith that lives in *expectation* of the advent of God, releasing itself to the passionate enjoyment of God. In the narrative of the Annunciation, the prayer of Mary's *fiat* is a "letting-be" that, in response to the advent of the divine, is infused with the expectation of possibilities. The Magnificat, as a *post-scriptum* in which Mary turns to address the community, celebrates the potential of these possibilities. The theological moment of these prayers is present in an excessive transgression: the moment in which the prayer addresses God in the piety of *Gelassenheit* is also a moment of faith opening "a passion to the enjoyment of God" in the *kardia* that is love of neighbor.

THE ANNUNCIATION: A MUTUAL GIFT OF *GELASSENHEIT*

The philosophical framework that I am interweaving in this paper provides a phenomenological approach to reading the text of the Annunciation. Husserl and Heidegger provide the foundational possibilities for thinking theologically through phenomenology about releasement (*Gelassenheit*) and openness to community. Irigaray emphasizes that Mary participates in a spiritual engendering through an attentive love; Marion suggests that the Annunciation is a gift of possibility; and Derrida provides a means to creatively read the speech of the Annunciation and the Magnificat. While each of these philosophers holds a different view of divinity, I would like to appropriate their thought in my own constructive proposal. From this framework, then, I propose an interpretation of the Annunciation as a joyful moment of *Gelassenheit* which is realized through a mutual promise of love and which overflows into an ethico-religious vision for the community. Through the divine gift of love to Mary, and through Mary's gift of love to the divine, there is a mutual releasement into transformative possibilities: just as the divine invites and enables Mary to become the mother of the Son of God, so too does Mary invite and enable the divine to become the Son of God.

Luce Irigaray suggests that spirituality is the sharing of breath which engenders life through attentive love. Mary, the woman who shares breath with the divine and shares life as well as breath with the divine Son, becomes divine herself through this sharing in love of breath and life. Through the interpenetrating fluidity of air, the breath that is shared between Mary and the divine—the breath of the question and the breath of the yes—is a spiritual breath leading to a spiritual engendering and an incarnation of divinity.

Intermingling with breath, life, and love is desire. In the narrative of the Annunciation, the desire of the divine for Mary is announced through the angelic messenger, and the echoing desire of Mary for the divine is announced through her response. Perhaps it is desire that allows the possibility for this sharing of breath and life and love. The invitation of the Most High invites Mary into a space of divine possibility. The desire of the divine, the "I desire you to desire me," beckons Mary to respond. Mary's "let it be" may be read as a response that desires the divine desire.

I propose, then, a slight revision of Irigaray's rendering of the question from the divine to Mary, "Do you want to be the mother of the/a savior?"[94] I would like to think of this question more in terms of a beckoning from the divine to Mary, an expression of the divine desire for Mary: "I desire you to desire to be the mother of the/a savior." Reading the Annunciation in this manner allows us to view the announcement of the angelic messenger as an invitation that springs from the overflowing desire of the divine for Mary, the human subject. Borrowing the words of Dionysius the Areopagite,

> [W]e must dare to affirm . . . that the Creator of the Universe Himself, in His Beautiful and Good Yearning towards the Universe, is through the excessive yearning of His Goodness, transported outside of Himself in His providential activities towards all things that have being.[95]

The divine yearns for Mary, and Mary responsively yearns for the divine, leading to a mutual gift of love that, as Irigaray might suggest, "mingles one term into another."[96]

This event—this event of Annunciation—is saturated with possibility: the possibility of an ecstatic union between Mary and the divine, a union in which one life flows into another through this mutual gift of love. As Karmen MacKendrick suggests, grace is an invitation into possibility: "Grace is the opening of spaces of possibility, an openness to the spaces of possibility which itself makes those spaces."[97] The words of the angelic messenger hail Mary into divine possibility; responding in grace, Mary invites the divine into possibility. Mary's response, her prayer of "let it be," enables the radical possibility of grace. Springing from desire, the desire of the divine as well as the desire of Mary, grace invites both Mary and the divine into the space of possibility it creates—the possibility for a joyful moment of *Gelassenheit*.

Transgressing language, the Annunciation slips into an apophatic moment of releasement. In the words of Meister Eckhart, it is through this *Gelassenheit* that "God must pour out the whole of himself with all his might so totally into every man who has utterly abandoned himself that God withholds nothing of his being or his nature or his entire divinity, but he must pour all of it fruitfully into the man who has abandoned himself for God."[98] Mary releases herself to the divine; and the divine pours the whole of the divine self into Mary, withholding nothing. This is a mutual sharing of the self: the call shares the divine self and the response shares the human self. Mary is blessed; she is filled with the fruitful possibilities of divinity, and the divine becomes incarnate as the Son.[99]

The gift of possibility is given through both the message of the angel and the response of Mary in the Annunciation. Following Jean-Luc Marion, it is Mary's "'Here I am!' of the responsal" that makes visible the "There you are!" of the address spoken by the angel.[100] Mary is called to possibility through a revelation of the divine that saturates intentionality, and, as Marion might suggest, "bedazzles the gaze."[101] The realm of the divine, for Marion, "starts where the impossible translates into the possible."[102] Mary's first response to the angel, "How can this be?" confines Mary to the impossible.[103] But the angel persuades Mary, "[N]othing will be impossible with God." The impossible is, as Marion observes, "the only indisputable sign by means of which God allows himself to be recognized."[104]

Mary recognizes the divine and responds by accepting the gift of radical possibility and extending her own gift of possibility to the divine: "[L]et it be with me according to your word."[105] Mary recognizes the possibility of the impossible: "[Y]ou will conceive in your womb and bear a son."[106] With the "let it be" of her response, Mary affirms the possible. While Marion emphasizes that the impossible becomes possible for Mary, I suggest that Mary gives a gift of possibility to the divine. Mary is called by the divine into the possibilities of grace, but she also extends a gift of possibility: she will bear the child who will be the son of the Most High.[107]

The speech of the Annunciation—the hailing of Mary by the divine, and the *fiat*, the "let it be," spoken by Mary in response to the divine—finds fulfillment in a moment of *Gelassenheit* through which the ineffable becomes the incarnate *Logos*: in the words of the angelic messenger, "[T]he child to be born will be holy; he will be called Son of God."[108] Following Jacques Derrida's understanding of prayer, we might interpret Mary's "let it be" as a prayer which addresses the divine, asking God "to give the promise of His presence."[109] The angelic messenger beckons Mary with the promise of divine presence; Mary's response invites the promised presence and promises her own presence. Through their shared promises—the promise of the divine, "I promise that you will be the mother of the/a savior" and the promise of Mary, "I promise that I will be the mother of the/a savior"—they unite in a mutual gift of love.[110] As the mystical theologian Angelus Silesius suggested, this gift of love is a shared gift:

> God loves me above all; if I love Him the same,
> I give Him just as much as I receive from Him.[111]
> The divine gives to Mary, and Mary in turn gives to the divine.

The Canticle of Mary, the Magnificat, speaks from this ineffable experience. The words of the Magnificat form a *post-scriptum* in which Mary turns for a moment to another addressee, bending her prayer.[112] Turning to Elizabeth, Mary's apophatic words of releasement become her kataphatic words of the Magnificat. The ineffable moment of excessive love becomes radically articulated in the Canticle of Mary, whose words, reminiscent of the song of Hannah, envision an ethical transformation of the social order.[113] The union of love with the divine becomes the inspiration for a theological language that participates constructively in the world: "My soul magnifies the Lord, and my spirit rejoices in God, my Savior."[114] The Magnificat celebrates a vision of divine liberation for the lowly, the oppressed, and the hungry through the overturning of the social and political order: "[H]e has scattered the proud. . . . He has brought down the powerful from their thrones and lifted up the lowly; he has filled the hungry with good things, and sent the rich away empty."[115]

Mary's words spring from the depths of *Gelassenheit*. As Silesius suggests,

> A man who is abandoned to God in all his ways
> He may already now to blessedness be raised.[116]

Mary is blessed, she shares a gift of love with the divine: "Surely," she declares, "from now on all generations will call me blessed."[117] Immersed in the possibilities of grace, Mary brings the message of that grace to Elizabeth. Borrowing again the poetic words of Silesius:

> If in your neighbor you but God and Christ will see
> Then you see with the light born from divinity.[118]

The moment of excessive love overflows into every future act of love for the neighbor.

When the angelic messenger hails Mary into the possibilities of divine grace, and when Mary responds with her own gift of possibility, these words become the prayerful promise of a *Gelassenheit* filled with grace. The Annunciation that Mary makes is one that proclaims the possibilities of this grace and celebrates the excess of divinity which speaks with and through her.[119] Through their mutual gift of *Gelassenheit*, the divine and Mary—the Lover and the Beloved—are transported into the possibilities of a mystical union overflowing with love.

Intimate Mysteries: The Apophatics of Sensible Love

KRISTA E. HUGHES

"I am a little discouraged," Hélène Cixous laments to her beloved; "I shall never have the strength nor the time to write something worthy of you. Would I do better to remain silent?" For "to say you, multimillionly of you, that goes beyond all possibilities, even the imaginary ones, of ever producing a successful stroke of writing. Yet," she confesses, "I do not have the courage not to write: I write to you, I write myself to you." Flowing from the most intimate of human love, this apophatic dilemma torments Cixous far more than cautious attempts to (not) speak of God; for, she wryly observes, "if one does not want to speak of God, it is permissible to not-speak of God with a perfect and definitive silence. . . . One can say nothing about God. And another way of speaking about God is to say God of him. . . . About God, one can say everything that is on the scale of impossibility, there is all nothing to say, which is obvious, and impossible but not difficult." The ease of these "divine mathematics" seems to Cixous insignificant and "really without relation to the torments that bring the need to speak to you absolutely non-absolutely, but absolutely faithfully . . . to say You, humanly infinite, inconclusive."[1]

Cixous's impassioned, agonizing, joyful struggle to write of and to her beloved poignantly depicts the theme of this volume, apophatic bodies. Her prayer of confession, lamentation, and praise celebrates precisely the incarnate infinity of the one whom she loves. An apophatic gesture at its emotional fullest, its appeal is strong: love, *eros*, rather than moral restraint or abstract speculative rigor, funds the utter unspeakability of the other. Within a discursive world replete with abstractions, Cixous's enfleshed apophasis of a particular intimate love stirs the theological air. Is this not what the genuine urge to unsay *the divine* should sound like—look, smell, feel like? Could Cixous's apophatic confession inspire *theology* toward more richly textured apophatic expression? Or, the inner voice cautions, would a theological appeal to her ebullient celebration of *human* love risk luring us into the very idolatries that theology's apophatic gestures are deployed to prevent? If we are reflecting on not simply apophasis but apophatic *bodies*, then Cixous's perspective, I believe, opens up something unique and something needed, particularly for a feminist theological contribution to the conversation on apophasis.

The reclamation of bodies and the senses has been one of feminist theology's central concerns, of course. Its relation to apophatic discourse, however, has been more ambiguous. On the one hand, the apophatic gesture has long been a potentially dangerous prospect for feminists: the call to unsay, or simply be silent, just as women (and historically silenced others) are finally finding their voices and being heard, poses a potential threat to the world's marginalized bodies. On the other hand, apophasis has played a significant role in prominent works of feminist theology. Elizabeth Johnson, for example, in her feminist systematic theology *She Who Is*, demonstrates how an apophatic posture toward the divine, by affirming God's ultimate unknowability, challenges the reification of masculine metaphors for God and opens the way for new and vibrant ones.[2] Similarly, philosopher of religion Grace Jantzen has underscored the fundamental ineffability of the divine in medieval mystical narratives, asserting that it is precisely the unspeakability of God that allows the mystics to plumb the "great fecundity and versatility" of language about the divine.[3]

Deploying the apophatic in the service of feminist scholarship is even more important given that women historically were denied the apophatic voice, as Amy Hollywood has argued in her work on mysticism and sexual difference. The modern study of mysticism, she notes, has asserted a simplistic and mistakenly gendered opposition between imagistic or kataphatic mystical texts, "by women," and ostensibly more sophisticated apophatic ones, "by men." She shows instead that both kataphatic language and apophatic language consistently occur *within* mystical texts (regardless of the gender of the author),[4] echoing both Jantzen's argument and Denys Turner's assertion that apophasis is "a moment of negativity within an overall theological strategy which is at once and every moment both apophatic and cataphatic."[5] In claiming the power and the necessity of the apophatic gesture, it is therefore key for feminists to interrogate apophasis as a discursive strategy: What is its purpose, and how do we perform it? Defining apophasis as a practice of temporary verbal restraint that gives birth to fresh images—a sort of discursive *tzimtzum*—allows feminist theologians to lay claim to the vital function of apophatic rhetoric without having to fear the loss of our voices or the dismissal of embodied needs and desires.

Although the French philosopher and literary theorist Hélène Cixous is not a theologian, her work suggests some of the contours of a specifically feminist expression of apophasis. In addressing the infinite mystery of her beloved's incarnate singularity, Cixous attends to the feminist concern that real bodies with unique needs and specific desires are often occluded by abstract principles of philosophical and theological discourse. Overcome by love both received and given, she models a kind of apophatic gesture that is rooted precisely in particular bodies and the love they share. This is good news for feminist theology insofar as she both acknowledges the needs and desires of real bodies *and* expands the possibilities of the apophatic gesture: the mysteries of *intimacy*, as it turns out, may exceed language no less than those of the *tout autre*.[6] A Cixousian apophasis, in other words, points feminist theology toward an apophatics of sensible love.

Feminist theology is ripe for a distinctive conception of apophasis that emerges out of intimacy. Many recent feminist thinkers have offered deeply pneumatological visions of the divine, emphasizing God's active presence *within* the dynamism of embodied relation. While Christianity has always confessed the providential movement of the Holy Spirit in the world, what is distinctive about certain feminist-relational theologies is their dual affirmation of God's radical immanence and the world's integrity vis-à-vis the divine. God is at once closer yet less coercive than many classic conceptions have allowed. Likewise, although these pneumatological portraits insist on God-in-the-world, they are also committed to protecting the irreducible difference of the divine other. Thus, even as they celebrate the body as a site of divine activity, this is a turn that, far from delimiting the divine, actually *frees* the divine to move in the world rather than simply beyond or above it. The divine Spirit is thus conceived not as a remote patriarch controlling the world and yet curiously untouched by it. Instead, Spirit is identified as a powerful force of compassion, love, and justice fostering the healing and vitality of all, human and nonhuman alike. Like wind and water, earth and fire, this is a divine who shapes and is shaped by all those she encounters, neither binding nor being bound—intimately close yet never captured . . . veiling and unveiling in a dance of retreat and revelation.[7]

In the light of these theological shifts, I wish to consider apophasis in a more sensible and erotic vein. I want to ponder how the task of constructive theology—which takes seriously both the theological and the ethical import of the apophatic gesture—might be informed by Cixous's struggle, one that is primarily grounded not in speculative, epistemological questions about the unknowability and incomprehensibility of the Other, but in the tender, agitating awe of intimate embodied love, in which proximity itself is the source of the other's mysteriousness. The Christian tradition already has its own witnesses to the sensible love of the divine, of course: the many medieval women mystics who pushed their era's boundaries of what constituted divine-human intimacy by refusing to dissociate body from spirit, even as they plumbed the inarticulable depths of divine mystery. They naturally ground any feminist articulation of apophatic theology. While claiming their bodies in ways largely unacceptable to their male counterparts, these women nevertheless experienced mystical intimacy as a self-annihilating fusion or union with the divine, a conception incompatible with many feminist commitments today. Cixous's depiction of sensible apophasis thus serves as a helpful postmodern *supplément* that, in insisting on *differánce*, offers an alternative to such fusion: an embodied intimacy that honors the integrity of both lovers precisely by acknowledging their *mutual* mysteriousness. While her portrait is of a human-human love, I propose that she models an apophasis of sensible intimacy that theologians might read as analogous to divine-human love and also supports the feminist theological affirmation that humans encounter the divine within embodied relations. God, while not possessing a discrete body, nonetheless both inspires and emerges from the multiple bodies of the cosmos and their interrelations. From Cixous's apophatic confession about and to her human beloved, we might then glean some theological insights beyond what even she herself intends.

Apophasis is not simply about mystery, of course: it is primarily about language. Thus a feminist theology of apophasis also needs to ask *how* it might best express the ineffability of embodied intimacy. Observing that apophasis is about the interplay of concealment and disclosure, about veiling by unveiling, Wolfson defines apophasis as "saying away," or "speaking away," instead of its standard locution, "unsaying." As he succinctly puts it, "apophasis as speaking-away . . . entails not-speaking by speaking rather than speaking by not-speaking,"[8] the latter of which would yield, of course, mere silence.[9] Cixous distinctively performs this practice of saying-away, of not-speaking by speaking: indeed, she writes voluminously about what she is *unable* to say in the face of her beloved's ineffability, even as she feels compelled to do so. This is perhaps one more gift that she might offer a feminist apophatic practice grounded in the sensible.

The testimonies of the medieval women mystics, supplemented by Cixous's apophatic confession, together inspire a distinctively feminist contribution to the theological question of apophasis: an apophatics of sensible love that flows from the mysteries of intimacy rather than just foreignness. This essay seeks to trace the contours of what that contribution might be, including a consideration of what kind of apophatic "practice" might best express such a sensible apophasis. I suggest that constructive theologians might strive to cultivate, in Wolfson's words, a certain "speaking away" that springs as much from the sensible, and its loves and delights, as from the invisible and untouchable.

MYSTICAL INTIMACIES: MEDIEVAL TESTIMONIES OF SENSIBLE LOVE

"God is love," testifies the writer of 1 John, "and those who abide in love, abide in God, and God abides in them" (4:16b, NRSV). As evinced by this New Testament verse, the category of intimacy is not new within theological discourse. It is, in fact, an originary confession of Christianity and one that took center stage in the testimonies of the tradition's so-called mystics. In their depictions of the divine-human encounter, both the speculative/intellectual and the affective strands of mysticism employed the language of divine-human intimacy. The former, exemplified in the works of Origen, Pseudo-Dionysius, and Meister Eckhart, emphasized cognition and revealed knowledge—union with God constituted unity with the mind of God—while the latter, most often identified with Bernard of Clairvaux, more centrally incorporated the language of *eros*, often linked to the love of Christ. Even affective mysticism, however, was not particularly embodied and in fact, as Grace Jantzen points out, tended at times to seem quite the opposite. Of Bernard she observes, "[I]f the weft of his sermons is the vocabulary of erotic love, the warp is a sharp denial of the body as having any part in it. The love with which the soul is to seek God is to be purely spiritual; the desire and passion and consummation are not to be thought of as in any sense engaging actual bodiliness and sexuality. . . . [In fact,] one of the most striking features is how unerotic they actually are."[10]

By contrast, many of the women mystics—such as Julian of Norwich, Hadewijch of Antwerp, Teresa of Ávila, and Hildegard of Bingen—who tended to be less formally trained than their male counterparts, portrayed their encounters with and visions of God using language that was not only affective but thoroughly sensible. Taking the Christian confession of divine incarnation deeply to heart, they refused to deny the body in favor or the mind or the spirit. Consciousness, Jantzen emphasizes, was certainly involved in these women's mystical encounters, but not at the expense of the body. She offers as an example fourteenth-century Julian of Norwich, whom she names "mystic of integration" for this anchorite's well-considered anthropology, which included both "the substantial and the sensual," the latter of which involves bodiliness as well as consciousness, "the life of the senses and the mind." "[We] are made sensual, [Julian] says, 'when our soul is breathed into our body'. . . . Our substance, on the other hand, is for Julian the essential part of ourselves, which she holds is directly united with God at all times, whether we are aware of it or not."[11] For Julian it was the fragmentation of the sensual and the substantial that constituted sin, rather than a fall away from God, which to her thinking was not even ontologically possible; and it was precisely their reintegration that constituted salvation. The body was never to be left behind in this process but in point of fact was at the very center of the process.

Christianity's incarnational confession shaped the women mystics' testimonies in another distinctive way: they portrayed their divine encounters as experiences that facilitated relation *with* the world rather than severing the mystic from her material context. Within modern philosophy, Jantzen notes, mystical encounters have been interpreted as those experiences that set the mystics apart from society, placing them in a position of singularity vis-à-vis the divine. But many of these women understood "union with God" as a sort of tutelage in Love, which fostered a sense of deep relation between themselves and the world around them. Citing the experiences and testimonies of Hadewijch of Antwerp, Jantzen explains that within the male mystical tradition, "deification meant the encounter of the mind and/or the affection with the mind of God, so that the deified person could come to think the thoughts of God," whereas "for Hadewijch 'becoming God with God' meant the encounter of the whole person with the love of God, so that the deified person could come to do the works of God. And these works were the works of love as demonstrated in the humanity of Jesus."[12] The mystical path, thus, "culminates in 'being love with Love' and thus doing the deeds of Love 'naturally.'"[13] This further meant that "to 'become God' is to become 'mighty and just,' strong in compassion and in the work for justice," not to become all-knowing—and certainly not "to escape from the body and its sensory needs and desires into the realm of the spirit."[14] While Hadewijch's tone is far more fiery and erotic than Julian's, which is notably pacific, both exemplify the incarnational lens by which women mystics tended to articulate their mystical insights, a lens that yielded testimonies of embodied sensibility and love, erotic and agapic, that encompassed both divine-human and human-human relations, spilling beyond a "private" experience of the divine into the world.[15]

Christianity's medieval women mystics, in attending to their own sensible experiences as well as the embodied circumstances of those whom they served, provide a rich and invaluable spring from which to pursue an apophatics of sensible love. We cannot leave intimacy untroubled as a theological or spiritual category, however. Internalized misogyny and images of self-annihilation in the face of the divine permeate the language of the women mystics. Therefore, even as we can allude to these mystical visionaries as examples of loving communion between divine and human, intimacy must not go unqualified. The divine-human intimacy that Beverly J. Lanzetta traces in the testimonies of Julian and Teresa raises potential red flags for feminist critical sensibilities. These women speak, after all, about the annihilation of the self, describing their marriage or union with God as total fusion (with a God, moreover, who is often figured as male). This seems to be a clear echo of the "soluble self," whom Catherine Keller and other feminist thinkers have diagnosed as a self-defeating tendency in women to be overly determined by their external relationships.[16] Lanzetta, while aware of this feminist concern, identifies a genuine experience of freedom for these women mystics, arguing that they are liberated through their mystical relation to God from the sociocultural constraints that defined what women were and ought to be. Thus, the sensation of nothingness that the women articulate in their testimonies is not, in Lanzetta's opinion, what modern feminism might call the soluble or fragmented self but a state in which the self, most joyfully, is absorbed through God into unity with all (in a manner similar to the Zen experience "no-self").[17] In other words, she propounds, oneness with God *equals* freedom of the self, and in "becoming 'nothing' one also becomes whole."[18] "The soul that is annihilated in love is finally whole, finally open to everything," declares Lanzetta, "and thus is the true source of women's freedom, strength, dignity, and empowerment."[19]

While Lanzetta's reading of these women's experiences is compelling, she perhaps too easily glosses over both the women's frequent use of self-deprecating language, often misogynist in tone—which she interprets as simply a rhetorical strategy—as well as the strong elements of self-mortification, bodily illness, and social isolation that, for Teresa and Marguerite Porete in particular, were part of the spiritual path toward union with God. That these women were unusually accomplished in their own time and that they conveyed a uniquely "female" spiritual wisdom that continues to speak today is not in question. It is with cautious care, however, that we should draw from them as models for a feminist-friendly understanding of intimate love today. We now recognize that both openness to others and an individual sense of cohesiveness are necessary for the healthy self-in-relation, as Luce Irigaray has proposed in the figure of the envelope, which, she explains, provides a "containing space" (particularly for women) without closing off either the world or the self.[20] Within their own contexts, this is perhaps what the women mystics were striving for, even as they employed the language of divine-human *union*: it is helpful to recall Jantzen's rendering that to "become one with God" was to become compassionate and loving toward the world as well as the divine, not simply to become intellectually enlightened or transcendently removed. Yet these women also worshipped a supremely powerful God while advocating a strong measure of worldly rejection, thereby attenuating their incarnational confession. Contemporary figurations of intimacy might benefit from a different vision of this confession, wherein incarnation and pneumatology interweave; wherein bodies are honored not simply as vessels or temples for the Spirit but as living manifestations of the divine; wherein the mysterious particularity of both lover and beloved is protected by the very space of difference that also renders intimate connection possible.

INCARNATE INTIMACIES: POSTMODERN TESTIMONIES OF SENSIBLE LOVE

Hélène Cixous offers a distinctive expression of apophasis that displays affinities with the women mystics' testimonies of sensible intimacy, while refusing (for her sake and that of her beloved) to define that intimacy as a desire for total union or fusion. In other words, she avows with her philosophical contemporaries an unqualified regard for the irreducibility of the other—an appreciation of the "to" or "toward" that at once links and differentiates (and thereby protects) lovers. Her work thus serves as a fitting *supplément* to Christianity's mystical foremothers, as we imagine a feminist apophasis of sensible love. Cixous's project is not theological, and as we have seen, her apophatic confession emerges from her intimate encounter with a *human* other. Yet the divine figures into her reflections with surprising frequency, both the God of speculative philosophy as well as her own more incarnate and "pneumatological" sense of the divine.[21] Her portrayal of intimate love, I therefore hope to show, might be read theologically as a reflection of a divine-human intimacy that frees the self to love and be loved in relation to all without self-annihilation—a sensible and joyful intimacy that embraces natality and life's continual graces rather than a singular "saving grace" of which death, in some form, is the prime requisite.[22] I attempt here a sketch of a Cixousian conception of apophasis by tracing how her thoughts on writing and otherness relate to the contemporary philosophical discourse on alterity. What I seek to show is that Cixous offers us an *apophatics of sensible love*, that is, a practice of "saying away" that finds its primary impetus, not in speculative or epistemological commitments, but instead in the inevitable mystery of intimate relationship with a sensible other—the mystery, moreover, that at once connects and protects lover and beloved.

Unlike some of her Parisian colleagues, Cixous's work has not tended to directly engage the discourse of negative theology, or even theology in general. It is celebrating life, rather than saving the name of God, that is her primary concern, an awareness that Jacques Derrida recognizes and honors.[23] And yet her close attention to the ways that writing and the power of language relate to issues of otherness brush her up against the discourse in notable ways. Cixous's concern with the limitations of language for representing reality manifests as a specific passion for the act of writing itself. Writing, for Cixous, is a vocation in the deepest sense of the word, for it is a way of living that draws our lives into the holy and the holy into our lives. She lives by and through writing: "I write celebrating living."[24] Accordingly, it is in the specific context of writing that she engages the postmodern philosophical discourse of alterity—the inability to capture or appropriate the other, linguistically or otherwise. Whether articulated as the Lévinasian stranger or the Derridean *tout autre*, this discourse attends to the ethical impulses and implications of apophasis, striving for the universal while also attempting to honor the particularity of every other.

The distinctiveness of Cixous's approach to these matters shines through in her essay "(With) Or the Art of Innocence," in which she explores and exposes an event of apophasis within the particular context of intimate love. Although Derrida does speak of love briefly in his plurivocal reflections "on the name" of God—offering a beautiful passage on *Gelassenheit* and loving as letting the other be[25]—his starting point seems to be more intellectual than sensible, a trait, as we have seen, that characterizes central (generally male) figures of the Christian mystical tradition. Likewise, the question of desire, *eros*-love, is never far from Derrida's talk of the apophatic. Yet in Cixous's joyful lamentations to her beloved, we hear her perform what Derrida seems only to speculate about (albeit multivocally)—that desire carries within itself an "extreme tension," one that, in the act of going toward the absolute other (in Cixous's case her beloved), "tries thereby to renounce its own proper momentum, its own movement of appropriation."[26] Giving voice to this paradoxical tension, Cixous confesses:

> [T]he feared truth is perhaps that it is not only difficult to speak to you, Antouylia, but absolutely non-possible to speak entirely simply of you. . . . [F]or all that concerns your humanity, I am not allowed to, even an allusion fills me with holy horror, I shall never sacrilege you. I have a dreamy, evasive humanity that is too pusillanimous ever to be worthy of giving an account of your obstinately, dangerously real humanity. Humanity maintained and non-denied moreover always puts all words to shame.[27]

Her only hope, therefore, is to say something that, while "written in [her] own sphere" and revolving around herself, "might have a chance . . . of approaching the edges of [her beloved's] mystery."[28]

Neither ethics nor metaphysics nor epistemology leads Cixous to this awareness, but rather her embodied experience of intimate love. It is *love* which reveals the limits of language and knowledge; it is *love* which grounds the apophatic, with only secondary linguistic and epistemological implications. Moreover, her reflections on the nonpossibility of speaking issues in the form of address: in speaking (or *not* speaking) *about* her beloved other, she finds herself speaking *to* her beloved, *toward* her, in a wave of emotion and insight that spills forth as confession, perhaps even prayer, in an echo of mystical practices that address God directly. Cixous's embodied, erotic reflections on the alterity of her beloved presage her Parisian contemporary Luce Irigaray's work on the intersection of otherness and love, the 1994 volume *I Love to You*, in which Irigaray considers how love might flourish across irreducible difference. Irigaray's addition of one small preposition, "to," renders an overworked and often diluted phrase both fresh and radical: "[T]he 'to' is the site of non-reduction of the other to the object."[29] Thus "*I love to you* means I maintain a relation of indirection to you. I do not subjugate you or consume you. I respect you (as irreducible). I hail you: in you I hail. I praise you: in you I praise. . . . I speak to you, not just about something, rather I speak *to* you."[30] Cixous likewise adopts the "to" as a way of expressing a love that is irresistible yet seeks to be nonappropriative—indeed which acknowledges that love that is vital and healthy cannot be appropriative. Thus, she seeks to "write only in drifting towards you, in To. . . . I write to you, I write myself to you, I fail, but at least it is to your address."[31]

Cixous and Irigaray, while embracing the ethical imperative of *differánce* at the heart of poststructuralist philosophy, use the lens of sexual difference to emphasize themes of embodiment, natality, and intimate love, thereby unveiling alternative dimensions of alterity and even apophatic practice. In their hands, both sensibility and love are declared central to the thinking and writing of alterity rather than hindrances, for embodied intimacy rather than foreignness funds the inappropriability of the other. "The mystery," Cixous says, "is that I do not understand the beings that I love the most," and yet she does not fear that strangeness, and it "does not hurt [her], does not plunge [her] into darkness."[32] It is precisely love's proximity that gives rise to mystery, strangeness, ineffability . . . and thus to the apophatic gesture.

If Cixous, with her notable grounding in love and sensibility, distinguishes herself from certain male philosophers of difference, it is precisely this grounding that she shares with the women mystics we have briefly explored. On the surface, she does not seem to be concerned with theology proper, particularly with the transcendent God (capital G) of speculative philosophy, with whom, unlike her beloved, she "never [risks] anything, either mistake, or an aside, or truth, and [does] not make him take any risk, [. . . in what] is sometimes a relationship of terrifying albeit imperturbable tranquility." Yet in her reflections we find ample evidence of a visceral understanding of the divine, as if, through the life which she counsels us to embrace, moves a dynamic, intensely vivifying power, that which the Christian tradition might name the Holy Spirit. Life for Cixous—that is, truly living rather than simply existing or surviving—happens within relationship, within the context of embodied love, and it is from this matrix that the divine emerges.[33] We thus might hear echoes of the Christian mystics in her writing to her beloved Antouylia: "My dazzled sentences revolve around your existence. I have to write to you with my eyes lowered, my body a little bent, I am writing almost blinded in your light, and I am shading myself with my own words on your hand."[34] This event of blinding revelation, while carrying the unique marks of Cixous's relation to writing, sounds markedly mystical.

It is therefore perhaps unsurprising to find that Cixous traces a conception of the divine that is deeply resonant with more explicit feminist pneumatologies: her awe in the face of her beloved is no less and no more ecstatically debilitating than her awe in the face of the divine—

because although Antouylia and God are not the same, neither can they be separated. Love's impossible call to write of and to her beloved, and all that their shared love brings to life, is a divine call issuing from countless directions. "When I have finished writing," Cixous declares,

> when I am a hundred and ten, all I will have done will have been to attempt a portrait of God. Of the God. Of what escapes us and makes us wonder. Of what we do not know but feel. Of what makes us live. I mean our own divinity, awkward, twisting, throbbing, our own mystery. . . . [w]e who are bits of sun, drops of ocean, atoms of the god, and who so often forget this, or are unaware of it.[35]

This is clearly not the God, dismissed earlier by Cixous, who gives rise to the easy and boringly obvious "divine mathematics" of classic speculative apophasis, the dispassion of which renders it all but irrelevant to Cixous's experience. Rather, in an echo of mystics such as Hadewijch and Julian, Cixous here lifts up the almost unthinkable intimacy that we humans share with the divine yet without losing the apophatic mystery of it all: there is still surprise and escape, yet it is likewise a completely visceral, enfleshed experience—"what makes us wonder" is also "what makes us live." Unlike the mystics, however, humanity and divinity are more mutually permeable, ever inseparable yet never dissolving one into the other. Her performative style of theorizing the Other, at once about human relations *and* the divinity that moves within and emerges out of those very connections, might be heard by theologians as a call back to the Church's incarnational confession, to the simultaneous proclamations of a God who cannot be appropriated, who surprises us time and time again, and yet with whom Christians claim to have a privileged intimacy.

Love, intimacy, and sensibility, as we have already noted, increasingly characterize reconfigurations of God-as-Spirit in constructive theology, particularly in its feminist-relational vein. In contrast to the hierarchical framework that traditionally has marked Christian thought, wherein the divine-human relation itself orders inter-human relations—a framework that also underpins the thought of the women mystics we have examined—divine-human and inter-human relations are now often viewed as being mediated within one another. Such reconceptualizations do not necessarily represent a collapse of the divine into the human, or the creaturely, but rather designate a freeing of the divine to move intimately and sacramentally among, within, and through the sensible bodies of the world, rather than relegating the divine primarily to a remote or ineffable realm. Accordingly, neither transcendence nor infinity nor mystery is lost, merely transformed and deepened . . . indeed, incarnated.

Cixous's unwitting contribution to these theological reconfigurations is a confession-cum-portrait of a particular intimate, embodied love that, I suggest, might be read theologically not only as a fresh metaphor for divine-human encounter[36] but, even more vital to the concerns of this volume, as a model for our endeavors to articulate that encounter. Thus, my theological intention in appealing to Cixous is to trace the markers of love, intimacy, and sensibility in her confession-lamentation yet also in turn to highlight how it is precisely these markers that engender her apophatic disposition toward her beloved. For Cixous, it is the process of bearing witness to this love, specifically through the act of writing, that brings her to the exhilarating, anguished—and utterly sensible—threshold of the apophatic. Might her testimony of a sensible, erotic apophasis help us to better understand our own attempts as theologians to articulate, by both speaking *and* speaking away, something of the loving-beloved, utterly mysterious, divine other we proclaim?

INTIMATE MYSTERIES: TOWARD AN APOPHATICS OF SENSIBLE LOVE

Theologians arrive at the threshold of the apophatic when we remember that our vocation requires us to strike a delicate, risky, crucial balance between audacity and humility: Who are we to speak of divine ways, to attempt our portrayals of God? Especially when we write, as Cixous quips, "with brushes all sticky with words."[37] And yet who are we to remain silent in the face of the myriad divine gifts offered to us, the divine invitations unceasingly issued? These questions-*sans*-answers should haunt our theological reflections, and goad them. At the same time, we are aware that our apophatic gestures function as more than mere intellectual insurance against claims of theological fraud. They are expressions of faith and gratitude, of awe and honor, of promise and dedication. Or they should be. Indeed, I aver, they *will* be if in fact we are paying attention to the sensible bodies that surround us, that make up our very lives, preceding and exceeding language and ever mediating whatever we can know of the divine or the infinite or the transcendent. Our apophatic practices are funded by apophatic bodies, those infinite incarnations that continually conceal and disclose the divine that moves among and within us. And thus we are called to speak . . . away—"drifting towards" the myriad singular others, divine and human, in a hopeful gesture that might, or might not, approach the edges of the other's mystery.

In its search for a sensible apophatics grounded in intimate love, this essay has appealed to both the Christian women mystics of old and the contemporary philosopher Hélène Cixous. The former constitute a mystical thread in the Christian tradition, women religious—from different places and eras—who embraced the body and its senses as central to their experience of intimacy with the divine. Their testimonies and teachings offer us an archive of "sensible" expressions of Christian spirituality and give us a window into how the role of the body was negotiated and understood in particular narratives of divine-human encounter. Infused body-and-soul with the Love of God, these women in turn sought to pour out love on other body-souls. Cixous, in her exploration of intimate human love, enhances this sensible-mystical thread with a contemporary *supplément*, painting a similar portrait of sensible intimacy, yet one that identifies and insists on the protective "distance" of difference and thereby marks the apophatic impasse as a continuous lure, never to be resolved by union or fusion. Drawing from these rich wells, we can envision a sensible apophatics of love for contemporary constructive theology, which increasingly emphasizes the intimate, sensible, and embodied closeness of the divine while retaining the mystery of the *deus absconditus* as well as the integrity of the human lover-beloved. As much as ever, theology needs the protective humility of the apophatic gesture. But I suggest that it may now flow from some additional fresh springs.

Within both Christian theology historically and postmodern philosophy contemporarily, apophasis in the face of the other has been, with a few notable exceptions, predicated on distance and foreignness: every other, and especially the divine, is wholly other. While honoring the wisdom of such insights, I am persuaded that Cixousian and Irigarayan reflections on the otherness of intimacy offer an equally fruitful theological resource—indeed, one that is perhaps even more faithful to the incarnational and pneumatological confessions of Christianity. Intimate love, marked as it is by spatial proximity and temporal longevity, begets mystery no less than utter foreignness does: closeness and the passage of time gradually reveal the innumerable intricacies of lover and beloved.[38] The love shared within intimate relationship, moreover, fosters even greater attention to these fine details that continually unveil and veil the beloved other. The foreigner is also mysterious in her strangeness, but any effort to be in relation with the total stranger frequently involves the search for *commonalities* across difference. In love, by contrast, where desire fires the drive for deeper intimacy, it is often *difference* that is cast in bold relief, as lovers encounter those inevitable barriers and gulfs that mark the more-than-one. "The mystery is that I do not understand the beings that I love the most," muses Cixous. "[What] I do not understand is their own mystery. . . . But I know their incomprehensibility well." Acknowledging the mystery, and hence ungraspability, of one's beloved is only the beginning of Cixous's insights into the foreignness that emerges from love, though: significantly, she goes on to say that her beloved's "strangeness does not hurt [her], does not plunge [her] into darkness."[39] The *amatrix abscondita* can be worthy of respect, awe, mystery—and therefore apophatic restraint—without necessarily instilling fear or dread. Mystery at its finest is not that which repels, stifles, or frightens, but that which lures, and possibly delights.

My hope is that theology, in the light of its revaluing of embodiment and the senses and its turn toward pneumatology, might in turn discover new modes of apophatic expression, fresh ways of not only unsaying but, in Wolfson's words, "speaking away" the intimate mysteries and mysterious intimacies of divine-human encounter and the love that mediates it. In particular, I wonder if a fuller embrace of theopoetics, with its aesthetic grounding in the sensible and its characteristic style of speaking away, might be one such approach. After all, while *Theologia* was once considered queen of the sciences, she is rooted in centuries of narrative, poetry, and music—and portraits of God, both painted and penned—that always already render our task an enterprise in *theopoesis* as much as *theologos*. A turn to poetics might make sense for an embodied apophasis, in which sensible love reveals the limits of language to witness to the divine, while paradoxically inviting the attempt to do so. Because this lure toward expressing the inexpressible is something that theologians and artists alike share, I suggest that nudging the *logos* a bit to make room for poetics might itself function as an expression of the apophatic, while simultaneously infusing our task with beauty and delight.

Cixous says that she would "like to write like a painter . . . to write like painting" and laments that she possesses a painter's intuitions but not the skills.[40] She admires painters' capacities to express the beauty of what they portray, by which she means not perfection in detail, form, or proportion but rather the "truth" of the painting's subject: "In writing as in painting," she says, "there is no other 'beauty' than fidelity to what is. Painting renders—but what it renders is justice. . . . Because everything that is loved, everything that finds grace, is equal to the 'beautiful.' Everything we don't reject." She goes on to note that "everything is equal to God and to the painter. And this is the lesson often given to the poet by painting. To love the ugly with an equal-to-equal love."[41] Such fidelity to "what is"—the grace of nonrejection and equal-to-equal love—seems like a worthy, and apt, standard for scholars of Christian God-talk, who are called to engage the world as it is: at once beautiful and broken. Painting with words, however, is hard, sometimes impossible, especially "at the extremity of life, at the nerve endings, around the heart"—the very realms in which theology is called to speak. "Words are our accomplices, our traitors, our allies," Cixous declares; "Words drive us mad." Indeed, "our problem as writers [is that we] must paint with brushes all sticky with words."[42] We too, as theologians, face the question of how to do theology with fidelity—how to simultaneously honor both the tradition which nourishes, or perhaps incites, our reflections as well as the world that is challenging us in ways pastoral and ethical—all the while dealing with brushes all sticky with doctrines, symbols, images, and narratives that sorely need unsticking, that they might flow with renewed vibrancy. Do we have the courage to write theology like painting? For are we not, like Cixous, in our various ways, attempting portraits of God—of "the God. Of what escapes us and makes us wonder. Of what we do not know but feel. Of what makes us live"?

Courage we need: "doing theology"—whether constructive or biblical, historical or philosophical—requires that we "sin boldly." This mandate from Reformer Martin Luther is not, and never was, a license to do, or say, whatever we please but rather an ironic locution for the good news: that divine grace invites us to take risks; that living fully bears a cost, but one that is worthwhile; that even with life's inevitable imperfections, accepting the invitation to "turn then and live" yields far more than remaining passive does. While Cixous and Luther would certainly make strange bedfellows, her hope that one day she will be daring enough to pursue "the most beautiful of all failures"[43]—that is, to attempt the portrait of that which constantly escapes her, of both her beloved and "the god," of what makes us live and what makes us wonder—resonates with Luther's counsel to sin boldly. Touched by the world's sensible bodies, at once intimate and mysterious, we seek the courage and the faith to write boldly, even as we attend with tenderness and tenacity to the questions at theology's apophatic threshold: Who are we to speak? Who are we to remain silent? Grace, I suggest, makes such courage possible, while love gives us inspiration and purpose.

Let us, then, wield our sticky brushes and speak . . . away . . .

NOTES

INTRODUCTION | CHRIS BOESEL AND CATHERINE KELLER

1. Meister Eckhart, *Sermon 83: Renovamini spiritu (ep. 4.23),* in *Meister Eckhart: The Essential Sermons, Commentaries, Treatises and Defense*, trans. Edmund Colledge, O.S.A., and Bernard McGinn (Mahwah, N.J.: Paulist Press, 1981), 207.
2. Franz Rosenzweig, *The Star of Redemption*, trans. William W. Hallo (New York: Holt, Rinehart and Winston, 1971), 23.
3. Meister Eckhart, *Meister Eckhart: The Essential Sermons, Commentaries, Treatises and Defense,* trans. Edmund Colledge, O.S.A., and Bernard McGinn. (Mahwah, N.J.: Paulist Press, 1981), 195.
4. Elliot R. Wolfson, *Language, Eros, Being* (New York: Fordham University Press, 2005), 289. Regarding extralinguistic expressions, note the source of this book's cover design.
5. Karl Barth, "The Word of God and the Task of the Ministry," in *The Word of God and the Word of Man*, trans. Douglas Horton (New York: Harper, 1957), 186.
6. Karl Barth, *Church Dogmatics* II/I, ed. G. W. Bromiley and T. F. Torrance, trans. G. W. Bromiley et al. (Edinburgh: T&T Clark, 1957), 203.
7. "The Mystical Theology," in *Pseudo-Dionysius: The Complete Works,* trans. Colm Luibheid (Mahwah, N.J.: Paulist Press, 1987), 135.
8. Nicolas of Cusa, *De docta ignorantia* 1440, in *Nicholas of Cusa: Selected Spiritual Writings*, trans. H. Lawrence Bond (Mahwah, N.J.: Paulist Press, 1997), I.26.86, 125.
9. Ibid., 104, 56.
10. Alfred North Whitehead, *Science and the Modern World* (New York: Free Press, 1967), 51f.

11. Augustine, *Sermon 52*, n. 16 in *Sermons* Vol. III, ed. John E. Rotelle, trans. Edmund Hill (Brooklyn, N.Y.: New York City Press, 1991), 57.
12. See John D. Caputo and Gianni Vattimo, *After the Death of God*, ed. Jeffrey W. Robbins (New York: Columbia University Press, 2007).
13. Jacques Derrida, "The Theater of Cruelty and the Closure of Representation," in *Writing and Difference*, trans. Alan Bass (London: Routledge, 2001), 307.
14. Elizabeth A. Johnson, *She Who Is: The Mystery of God in Feminist Theological Discourse* (New York: Crossroad, 2002), 117.
15. Trinh T. Minh-Ha, *Woman, Native, Other: Writing Postcoloniality and Feminism* (Bloomington: Indiana University Press, 1989), 2.
16. Trinh T. Minh-Ha, *When the Moon Waxes Red: Representation, Gender, and Cultural Politics* (New York: Routledge, 1991), 234.
17. Trinh, *Woman, Native, Other*, 2.
18. Michael A. Sells, *Mystical Languages of Unsaying* (Chicago and London: University of Chicago Press, 1994), 206.

THE CLOUD OF THE IMPOSSIBLE: EMBODIMENT AND APOPHASIS | CATHERINE KELLER

1. Nicholas of Cusa, *De visione Dei*, 1453, in *Nicholas of Cusa: Selected Spiritual Writings*, trans. H. Lawrence Bond (Mahwah, N.J.: Paulist Press, 1997), 9.36, 251.
2. If one looks for medieval antecedents of a flesh-affirmative theology, the more affective, erotically charged female mystics (Mechthild, Julian, Teresa, even Hildegard) hover closer to the flesh, to Christ's exceptional flesh first of all, but with no less ambivalence. See Amy Hollywood, *Sensible Ecstasy: Mysticism, Sexual Difference, and the Demands of History* (Chicago: University of Chicago Press, 2002), Caroline Walker Bynum, *Fragmentation and Redemption: Essays on Gender and the Human Body in Medieval Religion* (New York: Zone Books, 1982), and Grace M. Jantzen, *Power, Gender, and Christian Mysticism* (Cambridge: Cambridge University Press, 1995). Or one turns to Thomas Aquinas, with Denys Turner, juxtaposing his "thorough-going incarnational apophaticism" to the rhetorical radicalism of Meister Eckhart and other "over-enthusiastic apophaticists of his time" (Denys Turner, "Apophaticism, Idolatry and the Claims of Reason," in *Silence and the Word: Negative Theology and Incarnation*, ed. Oliver Davies and Denys Turner [Cambridge: Cambridge University Press 2002], 30, 34).
3. Amy Hollywood analyzes the mystical, and particularly apophatic, relation of the body as a matter of "the suffering that seems constitutive of embodiment." In relation to Porete and Eckhart, "[T]he desire to transcend such

suffering in body and soul leads to the primacy of apophasis" (*The Soul as Virgin Wife: Mechthild of Magdeburg, Marguerite Porete, and Meister Eckhart* [Notre Dame, Ind.: University of Notre Dame Press, 1995], 23).

4. Catherine Keller, "The Apophasis of Gender: A Fourfold Unsaying of Feminist Theology," *Journal of the American Academy of Religion* 76/4 (2008): 905–933; Catherine Keller, "Rumors of Transcendence: The Movement, State and Sex of 'Beyond,'" in *Transcendence and Beyond: A Postmodern Inquiry*, ed. John D. Caputo and Michael J. Scanlon (Indianapolis: Indiana University Press, 2007).
5. Elizabeth Johnson, *She Who Is: The Mystery of God in Feminist Theological Discourse* (New York: Crossroad, 1992); see also, more recently, Beverly J. Lanzetta, *Radical Wisdom: A Feminist Mystical Theology* (Minneapolis: Fortress Press, 2005).
6. Luce Irigaray explores the openings and envelopes of a "sensible transcendental," engaging the female mystics even in her early writing in *Speculum of the Other Woman*, trans. Gillian C. Gill (Ithaca, N.Y.: Cornell University Press, 1985). Later she would claim without disembodiment a spiritualized, even yogic, flesh. *I Love to You: Sketch for a Felicity within History*, trans. Alison Martin (New York: Routledge, 1996).
7. Judith Butler, *Bodies That Matter: On the Discursive Limits of Sex* (New York: Routledge, 1997), ix, 221.
8. "*Moments of unknowingness about oneself tend to emerge in the context of relations to others*, suggesting that these relations call upon primary forms of relationality that are not always available to explicit and reflective thematization" (Judith Butler, *Giving an Account of Oneself* [New York: Fordham University Press, 2005], 20 [emphasis mine]). Butler has no recourse, however, either to mystical clouds of unknowing or to current accounts of materiality, ecology, or cosmology.
9. As the handy title of a new anthology suggests: *Theology That Matters: Ecology, Economy, and God*, ed. Darby Kathleen Ray (Minneapolis: Fortress Press, 2006). As a recent example of a feminist incarnationalism at once aligned with the Christian doctrine and inflected by poststructuralism, see also Darby Kathleen Ray, *Incarnation and Imagination: A Christian Ethic of Ingenuity* (Minneapolis: Fortress Press, 2008).
10. Cusa, *De visione Dei*, 9.37, 252.
11. See Nelle Morton, *The Journey Is Home* (Boston: Beacon Press, 1985), 55.
12. Cusa, *De visione Dei*, 9.36, 251.
13. Caputo could have been alluding to Cusa's cloud, or the older *Cloud of Unknowing*: "Undecidability and substitutability do not form a bottomless

pit down which every decision is dropped never to be heard from again. They constitute rather the haze of indefiniteness . . . the gluey, glassy *glas* which conditions even very ordinary decisions, in which the urgency and passion of decision are nourished" (John D. Caputo, *The Prayers and Tears of Jacques Derrida: Religion without Religion* [Bloomington: Indiana University Press, 1997], 63). The Derridean/Caputan path of the impossible/impassable winds through the present essay.

14. Cusa, *De visione Dei*, 9.37, 251–2.
15. Karmen MacKendrick, *Word Made Skin: Figuring Language at the Surface of Flesh* (New York: Fordham University Press, 2004), 140, 150 (emphasis mine). Like Cusa, she is never far from an Eckhartian apophasis.
16. Cusa, *De visione Dei*, 9.37, 252.
17. For Cusa's debating skills in conciliar controversies early in his career Pius II had dubbed him "the Hercules of the Eugenians."
18. Cusa's *coincidentia* is not to be mistaken for a unifying Hegelian sublation, though Hegel does reflect extensively on Giordano Bruno's account of "the unity of opposites" (*die Einheit der Entgegengesetzen*) as an anticipation of his own understanding of the idea and its development in the unfolding of the universe (Hegel, *Lectures on the History of Philosophy*, sec. C). Hegel oddly does not seem aware of the origin of the *coincidentia oppositorum* in Cusa's thought, though Bruno cites Cusa often. For example, addressing one "Sophia," Bruno writes: "[I]f the matter be considered physically, mathematically and morally, one sees that that philosopher who has arrived at the theory of the 'coincidence of contraries' has not found out little" (Giordano Bruno, *The Expulsion of the Triumphant Beast*, ed. and trans. Arthur D. Imerti, with foreword by Karen Silvia de León-Jones [Lincoln: University of Nebraska Press, 1964/2004], First Dialogue, First Part, 90).
19. Nicholas of Cusa, *De docta ignorantia* 1440, in *Selected Spiritual Writings*, I.26.86, 126. Cusa's definition, spiraling back to the "brilliant darkness" of Pseudo-Dionysius, of negative theology continues: "[T]he precise truth shines forth incomprehensibly in the darkness of our ignorance" (I.26.89, 127). Of this passage Jean-Luc Marion writes: "[T]his infinity does not revert to affirmation after passing through negation, but lays bare and circumscribes the divine truth as the experience of incomprehension" ("In the Name," in *God, the Gift, and Postmodernism*, ed. John D. Caputo and Michael J. Scanlon [Bloomington: Indiana University Press, 1999], 25). For Cusa's darkness read through the lens of the "darkness on the face of the deep/*tehom*," see my *The Face of the Deep: A Theology of Becoming* (London: Routledge, 2003), 200–209.

20. "When, therefore, Moses grew in knowledge, he declared that he had seen God in the darkness, that is, that he had then come to know that what is divine is beyond all knowledge and comprehension, for the text says, Moses approached the dark cloud where God was." Gregory of Nissa, *The Life of Moses,* in *Gregory of Nyssa: The Life of Moses*, trans. Abraham J. Malherbe and Everett Ferguson (Mahwah, N.J.: Paulist Press, 1978), 95–97.
21. Indeed Cusa sent an actual icon along in the parcel with *De visione Dei*, the better to illustrate to the monks for whom he prepared the manuscript a certain point about the divine gaze.
22. Kevin Hart, *The Trespass of the Sign: Deconstruction, Theology, and Philosophy* (New York: Fordham University Press, 2000), 186.
23. Nicholas of Cusa, *Dialogue on the Hidden God,* 1444/5, in *Selected Spiritual Writings*, 12, 212f.
24. "Deconstruction comes not . . . 'before' or 'over' faith, but after God, after faith, in order to ask, with interest and admiration, 'what is happening?' Deconstruction does not think that 'God' is a bad name, even though its most assured secularist admirers would have it so" (Caputo, *Prayers and Tears of Jacques Derrida*, 67).
25. Elliot R. Wolfson, addressing a different but parallel tradition, puts this beautifully: "Traditional kabbalists (in line with the apophaticism of Neoplatonic speculation) assume there is a reality beyond language, a superessentiality that transcends the finite categories of reason and speech, but this reality is accessible phenomenologically only through language. Silence, therefore, is not to be set in binary opposition to language, but is rather the margin that demarcates its center" (*Language, Eros, Being: Kabbalistic Hermeneutics and Poetic Imagination* [New York: Fordham University Press, 2005], 289).
26. Caputo reassures us that this far-from-deconstructive aspect "does not have the effect of leveling or razing negative theology, but rather of liberating negative theology from the Greek metaphysics of presence in which it is enmeshed and forcing it to come up with a better story about itself than the hyperousiological one that it has inherited not from the Bible but from Neoplatonism" (*Prayers and Tears of Jacques Derrida,* 11). One might not so much force as permit this truth to do its own deconstructive work.
27. Hence the irresistible force of Eckhart's "therefore let us pray to God that we may be free of 'God'" (Meister Eckhart, "Sermon 52: Beati pauperes spiritu, quoniam ipsorum est regnum caelorum (Mt. 5:3)," in *Meister Eckhart: The Essential Sermons, Commentaries, Treatises and Defense*, trans. and with introduction by Edmund Colledge, O.S.A., and Bernard McGinn [Mahawh, N.J.: Paulist Press, 1981], 200). Sells insists ab origine on liberating

the text from the modern interpolation of inverted commas to distinguish God and "God," as "indicative of a pervasive modern dis-ease with the kind of mystical language composed by Eckhart" (Michael A. Sells, *Mystical Languages of Unsaying* [Chicago: University of Chicago Press, 1994], 1).

28. Franz Rosenzweig, *Star of Redemption*, trans. William Hallo (New York: Holt, Rinehart and Winston, 1970), 23.
29. Cusa, *Dialogue on the Hidden God*, 13, 212–13.
30. Sells, *Mystical Languages of Unsaying*, 3.
31. Cusa, *De docta ignorantia*, I.26.88, 126–27. For example, in the next paragraph the learned ignorance lets us "draw near the maximum and triune God of infinite goodness, according to the degree of our learning of ignorance, so that with all our strength we may always praise God for showing Godself to us as incomprehensible, who is over all things, blessed forever" (I.26.89, 127).
32. Negative theology, however, cannot be described as atheism in disguise, for atheism lacks the learned ignorance as surely as does orthodoxy. Even to address the positivisms of modernity, apophasis might need the partnership of deconstruction, which can always "pass for atheism" and thus burrow economically through the modernisms.
33. "But God is not in the sun 'sun' and in the moon 'moon'; rather God is that which is sun and moon without plurality and difference" (Cusa, *De docta ignorantia*, I.4.115, 139).
34. Cusa, *De visione Dei*, 13. 55, 259 (emphasis mine).
35. Johnson, *She Who Is*, 33. Raising her voice with "prophetic thinkers" "throughout the Jewish and Christian traditions," Johnson "challenge[s] the propensity of the human heart to evade the living God by taming the wildness of divine mystery into a more domesticated deity" (39).
36. Aquinas, not unlike current theologians of embodiment at least in this, was, as Denys Turner writes, "deeply suspicious of over-zealous negativities, of theological negations unsecured in the affirmation of human, carnal, worldly experience" ("Apophaticism, Idolatry and the Claims of Reason," in *Silence and the Word*, ed. Davies and Turner, 32). His concern is not motivated by feminist questions. But inasmuch as feminist theology has opened spaces in which women's bodies will not remain nobodies, premature auto-deconstruction is no doubt inadvisable.
37. See my "Returning God: The Gift of Feminist Theology," in *Feminism, Sexuality and the Return of Religion*, ed. John B. Caputo and Linda Martin Alcoff (Bloomington: Indiana University Press, forthcoming).

38. The ecological trajectory in feminist theology moves from Rosemary Radford Ruether's *New Woman, New Earth: Sexist Ideologies and Human Liberation* (New York: Seabury Press, 1975), through her *God and Gaia: An Ecofeminist Theology of Earth Healing* (San Francisco: HarperSanFrancisco, 1992) and numerous transnational anthologies, to Sallie McFague's numerous volumes including *The Body of God: An Ecological Theology* (Minneapolis: Fortress Press, 1993) and *A New Climate for Theology: God, the World, and Global Warming* (Minneapolis: Fortress Press, 2008). Similarly, Elizabeth Johnson's most recent volume of systematic theology, *Quest for the Living God: Mapping Frontiers in the Theology of God* (New York: Continuum, 2007), is substantively an ecological work.
39. For a discussion of the ecotheological implications of postcolonial discourse see *Planetary Loves: Gayatri Spivak, Postcoloniality, and Theology*, ed. Stephen D. Moore and Mayra Rivera (New York: Fordham University Press, forthcoming).
40. Cusa, *De visione Dei*, 13.55, 259.
41. Cf. Derrida's koan: *Tout autre est tout autre.* See also Caputo, on Derrida, on Levinas—on the problem of rendering the infinite merely Other. Caputo, *Prayers and Tears of Jacques Derrida*, 20ff.
42. Cusa, *De visione Dei*, 13.55, 259.
43. Cusa, *De docta ignorantia*, II.3.107, 135.
44. Cf. Arne Moritz, *Explizite Komplikationen: Der radikale Holismus des Nikolaus von Kues* (Münster: Aschendorff Verlag, 2006).
45. "The bottomless gulf between the infinite and the finite is bridged by the idea that the finite participates in the infinite." Thus Karl Jaspers wrote on the dominant idea of Cusa's thought in *Anselm and Nicholas of Cusa*, ed. Hannah Arendt, trans. Ralph Manheim (New York: Harvest, 1957/64), 87.
46. Cusa, *De docta ignorantia*, II.5.119, 141.
47. Derrida reflects on negative theology as a remarkable manifestation of a " 'self-difference' " within the history of Christianity, resisting "all the literal language of New Testament eventness (*événementialité*)," freeing its "language from all authority, all narrative, all dogma, all belief. . . . Whence the courage and the dissidence, potential or actual, of these masters (think of Eckhart), whence the persecution they suffered at times, whence their passion, whence this scent of heresy, these trials, this subversive marginality of the apophatic current in the history of theology and of the Church" (Jacques Derrida, "Sauf le nom," in *On the Name*, ed. Thomas Dutoit, trans. David Wood, John P. Leavey Jr., and Ian McLeod [Stanford, Calif.: Stanford University Press, 1995], 71).

48. Ibid., 73.
49. The taste for cosmology, respect for illiterate nonhumans, the difference between ground and foundation, or between ecology and "Nature" suggest underdeveloped potentials in poststructuralist thought. "Econstruction" names another possibility, or a decision taking place in the face of a conceptual impossibility, and the topic of last year's Transdisciplinary Theological Colloquium (TTC) at Drew Theological School. Cf. *Ecospirit: Religions and Philosophies for the Earth,* ed. Laurel Kearns and Catherine Keller (New York: Fordham University Press, 2007). See also Derrida's posthumously published *The Animal That Therefore I Am,* ed. Marie-Louise Mallet, trans. David Wills (New York: Fordham University Press, 2008), which reveals a rich ecological sensitivity, as well as a touching relation to his cat.
50. Cusa, *De docta ignorantia,* II.2.103, 133 (emphasis mine). "God is the form of being but not intermixed with creation? For a composite . . . who . . . can understand how the one, infinite form is participated differently by different creatures? . . . as if a work of art were to have no other being than that of dependency, for it would be totally dependent on the idea of the artist" (II.2.102–3, 133). "*Creating,*" worries Cusa "seems to be no different than *God's being* all things. If, therefore, *God is all things and if this means creating,* how can one understand the creation not to be eternal?" (II.2.101, 132 [emphasis mine]). He will reject that (impossible) outcome but not easily, engaging "Socrates and Plato" on the idea of participation.
51. Cusa, *De docta ignorantia,* II.2.104, 134 (emphasis mine). Cusa continues: "It is as if the Creator had spoken: 'Let it be made,' and because God, who is eternity itself, could not be made, that was made which could be made, which would be as much like God as possible. The inference, therefore, is that every created thing as such is perfect, even if by comparison to others it seems less perfect."
52. Ibid., 134.
53. Cusa, *De docta ignorantia,* II.1.97, 130 (emphasis mine).
54. Bruno, *On the Infinite Universe and Worlds: Fifth Dialogue.*
55. Like Bruno's, Cusa's cosmology is speculative rather than empirical. But his long friendship with the mathematician and physician Paolo del Pozzo Toscanelli supported this polymath's theology of nature.
56. Cusa, *De docta ignorantia,* II.12.162, 161. "Aided only by learned ignorance, you come to see that the world and its motion and shape cannot be grasped, for it will appear as a wheel in a wheel and a sphere in a sphere, nowhere having a center or a circumference" (II.11.161, 160f). He also precociously argues that the earth is not a true sphere, has no proper center, yet is nonetheless noble in form.

57. Current astrophysical ruminations on the shape of the universe resemble Cusa's acentrism, which is at the same time an omnicentrism, more than Copernicus's or Galileo's heliocentric models. Calculations of the accelerating expansion of the universe have it growing out in all directions from whichever point one is measuring. The big bang marks no center. "If the universe is spatially infinite, *there was already an infinite spatial expanse at the moment of the big bang*. . . . In this setting, the big bang did not take place at one point; instead, the big bang eruption took place everywhere on the infinite expanse" (Brian Greene, *The Fabric of the Cosmos: Space, Time, and the Texture of Reality* [New York: A. A. Knopf, 2004], 249). On Cusa's contribution to science, see Tamara Albertini, "Mathematics and Astronomy," in *Introducing Nicholas of Cusa: A Guide to a Renaissance Man*, ed. Christopher M. Bellitto, Thomas M. Izbicki, and Gerald Christanson (Mahwah, N.J.: Paulist Press, 2004).
58. The potential of this passageway is far from exhausted, as the work of quantum physicist David Bohm signals; he moves through the epistemological wall of the quantum wave/particle complementarity by translating it into "the implicate and the explicate orders." The implicate order is "undivided wholeness in flowing motion." David Bohm, *Wholeness and the Implicate Order* (London:Ark/Routledge,1980), 11; see also David Bohm and B. J. Hiley, *The Undivided Universe: An Ontological Interpretation of Quantum Theory* (London: Routledge, 1993), 350ff.
59. In Book One, on negative theology, "[I]t was shown that God is in all things in such a way that all things are in God," but now "it is evident that God is in all things, as if, *by mediation of the universe" (Cusa, De docta ignorantia*, II.5.117, 140 [emphasis mine]). This is Cusa's key replacement of the Platonic mediation through an abstract multiplicity of forms with the relation of folding. It is not that God is a substance who folds in and out of the world. God is the folding: "God is the enfolding and unfolding of all things" (II.3.111, 137).
60. Cusa, *De docta ignorantia*, II.5.118, 140 (emphasis mine).
61. Ibid., II.5.120, 141.
62. Process theology, an insistently kataphatic activity, benefits from an occasional unsaying. It provides the (often unnamed) depth-resource for a range of activist theologies whose future may depend on a certain mystical honesty, beyond or beneath the strategic rhetoric of doctrine and politics. Roland Faber outlines a negative process theology in *God as Poet of the World* (Louisville, Ky.: Westminster John Knox Press, 2008). He is currently developing a Deleuzian-Whiteheadian theopoetics of the manifold, with deep engagement of the apophatic tradition.

63. Alfred North Whitehead, *Science and the Modern World* (New York: Free Press, 1967), 91.
64. Bohm, *Wholeness and the Implicate Order*, 177.
65. For exploration of sacred folds as manifestation of nature's fecundity within a contemporary philosophical system see Robert S. Corrington's *Nature's Religion* (Lanham, Md.: Rowman & Littlefield, 1997).
66. Derrida, "Sauf le nom," 83. Derrida seems to be here paraphrasing Aristotle: "[N]o one has forged a path without first entering the pathless [aporia]."
67. Cusa, *De visione Dei*, 6.21, 245.
68. Smith, *White Teeth: A Novel* (New York: Random House, 2000), 445.
69. Cusa, *De visione Dei*, 7.25, 247 (emphasis mine); and 8.28, 248.
70. "The presence of God in grace is not the violence of the moment—but the unfolding of the divine maintenance and sustenance of the world." So Graham Ward wrote in a related register in "Language and Silence," which involves a rhythmic Derridean reading of the Sabbath, the silence or space for breathing, in *Silence and the Word*, ed. Davies and Turner, 176.
71. Cusa's characterization of divine influence as "continual urging" anticipates Whitehead's "initial aim" which as the "divine lure" John B. Cobb Jr. and David Griffin developed as the systematic alternative to divine coercive power. Cobb's *Grace and Responsibility: A Wesleyan Theology for Today* (Nashville: Abingdon Press, 1995) links the lure to Wesley's initiating, inspiring grace.
72. Hence the earlier thought of the relative perfection of each creature, by which "it prefers that which it itself holds, as if a divine gift" (Cusa, *De docta ignorantia*, II.2.104, 134).
73. See also Richard Kearney, *The God Who May Be: A Hermeneutics of Religion* (Bloomington: Indiana University Press, 2001); John Panteleimon Manoussakis, ed., *After God: Richard Kearney and the Religious Turn in Continental Philosophy* (New York: Fordham University Press, 2006).
74. The "rheomode (rheo is from a Greek verb, meaning 'to flow')" is presented as "an experiment in the use of language" that may elude the subject-verb-object form, which imposes "an inappropriate division between things" (Bohm, *Wholeness and the Implicate Order,* 31). Bohm thus advances the idea of the implicate order as a "holomovement," which "enfolds and unfolds in a multidimensional order, the dimensionality of which is effectively infinite" (189).
75. Gilles Deleuze, *The Fold: Leibniz and the Baroque*, trans. Tom Conley (Minneapolis: University of Minnesota Press, 1993), see chapter 6 on Whitehead,

"What Is an Event?" On the relation of Deleuze and Whitehead, see essays by Keller and Roland Faber in *Process and Difference: Between Cosmological and Poststructuralist Postmodernisms*, ed. Catherine Keller and Anne Daniell (Albany: State University of New York Press, 2002).

76. Pore (n) from Gk *poros*, lit. 'passage, way'; 1387L *'porus'*, pore; from PIE base por- 'going, passage.'
77. *Perein,* to pierce, run through. This porosity may be inviting, it may be sensual—but its softness exposes us to a bottomless vulnerability.
78. Cusa, *De visione Dei*, 17.71, 267.

SUBTLE EMBODIMENTS: IMAGINING THE HOLY IN LATE ANTIQUITY | PATRICIA COX MILLER

1. For discussion, see Patricia Cox Miller, "Visceral Seeing: The Holy Body in Late Ancient Christianity," *Journal of Early Christian Studies* 12 (2004): 391–411, and Rowan Williams, "Troubled Breasts: The Holy Body in Hagiography," in *Portraits of Spiritual Authority: Religious Power in Early Christianity, Byzantium and the Christian Orient*, ed. Jan Willem Drijvers and John W. Watt (Leiden: E. J. Brill, 1999), 63–78.
2. Marie-José Mondzain, *Image, Icon, Economy: The Byzantine Origins of the Contemporary Imaginary*, trans. Rico Franses (Stanford, Calif.: Stanford University Press, 2005), 81.
3. Averil Cameron, "The Language of Images: The Rise of Icons and Christian Representation," in *The Church and the Arts*, ed. Diana Wood, Studies in Church History 28 (Oxford: Blackwell, 1992), 4.
4. Peter Brown, *The Cult of the Saints: Its Rise and Function in Latin Christianity* (Chicago: University of Chicago Press, 1981), 51.
5. Ibid. See also Brown's "A Dark-Age Crisis: Aspects of the Iconoclastic Controversy," *English Historical Review* 88 (1973): 15, discussing the phenomenon of the holy man as "translating the awesomely distant loving-kindness of God into the reassuring precision of a human face."
6. *Life of Saint Symeon the Younger* 118, in *La vie ancienne de S. Syméon le Jeune*, ed. and trans. Paul Van den Ven, 2 vols. (Brussels: Société des Bollandistes, 1962, 1970), 1:98.
7. Louise Glück, *Proofs and Theories: Essays on Poetry* (Hopewell, N.J.: Ecco Press, 1994), 73.
8. Michael Sells, *Mystical Languages of Unsaying* (Chicago: University of Chicago Press, 1994), 2.
9. Claudia Rapp argues that hagiography is not a genre; see "'For Next to God, You are My Salvation': Reflections on the Rise of the Holy Man in

Late Antiquity," in *The Cult of the Saints in Late Antiquity and the Middle Ages: Essays on the Contribution of Peter Brown*, ed. James Howard-Johnston and Paul Antony Hayward (Oxford: Oxford University Press, 1999), 63–81.

10. On the human body as a site for the expression and enactment of meaning in Christianity, the classic study remains that of Peter Brown, *The Body and Society: Men, Women, and Sexual Renunciation in Early Christianity* (New York: Columbia University Press, 1988). For a recent study of divine presence and the use of the human senses to detect it, see Susan Ashbrook Harvey, *Scenting Salvation: Ancient Christianity and the Olfactory Imagination*, The Transformation of the Classical Heritage 42 (Berkeley: University of California Press, 2006).
11. *Life of St. Theodore of Sykeon* 39, in *Mnemeia Hagiologica*, ed. Theophilos Joannou (Leipzig: Zentralantiquiariat der Deutschen Demokratischen Republik, 1884; repr. ed. 1973), 397–98; trans. Elizabeth Dawes and Norman H. Baynes under the title *Three Byzantine Saints: Contemporary Biographies of St. Daniel the Stylite, St. Theodore of Sykeon, and St. John the Almsgiver* (Oxford: Blackwell, 1948), 115–16.
12. Bill Brown, "Reification, Reanimation, and the American Uncanny," *Critical Inquiry* 32 (2006): 199.
13. Ibid.
14. Ibid., 197. The quotation on the uncanny that Brown gives is from Ernst Jentsch, "On the Psychology of the Uncanny" (1906), trans. Roy Sellars, *Angelaki* 2, no. 1 (1995): 12.
15. *Life of Theodore of Sykeon* 139, ed. Joannou, 486; trans. Dawes and Baynes, 178.
16. Robin Cormack, *Writing in Gold: Byzantine Society and Its Icons* (New York: Oxford University Press, 1985), 39, 47.
17. Williams, "Troubled Breasts," 68, 73. See, for example, Athanasius's foundational hagiography, the *Life of Saint Antony*, in which Athanasius is careful (or anxious?) to specify that Antony's remarkable achievements were due not to his own agency but to Christ working through him. Athanasius seems to have been more wary of the localization of the holy—in geographical places as well as in the bodies of holy men—than later hagiographers. For discussion, see David Brakke, "'Outside the Places, Within the Truth': Athanasius of Alexandria and the Localization of the Holy," in *Pilgrimage and Holy Space in Late Antique Egypt*, ed. David Frankfurter (Leiden: Brill, 1998), 456–59.
18. The phrase in quotation is from Sells, *Mystical Languages of Unsaying*, 6.
19. The texts discussed here include *Historia monachorum in Aegypto* (hereafter *HM*), ed. A.-J. Festugière, Subsidia Hagiographica 34 (Brussels: Société des

Bollandistes, 1961), trans. Norman Russell under the title *The Lives of the Desert Fathers* (Kalamazoo, Mich.: Cistercian Publications, 1981); Theodoret of Cyrrhus, *Historia religiosa* (hereafter *HR*), ed. Pierre Canivet and Alice Leroy-Molinghen, 2 vols. (Sources Chrétiennes 234, 257 (1977, 1979), trans. R. M. Price under the title *Theodoret of Cyrrhus: A History of the Monks of Syria* (Kalamazoo, Mich.: Cistercian Publications, 1985); *Apophthegmata Patrum* (hereafter *AP*), trans. Benedicta Ward under the title *The Sayings of the Desert Fathers* (Kalamazoo, Mich.: Cistercian Publications, 1975). For discussion of the phenomenon of collective biography, see Patricia Cox Miller, "Strategies of Representation in Collective Biography: Constructing the Subject as Holy," in *Greek Biography and Panegyric in Late Antiquity*, ed. Tomas Hägg and Philip Rousseau, The Transformation of the Classical Heritage 31 (Berkeley: University of California Press, 2000), 209–54.

20. See Patricia Cox Miller, "Desert Asceticism and 'The Body from Nowhere,'" *Journal of Early Christian Studies* 2 (1994): 137–53; some of the material in this part of my discussion is drawn from this essay.
21. The literature on ancient Christian ascetic practice is voluminous. For a good discussion of the relation between bodily renunciation and spiritual well-being, see Elizabeth A. Castelli, "Mortifying the Body, Curing the Soul: Beyond Ascetic Dualism in *The Life of Saint Syncletica*," *differences* 4.2 (1992): 134–53. On fasting, see Teresa M. Shaw, *The Burden of the Flesh: Fasting and Sexuality in Early Christianity* (Minneapolis: Fortress Press, 1998).
22. For Symeon, see Theodoret, *HR* 26.23 (Canivet—Leroy-Molinghen ed.), 2:206; for Mary, see *Vita Mariae Aegyptae* 7 in *Harlots of the Desert, trans. Benedicta Ward* (Kalamazoo, Mich.: Cistercian Publications, 1987); for Pelagia, see *Vita Sanctae Pelagiae Meretricis* 14, in *Harlots of the Desert,* trans. Benedicta Ward (Kalamazoo, Mich.: Cistercian Publications, 1987). The two "harlot" hagiographies are not part of a collective biography, but they share a mind-set with that literature in terms of their presentation of ascetic rigor in the desert.
23. Brown, *Body and Society*, 31.
24. *AP*, prologue 4.
25. *AP*, Pambo 12; Sisoes 14.
26. *HM* 2.1.
27. *AP*, Silvanus 12; Arsenius 27.
28. Geoffrey Galt Harpham, *The Ascetic Imperative in Culture and Criticism* (Chicago: University of Chicago Press, 1987), 27.
29. For a list of the various charisms, see Russell, trans., *Lives of the Desert Fathers*, 175.

30. *HM* 10.20–21.
31. *HM* 2.9.
32. Harpham, *Ascetic Imperative in Culture and Criticism*, 43.
33. Stephen Crites, "Angels We Have Heard," in *Religion as Story*, ed. James B. Wiggins (New York: Harper and Row, 1975), 41–42.
34. Harpham, *Ascetic Imperative in Culture and Criticism*, 43.
35. On constant progress, see ibid. For the concept of the ascetic as emergent, see Richard Valantasis, "Constructions of Power in Asceticism," *Journal of the American Academy of Religion* 63 (1995): 801.
36. *AP*, Poemen 85. A particularly striking anecdote in this regard is the deathbed scene of Abba Sisoes (*AP*, Sisoes 14): "The old men asked [Abba Sisoes], 'With whom are you speaking, Father?' He said, 'Look, the angels are coming to fetch me, and I am begging them to let me do a little penance.' The old man said to him, 'You have no need to do penance, Father.' But the old man [Sisoes] said to them, 'Truly, I do not think I have even made a beginning yet.' "
37. As Karmen MacKendrick suggestively noted in her response to this paper when it was delivered at Drew University's Transdisciplinary Theological Colloquium 6, the fact that these ascetic bodies "hover between material and light, damage and healing," together with the hagiographical authors' emphasis on progress and action, suggests "that we might read their bodies not as entities but as processes or as events, as constant transitions always-coming, and going, rather than arrivals already-come. The body is fleeting without quite disappearing, incomplete but not simply disintegrated, in transformation but not wholly transformed." I thank Professor MacKendrick for her insightful comments.
38. See Williams, "Troubled Breasts," 75, and Miller, "Visceral Seeing," 405.
39. Athanasius, *Vita Antonii* 14. On Athanasius's view of holy places, see David Brakke, *Athanasius and Asceticism* (Baltimore: Johns Hopkins University Press, 1998), 36–41.
40. Brakke, "Outside the Places, Within the Truth," 459; see also 456–58.
41. See Williams, "Troubled Breasts," 76.
42. Peter Brown, "Arbiters of Ambiguity: A Role of the Late Antique Holy Man," *Cassiodorus* 2 (1996): 140.
43. See Gilbert Dagron, *Vie et Miracles de Sainte Thècle: Texte Grec, Traduction et Commentaire* (Brussels: Société des Bollandistes, 1978), 152, on miracles as repetitive like an incantation.
44. For a discussion of the rise in popularity of the cult of the martyrs and saints in the light of the felt remoteness of the "high gods," see Ramsay MacMullen, *Christianity and Paganism in the Fourth to Eighth Centuries* (New Haven, Conn.: Yale University Press, 1997), 119–39.

45. This phrase is from Daniel Tiffany, *Toy Medium: Materialism and Modern Lyric* (Berkeley: University of California Press, 2000), 23. For further discussion, see Miller, "Visceral Seeing," 395–96.
46. This is a revision of Ernst Kitzinger's argument that mediation of the divine by a human body requires dematerialization and abstraction. By arguing that saints and their images in art are "receptacles for divine substance," he comes close to erasing the saint's humanness. See Kitzinger, "The Cult of Images in the Age before Iconoclasm," *Dumbarton Oaks Papers* 8 (1954): 150 (for the quotation regarding divine substance). Full development of the idea of dematerialization is in Kitzinger, "Byzantine Art in the Period between Justinian and Iconoclasm," in his *The Art of Byzantium and the Medieval West: Selected Studies*, ed. W. Eugene Kleinbauer (Bloomington: Indiana University Press, 1976), 157–232.
47. For discussion of saints as epiphanies of saintly transfiguration, see Nicholas Constas, "An Apology for the Cult of the Saints in Late Antiquity: Eustratius Presbyter of Constantinople, On the State of Souls after Death (CPG 7522)," *Journal of Early Christian Studies* 10 (2002): 283–84.
48. The phrase in quotation is from Sells, *Mystical Languages of Unsaying*, 8.
49. *Life of Saint Symeon the Younger* 231; *La vie ancienne de S. Syméon le Jeune*, ed. Van den Ven, 1:205–6. For Barber's discussion of this miracle, see his *Figure and Likeness: On the Limits of Representation in Byzantine Iconoclasm* (Princeton, N.J.: Princeton University Press, 2002), 23.
50. I owe this insight to Karmen MacKendrick.
51. Sells, *Mystical Languages of Unsaying*, 7.
52. See Glück, *Proofs and Theories*, 73.
53. I have developed the idea of the ambiguous corporeality of the saints at length in "Visceral Seeing," 395–411.
54. *Miracles of Saint Thecla*, 38, *Vie et Miracles de Sainte Thècle*, ed. Dagron, 391–95.
55. *Miracles of Saint Thecla*, 46; *Vie et Miracles de Sainte Thècle*, ed. Dagron, 408.
56. I owe this observation to Scott Fitzgerald Johnson, *The Life and Miracles of Thekla: A Literary Study* (Cambridge, Mass.: Center for Hellenic Studies, 2006), 123.
57. See Sells, *Mystical Languages of Unsaying*, 8, which I am appropriating for my own purposes here.

"BEING NEITHER ONESELF NOR SOMEONE ELSE": THE APOPHATIC ANTHROPOLOGY OF DIONYSIUS THE AREOPAGITE | CHARLES M. STANG

1. Some scholars refrain from using the prefix "Pseudo-" on the grounds that it connotes an impostor. This convention unfortunately promotes the view

that pseudonymous writing amounts to little more than forgery. In what follows, I will follow the convention of referring to our author as "Dionysius" not because I wish to distance him from his pseudonymous enterprise—indeed I wish to draw attention to it—but because it is less unwieldy than "Pseudo-Dionysius."

2. For a survey, see the three introductions to the standard English edition: Jaroslav Pelikan, "The Odyssey of Dionysian Spirituality"; Jean Leclerq, "Influence and Noninfluence of Dionysius in the Western Middle Ages"; Karlfried Froehlich, "Pseudo-Dionysius and the Reformation of the Sixteenth Century"; all in *Pseudo-Dionysius: The Complete Works*, trans. Colm Luibheid (New York: Paulist Press, 1987), 11–46.

   All citations in English, unless otherwise noted, are from this edition and translation. Several scholars have noted that this translation contains problems. In the interests of the reader, however, I cite this widely available edition and note, where appropriate, those places in which I depart from its translation. All citations in Greek are from the standard critical edition: Beate Regina Suchla, *Corpus Dionysiacum* I (Berlin: de Gruyter, 1990) [*De divinis nominibus*]; Günter Heil and Adolf Martin Ritter, *Corpus Dionysiacum* II (Berlin: de Gruyter, 1991) [*De coelesti hierarchia, de ecclesiastica hierarchia, de mystica theologia, epistulae*]. In what follows, I refer to the entire *Corpus Dionysiacum* as the *CD* and its parts with the followed abbreviations: *DN* = *Divine Names*, *CH* = *Celestial Hierarchy*, *EH* = *Ecclesiastical Hierarchy*, *MT* = *Mystical Theology*, and *Ep.* = Letters.

3. See especially Jacques Derrida, "How to Avoid Speaking: Denials," in *Derrida and Negative Theology*, ed. Harold Coward and Toby Foshay (Albany: State University of New York Press, 1992).

4. Anders Nygren, *Eros and Agape* (New York: Macmillan, 1937), 576.

5. Paul Rorem, "The Uplifting Spirituality of Pseudo-Dionysius," in *Christian Spirituality: Origins to the Twelfth Century*, ed. Bernard McGinn and John Meyendorff in collaboration with Jean Leclerq (New York: Crossroad, 1985), 144. See also Jean Vanneste, S.J., "Is the Mysticism of Pseudo-Dionysius Genuine?" *International Philosophical Quarterly* 3 (1963): 286–306.

6. I must acknowledge my debt here to several scholars who do not share in this trend and instead insist on the robust Christology of the *CD*, including Alexander Golitzin, Andrew Louth, and Eric Perl.

7. For a subtle treatment of at least one Neoplatonic view of creation and embodiment, see Gregory Shaw's excellent study *Theurgy and the Soul: The Neoplatonism of Iamblichus* (University Park: Pennsylvania State University Press, 1995).

8. The order of the *CD* is a contested issue. There are many options: (1) the most common order in the Greek manuscript tradition is *CH, EH, DN, MT, Ep.*; (2) other orders from the Greek manuscript tradition include *CH, DN, EH, MT, Ep.*, and *DN, CH, EH, MT, Ep.*; (3) Sergius of Reshaina's Syriac translation is ordered *DN, CH, MT, EH, Ep.*; (4) the order of composition, as inferred from clues within the text, is: *DN, MT, CH, EH, Ep.* In what follows, I will adhere to (1).
9. This is clearest in *CH* 3.2 165A (*CD* II, 17.10–11): "the goal of a hierarchy, then, is to enable beings to be as like as possible to God and to be at one with him." See also *EH* 1.1 372A–B; *EH* 1.3 373D–376B; *EH* 2.1 392A. On deification in Dionysius, see Norman Russell, *The Doctrine of Deification in the Greek Patristic Tradition* (Oxford: Oxford University Press, 2005), 248–62.
10. *CH* 3.2 165B (*CD* II, 18.14–17): "Indeed for every member of the hierarchy, perfection consists in this, that it is uplifted to imitate God as far as possible and, more wonderful still, that it becomes what scripture calls a 'fellow workman for God' and a reflection of the workings of God."
11. For an excellent treatment of the ways in which spatial metaphors are deployed and then undermined in apophatic discourse, see Michael Sells's "Awakening without Awakener: Apophasis in Plotinus," in *Mystical Languages of Unsaying* (Chicago: University of Chicago Press, 1994), 14–33.
12. See Andrew Louth, *Denys the Areopagite* (London: G. Chapman, 1989), 105–6.
13. *DN* 4.14 713A (*CD* I, 160.14–15).
14. *DN* 4.13 712B (*CD* I, 159.12–1).
15. *DN* 4.10 705D (*CD* I, 154.20–22).
16. *EH* 3.3.11 441A (*CD* II, 91.2–4).
17. *DN* 1.5 593D (*CD* I, 117.12–13).
18. *DN* 1.1 585B.
19. Dionysius quotes 1 Cor 2:4: "My speech and my proclamation were not with plausible words of wisdom, but with a demonstration of the Spirit and of power, so that your faith might rest not on human wisdom but on the power of God" (*DN* 1.1 585B).
20. *DN* 1.1 588B (*CD* I, 109.16–110.1).
21. Dionysius mentions no fewer than seven works throughout the *CD*: *The Theological Representations, On the Properties and Ranks of the Angels, On the Soul, On Righteous and Divine Judgment, The Symbolic Theology, On the Divine Hymns, The Intelligible and the Sensible.* Although some believe them to be genuine works that did not survive, most scholars believe them to be fictitious, perhaps even mentioned to buttress the authenticity of its antiquity,

as if it suffered an incomplete transmission. See Louth, *Denys the Areopagite*, 19–20.

22. *MT* 3 1033C (*CD* II, 147.10–14); see also *Ep.* 9.
23. *MT* 1.3 1001A (*CD* II, 144.7–8).
24. *DN* 4.11 708D (*CD* I, 156,17–18).
25. Acts 17:23. All biblical citations drawn from the RSV.
26. In the opening prayer of *The Mystical Theology*, Dionysius addresses "Trinity!! Higher than any being, any divinity [*hyper-thee*], any goodness!" The term *hyper-theos* means literally "beyond god." And lest some suppose that the name "Trinity" suffices, recall *DN* 13.3 980D–981A (*CD* I, 229.9–10): "we use the names Trinity and Unity for that which is in fact beyond every name."
27. Proclus, *Commentary on the Parmenides*, trans. Glenn R. Morrow and John M. Dillon (Princeton, N.J.: Princeton University Press, 1987), 523, 523n. Proclus borrows the term from the Stoics (cf. Diog. Laert. VII, 69), for whom it was a double negative that simply equaled a positive: "it is not not day" = "it is night" ($--P = P$). But for Proclus, application of the double negative to the One signaled its transcendence of both sides of the opposition. For example, "the One is not not at rest" means that it transcends the opposition between rest and movement.

    As Carlos Steel reminds us ("'Negatio Negationis': Proclus on the Final Lemma of the First Hypothesis of the *Parmenides*," in *Traditions of Platonism*, ed. John C. Cleary [Aldershot, U.K.: Ashgate, 2004]), the phrase "the negation of negation" (*negatio negationis*) does not appear in Proclus. The phrase is in fact taken from Meister Eckhart but has come to stand for the view, expressed by Proclus and others, that the ineffable One transcends even all negations. See *Platonic Theology* 2.10: "It is likewise necessary, having attributed such a mode as this to the first God, again to exempt him from the negations also . . . [for] if no discourse belongs to it, it is evident that neither does negation pertain to it" (cited in Bernard McGinn, *The Foundations of Mysticism* [New York: Crossroad, 1991], 59).
28. See Sells, *Mystical Languages of Unsaying*, 3: "Any saying (even a negative saying) demands a correcting proposition, an unsaying. But that correcting proposition which unsays the previous proposition is in itself a 'saying' that must be 'unsaid' in turn. It is in the tension between the two propositions that the discourse becomes meaningful. That tension is momentary. It must be continually re-earned by ever new linguistic acts of unsaying."
29. Proclus, *Platonic Theology* 2.10, as cited in McGinn, *Foundations of Mysticism*.
30. *MT* 5 1048B (*CD* I, 150.6–7).

31. *CH* 2.2 137D (*CD* II, 11.6–7). For an insightful treatment of how *CH* 2 fits into (or rather subverts) the cycle as laid out in *DN* and *MT*, see Mary-Jane Rubenstein, "Unknow Thyself: Apophaticism, Deconstruction, and Theology after Ontotheology," *Modern Theology* 19, no. 3 (2003): 398.
32. *CH* 2.3 141A (*CD* II, —13.4–7).
33. *CH* 2.5 144C (*CD* II, 15.8–10).
34. *CH* 2.3 141B–C (*CD* II, 13.18–21).
35. *CH* 2.5 145A (Ps 22:6).
36. *Ep*. 9.1 1105B; 9.5 1112B–C (cf. Sg 5.1; Pss 44:23, 78:65).
37. *DN* 4.11 708C; cf. *CH* 8.4 305B.
38. *MT* 1.1 1000A (*CD* II 142.9–10).
39. Dionysius' theological enterprise, sketched above, is often characterized as "negative" or "apophatic." Obviously an "apophatic" enterprise presumes a "kataphatic" one—unsaying presumes saying. Dionysius prefers the term "mystical" to describe his own theology—that is, speech in praise of God—which says and unsays in perpetuity those names God has graciously revealed. To speak of the Dionysian vision as "apophatic," therefore, is warranted only if we understand that we are speaking *pars pro toto*. Accordingly, in what follows, I spell out the "apophatic anthropology" of the *CD* and demonstrating how crucial Paul is for this anthropology. And yet by "apophatic" I mean that anthropology that is implied by the entire mystical theological enterprise, which relies equally on the kataphatic and apophatic.
40. Thomas Tomasic, "Negative Theology and Subjectivity: An Approach to the Tradition of the Pseudo-Dionysius," *International Philosophical Quarterly* 9 (1969): 428: "a purgation, an asceticism, indispensable for attaining . . . the radical, ontological 'otherness' of subjectivity over against what it is not."
41. Eckhart's original prayer reads, "Therefore pray God that we may be free of God." Josef Quint and Josef Kock, eds., *Meister Eckhart: Die deutschen und lateinischen Werke* (Stuttgart and Berlin: Kohlhammer, 1936–), 2:493.
42. Bernard McGinn, *The Growth of Mysticism* (New York: Crossroad, 1994), 105–6; idem, "The Negative Element in the Anthropology of John the Scot," in *Jean Scot Erigène et l'histoire de la philosophie (Actes du II Colloque international Jean Scot Erigène,* Laon, 1975), ed. René Roques, 315–25; and McGinn, *The Mystical Thought of Meister Eckhart* (New York: Crossroad, 2001).
43. McGinn, *Growth of Mysticism*, 105.
44. Ibid., 106.
45. McGinn, *Mystical Thought of Meister Eckhart*, 48.
46. Ibid., 178.

47. *MT* 1.1 997B (*CD* II, 142.6–9).
48. *MT* 1.2 1000A (*CD* II, 142.14–15).
49. This is the Plotinian view, to which Iamblichus—and after him Pseudo-Dionysius—gives a sharp riposte.
50. This is especially clear in the case of Thomas Gallus and the author of *The Cloud of Unknowing,* who contend that midway along the mystical itinerary the intellect ceases and love completes the journey. See Denys Turner, *The Darkness of God* (New York: Cambridge University Press, 1995), 46–47.
51. *MT* 1.3 1001A (*CD* II, 144.10–11).
52. Ibid.
53. *DN* 4.13 712B (*CD* I, 159.12–14).
54. *DN* 4.13 712A (*CD* I, 159.6–8).
55. Ibid. (*CD* I, 159.3–6).
56. See, for example, Sermons 2 and 22 in Meister Eckhart, *The Essential Sermons, Commentaries, Treatises and Defense*, trans. Edmund Colledge and Bernard McGinn (New York: Paulist Press, 1981), 177–81, 19296. See also McGinn, "The Preacher in Action: Eckhart on the Eternal Birth," in *Mystical Thought of Meister Eckhart*, chap. 4.
57. *DN* 2.11 649D (*CD* I, 136.18–137.1).
58. See, for example: E. R. Dodds's comments on Pseudo-Dionysius in his introduction to Proclus' *The Elements of Theology* (Oxford: Clarendon, 1963); also Ronald F. Hathaway, *Hierarchy and the Definition of Order in the Letters of Pseudo-Dionysius* (The Hague: M. Nijhoff, 1969).

    There are at least three important exceptions to this rule: Alexander Golitzin, Andrew Louth, and Hans Urs von Balthasar all offer interesting explanations for the pseudonym. Golitzin argues that the author chose a sub-apostolic pseudonym in order to rebut wayward monastic movements in fifth-century Syria, which traced their own roots back to apostolic times through the apocryphal Thomas literature (Alexander Golitzin, "Dionysius Areopagita: A Christian Mysticism?" *Pro Ecclesia* 12, no. 2 (2003): 161–212). Louth argues that the pseudonym situates the author squarely in Athens and thereby suggests a synthesis between Christian revelation and pagan philosophy (Louth, *Denys the Areopagite*). Most intriguing, if cryptic, is von Balthasar's suggestion that the pseudonymous enterprise is based on a "mystical relationship" between the author and Paul (Hans Urs von Balthasar, "Denys," idem., *The Glory of the Lord: A Theological Aesthetics*, vol. 2 [Edinburgh: T. & T. Clark, 1984], 144–210).
59. The author quotes from and alludes to the Pauline material more than he does all the four gospels combined or the whole of the Johannine material.

See the approximate and conservative tabulations of the total quotations from the New Testament compiled by Paul Rorem, *Biblical and Liturgical Symbols within the Pseudo-Dionysian Synthesis* (Toronto: Pontifical Institute of Mediaeval Studies, 1984), 14n8.

60. Acts 9:3: "Now as [Saul] journeyed he approached Damascus, and suddenly [*exaiphnês*] a light from heaven flashed about him. And he fell to the ground and heard a voice saying to him, 'Saul, Saul, why do you persecute me?' And he said, 'Who are you, Lord?' And he said, 'I am Jesus, whom you are persecuting; but rise and enter the city, and you will be told what you are to do.'" It is Paul's encounter with the luminous Christ on the road to Damascus that is, along with John 1:1, the scriptural warrant for Dionysius' identification of Jesus with the light that moves through the hierarchies. See Dionysius' Third Letter on the word "suddenly" (*exaiphnês*), which has as much to do with the account in Acts of the "sudden" appearance of Christ to Paul as it does the legacy of "suddenly" in Platonism (see Alexander Golitzin, "'Suddenly, Christ': The Place of Negative Theology in the Mystagogy of Dionysius Areopagites," in *Mystics: Presence and Aporia*, ed. Michael Kessler and Christian Shepherd [Chicago: University of Chicago Press, 2003], 8–37).
61. The NRSV botches the translation of Paul's proclamation: "What therefore you worship as unknown [*agnoountes*], this I proclaim to you." The circumstantial participle *agnoountes* refers not to the object of worship, but to the implicit masculine plural subject of the verb "you worship," namely "you Athenians." Paul clearly meant something like, "What therefore you unknowingly worship, this I proclaim to you." But Dionysius could legitimately understand the same sentence to read: "I proclaim to you that which you therefore worship *through unknowing*."
62. Strangely, Dionysius never makes *direct* reference to any of these three episodes in the life of Paul. However, he refers *indirectly* to Paul's "sudden" blinding vision in the Third Letter regarding "suddenly." His entire treatment of "unknowing" derives, I submit, from Paul's admonition in Acts 17 that we worship God "through unknowing." We might think that Dionysius would draw on Paul's ascent to the third heaven so as to underwrite his account of the celestial orders and its organization into triads. When I say, then, that Dionysius apprentices himself to *this* Paul, I mean that Dionysius apprentices himself to the Paul who appears as an ecstatic mystic.
63. See Louth, *Denys the Areopagite*: "*The tendency to telescope the past*, so that the truth now is the truth affirmed at Nicaea, itself the truth of what had been believed and suffered for during the centuries when the Church had

been persecuted, was something that awakened an echo in the whole Byzantine world in a far more precise way than it would today. *And it is this conviction that underlies the pseudonymity adopted by our author*" (2, emphasis mine).

64. The four "treatises" (*CH*, *EH*, *DN*, *MT*) are in fact all letters addressed to Timothy, Paul's associate; Letters 1–4 are addressed to Gaius, another of Paul's associates (Rom 16:23, 1 Cor 1:14, Acts 19:29, 20:14); Letter 6 is addressed to Sosipater (Rom 16:21); Letter Seven is addressed to Polycarp, the bishop of Smyrna; Letter 9 is addressed to Titus (2 Cor 2:13, 7:6, 7:14f., 8:6, 8:23; Gal 2:1–3; 2 Tm 4:10); Letters 5 and 8 are addressed to Dorotheus and Demophilus, who do not appear to be associates of Paul; Letter 10, of course, is addressed to the apostle John on Patmos.
65. *DN* 3.2 681C–D.
66. Letter 10.
67. Most infamously, *DN* 4.19–35 is a paraphrase of Proclus' *On the Existence of Evils*. The simultaneous discovery of this fact in 1895 by Koch and Stiglmayr led to the end of the credibility of the pseudonym. See Hugo Koch, "Der pseudo-epigraphische Character der dionysischen Schriften," *Theologische Quartalschrift* 77 (1895): 353–421, and Josef Stiglmayr, "Der Neuplatoniker Proklos als Vorlage des sogen. Dionysius Areopagita in der Lehre von Übel," *Historisches Jahrbuch* 16 (1895): 253–73 and 721–48.
68. The Christology of Dionysius has been a vexed issue from its first appearance in the early sixth century. Dionysius is ambiguous, seeming to speak in places as a Chalcedonian ("[Christ] . . . remaining unmixed," *EH* 3.13 444C), and in others as a Monophysite ("theandric activity," *Ep*. 4. 1072C).
69. *MT* 1.2 1000A (*CD* I, 142.14–15).
70. Derek Krueger, *Writing and Holiness: The Practice of Authorship in the Early Christian East* (Philadelphia: University of Pennsylvania Press, 2004).
71. Ibid., 2. Krueger's debt to Michel Foucault—especially the late Foucault—is evidenced especially in the introduction in his discussion of writing as a "technology of the self." Krueger cites Foucault's famous essay "What Is an Author?" in *Language, Counter-Memory, Practice*, ed. Donald F. Bouchard, trans. Sherry Simon (Ithaca, N.Y.: Cornell University Press, 1977). Also relevant are Michel Foucault, *The Use of Pleasure*, trans. Robert Hurley (New York: Random House, 1985); Luther Martin et al., eds., *Technologies of the Self: A Seminar with Michel Foucault* (Amherst: University of Massachusetts Press, 1990); and David Brakke et al., eds., *Religion and the Self in Antiquity* (Bloomington: Indiana University Press,), 1–11.
72. Krueger, *Writing and Holiness*, 8, 3.

73. Ibid., 10, 9.
74. Ibid., 11.
75. My ellipsis, not Derrida's.
76. Jacques Derrida, *On the Name*, trans. David Wood, John P. Leavey Jr., and Ian McLeod (Stanford, Calif.: Stanford University Press, 1995), 35.
77. Jacques Derrida, "How to Avoid Speaking: Denials," in *Derrida and Negative Theology*, ed. Harold Coward and Toby Foshay (Albany: State University of New York Press, 1992).
78. *CH* 1.2 121A (*CD* II, 7.9).
79. On the predetermined addressee of negative theology, see Mary-Jane Rubenstein, "Unknow Thyself: Apophaticism, Deconstruction, and Theology after Ontotheology," *Modern Theology* 19, no. 3 (2003): 387–417.
80. *Ep.* 8.1 1092A (*CD* II, 180.1–3). This insistence recalls 1 Tim 4:16 ("watch yourself") and 1 Cor 7:26 ("it is well for you to remain as you are").
81. Von Balthasar remarks that with such an "objective hierarchical *taxis* . . . already we are moving toward the Byzantine and Carolingian world-order. . . . And if the earthly manifestation, the actual Church, is defective, then this never becomes for Denys (as it did for Augustine) an opportunity to distinguish between the carnal manifestation of the institution and the spiritual core of the 'pilgrim people of God'" (Hans Urs von Balthasar, "Denys," idem., *Glory of the Lord*, 166).
82. See Jonathan Lear, *Happiness, Death, and the Remainder of Life* (Cambridge, Mass.: Harvard University Press, 2000), 4. Lear confesses his own debt to Laplanche and Lacan and cites the following texts as representative of their historiography of psychoanalysis: Jean Laplanche, *Life and Death in Psychoanalysis* (Baltimore: Johns Hopkins University Press, 1985), and idem, "The Unfinished Copernican Revolution," in *Essays on Otherness* (London: Routledge, 1999); Jacques Lacan, *The Ego in Freud's Theory and in the Technique of Psychoanalysis, 1954–1955* (New York: W. W. Norton, 1988), and idem, *Freud's Papers on Technique, 1953–1954* (New York: W. W. Norton, 1988).
83. Arnold I. Davidson, "How to Do the History of Psychoanalysis: A Reading of Freud's *Three Essays on the Theory of Sexuality*," in *The Emergence of Sexuality* (Cambridge, Mass.: Harvard University Press, 2001).
84. Ibid., 91. On the concept of *mentalité*, see Jacques LeGoff, "Les Mentalités: *Une histoire ambigue*," in *Fair de l'histoire: Nouveaux objets*, ed. LeGoff and Pierre Nora (Paris, 1974), and Roger Chartier, "Intellectual History or Sociocultural History? The French Trajectories," in *Modern European Intellectual History: Reappraisals and New Perspectives*, ed. Dominick LaCapra and Steven L. Kaplan (Ithaca, N.Y.: 1982), 13–46.

85. Davidson, *Emergence of Sexuality*, 90.
86. Ibid., 82.
87. Ibid., 92.
88. For example, Dionysius makes unambiguously Monophysite comments: "[B]y the fact of being God-made-man he accomplished something new in our midst—the activity of the God man [literally, 'the theandric energy']" (*Ep.* 4 1072C). Nevertheless, John of Scythpolis overlooked this and other Christological missteps and chose instead to focus on another passage in which Dionysius sounds a more Chalcedonian tone: "Christ emerged from the hiddenness of his divinity to take on human shape, to be utterly incarnate among us while yet remaining unmixed" (*EH* 3.13 444C). See Jaroslav Pelikan, "The Odyssey of Dionysian Spirituality," in *Pseudo-Dionysius: The Complete Works* (New York: Paulist Press, 1987), 16–17. For a fuller treatment of the early reception and the process of rendering the *CD* palatable to sixth-century orthodox views, see Paul Rorem and John C. Lamoureaux, *John of Scythopolis and the Dionysian Corpus: Annotating the Areopagite* (Oxford: Clarendon Press, 1998).

BODIES WITHOUT WHOLES: APOPHATIC EXCESS AND FRAGMENTATION IN AUGUSTINE'S *CITY OF GOD* | VIRGINIA BURRUS AND KARMEN MACKENDRICK

1. Vladimir Lossky, "Elements of 'Negative Theology' in the Thought of St. Augustine," *St. Vladimir's Theological Quarterly* 21 (1977): 67–75. This essay first appeared in French in 1954.
2. See his *Letter to Proba* (cited by Lossky, in "Elements of 'Negative Theology,' in the Thought of St. Augustine," 71): "Est ergo in nobis quaedam, ut ita dicam, docta ignorantia, sed docta Spiritu Dei, qui adiuvat infirmatatem nostrum." ("There is therefore in us a certain learned ignorance, so to speak, but one learned from the Spirit of God, who aids our weakness.")
3. Lossky, "Elements of 'Negative Theology' in the Thought of St. Augustine," 73: "This 'spiritual touching' [Augustine, Sermon 117; PL 664], although it excludes comprehension, is not the transcendence of a thought in a mystical ignorance 'beyond the intellect,' nor the beginning of an 'infinite flight.' On the contrary, it is the limit of apophatic ignorance, the light of true knowledge attained without being acquired, in a passing contact of created thoughts always fleeing the present with the eternal Present of God."
4. David Dawson, "Transcendence as Embodiment: Augustine's Domestication of Gnosis," *Modern Theology* 10 (1994): 6.

5. Augustine's reference to "making truth" (*facere veritatem*) in confession fascinates (among others) Jacques Derrida, who returns to it repeatedly, e.g., "Circumfession," in Geoffrey Bennington and Jacques Derrida, *Jacques Derrida* (Chicago: University of Chicago Press, 1993), 47–48, 56, 137, 233, 300; "Typewriter Ribbon," in Jacques Derrida, *Without Alibi* (Stanford, Calif.: Stanford University Press, 2002), 109; "Composing 'Circumfession,'" in *Augustine and Postmodernism: Confessions and Circumfession,* ed. John D. Caputo and Michael J. Scanlon (Bloomington: Indiana University Press, 2005), 23. The relevant passage in Augustine is *Confessions* 10.1: "ecce enim veritatem dilexisti [Ps 50.8], quoniam qui facit eam venit ad lucem [John 3.21]. volo eam facere in corde meo coram te in confessione, in stilo autem meo coram multis testibus." ("For behold, you have loved truth, because the one who makes it comes to the light. I want to make it in my heart before you in confession, and in my book before a multitude of witnesses.") To suggest that Augustine understands the truth "made" in confession as a kind of fiction, even as ineradicably tainted with the possibility of perjury, may seem excessively perverse, especially as Augustine is known for his strong disapproval of lying; for a recent discussion of his position, see Paul J. Griffiths, *Lying: An Augustinian Theology of Duplicity* (Grand Rapids, Mich.: Brazos Press, 2004). At issue, however, is not only the performative (as opposed, in Austin's well-known terms, to the constative) character of confessional language but also the strict limits of self-knowledge: it is always possible that we are lying to ourselves. See the discussion of Derrida, "History of the Lie," in *Without Alibi,* 28–70.
6. Denys Turner, "The Darkness of God and the Light of Christ: Negative Theology and Eucharistic Presence," *Modern Theology* 15 (1999): 145. Dawson opposes apophatic to incarnational language (7), but we find Turner's sense of their necessary connection, even in their analytic distinguishability, more persuasive.
7. The relation of language and bodies at their limits is also of central concern in Karmen MacKendrick, *Word Made Skin: Figuring Language at the Surface of Flesh* (New York: Fordham University Press, 2004).
8. As Michael Sells puts it, "Apophasis can reach a point of intensity such that no single proposition concerning the transcendent can stand on its own. Any saying (even a negative saying) demands a correcting proposition, an unsaying" (*Mystical Languages of Unsaying* [Chicago: University of Chicago Press, 1994], 3).
9. An earlier reference to this theme of carnal and textual excess in the *City of God* can be found in Virginia Burrus, "An Immoderate Feast: Augustine

Reads John's Apocalypse," in *History, Apocalypse, and the Secular Imagination: New Essays on Augustine's City of God*, ed. M. Vessey, K. Pollmann, and A. D. Fitzgerald (Bowling Green, Ohio: Philosophy Documentation Center, 1999), 183–94.

10. This is rather precisely the temporal structure of his consideration of sexuality in Book 14. It may also apply in a looser way to the *City of God* as a whole, as well as to the structure of confession. Cf. Derrida, "Circumfessions," 142: "[F]or in drawing nonknowledge from the future of what happens, I find it nowhere other than in the confession of my memory."
11. In this they recall Augustine's failed attempt in *Confessions* to imagine the "nothing something" of formlessness from which he understands God to have created the cosmos. Making a mental effort to erase form, he merely manages to multiply it, picturing "numerous and varied" shapes that are "hideous and horrible," distortions so "bizarre and incongruous" that if they had actually manifested before his eyes he would have been psychologically undone. Exhausted by the visual shuffle of hybrid and unstable figures generated by his own imagination, he subsequently recognizes that mutability itself is the shifting substrate, the pretemporal (or, more properly, nontemporal) *nihil aliquid* around which he has been trying vainly to wrap his mind. If only he could capture the moment of transition between forms, he could see through time and know mutability in and as this betweenness that is the womb of time's eternity (12.6). The moment is always vanishing, however, and the mind cannot contain a truth that overflows time: thus Augustine here advocates "an ignorant knowledge or a knowing ignorance" (*vel nosse ignorando vel ignorare noscendo*) (*Conf.* 12.5). On Augustine's curious discussion of the *nihil aliquid*, see Catherine Keller, *Face of the Deep: A Theology of Becoming* (London: Routledge, 2003), 74–75. "Pure" matter, insofar as the notion can mean anything, is beyond both time and comprehension; in it, the excesses of space, not carved out into form, and time, not lined up into intervals, seem strangely to meet.
12. Thus Caroline Walker Bynum asserts that for Augustine "resurrection is restoration both of bodily material and of bodily wholeness or integrity, with incorruption (which includes—for the blessed—beauty, weightlessness, and impassibility) added on." She charges him with "a profound fear of development and process" that results in a view of "salvation as the crystalline hardness not only of stasis but of the impossibility of non-stasis." Admitting that "Augustine's insistence on keeping minute details of the heavenly body close to the earthly one" is quite striking, she notes again that he does so "while adding (a crucial addition of course!) stasis" (*The*

Resurrection of the Body in Western Christianity, 200–1336 [New York: Columbia University Press, 1995], 95, 97, 99). We question, however, whether "add stasis and stir" is a formula that adequately captures Augustine's approach, as if he were thereby seeking a recipe for balance between Neoplatonic transcendentalism and Christian incarnationalism.

13. The text overflows: "At Hippo Zaritus there is a man with feet shaped like a crescent, with only two toes on each, and his hands are similarly shaped. . . .

 "As for *Androgynes*, also called Hermaphrodites, they are certainly very rare, and yet it is difficult to find periods when there are no examples. . . .

 "Some years ago, but certainly in my time, a man was born in the East with a double set of upper parts, but a single set of the lower limbs. . . . And he lived long enough for the news of his case to attract many sightseers" (Augustine, *City of God* 16.8).

14. It appears to be Tertullian who first interpolated hair and nails into Deuteronomy 29:4, when he asserted that "the clothing and shoes of the children of Israel remained unworn and unwasted during the course of forty years; and that in their own bodies a just measure of aptness and propriety arrested the uninhibited growth of nails and hair, lest their unusual length be considered as some corruption" (*On the Resurrection* 58.6). Jerome reproduces the reading in his treatise against John of Jerusalem, noting that barbers (not to mention manicurists) would be out of work in heaven. David Satran suggests that two factors are at work for Tertullian: first, his awareness that hair and nails continue to grow after death, a potential problem for the argument that soul and body are necessarily separated at the moment of death (*On the Soul* 51.2); and, second, his interest in the debased figure of Nebuchadnezzar who performed penance by living in squalor for seven years, "his nails wild in the manner of a lion, his hair unkempt like that of an eagle" (*On Penitence* 12.7–8). Satran concludes: "These simple features of human anatomy become criteria of 'humanity' itself. Untempered, uncontrolled, they reduce man to the condition of a beast; held in check, mastered, they render him angelic" ("Fingernails and Hair: Anatomy and Exegesis in Tertullian," *Journal of Theological Studies* n.s. 40 [1989]: 120). Clearly Augustine is standing in this tradition when he asks, "Now, what reply am I to make about the hair and the nails?" Yet he chooses to cite a different biblical passage, namely Luke 21:18—"not one hair of your head will perish"—to marshal a rather different argument. According to Augustine, the excesses of physical growth are not held in check but incorporated in the resurrection. Note also that he has dislodged his argument from an

exegetical context that might have confined the issue to hair and nails by his resort to a scriptural passage that refers only to hair. If he's added nails to the list, why not other bodily products?

15. Consider also the puzzle of the Eucharist: What becomes of the ingested bread and wine, particularly if we consider them, as Augustine surely did, to be the body and blood of Christ? Problems beyond those of cannibalism are created here by the unusual temporality of the body of Christ and by its unusual spatiality in eucharistic multi-location.
16. This may be a case in point: a second problem that occurs to us is that of oral sex and the ingestion of bodily fluids, even if we don't add the Augustinian notion that the matter for the making of the human body is all contained within sperm. Like mother's milk, this seems to be a nondamaging fluid exchange in which it is unclear to whom the matter ultimately "belongs."
17. On the intersection of time with eternity, see Karmen MacKendrick, *Immemorial Silence* (Albany: State University of New York Press, 2001), with specific reference to Augustine at 71–80. See also Elliot R. Wolfson, *Alef, Mem, Tau: Kabbalistic Musings on Time, Truth, Death* (Berkeley: University of California Press, 2006), 92, with reference to a time intensely eternalized—"so fully in the moment that it can have no past or future and, consequently, no re/presentable present"—and an eternity equally richly temporalized. Wolfson offers a nuanced and innovative theory of time based on (but not confined to) kabbalistic texts that seems to capture very well the often underestimated complexities of Augustine's thought. See also his particular discussion of Augustine at 3–11, 16, 75.
18. On the beauty of resurrected bodies in Augustine, see Margaret R. Miles, "'Facie ad Faciem': Visuality, Desire, and the Discourse of the Other," *Journal of Religion* 87, no. 1 (2007): 43–58, and "Sex and the City (of God): Is Sex Forfeited or Fulfilled in Augustine's Resurrection of Body?" *Journal of the American Academy of Religion* 73, no. 2 (2005): 307–27.
19. Immanuel Kant, *The Critique of Judgment*, trans. Werner Pluhar (Indianapolis: Hackett, 1987), book 2, §§1–5; 43–53.
20. See Karmen MacKendrick, "Carthage Didn't Burn Hot Enough: Saint Augustine's Divine Seduction," in *Toward a Theology of Eros: Transfiguring Passion at the Limits of Discipline*, ed. Virginia Burrus and Catherine Keller (New York: Fordham University Press, 2006).
21. *Mystical Languages of Unsaying*, 6.
22. Ibid.
23. Ibid.

BODIES STILL UNRISEN, EVENTS STILL UNSAID: A HERMENEUTIC OF BODIES WITHOUT FLESH | JOHN D. CAPUTO

1. Biblical references are from the New Revised Standard Version (NRSV).
2. My thanks to Stephen Moore for his helpful comments on this section of the paper, which I have gratefully made use of in the revised version.
3. E. P. Sanders, *Paul* (Oxford: Oxford University Press, 1991), chap. 4.
4. B. Martin, *The Corinthian Body* (New Haven, Conn.: Yale University Press, 1995), 115 (glossing Cicero).
5. Throughout some eight hundred pages of exposition and interpretation, N. T. Wright in *The Resurrection of the Son of God* (Minneapolis: Fortress Press, 2003) manages to elude this question. After repeating what Luke 24 says, he says approvingly, "Luke makes no more effort to explain or justify this extraordinary innovation [the "transphysicality" of the risen body] than do any of the others" (661). That is, neither he nor Luke nor Paul nor anybody is willing to touch the subject of what bodies with transfigured, transformed, and glorified digestive tracts are doing eating bread or broiled fish, or with transfigured lungs and pancreas and all the other bodily organs are doing with these organs, since these organs have nothing to do. Through eight hundred pages there is a constant insistence that all of this is to be taken in most realistic and literal terms, which goes hand in hand with a resolute refusal to explain what that could literally mean. That all of this would have to do with another sort of discourse is anathema—the sort of thing you hear from the Jesus Seminar (656 n. 21). We do not get much closer to an explanation in Wright's *Surprised by Hope: Rethinking Heaven, the Resurrection, and the Mission of the Church* (New York: HarperOne, 2008); indeed in some ways it gets worse, because now we find that in the parousia, risen bodies will populate the planet earth. What will happen when, five hundred million years or so from now, the earth is toast is not addressed.
6. *The Corinthian Body*, 124. The paragraph that follows is a summary of chap. 5 of Martin.
7. 128–29.
8. Aquinas, *Summa Theologiae*, Part III, Question 55, art. 6, ad 1; see Tobias, 12:18–19; they only seem to eat an "invisible meat."
9. Thomas Aquinas, *Summa Theologiae*, III, Q. 54, art. 2 (in some editions art. 3); cf. I, Q. 51, art. 3, ad 5; on line at http://www.newadvent.org/summa/4054.htm.
10. *The Corinthian Body*, 115.

11. *A Midsummer Night's Dream*, 5.1.
12. The phenomenological sense of transcendence is not the passage beyond experience but the intensification of experience to the point that experience is forced to move on, to move up, to transcend, the stretching of experience beyond itself, so that experience is experience of the impossible. To lack transcendence is to remain within the parameters of the possible. If experience is equated with "immanence" in the widest sense, then transcendence is a modality of immanence, the chief way in which immanence becomes interesting, and so the operative distinction should be between regularized immanence and surprising immanence. Transcendence is not foreign to the materiality of the body but is a modality of the body, a dimension of bodily life that demands everything of us, or takes everything out of us. Transcendence is an irreducibly material image and hence a way of imaging bodily life as crossing or going beyond a spatial or temporal border. In that sense one cannot imagine, or rather one can only try to imagine, what it would be like for a being outside space and time to transcend. The body in all its materiality, its spatiality and temporality, is the primary site and reference for transcendence.

IN THE IMAGE OF THE INVISIBLE | KATHRYN TANNER

1. Gregory of Nyssa, "On the Making of Man," trans. H. A. Wilson, in *Nicene and Post-Nicene Fathers*, vol. 5, ed. Philip Schaff and Henry Wace (Peabody, Mass.: Hendrickson, 1994), chap. 11, sec. 4, 396; sections 2–3 are also relevant.
2. Augustine, "On the Holy Trinity," trans. A. W. Haddan, in *Nicene and Post-Nicene Fathers*, vol. 3, ed. Philip Schaff (Grand Rapids, Mich.: Eerdmans, 1956), book IX, chap. 11, sec.16.
3. See, for example, Romans 8:29; 2 Corinthians 4:4; and Colossians 1:15.
4. See, for example, Galatians 4:19; Ephesians 4:24; and Colossians 3:10.
5. Cyril of Alexandria, *Commentary on the Gospel according to John*, trans. P. E. Pusey (London: Walter Smith, 1885), book 5, chap. 7, 550.
6. See Colossians 1:15, New Revised Standard Version (NRSV).
7. Even in a theology like that of Athanasius, where the stress is on the pedagogical function of the Word's incarnation in a visible form, *what* is revealed in the contest with idolatry is the incomprehensible character of divinity.
8. Irenaeus, "Against Heresies," trans. Alexander Roberts and James Donaldson, in *Ante-Nicene Fathers*, vol. 1, ed. Alexander Roberts and James Donaldson (Grand Rapids, Mich.: Eerdmans, 1989), book 4, chap. 39, sec. 2, 523.

9. Gregory of Nyssa, "On the Soul and the Resurrection," trans. W. Moore, in *Nicene and Post-Nicene Fathers*, vol. 5, 452.
10. Gregory of Nazianzen, "Orations," trans. Charles Gordon Browne and James Edward Swallow, in *Nicene and Post-Nicene Fathers*, vol. 7, ed. Philip Schaff and Henry Wace (Grand Rapids, Mich.: Eerdmans, 1983), Oration 7, sec. 28, 237. I don't take this quotation (and others like it) to mean that what made you a man or a woman before is simply wiped out, along with your previous identities, but that those differences remain to be distinctively refashioned according to the same form of Christ; they become like diverse matters for a new fundamental reorganization that takes the same Christ-like shape each time. You are no longer identified as a man, say, rather than a woman, but what made you a man is still there as the material for the new organization of you that makes you Christ.
11. See Basil the Great, *On the Human Condition*, trans. and intro. Nonna Verna Harrison (Crestwood, N.Y.: St Vladimir's Seminary Press, 2005), 72.
12. See Harry G. Frankfurt, *The Reasons of Love* (Princeton, N.J.: Princeton University Press, 2006).
13. Augustine, "Holy Trinity," book X, chap. 5 , sec. 7, 138.
14. Gregory of Nyssa, "Fourth Homily," trans. and intro. Casimir McCambley, in *Commentary on the Song of Songs* (Brookline, Mass.: Hellenic College Press, 1987), 92.
15. Ibid.
16. Gregory of Nyssa, "On the Soul and Resurrection," 442.
17. Gregory of Nyssa, "On the Making of Man," chap. 18, secs. 3–4, 408.
18. Ibid., chap. 12, sec. 9, 399; the discussion continues into sections 10–11.
19. See Hilary Armstrong, "Spiritual or Intelligible Matter in Plotinus and St. Augustine," *Etudes Augustiniennes* (September 1954): 277–83.
20. Gregory of Nyssa, "An Address on Religious Instruction," trans. Cyril C. Richardson, in *Christology of the Later Fathers*, ed. Edward Hardy (Philadelphia: Westminster, 1953), sec. 6, 279.
21. Cyril of Alexandria, *Commentary on John*, book 9, chap. 14, sec. 9, 255.
22. Ibid., chap. 14, sec.7, 246, where Cyril is discussing Christ, but the point remains the same.
23. See Cornelio Fabro, *Participation et causalité selon S. Thomas D'Aquin* (Paris: Beatrice-Nauwelaerts, 1961), 468, 610.

"THE BODY IS NO BODY" | DAVID L. MILLER

1. See the magisterial treatment of this in the two-volume work by Raoul Mortley, *From Word to Silence: Volume I, The Rise and Fall of Logos; Volume II, The Way of Negation, Christian and Greek* (Bonn: Peter Hanstin Verlag, 1986).

2. Sarah Coakley, "The Eschatological Body," in *Powers and Submissions: Spirituality, Philosophy and Gender* (Oxford: Blackwell, 2002), 153–54.
3. Judith Butler, *Bodies That Matter: On the Discursive Limits of "Sex"* (New York: Routledge, 1993), ix.
4. Mary Douglas, *Purity and Danger: An Analysis of Concepts of Pollution and Taboo* (London: Routledge & Kegan Paul, 1966), 122.
5. Rafael López-Pedraza, *Hermes and His Children* (Zurich: Spring Publications, 1977), 70–74.
6. Picasso, *347 Gravures: 16.3.68–5.10.68*. Galerie Louise Leiris, Catalogue no. 23, serie A. Maîtres Imprimeurs, Draeger Frères, 1968. The relevant drawings—nos. 296–315—were not shown in the public exhibit!
7. Wallace Stevens, "Adagia," in *Opus Posthumous* (New York: Alfred A. Knopf, 1977), 173. For this reference and those that follow, I am indebted to Michael Sexson. See his book *The Quest of Self in the Collected Poems of Wallace Stevens* (Toronto: Edwin Mellen Press, 1981), 153. Cf. Michel de Certeau on "mystic speech" in *Heterologies: Discourse of the Other*, trans. B. Massumi (Minneapolis: University of Minnesota Press, 1986), 8–9: "The literature of mysticism provides a path for those who 'ask the way to get lost.' . . . It teaches 'how not to return.' Their [the mystics] goal is to disappear into what they disclose, like a Turner landscape dissolved in air and light." On the theme, see also David L. Miller, "Prometheus, St. Peter and the Rock: Identity and Difference in Modern Literature, " *Eranos 1988–57* (Frankfurt: Insel Verlag, 1989): 75–124.
8. Wallace Stevens, "Montrachet-le-Jardin," in *Collected Poems* (New York: Alfred A. Knopf, 1975), 264.
9. Stevens, "Adagia," *Opus Posthumous*, 158.
10. Wallace Stevens, "An Ordinary Evening in New Haven," in *Collected Poems*, 488.
11. *Enn.* 6.8.13.50, trans. A. H. Armstrong (Cambridge, Mass.: Harvard University Press, 1988). I am grateful to Patricia Cox Miller for this reference. See her "Plenty Sleeps There: The Myth of Eros and Psyche," in *The Poetry of Thought in Late Antiquity: Essays in Imagination and Religion* (Burlington, Vt.: Ashgate, 2001), 119 n.12.
12. Jacques Derrida, "Comment ne pas parler," in *Psyché: Inventions de l'autre* (Paris: Galilée, 1987), 577–78.
13. Raymond B. Blakney, trans., *Meister Eckhart* (New York: Harper and Row, 1941), 222–23.
14. Gaston Bachelard, *The Poetics of Space*, trans. M. Jolas (New York: Orion Press, 1964), 143–44.

15. Gaston Bachelard, *The Philosophy of No*, trans. G. C. Waterson (New York: Orion Press, 1968), 73.
16. Gaston Bachelard, *Water and Dreams,* trans. E. Farrell (Dallas: Institute of Humanities and Culture, 1983), 26 (translation corrected from *L'Eau et les rêves* [Paris: Librairie José Corti, 1942], 39).
17. Bachelard, *Water and Dreams,* 32.
18. Gaston Bachelard, *Earth and the Rêveries of Will,* trans. K. Haltman (Dallas: Institute of Humanities and Culture, 2002), 72.
19. Gaston Bachelard, *La Terre et les rêveries du repos* (Paris: Librairie José Corti, 1948), 83 (my translation).
20. Ibid., 89 (my translation).
21. Ibid. (my translation).
22. Ibid., 50 (my translation).
23. Gaston Bachelard, *Air and Dreams*, trans. E. Farrell and C. F. Farrell (Dallas: Institute of Humanities and Culture, 1988), 104. The original French publication of this work carries a 1943 copyright.
24. Gaston Bachelard, *The Flame of a Candle*, trans. J. Caldwell (Dallas: Institute of Humanities and Culture, 1988), 39. The original French publication of this work carries a 1961 copyright.
25. Bachelard, *Earth and Will*, 263; *La Terre et les rêveries de la volonté* (Paris: Librairie José Corti, 1948), 343.
26. Bachelard, *Earth and Will*, 280; *La Terre et volonté*, 364.
27. Bachelard, *The Flame*, 45.
28. Henry Corbin, "Pour l'anthropologie philosophique: Un traité persan inédit de Suhrawardî d'Alep," *Récherches philosophiques*, II (1932–33), 393.
29. This correspondence was kindly made available to me by Stella Corbin, the widow of Henry Corbin, and it is here published in my own translation with the permission of Mme Corbin, to whom I am most grateful.
30. Henry Corbin, "Sympathie et théopathie chez les 'Fidèles d'Amour' en Islam," *Eranos Jahrbuch 24–1955*, 199f. Corbin is citing Proclus.
31. Bachelard, *The Flame*, 60; *La Flame*, 87.
32. I have Mme Corbin's permission to share this paragraph in reporting this research.
33. This is provided by Mme Corbin (my translation).
34. This letter is previously published in Christian Jambet, ed., *Henry Corbin* (Paris: Éditions de L'Herne, 1981), 311–12 (my translation).
35. Henry Corbin, *Avicenna and the Visionary Recital*, trans. W. Trask (Dallas: Spring Publications, 1980), 238.
36. Cf. Patricia Cox Miller, "Dreaming the Body: An Aesthetics of Asceticism," in *Asceticism*, ed. Vincent Wimbush (Oxford: Oxford University Press, 1995),

281–300; "Desert Asceticism and 'The Body from Nowhere,'" *Journal of Early Christian Studies* 2 (1994): 137–53; and "'The Little Blue Flower Is Red': Relics and the Poetizing of the Body," *Journal of Early Christian Studies* 8 (2000): 213–36.

37. Justin Martyr, Theophilus of Antioch, Irenaeus, Hippolytus, Clement of Alexandria, and others as a description of the "true Christian," i.e., God became human so that human beings may be "made God" (*theopoein*). For example, in the *Stromata*, Clement wrote: "The 'theopoet' is the real human being who alone is wise while others flit about as shadows" (*Strom.* 4.317).
38. Amos Wilder, *Theopoetic: Theology and the Religious Imagination* (Philadelphia: Fortress Press, 1976).
39. Ibid., iv.
40. The proceedings of this consultation were published in *The New Hermeneutic,* ed. James Robinson and John Cobb (New York: Harper and Row, 1964).
41. The proceedings of this consultation were published in *Interpretation: The Poetry of Meaning,* ed. Stanley R. Hopper and David Miller (New York: Harcourt, Brace and World, 1967).
42. For a review of the first three of these consultations, see Stanley R. Hopper, "Introduction," to *Interpretation,* ix–xxii. Much of what follows in the next paragraphs is indebted to Hopper's account. Cf. David Miller, "Theopoiesis," in *Why Persimmons and Other Poems,* ed. Stanley R. Hopper (Atlanta: Scholars Press, 1987), 1–12; "Mythopoesis, Psychopoesis, Theopoesis: The Poetries of Meaning" (tape), *Panarion Conference 1976* (Jack Burkee, Box 9926, Marina Del Rey, Calif. 90291); *Christs: Meditations on Archetypal Images in Christian Theology* (New Orleans: Spring Journal Books, 2005); and *Hells and Holy Ghosts: A Theopoetics of Christian Belief* (New Orleans: Spring Journal Books, 2004).
43. Hopper, "Introduction," to *Interpretation,* ed. Hopper and Miller, xiv. This letter, without attribution of its context, appears in Martin Heidegger, *The Piety of Thinking: Essays by Martin Heidegger*, trans. James G. Hart and John C. Maraldo (Bloomington: Indiana University Press, 1976).
44. Beda Allemann, "Metaphor and Anti-Metaphor," in *Interpretation*, ed. Hopper and Miller, 103–24.
45. Stanley R. Hopper, *Way of Transfiguration*, ed. R. Melvin Keiser and Tony Stoneburner (Louisville: Westminster/John Knox Press, 1992), 166, 249, 288–90, 295, 298, 300.
46. Philip Wheelwright, *Metaphor and Reality* (Bloomington: Indiana University Press, 1962), 85, 88, 91.

47. Hopper, "Introduction," to *Interpretation,* ed. Hopper and Miller, xix. Compare Hopper's other writings on theopoetics, especially those collected in Hopper, *Way of Transfiguration,* viii, 1–4, 9, 12, 169, 298 and passim. For example: "Theo-logoi belong to the realm of mytho-poetic utterance and . . . theo-logos is not theologic but theopoesis" (225).
48. Wallace Stevens, "The Man with the Blue Guitar," in *Collected Poems*, 172. The lines concerning the vertical flame are: "A candle is enough to light the world. / It makes it clear. Even at noon / It glistens in the essential dark. / At night, it lights the fruit and wine, / The book and bread, things as they are, / In a chiaroscuro where / One sits and plays the blue guitar."
49. Ibid.
50. Wallace Stevens, *Letters of Wallace Stevens*, ed. H. Stevens (New York: Alfred A. Knopf, 1977), 783.
51. Ibid., 785.
52. Bachelard, *The Flame*, 40, 43, 59; *La Flame*, 58, 63, 85.
53. Gaston Bachelard, *The Psychoanalysis of Fire*, trans. A. C. M. Ross (Boston: Beacon Press, 1964), 41. Bachelard had said to Jean Lacroix, concerning this work "Tenez, Lacroix, j'ai fait ce qu'on ne devrait jamais faire, un livre autour d'une phrase qui chantait dan ma tête: elle est rouge, la petite fleur bleue!" See Gilbert Lascault, "Elle est rouge, la petite fleur bleue" ["Look here, Lacroix! I have created that which one ought never create! It is a book fashioned around a phrase that sang in my head: 'The little blue flower is red.'"]. *L'Arc*, 42: 32; and Vincent Therrien, *La revolution de G. Bachelard en critique littéraire* (Paris: Éditions Klincksieck, 1970).

REVISIONING THE BODY APOPHATICALLY: INCARNATION AND THE ACOSMIC NATURALISM OF HABAD HASIDISM | ELLIOT R. WOLFSON

1. Walter Benjamin in the 1916 essay "On Language as Such and on the Language of Man," in *Selected Writings,* vol. 1: *1913–1926*, ed. Marcus Bullock and Michael W. Jennings (Cambridge, Mass.: Harvard University Press, 1996), 63.
2. Habad follows a perspective that can be traced back to some kabbalists from the thirteenth century who began the counting of the ten *sefirot* with *Ḥokhmah* or *Maḥashavah*, adding *Daʿat* in place of *Keter*. This is not to say that *Keter* does not figure prominently in the teaching of Habad. The topic merits a separate investigation, but briefly it can be said that *Keter* is described variously as the nothing (*ayin*), the incomposite will (*raṣon pashuṭ*), the infinite light (*or ein sof*), the one in which opposites coalesce. The dimension of soul that corresponds to *Keter* is called *yeḥidah*, which connotes

unity and signifies the consubstantiality between divine and human. For a concise formulation, see the passage of Dov Baer Schneersohn cited below at note 38. Numerous texts could be adduced to substantiate the further assumption that *yeḥidah* is distinctive to the Jewish people, but this would take us too far afield. See below, note 14. I have discussed some of the relevant sources in the sixth chapter of *Open Secret: Postmessianic Messianism and the Mystical Revision of Menaḥem Mendel Schneerson* (New York: Columbia University Press, 2009).

3. The locus classicus for this terminology is Shneur Zalman of Liadi, *Liqquṭei Amarim: Tanya* (Brooklyn: Kehot, 1984), pt. 1, chap. 3, 7a–b.
4. The bibliography on the Besht is enormous, so I will here refer only to some of the more recent works where one can find ample reference to other relevant scholarship: Moshe Rosman, *Founder of Hasidism: A Quest for the Historical Baʿal Shem Tov* (Berkeley: University of California Press, 1996); Immanuel Etkes, *The Besht: Magician, Mystic, and Leader*, trans. Saadya Sternberg (Waltham, Mass.: Brandeis University Press, 2005); Rachel Elior, *The Mystical Origins of Hasidism* (Oxford: Litman Library of Jewish Civilization, 2006), 59–71; Netanel Lederberg, *Sod ha-Daʿat: Rabbi Israel Baʿal Shem Tov, His Spiritual Character and Social Leadership* (Jerusalem: Rubin Mass, 2007) (Hebrew).
5. On the seven masters of the Lubavitch sect, see the comprehensive analysis of Avrum M. Ehrlich, *Leadership in the HaBaD Movement: A Critical Evaluation of HaBaD Leadership, History, and Succession* (Northvale, N.J.: Jason Aronson, 2000), and idem, *The Messiah of Brooklyn: Understanding Lubavitch Hasidism Past and Present* (Jersey City, N.J.: Ktav, 2004), 51–80.
6. Joseph Weiss, *Studies in Eastern European Jewish Mysticism*, ed. David Goldstein (Oxford: Oxford University Press, 1985), 194–95; Naftali Loewenthal, *Communicating the Infinite: The Emergence of the Habad School* (Chicago: University of Chicago Press, 1990), 76.
7. In a number of passages, the seventh Rebbe explained the unique feature of Hasidism, by which he means most particularly Habad, in these terms. For example, see Menachem Mendel Schneerson, *Torat Menaḥem: Hitwaʿaduyyot 5714*, vol. 1 (Brooklyn: Lahak Hanochos, 1998), 271–72; idem, *Qunṭres Inyanah shel Torat ha-Ḥasidut* (Brooklyn: Kehot, 2004), 1.
8. Rachel Elior, "ḤaBaD: The Contemplative Ascent to God," in *Jewish Spirituality*, vol. 2: *From the Sixteenth-Century Revival to the Present*, ed. Arthur Green (New York: Crossroad, 1987), 160, 191–98; idem, *The Paradoxical Ascent to God: The Kabbalistic Theosophy of Habad Philosophy* (Albany: State University of New York Press, 1993), 138.

9. Rivka Schatz Uffenheimer, *Hasidism as Mysticism: Quietistic Elements in Eighteenth-Century Hasidic Thought*, trans. Jonathan Chipman (Princeton, N.J.: Princeton University Press, 1993), 256–60, and reference to other scholarly discussions cited on 256–57 nn. 2–3; Elior, *Paradoxical Ascent*, 167–72; Loewenthal, *Communicating the Infinite*, 77–86. Also relevant here is the discussion of two types of piety in Hasidism, the "mystical, contemplative piety" and the "piety of faith," the former represented by the Maggid of Mezeritch and the latter by Nahman of Bratslav, in Weiss, *Studies in Eastern European Jewish Mysticism*, 43–55. On the role of faith in early Hasidism, see Ron Margolin, "On the Substance of Faith in Hasidism: A Historical-Conceptual Perspective," in *On Faith: Studies in the Concept of Faith and Its History in the Jewish Tradition*, ed. Moshe Halbertal, David Kurzweil, and Avi Sagi (Jerusalem: Keter, 2005), 328–64 (Hebrew).
10. See the innovative analysis by Simeon Gershon Rosenberg, "Faith and Language according to the Admor ha-Zaqen of Habad from the Philosophical Perspective on Language of Wittgenstein," in *On Faith*, 365–87 (Hebrew).
11. Shneur Zalman of Liadi, *Torah Or* (Brooklyn: Kehot, 2001), 6a. On the literary history of this composition, see Rachel Elior, *The Theory of Divinity of Hasidut Habad* (Jerusalem: Magnes Press, 1982), 123 n. 12 (Hebrew).
12. The ideal of self-abnegation is presented as the mystical exegesis of the verse *ner yhwh nishmat adam*, "the soul of man is the lamp of the Lord" (Prov 20:27), which is applied specifically to Israel based on the older rabbinic idea that the word *adam* in its most exacting sense refers to the Jews and not to the nations of the world. For documentation of this theme in rabbinic and kabbalistic sources, see Elliot R. Wolfson, *Venturing Beyond: Law and Morality in Kabbalistic Mysticism* (Oxford: Oxford University Press, 2006), 42–57, 73–124. Since only the Jewish soul is rooted in the essence of the divine, the Jew alone has the possibility of drawing down the disclosure of the light of the essence of the Infinite into the world through the act of denegation of the self. The term *adam*, therefore, is related to the expression *eddammeh le-elyon* (Isa 14:14), which signifies the ontological similarity between human and divine as it is configured in the imagination. See, for instance, Menachem Mendel Schneerson, *Torat Menaḥem: Sefer ha-Maʾamarim Meluqaṭ*, vol. 1 (Brooklyn: Lahak Hanochos, 2002), 31–33: "Therefore Rosh ha-Shanah is precisely the day that he created the first Adam, for this power (to draw the disclosure of the essence of the light of the Infinite that is above the worlds, so that this expansion will be in the world) is in Israel especially, 'you are called Adam,' in the name of the first Adam. . . . Since the root of the soul of Israel is in his essence, blessed be

he, their capability is to draw into the world the disclosure of the essence of the light of the Infinite." In this essay, I will not qualify my use of the term "human" as denoting the Jew, but it should be understood that this qualification is in fact justified textually. A plethora of other sources could have been provided to substantiate my assertion, but it lies beyond the scope of this essay.

13. Shneur Zalman of Liadi, *Torah Or*, 6b.

14. The matter of the uniqueness of the Jewish soul, related especially to the aspect of *yeḥidah*, is a topic too complicated to discuss in this essay. Briefly, Habad thought has always accorded a distinctive ontological position to the Jews, as it is presumed that only they possess the aspect of the divine that is the essence of the Infinite, the "inner point of the heart" (*nequddat ha-lev penimit*), and therefore they alone are capable of *devequt* or *biṭṭul*, of being bound to and absorbed in the light beyond all boundaries. Nonetheless, the seeds to undermine this perspective are found in Habad teaching as well, since the light of the Infinite is characterized as nondifferentiated unity, a *coincidentia oppositorum* where there is no longer any basis to distinguish light and darkness, holy and impure, and, consequently, the hard-and-fast distinction between Jew and non-Jew is similarly challenged. For discussion on the status of non-Jews in Schneerson's teaching, see Alon Dahan, "'Dira Bataḥtonim': The Messianic Doctrine of Rabbi Menachem Mendel Schneersohn (The Lubavitcher Rebbe)," Ph.D. thesis, Hebrew University, 2006, 341–73, and the reference to my forthcoming book mentioned above at the end of n. 2.

15. As far as I could detect, the expression becomes prominent in sixteenth- and seventeenth-century sources, and from there passes into the Hasidic glossary. See, for example, Moses Cordovero, *Sefer Yeṣirah im Perush Or Yaqar* (Jerusalem, 1989), chap. 2, 122, chap. 5, 164, chap. 6, 169; Moses Ḥayyim Luzzatto, *Qelaḥ Pitḥei Ḥokhmah*, ed., Ḥayyim Friedlander (Benei-Beraq, 1992), chap. 96, 289, chap. 109, 311–12, chap. 110, 313; idem, *Adir ba-Marom*, pt. 2 (Jerusalem, 1988), 50; idem, *Sod ha-Merkavah*, in *Sefer Ginzei Ramḥal*, ed., Ḥayyim Friedlander, 2nd ed. (Benei-Beraq, 1984), 266, 267. The particular influence of Cordovero and Luzzatto on Hasidic masters has been well documented. See Schatz Uffenheimer, *Hasidism as Mysticism*, 263 n. 16; Bracha Sack, "An Investigation of the Influence of R. Moses Cordovero on Hasidism," *Eshel Beer Sheva* 3 (1986): 229–46 (Hebrew); idem, "The Influence of *Reshit ḥokhmah* on the Teachings of the Maggid of Mezhirech," in *Hasidism Reappraised*, ed. Ada Rapoport-Albert (London: Litman Library of Jewish Civilization, 1996), 251–57; Moshe Idel, *Hasidism: Between Ecstasy and*

Magic (Albany: State University of New York Press, 1995), 65–81, 86–89, 109–11, 159–62, 165–68, 178–80, 191–203, 215–16; Isaiah Tishby, *Messianic Mysticism: Moses Hayim Luzzatto and the Padua School*, trans. Morris Hoffman (Oxford: Littman Library of Jewish Civilization, 2008), 486–527.

16. The terms *mahut* (being) and *aṣmut* (essence) are used interchangeably to refer to that which we cannot know or name, the what-it-is-to-be, the light that is all things in virtue of being none of those things, the concealment revealed in the concealment of its revelation. See, for example, Shneur Zalman of Liadi, *Liqquṭei Amarim: Tanya*, pt. 2, chap. 7, 82a: "[T]he aspect of place and time are actually annihilated in existence in relation to his being and his essence, blessed be he [*beḥinat ha-maqom we-ha-zeman beṭelim bi-meṣiʾut mammash legabbei mahuto we-aṣmuto yitbarakh*], like the light of the sun in the sun."

17. Dov Baer Schneersohn, *Perush ha-Millot* (Brooklyn: Kehot, 1993), 112c: "'He draws mysteries out of darkness' (Job 12:22) . . . and the aspect of darkness is the black that is also above the aspect of the essential light of the resplendent luminosity [*or ha-aṣmi de-or ṣaḥ*], for the aspect of the essence [*ha-aṣmut*] is greatly above the aspect of the essential light [*or ha-aṣmi*]. However, that the darkness shines against its nature is also precisely the aspect of the essential light, as it says 'Darkness is not dark for You' (Ps 139:12)."

18. Shalom Dovber Schneersohn, *Be-Shaʿah she-Hiqdimu 5672*, 3 vols. (Brooklyn: Kehot, 1991), 1:134.

19. Shneur Zalman of Liadi, *Liqquṭei Torah*, vol. 2 (Brooklyn: Kehot, 1998), Waʾetḥanan, 8d. On the symbol of the supernal darkness, see ibid., 9a; Haʾazinu, 73a; Dov Baer Schneersohn, *Torat Ḥayyim: Bereʾshit* (Brooklyn: Kehot, 1993), 60c, 60d, 61a, 125a, 125b, 157c, 161c, 161d, 162b, 162d, 185c; idem, *Torat Ḥayyim: Shemot* (Brooklyn: Kehot, 2003), 16b, 343d; idem, *Derushei Ḥatunah*, vol. 2 (Brooklyn: Kehot, 1991), 547.

20. Shneur Zalman of Liadi, *Torah Or*, 14a.

21. Shalom Dovber Schneersohn, *Sefer ha-Maʾamarim 5678* (Brooklyn: Kehot, 1984), 99. See also Yosef Yitzchak Schneersohn, *Sefer ha-Maʾamarim 5692–93* (Brooklyn: Kehot, 2004), 165–66; Menachem Mendel Schneerson, *Torat ha-Menaḥem: Sefer ha-Maʾamarim 5717* (Brooklyn: Lahak Hanochos, 2006), 62.

22. Menachem Mendel Schneerson, *Torat ha-Menaḥem: Sefer ha-Maʾamarim 5717*, 63.

23. Dov Baer Schneersohn, *Shaʿarei Teshuvah* (Brooklyn: Kehot, 1995), 23c.

24. Schatz Uffenheimer, *Hasidism as Mysticism*, 263, grasped this essential dimension of Habad thinking from the writings of Shneur Zalman, though she does not use the precise language of incarnation. Thus, she noted that

the Lurianic notion of withdrawal (*ṣimṣum*) is no longer set in opposition to divine immanence, but it is rather a "form of revelation." Paradoxically, "the act of divine revelation is more likely in the world through His hiddenness and concealment and being embodied therein. . . . [T]he external act of Creation is an aspect of His concealment and hiddenness; the hiddenness and absorption of God within the world is itself an act of creation."

25. Shneur Zalman of Liadi, *Liqquṭei Torah*, vol. 1 (Brooklyn: Kehot, 1996), Beḥuqotai, 48b.
26. See discussion of this theme and citation of some relevant sources in Idel, *Hasidism*, 123–24.
27. Elior, *Paradoxical Ascent*, 185–89. For the background of the quietistic ideal and the annihilation of the self, see Schatz Uffenheimer, *Hasidism as Mysticism*, 65–79.
28. The technical term that can be rendered as "incorporation" is *hitkallelut*. See Moshe Idel, "Universalization and Integration: Two Conceptions of Mystical Union in Jewish Mysticism," in *Mystical Union and Monotheistic Faith: An Ecumenical Dialogue*, ed. Moshe Idel and Bernard McGinn (New York: Macmillan, 1989), 27–57, esp. 41–45; Elior, *Paradoxical Ascent*, 44–45; Loewenthal, *Communicating the Infinite*, 153, 170.
29. See above, nn. 12 and 14.
30. Shneur Zalman of Liadi, *Liqquṭei Amarim: Tanya*, pt. 1, chap. 19, 24a–b.
31. Ibid., 24b–25a. See also Shneur Zalman of Liadi, *Liqquṭei Torah*, vol. 2 (Brooklyn: Kehot, 1998), Re'eh, 18b. The theme is repeatedly emphasized in Habad literature. For example, see Menachem Mendel Schneerson, *Liqquṭei Siḥot*, vol. 12 (Brooklyn: Kehot, 2004), 408, and the Hebrew translation in idem, *Torat Menaḥem: Hitwaʿaduyyot 5712*, vol. 3 (Brooklyn: Lahak Hanochos, 1997), 187.
32. The point is made in numerous texts, but the source that is often mentioned in Habad literature is *Zohar* 1:12a, where the fourth of fourteen commandments is "to know that the Lord [YHWH] is God [Elohim], as it is written 'Know this day, and consider in your hearts that the Lord is God' (Deut 4:39), to contain the name Elohim in the name YHWH, to know that they are one and there is no division in them" (*Sefer ha-Zohar*, ed. Reuven Margaliot [Jerusalem: Mosad Ha-Rav Kook, 1960], 3 vols. [translations mine]).
33. Needless to say, this idiom appears frequently in Habad literature. Its locus classicus is Shneur Zalman of Liadi, *Liqquṭei Amarim: Tanya*, pt. 1, chap. 3, 7b.

34. See Menachem Mendel Schneerson, *Torat Menaḥem: Sefer ha-Maʾamarim 5716* (Brooklyn: Lahak Hanochos, 2006), 79: "By means of contemplation of matters that are suitable to the animal soul, that is, corporeal matters, the understanding and comprehension of the divine soul also takes on the aspect of an actual sensible comprehension [*hassagah muḥashit mammash*], as it is written 'Lift your eyes upward and see who created these' (Isa 40:26) . . . by way of sensible vision [*reʾiyyah muḥashit*], and by means of this the contemplation of the divine soul is in corporeal matters."
35. Shneur Zalman of Liadi, *Maʾamerei Admor ha-Zaqen 5565*, vol. 2 (Brooklyn: Kehot, 1981), 728–38.
36. The slogan "there is no thought that can comprehend him at all" (see below, n. 103) was a favorite among Hasidic masters. Ideally, the use of this dictum in Habad literature should be considered in relation to other sources, but that is a project that lies beyond the scope of this essay.
37. Shneur Zalman of Liadi, *Liqquṭei Torah*, vol. 1, Balaq, 69c.
38. Dov Baer Schneersohn, *Shaʿarei Orah* (Brooklyn: Kehot, 1979), 64a.
39. The locutions "place that is above place" and "time that is above time" were used by the seventh Rebbe to describe the holy of holies in the Jerusalem Temple. See Menachem Mendel Schneerson, *Liqquṭei Siḥot*, vol. 2 (Brooklyn: Kehot, 2004), 407–8, and idem, *Torat Menaḥem: Hitwaʿaduyot 5712*, vol. 3, 186–88.
40. Shneur Zalman of Liadi, *Maʾamerei Admor ha-Zaqen 5571* (Brooklyn: Kehot, 1995), 305.
41. Shneur Zalman of Liadi, *Liqquṭei Amarim: Tanya*, pt. 1, chap. 38, 50b. See reference to Idel cited above, n. 28.
42. On the role of the commandments and ritual, see Yitzchak Kraus, *The Seventh: Messianism in the Last Generation of Habad* (Tel Aviv: Yedioth Ahronoth, 2007), 132–76 (Hebrew).
43. For references to scholars who have discussed this motif, see Elliot R. Wolfson, *Language, Eros, Being: Kabbalistic Hermeneutics and Poetic Imagination* (New York: Fordham University Press, 2005), 422 n. 251.
44. Zalman of Liadi, *Torah Or*, 14a.
45. Menachem Mendel Schneerson, *Quntres Inyanah shel Torat ha-Ḥasidut*, 20.
46. *Midrash Tanḥuma*, Naso, 17. See ibid., Beḥuqotai, 3; *Numbers Rabbah* 13:6.
47. Shneur Zalman of Liadi, *Liqquṭei Amarim: Tanya*, pt. 1, chap. 36, 45b. For scholarly assessments of the importance of this motif, especially in the teaching of the seventh Rebbe, see Yitzchak Kraus, "'Living with the Times': Reflection and Leadership, Theory and Practice in the World of the

Rebbe of Lubavitch, Rabbi Menachem Mendel Schneerson," Ph.D. thesis, Bar Ilan University, 2001, 38–72 (Hebrew), and Dahan, "Dira Bataḥtonim." For a lucid but uncritical attempt to render this concept as the focal point of a unified system of thought—a "down to earth weltanschauung"—elicited from the Rebbe's talks and writings, see Faitel Levin, *Heaven on Earth: Reflections on the Theology of the Lubavitcher Rebbe, Rabbi Menachem M. Schneerson* (Brooklyn: Kehot, 2002).

48. Shneur Zalman of Liadi, *Liqquṭei Torah*, vol. 2, Ha'azinu, 75d.
49. Wolfson, *Venturing Beyond*, 22.
50. My view should be seen as a critique of the characterization of Hasidism by Buber, adopted by Scholem as well, as "Kabbalism turned Ethos," which was meant to insinuate that the originality of Hasidic thought was in transforming "the exploration of the theosophical mysteries" into the "quest for the true substance of ethico-religious conceptions" and "their mystical glorification." See Gershom Scholem, *Major Trends in Jewish Mysticism* (New York: Schocken, 1954), 342–43. The emphasis on the nexus between ontology and ethics challenges this portrayal of Hasidism.
51. Dov Baer Schneersohn, *Sha'arei Orah*, 9a.
52. Dov Baer Schneersohn, *Torat Ḥayyim: Bere'shit*, 185a. See n. 191 below.
53. Dov Baer Schneersohn, *Torat Ḥayyim: Shemot*, 292a. See idem, *Torat Ḥayyim: Bere'shit*, 49c, 219c.
54. Dov Baer Schneersohn, *Sha'arei Orah*, 39a. The concluding line is derived from the words *we-nafshi ke-afar la-kol tihyeh* from the meditation *yihyu le-raṣon imrei fi*, which is recited at the end of the standing prayer (*amidah*), the central part of the traditional liturgy.
55. Aaron Halevi Horowitz of Staroselye, *Sha'arei Avodah* (Jerusalem: Maqor, 1970), pt. 2, chap. 32, 46b. See Louis Jacobs, *Seeker of Unity: The Life and Works of Aaron of Starosselje* (London: Vallentine Mitchell, 1966), 107–8, 130–31.
56. Dov Baer Schneersohn, *Torat Ḥayyim: Bere'shit*, 65c.
57. Martin Heidegger, *Hölderlins Hymnen "Germanien" und "Der Rhein"* (Frankfurt am Main: Vittorio Klostermann, 1980), 293: "Echte Wiederholung entspringt aus ursprünglicher Verwandlung."
58. Martin Heidegger, *Elucidations of Hölderlin's Poetry*, trans. Keith Hoeller (Amherst, N.Y.: Humanity Books, 2000), 225. German original: *Erläuterungen zu Hölderlins Dichtung* (Frankfurt am Main: Vittorio Klostermann, 1981), 196. Significantly, the notion of the juxtaposition of the unfamiliar is expressed in Heidegger's gloss on the nature of intimacy (*Innigkeit*). See Peter Warnek, "Translating *Innigkeit*: The Belonging Together of the

Strange," in *Heidegger and the Greeks: Interpretive Essays*, ed. Drew A. Hyland and John Panteleimon Manoussakis (Bloomington: Indiana University Press, 2006), 57–82.

59. See Uffenheimer, *Hasidism as Mysticism*, 75–76.
60. My language is indebted to Heidegger, *Hölderlins Hymnen*, 250: "Wenn jedoch dieses Geheimnis als ein solches genannt und gesagt wird, dann ist es damit offenbar, aber die Enthüllung seiner Offenbarkeit ist gerade das Nicht-erklären-wollen, vielmehr das Verstehen seiner als der sich verbergenden Verborgenheit." For an English rendering and analysis, see Warnek, "Translating *Innigkeit*," 63.
61. Shalom Dovber Schneersohn, *Yom Ṭov shel Rosh ha-Shanah 5666* (Brooklyn: Kehot, 1999), 3a.
62. This principle is deployed in other hasidic texts with a meaning quite similar to Habad usage. For an illustration, see Moshe Hallamish, "The Teachings of R. Menahem Mendel of Vitebsk," in *Hasidism Reappraised*, 280.
63. Shalom Dovber Schneersohn, *Yom Ṭov shel Rosh ha-Shanah 5666*, 3a. In that context, human intellect (*sekhel enoshi*), which is said to derive from the tree of knowledge of good and evil, is contrasted with Torah, which emanates from the Supernal Wisdom (*ḥokhmah ilaʾah*), the something (*yesh*) whence one can discern the nothing (*ayin*).
64. Dov Baer Schneersohn, *Ner Miṣwah we-Torah Or* (Brooklyn: Kehot, 1995), 9b.
65. Menachem Mendel Schneerson, *Sefer ha-Maʾamarim 5711, 5712, 5713* (Brooklyn: Kehot, 1988), 103.
66. Shalom Dovber Schneersohn, *Be-Shaʿah she-Hiqdimu 5672*, 1:134.
67. Shneur Zalman of Liadi, *Torah Or*, 123d. It should be noted that this passage is from the supplements (*hosafot*) to the text that were apparently redacted by the Mitteler Rebbe. See also Dov Baer Schneersohn, *Shaʿarei Orah*, 33a.
68. Shneur Zalman of Liadi, *Liqquṭei Amarim: Tanya*, pt. 1, chap, 38, 50b. The expression *eḥad ha-shaweh* is based on the technical term *aḥdut ha-shaweh*, a locution attested in kabbalistic sources from the thirteenth century to denote the *coincidentia oppositorum*, that is, the indifferent one, or the one in which opposites are no longer distinguishable as discrete opposites. See Gershom Scholem, *Origins of the Kabbalah*, ed. R. J. W. Werblowsky, trans. Allan Arkush (Princeton: Princeton University Press, 1987), 312 and 439 n. 174, and analysis in Wolfson, *Language*, 99–105. For discussion of the coincidence of opposites in Habad speculation, see Moshe Hallamish, "The Theoretical System of R. Shneur Zalman of Liady (Its Sources in Kabbalah and Hasidism)," Ph.D. thesis, Hebrew University, 1976, 163–174 (Hebrew); Elior, *Paradoxical Ascent*, 25–31, 63–72.

69. Menachem Mendel Schneerson, *Torat Menaḥem: Hitwa'aduyyot 5745*, vol. 3 (Brooklyn: Lahak Hanochos, 1986), 1800.
70. See references in n. 68.
71. Schneerson, *Torat Menaḥem: Hitwa'aduyyot 5745*, vol. 3, 1800.
72. Menachem Mendel Schneersohn, *Derekh Miṣwotekha* (Brooklyn: Kehot, 1993), 121b.
73. Menachem Mendel Schneerson, *Qunṭres Inyanah shel Torat ha-Ḥasidut*, 20.
74. Many scholars have written on the apophatic elements of Maimonidean thought. For two recent treatments, see the innovative Wittgensteinian reading offered by Donald McCallum, *Maimonides' Guide for the Perplexed: Silence and Salvation* (London: Routledge, 2007), and Elliot R. Wolfson, "*Via Negativa* in Maimonides and Its Impact on Thirteenth-Century Kabbalah," *Maimonidean Studies* 5 (2008): 363–412 (a partial list of other scholarly contributions is given on 365–66 n. 6).
75. On the knowledge of God, the problem of attributes, and the *via negativa* in Habad thought, see Hallamish, "Theoretical System," 44–50. On the tendency to synchronize Maimonidean philosophy and Hasidic mysticism in the Lubavitch masters, see Jacob Gotlieb, "Habad's Harmonistic Approach to Maimonides," Ph.D. thesis, Bar-Ilan University, 2003 (Hebrew).
76. Shneur Zalman of Liadi, *Liqquṭei Amarim: Tanya*, pt. 4, 156b.
77. Shneur Zalman of Liadi, *Torah Or*, 111a. See also 55a.
78. Ibid., 66b.
79. Shneur Zalman's interpretation of the Lurianic concept of the break (*shevirah*) as the metaphoric trope to demarcate the transition from the aspect of boundlessness (*bilti ba'al gevul*) of the Infinite to the aspect of boundary (*gevul*) is expressed lucidly by his student Aaron Halevi Horowitz of Staroselye, *Sha'arei ha-Yiḥud we-ha-Emunah* (Shklov, 1820), pt. 3, 20b–21a: "Thus, in order for there be a disclosure of the potency for boundary in the power of the Infinite, blessed be he [*gilluy koaḥ ha-gevul she-be-khoḥo ha-ein sof barukh hu*], it was necessary for there to be the aspect of the break [*beḥinat shevirah*], that is, the light is removed so that there will be a disclosure from the aspect of the Infinite, blessed be he, so that there will be a place for the disclosure of the potency for boundary, for if there was not a removal of his light, blessed be he, in the aspect of the Infinite, then the boundary that is in his power, blessed be he, would not have been revealed even though in the power of his essence, blessed be he, everything was in complete equanimity." See Jacobs, *Seeker of Unity*, 90–112; Elior, *Theory of Divinity*, 72–73.
80. Shneur Zalman of Liadi, *Torah Or*, 111a.

81. The expression appears frequently in Habad literature. For example, see Shneur Zalman of Liadi, *Torah Or*, 22d, 90a, 90b, 90c, 92b, 109a, 109d, 114d; *Liqquṭei Torah*, vol. 1, Behar, 42b, 42d, Bemidbar, 12a, 12d; Dov Baer Schneersohn, *Shaʿarei Orah*, 35b, 39a, 54b, 55a, 56a, 79b, 124b; idem, *Shaʿarei Teshuvah*, 56d.
82. Shneur Zalman of Liadi, *Torah Or*, 111a.
83. Dov Baer Schneersohn, *Perush ha-Millot*, 79c.
84. Shneur Zalman of Liadi, *Liqquṭei Amarim: Tanya*, pt. 2, chap. 4, 79a. See also Menachem Mendel Schneerson, *Torat Menaḥem: Sefer ha-Maʾamarim Meluqaṭ*, vol. 2 (Brooklyn: Lahak Hanochos, 2002), 102.
85. Shneur Zalman of Liadi, *Torah Or*, 22c.
86. The conceptual point is bolstered by the numerological equivalence of the words *ha-ṭeva* (5 + 9 + 2 + 70 = 86) and *elohim* (1 + 30 + 5 + 10 + 40 = 86). Regarding the history of this numerology, see Moshe Idel, "*Deus sive Natura*—The Metamorphosis of a Dictum From Maimonides to Spinoza," in *Maimonides and the Sciences*, ed., Robert S. Cohen and Hillel Levine (Dordrecht: Kluwer Academic Publishers, 2000), 87–110.
87. Shneur Zalman of Liadi, *Liqquṭei Amarim: Tanya*, pt. 2, chap. 4, 78b–79a.
88. See n. 86.
89. Shneur Zalman of Liadi, *Liqquṭei Amarim: Tanya*, pt. 2, chap. 6, 80a–b.
90. Menachem Mendel Schneerson, *Torat Menaḥem: Sefer ha-Maʾamarim Meluqaṭ*, vol. 4 (Brooklyn: Lahak Hanochos, 2002), 114.
91. Ibid., 116.
92. Menachem Mendel Schneerson, *Sefer ha-Maʾamarim 5711, 5712, 5713*, 100.
93. Shalom Dovber Schneersohn, *Be-Shaʿah she-Hiqdimu 5672*, 2: 750, 751, 3:1404; Menachem Mendel Schneerson, *Torat Menaḥem: Hitwaʿaduyyot 5744*, vol. 1 (Brooklyn: Lahak Hanochos, 1990), 343. On occasion the abbreviated version *mafli laʿasot* is used. See Menachem Mendel Schneersohn, *Maʾamerei Admor ha-Ṣemaḥ Ṣedeq 5614–5615* (Brooklyn: Kehot, 1997), 214; Menachem Mendel Schneerson, *Torat Menaḥem: Hitwaʿaduyyot 5713*, vol. 3 (Brooklyn: Lahak Hanochos, 1998), 29.
94. Menachem Mendel Schneerson, *Sefer ha-Maʾamarim 5711, 5712, 5713*, 103.
95. Menachem Mendel Schneersohn, *Derekh Miṣwotekha*, 62a.
96. See, for instance, Lenn E. Goodman, "Maimonidean Naturalism," in *Maimonides and the Sciences*, 57–85.
97. Shneur Zalman of Liadi, *Maʾamerei Admor ha-Zaqen ha-Qeṣarim*, second edition (Brooklyn: Kehot, 1986), 469.
98. David R. Blumenthal, *Philosophic Mysticism: Studies in Rational Religion* (Ramat Gan: Bar-Ilan University Press, 2006).

99. Shneur Zalman of Liadi, *Liqquṭei Torah*, vol. 2, Shir ha-Shirim, 31b.

100. Menachem Mendel Schneersohn, *Derekh Miṣwotekha*, 71b. One should also bear in mind the two titles of another treatise by this author, *Sefer ha-Ḥaqirah* and *Derekh Emunah*. The implication of this dual title is that the exploration of creation, the central topic of the work, demands rational analysis (*ḥaqirah*) and belief (*emunah*). Not only are both necessary, but they are two sides of one coin or, utilizing a different metaphor, two byways on a single path that one must traverse. It is important to recall that, in spite of his philosophical inclinations, the Tzemach Tzedek was a strong opponent to the *haskalah*, Jewish enlightenment movement. The historical recounting of this opposition is the subject of the pamphlet by Yosef Yitzchak Schneersohn, *Admor ha-Ṣemaḥ Ṣedeq u-Tenuʿat ha-Haskalah* (Brooklyn: Oṣar ha-Ḥasidim, 1973), reprinted in Menachem Mendel Schneersohn, *Sefer ha-Ḥaqirah* (Brooklyn: Kehot, 1993), 427–79. Needless to say, the enlightenment is rejected not because of the value it placed on reason as an arbiter of truth but because of the secularization of reason and the consequent elimination of any place for faith in the equation. The faith affirmed by the Tzemach Tzedek, however, is not antithetical to reason, at least not in the way that he construes the intellectual capacity of the human soul, and one can even conjecture that the Habad emphasis on faith and reason is, at least in part, a response to the separation between the two suggested by Haskalah philosophers. The charge of rationalism against Habad by other Hasidic masters can also be seen in this light, as noted by Loewenthal, *Communicating the Infinite*, 173–75.

101. For discussion of some of the relevant Habad sources, see Elliot R. Wolfson, *Alef, Mem, Tau: Kabbalistic Musings in Time, Truth, and Death* (Berkeley: University of California Press, 2006), 107–17.

102. Menachem Mendel Schneersohn, *Derekh Miṣwotekha*, 72a.

103. *Tiqqunei Zohar*, ed., Reuven Margaliot (Jerusalem: Mosad ha-Rav Kook, 1978), Introduction, 17a, and see also the editor's note, ibid., sec. 70, 121a.

104. Menachem Mendel Schneersohn, *Derekh Miṣwotekha*, 71b.

105. Menachem Mendel Schneerson, *Iggerot Qodesh*, vol. 12 (Brooklyn: Kehot, 1989), 306–7.

106. Zohar 2:25a.

107. Herbert A. Davidson, "The Study of Philosophy as a Religious Obligation," in *Religion in a Religious Age: Proceedings of Regional Conferences Held at the University of California, Los Angeles, and Brandeis University in April, 1973*, ed. Sholmo D. Goiten (Cambridge, Mass.: Association for Jewish Studies, 1974), 53–68.

108. Shneur Zalman of Liadi, *Liqquṭei Amarim: Tanya*, pt. 4, chap. 19, 128a.

109. Shneur Zalman of Liadi, *Torah Or*, 11a. According to this passage, Abraham figuratively represents this aspect of intellect that is above rational comprehension.

110. Dov Baer Schneersohn, *Sha'arei Orah*, 63b.

111. Menachem Mendel Schneersohn, *Derekh Miṣwotekha*, 27b.

112. Menachem Mendel Schneersohn, *Or ha-Torah: Bemidbar*, vol. 3 (Brooklyn: Kehot, 1998), 1030. See also Shmuel Schneersohn, *Liqquṭei Torah: Torat Shmu'el 5633*, vol. 1 (Brooklyn: Kehot, 1994), 224, where mention is made of the "supernal knowledge before which everything is considered as naught" (*de'ah elyonah de-kholla qameih ke-lo ḥashiv*). The latter expression, which appears frequently in Habad literature, is based on Daniel 4:32.

113. Maimonides, *Mishneh Torah*, Yesodei Torah 2:10.

114. Dov Baer Schneersohn, *Torat Ḥayyim: Shemot*, 279c.

115. The language is closest to *Zohar* 2:60a. See Isaiah Tishby, *The Wisdom of the Zohar: An Anthology of Texts*, translated by David Goldstein (Oxford: Oxford University Press, 1989), 1085–86.

116. The reference is to a passage from the *Mishneh Torah* (see above, n. 113), which Shneur Zalman cites and interprets in *Liqquṭei Amarim: Tanya*, pt. 1, chap. 2, 6a–7a.

117. Shneur Zalman of Liadi, *Liqquṭei Amarim: Tanya*, pt. 1, chap. 4, 8a–b.

118. See, for instance, Shneur Zalman of Liadi, *Liqquṭei Amarim: Tanya*, pt. 4, chap. 18, 127a.

119. Shneur Zalman of Liadi, *Liqquṭei Amarim: Tanya*, pt. 3, chap. 7, 84a.

120. Shneur Zalman of Liadi, *Torah Or*, 110b.

121. *Zohar* 1:15a.

122. Shneur Zalman of Liadi, *Ma'amerei Admor ha-Zaqen 5567* (Brooklyn: Kehot, 1979), 392. See Loewenthal, *Communicating the Infinite*, 155. On the world being sustained through the letters by means of which it was created, see idem, *Liqquṭei Amarim: Tanya*, pt. 2, chap. 1, 76b–77a, which Idel, *Hasidism*, 216–17, presents as an example of "immanentist linguistic" orientation.

123. Elliot R. Wolfson, "Imago Templi and the Meeting of the Two Seas: Liturgical Time-Space and the Feminine Imaginary in Zoharic Kabbalah," *Res* 51 (2007): 125: "In the cultural ambiance of medieval kabbalah, language performs this function by expressing the inexpressible, rendering the invisible visible. The symbol brings the unknown into relation with the known, but without reducing the difference that binds the two incongruities into a selfsame identity. In the kabbalistic mind-set, accordingly, every signified becomes a signifier vis-à-vis another signified, which quickly turns into another signifier, and so on *ad infinitum*, in an endless string that winds its way

finally to the in/significant, which may be viewed either as the signified to which no signifier can be affixed or the signifier to which no signified can be assigned."

124. Shneur Zalman of Liadi, *Liqquṭei Torah*, vol. 1, Behar, 43b–c.
125. Dov Baer Schneersohn, *Torat Ḥayyim: Shemot*, 370c.
126. The source for the image of the curtain that divides is Hayyim Vital, *Eṣ Ḥayyim* (Jerusalem, 1963), 8:2, 36a: "After he constricted himself [*ṣimṣem aṣmo*], he left a curtain in the middle of his body, in the place of the navel, in order to create a barrier in the middle, and this is the secret of 'Let there be a firmament in the midst of the waters, and it shall separate the water from the water' (Gen 1:6)." On the identification of the curtain (*parsa*) as the parable (*mashal*), see Aaron Halevi Horowitz of Staroselye, *Shaʿarei ha-Yiḥud we-ha-Emunah* (Shklov, 1820), pt. 2, 19b–20a. See Elior, *Theory of Divinity*, 31–32. The metaphoric use of the image of the curtain to depict the nature of metaphor is related to the act of concealing (*hastarah*), which is connected to the former. On the image of the curtain (*parsa*) and the process of constriction (*ṣimṣum*), see Menachem Mendel Schneerson, *Torat Menaḥem: Hitwaʿaduyyot 5713*, vol. 3 (Brooklyn: Lahak Hanochos, 1998), 78.
127. Dov Baer Schneersohn, *Torat Ḥayyim: Shemot*, 194d. For further discussion of the status of the primordial Torah and the essence of the Infinite (*aṣmut ein sof*), see ibid., 183a–d, 370b–c.
128. Shneur Zalman of Liadi, *Liqquṭei Amarim: Tanya*, pt. 1, chap. 35, 44b.
129. Shalom Dovber Schneersohn, *Be-Shaʿah she-Hiqdimu 5672*, 3:1404.
130. Shneur Zalman of Liadi, *Torah Or*, 42b.
131. Yosef Yitzchak Schneersohn, *Sefer ha-Maʾamarim—Qunṭreisim*, vol. 1 (Brooklyn: Kehot, 1962), 204. The text, which is a meditation on the central tenet of Jewish monotheism, the proclamation of God's unity (Deut 6:4), was a discourse delivered in conjunction with 12–13 Tamuz 5790 (1930), the festival of redemption (*ḥag ha-geʾulah*) that commemorates his own release from imprisonment on 12–13 Tamuz 5687 (12–13 July 1927). Coincidentally, the sixth Rebbe's date of birth was 12 Tamuz 5640 (21 June 1880). On the depiction of the divine as being beyond time and place, see Shmuel Schneersohn, *Liqquṭei Torah: Torat Shmuʾel 5627* (Brooklyn: Kehot, 2000), 224. According to that passage, the eradication of the temporal and spatial is implied in the notion of God's unity, which is signified by the word *eḥad*. On the application of the term *yaḥid u-meyuḥad* to the divine prior to and after the creation, see Shneur Zalman of Liadi, *Liqquṭei Amarim: Tanya*, pt. 3, chap. 6, 110a.

132. Shneur Zalman of Liadi, *Torah Or*, 98b.
133. Wolfson, *Language, Eros, Being*, 190–260.
134. Elliot R. Wolfson, "Suffering Eros and Textual Incarnation: A Kristevan Reading of Kabbalistic Poetics," in *Theology of Eros: Transfiguring Passion at the Limits of Discipline*, ed. Virginia Burrus and Catherine Keller (New York: Fordham University Press, 2006), 341–65, esp. 342–53.
135. Menachem Mendel Schneerson, *Sefer ha-Ma'amarim: Ba'ti le-Ganni*, vol. 1 (Brooklyn: Kehot, 1988), 195. On the image of the primordial parable (*meshal ha-qadmoni*) in the teaching of Schneerson, see Dahan, "Dira Bataḥtonim," 59–64.
136. Kraus, "Living with the Times," 97–105; idem, *The Seventh*, 36–40; Dahan, "Dira Bataḥtonim," 147–196; Max Kohanzad, "The Messianic Doctrine of the Lubavitcher Rebbe, Rabbi Menachem Mendel Schneerson (1902–1994)," Ph.D. thesis, University of Manchester, 2006, 152–69.
137. Shneur Zalman of Liadi, *Ma'amerei Admor ha-Zaqen 5571*, 137.
138. Based on the formulation in *Tiqqunei Zohar*, Introduction, 5b.
139. This expression of Shneur Zalman (see following note) is based on the description of the *sefirot* of the world of emanation *Tiqqunei Zohar*, Introduction, 3b: *malka behon ihu we-garmeih ḥad behon ihu we-ḥayyoi ḥad behon*, "The king is in them, he and his self are one in them, he and his vitality are one in them." It is likely, however, that Shneur Zalman was more directly influenced by the paraphrase of the zoharic passage in Vital, *Eṣ Ḥayyim*, 42:4, 91c. In that context, Vital states that wisdom is the life (*ḥayyah*) that infuses all of the worlds, a theme that is central to Shneur Zalman's orientation as well.
140. Shneur Zalman of Liadi, *Torah Or*, 43b.
141. For discussion of the role of *mashal* in Dov Baer's thought, see Loewenthal, *Communicating the Infinite*, 154–57, 167–73.
142. Three studies that amply demonstrate the point are Loewenthal, *Communicating the Infinite*; Elior, *Paradoxical Ascent*; and Roman A. Foxbrunner, *Ḥabad: The Hasidism of R. Shneur Zalman of Lyady* (Northvale, N.J.: Jason Aronson, 1993).
143. For a lucid articulation, see Shneur Zalman of Liadi, *Torah Or*, 5d–6a; idem, *Liqquṭei Torah*, vol. 1, Shelaḥ, 37b–c. Countless other sources could have been cited.
144. Aviezer Ravitzky, *Messianism, Zionism, and Jewish Religious Radicalism*, trans. Michael Swirsky and Jonathan Chipman (Chicago: University of Chicago Press, 1996), 199, and, in much greater detail, Kraus, "Living with the

Times," and idem, *The Seventh.* On the controversies surrounding Habad Messianism, see also Menachem Friedman, "Habad as Messianic Fundamentalism: From Local Particularism to Universal Mission," in *The Fundamentalism Project*, ed. Martin E. Marty and R. Scott Appleby, vol. 4 (Chicago: University of Chicago Press, 1994), 328–57; idem, "Messiah and Messianism in Habad-Lubavitch Hasidism," in *The War of Gog and Magog: Messianism and Apocalypticism in Judaism in the Past and in the Present,* ed. David Ariel-Joel (Tel Aviv: Yedi'ot Aḥaronot–Sifrei Ḥemed, 2001), 174–229 (Hebrew); Naftali Loewenthal, "The Neutralisation of Messianism and the Apocalypse," in *Jerusalem Studies in Jewish Thought* 13 [*Rivkah Shatz-Uffenheimer Memorial Volume*] (1996): 59–73 (English section); idem, "Contemporary Habad and the Paradox of Redemption," in *Perspectives on Jewish Thought and Mysticism*, ed. Alfred L. Ivry, Elliot R. Wolfson, and Allan Arkush (Australia: Harwood Academic, 1998), 381–402; Aviezer Ravitzky, "The Messianism of Success in Contemporary Judaism," in *The Encyclopedia of Apocalypticism, Volume 3: Apocalypticism in the Modern Period and the Contemporary Age*, ed. Stephen J. Stein (New York: Continuum, 1998), 204–29; Rachel Elior, "The Lubavitch Messianic Resurgence: The Historical and Mystical Background, 1939–1996," in *Toward the Millennium: Messianic Expectations from the Bible to Waco*, ed. Peter Schäfer and Mark R. Cohen (Leiden: Brill, 1998), 383–408; David Berger, *The Rebbe, the Messiah, and the Scandal of Orthodox Indifference* (London: Littman Library of Jewish Civilization, 2001); Joel Marcus, "The Once and Future Messiah in Early Christianity and Chabad," *New Testament Studies* 47 (2001): 381–401; Shelly Goldberg, "The Zaddik's Soul after His 'Histalkut' (Death): Continuity and Change in the Writings of 'Nesiey' (Presidents of) Habad" (Ph.D. diss., Bar-Ilan University, 2003 [Hebrew]); Jan Feldman, *Lubavitchers as Citizens: A Paradox of Liberal Democracy* (Ithaca, N.Y.: Cornell University Press, 2003), 33–37.

145. Gershom Scholem, *The Messianic Idea in Judaism and Other Essays on Jewish Spirituality* (New York: Schocken Books, 1971), 223–27. Elior, "Ḥabad," 163–64, delineated seven "basic axioms concerning the relationship between God and world" in Habad: pantheism, acosmism, creation, immanence, panentheism, the world as manifestation of God, dialectical reciprocity between God and world such that the former has no separate existence without the latter.

146. Shneur Zalman of Liadi, *Torah Or*, 55c, 98b.

147. Yosef Yitzchak Schneersohn, *Sefer ha-Ma'amarim—Quntreisim*, vol. 1, 204. On the distinction between *yaḥid* and *eḥad*, see Shneur Zalman, *Torah Or*, 55b; Menachem Mendel Schneersohn, *Derekh Miṣwotekha*, 124a; Menachem

Mendel Schneerson, *Torat Menaḥem: Hitwaʿaduyyot 5712*, vol. 2 (Brooklyn: Lahak Hanochos, 1996), 200–1.

148. On the numerology of *elohim* and *ha-ṭeva*, see above, n. 86.
149. Yosef Yitzchak Schneersohn, *Sefer ha-Maʾamarim—Qunṭreisim*, vol. 1, 204.
150. Shneur Zalman of Liadi, *Liqquṭei Amarim: Tanya*, pt. 2, chap. 7, 82a–b.
151. Menachem Mendel Schneerson, *Iggerot Qodesh*, vol. 2 (Brooklyn: Kehot, 1987), 392. See n. 39 above.
152. Menachem Mendel Schneersohn, *Or ha-Torah: Siddur Tefillah* (Brooklyn: Kehot, 1984), 364.
153. Menachem Mendel Schneerson, *Torat Menaḥem: Sefer ha-Maʾamarim Meluqaṭ*, vol. 4, 119.
154. Menaḥem Mendel Schneerson, *Torat Menaḥem: Hitwaʿaduyyot 5715*, vol. 1 (Brooklyn: Vaad Hanochos BLahak, 1999), 127–28.
155. Catherine Keller, *Face of the Deep: A Theology of Becoming* (New York: Routledge, 2003), 219. My gratitude to Virginia Burrus for calling my attention to Keller's evocative discussion, which has helped me sort out my understanding of the complex cosmological patterns found in Habad.
156. The decoding of the word *ḥokhmah* as *koaḥ mah* to indicate the hylic nature of divine wisdom is attested already in kabbalistic sources from the thirteenth and fourteenth centuries. See, for example, Azriel of Gerona, *Commentary on Talmudic Aggadoth*, ed. Isaiah Tishby (Jerusalem: Magnes, 1983), 84 and 111; *Zohar* 3:28a (*Raʿaya Meheimna*), 220b, 235b (*Raʿaya Meheimna*); *Tiqqunei Zohar*, Introduction, 4a; sec. 19, 40a; sec. 69, 99b, 102b, 112b. This *jeu de mots* appears frequently in Habad literature, and here I offer only a small sampling from the writings of Shneur Zalman of Liadi: *Liqquṭei Amarim: Tanya*, pt. 1, chap. 3, 7b; idem, *Torah Or*, 12d, 73d; idem, *Liqquṭei Torah*, vol. 1, Pequdei, 6b, 8b, Aḥarei, 27c; Bemidbar 14a; Qoraḥ 55b; Ḥuqat 61a; Maṭot 87b; Masʿei 90a; vol. 2, Eqev 16c, 17d; Reʾeh 29b; Ki Teṣe 37b; Derushim le-Rosh ha-Shanah 56b; Haʾazinu 77c; Shir ha-Shirim 26d.
157. Shneur Zalman of Liadi, *Torah Or*, 61b; idem, *Liqquṭei Torah*, vol. 1, Shelaḥ, 46d; vol. 2, Reʾeh, 19c.
158. Elior, *Paradoxical Ascent*, 62, seems to be expressing a similar sentiment: "However, Hasidic thought is strained to the ultimate stage in a dialectical way, just as there is no separate reality and no discriminate essence in the world without God, so also God has no revealed and discriminate existence without the world. That is, just as one cannot speak of the existence of the world without God, so too one cannot speak of the existence of God without the world."
159. Shneur Zalman of Liadi, *Liqquṭei Torah*, vol. 2, Devarim, 42d, 43c.

160. Shmuel Schneersohn, *Liqquṭei Torah: Torah Shmu'el 5633*, vol. 1, 284. See idem, *Liqquṭei Torah: Torah Shmu'el 5631*, vol. 1 (Brooklyn: Kehot, 2004), 132; idem, *Liqquṭei Torah: Torah Shmu'el 5633*, vol. 2 (Brooklyn: Kehot, 1994), 498–99.
161. The allusion is to the Lurianic doctrine of the trace or vestige (*reshimu*) of light that remains in the space from which the Infinite withdraws its light. From that residue, the aspect of the shell, which is the darkness that stands over and against the light, eventually comes forth from that trace, but in its root, it is itself light. On the Lurianic conception of the *reshimu*, see Scholem, *Major Trends in Jewish Mysticism*, 264; Isaiah Tishby, *The Doctrine of Evil and the "Kelippah" in Lurianic Kabbalism* (Jerusalem: Magnes Press, 1984), 24–25 (Hebrew); Lawrence Fine, *Physician of the Soul, Healer of the Cosmos: Isaac Luria and His Kabbalistic Fellowship* (Stanford, Calif.: Stanford University Press, 2003), 130–31, 147–48. For a different emphasis, see Wolfson, "Suffering Eros," 362–65.
162. Shalom Dovber Schneersohn, *Be-Sha'ah she-Hiqdimu 5672*, 1:257; see also 3:1346.
163. Menaḥem Mendel Schneerson, *Torat Menaḥem: Hitwa'aduyyot 5711*, vol. 1, 202.
164. Shneur Zalman of Liadi, *Torah Or*, 12a–b, 46b, 63a.
165. Shneur Zalman of Liadi, *Liqquṭei Amarim: Tanya*, pt. 1, chap. 33, 42a.
166. Shneur Zalman of Liadi, *Liqquṭei Torah*, vol. 1, Bemidbar, 18d.
167. The identification of nature as an expression of the divine is reinforced by the numerical equivalence of the name *elohim* (1 + 30 + 5 + 10 + 40 = 86) and the word *ha-ṭeva* (5 + 9 + 2 + 70 = 86).
168. Shneur Zalman of Liadi, *Liqquṭei Amarim: Tanya*, pt. 3, chap. 29, 149b. On the future disclosure of the "substance of the supernal delight" (*mahut ta'anug ha-elyon*), which is linked exegetically to the verse "Oh, give me of the kisses of your mouth" (Song 1:2), see Shneur Zalman of Liadi, *Torah Or*, 8c. On the role of eros in Ḥasidic lore, with special reference to the concept of delight (*ta'anug*), see Idel, *Hasidism*, 133–140, 234–235; idem, *Kabbalah and Eros* (New Haven: Yale University Press, 2005), 228–229; idem, "Ta'anug: Erotic Delights From Kabbalah to Hasidism," in *Hidden Intercourse: Eros and Sexuality in the History of Western Esotericism*, ed. Wouter J. Hanegraaff and Jeffrey J. Kripal (Leiden: Brill, 2008), 131–145.
169. Elliot R. Wolfson, *Circle in the Square: Studies in the Use of Gender in Kabbalistic Symbolism* (Albany: State University of New York Press, 1995), 69–72, 189–92 nn. 174–80.
170. Shneur Zalman of Liadi, *Liqquṭei Torah*, vol. 1, Bemidbar, 18c.

171. Shneur Zalman of Liadi, *Torah Or*, 22c.
172. On the distinction between *ithafpkha* and *itkafya*, especially in the seventh Rebbe's thought, see Hallamish, "Theoretical System," 374–82; Goldberg, "Zaddik's Soul," 176–77; Dahan, "Dira Bataḥtonim," 119–28; Levin, *Heaven on Earth*, 65–71.
173. On the distinction between "origin" and "beginning" in early kabbalistic symbolism, see Wolfson, *Alef, Mem, Tau,* 119–26; Cristina Ciucu, "Neo-Platonism and the Cabalistic Structure of the Divine Emanation," *Echinox Notebooks* 12 (2007): 184–93.
174. Menachem Mendel Schneerson, *Qunṭres Inyanah shel Torat ha-Ḥasidut*, 20.
175. See Shneur Zalman of Liadi, *Liqquṭei Torah*, vol. 1, Shemini, 18b; Menachem Mendel Schneerson, *Torat Menaḥem: Hitwaʿaduyyot 5712*, vol. 2, 162.
176. Menachem Mendel Schneerson, *Torat Menaḥem: Hitwaʿaduyyot 5713*, vol. 3, 80.
177. Ibid.
178. Scholem, *Messianic Idea*, 224. See Jacobs, *Seeker of Unity,* 65–66, who expressed the view that the Habad interpretation of the Lurianic conception of divine withdrawal is reminiscent of Far-Eastern notions on the illusory nature of the universe.
179. Menachem Mendel Schneerson, *Reshimot*, vol. 4 (Brooklyn: Kehot, 2003), sec. 136, 238.
180. Shneur Zalman of Liadi, *Torah Or*, 18d.
181. The expression to denote the indifference, *shaweh u-mashweh*, is derived from the description of God's judicial impartiality as *ha-shaweh u-mashweh qaṭon we-gadol*, "he renders the small and great as equal," in the liturgical poem *ha-oḥez be-yad middat mishpaṭ*, composed by the sixth-century Palestinian poet Yannai. See *Piyyute Yannai: Liturgical Poems of Yannai*, ed. Menahem Zulay (Berlin: Schocken, 1938), 338 (Hebrew).
182. This is the view of Lurianic kabbalah promulgated by Scholem, *Major Trends in Jewish Mysticism*, 274. For a critique of Scholem, see Dahan, "Dira Bataḥtonim," 197 n. 1.
183. Menachem Mendel Schneerson, *Torat Menaḥem: Hitwaʿaduyyot 5712*, vol. 2, 201.
184. Menachem Mendel Schneerson, *Torat Menaḥem: Hitwaʿaduyot 5750*, vol. 3 (Brooklyn: Lahak Hanochos, 1991), 21.
185. Yosef Yitzchak Schneersohn, *Sefer ha-Maʾamarim 5700* (Brooklyn: Kehot, 1986), 26.
186. Dov Baer Schneersohn, *Torat Ḥayyim: Bereʾshit*, 134a; Menachem Mendel Schneerson, *Torat Menaḥem: Hitwaʿaduyyot 5713*, vol. 3, 79.

187. On the portrayal of the revelation of God as one in which the visual and auditory modes are not differentiated, see Shmuel Schneersohn, *Liqquṭei Torah: Torat Shmuʾel 5627*, 118. The separation of vision and hearing is indicative of an exilic state.

188. Loewenthal, *Communicating the Infinite*, 137.

189. Dov Baer Schneersohn, *Shaʿarei Orah*, 59b.

190. Menachem Mendel Schneerson, *Liqquṭei Siḥot*, vol. 17 (Brooklyn: Kehot, 2000), 92–99, esp. 93. These descriptions are taken from a literary account of talks given by the Rebbe in 5731 (1971) and 5736 (1976) on the Sabbath when the section Shemini (Lev 9:1–11:47) was read liturgically. As one would expect from the fact that the narrative in the Torah portion is set on the eighth day after the dedication of the Tabernacle, the focus of the meditation is on the number eight, in particular its messianic valence, inspired by the rabbinic tradition that the harp of David had seven strings in contrast to the harp of the Messiah, which has eight strings. See Menachem Mendel Schneerson, *Torat Menaḥem: Hitwaʿaduyyot 5748*, vol. 2 (Brooklyn: Lahak Hanochos, 1990), 115–16. On the topos of the messianic harp, see Louis Ginzberg, *The Legends of the Jews* (Philadelphia: Jewish Publication Society of America, 1968), 6:262 n. 81. The eschatological significance of the number eight is obviously not unique to Habad hasidism, or even to hasidism more generally, as it assumed that relevance in much earlier kabbalistic sources, reflected, for instance, in the identification of *Binah*, the eighth emanation counting from the bottom, as the world-to-come. The messianic import of the number is also enhanced by the identification of *Yesod*, the eighth emanation counting from *Ḥokhmah* downward, as the *ṣaddiq*, the righteous one, who is the foundation of the world (Prov 10:25). For an alternative illustration of this symbolism, see Elliot R. Wolfson, "The Cut That Binds: Time, Memory, and the Ascetic Impulse (Reflections on Bratslav Hasidism)," in *God's Voice from the Void: Old and New Studies in Bratslav Hasidism*, ed. Shaul Magid (Albany: State University of New York Press, 2002), 103–54.

191. Dov Baer Schneersohn, *Torat Ḥayyim: Bereʾshit*, 185a. In that context, the "essential nothing" (*ha-ayin ha-aṣmi*) is classified as one of two aspects of the "aspect of nothingness" (*beḥinat ha-ayin*), the other being the "nothing of the something" (*ayin shel ha-yesh*). The latter is further delineated as the darkness that God places as his mystery (Ps 18:12) or the darkness that precedes the light of creation (Babylonian Talmud, Shabbat 77b), the aspect of the withdrawal (*beḥinat ha-ṣimṣum*), which is linked to the name *elohim* or to the attribute of judgment. On the use of the term *ha-ayin ha-aṣmi,* see also ibid., 18c, 27b, 48b, 65c.

192. Yosef Yitzchak Schneersohn, *Sefer ha-Maʾamarim 5689* (Brooklyn: Kehot, 1990), 64. The expression *heʿlem ha-aṣmi* is used frequently by exponents of Habad philosophy. See, for instance, Dov Baer Schneersohn, *Shaʿarei Orah*, 111a, 134a; idem, *Torat Ḥayyim: Bereʾshit*, 161b; idem, Dov Baer Schneersohn, *Torat Ḥayyim: Shemot*, 96b, 229b, 298b; idem, *Perush ha-Millot*, 26c, 69d, 103d; idem, *Derushei Ḥatunah*, vol. 2 (Brooklyn: Kehot, 1991), 476; Shmuel Schneersohn, *Liqquṭei Torah: Torat Shmuʾel 5627*, 412; idem, *Liqquṭei Torah: Torat Shmuʾel 5632*, vol. 1 (Brooklyn: Kehot, 1999), 136, 137; idem, *Liqquṭei Torah: Torat Shmuʾel 5633*, vol. 2 (Brooklyn: Kehot, 1994), 510; Shalom Dovber Schneersohn, *Be-Shaʿah she-Hiqdimu 5672*, 1: 82, 404, 417, 420, 421, 460, 461, 474, 482, 586, 2: 644, 663. 900, 905, 906, 3: 1270, 1271, 1276, 1277, 1287, 1298, 1299; Menachem Mendel Schneerson, *Torat Menaḥem: Hitwaʿaduyyot 5712*, vol. 2, 179; idem, *Torat Menaḥem: Hitwaʿaduyyot 5712*, vol. 1 (Brooklyn: Lahak Hanochos, 1997), 129; idem, *Torat Menaḥem: Hitwaʿaduyyot 5713*, vol. 2 (Brooklyn: Lahak Hanochos, 1997), 113; idem, *Torat Menaḥem: Sefer ha-Maʾamarim 5714* (Brooklyn: Vaad Hanochos BLahak, 2006), 9, 41–42.
193. Shneur Zalman of Liadi, *Liqquṭei Torah*, vol. 1, Pequdei, 3d. The idea is linked exegetically to the verse *yashet ḥoshekh sitro* (Ps 18:12), which is rendered theopoetically as "He made darkness his mystery," and to the rabbinic dictum describing the creation "at first darkness and afterwards light," *be-reisha ḥashokha we-hadar nehora* (Babylonian Talmud, Shabbat 77b).
194. Yitzchak Schneersohn, *Sefer ha-Siḥot 5688–5691* (Brooklyn: Kehot, 2002), 153.
195. Menachem Mendel Schneerson, *Liqquṭei Siḥot*, vol. 17, 95.
196. Menachem Mendel Schneerson, *Torat Menaḥem: Sefer ha-Maʾamarim Meluqaṭ*, vol. 2, 102–3.
197. Joseph Ben-Shlomo, *The Mystical Theology of Moses Cordovero* (Jerusalem: Mosad Bialik, 1965), 95–100 (Hebrew); Elliot R. Wolfson, "Divine Suffering and the Hermeneutics of Reading: Philosophical Reflections on Lurianic Mythology," in *Suffering Religion*, ed. Robert Gibbs and Elliot R. Wolfson (New York: Routledge, 2002), 110–15; idem, *Language, Eros, Being*, 27. For the impact of the dialectic of disclosure and concealment on Habad, see Elior, *Theory of Divinity*, 67–71; idem, *Paradoxical Ascent*, 116–17, 121–22.
198. Menachem Mendel Schneerson, *Iggerot Qodesh*, vol. 18 (Brooklyn: Kehot, 2003), 281.
199. Shneur Zalman of Liadi, *Liqquṭei Torah*, vol. 2, 62a.
200. As I have noted elsewhere, this way of thinking brings to mind the Heideggerian *Lichtung*, which similarly is imagined to be a clearing that manifests by concealing; this clearing is the mythopoeic equivalent to the scientific category of world. See Wolfson, "Divine Suffering," 154 n. 112; idem, *Language, Eros, Being*, 18–19, 412 n. 155.

201. Shneur Zalman of Liadi, *Liqquṭei Amarim: Tanya*, pt. 1, chap. 21, 27a. For a slightly better reading, see idem, *Liqqutei Amarim—First Edition (Based on the Earliest Manuscripts)* (Brooklyn: Kehot, 1981), 151–52.
202. *Zohar* 1:11b.
203. Yosef Yitzchak Schneersohn, *Sefer ha-Maʾamarim 5700*, 24.
204. Dov Baer Schneersohn, *Shaʿarei Orah*, 86b; idem, *Shaʿarei Teshuvah*, 12b; Menachem Mendel Schneerson, *Torat Menaḥem: Hitwaʿaduyyot 5712*, vol. 1, 6.
205. Yosef Yitzchak Schneersohn, *Sefer ha-Maʾamarim 5700*, 22.
206. On the thematic and linguistic link between the traditional expression "yoke of the kingdom of heaven" (*ol malkhut ha-shamayim*) and the kabbalistic symbol of the "kingship of the Infinite" (*malkhut de-ein sof*), see Shmuel Schneersohn, *Liqquṭei Torah: Torat Shmuʾel 5629* (Brooklyn: Kehot, 1992), 246.
207. Menachem Mendel Schneerson, *Torat Menaḥem: Hitwaʿaduyyot 5712*, vol. 2, 168.
208. Menachem Mendel Schneersohn, *Derekh Miṣwotekha*, 136a.
209. *Pirqei Rabbi Eliʾezer* (Warsaw, 1852), chap. 3, 5b.
210. Shneur Zalman of Liadi, *Liqquṭei Torah*, vol. 2, Shir ha-Shirim, 5a. The potentiality of the divine to emanate its light is identified as "the aspect of his name that is contained in his essence" (*shemo ha-kalul be-aṣmuto*). See also Shalom Dov Baer Schneersohn, *Be-Shaʿah she-Hiqdimu 5672*, 1: 138, 139, 417, 569, 3:1270, 1287, 1346, 1407, 1408, 1415, 1421, 1422, 1423.
211. Menachem Mendel Schneerson, *Sefer ha-Maʾamarim 11 Nisan*, vol. 2 (Brooklyn: Kehot, 1999), 398.
212. Menachem Mendel Schneerson, *Torat Menaḥem: Hitwaʿaduyyot 5712*, vol. 2, 165.
213. Yosef Yitzchak Schneersohn, *Sefer ha-Maʾamarim 5700* , 23.
214. Ibid., 21.
215. On occasion the expression *heʿlem de-heʿlem*, "concealment of concealment," designates the Infinite in its essential hiddenness. See Dov Baer Schneersohn, *Perush ha-Millot*, 24a.
216. Aaron Halevi Horowitz of Staroselye, *Shaʿar ha-Tefillah* (Jerusalem: Maqor, 1972), 49a.
217. Aaron Halevi Horowitz of Staroselye, *Shaʿarei Avodah*, pt. 1, chap. 32, 44a.
218. There are numerous studies of the Mādhyamika, the Mahāyāna Buddhist school of the middle. I will mention here only a few examples that have been useful to me as a nonspecialist: Theodore Stcherbatsky, *The Conception of Buddhist Nirvāna* (New York: Samuel Weiser, 1968), 36–44; David J. Kalupahana, *Nāgārjuna: The Philosophy of the Middle Way* (Albany: State University of New York Press, 1986); C. W. Huntington Jr. with Geshé Namgyal

Wangchen, *The Emptiness of Emptiness: An Introduction to Early Indian Mādhyamika* (Honolulu: University of Hawaii Press, 1989); Tachikawa Musashi, "Mahāyāna Philosophies: The Mādhyamika Tradition," in *Buddhist Spirituality: Indian, Southeast Asian, Tibetan, Early Chinese*, ed. Takeuchi Yoshinori, in association with Jan Van Bragt, James W. Heisig, Joseph S. O'Leary, and Paul L. Swanson (New York: Crossroad, 1993), 188–202; Thomas E. Wood, *Mind Only: A Philosophical and Doctrinal Analysis of the Vijñānavāda* (Honolulu: University of Hawaii Press, 1991); idem, *Nāgārjunian Disputations: A Philosophical Journey through an Indian Looking-Glass* (Honolulu: University of Hawaii Press, 1994); *The Fundamental Wisdom of the Middle Way: Nāgārjuna's Mūlamadhyamakakārikā*, trans. and commentary by Jay L. Garfield (Oxford: Oxford University Press, 1995); David Burton, *Emptiness Appraised: A Critical Study of Nāgārjuna's Philosophy* (London: RoutledgeCurzon, 1999); Elizabeth Napper, *Dependent-Arising: A Tibetan Buddhist Interpretation of Mādhyamika Philosophy Emphasizing the Compatibility of Emptiness and Conventional Phenomena* (Boston: Wisdom Publications, 2003). For a lucid discussion of the Mādhyamika logic, see Matthew Bagger, *The Uses of Paradox (Religion, Self-Transformation, and the Absurd)* (New York: Columbia University Press, 2007).

219. Shōryū Katsura, "Nāgārjuna and the Tetralemma (*Catuṣkoṭi*)," in *Wisdom, Compassion, and the Search for Understanding: The Buddhist Studies Legacy of Gadjin M. Nagao*, ed. Jonathan A. Silk (Honolulu: University of Hawaii Press, 2000), 201–20; Jay L. Garfield, *Empty Words: Buddhist Philosophy and Cross-Cultural Interpretation* (Oxford: Oxford University Press, 2002), 99–104.

220. My attempt to interpret the Habad material through the prism of the *madhyamaka* shares the same methodological orientation of scholars of Mahāyāna Buddhism, who have compared the tetralemma logic to Derridean deconstruction, especially to his conception of the tetrapharmakon. For a representative list of relevant studies, see Robert Magliola, *Derrida on the Mend* (West Lafayette, Ind.: Purdue University Press, 1984); David Loy, *Nonduality: A Study in Comparative Philosophy* (New Haven, Conn.: Yale University Press, 1988), 248–60; idem, "The Deconstruction of Buddhism," in *Derrida and Negative Theology*, ed. Harold Coward and Toby Foshay (Albany: State University of New York Press, 1992), 227–53; Carl Olson, *Zen and the Art of Postmodern Philosophy: Two Paths of Liberation from the Representational Mode of Thinking* (Albany: State University of New York Press, 2000); idem, *Indian Philosophers and Postmodern Thinkers: Dialogues on the Margins of Culture* (Oxford: Oxford University Press, 2002); Youxuan Wang, *Buddhism and Deconstruction: Towards a Comparative Semiotics* (Richmond, U.K.: Curzon

Press. 2001); and the essays in *Buddhisms and Deconstructions*, ed. Jin Y. Park, afterword by Robert Magliola (Lanham, Md.: Rowman & Littlefield, 2006). The reader should be apprised of the select bibliography prepared by William Edelglass in *Buddhisms and Deconstructions*, 271–79. For a different approach, which is based on a comparison of the Buddhist Centrist philosophy (especially as it is enunciated by Nāgārjuna and Chandrakīrti) to the thought of Wittgenstein, see the "Introduction" to *Nāgārjuna's Reason Sixty with Chandrakīrti's Commentary*, trans. with introductory study by Joseph John Loizzo (New York: American Institute of Buddhist Studies, 2007), 3–116. On the use of Wittgenstein to illumine the implications of the *madhyamaka*, see also Garfield, *Empty Words*, 88–90, 98–99.

221. Bagger, *Uses of Paradox*, 88–89, compares the Madhyamika doctrine of emptiness to the Liar Paradox of Epimenides the Cretan, "All Cretans are [always] liars." Clearly, for this statement to be true, it must be false, but it can be false only if it is true. Other scholars have noted the relevance of this comparison. See, for instance, Garfield, *Empty Words*, 89, 104–5. Also relevant and worthy of consultation is Robert Lawson Slater, *Paradox and Nirvana: A Study of Religious Ultimates with Special Reference to Burmese Buddhism* (Chicago: University of Chicago Press, 1951), 65–111.

222. Garfield, *Empty Words*, 96–99.

223. *Fundamental Wisdom of the Middle Way*, trans. Garfield, 282. Bagger cites the passage in *Uses of Paradox*, 89.

224. Text cited in Döl-b̄o-b̄a Ṡhay-rap-gyel-tsen, *Mountain Doctrine: Tibet's Fundamental Treatise on Other-Emptiness and the Buddha Matrix*, ed. Kevin Vose, trans. and introduced by Jeffrey Hopkins (Ithaca, N.Y.: Snow Lion Publications, 2006), 328.

225. Ibid., 328–29. Part of the passage is cited in T̄āranātha, *The Essence of Other-Emptiness*, trans. and annotated by Jeffrey Hopkins in collaboration with Lama Lodrö Namgyel (Ithaca, N.Y.: Snow Lion Publications, 2007), 83.

226. Ḥayyim Vital, *Eṣ Ḥayyim*, 42:1, 89b: "That which precedes the void [*tohu*] is called *efes*, as [in the verse] 'they are considered by him to be from nothing and the void [*me-efes wa-tohu neḥshevu lo*]' (Isa 40:17). And the matter is that the Infinite [*ein sof*] is called *efes*, for there is no comprehension of it, since there is no matter or form there at all, and after it came forth the void [*tohu*], which is *Keter*, and afterwards came forth the chaos [*bohu*], which comprises the four elements, *Ḥokhmah* and *Binah*, *Tif'eret* and *Malkhut*." A parallel version appears in Ḥayyim Vital, *Adam Yashar* (Jerusalem, 1994), 46. The only notable variation is the inclusion of the remark "there is the negation of the material" (*sham afisat ha-ḥomer*) prior to "since there is no matter or form there at all."

227. Shneur Zalman of Liadi, *Torah Or*, 114c.

228. Menachem Mendel Schneerson, *Or ha-Torah: Devarim*, vol. 6 (Brooklyn: Kehot, 1984), 2204; Shmuel Schneersohn, *Liqquṭei Torah: Torat Shmu'el 5627*, 413. The expression *afisat ha-ra'yon* as a designation of *Keter* is found in Moses Cordovero, *Pardes Rimmonim* (Jerusalem, 1962), 23:1, 7c, 23:8, 18c; idem, *Or Ne'erav* (Jerusalem, 1974), chap. 7, 57. But the source cited by both Menachem Mendel and his son Shmuel is Meir Poppers, *Me'orot Natan* (Frankfurt am Main, 1709), 10b: "*Efes* [is the name by which] the Infinite is called, for there is no comprehension of it [*ki ein bo tefisah*], and in it is the negation of thought [*u-vo afisat ha-ra'yon*]." The work of Poppers is referred to as *Me'orei Or*. The passage is mentioned as well in the addenda to Shneur Zalman of Liadi, *Torah Or*, 114c (from the supplements edited by his son, Dov Baer).

229. Shalom Dov Baer Schneersohn, *Sefer ha-Ma'amarim 5652–5653* (Brooklyn: Kehot, 1987), 10.

230. Maitreya, *Middle Beyond Extremes: Maitreya's Madhyāntavibhāga with Commentaries by Khenpo Shenga and Ju Mipham*, trans. Dharmachakra Translation Committee (Ithaca, N.Y.: Snow Lion Publications, 2006), 25.

231. Ibid., 37.

232. Döl-bo-ba Shay-rap-gyel-tsen, *Mountain Doctrine*, 329.

233. Menachem Mendel Schneersohn, *Or ha-Torah: Siddur Tefillah*, 352.

234. Menachem Mendel Schneersohn, *Derekh Miṣwotekha*, 62a.

235. Ibid., 136a.

236. Menachem Mendel Schneersohn, *Or ha-Torah: Siddur Tefillah*, 364. See also Shalom Dov Baer Schneersohn, *Sefer ha-Ma'amarim 5654* (Brooklyn: Kehot, 1991), 40; idem, Shalom Dov Baer Schneersohn, *Be-Sha'ah she-Hiqdimu 5672*, 1:569.

237. Shmuel Schneersohn, *Liqquṭei Torah: Torat Shmu'el 5633*, vol. 2 (Brooklyn: Kehot, 1994), 493.

238. Shalom Dov Baer Schneersohn, *Be-Sha'ah she-Hiqdimu 5672*, 1:569; see also 2:1158.

239. Aaron Halevi Horowitz of Staroselye, *Sha'arei Avodah*, pt. 2, chap. 31, 45b. Compare idem, *Sha'arei ha-Yiḥud we-ha-Emunah*, pt. 2, 47b: "in relation to him, blessed be he, the something and nothing are equal" (*ha-yesh we-ha-ayin shawwin*).

240. Here I follow the view of Garfield, *Fundamental Wisdom of the Middle Way*, 94–95, 176–77. See further references in the following note.

241. Wood, *Nāgārjunian Disputations*, 124–25, 194–99. On the compatibility of emptiness and dependent-arising, see also Napper, *Dependent-Arising*, 126–33, 149–50.

242. The words *mahut* and *tehom* are made up of the same letters.
243. For instance, see Shneur Zalman of Liadi, *Liqquṭei Amarim: Tanya*, pt. 1, chap. 36, 46a–b; idem, *Seder Tefillot mi-kol ha-Shanah* (Brooklyn: Kehot, 1986), 132a; Dov Baer Schneersohn, *Shaʿarei Teshuvah*, 142d; Menachem Mendel Schneerson, *Liqquṭei Siḥot*, vol. 9 (Brooklyn: Kehot, 2000), 63–64.
244. Yosef Yitzchak Schneersohn, *Sefer ha-Maʾamarim 5700*, 26.
245. Shneur Zalman of Liadi, *Torah Or*, 114c.
246. Yosef Yitzchak Schneersohn, *Sefer ha-Maʾamarim: Quntreisim*, vol. 2 (Brooklyn: Kehot, 1986), 826.
247. Menachem Mendel Schneersohn, *Or ha-Torah: Siddur Tefillah*, 364.
248. Shneur Zalman of Liadi, *Liqquṭei Torah*, vol. 2, Derushim le-Rosh ha-Shanah, 62a.
249. Shalom Dov Baer Schneersohn, *Sefer ha-Maʾamarim 5654*, 40.
250. Yosef Yitzchak Schneersohn, *Sefer ha-Maʾamarim 5711* (Brooklyn: Kehot, 1986), 159–61.
251. I have elaborated on this topic in the "Postface" to *Open Secret*.
252. Shneur Zalman of Liadi, *Maʾamerei Admur ha-Zaqen: Maʾarz"l* (Brooklyn: Kehot, 1984), 474.
253. Menachem Mendel Schneersohn, *Or ha-Torah: Siddur Tefillah*, 364. On the theme of two opposites in one subject, see Elior, *Paradoxical Ascent*, 97–100, 135, 176–77, 179–82, 220.
254. Shalom Dov Baer Schneersohn, *Sefer ha-Maʾamarim 5652–5653*, 10.
255. Aaron Halevi Horowitz of Staroselye, *Shaʿarei Avodah*, pt. 2, chap. 32, 48b.
256. Menachem Mendel Schneerson, *Liqquṭei Siḥot*, vol. 5 (Brooklyn: Kehot, 1972), 386.
257. Menachem Mendel Schneerson, *Torat Menaḥem: Hitwaʿaduyot 5752*, vol. 2 (Brooklyn: Lahak Hanochos, 1994), 242.
258. Menachem Mendel Schneerson, *Torat Menaḥem: Hitwaʿaduyot 5750*, vol. 3, 23.
259. Ibid., 23–24.
260. See above, n. 209.
261. Menachem Mendel Schneerson, *Torat Menaḥem: Hitwaʿaduyyot 5712*, vol. 2, 169.
262. Ibid., 170.
263. Menachem Mendel Schneerson, *Torat Menaḥem: Hitwaʿaduyyot 5745*, vol. 4 (Brooklyn: Lahak Hanochos, 1986), 2494.

BODIES OF THE VOID: POLYPHILIA AND THEOPLICITY | ROLAND FABER

1. The language of "bodying" indicates the necessary openness of the otherwise problematic introduction of a hidden dualism of body *and something*

else included in the metaphor of "embodying" and "un-bodying"—like a "soul" or an "essence" that is *em*bodied or *un*bodied. Countering any dualism, the apophatic move—as will be elaborated in the following considerations—precisely *inscribes itself* and not by negating or realizing "something else" like an essence that is negated or realized.

2. See Edward S. Casey, *The Fate of Place: A Philosophic History* (Berkeley: University of California Press, 1998),103–29.
3. See Werner Beierwaltes, *Identität und Differenz*, Philosophische Abhandlungen 49 (Frankfurt am Main, 1980), 104 n. 34.
4. Johannes Duns Scotus, *God and Creatures: The Quodlibetal Questions*, ed. Felix Alluntis and Allan B. Wolter (Princeton, N.J.: Princeton University Press, 1975), 112.
5. See Th. Carlson, "Postmodernity's Finitude and Apophatic Unknowing of Dionysian Traditions," in AAR/SLB-Abstracts 1996, 33.
6. See Meister Eckhart, *Deutsche Predigten und Traktate*, 3rd ed., ed. Josef Quint (München, 1969) und ders. (Hg.), Meister Eckharts Predigten, Stuttgart 1959. Roman numbers Quint (1959), arabic numbers Quint (1969), 26, 273.10–28.
7. See Beierwaltes, *Identität und Differenz*, 117.
8. See L. Gabriel, ed., *Nikolaus von Kues: Philosophisch-theologische Schriften*. vol. 1 (Vienna, 1989), 65.
9. See Roland Faber," 'Gottesmeer'—Versuch über die Ununterschiedenheit Gottes," in"*Leben in Fülle": Skizzen zur christlichen Spiritualität*, ed. Thomas Dienberg and Michael Plattig (Münster, 2001), 64–95.
10. See Gilles Deleuze, *Difference and Repetition*, trans. Paul Patton (New York: Columbia University Press, 1994), 207–20: The differentiated presupposes unity, as in the difference of things from one another, differenciation does not, intellectually, conceptually, or materially, presuppose any "unity," it is the pure process of difference that is "prior" and constituting shifting "unities."
11. See Judith Butler, *Gender Trouble: Feminism and the Subversion of Identity* (New York: Routledge, 2006), chap. 1, 5.
12. See Alain Badiou, *Infinite Thought: Truth and the Return to Philosophy* (New York: Continuum, 2003), 3–4.
13. See Luce Irigaray, *This Sex Which Is Not One* (Ithaca, N.Y.: Cornell University Press, 1985).
14. See Thomas Walter Laquer and Catherine Gallagher, *The Making of the Modern Body: Sexuality and Society in the 19th Century* (Berkeley: University of California Press, 1987).
15. See Casey, *Fate of Place*, 151–61.

16. See Gilles Deleuze and Félix Guattari, *What Is Philosophy?* trans. Hugh Tomlinson and Graham Burchell (New York: Columbia University Press, 1994), chap. 2. For Derrida see I. Almond, "How *Not* to Deconstruct a Dominican: Derrida on God and 'Hypertruth,'" *Journal of the American Academy of Religion* 68/2 (2000): 329–44.
17. See Irigaray, *This Sex Which Is Not One.*
18. See Julia Kristeva, *Revolution in Poetic Language* (New York: Columbia University Press, 1984).
19. See Catherine Keller, "The Process of Difference, the Difference of Process," in *Process and Difference: Between Cosmological and Poststructuralist Postmodernisms*, ed. Catherine Keller and Anne Daniell (Albany: State University of New York Press, 2002), 16.
20. Alfred North Whitehead, *Process and Reality: An Essay in Cosmology*, corr. ed., ed. David Ray Griffin and Donald W. Sherburne (New York: Free Press, 1978), 121.
21. See Gilles Deleuze and Félix Guattari, *A Thousand Plateaus: Capitalism and Schizophrenia*, trans. Brian Massumi (Minneapolis: University of Minnesota Press, 1987), 84.
22. Whitehead, *Process and Reality*, 176.
23. See Tamsin Lorraine, *Irigaray and Deleuze: Experiments in Visceral Philosophy* (Ithaca, N.Y.: Cornell University Press, 1999).
24. See Jacques Derrida, "Geschlecht: Sexual Difference, Ontological Difference," *Research in Phenomenology* 13 (1983): 65–83.
25. Martin Heidegger, *The Metaphysical Foundation of Logic*, trans. Michael Heim (Bloomington: Indiana University Press, 1984), 136–37.
26. Derrida, "Geschlecht," 71.
27. Ibid., 72.
28. E. A. Grosz, *Space, Time, and Perversion: Essays on the Politics of Bodies* (New York: Routledge, 1995), 78.
29. See Casey, *Fate of Place*, 202–10.
30. See Whitehead, *Process and Reality*, 113, where Whitehead in relation to Kant's *Critiques* makes the paradigm shift by inversion of their interest in the transcendental subject and proposing a "critique of pure feeling," which is nothing but a systematic statement of the *body-apriori.*
31. Alfred North Whitehead, *Science and the Modern World* (New York: Free Press, 1967), 91.
32. Whitehead, *Process and Reality*, 119.
33. Whitehead, *Science and the Modern World*, 92.
34. Alfred North Whitehead, *Modes of Thought* (New York: Free Press, 1966), 163–64.

35. Alfred North Whitehead, *Adventures of Ideas* (New York: Free Press, 1967), 197.
36. Whitehead, *Science and the Modern World*, 51.
37. Ibid., 91.
38. See Michel Foucault, *Überwachen und Strafen* (Frankfurt am Main, 1977), 41–42.
39. See Butler, *Gender Trouble*, chap. 5.
40. Whitehead, *Modes of Thought*, 162.
41. Ibid., 29.
42. For the interaction of life and consciousness but also the mutual evolutionary dependence of both modes of mutual obstruction in Whitehead see Elizabeth Kraus, *The Metaphysics of Experience: A Companion to Whitehead's* Process and Reality (New York: Fordham University Press, 1998), 65–75.
43. Whitehead, *Process and Reality*, 104.
44. Whitehead, *Modes of Thought*, 124.
45. See Butler, *Gender Trouble*, chap. 5.
46. See Casey, *Fate of Place*, 79–84.
47. Kristeva, *Revolution in Poetic Language*, 19–106.
48. See Jacques Derrida, "Khora," in *On the Name*, ed. Thomas Dutoit, trans. David Wood, John P. Leavey Jr., and Ian McLeod (Stanford, Calif.: Stanford University Press, 1995), 89–127.
49. Whitehead, *Adventures of Ideas*, 134.
50. Deleuze and Guattari, *A Thousand Plateaus*, 260.
51. See Gilles Deleuze, *The Fold: Leibniz and the Baroque*, trans. Tom Conley (Minneapolis: University of Minnesota Press, 1992).
52. See Roland Faber, *Gott als Poet der Welt: Anliegen und Perspektiven der Prozesstheologie*. 2nd ed. (Darmstadt: WBG, 2004), §40.
53. Alain Badiou, *Being and Event* (New York: Continuum, 2005), 55.
54. See Roland Faber, "Whitehead at Infinite Speed: Deconstructing System as Event," in *Schleiermacher and Whitehead: Open Systems in Dialogue*, ed. Christine Helmer, Marjorie Suchocki, John Quiring, and Katie Goetz (Berlin: Walter de Gruyter 2004), 39–72.
55. See Whitehead, *Process and Reality*, 21.
56. See Whitehead, *Adventures of Ideas*, 203.
57. Whitehead, *Process and Reality*, 103–7.
58. Deleuze and Guattari, *A Thousand Plateaus*, 149–60.
59. See Roland Faber, "'O Bitches of Impossibility!'—Programmatic Dysfunction in the Chaosmos of Deleuze and Whitehead," in *Deleuze, Whitehead and the Transformations of Metaphysics*, ed. A. Cloots and K. Robinson (Brussels: Contactforum, 2005), 117–28.

60. *Process and Reality*, 103; Deleuze and Guattari, *A Thousand Plateaus*, 165.
61. Deleuze, *Difference and Repetition*, 42.
62. Whitehead, *Process and Reality*, 104.
63. Ibid., 339.
64. See Whitehead, *Adventures of Ideas*, 11, 198, 253.
65. See Deleuze and Guattari, *Philosophy*, 32.
66. See 1 Cor 15. Biblical references are from the New Oxford Annotated Bible.
67. Whitehead, *Adventures of Ideas*, 25–26; Category of Explanation, xxv.
68. See Maurice Merleau-Ponty, *The Visible and the Invisible*, ed. Claude Lefort, trans. Alphonso Lingis (Evanston, Ill.: Northwestern University Press, 1968), 133–34.
69. Glen Mazis, *Emotion and Embodiment: Fragile Ontology* (New York: Peter Lang, 1993), 129.
70. Whitehead, *Process and Reality*, 119.
71. Deleuze, *Essays: Critical and Clinical*, trans. Daniel W. Smith and Michael A. Greco (Minneapolis: University of Minnesota Press, 1997), 131.
72. Whitehead, *Adventures of Ideas*, 186.
73. Whitehead, *Process and Reality*, 72.
74. Deleuze, *Difference and Repetition*, 42.
75. Ibid., 262; see Whitehead, *Process and Reality*, 156.
76. See Exodus 33:20–23.
77. See Deleuze, *Difference and Repetition*, 1: "The exchange . . . of particulars defines our conduct in relation to generality. . . . By contrast, we can see that repetition is a necessary . . . conduct only in relation to that which cannot be replaced. Repetition as a conduct . . . concerns non-exchangeable and non-substitutable singularities. . . . Generality, as generality of the particular, thus stands opposed to repetition as universality of the singular."
78. Deleuze and Guattari, *A Thousand Plateaus*, 154.
79. Gilles Deleuze and Claire Parnet, *Dialogues*, trans. Hugh Tomlinson and Barbara Habberjam (New York: Columbia University Press, 1997), xxxvii.
80. Gilles Deleuze, "Immanence: A Life—. . . ," in *Pure Immanence: Essays on a Life*, trans. Anne Boyman (New York: Zone Books, 2005), 27.
81. Alfred North Whitehead, "Immortality," in *Essays in Science and Philosophy* (New York: Greenwood Press, 1968), 79.
82. Ibid., 82.
83. That Deleuze, despite his critique of the scheme actual-possible, himself was inclined to subscribe to such a resonance as this can be seen in his own words in *The Fold*, chap. 6.
84. Whitehead, "Immortality," 90.

85. Ibid., 81.
86. Deleuze, "Immanence," 29–30.
87. Whitehead, "Immortality," 88 (emphasis mine).
88. Ibid., 90.
89. Ibid., 88.
90. The mutual determination between virtuality and actuality being differentiation and differenciation. See J. Williams, "Deleuze and Whitehead: The Concept of Reciprocal Determination," in *Deleuze, Whitehead and the Transformations of Metaphysics*, ed. Cloots and Robinson, 89–106.
91. See C. Stagoll, "Becoming," in *The Deleuze Dictionary*, ed. Adrian Parr (Edinburgh: Edinburgh University Press, 2005), 21.
92. See Whitehead, *Process and Reality*, 73: "I shall use the term 'event' in the more general sense of a nexus of actual occasions."
93. Ibid.
94. Ibid., 80.
95. Ibid., 90.
96. Ibid., 87.
97. Ibid., 90.
98. Deleuze, "Immanence," 30.
99. Deleuze, *Essays: Critical and Clinical*, 131.
100. Gilles Deleuze and Félix Guattari, *Anti-Oedipus: Capitalism and Schizophrenia*, trans. Robert Hurley, Mark Seem, and Helen R. Lane (Minneapolis: University of Minnesota Press, 1996), 13.
101. Whitehead, *Process and Reality*, 105.
102. Ibid., 350.
103. Whitehead, "Immortality," 90.
104. Deleuze, "Immanence," 30.
105. Whitehead, *Process and Reality*, 351.
106. Luke 18:16. In some Gnostic gospels, like the *Gospel of Judas*, Christ appears to his disciples as a child! See Rodolphe Kasser, Marvin W. Meyer, and Gregor Wust, eds., *The Gospel of Judas from Codex Tchacos* (Washington D.C.: National Geographic: 2006), 20.
107. Whitehead, "Immortality," 90.
108. Ibid., 94.
109. Alfred North Whitehead, *Religion in the Making* (New York: Fordham University Press, 1996), 57.
110. Deleuze, "Immanence," 30.
111. Ibid.
112. Whitehead, "Immortality," 94.
113. See 1 Cor 15:44.

THE METAPHYSICS OF THE BODY | GRAHAM WARD

1. Judith Butler, *Bodies That Matter: On the Discursive Limits of "Sex"* (New York: Routledge, 1993), 27–56.
2. Annemarie Mol, *The Body Multiple: Ontology in Medical Practice* (Durham, N.C.: Duke University Press, 2002), 10. Mol's work is fascinating for the way in which she tries to overcome the notion of the "body" as a single object, in fact, for raising the question of what an object is as such.
3. Bret Easton Ellis, *American Psycho* (London: Picador, 1991), 370.
4. See the highly controversial exhibition *Bodies* recently put on at Earls Court. The program notes announce: "A collection of 22 life-sized, whole human bodies are on display in Bodies The Exhibition, accompanied by 260 assorted organs and body parts. Stripped of their skin and plastinated in various poses, the exhibits are intended to show the science of human biology up close and personal."
5. More recently, Giorgio Agamben has examined this reduction in terms of "bare life" and views the creation of "bare life" as endemic to contemporary political living. See *Homo Sacer: Sovereignty and Bare Life*, trans. Daniel Heller-Roazen (Stanford, Calif.: Stanford University Press, 1998).
6. Ellis, *American Psycho,* 374–75.
7. Agamben, *Homo Sacer*, 123–24.
8. Henri de Lubac, *Corpus Mysticum: l'Eucharistie et l'Église au Moyen Âge* (Paris: Aubier-Montaigne, 1944).
9. Ernst Hartwig Kantorowicz, *The King's Two Bodies: A Study of Mediaeval Political Theology* (Princeton, N.J.: Princeton University Press, 1957).
10. Bruno Latour, *Reassembling the Social: An Introduction of Actor-Network Theory* (Oxford: Oxford University Press, 2005), 162.
11. Benedict Anderson, *Imagined Communities* (London: Verso, 1991).
12. Michael Hardt and Antonio Negri, *Multitude* (New York: Penguin Press, 2004), 56.
13. Ibid., 59.
14. Quoted in F. A. Hayek, *The Road to Serfdom* (London: Routledge, 2001), 188–89.
15. Jürgen Habermas, *The Structural Transformation of the Public Sphere: An Inquiry into a Category of Bourgeois Society*, trans. Thomas Burger (Cambridge, U.K.: Polity Press, 1989).
16. Colin Crouch, *Post-Democracy* (Cambridge: Polity Press, 2004).
17. Hayek, *Road to Serfdom*, 179.
18. Louis Althusser, *Lenin and Philosophy and Other Essays*, trans. Ben Brewster (New York: Monthly Review Press, 2001).

19. G. W. F. Hegel, *Elements of the Philosophy of Right*, trans. H. B. Nisbet (Cambridge: Cambridge University Press, 1991), 20.
20. Ibid., 25.
21. Ibid., 22.
22. In the Preface to *Elements of the Philosophy of Right*, Hegel argues polemically for the role philosophy has to play in understanding the state and the political. He counters contemporary suggestions about the secularity of the state and the denigration of metaphysics in political science, speaking of the need to establish any thinking about the state in terms of "universal principles" (18). For such people "the claims of the concept constitute an embarrassment," but, Hegel adds, this is an embarrassment "from which they are nevertheless unable to escape" (19).
23. Ibid., 19.
24. Ibid., 21.
25. Ibid., 373.
26. Ibid., 371.
27. Ibid., 380.
28. Fukuyama, *The End of History and the Last Man* (Harmondsworth, U.K.: Penguin Books,1992).
29. G. W. F. Hegel, *Phenomenology of Spirit*, trans. A. V. Miller (Oxford: Oxford University Press, 1977), 20.
30. Hegel, *Philosophy of Right* , 308.
31. Ibid., 319.
32. Ibid., 38.
33. Ibid.
34. Ibid., 39.
35. Ibid., 40.
36. Ibid., 397.
37. Walter Kaufmann quotes Heinrich Heine as Nietzsche's source for the idea of "eternal reoccurrence." Heine sums this idea up in his famous words: "time is infinite, but the things in time, the concrete bodies are finite. . . . Now, however long a time may pass, according to the eternal laws governing the combinations of this eternal play of repetition, all configurations that have previously existed on this earth must yet meet, attract, repulse, kiss, and corrupt each other again." Cited in Walter A. Kaufmann, *Nietzsche: Philosopher, Psychologist, Antichrist* (Princeton, N.J.: Princeton University Press, 1959), 276.
38. Hegel, *Philosophy of Right*, 362.
39. For Hegel's exposition of the relations between Church and State, see *Philosophy of Right,* 291–304. His views are based on the premise that "religion

is that moment which integrates the state at the deepest level of the disposition [of the citizens], the state ought even to require all its citizens to belong to such a [religious] community" (295).

40. Richard Horsley, ed., *Paul and Empire: Religion and Power in Roman Imperial Society* (Harrisburg, Penn.: Trinity Press International, 1997), and idem, *Paul and Politics: Ekklesia, Israel, Imperium, Interpretation* (Harrisburg, Penn.: Trinity Press International, 2000).
41. Neil Elliot, "Paul and the Politics of Empire," in *Paul and Politics*, 15–39, and *Liberating Paul: The Justice of God and the Politics of the Apostle* (Minneapolis: Fortress Press, 2005).
42. Bruno Blumenfeld, *The Political Paul: Justice, Democracy and Kingship in a Hellenistic Framework* (Sheffield, U.K.: Sheffield Academic Press, 2001).
43. Alain Badiou, *St. Paul: The Foundation of Universalism*, trans. Ray Brassier (Stanford, Calif.: Stanford University Press, 2003).
44. Giorgio Agamben, *The Time That Remains: A Commentary on the Letter to the Romans*, trans. Patricia Dailey (Stanford, Calif.: Stanford University Press, 2005).
45. Slavoj Žižek, *The Puppet and the Dwarf: The Perverse Core of Christianity* (Cambridge, Mass.: MIT Press, 2003).
46. Blumenfeld, *The Political Paul*, 383.
47. Ibid., 299–300.
48. Ibid., 383.
49. Elliot, *Liberating Paul*, 13.
50. The literature is expansive, but a chain of inquiry often goes back to Schmidt's *Der Leib Christi* (Leipzig: A. Deichert, 1919) and continues through Ernst Käsemann, *Leib und Leib Christi* (Tübingen: J. C. B. Mohr, 1933) to such class studies in English as John A. T. Robinson, *The Body: A Study in Pauline Theology* (London: SCM Press, 1952) and Ernst Best, *One Body in Christ* (London: SCM Press, 1955). The most recent studies would include Gosnell L. O. R. Yorke, *The Church as the Body of Christ in the Pauline Corpus* (Lanham, Md.: University Press of America, 1991); Dale Martin, *The Corinthian Body* (New Haven, N.J.: Yale University Press, 1995); and Michelle V. Lee, *Paul, the Stoics, and the Body of Christ* (Cambridge: Cambridge University Press, 2006).
51. Michelle V. Lee refers to the famous fable by Dionysius of Halicarnassus (in *Antiquitates Romanae*, 6.83.2) in which the body is likened to a commonwealth, and Livy, *History of Rome* 2.328–12, where it is likened to the state (*Paul, the Stoics, and the Body of Christ*, 9). But this is very different to the Pauline emphasis that the kingdom of God *is* a body. As she points out,

Paul's use is much closer to Stoics like Seneca and Cicero who also both employ the body analogy politically to speak of a universal humanity.

52. Robinson, *The Body: A Study in Pauline Theology*, 51.
53. Baptism functions as a liturgical practice signifying what Paul elsewhere calls "adoption" (Gal 4:5)—by nature we are not children of God. This "adoption" marks a difference between teleology (as in Aristotle and Hegel) in which an efficient cause moves the final cause, that for which it was created, and eschatology in which there is a shift to another order of being wrought by divine grace.
54. Talal Asad, *Genealogies of Religion: Disciplines and Reasons of Power in Christianity and Islam* (Baltimore: John Hopkins University Press, 1993).
55. Dale Martin, *The Corinthian Body*.
56. Robinson, *The Body: A Study in Pauline Theology*, 53.
57. Ibid., 76.
58. Ibid., 79.
59. Ibid., 63.
60. Hegel, *Philosophy of Right*, 380.

EMPTYING APOPHASIS OF DECEPTION: CONSIDERING A DUPLICITOUS KIERKEGAARDIAN DECLARATION | T. WILSON DICKINSON

1. *Kierkegaard's Writings*, IV, *Either/Or: Part II*, trans. Howard V. Hong and Edna Hong (Princeton, N.J.: Princeton University Press, 1987), 339.
2. John D. Caputo describes the movement of a "demystifying analysis" as an attempt "to force out into the light of day the secret contract that allows one to do one thing under the cover of its opposite, e.g., to reap the rewards under the cover of giving" (*The Prayers and Tears of Jacques Derrida* [Bloomington: Indiana University Press, 1997], 218).
3. Michael Sells, *Mystical Languages of Unsaying* (Chicago: University of Chicago Press, 1994). See 187–92 for his discussion of the modern insertion of quotation marks around "God" in Meister Eckhart's famous 52nd sermon, and, even more important, his translation of Ibn al-'Arabi's "Ringstone" on Adam in "Towards a Poetic Translation of the *Fusus al-Hikam*," in *Muhyiddin Ibn 'Arabi: A Commemorative Volume*, ed. Stephen Hirtenstein and Michael Tiernan (Shaftesbury, U.K.: Element, 1993) 124–39.
4. Sells, *Mystical Languages of Unsaying*, 3.
5. William Franke, *A Philosophy of the Unsayable* (forthcoming).
6. Moving into the space of the performative thereby extends beyond Raoul Mortley's description of the role of apophasis in the Greek tradition—as a

negative that is not in opposition to the term it is negating, but as the opening of everything other than that term. Raoul Mortley, *From Word to Silence,* vol. 1: *The Rise and Fall of Logos* (Bonn: Hanstein,1986), 137.

7. This is especially the case insofar as truth is understood in terms of representation.
8. Some of those who have objected to the critical reading of apophasis have done so through an appeal to performance that imagines a stark if not essential distinction between theological discourse and prayer and praise. This essay seeks a middle (or doubled) path between these two approaches that doubts its own ability to so clearly identify mystification, while also not making the ironic mistake of designating the purity of prayer and praise with the speculative discourse that it supposedly overcomes.
9. Kierkegaard, *Either/Or,* 338.
10. Though the role that a Jewish other plays in this discourse is significant, it cannot be adequately addressed within the space of this essay. The caricaturing of Jewish identity through the condemnation and destruction of Jerusalem and the supposed arrogance of the chosen people has a serious and bloody history in Protestant theology. I would, however, direct the reader to George Pattison's examination of the "Wandering Jew" in Kierkegaard's thought in *Kierkegaard, Religion, and the Nineteenth-century Crisis of Culture* (Cambridge: Cambridge University Press, 2002), 81–95. I agree with Pattison's argument that it is the figure's nihilism and not his Jewishness that is primary (much like Jacques Derrida's meditations on Jerusalem). This point is given further credence within the context of Kierkegaard's larger theological criticism of culture that focuses on those who are in power in Europe and Christendom and not external others.
11. Kierkegaard, *Either/Or,* 341.
12. Ibid., 343.
13. Ibid., 344. Robert Perkins interprets this paragraph differently, arguing that the Preacher is positively employing justice in the sermon when he writes: "[J]ustice you will love, justice you will practice early and late." "Either/Or/Or: Giving the Parson His Due," in *International Kierkegaard Commentary,* vol. 4: *Either/Or Part II,* ed. Robert L. Perkins (Macon, Ga.: Mercer University Press, 1995), 224. I, however, take this paragraph to be one of condemnation, not recommendation, as it ends by noting that the "you" being addressed "will contend with God." Given that the next paragraph begins with "You are not to argue with God" and the central thought of the sermon is that one is always wrong in relation to God (though I find Perkins's reading plausible and do not think that the Preacher is condemning justice as such), it would seem that within the context of this sermon,

God and other people, and not justice, should be the objects of love. Therefore, it is the assurance and priority given to justice and one's own understanding of it that is being critiqued.

14. In particular he notes the possible mystification of negative theology whose thought could be considered as "a logic, a rhetoric, a topology, and a tropology of Jerusalem." Jacques Derrida, "How to Avoid Speaking," in *Derrida and Negative Theology*, ed. Howard Coward (Albany: State University of New York Press, 1992), 83. The line of thought that I hope to open here does not await the realization of the place or seek to possess its actuality.
15. It is the war over this place, of the taking place of fullness, of the ability to bring God into the system, that characterizes the current political reality of Jerusalem, and the notion of the chosen people. Derrida writes, "It is therefore a holy place but also a place that is in dispute, radically and rabidly, fought over by all the monotheisms . . . each claiming its particular perspective on this place and claiming an original historical and political interpretation of Messianism and the sacrifice of Isaac" (Jacques Derrida, *The Gift of Death* [Chicago: University of Chicago Press, 1996], 70). Derrida notes humanism's particular and similar role in this drama by quoting Victor Hugo: "Paris, the place of revolutionary revelation, is the human Jerusalem" (Jacques Derrida, *The Politics of Friendship* [London: Verso, 1997], 266).
16. Derrida, "How to Avoid Speaking," 118.
17. Kierkegaard, *Either/Or,* 343.
18. I am alluding here not only to 1 Corinthians 2:6–16 but also to John D. Caputo's reading of it in *The Weakness of God* (Bloomington: Indiana University Press, 2006), 45–48. Biblical references are drawn from the New Revised Standard Version (NRSV) unless otherwise indicated.
19. Luke 19:45–46.
20. Though Paul does speak of the knowledge of the Christian in this letter, it would seem as though it is a transformed knowledge that would not resemble that of the autonomous self, but would more closely resemble the love relation, as the next two verses read: "If any one imagines that he knows something, he does not yet know as he ought to know. But if one loves God, one is known by him" (1 Cor 8:1–3). The Revised Standard Version (RSV) translation takes the liberty of distinguishing between these two types by inserting quotation marks around this first sense of knowledge.
21. Kierkegaard, *Either/Or,* 348.
22. The call for the lover to search for his or her own fault becomes greatly problematic when considered within the context of domestic violence, for example. Though the shape of ethics that would follow the practice of this

self-emptying cannot provide us with adequate assurance in regards to this question, it does not call for an absolute passivity, quietism, veneration of suffering, or disconnection from all concepts of justice. Rather, as I will try to clarify, the upbuilding of this thought moves one to action and relationship, and, therefore, is an activity of resistance and change. That being said, this is not an issue that I seek to fortify my position against, but it is an important problem that demands continued struggle and consideration.

23. Kierkegaard, *Either/Or*, 349.
24. Perkins, however, affirms this statement as a fact assumed in the "absolute and qualitative difference between persons and God" (Perkins, "Either/Or/Or," 229). For the Preacher this declaration is neither an upbuilding thought nor within our capabilities of knowing. The Preacher continually emphasizes the free and loving acknowledgment of being wrong over the necessity of God's being right. Therefore, I am arguing here that the Preacher's concern is not with the accuracy of this or that speculative claim about God, but the performance and utterance of what we are saying. He writes, "[W]hen you acknowledge that God is always in the right, you stand outside of God," which is contrasted with being wrong in which "you are hidden in God" (Kierkegaard, *Either/Or*, 350).
25. Such an affirmation would necessitate an acceptance or confession of doctrine or a speculative metaphysics. However, as George Pattison points out, Kierkegaard does not make this appeal but locates it at the site of the subject and human experience, and articulates a philosophical and rhetorical theology, which I am arguing is also apophatic (*Kierkegaard: The Aesthetic and the Religious: From the Magic Theatre to the Crucifixion of the Image* [New York: St. Martin's Press, 1992], 64).
26. Edward Mooney gives a helpful and far more nuanced reading of the Judge's account of the self in "Self-Choice or Self-Reception: Judge Wilhelm's Admonition," in *Selves in Discord and Resolve: Kierkegaard's Moral-Religious Psychology from* Either/Or *to* Sickness unto Death (New York: Routledge, 1996), 11–27.
27. Kierkegaard, *Either/Or*, 213.
28. Mooney, "Self-Choice or Self-Reception," 18.
29. Kierkegaard, *Either/Or*, 236.
30. Ibid., 323. The Latin phrase is a quote from Horace.
31. Ibid., 350. Pattison captures this quite well, writing, "the 'victory' that God wins over the self is that what is finally offered is not an 'explanation' of a cognitive kind but an existential reordering of the self that Kierkegaard calls a 'transfiguration'" (George Pattison, *The Philosophy of Kierkegaard* [Montreal: McGill–Queen's University Press, 2005], 141).

32. The Danish word is "*mod*" meaning "against," denoting struggle. I thank Edward Mooney for his insight into this issue.
33. Kierkegaard, *Either/Or,* 246.
34. Ibid., 249.
35. Ibid., 247.
36. I am trying merely to describe two different sensibilities here, and I do not seek to organize them under the headings of "Roman" and "Christian" (I have tried to make this clear by alluding to Augustine's definition of peace). Rhetoric which moves under the banner of such oversimplified headings and does not acknowledge the heuristic and generalized purposes of the distinction, like the binary of "the Jew" and "the Greek," seems reckless on both historical and philosophical accounts.
37. Kierkegaard, *Either/Or,* 323. The passage continues: "Anyone who refuses to struggle with actualities acquires phantoms to struggle against." There is something spiritual and spectral at stake in embodied apophasis, but I do not think this calls for the demystification of pure fantasy, but rather leads to a postsecular space of a critical re-enchantment of the world and "matter."
38. Ibid., 351.
39. Ibid., 345.
40. Ibid., 341.
41. Ibid., 353.
42. For exemplary, but quite different, examinations of the deep connections between apophasis and contemporary issues of justice, see Catherine Keller, "*Docta ignorantia:* Darkness on the Face *pne choshekh* in *Face of the Deep: A Theology of Becoming* (Routledge: New York, 2003), 200–12, and Denys Turner, "Material Poverty or Poverty of Spirit? Holiness and the Liberation of the Poor," in *Holiness, Past and Present*, ed. Stephen C. Barton (London: T & T Clark, 2003), 441–59.
43. Kierkegaard, *Either/Or,* 353.
44. I do not seek here, by emphasizing the roles of these two pseudonyms, to drive a wedge between the religious and secular. As Kierkegaard's later criticism will illustrate, the division between Christendom and modernity is often deceptive (as a judge could be a "knight of faith" and preachers are much maligned figures in many of his other works). The duplicity that is at work in apophatic performance seems, instead, to rupture this dualism and call into question the boundaries we might draw to protect the one from the other.
45. Kierkegaard, *Either/Or,* 248.

46. Ibid., 13–16. He is citing Philippians 2:6 in particular.
47. 47. This is my formulation and not the Preacher's.
48. Catherine Keller, quite aptly, challenges "the patriarchal implication of the kenotic Christ idea," calling into question in particular the veneration of suffering and the emptying of the self. Noting that the latter is a reaction against an extreme articulation of the masculine ego, Keller wonders if the movement of self-emptying is not negatively defined by, and thereby a simple repetition of, the problematic of patriarchy. In opposition, she proposes a relational, dynamic, and embodied understanding of the self. See Catherine Keller, "Scoop up the Water and the Moon Is in Your Hands: On Feminist Theology and Dynamic Self-Emptying," in *The Emptying God: A Buddhist-Jewish-Christian Conversation*, ed. John B. Cobb Jr. and Christopher Ives (Maryknoll, N.Y.: Orbis Books, 1990), 104. This criticism does not, however, close down the affirmative possibilities of kenosis for Keller, as she notes that the traditional doctrinal formulation of self-emptying is in need of a "gentle . . . iconoclasm" (111). In a later essay, Keller seems to follow through on this iconoclasm in showing how apophatic theology can provide an opening in the work for justice, going so far as to positively employ the phrase "kenotic subjectivity" (Keller, "Docta Ignorantia," 203). Accordingly, I hope to follow a similar trajectory by shifting away from understanding kenosis in speculative Christological terms and toward an emphasis upon apophatic performance. In doing so, however, I would also want to heed Sarah Coakley's warning that one need not repress vulnerability. See Coakley, "*Kenosis* and Subversion: On the Repression of 'Vulnerability' in Christian Feminist Writing," in *Powers and Submissions: Spirituality, Gender and Philosophy* (Malden: Blackwell, 2002), 33.
49. Søren Kierkegaard, *Practice in Christianity*, trans. Howard V. Hong and Edna Hong (Princeton, N.J.: Princeton University Press, 1991). Though I do not seek to treat Kierkegaard's authorship as a coherent whole, I am drawing a connection between the early "religious" pseudonym of the Jutland Pastor and the later Anti-Climacus, particularly given Kierkegaard's characterization of the latter's "poetic-communication" (293). Though I shall return to the issue of the authorship at the conclusion of this essay, it seems as though it is a duplicitous tension that neither can nor should be resolved in footnotes (or monographs for that matter). My reading of *Practice in Christianity* draws from both Merold Westphal's essay "Kenosis and Offense: A Kierkegaardian Look at Divine Transcendence," in *International Kierkegaard Commentary*, vol. 20: *Practice in Christianity*, ed. Robert L. Perkins (Macon, Ga.: Mercer University Press, 2004), 19–46, and Pattison's reading in *Kierkegaard: The Aesthetic and the Religious*, 87–94, 174–88.

50. Kierkegaard, *Practice in Christianity,* 238.
51. Ibid., 123.
52. Ibid.
53. Ibid., 125.
54. David Law also notes the apophatic character of Kierkegaard's Christology, though he is using apophasis in a more scientific sense: "The underlying apophatic structure of Kierkegaard's Christology can be detected in his denial that we can acquire knowledge of Christ either through immediate contemporaneity or on the basis of historical information. . . . Christ is simply inaccessible to those principles upon which knowledge is constructed. . . . In this transferral of knowledge of Christ from the epistemological sphere to the realm of faith, the underlying apophaticism of Kierkegaard's thought again becomes apparent" (David R. Law, *Kierkegaard as Negative Theologian* [Oxford: Oxford University Press, 1993], 198).
55. Kierkegaard, *Practice in Christianity,* 133.
56. Pattison observes the imagistic component (*-billede*) lost in the English translation of "prototype" or "pattern" for "*forbillede*" and thereby opens a necessarily embodied aspect to it that pushes beyond a merely representational understanding. "As 'image' alone, Christ would mean the *presence* of God to humanity, and as 'prototype' this presence is brought into relation to the requirement of a future directed askesis which, by virtue of this futurity decompresses the fullness of presence implied in the concept of the 'image'" (Pattison, *Kierkegaard: The Aesthetic and the Religious,* 176).
57. My reading of the kenotic hymn in Philippians partially draws from Graham Ward's account, though we ultimately reach quite different conclusions. See Graham Ward, "Kenosis: Death, Discourse, and Resurrection," in *Balthasar at the End of Modernity*, ed. Lucy Gardner et al. (London: T. & T. Clark, 2001), 15–68.
58. This is the King James Version (KJV) translation. *Schemati* is not differentiated from *morphe* in the New Revised Standard Version (NRSV), as both are translated as "form."
59. Ward makes the same observation: "[T]he repetition of [form] identifies the two in the way that John in his gospel identifies crucifixion with exaltation" (Ward, "Kenosis," 22).
60. Caputo, *Weakness of God,* 48.
61. Jean-Louis Chretien offers a similar reading of Kierkegaard in which subjectivity is not centered on the epistemological confines of necessity or the isolation of autonomy, but issues from the structure of the call and the response. In this sense, the task of speaking (the Preacher's utterance for

example) is not an attempt to explain and describe existence from a position of autonomy and isolation, a project that leads to the loss of speech, but it is the response-ability to the other. Jean-Louis Chretien, "Perdre la parole: La demoniaque selon Kierkegaard," in *Le Regard de l'Amour* (Paris: Desclee de Brouwer, 2000), 95.

62. *Either/Or*, 352.
63. As I have already cited, one remains "happy in their work" even if "heaven was shut" (ibid., 353). Though as John D. Caputo has pointed out to me, in his later work Kierkegaard develops a very negative view of the body in general, and sex and marriage in particular.
64. Ibid., 348.
65. Jean-Luc Nancy is not an unproblematic figure to evoke in a theological discourse, even one attempting to think the impossibility of apophatic bodies. In *Corpus* (Paris: Métaillé, 2000) he carries out a rather strong reading against much of the Christian theological tradition, noting what could be called in this context the mystification of the incarnation that trades on the conflation of the transcendent and the immanent. Instead of this, Nancy seems to be proposing a dissemination of "carnations," a reading of the body that escapes the appropriation of transubstantiation, "*this is my body.*" Read next to Kierkegaard's apophatic Christology, however, the two might not be in such stark opposition as it appears.
66. Ibid., 19–21.
67. 67. Many discourses that emphasize embodiment appeal to markers that are themselves abstractions as they demand a substratum, effacing the occurrence and singularities of bodies and utterances. Though these particularities certainly remain meaningful, their dynamic and abstract character cannot be muted.
68. Ibid., 36–39. Through the negativity of these statements, I have not been trying to describe the reality of the body, but merely to disrupt any simple effort at doing so.
69. Pattison, *Kierkegaard, Religion, and the Nineteenth-century Crisis of Culture*, 175.
70. It accordingly seems to call into question the famous typology of the three stages (of the aesthetic, ethical, and religious) that it seems to confirm, and that have so often been used to organize and control Kierkegaard's discourse.
71. Søren Kierkegaard, "The Point of View for My Work as an Author," in *A Kierkegaard Anthology*, ed. Robert Bretall, trans. Walter Lowrie (Princeton, N.J.: Princeton University Press, 1973), 324.

FEMINIST THEOLOGY AND THE SENSIBLE UNSAYING OF MYSTICISM | SIGRIDUR GUDMARSDOTTIR

1. Ann-Marie Priest, "Woman as God, God as Woman: Mysticism, Negative Theology, and Luce Irigaray," *Journal of Religion* 83:1 (Jan. 2003): 4.
2. Laurel Schneider, *Re-Imagining the Divine: Confronting the Backlash Against Feminist Theology* (Cleveland, Ohio: Pilgrim Press, 1998), 18–19.
3. Ibid., 20.
4. Grace M. Jantzen, *Power, Gender, and Christian Mysticism* (Cambridge: Cambridge University Press, 1995), 23.
5. Amy Hollywood, *Sensible Ecstasy: Mysticism, Sexual Difference, and the Demands of History* (Chicago: University of Chicago Press, 2002), 21.
6. Ibid., 18.
7. Mary Daly, *Gyn/Ecology: The Metaethics of Radical Feminism* (Boston: Beacon Press, 1978), 8.
8. Mary Daly and Jane Caputi, *Webster's First New Intergalactic Wickedary of the English Language* (Boston: Beacon Press, 1987), 82.
9. Daly, *Gyn/Ecology*, 2, 6.
10. Mary Daly, *Beyond God the Father: Toward a Philosophy of Women's Liberation* (Boston: Beacon Press, 1973), 34; Daly, *Gyn/Ecology*, 4.
11. Daly, *Gyn/Ecology*, 4.
12. Charlene Spretnak, "The Politics of Women's Spirituality," introduction to *The Politics of Women's Spirituality: Essays on the Rise of Spiritual Power within the Feminist Movement*, ed. Charlene Spretnak (Garden City, N.Y.: Anchor Press/Doubleday, 1982), xv.
13. Daly, *Gyn/Ecology*, 1.
14. Judith Plaskow and Carol P. Christ, eds., introduction to *Weaving the Visions: New Patterns in Feminist Spirituality* (San Francisco: HarperSanFrancisco, 1989), 3.
15. Rosemary Radford Ruether, "Sexism and God-Language," in *Weaving the Visions*, 158.
16. Cf. Elizabeth A. Johnson, *She Who Is: The Mystery of God in Feminist Theological Discourse* (New York: Crossroad, 1992).
17. Beverly J. Lanzetta, *Radical Wisdom: A Feminist Mystical Theology* (Minneapolis: Fortress Press, 2005), 1.
18. Schneider, *Re-Imagining the Divine*, 75.
19. See the second chapter of my doctoral dissertation: Sigridur Gudmarsdottir, "Abyss of God: Flesh, Love and Language in Paul Tillich" (Ph.D. diss., Drew University, 2007).
20. Schneider, *Re-Imagining the Divine*, 176.

21. Cf. Gianni Vattimo, cited in Judith Butler, "Bodies That Matter," in *Engaging with Irigaray: Feminist Philosophy and Modern European Thought*, ed. Carolyn Burke, Naomi Schor, and Margaret Whitford (New York: Columbia University Press, 1994), 141, 166.
22. Françoise Meltzer describes the generalizations of French-speaking feminists in this way. Françoise Meltzer, "Transfeminisms," in *Transfigurations: Theology and the French Feminists*, ed. C. W. Maggie Kim, Susan M. St. Ville, and Susan M. Simonaitis (Eugene, Ore. : Wipf and Stock, 1993), 4.
23. Many books and articles in feminist theory and feminist theology alike especially in the Anglo-American world-zone have been written about the "French feminists" and their alleged essentialism. Four concise essays arguing on Irigaray and essentialism are found in the anthology *Engaging with Irigaray: Feminist Philosophy and Modern European Thought,* ed. Carolyn Burke, Naomi Schor, and Margaret Whitford (New York: Columbia University Press, 1994), 37–140. Toril Moi, *Sexual/Textual Politics: Feminist Literary Theory* (London: Methuen, 1985) gives an account on the debate on Kristeva and essentialism. Feminist theologians who have accused Irigaray and Kristeva of essentialism are, among others, Susan Thistlethwaite and Elisabeth Schüssler Fiorenza. See also St. Ville, Kim, and Simonaitis, *Transfigurations,* for short essays on feminist theology and "French" theory.
24. See especially Julia Kristeva, *In the Beginning Was Love: Psychoanalysis and Faith*, trans. Arthur Goldhammer (New York: Columbia University Press, 1987), and Julia Kristeva, *Tales of Love*, trans. Léon Roudiez (New York: Columbia University Press, 1987).
25. Luce Irigaray, *Speculum of the Other Woman*, trans. Gillian C. Gill (Ithaca, N.Y.: Cornell University Press, 1989), 191–92.
26. 26. Jantzen, *Power, Gender and Christian Mysticism* 108–9; Hollywood, *Sensible Ecstasy*, 8–10.
27. Amy Hollywood, "Justice and Gender in Mysticism," *Christian Spirituality Bulletin* 4:2 (Fall 1996): 28–29.
28. Daly, *Gyn/Ecology*, 4.
29. Luce Irigaray, "La Mysterique," in *Speculum of the Other Woman*, 200.
30. Priest, "Woman as God, God as Woman" 8.
31. Luce Irigaray, "Divine Women," in *Sexes and Genealogies*, trans. Gillian C. Gill (New York: Columbia University Press, 1993), 71.
32. Ibid., 67.
33. Serene Jones, "This God, Which Is Not One" in *Transfigurations*, 138. Jones's own metaphors sound strangely biblical here in relating divinity to a devouring fire or a burning bush (Ex 3:2, 24:17; Dt 4:24, 9:3; Is 30:27, 30, 33:14; Heb 12:29).

34. Lanzetta, *Radical Wisdom*, 16–17.
35. Catherine Keller, *Face of the Deep: A Theology of Becoming* (New York: Routledge 2002), 207.

THE INFINITE FOUND IN HUMAN FORM: INTERTWININGS OF COSMOLOGY AND INCARNATION | PHILIP CLAYTON

1. Etymologically, *apophasis* means "saying away;" *kataphasis* means "saying with." I take both to be claims about the nature of religious language: To what extent can it correspond to the religious object, and to what extent is it altogether ineffable, eluding all attempts to give it voice?
2. I think there are good reasons to eschew radical skepticism, the attempt to rend asunder knowledge and religion. But for purposes of this essay this claim will have to be taken as a postulate. My primary goal is to explore a kataphatic theory of religious language in the context of more nuanced religious claims to knowledge.
3. John Rawls, *A Theory of Justice*, 2nd ed. (Cambridge, Mass.: Harvard University Press, 1999); idem, *Political Liberalism* (New York: Columbia University Press, 1996); idem, *Justice as Fairness: A Restatement* (Cambridge, Mass.: Harvard University Press, 2001); idem, "Outline of a Decision Procedure for Ethics," reprinted in *Collected Papers*, ed. Samuel Freeman (Cambridge, Mass.: Harvard University Press, 1999), 1–19; and idem, "The Independence of Moral Theory," in *Collected Papers*, 286–302. See also S. Freeman, ed., *The Cambridge Companion to Rawls* (Cambridge: Cambridge University Press, 2002), esp. 139–67.
4. There are even some very explicit comparisons in the early Vedic literature about the beginnings of bhakti. Rig Veda I.62.11 says, "[P]rayers are said to touch Indra who is longing just as a wife with desires gets her husband." Another hymn says, "All my hymns in unison praise Indra; as wives embrace their husbands so do my thoughts embrace Indra the divine bestower of gifts" (Rig Veda X.43.1). The Katha Upanishad treats this knowledge as a sort of grace: "The Atman is not to be obtained by exposition / Nor by intellect, nor by much learning / He is to be obtained only by the one whom He chooses / To such a one only doth He reveal his own person" (I.2.23).
5. I am grateful to Professor Sangeetha Menon of the National Institute for Advanced Studies (NIAS) in Bangalore for helpful discussions of these concepts, as well as for Sanskrit instruction and guidance in the secondary literature.

6. Available at http://vedabase.net/cc/en, verified September 11, 2006. This particular text is at http://vedabase.net/cc/adi/3/18/en. A more primary reference might be:

    sālokya-sārṣṭi-sāmīpya-
    sārūpyaikatvam apy uta
    dīyamānaṁ na gṛhṇanti
    vinā mat-sevanaṁ janāḥ

    A pure devotee does not accept any kind of liberation—sālokya, sārṣṭi, āmīpya, sārūpya or ekatva—even though they are offered by the Supreme Personality of Godhead. (Śrīmad Bhāgavatam 3.29.13)

   See also the analysis of the Brahma Sutra by Swami Krishnananda, now available online at http://www.swami-krishnananda.org/brahma/brahma08a.html.
7. Thus one commentary explains, "The Supreme Person, in His different plenary expansions, lives on innumerable Vaikuṇṭha planets, and the chief planet is Kṛṣnaloka. Just as within the material universe the chief planet is the sun, in the spiritual world the chief planet is Kṛṣnaloka. From Kṛṣnaloka, the bodily effulgence of Lord Kṛṣna is distributed not only to the spiritual world but to the material world as well; it is covered by matter, however, in the material world. In the spiritual world there are innumerable Vaikuṇṭha planets, and on each one the Lord is the predominating Deity. A devotee can be promoted to one such Vaikuṇṭha planet to live with the Supreme Personality of Godhead" (http://vedabase.net/sb/3/29/13/en).
8. Following a suggestion from Professor Menon.
9. Hans Frei was famous among his doctoral students at Yale, and beyond, for his impatience with the methodology debates in theology. He would list off the great methodological texts—Langdon Gilkey, David Tracy, Schubert Ogden, and so forth—with a certain disdain. Frei's exhortation to his students was always to move beyond the methodology disputes that take place in the antechamber to theology and to grapple with the actual issues of constructive theology. Applied in the present context, Frei's call is to (attempt to) move beyond the comfortable space of *sālokya* toward the stages that follow.
10. See, for example, Peter Berger, *A Rumor of Angels* (Harmondsworth, U.K.: Penguin Books, 1971): "By signals of transcendence I mean phenomena that are to be found within the domain of our 'natural' reality but that appear to point beyond that reality. In other words, I am not using transcendence

here in a technical philosophical sense but, literally, as the transcending of the normal, everyday world that I earlier identified with the notion of the 'supernatural'" (70).

11. The claim of epistemic privilege for the poor and the oppressed goes back to Gustavo Gutiérrez, *A Theology of Liberation: History, Politics, and Salvation* (Maryknoll, N.Y.: Orbis Books, 1988).
12. Gustaf Aulén, *Christus Victor: An Historical Study of the Three Main Types of the Idea of Atonement* (New York: Macmillan, 1951).
13. From the commentary on *Śrīmad Bhāgavatam* 3.29.13, available at http://vedabase.net/sb/3/29/13/en. This response of pulling back from final union mirrors the description of Brahman in Taittiriya Upanishad 2.4.1 as "that before which words are turned away, it not having been grasped by the mind" (*yato vaco nivartante, aprapya manasa saha*). As Ramanuja repeatedly insisted, it's not possible to pray to a God with whom you have become one.
14. See W. T. Stace, *Mysticism and Philosophy* (London: Macmillan, 1980); and idem, *The Nature of the World: An Essay in Phenomenalist Metaphysics* (New York: Greenwood Press, 1969), and, on this topic in particular, Louis Dupré, "*Unio mystica*: The State and the Experience," in *Mystical Union in Judaism, Christianity, and Islam*, ed. Moshe Idel and Bernard McGinn (New York: Continuum, 1989), 3–23.
15. Cusa, *De docta ignorantia*, in *Nicholas of Cusa: Selected Spiritual Writings*, trans. H. Lawrence Bond (New York: Paulist Press, 1997), 133. Readers will note the subtle differences between my reading of this text and the reading Catherine Keller provides in her chapter.
16. Ibid.
17. Ibid., 132 (emphasis mine).
18. Cusa, *De visione Dei* 13, in Jasper Hopkins, *Nicholas of Cusa's Dialectical Mysticism: Text, Translation, and Interpretive Study of De visione Dei*, 3rd ed. (Minneapolis: Arthur J. Banning Press, 1985), 705f. I offer a fuller treatment in *The Problem of God in Modern Thought* (Grand Rapids, Mich.: Eerdmans, 2000), chap. 3.
19. In an issue of the *American Catholic Philosophical Quarterly* (64, no. 1 [Winter 1990]) entirely devoted to the work of Nicholas of Cusa, Thomas P. McTighe argues convincingly from Cusa's texts that for Cusanus the only distinction between God and creature consists in the creature's finitude, which would mean that the distinction is a purely negative one.
20. Clayton, *The Problem of God*, esp. chap. 1.
21. "This infinity is the 'bad' or negative infinity, insofar as it is nothing more than the negation of the finite. [When it is understood in this way] the

finite arises again, and thus to that extent has not been sublated. Put differently, this [type of] infinity only expresses that the finite *should* be sublated" ("Diese Unendlichkeit ist die schlechte oder negative Unendlichkeit, indem sie nichts ist als die Negation des Endlichen, welches aber ebenso wieder entsteht, somit ebensosehr nicht aufgehoben ist,—oder diese Unendlichkeit drückt nur das Sollen des Aufhebens des Endlichen aus") (G. W. F. Hegel, *Enzyklopädie der philosophischen Wissenschaften im Grundrisse . . .*, § 94).

22. "This progress into [or: toward] the infinite is however not the truly infinite, which instead consists of being by itself through its other or—when one formulates it as process—to come to itself in [or: through] its other" ("Dieser Progreß ins Unendliche ist nun aber nicht das wahrhaft Unendliche, welches vielmehr darin besteht, in seinem Anderen bei sich selbst zu sein oder, als Prozeß ausgesprochen, in seinem Anderen zu sich selbst zu kommen") (ibid.).
23. Cusa, *De docta ignorantia*, 135.
24. See John Polkinghorne, ed., *The Work of Love: Creation as Kenosis* (Grand Rapids, Mich.: W. B. Eerdmans, 2001), and Jürgen Moltmann, *God in Creation: A New Theology of Creation and the Spirit of God* (Minneapolis: Fortress Press, 1993).

THE APOPHASIS OF DIVINE FREEDOM: SAVING "THE NAME" AND THE NEIGHBOR FROM HUMAN MASTERY | CHRIS BOESEL

1. Jacques Derrida, "*Sauf le nom* (Post-Scriptum)," trans. John Leavey, in *On the Name*, ed. Thomas Dutoit (Stanford, Calif.: Stanford University Press, 1995). See also Pseudo-Dionysius, "How Then Can We Speak of the Divine Names?" from *The Divine Names*, in *Pseudo-Dionysius: The Complete Works*, trans. Colm Luibheid (New York: Paulist Press, 1987), especially 53ff.
2. Several leading voices in the specific engagement of deconstruction and theology are John D. Caputo, see especially *The Prayers and Tears of Jacques Derrida* (Bloomington: Indiana University Press, 1997); Graham Ward, see especially *Barth, Derrida, and the Language of Theology* (Cambridge: Cambridge University Press, 1995); Walt Lowe, see especially *Theology and Difference* (Bloomington: Indiana University Press, 1993). Caputo's work, together with Kevin Hart's *The Trespass of the Sign* (Cambridge: Cambridge University Press, 1989), is particularly in the background of this introductory sketch of deconstruction's engagement with negative theology. Likewise, Ward and Lowe are significantly in the background of my reading of a Barthian resonance—yet, entailing significant distinctions—with Derridean deconstruction.

3. Pseudo-Dionysius, *The Mystical Theology*, in *Pseudo-Dionysius: The Complete Works*, trans. Colm Luibheid (New York: Paulist Press, 1987), 135–36.
4. "Negative theology would have managed to lift itself up into a pure presence above time and history, above language and the play of the trace, above the mediation of the trace and *différance*. Now apart from the fact that such an excessively hyper-logocentric hyper-essentialism is incoherent, since it will have already begun to speak in language and in time, it is also something that lends itself to a consummately dangerous political and ecclesiastical absolutism, to a politics of negative theology that is a threat to everyone. . . . Then negative theology would not save the name of God, or its own name, but would endanger everybody with a dangerous absolutism" (Caputo, *Prayers and Tears of Jacques Derrida*, 47).
5. Pseudo-Dionysius, *The Mystical Theology*, in *Pseudo-Dionysius: The Complete Works*, 137.
6. Ibid., 135–36.
7. Deconstruction can help theology (and philosophy) distinguish God from any "*concept* of God to which one can appeal that can ground one's discourse about God and the world," and in so doing "suggest the possibility of re-thinking the divine in a discourse which, while it cannot abolish metaphysics, is no longer governed by metaphysics" (Hart, *Trespass of the Sign*, 28, 47).
8. This deconstructive "saving the name" of God is to "save the name of God *for everybody*, not just the faithful in the determinable faiths" (Caputo, *Prayers and Tears of Jacques Derrida*, 43 [emphasis mine]).
9. To say "what the Word of God is. The goal of all yearning in theology is to be able to do this, but this is the goal of an illegitimate yearning [i.e., sin]" (Karl Barth, *Church Dogmatics*, I/1, ed. G. W. Bromiley and T. F. Torrance, trans. G. W. Bromiley et al. [Edinburgh: T&T Clark, 1957], 164).
10. Ward and Walt Lowe were first to explore the resonance between Derridean deconstruction and the theological assumptions of Karl Barth.
11. Søren Kierkegaard, *Philosophical Fragments*, trans. Howard V. Hong and Edna H. Hong (Princeton, N.J.: Princeton University Press, 1985), 14ff.
12. Kierkegaard, *Philosophical Fragments*, 24–25.
13. The Socratic also frames knowledge in terms of love, e.g., the learner, or knower, is a lover of wisdom, the journey of knowledge is a journey of love for the eternal, the good, beauty, etc. What is distinct about Climacus's thought experiment—how it is a change of context, putting the question of knowledge in a different kind of "love" context—is the emphasis on the love of the eternal, of the god, for the learner; a divine love which moves the god to descend to the learner, in contrast to the love of the

learner which ascends to the divine. This change of context is also, then, a change of direction and a change of subject.

14. Kierkegaard, *Philosophical Fragments*, 25.
15. Two things to note here: 1. This concern that the god cannot reveal herself, make herself understood to the creature, without destroying the creature, due to the radical difference, incommensurability between them—due to the Holiness, or wholly otherness of the god—is a classic feature of the witness of the Hebrew scriptures. Climacus notes this himself: "There was a people with a good understanding of the divine; this people believed that to see the god was death" (32). This latter phrasing is almost identical with Derrida's critique of Levinas's early stress on the absolute alterity of "the other." 2. It is resonant with Derrida's critique, in "Violence and Metaphysics," of Levinas's view of the radical alterity of the other: if the other is wholly other, then the address of that other would annihilate the addressee—would be an absolute violence—for both the addressee and "the third," the other other, the neighbor of the other who is also the addressee's neighbor. This critique can be traced through to Derrida's "every other is wholly other" refrain in *The Gift of Death*; for there to be an (ethical) relation of any kind, without the destruction of the addressee and the other other, there cannot be absolute otherness—a wholly other, an absolute other. In other deconstructive language, there is no absolute outside, no absolute boundary or difference: there is always difference, but no (single) absolute difference, ergo, the concepts of supplement, iterability, repeatability, etc. See also David Wood's critical reading of Levinas on this point in *The Step Back: Ethics and Politics after Deconstruction* (Albany: State University of New York Press, 2005).
16. Kierkegaard, *Philosophical Fragments*, 29.
17. Ibid., 34, 31.
18. Ibid., 32–33. "Therefore the god must suffer all things, endure all things, be tried in all things, hunger in the desert, thirst in his agonies, be forsaken in death, absolutely the equal of the lowliest of human beings." To become what the god is not—creature—is also part of Barth's understanding of omnipotence; again, an understanding determined by the context of a love relation between God and the creature.
19. This, of course, assumes that the god *wants* to be loved, and so known; if this is not the case, if the god is indifferent, or content with the intimacy of the cause-and-effect relation, of the relation of the fish to the water, of the fetus to the womb, of creature to the creator and nothing more, then there is no problem (and Kierkegaard would say, no Christianity). *Whether* this is

or is not the case is not to be argued or decided here (this is just a "thought experiment"), and I would suggest cannot be decided publicly, once and for all, anywhere at any time. Here, as both Derrida and Barth would agree, there can only be contesting testimony, and that's all—no proof, no conclusive ending of the dialogue, discourse, conversation, etc., that is possible *for us*.

20. Kierkegaard, *Philosophical Fragments*, 33.
21. The event of "knowing otherwise"—the event of faith, in which the "eyes" of faith are opened—is more properly, then, an event of hearing the Word, of having our ears opened, than an event of seeing. This is an interesting point of contact with Levinas's critique of Greek philosophy as too focused on seeing, sight, and vision, which he feels more easily plays into control and mastery of "the object" seen than does hearing.
22. Barth, *Church Dogmatics* I/1, 176. Although I find it easy to approve of the first assertion of this last phrase, it is another matter whether I approve equally, or as comfortably, of the second.
23. Barth, *Church Dogmatics* I/1, 162. The movement of deconstruction shows how, in fact, we cannot become "master" of any object of thought or speech. This is its critique of modernity and of "philosophy" in general. The consequences for the nature of our relation to the Word of God (as object of our thought and speech): 1. We can "master" this object even less than everything else; this is the least possible human place for confidence, power, control, certainty—the "weakest," most helpless and insufficient of all possible human positions and provisional forms of "knowledge." 2. This does not necessarily mean that it cannot "master us." A radical philosophical rendering of the radical limits of *all* human possibility with regard to thought and speech, knowing and speaking, is not necessarily identical with a rendering of the limits of divine possibility, precisely as divine and not human. But about the existence, the actuality of this divinity, this Word of God that can address and master us in a free event, nothing can be said but the worst, weakest, most vulnerable and insufficient human witness—"believe me as you would a miracle," indeed, not "as you would," but, "believe me, a miracle *has occurred*," or even, "a miracle has occurred: God with us, sinners; there and then, here and now."
24. Barth, *Church Dogmatics* I/1, 249.
25. It is not "inaccessible" in the transcendental or phenomenological sense, i.e., in the sense of the structures of the conditions of possibility that do not "exist," e.g., are not encountered and experienced in time and space, yet are necessary for things to "exist," for phenomena to occur and be encountered, experienced. So there may be an important difference here from the

"immemorial" address of alterity in Levinas, one that never occurs as a "present," likewise in relation to self-effacing *différance* that, for Derrida, constitutes the possibility of difference without itself "being" a difference, without "being" at all.

26. Barth, *Church Dogmatics* I/1, 237. Also: "He will not want to reflect upon it but will simply be in it" (220).
27. Ibid., 90, 91–92 (emphasis mine). As regards the human possibility, or capacity, for hearing and receiving the self-giving of God in her Word: "As we hear it, we have the possibility of hearing it" (237). In other words, it is not an innate capacity; God Herself must give us "the condition" (Kierkegaard) of hearing the Word in her very giving, or speaking, of the Word.

    This slippery passivity of receptivity to address in the moment moves Barth to employ his own strikingly apophatic language of "unknowing" when he asserts that "human experience of God's Word, will never be able to see, perceive, or understand itself, if it is real, as determined by the Word of God." He goes on: "It will be this without seeing or understanding itself in this being. It will just be true *from God* that human existence is engaged here in acknowledgment of the Word of God" (Barth, *Church Dogmatics* I/1, 222 [emphasis mine]). The "from God" is both what determines the "knowing otherwise" as analogous to deconstruction's own critique of negative theology, i.e., its own apophatic desire, and what is also contra to it, if not anathema—or at least, beyond its ken.
28. Barth, *Church Dogmatics* I/1, 91, 220 (my emphases). Note the significance of the New Testament account of Peter's confession of Jesus as Messiah. It is "given" to him from God; he "knows" it in the moment of confessing it. But it is a "knowledge" that appears to be gone as quickly as it came, for in the very next episode of the story Jesus is calling him "Satan" and telling him to stop obstructing the will of God.
29. Karl Barth, "The Authority and Significance of the Bible," in *God: Here and Now*, trans. Paul van Buren (London: Routledge, 1964), 39.
30. The echoes of deconstruction: our "knowing otherwise" structured as futurity, as structure of our finitude (e.g., justice is always to come; the other that is always to come and who never actually comes). Contra deconstruction: it *has occurred*; the Word of God, God herself, has and does come, in a present occurrence of "fulfillment"—really God with us, God really with us, despite our finitude, but precisely as miracle, as divine possibility and actuality. But precisely as such, as divine occurrence in the creaturely realm, it is never ours to possess, but only to receive, recollect, and await anew.

31. Barth, *Church Dogmatics,* I/1, 228. "We cannot produce this event and so we cannot give a basis for our reference. . . . [W]e could do so only by producing the event to which it points and letting it speak for itself."
32. Ibid., 92. It is an event "which comes upon us and the whole world of our motivations absolutely from without" (90).
33. Ibid., 67 (emphasis mine).
34. Ibid., 90 (emphasis mine). See also *Church Dogmatics,* II/1, 22. "He always gives Himself to be known so as to be known by us in this giving, which is always a bestowal, always a free action."
35. Barth, *Church Dogmatics,* I/1, 249.
36. Ibid., 181.
37. Ibid., 120 (emphasis mine).
38. Ibid., 92 (emphasis mine).
39. We "cannot get round this twofold barrier . . . even in [attending] to the concrete content of the Word of God" (ibid., 249).
40. Karl Barth, "The Sovereignty of God's Word and the Decision of Faith," in *God: Here and Now,* 27.
41. Postmodern discourse on "the gift" is obviously pertinent here, especially in the work of Derrida and Jean-Luc Marion.
42. Barth, *Church Dogmatics,* I/1, 165.
43. The question is raised: Is God then unfair, unjust, to do such a thing, to behave in such a manner, to come to the human creature by giving Godself to be known within the limits of the creaturely sphere given these very consequential limitations? It is perhaps not irrelevant to note that the apostle Paul wrestled with this question on occasion, particularly in regard to God's choosing, for example, Jacob over Esau (in the epistle to the Romans). His answer to this question, of course, is simply to point to divine mystery—the mystery of God's way with creation and the human creature. What else could his answer be? What would the answer of, "Yes, God is unjust!" imply about our—or Paul's—limits (of ethical capacity and judgment, as distinguishable from epistemological capacity, if they are distinguishable) in relation to divine mystery? Are we less radically limited, less in the dark, ethically than we are epistemologically in relation to divine mystery? How is this related to whether the "subject" of divine mystery is taken to be divine nature/being/essence or divine act and behavior? If God is just "sitting there," there is no mystery to confront our ethical capacity and judgment, only the task of policing the boundaries of human finitude in relation to the divine, as if we knew what those were. But what if God should suddenly awake from benign meditation, or, to borrow a powerful

phrase from feminist theology, what if she should speak? Is it possible, is God mysterious enough, that she might say something, or do something, we don't like, approve of, are confounded and offended by—that confronts our creaturely *ethical* as well as epistemological capacity and judgment as impenetrable mystery?

44. In Barth's view of revelation as a trinitarian event, the First Person corresponds to the speaking of the Word, the Second Person corresponds to the Word spoken, and the Third Person corresponds to the miraculous enabling of the human creature to hear the Word in faith.
45. Romans 9:20 and 11:33–34, RSV.
46. Jacques Derrida, "Faith and Knowledge: The Two Sources of 'Religion' at the Limits of Reason Alone," in *Acts of Religion*, ed. Gil Anidjar (New York: Routledge, 2002), 98. Derrida uses this phrase as a figure for the way in which the fundamental nature of all knowledge, even that which attempts to distinguish itself from faith with regard to certainty, is structurally determined as a form of faith, that is, as a form of witness and testimony.
47. Barth, *Church Dogmatics,* I/1, 163. In addition, on the mystery of divine freedom in relation to the neighbor, I simply submit some suggestive and perhaps surprising sentences from Barth. "Moreover, it could hardly be denied that God can speak His Word to man quite otherwise than through the talk about Himself that is to be found in the Church as known or as yet to be discovered, and therefore quite otherwise than through proclamation. He can establish the Church anew and directly when and where it pleases Him" (54). "Hence, it can never be the case that the Word of God is confined to the proclamation of the existing Church. . . . Church proclamation itself, in fact, regards itself only as . . . a means of grace in God's free hand. Hence it cannot be master of the Word, nor try to regard the Word as confined within its own borders" (54). "God may speak to us through Russian Communism, a flute concerto, a blossoming shrub, or a dead dog. We do well to listen to Him if He really does. . . . God may speak to us through a pagan or an atheist, and thus give us to understand that the boundary between the Church and the secular world can still take at any time a different course from that which we think we discern" (55).
48. This notion of resistance to the way in which God chooses to come to us in and for love raises another level at which the "subject is changed" within the "thought experiment." The identity of the creature changes from finite to sinful. The nature of the limit, then, from finitude to sin; the character of the relation, from metaphysical/ontological (or, structural, in the case of deconstruction)—e.g., finitude in relation to infinity—to personal. The

creature is not simply ignorant of God, incapable of knowing God; the creature does not *want* to know God as God has given herself to be known. I do not want God to be God when, where, and how it pleases God to be God; I want God on my own terms. Again, I want to legislate what God can and cannot do (or be).

49. Derrida, "Passions: 'An Oblique Offering'," trans. David Wood, in *On the Name*, 31, as quoted by John Caputo, *Prayers and Tears of Jacques Derrida*, 112.
50. Barth, *Church Dogmatics*, I/1, 83 (emphasis mine).

LET IT BE: FINDING GRACE WITH GOD THROUGH THE *GELASSENHEIT* OF THE ANNUNCIATION | ROSE ELLEN DUNN

1. Richard Kearney, "Hermeneutics of the Possible God," in *Givenness and God: Questions of Jean-Luc Marion*, ed. Ian Leask and Eoin Cassidy (New York: Fordham University Press, 2005), 223.
2. Edmund Husserl, *Ideas Pertaining to a Pure Phenomenology and to a Phenomenological Philosophy: First Book: General Introduction to a Pure Phenomenology*, trans. F. Kersten (The Hague: Martinus Nijhoff, 1982), §27, p. 51.
3. Edmund Husserl, *Ideen zu einer reinen Phänomenologie und phänomenologischen Philosophie: Drittes Buch: Die Phänomenologie und die Fundamente der Wissenschaften* (The Hague: Martinus Nijhoff, 1952), §12, p. 75.
4. Edmund Husserl, *Formal and Transcendental Logic*, trans. Dorion Cairns (The Hague: Martinus Nijhoff, 1967), §99, p. 251.
5. Steven W. Laycock, "The Intersubjective Dimension of Husserl's Theology," in *Essays in Phenomenological Theology*, ed. Steven W. Laycock and James G. Hart (Albany: State University of New York Press, 2001), 172. See also 185–86 n. 6. See also Stephen Strasser, "History, Teleology, and God in the Philosophy of Husserl," in *The Teleologies in Husserlian Phenomenology: The Irreducible Element in Man Part III 'Telos' as the Pivotal Factor of Contextual Phenomenology, Analecta Husserliana*, vol. 9, ed. Anna-Teresa Tymieniecka (Holland: D. Reidel, 1976), 325–26.
6. Steven W. Laycock, "Introduction: Toward an Overview of Phenomenological Theology," in *Essays in Phenomenological Theology*, ed. Steven W. Laycock and James G. Hart (Albany: State University of New York Press, 2001), 1–2.
7. Edmund Husserl, *Cartesian Meditations: An Introduction to Phenomenology*, trans. Dorion Cairns (The Hague: Martinus Nijhoff, 1960), §43, p. 91.
8. James Hart, "Divine Truth in Husserl and Kant: Some Issues in Phenomenological Theology," in *Phenomenology of the Truth Proper to Religion*, ed.

Daniel Guerrière (Albany: State University of New York Press, 1990), 221. Husserl quoted from the *Nachlass* MSS B I 4.

9. Strasser, "God in the Philosophy of Husserl," *Analecta Husserliana* 9:328.
10. James Hart, "A Précis of an Husserlian Philosophical Theology," in *Phenomenology of the Truth Proper to Religion*, ed. Daniel Guerrière (Albany: State University of New York Press, 1990), 148. Husserl quoted from the *Nachlass* MSS (165, n. 76).
11. Ibid., 137–38. Husserl quoted from the *Nachlass* MSS (164 n. 66).
12. Ibid., 149. Husserl quoted from the *Nachlass* MSS (165 n. 81).
13. Martin Heidegger, "Letter on Humanism," in *Basic Writings from Being and Time (1927) to The Task of Thinking (1964)*, ed. David Farrell Krell (New York: Harper and Row, 1977), 230.
14. Kearney, "Possible God," 228.
15. Martin Heidegger, "Postscript to 'What Is Metaphysics?'" in *Pathmarks*, ed. William McNeill (Cambridge: Cambridge University Press, 1998), 234.
16. Martin Heidegger, *What Is Called Thinking?* trans. Fred D. Wieck and J. Glenn Gray (New York: Harper and Row, 1968), 121.
17. Martin Heidegger, *The Principle of Reason*, trans. Reginald Lilly (Indianapolis: Indiana University Press, 1991), 46–7.
18. Heidegger, *Poetry, Language, Thought*, trans. Alfred Hofstader (New York: HarperCollins, 1971), 221.
19. Martin Heidegger, *Discourse on Thinking*, trans. John M. Anderson and E. Hans Freund (New York: Harper and Row, 1966), 87.
20. John D. Caputo, *The Mystical Element in Heidegger's Thought*, 2nd rev. ed. (New York: Fordham University Press, 1986), 174.
21. George Kovacs, *The Question of God in Heidegger's Phenomenology* (Evanston, Ill.: Northwestern University Press, 190), 258.
22. Caputo, *The Mystical Element in Heidegger's Thought*, 144.
23. John D. Caputo, *Demythologizing Heidegger* (Bloomington: Indiana University Press, 1993), 184.
24. Ibid.
25. Luce Irigaray, *Between East and West: From Singularity to Community*, trans. Stephen Pluhacek (New York: Columbia University Press, 2002), 52.
26. Ibid.
27. Ibid., 78.
28. See Irigaray, *Marine Lover of Friedrich Nietzsche*, trans. Gillian C. Gill (New York: Columbia University Press, 1991).
29. Luce Irigaray, "Divine Women," in *Sexes and Genealogies*, trans. Gillian C. Gill (New York: Columbia University Press, 1993), 71.

30. Irigaray, *Between East and West*, 52.
31. Ibid., 53.
32. Ibid.
33. Ibid., 76.
34. Irigaray, *Marine Lover of Friedrich Nietzsche*, 176.
35. Cf. ibid., 177.
36. The first phenomenological reduction is the transcendental reduction proposed by Edmund Husserl, which gives to the experiencing I the intended object and the transcendental *I*. The second reduction is the existential/ ontological reduction proposed by Martin Heidegger which reduces to *Dasein*, There-Being as being-in-the-world, while asking the question of Being. See Jean-Luc Marion, *Reduction and Givenness: Investigations of Husserl, Heidegger, and Phenomenology*, trans. Thomas A. Carlson (Evanston, Ill.: Northwestern University Press, 1998).
37. Jean-Luc Marion, "The Saturated Phenomenon," in *Phenomenology and the "Theological Turn": The French Debate,* by Dominique Janicaud, Jean-François Courtine, Jean-Louis Chrétien, Michel Henry, Jean-Luc Marion, and Paul Ricoeur (New York: Fordham University Press, 2000), 184.
38. Marion, *Reduction and Givenness*, 204.
39. Ibid., 203.
40. Ibid., 204–5.
41. Ibid.
42. Jean-Luc Marion, *Being Given: Toward a Phenomenology of Givenness*, trans. Jeffrey Kosky (Stanford, Calif.: Stanford University Press, 2002), 321.
43. Ibid., 320–21.
44. Jean-Luc Marion, "The Event, the Phenomenon, and the Revealed," in *Transcendence in Philosophy and Religion*, ed. James E. Faulconer (Bloomington: Indiana University Press, 2003), 102.
45. Marion, *Reduction and Givenness*, 205.
46. Marion, "The Event, the Phenomenon, and the Revealed," 103.
47. Marion, *Being Given*, 288.
48. Ibid.
49. Ibid., 298.
50. Marion, "The Saturated Phenomenon," 184.
51. Ibid.
52. Ibid.
53. Ibid., 188.
54. Ibid., 213.
55. Ibid., 215.

56. See Marion, *Being Given*, 225–33.
57. Ibid., 236.
58. Ibid., 241.
59. Ibid., 243.
60. See Jean-Luc Marion, "The Impossible for Man—God," in *Transcendence and Beyond: A Postmodern Inquiry*, ed. John D. Caputo and Michael J. Scanlon (Bloomington: Indiana University Press, 2007).
61. Marion, "The Impossible for Man—God," 26.
62. Ibid., 33–34.
63. See ibid., 34.
64. Ibid., 27.
65. See ibid., 27, 34.
66. See ibid., 34.
67. Ibid., 27.
68. Jacques Derrida, "*Circumfession*," in *Jacques Derrida*, ed. Geoffrey Bennington and Jacques Derrida (Chicago: University of Chicago Press, 1993), 56.
69. Jacques Derrida, *Of Grammatology*, corrected edition, trans. Gayatri Chakravorty Spivak (Baltimore: Johns Hopkins University Press, 1997), 47.
70. Jacques Derrida, "*Différance*," in *Margins of Philosophy*, trans. Alan Bass (Chicago: University of Chicago Press, 1984), 11.
71. Jacques Derrida, "At This Very Moment in This Work Here I Am," in *A Derrida Reader: Between the Blinds*, ed. Peggy Kamuf (New York: Columbia University Press, 1991), 406.
72. Jacques Derrida, "*Sauf le nom*," in *On the Name*, trans. David Wood (Stanford: Stanford University Press, 1995), 35.
73. Jacques Derrida, *The Gift of Death*, trans. David Willis (Chicago: University of Chicago Press, 1995), 67.
74. Jacques Derrida, "I Have a Taste for the Secret," in *A Taste for the Secret*, by Jacques Derrida and Maurizio Ferraris, ed. Giacomo Donis and David Webb, trans. Giacomo Donis (Cambridge: Polity Press, 2001), 57.
75. Derrida, "*Sauf le nom*," 79.
76. Ibid. Derrida is quoting Meister Eckhart.
77. Jacques Derrida, "How to Avoid Speaking: Denials," in *Derrida and Negative Theology*, ed. Harold Coward and Toby Foshay, trans. Ken Frieden (Albany: State University of New York, 1992), 74.
78. Derrida, "*Sauf le nom*," 43.
79. Ibid.
80. Ibid., 78–79.
81. Ibid., 69.

82. Ibid., 83.
83. Ibid., 58.
84. Ibid., 40.
85. Ibid., 38.
86. Augustine. *Confessions*, trans. R. S. Pine-Coffin (New York: Penguin Books, 1961), II.3.45.
87. Derrida, "How to Avoid Speaking: Denials," 110–11.
88. Ibid., 112.
89. Ibid., 117.
90. Ibid.
91. Ibid., 130–31.
92. Derrida, "*Sauf le nom,*" 56.
93. Ibid.
94. Irigaray, *Between East and West*, 52.
95. Dionysius the Areopagite, *The Mystical Theology; and, The Divine Names*, trans. C. E. Rolt (Mineola, N.Y.: Dover Publications, 2004), 106.
96. Luce Irigaray, "*La Mystérique,*" in *Speculum of the Other Woman*, trans. Gillian C. Gill (Ithaca, N.Y.: Cornell University Press, 1985), 191.
97. Karmen MacKendrick, *Immemorial Silence* (Albany: State University of New York Press, 2001), 111.
98. Meister Eckhart, *The Essential Sermons, Commentaries, Treatises, and Defense*, trans. Edmund Colledge, O.S.A., and Bernard McGinn (Mahwah, N.J.: Paulist Press, 1981), 197.
99. Luke 1:35, 42, 45, 48, *The New Oxford Annotated Bible with the Apocryphal/Deuterocanonical Books*. New Revised Standard Version, ed. Bruce M. Metzger and Roland E. Murphy (New York: Oxford University Press, 1994). Unless otherwise cited, this edition is used throughout this essay.
100. Marion, *Being Given*, 298.
101. Jean-Luc Marion, "Introduction: What Do We Mean by 'Mystic'?" in *Mystics: Presence and Aporia*, ed. Michael Kessler and Christian Sheppard, trans. Gareth Gollrad (Chicago: University of Chicago Press, 2003), 5.
102. Marion, "The Impossible for Man—God," 27.
103. Luke 1:34.
104. Marion, "The Impossible for Man—God," 12.
105. Luke 1:38.
106. Luke 1:31.
107. Luke 1:31–32.
108. Luke 1:35.
109. Derrida, "How to Avoid Speaking: Denials," 110–11.

110. Irigaray, *Between East and West*, 52.
111. Angelus Silesius, *The Cherubinic Wanderer*, trans. Maria Shrady (Mahwah, N.J.: Paulist Press, 1986), 40.
112. Derrida, "How to Avoid Speaking: Denials," 130–31.
113. See Luke 1:46–55 and 1 Samuel 2:1–10.
114. Luke 1:46–47.
115. Luke 1:51b–53.
116. Silesius, *Cherubinic Wanderer*, 89.
117. Luke 1:48b.
118. Silesius, *Cherubinic Wanderer*, 48.
119. See Irigaray, *Marine Lover of Friedrich Nietzsche*, 172.

INTIMATE MYSTERIES: THE APOPHATICS OF SENSIBLE LOVE | KRISTA E. HUGHES

1. Hélène Cixous, "(With) Or the Art of Innocence," in *The Hélène Cixous Reader*, ed. Susan Sellers (New York: Routledge, 1994), 99–100.
2. Elizabeth A. Johnson, *She Who Is: The Mystery of God in Feminist Theological Discourse* (New York: Crossroad, 1992), 104–12.
3. Grace Jantzen, *Power, Gender, and Christian Mysticism* (Cambridge: Cambridge University Press, 1995), 284. One of Jantzen's key points is that ineffability refers to *the divine*, and not to the subjective experience of the so-called mystic, as modern philosophy has asserted in the wake of William James.
4. Amy Hollywood, *Sensible Ecstasy: Mysticism, Sexual Difference, and the Demands of History* (Chicago: University of Chicago Press, 2002), 97–98.
5. Denys Turner, *The Darkness of God: Negativity in Christian Mysticism* (Cambridge: Cambridge University Press, 1995), 265.
6. Mayra Rivera has named this "relational transcendence." See *The Touch of Transcendence* (Louisville: Westminster/John Knox Press, 2007).
7. For just a few diverse manifestations of this "pneumatological turn" in feminist theology, see Johnson, *She Who Is*; Catherine Keller, *Face of the Deep: A Theology of Becoming* (London: Routledge, 2003); Rita Nakashima Brock, *Journeys by Heart: A Christology of Erotic Power* (New York: Crossroad, 1988); and Ivone Gebara, *Out of the Depths: Women's Experience of Evil and Salvation*, trans. Ann Patrick Ware (Minneapolis: Fortress Press, 2002).
8. Elliot R. Wolfson, *Language, Eros, and Being: Kabbalistic Hermeneutics and Poetic Imagination* (New York: Fordham University Press, 2004), 220.
9. Oliver Davies, in his essay "Soundings: Towards a Theological Poetics of Silence," explores apophasis in this latter vein, arguing that there are different types of silence. In an appeal to the Russian language, he identifies

tishina—primordial silence, "the silence of the forest"—and *molchanie*—the silence maintained by one who speaks; while the former is the *condition* of speech, the latter is a *type* of speech, or in Wolfson's locution, speaking by not-speaking. Moreover, *molchanie* can convey many things: anger, embarrassment, comfort, reflection, compliance. *Silence and the Word: Negative Theology and Incarnation*, ed. Oliver Davies and Denys Turner (Cambridge: Cambridge University Press, 2002), 222.

10. Jantzen, *Power, Gender, and Christian Mysticism*, 128.
11. Ibid., 148.
12. Ibid., 142.
13. Ibid., 143.
14. Ibid., 145. Naming it the "inner monastery," Beverly J. Lanzetta similarly explores this distinctive aspect of the women mystics' spirituality in *Radical Wisdom: A Feminist Mystical Theology* (Minneapolis: Fortress Press, 2005), 91–93. Based on her reading of Julian and Teresa of Ávila, she constructively develops a feminist mystical theology for today, in which contemplation "builds an inner hermitage in the person's core—a holy respite free from everyday antics and daily distractions—where one does not flee from the world but rather finds it anew. As a return to the center point of love, contemplation touches an inexhaustible ocean of compassion from which all external works of mercy are generated" (196).
15. This is not to say that these women were perfect in their piety. Like so many influential Christian practitioners, "love for all" was often limited to Christian circles.
16. Catherine Keller, *From a Broken Web: Separation, Sexism, and the Self* (Boston: Beacon Press, 1986). Judith Plaskow early identified "woman's sin" as passivity rather than pride. *Sex, Sin, and Grace: Women's Experience and the Theologies of Reinhold Niebuhr and Paul Tillich* (Washington, D.C.: University Press of America, 1980). Serene Jones has similarly noted the fragmentation of woman's "self" in *Feminist Theory and Christian Theology: Cartographies of Grace* (Minneapolis: Fortress Press, 2000).
17. Lanzetta, *Radical Wisdom*, 95–98.
18. Ibid., 101, 96.
19. Ibid., 97.
20. Luce Irigaray, *An Ethics of Sexual Difference*, trans. Carolyn Burke and Gillian C. Gill (Ithaca, N.Y.: Cornell University Press, 1993). Serene Jones has explored this figure from a theological perspective. See *Feminist Theory and Christian Theology*, especially "Sanctification and Justification: Lived Grace," 49–68.

21. Neither a theologian nor a Christian, Cixous would not name her notion of divinity a pneumatology. Her descriptions of the divine are nonetheless resonant with certain feminist-relational pneumatologies, and she is therefore a promising interlocutor for a feminist conception of apophasis that flows from a strongly pneumatological figuration of the divine.
22. Recall Teresa's famous acclamation, *Muero porque no muero:* "I die because I do not die."
23. "I do not know," Derrida says, "whether, more than her, sooner than her, better than her, anyone will have ever given me to think what *to live* means." *H.C. for Life: That Is to Say . . .* , trans. Laurent Milesi and Stefan Herbrechter (Stanford, Calif.: Stanford University Press, 2006), 16. Cixous, however, is not uninterested in the name of God. With Derrida, she shares the conviction, notably Jewish, that the true name of God bears untold power: "[E]ver since the beginning we have guessed that if we ever managed to pronounce just once the true name of God, all the truth dispersed in all languages and all the truth of lives that is concentrated in the body and reserved for love, would shatter in a single breath, just as if god, who ever since the beginning has not spoken to anyone, had always made our name resound in His language, and once the true name rang out, all words in all languages would become unusable, so weak, false, bare, impotent, unforgettably merely words, the straw of thought, that we would not longer wish to speak." Cixous, "(With) Or the Art of Innocence," 96.
24. While Cixous is renowned in Anglo-American academic circles primarily as a theorist, she is also a novelist, memoirist, and dramatist and currently is perhaps most well known in France for her theater work: not theory, but writing in all its various forms is her *vocation*. "I need writing; I need to surprise myself living: I need to feel myself quiver with living: I need to call myself into living and to answer myself by living: I need to be living in the present to the present: I need double-living: I need to come into life: I am afraid that writing will take the place of living: I need writing thinking of living: I write celebrating living: I need to accompany living with music: I need writing to celebrate living." "(With) Or the Art of Innocence," 95–96.
25. "As you describe this *Gelassenheit*, you are very careful not to talk about love, and here love is probably only a particular figure for all that this letting be can affect (without, however, affecting it). But why not recognize there love itself, that is, this infinite renunciation which some *surrenders to the impossible* [*se rend à l'impossible*]. To surrender to the other, and this is the impossible, would amount to giving oneself over in going toward the other, to coming toward the other, but without crossing the threshold, to

respecting, to loving even the invisibility that keeps the other inaccessible." Derrida, "Sauf le Nom" in *On the Name*, ed. Thomas Dutoit (Stanford, Calif.: Stanford University Press, 1995), 73–74.

26. Ibid., 37.
27. Cixous, "(With) Or the Art of Innocence," 101.
28. Ibid., 100.
29. Luce Irigaray, *I Love to You: A Sketch of Possible Felicity in History*, trans. Alison Martin (New York: Routledge, 1996), 110.
30. Ibid., 109.
31. Cixous, "(With) Or the Art of Innocence," 96, 100.
32. Ibid., 101.
33. "Truth is the matrix for what I would call life, that is life worth living. I am, again, referring to intimate relations between human beings," Cixous states. She further notes that the life and love to which she refers is not utopic or pure: "Because we want to avoid the difficulties of the exchanges, most of the time we simplify the relations and we think of love as a whole, love as a sphere that is full of love. That is not true of course. Love is full of separation, of anguish." "Difficult Joys," in *The Body and the Text: Hélène Cixous, Reading, and Teaching*, eds. Helen Wilcox, Keith McWatters, Ann Thompson, and Linda R. Williams (New York: Harvester Wheatsheaf, 1990), 28.
34. Cixous, "(With) Or the Art of Innocence," 99.
35. Helene Cixous, "The Last Painting or the Portrait of God," in *"Coming to Writing" and Other Essays*, ed. Deborah Jenson, trans. Sarah Cornell, Deborah Jenson, Ann Liddle, and Susan Sellers (Cambridge, Mass.: Harvard University Press, 1991), 129–30.
36. The metaphor of lover for divine-human encounter is not new. Sallie McFague proposes lover, along with mother and friend, as a Trinitarian metaphor for divine-human relations in *Models of God: Theology for an Ecological, Nuclear Age* (Philadelphia: Fortress Press, 1987).
37. Cixous, "The Last Painting," 127.
38. While my description may most immediately call to mind lovers, I intend intimacy in the broadest of terms, to include also love between parent and child, siblings and other family members, and friends.
39. Cixous, "(With) Or the Art of Innocence," 101.
40. Cixous, "The Last Painting," 104.
41. Ibid., 119–20.
42. Ibid., 127.
43. Cixous, "(With) Or the Art of Innocence," 100.

CONTRIBUTORS

Chris Boesel is Associate Professor of Christian Theology at the Theological School and Graduate Division of Religion of Drew University. His publications include *Risking Proclamation, Respecting Difference: Christian Faith, Imperialistic Discourse, and Abraham* (2008). He is currently working on an intervention in postmodern theology, tentatively titled *The Postmodern "Turn" to Religion as Return to Modernity.*

Virginia Burrus is Professor of Early Church History at Drew University. Her publications include *"Begotten, Not Made": Conceiving Manhood in Late Antiquity* (2000), *The Sex Lives of Saints: An Erotics of Ancient Hagiography* (2004), *Toward a Theology of Eros: Transfiguring Passion at the Limits of Discipline* (co-edited with Catherine Keller) (2006), *Saving Shame: Martyrs, Saints, and Other Abject Subjects* (2008), and *Seducing Augustine* (co-authored with Mark Jordan and Karmen MacKendrick) (forthcoming).

John D. Caputo is Thomas J. Watson Professor of Religion and Humanities and Professor of Philosophy at Syracuse University. His most recent publications include *The Weakness of God: A Theology of the Event* (2006), winner of the AAR book award in Constructive Theology, and *What Would Jesus Deconstruct?* (2007), winner of the *ForeWord Magazine* award for the best book in philosophy in 2007; and *After the Death of God* (with Gianni Vattimo). He is currently preparing a book on the theology of the flesh.

Philip Clayton is Ingram Professor of Theology at the Claremont School of Theology. His publications include *Mind and Emergence: From Quantum to Consciousness* (2004), *Adventures in the Spirit: God, World, Divine Action* (2008), and *In Quest of Freedom: The Emergence of Spirit in the Natural World* (forthcoming).

T. Wilson Dickinson is a doctoral candidate in the department of Religion at Syracuse University. His work focuses on nineteenth- and twentieth-century continental philosophy and Christian theology, particularly as they address issues that arise from globalization. His dissertation is titled "Specters of Truth: Exercising Philosophy and Theology."

Rose Ellen Dunn is completing her Ph.D. in New Testament and Early Christianity at Drew University. Her research interests currently center on the theological possibilities of phenomenology and the rich potential for these possibilities to enter into conversation with the biblical text. Her dissertation is titled "Finding Grace with God: A Phenomenological Reading of the Annunciation."

Roland Faber is Professor of Process Theology at the Claremont School of Theology, Professor of Religion and Philosophy at the Claremont Graduate University, and Co-Director of the Center for Process Studies and Executive Director of the newly founded Whitehead Research Project (2007). His publications include *Gott als Poet der Welt: Anliegen und Perspektiven der Prozesstheologie* (2003), *Prozesstheologie: Zur ihrer Würdigung und kritischen Erneuerung* (2000), and *God as Poet of the World: Exploring Process Theologies* (2008).

Sigridur Gudmarsdottir has taught theology at the University of Winchester, U.K., and Drew University. She currently works as an ordained minister and independent scholar in her native country, Iceland. Her research interests are in the field of constructive theology with special interests in ecofeminist, poststructuralist and mystical theology. She is currently working on a book on Paul Tillich and the abyss of God.

Krista E. Hughes is Assistant Professor of Theological Studies at Hanover College (Havover, Indiana). A constructive theologian, she works at the intersection of feminist and process theologies, history of doctrine, and continental philosophy. Her dissertation, titled "The Dance of Grace: A

Feminist Theology of Reciprocity," explored questions of agency, gift, corporality, and aesthetics in the movement of grace. She is currently working on a manuscript tentatively titled *In the Flesh: A Feminst Vision of Hope.*

Catherine Keller is Professor of Constructive Theology in the Theological School and Graduate Division of Religion of Drew University. Her publications include *From a Broken Web: Separatism, Sexism, and Self* (1986), *Apocalypse Now and Then: A Feminist Guide to the End of the World* (1996), *Face of the Deep: A Theology of Becoming* (2003), *God and Power: Counter-Apocalyptic Journeys* (2005), and *On the Mystery: Discerning God in Process* (2008). She has also co-edited several volumes in the present Fordham Transdisciplinary Theological Colloquia series.

Karmen MacKendrick is Professor of Philosophy at LeMoyne College in Syracuse, New York. Her publications include *Conterpleasures* (1999), *Immemorial Silence* (2001), *Word Made Skin: Figuring Language at the Surface of Flesh* (2004), and *Fragmentation and Memory: Meditations on Christian Doctrine* (2008). She is currently working on a project on seductive theology.

David L. Miller is Watson-Ledden Professor of Religion, Emeritus, at Syracuse University. His publications include *Christ: Meditations on Archetypal Images in Christian Theology* (1981, 2005), *Three Faces of God: Traces of the Trinity in Literature and Life* (1986, 2005), and *Hells and Holy Ghosts: A Theopoetic of Christian Belief* (1989, 2004).

Patricia Cox Miller is the W. Earl Ledden Professor of Religion at Syracuse University. Her publications include *Biography in Late Antiquity: A Quest for the Holy Man* (1983), *Dreams in Late Antiquity: Studies in the Imagination of a Culture* (1994), *The Poetry of Thought in Late Antiquity: Essays in Imagination and Religion* (2001), and *The Corporeal Imagination: Signifying the Holy in Late Ancient Christianity* (2009).

Charles M. Stang is Assistant Professor of Early Christian Thought at Harvard Divinity School. His research interests are in the field of late antique Eastern Christianity. He is coeditor of *Rethinking Dionysius the Areopagite* (2008) and is currently working on another book on Dionysius.

Kathryn Tanner is Dorothy Grant Maclear Professor of Theology at the University of Chicago Divinity School. Her publications include *God and Creation in Christian Theology: Tyranny or Empowerment?* (1988), *The Politics of God: Christian Theologies and Social Justice* (1992), *Theories of Culture: A New Agenda for Theology* (1997), *Jesus, Humanity, and the Trinity: A Brief Systematic Theology* (2001), and *Economy of Grace* (2005).

Graham Ward is Head of the School of Arts, Histories and Cultures and Professor of Contextual Theology and Ethics at the University of Manchester. His publications include *Barth, Derrida, and the Language of Theology* (1995), *Cities of God* (2000), *True Religion* (2003), *Cultural Transformation and Religious Practice* (2005), *Christ and Culture* (2005) and *The Politics of Discipleship* (2009).

Elliot R. Wolfson is the Abraham Lieberman Professor of Hebrew and Judaic Studies at New York University. His publications include *Through a Speculum That Shines: Vision and Imagination in Medieval Jewish Mysticism* (1994), winner of the AAR's Award for Excellence in the Study of Religion in the Category of Historical Studies and the National Jewish Book Award for Excellence in Scholarship, *Pathwings: Poetic-Philosophic Reflections on the Hermeneutics of Time and Language* (2004), *Language, Eros, Being: Kabbalistic Hermeneutics and the Poetic Imagination* (2005), winner of the Jewish Book Award for Excellence in Scholarship, *Venturing Beyond: Law and Morality in Kabbalistic Mysticism* (2006), *Alef, Mem, Tau: Kabbalistic Musings on Time, Truth, and Death* (2006), *Luminal Darkness: Imaginal Gleanings from Zoharic Literature* (2007), *Footdreams and Treetales: 92 Poems* (2007), and *Open Secret: Post-Messianic Messianism and the Mystical Revision of Menahem Mendel Schneerson* (2009).